FRANK

FRANK

The Voice

||||||||||||||||||||||||||||||||||||||||||||||||||||||||||

JAMES KAPLAN

DOUBLEDAY

NEW YORK LONDON TORONTO

SYDNEY AUCKLAND

DD
DOUBLEDAY

Copyright © 2010 by James Kaplan

All rights reserved. Published in the United States by Doubleday,
a division of Random House, Inc., New York, and in Canada by
Random House of Canada Limited, Toronto

www.doubleday.com

DOUBLEDAY and the DD colophon are registered trademarks of
Random House, Inc.

LIBRARY OF CONGRESS CATALOGING-IN-PUBLICATION DATA
Kaplan, James, 1951–
Frank : the voice / by James Kaplan.—1st ed.
p.   cm.
1. Sinatra, Frank, 1915–1998. 2. Singers—United States—
Biography. I. Title.
ML420.S565K35 2010
782.42164092—dc22
[B]   2009031046

ISBN 978-0-385-51804-8

PRINTED IN THE UNITED STATES OF AMERICA

1 3 5 7 9 10 8 6 4 2

First Edition

FOR MY MOTHER

What is a poet? A poet is an unhappy being whose heart is torn by secret sufferings, but whose lips are so strangely formed that when the sighs and the cries escape them, they sound like beautiful music . . . And men crowd about the poet and say to him: "Sing for us soon again"; that is as much as to say: "May new sufferings torment your soul."

—Kierkegaard, Either/Or

Just because you asked for your contract back, there's no reason why you should get it. We don't do business that way. I don't know who has been putting these ideas into your head or where you're getting them from. They don't sound like Sinatra . . . I had an operation, it took a lot out of me, I've had family difficulties of which you're well aware. But nothing has hurt me as much as the wire I received from you. Don't friendship and sincerity mean anything to you? Or is it that, when you make up your mind to do something, that's the way it has to be? I'm telling you, I've seen it happen and so have you. *If this is the attitude you want to adopt, it's got to hit you— you just can't get away with it; life itself won't permit it* [italics mine]. Love, Manie.

— August 1945 letter to Sinatra from his close friend Emanuel Sacks,
manager of popular repertoire at Columbia Records

There is no excellent beauty that hath not some strangeness in the proportion.

—Francis Bacon

CONTENTS

———

Act One

FRANKIE
AND
DOLLY

||||||||||||||||||||

The only two people I've ever been afraid of are my mother and Tommy Dorsey.
—Frank Sinatra

=

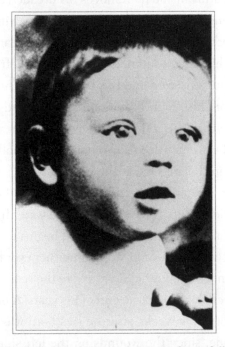

The child is the father to the man: a beautifully
formed mouth, an avid blue-eyed gaze. Undated
photo of Frank at about six months.

A raw December Sunday afternoon in 1915, a day more like the old
century than the new among the wood-frame tenements and
horse-shit-flecked cobblestones of Hoboken's Little Italy, a.k.a.
Guinea Town. The air smells of coal smoke and imminent snow. The
kitchen of the cold-water flat on Monroe Street is full of women,
all gathered around a table, all shouting at once. On the table lies a
copper-haired girl, just nineteen, hugely pregnant. She moans hoarsely:
the labor has stalled. The midwife wipes the poor girl's brow and

motions with her other hand. A doctor is sent for. Ten long minutes later he arrives, removes his overcoat, and with a stern look around the room—he is the lone male present—opens his black bag. From the shining metallic array inside he removes his dreaded obstetric forceps, a medieval-looking instrument, and grips the baby with it, pulling hard from the mother's womb, in the violent process fearfully tearing the left side of the child's face and neck, as well as its left ear.

The doctor cuts the cord and lays the infant—a boy, huge and blue and bleeding from his wounds, and apparently dead—by the kitchen sink, quickly shifting his efforts to saving the nearly unconscious mother's life. The women lean in, mopping the mother's pallid face, shouting advice in Italian. One at the back of the scrum—perhaps the mother's mother, perhaps someone else—looks at the inert baby and takes pity. She picks it up, runs some ice-cold water from the sink over it, and slaps its back. It starts, snuffles, and begins to howl.

Mother and child both survived, but neither ever forgot the brutality of that December day. Frank Sinatra bore the scars of his birth, both physical and psychological, to the end of his years. A bear-rug-cherubic baby picture shot a few weeks after he was born was purposely taken from his right side, since the wounds on the left side of his face and neck were still angry-looking. Throughout Sinatra's vastly documented life, he would rarely—especially if he had anything to do with it—be photographed from his left. One scar, hard to disguise (though frequently airbrushed), ran diagonally from the lower-left corner of his mouth to his jawline. His ear on that side had a bifurcated lobe—the classic cauliflower—but that was the least of it: the delicate ridges and planes of his left outer ear were mashed, giving the appearance, in early pictures, of an apricot run over by a steamroller. The only connection between the sonic world and the external auditory meatus—the ear hole—was a vertical slit. Later plastic surgery would correct the problem to some extent.

That wasn't all. In childhood, a mastoid operation would leave a thick ridge of scar tissue on his neck behind the ear's base. A severe case of cystic acne in adolescence compounded his sense of disfigurement: as an adult, he would apply Max Factor pancake makeup to his face and neck every morning and again after each of the several showers he took daily.

Sinatra later told his daughter Nancy that when he was eleven, after some playmates began to call him "Scarface," he went to the house of the physician who had delivered him, determined to give the good doctor a good beating. Fortunately, the doctor wasn't home. Even when he was in his early forties, on top of the world and in the midst of an artistic outpouring unparalleled in the history of popular music, the birth trauma—and his mother—were very much on Sinatra's mind. Once, in a moment of extraordinary emotional nakedness, the singer opened up very briefly to a lover. "They weren't thinking about me," he said bitterly. "They were just thinking about my mother. They just kind of ripped me out and tossed me aside."

He was talking to Peggy Connelly, a young singer whom he met in 1955 and who, for almost three years at the apex of his career, would be as close to him as it was possible for anyone to be. The scene was Madrid, in the spring of 1956: Sinatra was in Spain shooting a movie he had little taste for. One night in a small nightclub, as he and the twenty-four-year-old Connelly sat in the dark at the edge of the dance floor, she caressed his left cheek, but when her fingertips touched his ear, he flinched. She asked him what was wrong, and he admitted he was sensitive about his deformity.

"I really don't think I had ever noticed it, truly," Connelly said many years later. "This was early on in our relationship." Sinatra then went on to spill out the whole story of his birth: his great weight (thirteen and a half pounds), the ripping forceps, the way he'd essentially been left for dead. "There was no outburst of emotion," Connelly recalled. "There was [instead] an obvious lingering bitterness about what he felt had been a stupid neglect of his infant self to concentrate only on [his] mother, intimating that he was sort of 'ripped from her entrails' and tossed aside; otherwise his torn ear might have been tended to."

In the years immediately following the harrowing birth of her only child, Dolly Sinatra seems to have compensated in her own way: she became a midwife and sometime abortionist. For the latter activity she got a nickname ("Hatpin Dolly") and a criminal record. And while she sometimes refused to accept payment for terminating pregnancies, she could afford the generosity: her legitimate business of midwifery, at $50 per procedure, a substantial sum at the time, helped support her family in handsome fashion. Strikingly, two of her arrests, one in late 1937 and one in February 1939 (just three weeks after her son's wedding), neatly bracketed Frank Sinatra's own two arrests, in November and December 1938, for the then-criminal offenses of (in the first case) seduction and (in the second) adultery. Also remarkable is that all these Sinatra arrests were sex related—and that none of them would have occurred today.

What was happening in this family? To begin to answer the question, we have to cast ourselves back into the knockabout Italian streets of Hoboken in the 1920s and 1930s—and into the thoroughly unpsychological household of Dolly and Marty Sinatra. But while it's easy to wonder what effect growing up in such a household could have had on an exquisitely sensitive genius (which Frank Sinatra indisputably was), we must also remember that he was cut from the same cloth as his parents—especially his mother, a woman he seems to have hated and loved, avoided and sought out, in equal measures, throughout his life; a woman whose personality was uncomfortably similar to his own.

The first mystery is what brought two such disparate characters as Natalina Garaventa and Anthony Martin Sinatra together in the first place. Dolly (she acquired the nickname as a little girl, for being so pretty) was, even as a very young woman, loud, relentlessly foulmouthed, brilliant (she had a natural facility for languages), and toweringly ambitious. So—to what kind of star did she imagine she was hitching her wagon when she went after (for she must have been the aggressor in the relationship) Marty Sinatra?

For he was a lug: a sweet lug, maybe, but a lug nevertheless. Short, with an obstinate-looking underbite and an early-receding hairline. A fair bantamweight prizefighter (he billed himself as Marty O'Brien, because of the anti-Italian prejudice of the times), frequently unemployed, who sometimes moonlighted as a chauffeur to make ends meet. A little man who had his arms covered in tattoos to try to look tough. Asthmatic; illiterate all his life. And exceedingly stingy with words. In his sixties, Frank Sinatra recalled listening to his parents through the bedroom wall. "Sometimes I'd be lying awake in the dark and I'd hear them talking," he said. "Or rather, I'd hear her talking and him listening. Mostly it was politics or some worthless neighbor. I remember her ranting about how Sacco and Vanzetti were framed. Because they were Italians. Which was probably true. All I'd hear from my father was like a grunt . . . He'd just say, Eh. Eh."

It's difficult to extract much personality from the few stories told about the elder Sinatra. He seems to have had a wry and quiet sense of humor, and photographs of him as a young man appear to bear this out—it's a sweet, though dim, face. Nancy Sinatra, in *Frank Sinatra, My Father,* tries to paint her grandfather as a lovable practical joker: There was the time Marty gave a pal a laxative and spread glue on the outhouse toilet seat. And then there was Marty's revenge on a deadbeat barkeep who tried to pay off a debt to him with a sick horse instead of cash: her grandfather, Nancy says, walked the horse to the saloon in the middle of the night and shot it dead in the doorway, leaving the carcass as a discouragement to business.

Rough humor! The joke has a Sicilian tinge to it, and Sicily is where Marty came from, in 1903, aged nine, when he landed at Ellis Island with his mother and two little sisters to join his father, Francesco Sinatra, who—in the common practice of the day—had arrived in America three years earlier to establish himself.

Dolly Garaventa's people were from the north of Italy, near Genoa. And the ancient, deeply held social prejudice on the part of northern Italians toward southerners makes it doubly difficult to imagine what was on her mind when, at sixteen, she set her cap for the eighteen-year-old Marty. Was it irresistible attraction? Or adolescent rebellion—the chance to stick it to her parents, the lure of the bad boy? It's said that little Dolly (she was under five feet, and just ninety pounds) used to disguise herself as a boy to sneak into Marty's prize-fights, her strawberry blond hair stuffed into a newsboy cap, a cigar stuck in her mouth: a sweet story, with a ring of truth about it, bespeaking her willfulness, her force. And her originality.

Against her family's outcry (and probably at her urging), the two eloped, ages seventeen and nineteen, and were married at the Jersey City city hall on Valentine's Day (a holiday that would loom large at two junctures in Frank Sinatra's first marriage) 1913. On the marriage certificate, Marty gave his occupation as athlete. In truth, he only ate regularly because his parents owned a grocery store. Soon the couple made it up with her parents, got remarried in the church, and set up housekeeping in the cold-water flat at 415 Monroe Street.

Every family is a mystery, but some are more mysterious than others. After Dolly and Marty Sinatra's only child was born, theirs was a centrifugal household. Family lore says that the birth rendered Dolly unable to have more children, but it seems equally likely she simply decided—she was a decider—she didn't want to go through *that* again. Besides, she had many other fish to fry. Her skill with Italian dialects and her fluency in English led her to become a facilitator for new immigrants who had court business, such as trying to get citizenship papers. Her appearances in court brought her to the attention of local Democratic politicians—the Irish bosses of Hoboken—who, impressed by the force of her personality and her connection with the community, saw in her a natural ward leader. Soon she was getting out votes, petitioning city hall (as part of a demonstration for suffrage in 1919, she chained herself to the building's fence), campaigning for candidates, collecting favors. All the while roaming the streets of Hoboken with her black midwife's bag.

It all meant she simply wasn't at home very much. In any case, home wasn't the place for Dolly: she was *out*, not in; she had the politician's temperament—restless, energetic, unreflective. And she had unique ideas about child rearing. Of course, to present-day sensibilities filled with the art and science of what we now call parenting, child rearing in the early twentieth century has a distinctly primitive look to it. Poor and lower-middle-class families were large, and with the parents either working or simply exhausted, the older children—or the streets—frequently raised the young.

Neither was an option for Frank Sinatra. As an only child in Hoboken in the 1920s and 1930s, he was an anomaly. His mother paid him both too much attention and too little. Having wanted a girl, she dressed him in pink baby clothes. Once he was walking, there were Little Lord Fauntleroy outfits.

He was the apple of his parents' eye and their ball and chain. Dolly had babies or votes to deliver; Marty had things to do. Italian men left the house whether they were employed or not, if only to sit somewhere and sip a beverage with pals. Late in the second decade of the twentieth century, Dolly borrowed money from her family, and she and Marty bought a bar, on the corner of Jefferson and Fourth, which they called Marty O'Brien's. While they ran the place, little Frankie was looked after by his grandmother or a cousin or, most regularly, a nice Jewish neighbor named Mrs. Golden. She taught him Yiddish.

When Dolly was with her son, she alternately coddled him—beautiful clothes continued to be a theme—and abused him. In those days it was known as discipline. The child was spirited, and so was the mother. It's a miracle the child kept his spirit. Dolly once pushed her son down a flight of stairs, knocking him unconscious. She playfully ducked his head under the ocean waves, terrifying him (remarkably, he became an expert swimmer). And most regularly, she hit him with a stick. It was a small bat, actually, something like a policeman's nightstick: it was kept behind the bar at Marty O'Brien's.

"When I would get out of hand," Sinatra told Pete Hamill, "she would give me a rap with that little club; then she'd hug me to her breast."

"She was a pisser," he recollected to Shirley MacLaine. "She scared the shit outta me. Never knew what she'd hate that I'd do."

If the primary intimacy was up for grabs, so was every subsequent relationship: Sinatra would feel ambivalent about women until the end of his days. He would show every lover something of what Dolly had shown him.

It seems straight out of a textbook: an only child, both spoiled and neglected, praised to the skies and viciously cut down when he fails to please, grows up suffering an infinite neediness, an inability to be alone, and cycles of grandiosity and bottomless depression.

"I think my dad desperately wanted to do the best he could for the people he loved," Tina Sinatra writes, "but ultimately he would do what he needed to do for *himself*. (In that, he was his mother's son.)"

Yet that doesn't quite tell the whole story. Yes, Frank Sinatra was born with a character (inevitably) similar to Dolly's, but nature is only half the equation. Frank Sinatra did what he needed to do for himself because he had learned from earliest childhood to trust no one—even the one in whom he should have been able to place ultimate trust.

And then there is the larger environment in which Sinatra grew up, those knockabout streets of Hoboken during Prohibition and the Depression.

By some accounts, the Square Mile City was a pretty mobbed-up place in those days. Some say even Marty O'Brien's little tavern was a hotbed of crime. We hear about big Mob names like Meyer Lansky and Bugsy Siegel and Joe Adonis and Johnny Torrio and the Fischetti brothers and Longy Zwillman and Willie Moretti and Dutch Schultz and Frank Costello and—of course—Lucky Luciano, who, as fate would have it, was born in the same Sicilian village as Frank Sinatra's grandfather, Lercara Friddi.

What business could all these big cheeses of organized crime possibly have had with the small-time Sinatras of Hoboken? It all had to do (we're told) with liquor. The Mob made millions from rum-running; Dolly and Marty Sinatra bought illegal booze from their lieutenants, or the lieutenants' lieutenants. Poor Marty, it seems, once got hit, knocked unconscious, when he tried to make some pin money riding shotgun for a liquor shipment. The big-time bootlegger Waxey Gordon (identified in Nancy Sinatra's book as "Sicilian-born," which must mean a very odd neighborhood in Sicily, for he was born Irving Wexler) was said to be a regular at Marty O'Brien's.

Meanwhile, by his own later account, little Frankie also hung out at the bar, doing his homework and, now and then at the urging of the clientele, climbing up on top of the player piano to sing a song of the day for nickels and quarters: *Honest and truly, I'm in love with you . . .*

It appears that Dolly's brothers Dominick and Lawrence were both involved in shady activity. Both had criminal records; Lawrence, a welterweight boxer under the name Babe Sieger, dabbled in crime, sort of. "He was a hijacker with Dutch Schultz with the whiskey and stuff," Dolly's sister's son recalled, somewhat vaguely. And, of course, Dutch Schultz did business with Lucky Luciano, and we can fill in the blanks from there.

But to understand the effect of organized crime on the evolving psyche of young Frank, we need look no further than Dolly herself—at least if we consider the writings of Mario Puzo.

In 1964, Puzo published his second novel, the highly autobiographical *The Fortunate Pilgrim*. Critics hailed it as a minor classic—much as they had hailed his first book, a World War II novel called *The Dark Arena*. After those two books, Puzo, unable to make a living from his writing, decided he was tired of creating minor classics. And so he wrote *The Godfather*.

The Fortunate Pilgrim is a beautiful, harrowing story, depicting the travails of an Italian-American family living in Hell's Kitchen in the depths of the Depression. When the father, the family's breadwinner, has a breakdown and is institutionalized, the mother, Lucia Santa Angeluzzi-Corbo, takes matters into her own hands, deciding she will not let her six children go hungry or be farmed out to other households. She learns how to earn a living; she holds the family together by the sheer force of her will.

The book was based on Puzo's own childhood, and he would later make an amazing admission: he had based the character of Vito Corleone, the Godfather, on the very same person who had been the model for Lucia Santa Angeluzzi-Corbo—his own mother. Just like Lucia Santa and Don Corleone, Mother Puzo had been benevolent but calculating, slow to anger but quick to decide: the ultimate strategist.

Like Lucia Santa Angeluzzi-Corbo, Dolly Sinatra managed, by sheer force of will, to make a life for her little family in the years leading up to, and into the teeth of, the Depression. It wasn't easy.

She was a politician and a master strategist: endlessly ambitious, fiercely determined, utterly pragmatic. She was also abusive, violent, and vengeful. It was quite a different version of the godfather from Mario Puzo's. But it was a cogent version nonetheless. Frank Sinatra

A heavy hand. "She scared the shit outta me," Sinatra recollected to Shirley MacLaine. "Never knew what she'd hate that I'd do." Frank and Dolly on a trip to the Catskills, circa 1926.

may have grown up with Fischettis down the street, Dutch Schultz around the corner, Waxey Gordon on the next bar stool at Marty O'Brien's, but he had his own model for a Mafia chief right inside his house. Small wonder that when he eventually met the real thing, he felt a shot of recognition, an instant pull. And small wonder that when the real mafiosi met Sinatra, they smiled as they shook his hand. It wasn't just his celebrity; celebrities were a dime a dozen. It was that part of Dolly that her son always carried with him: his own inner godfather. He both wanted to be one of them and—in spirit and in part— really was.[1]

First Communion, 1924.

Even with Dolly's Napoleonic drive, moving up from Guinea Town was no simple matter. She and Marty endured 415 Monroe Street for fourteen years, Frankie, almost twelve. A long time.

Toward the end of their tenure there, another joined them.

It was a strange little ménage, the precise sleeping arrangements lost to history: Dolly and Marty in one bed, Frankie in another, and somewhere Marty's cousin from the Old Country, one Vincent Mazzola. In her memoir, Tina Sinatra remembers "Uncle Vincent, a tiny,

darling man with a severe limp from World War I, where he'd earned a
Purple Heart. With no family of his own, he'd lived with my grandpar-
ents since the late thirties."

In fact, according to a family friend, it was a dozen years earlier,
around 1926, when Vincent Mazzola moved into the little flat with Dolly
and Marty and Frankie. Mazzola's mysterious nickname was Chit-U.
Nobody seems to know what it meant, but one wonders if it was in
any way related to *citrullo,* an Italian word for simpleton, or fool. (Or a
crude joke—shit-you-pants?) In any event, Chit-U seems not to have
had much going on upstairs. In all likelihood he was shell-shocked.

His arrival at Monroe Street came at a particularly inopportune
moment for the family: Marty could no longer box, having broken both
wrists in the ring,¹ and had lost his job as a boilermaker because of his
asthma. Between the fees she earned from midwifery and abortion and
a weekend job dipping chocolates in a candy store, Dolly was holding
the Sinatras' fortunes together. Imagine her delight at having to take in
a slow-witted cripple.

But she pulled up her socks and put Chit-U to work, using her
political influence in the Third Ward to get him a job on the docks.
Every week, he meekly handed his paycheck to her. She also took out a
life-insurance policy on the little man, listing herself as the beneficiary.

And not long after setting Cousin Vincent to work, she got busy
with Marty, marching to city hall and calling in some Democratic
Party chits to demand for her husband a coveted spot in the Hoboken Fire Department. Since the HFD (a) was predominantly Irish and
(b) required a written test of all applicants, and since Marty Sinatra
was (a) Irish in nickname only and (b) illiterate, one would imagine
his chances to have been slim. But *no,* to Dolly Sinatra, was an inau-
dible syllable. Presto, Marty was a fireman! And now, with her husband
established in a rock-solid and well-paying (and as a bonus, not exces-
sively labor-intensive) position, and Chit-U's income from the docks
added to Marty's pay and Dolly's own, escape from Guinea Town was
at long last possible.

He was a lonely boy, by turns timid and overassertive. He desperately wanted to be "in"—part of a gang or group of any sort. Pampered and overprivileged, he used the money Dolly gave him to try to buy friendship with gifts, with treats. Still, as in the early Hal Roach *Our Gang* films in which the prissily dressed stock character of the rich boy is pushed into mud puddles, he was mocked: for his outfits, his oddity.

And his emotionalism. He would never be one of the cool kids—he was hot, and his anger and laughter and tears came too easily.

Yet this was not the rich boy in *Our Gang*. The damaged left ear was clearly visible, as was a scar at the top of the philtrum. This was a face to be reckoned with—a startling face, not least because of the similarity to what it would become; but also in itself: serene, mischievous, beautiful. Late in life Sinatra told a friend that as a child he had heard the music of the spheres.

He may have been timid and babyish and spoiled; he may even, as some accounts suggest, have played with dolls as late as age twelve. But he seems from early years to have had the strong sense that he was Someone—a sense that would have been encouraged by the material things lavished on him, and undercut by the attention that was denied. Not to mention the billy club.

Still, if there's any truth to the idea of victims' identifying with the oppressor, it can be found in young Frank Sinatra's face. Dolly wanted and expected things: things material and immaterial, possessions and power. She wanted the world. Her son may have been uncertain of the ground he walked on where she was concerned, but if there was one thing he was absolutely sure of, it was that he had big things coming to him.

And in early adolescence (just as his family was beginning to bootstrap itself out of the ghetto) he began to dress the part. Frankie had a charge account at the local department store, Geismar's, and a wardrobe so fabulous that he acquired a new nickname: "Slacksey O'Brien." A lesser boy might have become just a well-tailored layabout, a Hoboken *vitellone,* but young Frank's splendor was much more than skin-deep. And his large sense of himself derived not only from his identification with Dolly's voracious sense of entitlement but also from the Secret he entertained, the sounds he heard in his head.

In September 1927 the Sinatras made their big move east, from Monroe Street across the super-significant border of Willow Avenue and into a three-bedroom apartment, at $65 a month, in a German-Irish neighborhood on the tony-sounding Park Avenue.² Later in life, Frank Sinatra liked to foster the impression that he'd led a pretty rough-and-tumble boyhood among the street gangs of Hoboken. More likely, he spent his early years dodging the gibes and brickbats of the tougher boys of Guinea Town. Now, however, he and his family had crossed a crucial line, into their new life in the high-rent district: every morning, Marty went off to the firehouse to roll up his sleeves (revealing those impressively tattooed arms) and play pinochle; Dolly roamed Hoboken with her black bag; Chit-U limped off to the docks (in his spare time, he limped around the new apartment, mopping and dusting); and Frankie, once school was done for the day (thank God—he hated every minute of it), dreamed by the radio.

It was the centerpiece of any bourgeois or aspiring-bourgeois household in the mid-1920s: the more elaborate and fine-furniture-like, the better. And the Sinatras owned not just one radio but two. For eleven-year-old Frankie had his own bedroom (at a time when entire families in Hoboken slept in a single room) and his very own Atwater Kent, an instrument he would later recall resembling "a small grand piano."

Radio was just coming into its own as a medium. The linkage of local transmitters by telephone lines had led, in 1926 and 1927, to the formation of the first two networks, NBC and CBS. Suddenly a wondrous world of faraway news, drama, and sports opened up, emanating from the magical cabinet. Alone in his bedroom, young Frankie would have listened hungrily, passionately. But to his ears, the most miraculous sounds of all were musical: the operatic voices of Lauritz Melchior and Lily Pons and Amelita Galli-Curci; the jazz rhythms of the Roger Wolfe Kahn and Ted Fio Rito and Paul Whiteman orchestras.

And then there were the crooners.

The recent perfection of the electronic microphone had led to a sea change in the art of popular singing. Music had been recorded since the 1870s and broadcast since 1920, but prior to 1924 singers had to project through megaphones or into acoustical microphones that provided scarcely greater amplification than cardboard cones. The art of popular singing had therefore been an art of projection, and higher voices—female or tenor—simply carried better.

Now with the modern microphones came a new generation of baritones, men who leaned in and sang softly, intimately, to millions of listeners. There was Gene Austin and Art Gillham and Cliff "Ukulele Ike" Edwards (later the voice of Jiminy Cricket) and Rudy Vallée and Russ Columbo. But most startlingly, there was Bing Crosby.

Crosby, out of Spokane, Washington, had come up through vaudeville, singing as part of a trio called the Rhythm Boys, first with Paul Whiteman, then with the Gus Arnheim Orchestra. But Crosby quickly overshadowed his singing partners—and then even the orchestras that accompanied him—by bringing something entirely new to the art of the popular song: himself.

Prior to the age of the new microphone, popular singing had been, of necessity, a declamatory art: singers literally had to reach the back rows. Crosby's idol, Al Jolson, electrified the Jazz Age with his overpowering pipes and incandescent theatricality. Artifice was an essential part of show business.

The new crooners were more laid-back, but equally artificial. Under the old show-business conventions, a certain remove from the audience, in the form of "classiness," as exemplified by heightened diction, was a quality to be cultivated. Bing Crosby captured America's heart as no entertainer had ever done before by removing the remove, by seeming the most common of men.

Of course he wasn't that by a long shot. He was a one-of-a-kind phenomenon, a single figure as transforming of the American cultural landscape as Jolson had been, and as Frank Sinatra himself—or Elvis Presley, or Bob Dylan—would be in decades to come. Crosby was, first and foremost, a musical genius, a quality that underlay all his other contradictions, which were plentiful. He was a Jesuit-educated intellectual and a ne'er-do-well; he was at once lovably warm and unreachably cool. He was, with his English-Irish background and ice blue eyes, the whitest of white men and, with his fondness for hard liquor (and, now and then, marijuana) and his incomparable talents for melodic and rhythmic improvisation, a great jazz musician to the core of his being. As Artie Shaw memorably put it: "The thing you have to understand about Bing Crosby is that he was the first hip white person born in the United States."

In other words, Crosby came along (as Elvis would a quarter century later) at precisely the tick of time when the vast white music-listening audience of the United States was primed for hipness—as long as it came in white form. As Gary Giddins reminds us in his superb biography of Bing, *A Pocketful of Dreams,* the definition of jazz in the Jazz Age was far looser than it would come to be later: witness the above-mentioned Kahn, Fio Rito, and Whiteman orchestras, which were stately and lily-white but agreeably peppy.

Meanwhile, truly transformational musicians, both black and white—the likes of Fletcher Henderson, Bix Beiderbecke, Duke Ellington, Bubber Miley, Chick Webb, and Benny Goodman—were creating genuine jazz. It was an age of intense cross-fertilization in popular music, and an age of great excitement, when anyone who was paying attention could hear new and wonderful things.

And Bing Crosby had big ears, literally and figuratively. He heard jazz, and for a few years at the beginning of his career he projected something earthshakingly new through the speakers of those Zeniths and Crosleys and Philcos, something that set him quite apart from all the other crooners.

First came the voice itself, deep and rich and masculine, though not ostentatiously so. Crosby was also pitch-perfect and wonderfully adventurous rhythmically—but again, these are the last things most listeners would have noticed. What was most thrilling about Bing Crosby's voice to radio listeners of the 1920s and 1930s was its warmth and directness: unlike other singers, who seemed to be contriving a character as they vocalized, Crosby appeared to be *himself,* speaking straight to the listener in the most casual possible way. It sounded almost as if he were making up the song on the spot.

How did he accomplish this? Remarkably, his Jesuit education had much to do with it. Crosby had been born with a gift for language and a love for words, qualities that were especially encouraged at Spokane's Gonzaga High and Gonzaga University. Giddins writes: "Bing Crosby is the only major singer in American popular music to enjoy the virtues of a classical education . . . Classes in elocution, in which he excelled, taught him not only to enunciate a lyric but to analyze its meaning. At Gonzaga High, education was idealized in the phrase *eloquentia perfecta* (perfect eloquence). Students coached in literature were expected to attain rhetorical mastery as well."

Crosby did well in his studies; at the same time, he was a deeply ambivalent student who, lured by popular music's siren call, dropped out of his pre-law course at Gonzaga in his senior year to go on the road—for the rest of his life, as it turned out. His intellectual half-heartedness forever saved him from pedantry and lent a sense of playfulness to his verbal theatrics.

That he was smart and funny on his own terms raised him above the pack. The popular music of Crosby's early career was a very mixed bag, containing both great standards that would endure the test of time and some of the schmaltziest tunes ever written. As Bing approached the peak of his movie success in the 1930s, he would have the power and the good sense to simply command his songwriters to leave out the schmaltz. Early on, though, he had to sing plenty of it. This is where his fabled coolness stood him in good stead: Crosby possessed the unique ability to make a number like "Just One More Chance" ("I've learned the meaning of repentance/Now you're the jury at my trial") work by sounding wholehearted and ever so slightly skeptical at the same time.

The effect was electric. To women, he sounded romantic, vulnerable, and faintly mysterious; to men, he conveyed emotions without going overboard. He was one of them: a *man,* not some brilliantined eunuch. And the seeming casualness of his vocal style made every man feel he could sing like Bing.

Little Frankie was no exception. But he came by the idea honestly: as it happened, both his parents could also sing. Marty had wooed Dolly by serenading her with an old-fashioned number called "You Remind Me of the Girl Who Used to Go to School with Me." For her part, Dolly used to love to gussy herself up on Saturday nights, bounce around to Hoboken's many political meetings, get loaded on beer, and warble "When Irish Eyes Are Smiling" over and over and over again. No wonder Frankie got up on the piano at the bar.

Still, Crosby's influence on him cannot be underestimated. The period of Bing's explosion into the American consciousness, propelled by radio's beginnings as a truly mass phenomenon, precisely coincided with Frank Sinatra's emergence as a sexual being. There he was alone in his room, just him and his radio—with *that voice* coming out of it. (Talk about masculine role models: poor grunting Marty couldn't have compared well.) Anyone who came of age in the early 1960s, hearing Dylan and the Beatles for the first time, can remember the feeling: There you are with your hormones aboil, and someone is speaking, really speaking, to you . . . And if that someone who's speaking happens to possess genius, interesting things percolate in your mind.

Even in early adolescence, Frank Sinatra's mind was an exceedingly interesting one. He was already aware of something that set him apart from others his age: an inner riot of constantly flowing emotions, happy to sad to miserable to ecstatic to bored, sometimes all within the space of a minute, each shift hanging on the precise character of the daylight, the look of the clouds, a sharp sound in the street, the smell of the page of a comic book . . . He might have been ashamed of his inner chaos at times—weren't these kinds of feelings for girls?—or he might've been proud. In any case, he kept this part of himself to himself.[3]

As—for now—he kept secret the thrill he felt at the sound of Crosby's voice, couched in the certainty that Bing was *speaking to him*. In fact, in the case of Crosby and Sinatra, genius was speaking to genius—though in Sinatra's case, the genius was very much nascent. Frank Sinatra was a slow bloomer. With his feet rooted firmly in the soil of New Jersey. When a *Life* magazine writer asked him, in the early 1970s, if he could recall the first time he ever sang in public, Sinatra said, "I think it was at some hotel in Elizabeth, New Jersey. Late 20s . . . I probably sang 'Am I Blue?' and I probably got paid a couple of packs of cigarettes and maybe a sandwich."

Which begs the question of those piano-top performances at Marty O'Brien's, but still—he was singing. Unlike school, this was something he could do.

———

In June 1931, he graduated from Hoboken's David E. Rue Junior High School; around that same time—perhaps as a graduation present—his mother, always looking to boost his popularity, bought him a used Chrysler convertible for $35. That fall, she had reason to regret her generosity: after a mere forty-seven days' attendance at A. J. Demarest High, Frankie either dropped out or, as he later claimed—probably in another attempt to bolster his bad-boy credentials—was expelled, "for general rowdiness." He was not quite sixteen.

According to some sources, Dolly, who'd dreamed of Frankie's becoming a doctor or a civil engineer, was furious. "If you think you're going to be a goddamned loafer, you're crazy!" she is said to have screamed. According to other accounts, however, Dolly was unperturbed ("Her way of thinking," a niece recalled, "was that Italians didn't need an education to get a job"), even if Marty's plans for his son to attend Stevens Institute had hit a rough patch. In any case, some-body was disappointed.

If Frank Sinatra's boyhood were a movie, a continuing visual theme would have to be Dolly marching around Hoboken, her firm jaw set, bent on accomplishing for the powerless males around her what they seemed unable to accomplish for themselves. This time she marched straight over to the offices of the *Jersey Observer* and buttonholed Frankie's godfather and namesake, the *Observer's* circulation manager, Frank Garrick, refusing to leave the premises until she had secured for her son a job bundling newspapers on a delivery truck.[4]

A famous story ensues: Frankie, restless and smart and intellectu-ally ambitious, though also possessing a strong streak of intellectual laziness, didn't like bundling newspapers on a delivery truck. Instead, he got it into his head that he would prefer to be a sportswriter. Not become a sportswriter—*be* a sportswriter. And so one day, after some poor cub reporter on the *Observer's* sports desk got himself killed in a car wreck, Dolly ordered her thoroughly unqualified son to march into Garrick's office and demand the job. Not finding Garrick present, Frankie went over to the dead boy's desk and simply sat down, doing things he imagined an actual sportswriter might do: sharpening pen-cils, filling the glue pot—everything, in short, but writing about sports.

When the *Observer's* editor saw Frankie at the dead kid's desk, he quite reasonably asked him what he was doing there. Frankie responded that Mr. Garrick had given him the job. The editor asked Mr. Garrick if this was the case. Garrick said it was not. The editor told Frank Garrick to let Sinatra go. More likely—with what one knows of editors, and the time and the territory—he told him to let the lying little son of a bitch go.

Garrick regretfully informed his godson that he, Frankie, had put him in an untenable position, and that it would be impossible for him, Frankie, to stay in the *Observer's* employ.

Whereupon Frankie lost it.

Screaming, red faced, veins pounding, he cursed out his godfather, dredging up every scrap of gutter talk he'd learned on the sidewalks of Hoboken. A sixteen-year-old high-school dropout cursing out a grown man, a figure of benevolence and authority: *the man who had given him his name.*

"Like Dolly, he resented authority in any guise—especially when he knew he was wrong," Sinatra's daughter Tina wrote. "The more you yanked him by the neck, the less he liked it, and the more he'd dig in his heels."

The Garrick episode has a whiff of sulfur about it. It speaks of the Old World spirit—the true, violent spirit—of vendetta. But even worse: if true—and there's no reason to suppose it isn't, since both Garrick and, later, his widow recalled the incident—it says not-so-good things about the teenage Sinatra. Does this make him a tougher customer than we'd first suspected?

Probably not. For all Sinatra's claims that he'd run with a rough crowd, carried around a length of lead pipe, and so on—not to mention his stories about Marty teaching him to fight—there are too many accounts from Hoboken contemporaries that portray him as a natty little weakling who couldn't punch his way out of a paper bag, who tried desperately to bribe bigger, tougher boys to be his friends. An old photograph in Nancy Sinatra's second book about her father, *Frank Sinatra: An American Legend,* shows Frankie, aged about twelve, looking rather timid as he stands on the sidewalk with his big, expensive bicycle. He's wearing a newsboy cap, beautifully pressed trousers, and a jacket marked "TURKS." "Frank, sporting the T-shirt of his street gang, the Turks," Ms. S.'s caption reads. "Just like they do today, street gangs protected their territory."

But it turns out the gang wasn't a gang at all: it was an after-school club called the Turk's Palace. The Turks had secret handshakes, they played a little baseball, they wore flashy orange and black jackets with a half-moon and dagger on the back.[5] And Dolly was the one who bought the jackets, thus ensuring that Frank would be the club's manager and the baseball team's pitcher. Which makes it hard to credit the idea that the Fauntleroy of Park Avenue had suddenly turned into a hard guy as he entered adolescence.

Instead, what we see is a type: the overaggressive, loud-talking bantamweight who snarls to hide his terrors. Sinatra's explosion shows a ferocious sense of entitlement, built on a foundation of sand. (It also shows a deep fear of his mother, and how she might feel about his losing his job.) Frankie had to have known that he was in the wrong, and the resulting self-dislike would have stoked his tantrum. He then would have felt furious at himself for losing his temper, and further furious at Frank Garrick for *making* him lose his temper. A nuclear chain reaction.

There would be many such exhibitions in Sinatra's life.

(In later years—perhaps abetted by his publicist George Evans— he liked to let it slip that he had once worked as a sportswriter for the *Jersey Observer.*[6] The assertion found its way, unchallenged, into many later accounts of his life. Once he was famous, he found a way to *have been* a sportswriter.)

We are told that after Frankie recounted the Garrick incident to Dolly (no doubt carefully spinning it in his favor), she never spoke to the man again. For his part, Sinatra didn't talk to his godfather for close to five decades. He failed to invite Garrick to his first wedding, to the baptisms of any of his children, or to Dolly and Marty's fiftieth-anniversary party.

Then, out of the blue, not long after Dolly died (in 1977), Sinatra phoned Garrick, asking if he could come by to visit. Generously, Garrick told him that would be fine. Sinatra didn't show up.

He called several more times, but each time failed to appear.

Finally, in 1982, the sixty-six-year-old Sinatra went to see the eighty-five-year-old Garrick and his wife in their three-room apartment in a senior citizens' building in Hoboken. Not alone—he brought along his secretary, Dorothy Uhlemann, and his best friend, Jilly Rizzo, as insulation. Picture the commotion in the tiny apartment as, amid cooking smells and a barking television, the tanned and bewigged superstar and his retinue enter. Sinatra surprisingly timid at first, Dorothy's sweetness and Jilly's gruff bonhomie covering the initial awkward silences. Frank then presents the elderly couple with an elaborate fruit basket and an envelope containing five $100 bills. Much more is to come, he promises. Finally, all material gestures having been exhausted, Sinatra and Garrick embrace, and both men weep. Sinatra tells his godfather he has never gotten in touch because he was scared.

But now Dolly Sinatra is in the grave, and it's safe.

Even then he could wear a hat. Frankie had a charge account at
Geismar's, a Hoboken department store, and a wardrobe so fabulous
that he acquired a new nickname: "Slacksey O'Brien." Circa 1929.

On the sheer strength of her chutzpah, young Dolly moved her little family ever farther from Guinea Town and toward the plusher
districts closer to the Hudson. In December 1931, as former
business executives stood on breadlines and sold apples, the Sinatras (and ever-present Uncle Vincent) relocated again, this time to
an honest-to-God four-story house at 841 Garden Street (a very nice
address), replete with central heating, several bathrooms, a gold bird-

bath at the entrance, a mahogany dining-room set, a baby grand piano, and—like something out of *Dinner at Eight*—a chaise longue and gold and white French telephone (number: HOboken 3–0985) in the master bedroom.

True, Dolly would need to scrape every nickel and dime, not to mention take in boarders, to pay the substantial mortgage (the house cost over $13,000, a bloody fortune in those days), but that was part of her master plan. She had already lifted the Sinatras out of the lower middle class. And she announced as much in the society pages of the *Jersey Observer:* "[A] New Year's Eve party was given at the home of Mr. and Mrs. M. Sinatra of upper Garden Street in honor of their son, Frank. Dancing was enjoyed. Vocal selections were given by Miss Marie Roemer and Miss Mary Scott, accompanied by Frank Sinatra."[1]

Upper Garden Street.

Accompanied by Frank Sinatra.

It isn't so hard to imagine that the musical portion of the festivities had initially been planned for the two young ladies alone, and that headstrong Frankie had shoehorned himself in, to Marty's displeasure and Dolly's ambivalent approval. That she commemorated his participation afterward doubtless had more to do with wanting to wring every possible drop of family glory out of the event than with a sudden acceptance of his boyish dream. He was still a dropout and a ne'er-do-well, drawing free room and board under the expensive roof of 841 Garden Street.

Since there was a depression on and no loafing was countenanced in Dolly's house, he was put to work. His mother got him jobs and he took them—briefly, and with maximum reluctance. He caught hot rivets at the Tietjen and Lang shipyards in Hoboken, swinging terrified (he was afraid of heights) on a harness over a four-story shaft. That lasted three days. He unloaded crates of books at a Manhattan publisher's office until the futility of it all got to him—and he wound up back on the Hoboken docks. This time, at least, tedium replaced terror. Here was a foretaste of a dropout's future: In United Fruit's freighter holds, on the night shift and in the dead of winter, Frank removed parts of condenser units, cleaned and replaced them. Over and over again. For anyone who's ever done physical labor for hourly pay, Sisyphus is no myth. Did he gaze across the river at the brilliant towers, lit from beneath in Art Deco fashion, dreaming of the justice that would be his when he was rich and powerful? Did he hear Bing's golden voice in his head as he unscrewed and re-screwed the condenser tubes?

Of course he did. He was frequently seen, in those days, not only smoking a pipe like his idol but also wearing a white yachting cap with gold filigree.[2] In addition, according to a female friend of the time, Frankie, in his nonworking hours, dressed in much the same style as, and every bit as well as, the college boys at Stevens Institute, up on the hill. (One of the more unpleasant features of manual labor, for him, must have been the dirt. Like Dolly, who had Chit-U on tap to mop and dust, Frank was a neat freak.[3] One good reason for a large wardrobe was that he always had something clean to wear.)

In his mind he was a Personage. He had wheels, he had threads, he had a dream. In his mind, all that business on the docks, the drudgery, was just an illusion, like some dingy version of the veil of Maya.

He didn't last long at any of the jobs, but he wasn't idle. Even if he was only a singer by his own nomination, a singer had to sing. It was an era of live music, and Hoboken was full of bands: at school dances, political clubs, taverns. Frankie idolized real musicians, sought their company constantly. Sometimes they brushed him off; sometimes they indulged him. He had a way of insinuating himself; Dolly helped him out. She could never help spoiling him. He knew instrumentalists were always hungry for orchestrations, and so he hit her up for them. A dollar here, a dollar there—soon he had a sheaf of arrangements. And if he provided the charts, occasionally the bands were kind enough to let him sing along.[4] Just like Rudy Vallée (and like Crosby in his early days), Frankie vocalized through a megaphone, microphones being an expensive rarity then. The neighborhood boys used to try to pitch pennies into his mouth through the megaphone—a fat target.

His pretensions didn't sit well with a lot of people. Who the hell did he think he was, strutting around Hoboken in fancy duds and a yachting cap? (He also used to loll around on the stoop plunking on the ukulele that an uncle had given him.) When he brought home musicians to jam, Marty made them play in the basement. Even Dolly got fed up. "When she saw Crosby's picture on Frank's bedroom wall," a relative recalled, "she threw a shoe at her son and called him a bum."

Marty went her one further. One morning at breakfast, he looked coolly at his son and told him to get out of the house. "I remember the moment," Sinatra told Bill Boggs in a 1975 television interview. "He got a little bit fed up with me, because I just wasn't going out looking for work. [Instead] at night, I [was], you know, singing with the bands— for nothing, so I could get the experience. And he, on this particular morning, said to me, 'Why don't you just get out of the house and go out on your own.' That's really what he said. 'Get out.' I think the egg was stuck in here for about twenty minutes . . . My mother, of course, was nearly in tears. But we agreed that it might be a good thing. Then I packed up the small suitcase that I had and I came to New York."

My mother, of course, was nearly in tears. We agreed that it might be a good thing. I packed up the small suitcase that I had . . . Here is a scene from an old family melodrama: the mother dabbing her eyes with her apron; the implacable father, an arm thrown out to one side, index finger pointed at the door; the shamefaced son standing with his head bowed. (That small suitcase is the real killer.) The actual scene was probably slightly less genteel: more likely, Dolly's mouth fell open with surprise at the sound of Marty speaking up. Those two words, however—"Get out"—ring absolutely true.

Where, exactly, Frankie went after he stepped off the Hoboken Ferry (fare, four cents) at Twenty-third Street and what, precisely, he did during his mini-exile—not to mention just how long he was gone—remain a mystery. It seems certain he crossed the river to the Emerald City for a short spell, that he made some sort of stab at singing there, and that he failed miserably. He returned home with his tail between his legs. In 1962, Sinatra laid down a considerably more glamorous-sounding official version for the starry-eyed English writer Robin Douglas-Home. "It was when I left home for New York that I started singing seriously," he said—perhaps giving Douglas-Home a piercing glance with those laser-blues to make sure he was getting it all down. "I was seventeen then, and I went around New York singing with little groups in road-houses. The word would get around that there was a kid in the neighborhood who could sing. Many's the time I worked all night for nothing. Or maybe I'd sing for a sandwich or cigarettes—all night for three packets. But I worked on one basic theory—stay active, get as much practice as you can. I got to know a song-plugger called Hank Sanicola . . . and he used to give me fifty cents or a dollar some weeks to buy some food. For some reason he always had terrific faith in me."

Looking beyond the improbability of roadhouses in New York (at least after the nineteenth century) and the self-aggrandizement of the word's supposedly getting around, what seems most clear from this slightly jumbled account is that Sinatra was rewriting his past to make himself look more precocious than he actually was.[5] The little groups, the roadhouses, meeting Sanicola—all this would happen, but not for a couple more years, when Sinatra was closer to twenty. At seventeen, he may have been cocky, but he couldn't have been very confident; on his own in the big city, he wouldn't have had the emotional wherewithal or the professional smarts to figure out how to get much practice. The Apple was the toughest of tough towns, especially in the Depression, and he would have to go at it several times before he made any inroads.

As a Grand Old Man holding forth to the journalist Sidney Zion, on the occasion of the first Libby Zion Lecture at Yale Law School in 1986, Sinatra painted the perfect motion-picture ending to his brief foray into Manhattan: "On Christmas Eve I went home to visit my folks and there was the hugging and the make-up."

Perhaps it really was a visit and not an abject (and probably famished) retreat. Perhaps it was a beautiful combination of the Return of the Prodigal and *It's a Wonderful Life*—though it's much easier to imagine Dolly giving him a sharp slap (now that he was too old for the billy club). Marty would have felt guilty about losing his temper with the boy; Dolly (after the slap) would have fixed him a hell of a meal.

Yet what seems certain is that both parents had come to a realization: they had a strange duck on their hands. The boy, God help him, really did want to sing. There would be no further trips to the docks or the publisher's warehouse.

———

Some say he borrowed the $65 from Dolly; some say, more convincingly, that she simply gave it to him. In any case, $65 was a lot of money in 1934, the equivalent of over a thousand today, a very decent couple of weeks' wages for anybody fortunate enough to be employed in that very unfortunate year. The money went for a sound system: a microphone connected by a cable to a small amplifier. The amplifier had vacuum tubes inside: after you clicked the on switch, the tubes took a minute or so to warm up, the tiny filaments gradually glowing bright orange. The speaker was covered with sparkly fabric—very classy-looking. At the height of his career, Sinatra liked to use a mike that was as unobtrusive as possible—black was the preferred color— to give the illusion that his hand was empty, that he was connecting directly with the audience. That was at the height of his career. This early microphone would have been neither black nor unobtrusive. But it was a microphone.

It meant so much more than not getting any more pennies thrown into his mouth. It meant power. Dressing like Bing was just the beginning of his transformation: what Frankie discovered, as he used the mike, was that it *was* his instrument, as surely as a pianist's piano or a saxophonist's sax. It carried his voice, which was still relatively thin and small, over the big sound of the band, straight to the kids in the back of the room—particularly the female kids in the back of the room.

For that was the power of the microphone: not just its symbolic force as an object, but the literal power it projected. Like a gun, it made the weak strong; it turned a runt with scars and a starved triangular face into . . . what?

Into a dream lover, was what. The quality of a man's voice is one of the primal signals to a woman's brain—it goes right in there and messes with the circuitry. It tells her stories, stories about all the wondrous things he'll do for her . . . and to her. All at once, this dropout, this punk who was so going nowhere that Marie Roemer turned up her turned-up nose at him, had been alchemized into—well, into something else. Those blue eyes, formerly merely insolent, were suddenly compelling . . . And he was so thin! One night at a school dance, while he was trying to hold a note, his voice caught out of sheer nervousness, and—ever watchful—he got a load of what it did to the girls: they melted. This was a boy who clearly needed to be taken care of.

He filed away the memory.

Little Frankie wasn't going nowhere anymore. Even though it was still far from clear just where he might be going.

When Marty wasn't looking, Dolly slipped him a few more dollars for additional orchestrations. Now the musicians, hesitant at first, began to flock to him. He had charts, he had equipment, he had a car. He didn't have much of a voice, but things being what they were, he played school dances and social halls and Democratic Party meetings and the Hoboken Sicilian Cultural League, singing mostly Crosby numbers: "Please" and "I Found a Million-Dollar Baby (in a Five-and-Ten-Cent Store)" and "June in January" and "Love in Bloom." And—in his head at least—he really did feel like Bing up there, the mike allowing his voice to glide smoothly over the horns and piano and drums . . .

That summer he took a vacation. Not that he was exactly working his fingers to the bone, but it was summertime, vacation time, so he went to the beach—*down the shore,* as they say in Jersey: to Long Branch, where Dolly's sister Josie Monaco was renting a place. It was his nineteenth summer, and he was finally a young man, no longer a boy—broader in the shoulders, deeper voiced. With a dark tan (he loved the beach and the sun) setting off those eyes, his hair floppy on top and razor trimmed on the sides, he cut a striking figure.

Across the street was a girl.

"All life's grandeur," Robert Lowell wrote, "is something with a girl in summer." She was a little thing, dark haired, tan, and cute.

Nanicia—Americanized to Nancy Rose. Just seventeen that summer.

The clingy tang of salt air, the pearly morning light, the faint sound of someone's radio carrying on the breeze. Bing. Oh God, that voice of his. The feeling of the warm, pebbly asphalt on the bare soles of his feet. She sat on the porch of the big house, watching him.

Maybe he called to her; maybe she pretended not to notice.

Later in the day, after the beach, he stopped by again, and there she was again, same wicker rocking chair, same nail file.

He ducked into Josie's house and returned holding something behind his back. Now he brought out the ukulele, strummed, and sang:

> It was a lucky April shower,
> It was a most convenient door.

It wasn't a bad voice at all: boyish, yearning. It made her feel nice to listen to it. In a minute her sisters and cousins were staring out the windows.

Frankie had never had a steady girl before. This one came with a lot of strings attached: strict father; big, noisy family. Lots of people at the dinner table, lots of questions. Opera always playing somewhere. He loved it. He felt as if he'd finally come indoors from the cold, into a warm, crowded room. Home.

He would have whispered his most deeply held dream to her: he wanted to be a singer.

And she would have responded, instantly and sincerely, that she believed in him.

In September, back home, he had to keep seeing her. Her and that big household, five sisters and a brother, just a hop, skip, and a jump away, in a nice big house, with a front porch, on Arlington Avenue in Jersey City. The house and the girl: both pulled him equally. But with sisters giggling behind hands and furtive necking on the couch after the house was quiet—with all this came assessment, and rules.

Mike Barbato, a plastering contractor and self-made man, looked the world right in the eye, and he knew that ukulele strumming did not make the world go around. This Sinatra kid was cute, and respectful enough when he talked to Mike. But real respect would mean holding down a steady job—which, it looked like, the kid had absolutely no intention of doing. Mike popped the question one night after dinner, leaning back in his chair at the head of the big table, loosening his belt, and picking at his eyetooth, where the meat always caught.

So, Frankie (he'd certainly have asked). What are you doing for work these days?

A proud smile: he had a job singing at the Cat's Meow Friday night, Mr. B.

Mike gave him that dark-eyed stare. And what about Monday morning?

This stopped him for a second. He didn't like mornings. Or Mondays, for that matter.

The women were in the kitchen; for the moment it was just the two of them at the table. Mike leaned toward the kid with a regretful smile. No work, no Nancy.

And so, at an ungodly hour on Monday morning, Frankie reported for duty as a plasterer's assistant on a repair job in Jersey City. Wearing a white hat and overalls, gamely laboring alongside Nancy's brother, Bart. And Monday afternoon, he limped home, covered head to toe with the smelly white stuff and hurting in every part of his body.

He went through two weeks of it, doing work that Mike always had to do over. Then, one morning, he accidentally overslept. He decided to take the day off. The next one too.

It was the last day job he would ever have.

But now he was no longer welcome at Arlington Avenue. Now he and Nancy had to neck in his car, which was cramped and embarrassing—once a Jersey City cop rapped on the glass with his nightstick at the worst possible moment—or down in his basement, with Dolly clomping around upstairs.

In the meantime, he wasn't letting the grass grow under his feet. He kept foisting himself on the attention of every musician in Hoboken. He entered an amateur contest at the State Theater in Jersey City, and won. He darkened the door of radio station WAAT, also in Jersey City, until, in April 1935, they vouchsafed him a precious (and unpaid) weekly fifteen minutes of airtime. He took along a pal, guitarist Matty Golizio, as an accompanist. (In a few years Golizio would be playing on Sinatra's Columbia recordings.) We'll never know just what he sang, but we do have the testimony of his oldest friend, Tony Macagnano, as to how he sounded. "You'd better quit," Tony Mac told his pal. "Boy, you were terrible."

Maybe he was; maybe he wasn't. His voice was thin and high, but he had nerve and a sense of style and—you're born with it or you're not—he could sing on key. He was unformed, but he wasn't clueless. Maybe Tony Mac was just jealous.

And maybe if the right someone heard him on the air, big things would happen.

Dolly, touched by his initiative, leaned hard on Joseph Samperi, the owner of the Union Club, a big, classy nightspot on Hudson Street, to give her son a regular singing job. Samperi, owing her a favor or two, relented. For a while, Frankie crooned there five nights a week, but he was more impatient than grateful: The place lacked what the top clubs had then, a telephone-wire hookup to a New York radio station. None of the Jersey couples out on that dance floor was in a position to advance his career.

Three of the musicians Frankie pestered that spring had a much better gig. They were a singing trio, Italian boys known all too presciently as the Three Flashes: Fred Tamburro, James "Skelly"

Petrozelli, and Pat Principe were their names. Lost to history except as Sinatra witnesses. For a minute and a half in the mid-1930s they were hot stuff. Warm, anyway. Every weekend the Flashes traveled up the road to Englewood Cliffs, just north of the spanking-new George Washington Bridge, to perform with Harold Arden and His Orchestra at a western-style nightclub on the Palisades called the Rustic Cabin. The Cabin didn't pay much, but what it did have was a wire hookup to WNEW, which—with its live remote broadcasts from New York–area nightclubs, as well as Martin Block's *Make-Believe Ballroom*—was, by its own admission, "The NEWest Thing in Radio!"[6] For their gigs, the Flashes borrowed a car or, more frequently, hitched a ride with an indulgent musician. Still, indulgence had a way of wearing thin. Once or twice they'd had to take a cab all the way from Hoboken, eating up the evening's profits. With what they were making, it would be a long time before any of them could afford wheels of his own.

Then came salvation, in the form of this pesky runt.

Little Frankie wanted in the worst way to become the fourth Flash. Sure—like that was about to happen. But when it turned out that Frankie Boy had a green Chrysler convertible, the Flashes got a lot more encouraging.

Watch and learn. Soak it all in for a little while.

He saw it and he wanted it: saw himself, so clearly, standing center stage in the Cabin, the mike beaming his voice to millions of people out in the night, including, of course, People Who Mattered.

Then a remarkable thing happened.

One Friday night while the Flashes were taking five, a sharply dressed fellow came up and handed them a business card. The card belonged to Major Bowes, who, with his *Original Amateur Hour*— the *American Idol* of the day—was the hottest thing on radio, all over the country, not just in New York. The Major was going to shoot some movie shorts, at the Biograph Studios in the Bronx, and he wanted the Flashes, who had cute, guinea-boy face appeal (not that he would have put it in precisely those terms to their faces[7]), to appear in one or two.

They slapped each other on the back in the parking lot. Frankie watched enviously, his pulse racing. This was It.

He piped up and asked them to give him a shot.

They looked at each other. Well, they needed a ride home, anyway. They'd think about it.

He knew how long they'd think about it.

He told Dolly the next morning that he wanted this more than anything he'd ever wanted before. Anything.

And what did the fucking no-good bastards tell him?

They told him they'd think about it.

Dolly marched. The Tamburros—eight kids and two exhausted, non-English-speaking parents—lived in a railroad flat on Adams Street in Little Italy. Freddie, with his crazy singing, was kicking a little money into the family till. Dolly paid Mr. and Mrs. T. a visit, to make sure they fully understood the value of her good works—translation, authoritative intercession with landlords, school officials, cops, and so on. Except that this time it wasn't a Democratic vote she was seeking.

Frankie was in.

Every day for a week, grinning at the wheel of the Chrysler, he drove his fellow Flashes over the great shining bridge (just four years old; an architectural marvel) to Tremont Avenue in the Bronx, home of Biograph. The movie shorts in question—it was an unapologetic era— were a filmed minstrel show. Every day Frankie painted on blackface and big white lips and donned a top hat. He didn't sing, but he acted (playing a waiter), and *he was in the movies!*

But that was only the beginning. After seeing the footage, the Major himself sent word up to the Bronx: he wanted to audition the Flashes for his nationally broadcast radio show.

Tamby, Skelly, and Pat talked among themselves, grumbled. They wanted in the worst way to shake this superfluous banana off the tree. Across the studio floor, Frankie got a gander at the confab, knew at once what was going on.

This time Dolly didn't have to march. She sent word via drugstore telephone to a friend on Adams Street, who passed the word to the phone-less Tamburros, in Mezzogiorno dialect: *Dolly Sinatra would be very disappointed if her son were not included in the audition for the great Major Bowes.* No visit necessary this time; her absence as effective as her presence.

And so the four of them gathered, wearing budget-busting white suits with black silk pocket squares, in Major Bowes's midtown office, in—of course—the Chrysler Building. As they cooled their heels nervously in the waiting room, the door popped open, startling them all. It was the Major himself, gray haired and dyspeptic, with a big red nose and a square jaw and a dark three-piece suit like a senator in the movies. Like W. C. Fields without a sense of humor. His eyes were old and watery; a faint distillery smell hung about him.

They jumped to their feet, shook his hand.

And what did the boys call themselves again?

The Thr—— uh, Four Flashes.

Hmm.

They looked at each other while he stroked his chin. And shook his head. His personality, all business, was not what you'd call electric. But he was *Major Bowes.*

The Four Flashes sounded like the Hot Flashes. Or the Four-Flushers. Where were they from?

Thus the freshly christened Hoboken Four (though tiny Patty Principe was technically from West New York) filed into Bowes's office and cleared their throats to sing. Their audition piece was "The Curse of an Aching Heart," a syrupy, barbershop relic from 1913.[8] The Major liked them but hated the song.

He'd put them on. But they'd need something more up-to-date. Something to lift the hearts of Mr. and Mrs. America.

When they reconvened, Frankie pulled out his ace in the hole, sheet music for "Shine," a big hit for Bing Crosby and the Mills Brothers a couple of years earlier. It was a minstrel song, all about curly hair and pearly teeth and shiny shoes and not much else, an ideal vehicle for the wildly talented, instrument-imitating (and African-American) Millses, who pumped along in close-harmony background while Bing led, then scatted his fool head off. A white man scatting!

Frankie told his fellow Flashes that he could do Bing's part.

The other three looked at each other. He had them over a barrel and they knew it. He had the sheet music and the car and he could sing. The worm had officially turned.

On September 8, 1935, a Sunday evening, Frankie stood in the wings of the Capitol Theater at Fifty-first and Broadway with the other former Flashes, literally unable to stop his knees from shaking. It was the second-largest theater in the entire world, at fifty-three hundred seats—five aisles in the orchestra, an ocean of faces out there. The fact that the Roxy, a block south, was a few hundred seats bigger was no consolation. Frankie's nerves were like nothing he had ever felt before. Even the stolid Major, he'd noticed before the show, was giving off an extra-strong whiskey odor.

But once the show began, Major Edward Bowes strode out to the center of the stage as if he owned the place (which, in point of fact, he did), took his position beside the big gong,[9] and—as the buzzing crowd obediently went dead silent—spoke firmly into the microphone. "Good evening, ladies and gentlemen, and welcome to the *Original Amateur Hour*." He sounded like a tired old insurance salesman, but—Frankie peeped out through a crack in the curtain—the audience gazed up at him as if he were Jesus Christ himself. It hit him: Every goddamn sound that went into that big square mike was emanating out to the whole goddamn country. And half the people in the goddamn country wanted to be where he was right now. When their turn came, Frankie's stomach rose up and fluttered away like a little bird. He wanted to flee, but didn't think his legs would carry him.

". . . Hoboken Four, singing and dancing fools," the Major announced.

A little wise guy they'd met before the show, his name lost to history, piped up from the wings: Why did the Major call them fools?

The sour-faced Bowes actually gave a half smile. "I don't know," he said. "I guess 'cause they're so happy."

And with that as their cue, Fred, Skelly, and Pat skipped out onto the giant stage like schoolboys on holiday, Frankie trying his best to walk along behind them.

The Major greeted them. Why not introduce themselves and tell the folks where they worked? This last, of course, was key to establishing their amateur status. Frankie saw Tamby taking charge, doing all the talking, but didn't hear the words that were coming out. All he was aware of was the roar of blood in his ears and the voice in his head: *What, in Christ's name, could Tamby say about* him?

Nothing, as it turned out. After a deadly second of dead air, suddenly ten thousand eyes were staring at little Frank Sinatra.

"What about him?" the Major said.

"Oh, he never worked a day in his life," Tamby said.

4

||||||||||||

The Hoboken Four on Major Bowes's *Original Amateur Hour,* circa 1935. Left to right: Fred Tamburro, Pat Principe, Bowes, "Skelly" Petrozelli, Frank.

And then they sang, thank God, for that was one thing Frank knew how to do. Or thought he did: while the other three tootled along, doing their best Mills Brothers imitation, Frankie, trying to keep the smile fixed on his lips, jumped in with the nearest thing to Bing's improvising he could muster:

Just because—my hair is curly
Just because—my teeth are pearly.

And yet, more clearly than ever, he realized that what Crosby made sound like falling off a log was in fact nigh unto unattainable: the absolute ease and richness of the voice, the effortless skipping around the beat, never ever putting a foot wrong.

It simply wasn't Frank. Ease wasn't his to feel or feign; singing was an urgent matter. A personal matter. Vocalizing in chorus was possible, though not desirable. Skipping around the beat was somebody else's idea of fun.

He did his best.

Which, miraculously, was all right. The gong never sounded! And when the four of them finally finished, the gigantic beast out in the dark—ten thousand eyes, ears, hands—exploded with delight, sending the needle on the big onstage applause meter far over to the right and keeping it there. The Major looked pleased. He kept nodding, like the old snake-oil salesman he was. These fellows had "walked right into the hearts of their audience."

═══

Amazingly enough, they had. They had won the contest. The radio-audience votes out in America agreed with the meter: the night of September 8, 1935, belonged to the Hoboken Four. Which entitled them to become a cog in the great Bowes machine. Entertainment colossus that he was, the Major ran a small army of *Original Amateur Hour* companies, conglomerations of acts that had succeeded on the show, whom he then signed to crisscross the nation by bus and train, entertaining burgs large and small, generating a steady river of cash, and keeping the Bowes brand name ever fresh. It was a brilliant idea, allowing the Major to stay close to the home office in New York while he raked in the hundreds of thousands. Fifty simoleons per week of which, apiece, now went to the Hoboken Four—meals, accommodations, and travel included. One week after their radio performance, they joined the Major Bowes Number Five tour unit, a motley troupe of bell ringers, jug blowers, harmonica players, yodelers . . . hard-r'd characters from out in the country someplace, among whom four Italian boys from Hoboken, New Jersey, might as well have come from— well, from Italy.

Which was not necessarily a bad thing, at least in Frankie's case. After a couple of stops he learned to tell people—girls especially—that Hoboken was really, basically, the same thing as New York City. It was a big, wide, lonely country in those days, a poor one too, and folks out in the hinterlands were starving for any diversion from their stifling, peeling-wallpaper-and-coal-stove lives. New York was magic; New York was the theater and radio, men in tuxedos and women in clinging white silk. Frankie may not have looked like Gary Cooper or Dick Powell—he looked like he could use a meal, and a hug. But he was from New York.

And he could sing. Even the original Flashes finally had to admit that: the farther they got on this cockamamie bus-and-train tour—Des Moines and Wichita and Oakland and Vancouver and Bellingham, Washington—the farther they got, the more comfortable Frankie became with his voice, and the more they realized he really *should* be the one in front. He felt what he sang, he had a way of getting inside it—which translated, once the evening's entertainment was over, into a way of getting into the pants of the hick girls that gathered down at the front of the orchestra.

Oddly enough, this was all new to Frank. He may have lost his cherry to some girl on a Hoboken roof or on the beach down the shore in Long Branch, but he had certainly never had intercourse with a woman in a bed before. Now he was having a lot of it, in a lot of beds, with a lot of women—young ones mainly, but some older ones too, including married ones whose husbands happened to be out during the day. Now and then he thought about Nancy—with whom he'd gone just a little way down this road—but her image was quickly dimming. He was getting a rapid education in the wide range of female sexual response and emotional variability. There was just one common denominator: they all liked him, a lot.

He wasn't much to look at—beyond the facial scars, he was still plagued with fairly severe acne—but his mouth, with its slight up curve at the corners and its extravagantly rich and wide, slightly jutting lower lip, was beautifully formed, and his eyes—those eyes!—were a little bit wild. None of the boys in Des Moines or Oakland or Bellingham looked like that.

The question of his body must also be addressed, now being as good a time as any.

Naked, Frank Sinatra stood five feet seven and a half inches tall. This was his full adult stature; he would never grow even a quarter inch more, though in later years he would give his height variously as five nine, five ten, even five eleven—the maximum he could stretch the truth without pretending to a patently absurd six feet. In later years, he wore lifts in his shoes that got him up to five nine or so; his fearsome presence, and the intense reluctance of the world at large to challenge him on any matter, made up the difference.

In an era when the average height of an adult male was five nine, there was nothing very wrong with five feet seven and a half inches. But he was also skinny, so skinny, with the kind of metabolism—as a young man, at least—that made it difficult to keep weight on, let alone gain it. He was not especially broad shouldered. He was also narrow at the hips, and his gluteus maximus was *minimus*—he was completely flat fannied. (And, throughout his young manhood and early middle age, self-conscious about it.) His hands and feet were well formed; in fact his hands—unlike, say, Mike Barbato's—were soft, padded, artistic-looking: most definitely not made for manual labor. Clean, always. Sometimes they grew chapped from the many times he washed them throughout the day. His fingernails, throughout his life, were always exquisitely manicured.

Naked, Frank Sinatra was a fairly unexceptional specimen. Except.

It is literally central, an integral part of the lore, beginning with the frequently disinhibited Ava Gardner's legendary comment (so good that she must have said it—or someone improved it along the way)—"There's only ten pounds of Frank, but there's a hundred and ten pounds of cock"—and continuing, in later years, with the graphic and admiring testimony of Sinatra's valet, George Jacobs, who revealed in his charming memoir that the thing was so big, Mr. S. had to have special underwear made to keep it in check.

Macrophallus is the medical term: a peculiar condition, ostensibly enviable. Every man has witnessed it at one time or another: that college acquaintance, say, a small and skinny and otherwise totally unprepossessing fellow, emerging quite startlingly from the shower in a dorm bathroom . . .

By some evidence, Sinatra was proud of his extraordinary endowment: he is even said to have called his penis Big Frankie. (Unlike the little Frankie it hung from.) On the other hand, much testimony suggests that throughout his life, he was ambivalent at best about his physical self. His height. His flat behind. His facial scars. His receding, then vanishing, hairline. "I hate your husband," he once told the actress Betty Garrett, who was married to the actor Larry Parks. "He has what I call a noble head. I've got a head like a walnut."

He may have had similarly mixed feelings about Big Frankie. After all, the special underwear cited by George Jacobs was a cosmetic as well as a physical accommodation: Sinatra didn't want to attract undue attention while wearing close-cut tuxedo trousers.

Sinatra's lovers, too, may have had mixed feelings: contrary to the worries of insecure men (in other words, most men), not every woman is crazy about the idea of a big member, which, even if visually stimulating, can be an impediment to lovemaking. History itself is indecisive on the subject. None of the Don Juan stories seem to be anatomically specific. Greek myth, on the other hand, rarely holds back—the god Priapus is said to have had a penis so large that no woman wanted to sleep with him. On the other hand, Petronius's *Satyricon* tells of a rural youth so well-endowed that the locals revered him, literally tripping over each other to touch it for good luck.

Oh, Frankie . . .

But Frankie had something more than physical presence: when he was onstage, every one of them, every last one, believed, to the core of her being, that he was singing to her and her alone.

═══

The Hoboken Three, the original Flashes, didn't like that very much. They weren't liking Frankie Boy too much in general, if the truth be told. Especially Tamby and Skelly. Patty Principe, just five one in his shoes, was cheerful and even tempered. But Freddie Tamburro and Skelly Petrozelli were bruisers, truck drivers both of them, and not at all bad-looking, either. What was the skinny runt with the pizza face doing outshining them on the stage and getting all the tail afterward? They took to laying a beating on him now and then, just to show him who was boss. Once, Tamby knocked him out cold. So much for Marty's boxing lessons.

And Frankie—you could hardly blame him—didn't enjoy it at all. In fact he was pretty damn sick of the Number Five tour unit: of living in YMCAs and cheap rooming houses and fleabag hotels, of eating lunch-counter food for dinner. He liked all the sex just fine, but the beatings pretty much counterbalanced that.

And another thing: the original Flashes weren't doing too much for him professionally anymore. He knew (and the audiences' reactions, especially the women's, confirmed it for him) that he had more talent in his left pinkie than all three of them put together. They could beat him up all they wanted, but they couldn't beat that out of him.

In mid-December, soon after his twentieth birthday, he left the tour in Columbus, Ohio, and went back home to Hoboken. Just in time, once more, for Christmas.

It wasn't a defeat but a strategic withdrawal. For four years he had been chasing after far lesser musicians like a pesky mascot. Now—in his mind, at least—the shoe was on the other foot.

═══

His homecoming this time was a good deal more subdued. He was back, he was twenty, and he was unemployed—a potentially volatile situation, as we've seen, at 841 Garden Street. Dolly was moderately impressed by his run with Bowes, but What Have You Done for Me Lately? could have been the woman's middle name. That big mortgage still needed paying, there was still a depression on, and everyone on the premises still had to pull his weight, and then some. As for Marty, what he thought (as far as anybody could tell) was: radio or no radio, the kid continued to stand a good chance of turning into a bum.

Amazingly, Frankie would live under his parents' roof for three more years.

But he wasn't malingering—quite the opposite. Motivated as much by anxiety as ambition, he shifted into high gear, exploring every conceivable singing opportunity in North Jersey, paid and unpaid—and in the process, staying out of the house as much as possible. He did $2-a-night gigs at the Elks; he worked again at the Cat's Meow and the Union Club (whose owners could now advertise "Major Bowes Radio Winner"[1]); he took his mike and sparkly speaker to political rallies and weddings; he dragged Matty Golizio back to WAAT in Jersey City.

But, most important, he now had the maturity and knowledge to begin his assault on Manhattan. If the years 1935 through 1937 were, as Sinatra later said, his "panic period," they were also a time of intense connection—the kind of connection that simply wasn't possible on the left bank of the Hudson. Jersey certainly had talented musicians, but the Big Apple was a different universe, and Tin Pan Alley, just north of Times Square, was the red-hot center of it.

It was also a moment of intense transition for the music business: a business that, for over half a century, had been built upon the sale of sheet music—the content of the day—to the piano-playing, parlor-singing American public. Now, with the rise of radio and phonograph records, power had shifted to the bandleaders who conveyed the content—and, still to a lesser extent in the 1930s, the band singers. Few, if any, important vocalists were out on their own yet. The music publishers of Tin Pan Alley employed singer–piano players (the so-called song pluggers, most of them themselves aspiring songwriters) to sell the publishers' songs to the performers.

Sinatra was barely a performer. In the universe of the music business, he was just a cosmic speck, one of the hundreds of "kolos"—the term of art in those days for wannabe singers and musicians—who haunted Tin Pan Alley music publishers, hoping to latch onto hot new material. In the usual food chain of the business, kolos pestered song pluggers, and song pluggers looked over the kolos' shoulders for somebody really important. But here was a kolo who acted as if he already were important, strutting around announcing to one and all that whatever the current reality, he was going to be the next big singer.

Two pluggers in particular were impressed. One, a short, stocky kid from the Bronx with a prematurely receding hairline and the arms of a blacksmith, was named Hank Sanicola. The other, a tall kid from upstate New York with a brilliant keyboard technique and an equally recessive hairline, had the improbable moniker of Chester Babcock. His *nom de piano* was Jimmy Van Heusen.

Both, like Sinatra, were in their early twenties; each would become central in the singer's life. Sanicola was a salt-of-the-earth character, a workmanlike aspiring songwriter who knew enough about music to understand his limitations, and to recognize real talent when he heard it. Van Heusen had real talent.

Edward Chester Babcock, of Syracuse, was a paradox: foul-mouthed, obsessed with sex and alcohol, but a songwriter of deep and delicate gifts, verging on genius. Some of the melodies that would one day make his reputation had been in his head since puberty. Meanwhile, he bided his time trying to sell other men's tunes at Remick and Company, the music publisher.

While Van Heusen watched for his shot as an in-house songwriter, he sat at his piano facing a daily tide of would-be bandleaders and vocalists. One of the latter was this starved-looking kid from Hoboken, so cocky he walked around in a yachting cap in imitation of his idol Bing Crosby. Van Heusen listened to the kid, and liked what he heard. He liked Frank Sinatra, period. The two young men (Jimmy was about three years older) had much in common: an eye for the ladies, a night-owl disposition, a sardonic sense of humor. Soon Chester (as Jimmy's close friends called him) was running with Sinatra and Sani- cola.

Physically speaking, either Hank or Chester could have snapped Frank in two, could have wiped the floor with him the way Tamby and Skelly had, if they felt like it. But they didn't feel like it.

Instead, they listened to him, smiled when he barked. The guy was a pussy magnet, it was as simple as that.

Manhattan in those days was a hotbed of great jazz: Jimmy Dorsey at the New Yorker Hotel, Tommy Dorsey and Artie Shaw at the Manhattan Room of the Hotel Pennsylvania. You could stroll down Fifty-second Street at 2:00 a.m. and pop into Leon and Eddie's or the Famous Door or the Onyx Club, and see, and hear, Fats Waller, Art Tatum, Count Basie, Louis Prima. This was Sinatra's Moveable Feast, a time and place he would remember forever.

The jazz was thrilling, but what he loved most were the singers. The clubs on Fifty-second Street, most of them small and intimate, featured them heavily. He heard the great Ethel Waters, who could break your heart with a ballad or scat like Louis Armstrong; there was a young black Englishwoman named Mabel Mercer who spoke the lyrics more than sang them, and with such beautiful diction. And then there was Billie Holiday. Just twenty, only eight months older than Sinatra, she was—quite unlike him—an astonishingly mature artist, with a fully formed style. Barely out of her teens, she sang like a woman who had been around awhile, and in fact she had: her history made Sinatra look like the spoiled rich boy he almost was. She had been born out of wed- lock to a thirteen-year-old mother impregnated by a sixteen-year-old banjo player, had been brought up in a Baltimore slum, been raped twice before the age of fifteen, had worked as a prostitute and done jail time. She began singing for tips in Harlem clubs; in 1933, the Columbia Records artists and repertoire man John Hammond discovered her at one of them, and immediately started her recording with Benny Goodman. She was eighteen. Two years later, when Sinatra first saw her, probably at the Famous Door, she was singing with Jimmy Van Heusen's idol the great pianist Teddy Wilson. Chester boasted he could play almost as well as Teddy.

Frankie wished he could sing like Billie. He gazed at her. She was extraordinary-looking: slim and straight, with honey-colored skin, high cheekbones, something Indian around the flashing eyes. Dark lipstick and white white teeth. Perhaps by merging with her, he could somehow take in her sorcery. Even more than Waters or Mercer, she lived in the lyric, made you ache its ache, while skipping around the music's beat like some kind of goddess of the air, landing just where she pleased. And as was not the case with Ethel Waters or Mabel Mercer, Billie Holiday brought sex—painful, longing sex—into every syllable of her songs.

He wanted her even though (maybe a little because) she was what Marty would call a *mulignane.* A *moolie,* an eggplant. His eyes stung at the sheer stupidity of it, boiling someone down to the color of her skin—and eggplant was all wrong anyway. He'd been called wop and dago enough times to know all the names were bullshit. He knew dumb wops and micks and kikes and niggers, and he knew plenty of smart ones too—and there was brown-skinned Teddy Wilson, with his mustache and cigarette and haughty squint, sitting like a king at his keyboard. And Billie, making everyone in the joint fall in love with her.

Someday, someday, maybe he could sing like that.

===

Not yet, though. His voice was still thin and high, stuck in his throat. Sanicola, who had a little money in his pocket (and slipped Frankie a buck or two here and there), told him he knew a singing teacher, said he would stake him to a lesson or two. He had to get that voice down into his chest somehow.

The teacher had him sing scales while he, the teacher, played the piano—boring but necessary—and taught him where his diaphragm was. But it turned out the lessons were $2 for forty-five minutes: a fucking fortune, the price of a good meal at Horn & Hardart's Automat, and Frank didn't want to have to choose between eating and singing.

The teacher passed him along to another coach desperate enough to charge half the price.

John Quinlan had sung tenor for the Metropolitan Opera before getting bounced for drinking. Even now, at 10:00 a.m., he had that Major Bowes barroom bouquet about him. He was a big, solid fellow, his thin sandy hair slicked straight back from a high forehead, his collar slightly askew around a meager tie knot, plenty of dandruff on his shoulders. He spoke with an English accent that wasn't quite English—there was something tough about it. Irish? Turned out he was Australian, far from home. Quinlan listened to Frank sing, and nodded.

There was something to work with; that was a relief. But the first thing they *had* to do was get him to stop sounding like a stevedore from—where the Christ did he say he was from?

Week in and week out, Frankie did the vocal exercise: "Let us wander by the bay," running up the scale and back down, in all twelve keys. Quinlan could do accents, could mimic Caruso in perfect Italian, sing *Carmen* in French, speak the King's English. He taught Sinatra that "brother" had an *r* at the end, a *th* in the middle. "While" began with an exhalation, as if the *h* came first.

Puff the air out, Frank.

Frank needed to work on his *t*'s—the tip of his tongue was touching the back of his teeth instead of the roof of his mouth. Crisp *t*'s, Frank. Tut tut tut.

Dut dut dut.

And so—even though his *t*'s, over the next sixty years, would never become entirely crisp—the Hoboken began to drain from his voice.

Not in day-to-day speech; rather, it was a trick, something he could, increasingly, do at will. At first, though, it drew the discomfiture of old friends and acquaintances. But even as they mocked him, they envied him. Suddenly he could sound almost like the people in the movies and on the radio: people who were never without a trenchant observation or a witty rejoinder, people who were never sad or hard up or horny or just sitting around picking their noses, bored. Most especially, people in the movies and on the radio were never, ever bored.

Frank was singing with more confidence. He'd begun to find regions of his chest he never knew existed; his increasing poise with diction was bringing the words alive a little bit.

He learned to look at the lyric on paper and think about it. Somebody had written those words for a reason—he tried to imagine what that reason might have been. He began to see: you can't sing it if you don't understand it.

I don't want you
But I hate to lose you.

The songs were almost all about love, but the implicit and compelling argument—in that era—was that love was the ultimate human subject, and could therefore encompass absolutely any idea or shade of emotion: euphoria, sorrow, lust, hate, ambivalence, cynicism, naughty fun, surprise, surrender. The best lyricists were akin to poets. A singer who could comprehend their work would understand their brilliance and polish it, even add to it. Would, in optimal circumstances, take temporary possession of the song, making it seem like something that had just been thought up and uttered, most compellingly.

For the time being, the best Frank could hope for was to begin to understand. He saw now how hollow his earlier efforts had been—trying to ape Bing and Rudy and Russ Columbo, wanting the rewards of acclaim without truly comprehending what he was doing. He began to see the differences between poor and fair and good and great songs.

But it seemed the more he learned and the harder he tried, the less work he could find. Sometimes it felt as if he had had his shot, his moment in the national sun with the Major, and maybe it would all be downhill from there. He spent his nights at the Onyx Club and the Three Deuces on Fifty-second Street strictly as a spectator, a nobody from nowhere, his nose pressed against the glass. He was stuck in Hoboken like a fly on flypaper, still singing for chump change at bars and social clubs and weddings, and even in blackface—again—at a minstrel show sponsored by Marty's fire company. (Marty looked all too entertained.) He kept dogging the radio stations, WAAT and WOR and WNEW, offering to work for free, or for carfare, and being taken up on the offer—and then having to put his hand out to Sanicola or Dolly for walking-around money. Two breaks raised his hopes: First, his cousin Ray Sinatra, an arranger for the NBC radio house band, wangled him an audition, and he got a job on a daily fifteen-minute spot on the network—for seventy cents a week. Then he sang "Exactly Like You" (accompanying himself on the ukulele) on another amateur hour, *Town Hall Tonight,* hosted by the vinegar-pussed Fred Allen. Nothing came of it.

Then he heard about something he really wanted.

The Rustic Cabin, whose parking lot he knew all too well from his days chauffeuring the Flashes, had an opening for a singing waiter and emcee. Fifteen dollars a week—not so great, even at the bottom of the Depression. But the wire to the radio station was still there, and now the station had a new broadcast, WNEW *Dance Parade,* featuring the Cabin's band and singer. A golden opportunity. Frankie drove the familiar route up to Englewood Cliffs, strolled into the club—the dark interior had log-cabin walls, booths with high split-log partitions (ideal for tête-à-têtes and trysts), a dance floor, and a bandstand—and found himself face-to-face with Harold Arden. Not Harold Arlen the immortal songwriter, but Harold Arden the bush-league bandleader, who wore a mustache with long waxed tips and bore a passing resemblance to the supercilious actor Franklin Pangborn. Arden, for some reason, had taken an instant dislike to Sinatra: maybe it was the yachting cap; maybe it was the way he carried himself. In any case, as soon as Frankie, standing by the bored piano player, had finished singing his latest hit, "Exactly Like You," Arden gave the owner, Harry Nichols, a lemon-sucking look. Nichols took out his cigar.

They'd keep him on file.

Dolly, of course, was standing by the door when he got home, waiting to ask if he'd gotten the job. Girlie, his miniature collie, came up to greet him, and before Dolly could get the question out, Frank swooped the dog into his arms, pounded up the stairs to his room, and slammed the door.

Dolly stood in the front hall, stymied. Twenty-two years old, living at home, no trade, no money in his fucking pocket except what she put there—useless for everything, in short, except warbling tunes for spare change.

And bawling like a little girl.

Yet she knew not what he could be—she hadn't the ear for that—but that there was nothing else he could be. So he was high-strung. So what?

This time she picked up her white telephone and rang a Democratic Party pal named Harry Steeper, who was the mayor of North Bergen, between West New York and Cliffside Park. He was also head of the New Jersey musicians' union—and, as such, a good pal to James Caesar Petrillo, the man who was swiftly rising toward absolute power in the American Federation of Musicians. Petrillo was a mediocre trumpet player but, as his middle name foreordained, a vastly ambitious man whose chief abhorrence in life was the phonograph record. As James Caesar Petrillo saw it, the phonograph was an invention whose sole purpose was to put honest musicians out of work. And Petrillo (whose path would cross with Frank Sinatra's in an important way in just a few years) was a Friend of the Musician, and Harry Steeper was a friend of James C. Petrillo's.[2]

So—surprise—Frankie got the job. Harold Arden could wax the tips of his mustache with *that*.

Frank fronting Bill Henri and His Headliners at the Rustic Cabin, early 1939.
Harry James would discover Sinatra here in June.

The universe, in Dolly Sinatra's view, was a well-ordered place as
long as she had anything to do with it. Within her realm, she could
control the miracle of birth itself and all the machinations of the
day-to-day world. But certain areas threatened her: Frankie's temperament, for one. She possessed the same volcanic center, but she could
keep a lid on it. The thought of living without that control perplexed
and, at times, terrified her.

Sex was another matter, a dark force that had to be contained at all costs. With Marty, the question had long since been put to rest, but poor Chit-U was another story. Poor Chit-U, slow-witted and gimpy, was forty, well past the age when a man should have a wife. Still, one day Chit-U found a woman: a poor little wounded duck who worked behind the counter at the greengrocer, so shy she herself could barely speak. Within a few weeks he was taking her out for beers on Friday nights.

Dolly saw where it was going.

The man lived under her roof, mopped her floors, dusted her vases, and put his salary from the docks into her pocket. If a piece of heavy equipment, a pallet, or a shipping crate, God forbid, fell on Chit-U's head, the life-insurance money was hers.

Now he was using his money—which was her money—to buy drinks for this woman. Dolly knew meals and gifts would follow, and soon enough, a ring, and brats, and then his insurance would be signed over to *them*.

Dolly found out where the woman lived and went there one night, stood under her window, and shrieked abuse and obscenities at the top of her precinct captain's voice. The whole neighborhood heard the racket, the cop on the beat came by—but one sharp look from Dolly took care of *him*. She continued her shrieking; the poor little wounded bird shivered in her rented room, making the only possible assumption: *Chit-U must have a wife*.

But Frankie's stream of girls would not be stopped so easily.

A few years earlier, just before he dropped out of high school, he had gone out for a while with Marian Brush, a cute, smart Garden Street neighbor. One afternoon when the two of them came home from school, Dolly was there. Frankie, in all innocence, said he wanted to show Marian something amazing: his new radio that could pick up *Pittsburgh*.

Marian, glancing back over her shoulder as they went up the stairs, saw Dolly staring after them with an expression the girl would remember until she was an old lady: *She thought we were going up there to do it*. Just the look in Dolly's eyes made Marian feel dirty.

But Frankie would always have girls pursuing him. And the Cabin was an ideal base of operations: it was a sneak joint, a place where married men brought their girlfriends. The place oozed sex, and Frankie, showing the giggly couples to their booths in his waiter's outfit, felt horny just being there. It showed in his voice.

The lyrics had begun to mean something. *Somebody wrote that for a reason—try to imagine what that reason might have been.* The better the song, the deeper the meaning.

> *What is this thing called love?*
> *this funny thing called love?*

Feeling the words, and remembering how Billie could tell you her whole life story in the glide of a note, Frank began to sing the lyrics as if he really meant them, and something happened.

The girls, dancing with their dates, began to stop mid-step and stare at him.

═══

And Dolly knew. Which was why it was so important to push forward the Plan. She'd thought of it more than two years before, when he first brought the little mouse home: Frankie had to marry her.

She was from a good family, a family with money, with a big wooden house and five sisters who had married lawyers or accountants. Even if she wasn't beautiful, she was pretty, with a quiet dignity about her: She would make good babies; she would take care of a household.

And Nancy Barbato would never threaten Dolly's supremacy.

The Plan was accelerated when Frank met the older one. The truth of it was that there were many girls now, coming out of the cursed knotty-pine woodwork of the Rustic Cabin, bewitched by the sound of his voice. They were writing letters to him, mash notes in perfumed envelopes—Dolly stuffed them straight into the garbage, with the coffee grounds and grapefruit rinds. They were storming his front door, just as she had known they would. And the older one was the most dangerous of all: cheap trash from Lodi—her father was a rumrunner or something. She was three years Frankie's senior, Antoinette Della Penta, and pretty, but with a fucked-out look about her—she might as well have been a whore as far as Dolly was concerned. Mrs. M. Sinatra of upper Garden Street hadn't pulled her little clan up from Guinea Town to have her only son grabbed by a gold-digging hussy.

There had been a dinner between the two families, Dolly and Marty generously making the trip to Lodi, but it had not gone well. Dolly—no surprise—had spoken her mind.

Still, Toni kept coming on strong even as Frankie continued to woo Nancy. For a while it was fun, Nancy and Toni coming alternate nights to the Cabin, Nancy the good girl sitting uneasily as the other women stared openmouthed at her Frankie. Nancy the good girl, with her sweet face and sweet hair and sweet kisses—and kissing was where it stopped.

Then, on the other nights, Toni the bad girl, or the girl with the promise of badness anyway. He couldn't help himself; he was so desperate to have her that he gave her a ring, not a big stone, a cheap chip of diamond, but it did the trick. She let him take her to a hotel, and they registered as Mr. and Mrs. Sinatra. She teased him mercilessly as he lay there with his eyes rolled back in his head. Had anyone ever done that for him?

Certainly not Nancy. But then came the night after Thanksgiving, when Nancy and Frank were sitting in a booth between sets and Freddy the busboy brought the black telephone to the table. Freddy gave Frankie a funny look: *For you, kid.* Nancy, giving him her own look, a look of power and ownership, pushed Frank's hand away from the phone and picked up the receiver.

He sat there with his hand over his eyes as she went at it pretty good. He was surprised at how tough she was. She'd pull Toni's hair out by the roots if she ever caught her anywhere near her Frank.

His stomach warmed to hear that, but then, after she slammed down the receiver, he knew he was in for it. The bawling out, though, that was the easy part. The hard part was dealing with the other one.

Half an hour later, she stomped into the Cabin as he was about to start singing and walked toward him, but Nancy stopped her. Then they were flailing at each other like two cats. The music stopped and everyone stared. Before Frank and the other waiters and the busboys could get between the women, Toni had ripped Nancy's good white dress.

It was a long night, but he stuck to his story: The woman was nothing to him. It had been a flirtation, and it was over. The woman couldn't face the facts.

The next night, Saturday, things got worse. After he'd sung "Night and Day," there was a stirring on the dance floor, and two cops in motorcycle boots stomped in and arrested him right in front of everyone.

Frankie tried to bluff it out. Mistaken identity, he announced, as they led him to the door, to scattered applause (which began with the band).

They took him to the county clink, in Hackensack—it was two in the morning—and booked him.

Even in a mug shot it is an astonishing face. The extravagantly sensual lower lip. The intelligence of the pale, wide-set eyes. The greasy hank of hair over the left eyebrow—he could have flicked it out of the way; he chose not to—is a rebellious 1930s touch worthy of a Dillinger or Pretty Boy Floyd. It is a sensitive face, but one of a man with full knowledge of his own importance.

Full-face he looked defiant, but in profile he looked weary. A night in jail had taken the starch out of Frank. Now he was allowed to make his single phone call. Dolly answered, and told him she would have him out in an hour.

It took a bit longer than that. The whole episode was an operetta in three acts, playing out over months, each part taking its own sweet time. The original arrest warrant stated that on November 2 and 9, 1938, Frank Sinatra, "being then and there a single man over the age of eighteen years, under the promise of marriage, did then and there have sexual intercourse with the said complainant who was then and there a single female of good repute for chastity whereby she became pregnant." Then and there. Good repute for chastity. Old English language aside, the warrant had a couple of holes in it. The beginning of November sounds like very quick work if indeed she did become pregnant; some have speculated the affair actually began in the spring and was consummated during the summer, which sounds more plausible. And there was this small detail: The female was not single. She was legally separated, but still married.

The case fell apart like the house of cards it was, except that it fell in slow motion. First, Dolly sent Marty to call on Toni's father. Marty had such a hangdog expression—"He looked like a hobo at the door begging for something to eat," Toni recalled many years later—that her father offered the poor old pug a shot of booze. The two men drank together—sacred bond—and finally Toni was persuaded to go spring Frankie herself.

According to Toni, Frankie sobbed when she confronted him in his cell. She withdrew the charges, but only after (she remembered) she made her lover promise that his mother would apologize for the mean things she'd said. Dolly apologize! Three weeks later, no apology having occurred, Toni went to Garden Street to confront Mrs. Sinatra. After a screaming fight that brought the neighbors out of their houses, the forty-two-year-old, four-foot-eleven Dolly somehow managed to throw the young woman into the basement. The police arrived. This being Dolly Sinatra's turf, Toni was arrested and given a suspended sentence for disorderly conduct. She thereupon swore out a *second* warrant against Frank Sinatra: not having been able to make seduction stick, this time she owned up to her non-single status and went for adultery. Three days before Christmas, he was arrested once more—again at the Cabin, this time by court officers purporting to be bearing a Christmas gift from admirers. Dolly once more arrived with bail, and Frankie was once again released on his own recognizance. A headline in the next day's *Jersey Observer* read: SONGBIRD HELD IN MORALS CHARGE.

It may have been North Jersey light opera, a tempest in a 1930s teapot, but Mike Barbato can't have failed to notice that his prospective son-in-law was neither a lawyer nor an accountant nor even a plasterer, but, well, a songbird and a perp. (Though Toni eventually dropped these charges as well because, she claimed, she'd found out about *Dolly's* arrest record, for abortion.) Nancy Rose might have looked like a terrific match to Dolly, but things can't have appeared quite so rosy from the Jersey City side. And what did Nancy herself think about all this? Her boyfriend's stonewalling wasn't helped by a second arrest, not to mention newspaper headlines.

But she loved him. And he loved her. It was the God's honest truth. She knew him to the bottom of his soul, and loved him for it and in spite of it. What's more, she knew he contained that strangest of all quantities, there among the frame row houses and brownstone tenements of blue-collar, bill-paying Hudson County: greatness. And he loved that she knew it, and he loved that she loved him, and he loved her goodness, her wisdom, and her sweet kisses.

It was just that he needed so much more . . .

It was time to put a cap on things. There were more Tonis out there. Dolly came up with a 1930s solution: against the Barbatos' grave misgivings, Frank and Nancy would be married. It happened just a little over a month after his second arrest—Saturday, February 4, 1939, at Our Lady of Sorrows Church in Jersey City. A small wedding, in the Barbatos' territory; few Hobokenites in attendance. The bride's white dress was as true as the tears that flowed from her eyes as her father, guardedly happy, walked her down the aisle: she did love Frank Sinatra, but now she was joined to him forever, with all that entailed.

Three weeks later, Dolly was arrested once more, for performing another abortion. This too made the papers. The Sinatras were famous all over Hudson County.

So the boy left his mother (sort of: he was commanded to visit Garden Street at least once a week—alone, if possible) and settled, uneasily, into married life, in a $42-a-month, third-floor walk-up on Garfield

Avenue in Jersey City. As cozy as the little apartment was, the new-lyweds didn't see much of each other. Weekdays, Nancy worked as a $25-a-week secretary at American Type Founders in Elizabeth, rising early to the sight of her skinny young husband still snoring, exhausted from his labors at the Cabin. The club—on-site arrests notwithstand-ing—had given him a raise to $25 a week. He often spent more than that on clothes. His practical young wife fretted about his predilection for budget-busting $35 Woodside suits. She skimped on her own cloth-ing, made him silk bow ties so he wouldn't have to spend the money. His wardrobe took up what little closet space they had, and then some.

She coped. She wanted stability, and a family; she still worried about his mercurial nature. As far as other women were concerned, she knew it was not a question of if, but—Italian men being Italian men—when and how. (Mike Barbato, the tough paterfamilias, the paragon of respectability, was no exception in this regard.) But Nancy loved Frank desperately. He was infinitely sensitive; he could be so sweet and funny. And she knew he loved her. Then the slightest thing—there was no predicting—could set him off. And she had backbone: she would stand up to him. They had some terrible blowouts (the neighbors below banged on their ceiling). Then they made up. That was nice.

She wanted children. What else was marriage for? He was reluc-tant at first: they couldn't afford them yet. She did everything she could to hold him—cooked him spaghetti just the way he liked it, baked him lemon-meringue pies. He loved her meals, and he loved her, but he was elusive. He had important places to go, people to see. He would rise in the afternoon and gather up his Hoboken pal Nick Sevano before getting on the ferry to Manhattan and making the rounds of radio sta-tions and music publishers. Sanicola and Van Heusen would often join him for the evening, along with a new friend, a fast-talking, wisecrack-ing, breathtakingly talented little lyricist named Sammy Cahn. Nobody else in the crew was married. Why were the chicks always drawn to the one that was?

He felt stalled that spring, a fly trapped in amber. He had married in haste; he wasn't cut out for it. He loved her so much, but he wasn't cut out for it. Much of the time—he hated himself for thinking it—Nancy was a millstone around his neck. He wasn't getting any younger, and his career wasn't going anywhere. The radio stations still weren't paying, and nerves caused him to blow two important occasions: Once when he was trying out for a band run by a new leader, a rich kid from Detroit named Bob Chester, Tommy Dorsey stopped by. Tommy fucking *Dorsey.* Sinatra got so flustered at the sight of that cold Irish puss (he looked like a goddamn emperor or something) that he forgot the lyrics of the song he was singing and froze—literally opened his mouth and nothing came out.

And the same damn thing happened again one night at the Cabin: almost fifty years later, the horror of it would still live with him. "On a Sunday evening during the summer months, people would come back from the countryside, and stop and have a little nip before they went over the bridge to go back into New York," Sinatra recalled, at Yale Law School in 1986.

> There were about seven people in the audience, and the trumpet player—we had a six-piece "orchestra"; big sound, beautiful—the trumpet player, named Johnny Buccini, said to me, "Do you know who this is sitting out there?" I said, "No. Where?" He said, "Right out there, you dummy. Look straight ahead." I said, "Yeah, I know that face." He said, "That's Cole Porter."
>
> I had been so infatuated with his music that I couldn't believe he was sitting out in the audience with four or five people. I said to the orchestra leader, "I'd like to do one of Cole Porter's songs . . . Let's do 'Night and Day' for them, and I'll talk about it." So I said, "Ladies and gentlemen, I'd like to sing this song and dedicate it to the greatly talented man who composed it and who is maybe one of the best contributors to American music at this particular time in our lives." I said that

Mr. Porter was in the room, and the orchestra played the introduction—and I proceeded to forget all the words. I swear to
God. I couldn't think. I kept saying "night and day" for fifteen
bars!

But with Sinatra, ambition trumped shame every time. And twenty
years later, during the making of *High Society,* Porter would recall the
night, and smile.

One afternoon that winter, Frankie stopped by the Sicilian Club
in Bayonne and found Frank Mane, an alto sax player he knew from
WAAT, rehearsing some songs with a ten-piece pickup band. When he
asked Mane what he was practicing for, the sax player told him he was
trying out for a spot with a Los Angeles outfit, Clyde Lucas and His
California Dons. He was going over to Manhattan to make an audition
record.

"Cheech, could I go to New York with you and sing with the band?"
Frankie asked.

Mane shrugged. "Sure, why not?"

And so on March 18, all atingle, Frankie set foot for the first time
in a recording studio—Harry Smith's, 2 West Forty-sixth Street, a large
office tower today. It was a Saturday afternoon: the city was quiet; studio time was cheap. After Mane and his band cut a couple of instrumentals, the musicians took out the sheet music to something called
"Our Love"—corny lyrics grafted onto Tchaikovsky's theme for *Romeo
and Juliet.* Then, with a nod from the guy in the glass booth, the band
hit the first notes and Frankie began to sing. He couldn't help grinning
at the freedom and ease, the *rightness* of it: he was making a record!

Our love, I feel it everywhere . . .
Our love is like an evening prayer.

A little while later, he was able to listen to a 78-rpm demo platter
with his very own voice on it. It was a respectable-enough debut: the

sound was a little scratchy, the band's tempo plodding, but Frankie had sung on key and hit all the high notes. To him it was a miracle: he would have listened to the disc over and over again if Frank Mane had let him, so entranced was he at the sound of his own voice.

———

It wasn't just narcissism. His ear, after all, was part of his genius. He was literally amazed at himself—the voice *worked*. Technically speaking, there were much better instruments out there: the Eberle brothers, Bob (who spelled it "Eberly") and Ray; Dick Haymes—all, at that point, could sing circles around him. They had bigger, richer baritones; they sounded like men. He still sounded like a boy.

But this was what worked for him—he didn't sound like anyone else. He *was* a boy, and he was vulnerable (and would remain so, as long as Dolly was alive), and he could carry a tune, in both senses of

The iconic mug shot. Defiance, style, and the astonishing intelligence of the pale, wide-set eyes. A man with full knowledge of his own importance.

both words. He made good and goddamn sure that he understood the words to every song he sang, made sure (like Mabel, like Billie) that his audiences knew he was telling a story. And his audiences (and especially the women in them) wanted to hear him telling it.

A woman happened to hear him on the radio one night that spring—the WNEW wire from the Rustic Cabin, the *Dance Parade*. Her name was Louise Tobin, and she was a band singer herself—young, black haired, gorgeous, and newly married to a freshly minted young bandleader, a tall, rail-thin, hatchet-headed Texas trumpeter named Harry James. Tobin and James were in their room at the Lincoln Hotel, at Eighth Avenue and Forty-fourth Street; Tobin was preparing to catch a late train for a gig in Boston; James was lying on the bed, resting up after his appearance at the Paramount.

Tobin was standing at the mirror, watching herself putting in an earring, wearing that abstracted look women get, holding the earring post in her mouth, when she heard this kid singing "Night and Day" through the Philco's cheesy speaker. (This time he knew the words.) The voice stopped her. The kid had something. It wasn't the most stupendous voice she had ever heard—the earring post didn't fall from her lips—but he sounded awfully self-assured for however the hell old he was.

"So," Tobin recalled many years later, "I woke Harry and said, 'Honey, you might want to hear this kid on the radio.'"

Act Two

HARRY AND TOMMY

Frank broadcasting with the Harry James Orchestra, August 1940, at the Roseland Ballroom, New York City. Left to right: Frank, unidentified, band manager Pee Wee Monte, Harry James, vocalist Bernice Byers.

It was a typical day in the life of a touring swing band: *long*. Motor down the pike from New York to Philadelphia, play a tea dance at the Benjamin Franklin Hotel, turn around, and head home. On the way out of Manhattan that morning, riding ahead of the band bus in his big Chrysler, Harry James had stopped on Riverside Drive to pick up his new girl singer, a petite seventeen-year-old dynamo from Florida with a big voice, a sparkly personality, and a laughably impossible name: Yvonne Marie Antoinette JaMais. As they rolled south through the Jersey farmlands with the band manager, Pee Wee Monte, at the wheel, James clacked a stick of Black Jack gum and squinted in deep thought at the problem of rechristening her for the stage. *Rhymes with Yvonne* . . . In a moment, he had it: Connie!

Connie what?

"Connie Haines!" he suddenly crowed. He had a high, squeaky voice and a Texas accent. The bandleader smiled in triumph: it went perfectly with Harry James.

So Connie Haines it was, and as the Chrysler sped north through the New Jersey night, the newly named singer, exhausted and elated after a successful first engagement with the band, was amazed to see that Harry was still full of beans, bouncing around in the front passenger's seat, clacking his gum, tapping in time on the dashboard to the staticky song on the radio. Suddenly he turned around, resting his long chin on his long fingers on the back of the seat.

"Hey, Connie Haines," he said with a wink. "How you doin' back there?"

Fine, she told him. Maybe a little tired.

That was just what he wanted to talk to her about, he said. He wanted to make one little stop before they crossed the bridge. There was this boy singer he wanted to hear.

<hr />

Harry James was the same age as Frank Sinatra—in fact he was three months younger. But even given Sinatra's tour with Major Bowes, all the gigs in dumps and dives, the radio shows, the women, the arrests— James had done a lot more living in his twenty-three years than Sinatra had in his. To begin with, Harry Haag James was a son of the circus. His mother was a trapeze artist whose specialty ("The Iron Jaw") was dangling from a wire far above the sawdust by her teeth; his father was a cornetist and bandmaster. Harry himself had started performing as a drummer for the Christy Brothers Circus at age three; at the tender age of five, he became a contortionist known as the Human Eel. At eight he began playing the trumpet, and by the time he was twelve, he was leading the circus's number-two band. At fourteen, young Harry was drinking hard and taking his pick of the innocent girls who came to gawk at the big top's spectacles.

James was a superbly gifted natural musician whom the circus had schooled to play loud, hard blues. It was a style equally apt for the midway and the dawning of the Swing Era in the mid-1930s. By 1935, the nineteen-year-old James was married to the seventeen-year-old Louise Tobin (and cheating on her every chance he could get) and playing with a band led by the Chicago drummer Ben Pollack; by the end of 1936, he had signed with Benny Goodman, the *capo di tutti capi* of American bandleaders. They made a formidable combination. On the occasion of the great clarinetist's death in 1986, the *San Francisco Chronicle* columnist Herb Caen vividly recalled a Goodman concert of fifty years earlier as "bedlam. Gene Krupa riding his high hat like a dervish. Harry James puffing out his cheeks till surely they must burst, the rhythm always burning and churning and driving you out of your mind, and then, just when you thought nothing could get hotter, Benny's clarinet rising like a burnished bird out of the tightly controlled maelstrom and soaring to the heavens, outscreaming even the crowd."

It was rock 'n' roll with big-band arrangements. And two years of maximum national prominence with Goodman had turned Harry James into the 1930s equivalent of a rock star. He was itching to fly on his own. At the end of 1938, bankrolled by Goodman, the trumpeter started his own outfit, Harry James and His Music Makers.

Musical gods were different then. For one thing, teenagers of that era didn't demand that their musical idols be, or look like, teenagers. By the spring of 1939, Harry James was a very famous, accomplished, and self-assured twenty-three-year-old—and with his hawk nose, piercing blue eyes, pencil mustache, and big-shoulder suits, he didn't remotely resemble any twenty-three-year-old we would recognize today. At twenty-three he looked as if he were well into his thirties. He had star quality to burn, and when he strode into the Rustic Cabin that blossom-heavy night in early June 1939, the crowd parted before him like the Red Sea before Moses.

The Cabin's owner, Harry Nichols, came up, grinning, his cigar hanging from his lower lip, and told James to take any table he'd like. Drinks on the house, of course.

James winked at him. How about that boy singer his wife had heard on the radio the other night? Was he here?

Nichols frowned. "We don't have a singer," he said.

James frowned back. "That's not what I heard."

"Well, we do have an emcee who sings a little bit . . ."

"This very thin guy with swept-back greasy hair had been waiting tables," James recalled many years later. "Suddenly he took off his apron and climbed onto the stage. He'd sung only eight bars when I felt the hairs on the back of my neck rising. I knew he was destined to be a great vocalist."

This has all the verisimilitude of an MGM musical, and the tin-can ring of hindsight, but Harry James surely heard something that night, especially if, as he later reported, Sinatra really performed Cole Porter's notoriously difficult, 108-bar epic "Begin the Beguine." Any twenty-three-year-old who could bring *that* off would indeed be something special. But in a way it doesn't matter what Sinatra sang that night—it was the way he sang it, the voice itself, that got Harry James where he lived.

"It's an interesting thing," the singer and musicologist Michael Feinstein says. "You can look at the vibration of somebody's voice on a machine—whatever the machines are called—and it looks like this; someone else's voice will look the same. You can match up graphs that look the same, but they don't sound the same. The point is that there is something that cannot be defined in any way scientifically.

"You can't explain what it is about the sound of Sinatra's voice," Feinstein says. "I mean, you can try, and you can get very poetic in describing it. But there is something there that is transcendent, that simply exists in his instrument. He developed it, he honed it, he understood it himself, he knew what he could do, and he used it to his best advantage. That was something that people responded to."

The voice was still developing in the spring of 1939—it would continue to develop for the next fifty years. It wasn't as rich as it would be even five years later. But its DNA was there, the indefinable something composed of loneliness and need and infinite ambition and storytelling intelligence and intense musicality and Hoboken and Dolly herself, the thing that made him entirely different from every other singer who had ever opened his mouth.

And Frank Sinatra had one more astounding thing at twenty-three: a plan. He was going to knock over Crosby. He knew it in the pit of his gut. Not even Nancy knew the true height of his hubris.

Harry James, believing that whatever Sinatra had was worth signing him up for, offered him a contract on the spot: $75 a week. It was quite an offer: three times what Sinatra was currently making, more than he and Nancy were earning together. What James neglected to mention was that there were some weeks (he wasn't especially good with money) when he didn't have $75 to his name.

Since Harry had created Connie Haines that morning, he was feeling lucky. Sinatra was too Eye-talian, he said. How about Frankie Satin? It went nice with that nice smooth voice of his.

Just a moment before, Sinatra recalled in later years, he had been grasping James by the arm, incredulous at the offer, making sure his main chance didn't get away. Now, as Connic Haines remembered sharply sixty-seven years after that night, the singer's eyes went cold. "Frank told Harry, 'You want the singer, take the name,'" Haines said. "And walked away."

Sinatra had good reason to be insulted. His father's boxing alias, Marty O'Brien, had been not a whim but a forced decision: an Italian surname would have gotten him barred from training gyms. In perception and reality, the Irish stood above the Italians on the American social ladder, a heavy foot firmly planted on all upturned faces. Even as late as the 1940s, the Italian-American author Gay Talese recalled, "The Irish kids were the ones who called me 'wop.'" And as Pete Hamill, a Sinatra friend who has analyzed the underheated melting pot from the Irish-American point of view, wrote: "In those days it would not have been strange for a boy to believe that the man was ashamed of being Italian. His father's split identity surely explains, at least in part, Sinatra's . . . vehemence about keeping his own name when Harry James wanted to change it."

Sinatra had already tried an anglicized stage name—Frankie Trent—very briefly, a couple of years before. Very briefly because once Dolly got wind of it, she gave him both barrels—maybe she hit him with the bat. In any case, while "Frankie Trent" was bad enough, "Frankie Satin" was much, much worse—it made "Connie Haines" look like sheer genius. It wasn't even anglicized; it was 100 percent corn oil. As Sinatra told Hamill, "Can you imagine? Is that a name or is that a name? 'Now playing in the lounge, ladies and gennulmen, the one an' only Frankie Satin' . . . If I'd've done that, I'd be working cruise ships today."

But when Frank walked away, James came right after him. The defiantly unrenamed Frank Sinatra joined the Music Makers on June 30, as they opened a weeklong engagement at the Hippodrome in Baltimore. He was so new that he wasn't even listed on the bill. Still, some girls in the audience quickly got the idea. "After the first show, the screaming started in the theater, and those girls came backstage," Connie Haines told Peter J. Levinson for his Harry James biography, *Trumpet Blues.* "There were about twenty of them . . . it happened, it was real, it was not a gimmick."

Not a gimmick at all. The Voice—might as well start capitalizing it here—was simply working its spooky subliminal magic. Did it help that the singer was clearly in need of a good meal, that his mouth was voluptuously beautiful, that his eyes were attractively wide with fear and excitement, that he knowingly threw a little catch, a vulnerable vocal stutter, into his voice on the slow ballads? It helped. It whipped into a frenzy the visceral excitement that his sound had started. But the sound came first. There was simply nothing like it.

———

The singer was a genius, the trumpeter-leader a kind of genius. The band was terrific (and light-years from the rinky-dink six-piece outfit at the Rustic Cabin). The world would fall at both men's feet in a few years. But not everyone was thrilled at first: both Sinatra and Harry James seemed to be simply ahead of their time. James blew hot and hard, a style that delighted critics—*Down Beat* had voted him America's number-one trumpeter in 1937, over the headiest of competition: Louis Armstrong, Bunny Berigan, and Roy Eldridge—but didn't always sit well with country-club and society-ballroom and nightclub audiences. They didn't want to *listen;* they wanted to dance close and slow, and go home and make babies who would grow up and go to country clubs and society ballrooms and dance close and slow . . . A nice society band, a Lawrence Welk or an Eddy Duchin outfit, was simply more adequate to the purpose than a group that made you sit up and take notice.

And Frank Sinatra—well, Sinatra, for his part, was an acquired taste at first. Especially for the critics. When the band played the Roseland Ballroom on West Fifty-second Street in the summer of 1939, Sinatra begged the Music Makers' road manager, Gerry Barrett, to beg George T. Simon, *Metronome's* influential critic, for a decent review. The dutiful Barrett all but tackled Simon as he was leaving the building. "Please give the new boy singer a good write-up because he wants it more than anybody I've ever seen and we want to keep him happy," he said.

Simon (whose brother Richard would found Simon & Schuster, and in a few years father a daughter named Carly, who would herself grow up to do some singing) more or less complied. In his review he effused over James's "sensational, intense style," and went on to praise the saxophonist Dave Matthews, the drummer Ralph Hawkins, and the arranger Andy Gibson. Then and only then did Simon give a nod to "the pleasing vocals of Frank Sinatra, whose easy phrasing is especially commendable."

But even if the mention was obligatory (and lukewarm), it contained an important kernel of truth. When it came to that mysterious quantity known as phrasing—the emotional essence of all speech, sung or spoken—Frank Sinatra had a unique ability, composed of innate talent, very hard work, and the irrepressible obtrusion of his unruly soul. Easy? There was nothing remotely easy about any molecule of his being, especially his phrasing. Maybe what George T. Simon should have said was that, like Joltin' Joe DiMaggio swinging a bat, Sinatra made it *look* easy.

A quarter century later, Simon wrote in *Billboard* what he really thought of Sinatra that night: "He sounded somewhat like a shy boy out on his first date—gentle, tender but frightfully unsure of himself." Be that as it may, when the Music Makers hit the Panther Room of the Hotel Sherman in Chicago a couple of weeks after the Roseland gig, Betty Grable, whose star was rising in Hollywood (and who would in a few years replace Louise Tobin as Mrs. Harry James), dragooned a young reporter named James Bacon into going to hear Sinatra. Bacon had never heard of the guy. "I'll never forget," he recalled years later. "The minute Sinatra started singing, every girl left her partner on the dance floor and crowded around the microphone on the bandstand. He was so skinny, the microphone almost obscured him."

Afterward, Bacon congratulated Harry James on his new boy singer. "Not so loud," James replied. "The kid's name is Sinatra. He considers himself the greatest vocalist in the business. Get that! No one ever heard of him. He's never had a hit record. He looks like a wet rag. But he says he is the greatest. If he hears you compliment him, he'll demand a raise tonight."

Frank Sinatra was anything but unsure of himself. Along with his abilities, the other thing he was certain of was precisely how the girls liked him to sound. The boys didn't always agree. During the Chicago stand, a *Billboard* reviewer wrote that Sinatra sang "the torchy ballads in a pleasing way in good voice," but then went on: "He touches the songs with a little too much pash, which is not all convincing."

Or maybe all that pash was simply unsettling because it was so new. Among the smooth-as-silk baritones of the day, led by Crosby, Sinatra was an anomaly, a hot artist rather than a cool one, a harbinger of his own singular future.

Harry James, too, was a hot artist: a hepcat, a weed-puffing wild man. He was also a strangely self-defeating character—alcoholic, remote, and persistently broke. That summer, he lost everything he had in a settlement over an auto accident. (Connie Haines, whose salary he could no longer afford, had to leave.) And in a country crowded with big-band talent—Tommy Dorsey, Benny Goodman, Charlie Barnet, Count Basie, Jimmy Dorsey, Duke Ellington, Bob Crosby, Jimmie Lunceford, Glenn Miller, and Artie Shaw were all crisscrossing the land with their outfits in the swinging late 1930s—James was having a hard time making a go of it. Some nights, as the Music Makers worked their way westward, the band only pulled down $350—and that had to pay seventeen band members and a bus driver, not to mention defray food, gas, and accommodations. There were times the outfit seemed snakebit. Other bands had hit records; Harry James couldn't catch a break. Meanwhile, a music-business brouhaha—the three-way royalty beef between ASCAP, the American Federation of Musicians, and the radio stations, a dispute that led ASCAP to ban radio performances of all the songs it licensed—didn't help.

Frank Sinatra, who would record over thirteen hundred songs in his career, cut just ten sides in his six months with the Harry James band. The first time he went into the Brunswick studios at 550 Fifth Avenue—the date was July 13, 1939—was only the second time he had ever set foot in a recording studio. In all, Sinatra and James recorded three times in New York that summer (subsequent sessions would take place in Chicago in October and Los Angeles in November), on each occasion laying down two sides of a 78-rpm platter. The third session took place on Thursday, August 31, the day before the Nazis stormed through Poland—cool and cloudy in Manhattan; double-decker buses cruising up Fifth Avenue; big fans whirring in the studio. That day the Music Makers recorded one take of a soupy, utterly forgettable Frank Loesser ballad called "Here Comes the Night" ("Here comes the night, my cloak of blue / Here comes the night, with dreams of you") and two takes of a new song by Arthur Altman and Jack Lawrence. The number was called "All or Nothing At All."

It is impossible to listen to the song today and not think of all it would become: a huge hit, a trademark tune for Sinatra, a cliché so delicious that the animator Tex Avery would put singer and song in an MGM cartoon (in which a skunk dressed as Frankie croons it to a bunch of swooning bunnies).

It was not a great song. But it was a powerful song of the period, and an exceptional one: rather than just taking a chorus in the middle, as was customary with band vocalists of the era, Sinatra vocalized all the way through, to powerful and passionate effect. He was in great voice, his breath control was superb, and the twenty-three-year-old's assurance, against the rock-solid background of James's band, was extraordinary. There were minor gaffes: On both "half a love never appealed to me" and "if your heart never could yield to me," his den- talization of the *t* in "to" is so extreme as to be laughable—that *t* could have walked straight off the graveyard shift at the Tietjen and Lang shipyards. And for a heart-stopping half second on the final, operatic high F ("all—or nothing at *alllllll!*"), Sinatra's voice, at the height of passion, slips upward, a half note sharp.

And yet he had laid down a track for the ages, and on his seventh time out.[1]

Meanwhile, his boss simply couldn't catch a break. Harry James's management, the Music Corporation of America, didn't know what to do with him. Bookings were scattershot. The band's morale was sinking fast. Then, while the Music Makers played the Hotel Sherman, James finally got some good news: MCA had landed them a big gig at a big venue, the famed Palomar Ballroom in Los Angeles, where Benny Goodman and his band had started the Swing Era overnight with a fabled performance in August 1935. There were smiles on the bandstand at last.

On October 4, 1939, the Palomar burned to the ground. (Charlie Barnet lost all his orchestrations, barely escaped with his life.) When Harry James's band bus pulled out of Chicago ten days later, it must have felt a little like the Flying Dutchman.

Frank Sinatra wasn't on the bus. Rather, he and his young wife had traveled west in his green Chrysler convertible. As the self-professed greatest vocalist in the business, Sinatra would have appreciated the symbolic value of separateness, not to mention the convenience of having his own wheels. Yet as an already established cocksman, with an already shaky commitment to the institution of marriage ("an institute you can't disparage," he would sing, jauntily, in 1955—at a moment when his second marriage had collapsed irreparably and he was entering his longest period of bachelorhood), he had to have felt ambivalent, at the very least, about taking the little woman along on the road.

But there is every likelihood that the dignified and self-assured Nancy Sinatra simply demanded it. She had seen the girls clustering around the microphone. And there was something else: in October 1939, she was just a little bit pregnant.

———

The band's spirits had nowhere to go but up. And morale soared when, after the Palomar fire, MCA snagged the Music Makers an alternate engagement, at a Beverly Hills dining and dancing establishment called Victor Hugo's, run by a character named Hugo Aleidas. Unfortunately, the restaurant turned out to be a small stuffy joint, with canaries in gilt cages decorating the room: the kind of place where dulcet society bands like Guy Lombardo's fit in just fine. Harry's band didn't just play hot and sweet, they played *loud*. At first the management tried erecting a canopy over the bandstand to muffle the sound. When that proved insufficient, the horn players were asked to stuff cloth napkins into the bells of their instruments. By the end of the week, customers were voting with their feet—James, Sinatra, and company were playing to half-full houses. Finally, even Sinatra's ballads were to no avail: one night, while he was in the middle of "All or Nothing At All," no less, Aleidas ran out onto the dance floor, waving his arms and shouting, "Stop! No more! Enough!" To add insult to injury, and to underline Harry James's perfectly bad business luck, the owner refused to pay the band.

Things were so bad that the Music Makers had to bunk together, wherever they could hang their hats. Frank and Nancy shared a two-bedroom apartment in Hollywood with the diminutive drummer Mickey Scrima. The whole band came over for meals. Nancy cooked spaghetti and franks and beans for the musicians, including Harry. It was a desperate period; strikingly, though, both Nancy and Frank would also later remember it as one of the happiest times of their life together.

And, seen through the lens of nostalgia, it was. Everything was simple, because they had nothing. The road lay ahead of them—beckoning, shining.

But in that moment of loving his wife and the baby inside her, Sinatra felt a growing desperation. He had the goods and he knew it, and here he was eating franks and beans with Harry James, who weighed what he did but was six inches taller. He had learned a lot from Harry James—he loved Harry James. But he knew he needed to get out.

He dreamed of singing with Benny Goodman or Count Basie, the way Billie had, or even Tommy Dorsey, who ran the Rolls-Royce of bands and really knew how to feature singers.

In the meantime, the road was no place for a young wife—especially if the wife was pregnant and the band was broke. Frankie sold the Chrysler and, amid many tears, put Nancy on a train back east.

Every penny they had after buying her ticket was in her purse. As the Super Chief pulled out of Union Station, she pointed at him, crying: he'd better be good.

He nodded, crying too. He would try, for her and the baby. In his fashion.

The Music Makers were limping home. MCA managed to get them a week at a Los Angeles movie house and another week at the Golden Gate Theatre in San Francisco, but then came the interminable drive over the Rockies and the Great Plains, the one-nighters in Denver and Des Moines and Dubuque. They lived on hot dogs and Cokes and candy bars, flirted halfheartedly with the local girls as they headed toward their next stand: a week at the Chicago Theatre, and a Christmas benefit thrown by the mayor of the Windy City, Boss Edward J. Kelly. Riding, riding through the night. As the rest of the band played cards and laughed or told dirty jokes or slept and snored, Sinatra sat by himself in the back of the bus, his jacket folded over his eyes, with one thought in mind, over the Rockies, across the Great Plains, across the unendingly huge country that did not yet lie at his feet but would: on the bill at the Chicago Theatre would be Tommy Dorsey.

Summit. Frank, Buddy Rich, Tommy Dorsey, circa 1941.

He was one tough son of a bitch, the second son of a horn-playing family from the coal-mining hills of eastern Pennsylvania, one of the starkest places on earth. His father, Tom Dorsey Sr., was self-taught on cornet and four other instruments, and an even tougher son of a bitch than his sons. Pop Dorsey had used his musical skills to escape the mines, had dragged himself up by his bootstraps from the worst job in the world, and was damned if his sons would have to go down in those black pits. So he pushed them, bullied them really, to learn their instruments: Jimmy, the saxophone, and Tom junior, the trombone. And they learned well, both boys, they were brilliant musicians like their dad, but like their dad they also had the devil in them, a taste for alcohol and a deep black anger, as black as the coal in the mines, as old as Ireland, as explosive as TNT. They got into fistfights with anyone they had to, and many they didn't have to, and they fought each other, too. They vied for supremacy, Tommy refusing to accept the role of the second son, giving his older brother no deference. They loved each other, but perhaps hated each other a little more.

The brothers played together (and fought together) in dozens of bands as they came up during the 1920s and 1930s: the Scranton Sirens and Jean Goldkette's band (with an insanely talented, desperately alcoholic cornetist named Bix Beiderbecke) and Paul Whiteman's; then, against all emotional logic, they formed their own outfit, the Dorsey Brothers Orchestra, and fought some more, and then, as the Swing Era was getting started in 1935, Tommy couldn't take the fighting anymore, and walked out to start on his own.

He was just thirty, but thirty was more like forty in those days, and coming from where he'd come from, and having done what he'd done, Tommy Dorsey had a hundred thousand miles on him. He was five ten and ramrod straight, with a square, pitiless face, a hawk nose, cold blue eyes behind little round glasses. He looked just like a high-school music teacher—he knew it, others knew it, and he tried to shift the impression by dressing more elegantly than other bandleaders (he had an immense wardrobe, over sixty suits) and standing taller (he wore lifts in his shoes, and tended to pose for the camera with his trombone slide extended alongside himself, to emphasize the vertical line). His ambition was titanic, his discipline incomparable. He could (and often did) drink himself into a stupor after a gig, sleep three hours, then get up at 6:00 a.m., play golf, and be fresh as a daisy for the day's work. No matter how long the road trip or how taxing the engagement, he was never seen in rumpled clothes. He did precisely what he wanted, when he wanted, took shit from nobody, and played an absolutely gorgeous trombone. "He could do something with a trombone that no one had ever done before," said Artie Shaw, who was stingy with compliments. "He made it into a singing instrument . . . Before that it was a blatting instrument."

Dorsey had a massive rib cage and extraordinary lung power. He could play an unbelievable thirty-two-bar legato. And yet he hopelessly idolized the legendary Texas trombonist and vocalist Jack Teagarden, a great jazz artist, a man who could transform a song into something new and sublime and dangerous. Dorsey didn't transform: he ornamented; he amplified. It was a quibble, really, but not in Dorsey's mind. There was something about himself—there were a few things—that he didn't like. When he thought about Teagarden, the pure artist, he would pour himself another drink, turn mean as a snake, go looking for somebody to punch out.¹ But when he blew those glorious solos, measure after silken measure seemingly without a pause for breath, you forgot about jazz: Tommy Dorsey made his own rules.

Still, jazz dominated the mid-1930s. The bad, scared days of the Depression were starting to give way to the optimism of the New Deal; people wanted to dance. The black bands of Count Basie, Duke Ellington, and Jimmie Lunceford were wildly swinging and innovative, and Benny Goodman—who was soon to break the color barrier by hiring Teddy Wilson, Lionel Hampton, and Charlie Christian—wasn't far behind.

Then there was Tommy Dorsey, whose theme song, "I'm Getting Sentimental over You," spoke for itself; he also had a deliciously corny nickname, the Sentimental Gentleman of Swing. For three years he entranced the fox-trotting masses with his long sweet solos. But swing grew hotter as the 1940s approached—even Glenn Miller's band was starting to sound punchier—and the critics began to carp about Dorsey's monotonous mellowness. The truth is, Tommy Dorsey was starting to get bored with himself. Any sentimentality that he possessed was buried under layers of toughness and anger. Nor was he—except when the microphone was on—particularly gentlemanly. Before his public grew bored too, the ever restless, insatiably ambitious bandleader decided to make some changes.

And 1939 was a year for change. Dorsey's first move was his most radical: that summer, he hired away Jimmie Lunceford's genius arranger, Melvin James "Sy" Oliver. Other white bands had used black arrangers before: Fletcher Henderson was the secret of Benny Goodman's success. Tommy Dorsey needed some similar magic, and with Sy Oliver he got it. The immediate and dramatic result of the new acquisition, as Peter J. Levinson noted in *Tommy Dorsey: Livin' in a Great Big Way,* was that "the Dorsey band . . . became a magnet for jazz musicians who noticed the difference Oliver's presence made."

One of those musicians was the ace trumpeter Zeke Zarchy. Another was the percussively and temperamentally explosive twenty-two-year-old drummer Buddy Rich, who had become a national phenomenon that year while playing for Artie Shaw's band. Rich had first performed onstage at the age of eighteen months, a percussion prodigy of Mozartean éclat (complete with a pushy, less-talented stage father) known as Traps, the Drum Wonder. The famously temperamental Shaw and the volatile, egomaniacal Rich were bound to clash, and clash they did, when Shaw accused Rich—of all things—of not being a team player. Of course Buddy Rich wasn't a team player: he was a force of nature, a law unto himself, a hard-drumming whirlwind who could give Gene Krupa a run for his money anytime. In November, Rich magnanimously accepted Dorsey's offer of $750 a week—a fortune then—and joined the band at its engagement at the Palmer House in Chicago.

Buddy Rich loved Tommy Dorsey's playing ("the greatest melodic trombone player that ever lived. Absolutely") and detested him personally. Many others felt the same way. Dorsey was really more a dictator than a leader, a martinet who ran an almost militarily rigid organization, enforcing proper dress and decorum, fining or firing violators for drinking or smoking marijuana. (Dorsey's own heavy drinking and womanizing—he had a wife at home in New Jersey, but was carrying on an affair with his girl singer, Edythe Wright—were theoretically beside the point.) Physically powerful and fearless, he had literally thrown offenders off the band bus. The object wasn't petty discipline but tight playing and—always—commercial success. He was renowned for firing his entire trumpet section (somehow it was always the trumpet section) if their playing didn't come up to snuff. His musicians, most of them in their twenties, called him the Old Man. In November 1939, Tommy Dorsey had just turned thirty-four.

In his own way, Jack Leonard was another part of the musical storm forming around the Dorsey band in the late fall of 1939. Over the years, it has become accepted wisdom that Dorsey's silky-voiced young baritone had grown restless and wanted to go out on his own. In fact Leonard was restless with his domineering boss. Dorsey had learned a cold and cutting wit from his tough family, and was free with it on and off the bandstand. His musicians learned to take it when he dished it out. But one night at the Palmer House, Jack Leonard, who had been with the band since he was nineteen, who had crisscrossed the country many times, his bladder ready to burst (it was rumored Dorsey didn't have one) in the ice-cold or baking-hot band bus, who had dutifully laid down the workmanlike vocals on forty-two Dorsey recordings, who had felt the Old Man's occasional warmth, but—more often—suffered his tongue-lashings, had simply had it. He walked off the bandstand, took a deep breath—free!—and left for good.

It wasn't easy: at times, Dorsey had been like a father to him. They'd had one of their warm moments a couple of months before, as leader and singer drove out to Dorsey's country house in New Jersey after a gig at the Hotel Pennsylvania roof in Manhattan. Basking in the Old Man's presence, late at night in the car, Leonard felt expansive. He asked Dorsey if he'd happened to catch Harry James's new boy singer on the radio—each afternoon, before the evening gig at the Roseland, the Music Makers were broadcasting from the World's Fair, out in Flushing. "They've got this new kid, Tommy, singing 'All or Nothing At All.' Have you heard him?"

At the wheel, Dorsey shook his head. "Uh-uh."

"Well," Leonard said, "this kid really knocks it out of the park. In fact, if you want to know the truth, he scares the hell out of me. He's that good."

Dorsey had cause to remember the conversation soon after Leonard walked out. One night in Chicago, the bandleader was having dinner with a pal named Jimmy Hilliard, the music supervisor for CBS, and bemoaning his boy-singer problem. "Have you heard the skinny kid who's singing with Harry James?" Hilliard asked. "He's nothing to look at, but he's got a sound! Harry can't be paying him much—maybe you can take him away."

Dorsey had quickly filled the breach caused by Leonard's departure with a baritone named Alan DeWitt. But DeWitt was merely adequate, and Tommy Dorsey wasn't interested in adequacy.

Then he heard Sinatra for himself.

The band was filing through the lobby of the Palmer House when a radio playing stopped Dorsey in his tracks. The song was "All or Nothing At All." He beckoned to his clarinetist, Johnny Mince. "Come here, Johnny, I want you to hear something," Dorsey said. "What do you think?"

The next night he sent his manager, Bobby Burns, to Mayor Kelly's Christmas party to hear the Music Makers. After the performance, Burns slipped Harry James's boy singer a note scribbled on a strip torn from a sandwich bag. Frank Sinatra's heart thumped hard when he saw the pencil scrawl on the grease-spotted brown paper: the note indicated Dorsey's suite number at the Palmer House and the time Frank should show up. Sinatra saved that scrap of paper for a long time.

It was a careful dance, the kind of unspoken minuet men do when approaching each other on a matter of importance. Sinatra had been aware, with each mile Harry James's rickety band bus traveled eastward, of Dorsey's looming presence in Chicago: it was like entering the gravitational field of an enormous dark star. And Dorsey, always calculating, had registered something when Jack Leonard made his offhand comment that night in the car on the way to Bernardsville.

The something moved a click when Jimmy Hilliard mentioned Sinatra, then clicked into place when Dorsey heard that song on the radio: he had already met this kid once.

Sinatra, of course, remembered the occasion intimately, as one of his great gaffes, like spilling a drink on a pretty girl's dress or calling someone important by the wrong name: he had frozen up in the great man's presence. It was one thing to be trying out for a new band—Bob Chester was a nice kid—it was quite another to have Himself walk in. He could freeze you with a stare, that cold puss of his. Sinatra still blushed just thinking about it.

This would be Frank's one and only chance to set things right, his one and only second chance with the great man, and it must, it must go right. There would be no third chance. He slept barely at all that night, for thinking of Tommy Dorsey's tough face and his perfect suits and, most of all, his gorgeous sound, those long, beautiful melody lines that backed a singer the way the purple velvet in a jewel box backed a diamond bracelet . . .

At 2:00 p.m. on the dot, Dorsey greeted Frank at the door of his suite, wearing a silk dressing gown over suit pants, shirt, and a tie. He exuded a manly whiff of Courtley cologne. His square gold cuff links were engraved TD.

Sinatra felt weak in the knees.

A strong handshake and that icy stare, from slightly above, with the very faintest of smiles. "Yes, I remember that day when you couldn't get out the words."

And damned if it didn't almost happen again: Frank's mouth fell open, and for a second nothing came out. He had to clear his throat to get his heart started again, and with that sound, miraculously, a sentence emerged.

Well, he'd been pretty nervous that day. He was pretty nervous today, too.

The smile warmed just a degree or two.

Dorsey told Frank to call him Tommy. He told him he'd like to hear him sing. Did Frank think he could manage that?

He had a few of the boys waiting up in the ballroom, Dorsey said. Did Frank know "Marie"?

Frank had only heard Jack Leonard sing it about a million times with that band behind him, had only imagined himself in Leonard's place about a million times. And Sinatra knew he could leave Jack Leonard in the dust. If he could get the words out.

And that was what Tommy Dorsey heard that afternoon in the Palmer House ballroom, as Sinatra stood by the piano, not nervous at all now, but as excited to be following Dorsey's dazzling trombone lead-in as he had ever been excited by a widespread pair of silky thighs . . . And you can hear it too, if you listen, back-to-back, to Jack Leonard performing "Marie" on disc 2 of the Tommy Dorsey *Centennial Collection* and Frank Sinatra singing the number with the Dorsey band on disc 5 of *The Song Is You*. First comes Leonard's strictly serviceable, utterly forgettable vocal, a pallid instrument among more interesting instruments, a lead-in, really, to the main event, Bunny Berigan's astonishing trumpet solo.

Then comes Sinatra. Or rather, first comes Dorsey's trombone chorus, and then the rather startling sound of the bandleader's waspish voice speaking a corny intro: "Fame and fortune. [*Fame and Fortune* was the name of the NBC radio show on which the song was being broadcast.] One simple little melody may turn the trick. I know—for you're listening to the tune that had a great deal to do with sending us on our way to fame. And here to bring you a listening thrill is Frank Sinatra, to sing the ever-popular 'Marie.' All right, Frank, take it."

Frank takes it. Crooning the melody against the rollicking background of the band's chanted antiphony ("On a night like this/We go pettin' in the park . . . Livin' in a great big way/Oh, mama!"), a background that would have overwhelmed a lesser artist, Sinatra sings with superb authority and subtle swing, having his sweet way with the rhythm and generally making you feel as if he were letting you in on a story he might have just made up then and there.

Dorsey nodded, almost smiling, as Sinatra sang his audition; seeing his reaction, Sinatra smiled and sang even better.

When Frank was done, Tommy told him he wanted him to come sing with the band. If Harry would let him go. Dorsey couldn't pay him a lot to begin with—just seventy-five a week—but they could talk later.

Sinatra didn't even hear the figure. He only registered the first sentence: *I'd like you to come sing with the band.* The Dorsey band. He called Nancy from a phone booth in the Palmer House lobby. The distant phone rang, then Nancy answered, far away. She sounded alarmed to hear his voice—but it was good news, he told her. The best.

What about Harry? she asked.

And of course she was right. Nancy, ever practical and straightforward, was always right. And he was wrong so much of the time . . . except about what he knew he needed.

Harry was in his hotel room with the door open, sitting back in an easy chair reading *Metronome,* his long legs resting on the bed. His socks had pictures of clocks on them. Sinatra walked right in. A room-service tray full of dirty dishes sat on the table. Through the bathroom door, Frank noticed—though Louise was still on the road—a pair of nylons hanging on the shower-curtain rod. The bandleader turned the pages of the magazine and chewed his Black Jack gum, not looking up. Frank stood for a moment, then walked out in the hall and came back in. No response. He left, counted to twenty, and entered again.

Finally, James put down the magazine and asked his singer what was eating him.

Sinatra told Harry that he'd rather open a vein than say what he was about to say. Then he said it.

James whistled, soft and low. He reached out a bony hand. Sinatra took it. James smiled and told Frank he was free. "Hell, if we don't do any better in the next few months, see if you can get me on, too."

It was a bittersweet moment. At not quite twenty-four, Harry James was nothing like the father figure Dorsey was to Dorsey's band—to Sinatra, he was more like a brother. Still, the singer, who always had vast respect for musical talent, and was voraciously open to musical influences of all kinds, "learned a lot from Harry," Louise Tobin said many years later. "He learned a lot about conducting and a lot about phrasing."

He'd also learned a lot about jazz, and how to sing up-tempo numbers. But Sinatra also knew—as he would his whole life—precisely when to move on.

There was one final gig with the Music Makers, two weeks in late December and early January at Shea's Theatre in Buffalo (also on the bill were Red Skelton and Sinatra's co-star-to-be in *From Here to Eternity*, Burt Lancaster, a grinning young acrobat at the time, half of a trampoline act, dreaming of being in the movies someday). And even though Frank Sinatra had learned what he could from Harry James, and even though by some accounts Frank had been a loner on the Music Makers bus ("he dozed, read magazines, and seldom said anything," one bandmate recalled)—despite all this, in later years Sinatra would recall his parting from the band with nostalgia and regret. "The bus pulled out with the rest of the boys at about half-past midnight," he said. "I'd said goodbye to them all and it was snowing. There was nobody around, and I stood alone in the snow with just my suitcase and watched the taillights disappear. Then the tears started, and I tried to run after the bus. There was such spirit and enthusiasm in that band, I hated leaving it."

It's a beautiful description, snow and taillights and tears. For whom, and about what, precisely, was he crying?

===

Dry-eyed and with an entourage yet, Sinatra joined the Dorsey band on the road just a few days later. Accompanying him were his old pal Hank Sanicola, to play rehearsal piano and swat off pests, and his Hoboken friend named Nick Sevano, to lay out Frank's clothes and run for coffee. How the singer could afford not one but two hangers-on at $75 a week is an almost theological question, answered nowhere in the vast body of Sinatriana—did Christ pay the disciples? And as to whether Sinatra met up with his new boss in (as has variously been reported)

Minneapolis or Sheboygan or Milwaukee or Rockford, Illinois, there is no consensus. This much is universally agreed, however: he knocked the socks off of all who were fortunate enough to be present.

"The first time I heard him, we were on stage in Milwaukee, and I had not even met him," Jo Stafford recalled. "Tommy introduced him and he came out and sang 'South of the Border.'"

Her visitor was perplexed. Many accounts said the number was "Star Dust."

Stafford, though a very old lady now, shook her head vigorously. " 'South of the Border,'" she insisted.

Almost seventy years earlier, at twenty-two, she had helped form Tommy Dorsey's perfect storm. It began for Stafford during the summer of 1938, when Dorsey tried out a young singing octet called the Pied Pipers on his radio show in New York. The lead singer and the group's only girl, Stafford had the purest soprano Tommy had ever heard. But the show's sponsor, an Englishman, threw a hissy fit when the kids sang a slightly risqué Fats Waller number called "Hold Tight (Want Some Sea Food, Mama!)," and fired them on the spot. Still, that girl's amazing voice stayed with Tommy. And so in December 1939, in Chicago, having hired Sy Oliver and Zeke Zarchy and Buddy Rich, and now Sinatra, Dorsey phoned Jo Stafford at home in California and told her he wanted the Pipers back.

"The only problem, Jo, is, I can't afford eight singers," he said.

Stafford laughed. "That's OK, Tommy. Four quit to try and earn an honest living. There are only four of us now."

The Pipers joined the band in December 1939, while Sinatra fulfilled his obligation to Harry James. And they were sitting on the stage in Milwaukee or Sheboygan or Minneapolis or Rockford when he appeared, straight out of the blue.

Had Stafford even heard him on the radio at that point?

"Never even heard *of* him," she said. "But I sure knew this was something. Everybody up until then was sounding like Crosby, but this was a whole new sound."

Was it ever. To get a sense of what Stafford heard that night, skip forward a few months and listen, side by side, to Bing's version of a corny yet completely seductive number called "Trade Winds" and then Frank's. The two recordings were made just four days apart—and Sinatra's was first, on June 27, 1940, in New York City, with Dorsey and orchestra, including the still-unfired Bunny Berigan (like Beiderbecke, a fatally self-destructive lush) on trumpet, Joe Bushkin on piano, and Buddy Rich on drums. Crosby laid down his track the following Monday, July 1, in Los Angeles, with Dick McIntire and His Harmony Hawaiians.

Amazingly, both versions are equally strong. The thirty-seven-year-old Bing had been at the very top of his game for the better part of a decade, the biggest star in America and a vocal force of nature. On this number, as always, his matchlessly rich baritone was simultaneously romantic and (ever so slightly) ironic. Other men could try to sing like him—and many did try—but that voice, utterly of a piece with his elusive personality, was simply inimitable.

As was Sinatra's.

As young as he was—not yet twenty-five—he carried the flyweight tropical number off with complete aplomb. Unlike Crosby's version, which, as a superstar deserved, was an out-and-out vocal from beginning to end, Sinatra's was a band singer's dutiful turn, coming on the heels of Dorsey's supersmooth trombone intro. His voice was nowhere near as deep and rich an instrument as it would become in the 1950s, and the Hoboken accent was still defiantly unreconstructed, the *r*'s dicey and the *t*'s a little adventure in themselves ("trade" became "chrade").

Yet Frank was lilting, persuasive, and assured. He didn't sound remotely like anyone else—and he knew it. Even that Hoboken accent was part of his arsenal. While Bing's power was his cool warmth, Frank's was his unabashed heat.

In fact, Bing's days were numbered.

Not commercially. Buoyed by his movie career, his matchless radio presence, and his ever-rising record sales, Crosby's stock was headed nowhere but up, and would continue to flourish for more than twenty years. But a new ballad singer had taken the field, and though America didn't know it yet, its heart hung in the balance. Bing had specifically instructed his lyricist, the great Johnny Burke, never to put the words "I love you" into any of his numbers: It simply wasn't a sentiment the star could carry off head-on. His humor—America loved him for his dry humor—would have been undercut by it. His wooing was more oblique. There was nothing oblique about Frank Sinatra.

"Frank really loved music, and I think he loved singing," Jo Stafford said. "But Crosby, it was more like he did it for a living. He liked music well enough. But he was a much colder person than Frank. Frank was a warm Italian boy. Crosby was not a warm Irishman."

So, suddenly, in the land of Crosby sound-alikes, in the year of Our Lord 1940, when Americans heard their president speak on the radio in godlike aristocratic tones, when they heard American movie actors declaiming in indeterminate English-y accents—here was something utterly new: a warm Italian boy. A boy with a superb voice that was also a potent means of communicating all kinds of things that white popular singers had never come close to: call it romantic yearning with hints of lust behind it, or call it arrogance with a quaver of vulnerability. In any case, it was a formula absolutely irresistible to blindsided females—not to mention to impressed males, who very quickly began using Sinatra as background to their wooing. As Daniel Okrent wrote in a 1987 *Esquire* article, "Sinatra knew this: the male of the species has never developed a more effective seduction line than the display of frailty."

And Jo Stafford, as levelheaded as they come, was seduced. Not sexually (though, as a woman, she had to have felt *that thrum*), but musically. She was operatically trained, a coloratura soprano, a great ear as well as a great voice, and very far from an easy sell. But she knew within a couple of bars of "South of the Border," there in Minneapolis or Milwaukee or Rockford or wherever the hell it was, when Sinatra was so new on the band that no charts had been written for him yet, that the entire game had changed, then and there.

"Well, see," she said, "he was doing what we call hitters. I mean, there was no arrangement for him. He just sang it, and the band picked up. So it was very impromptu. But of course, you heard the sound of the voice."

Leaving Crosby aside, her visitor asked, could she say how Jack Leonard or Bob Eberly, for example, were different from Sinatra?

Stafford shook her head. "I don't know. I think they made their own sounds, and they were good. They just weren't as good as Frank."

Why?

"There's a whole round sound of a beautiful voice with a great tone, singing straight down the middle of that note," Stafford said. She frowned. "I don't think I'm very good at describing it."

Was she aware of his expressiveness right away, the feeling that he brought to the song?

She shook her head again. "I don't think so," she said. "I just knew it was a wonderful, great sound, and it was not Crosby. It was a new sound and a good one, a very musical sound."

What did Sinatra look like then? her visitor asked.

"Young." She laughed, a surprisingly strong laugh. Even at close to ninety, she still had a beautiful voice. "Young with lots of hair, and very thin."

===

She was sold; most in the band weren't. At first the veterans, who had all been fond of the sweet-tempered Jack Leonard, simply froze the newcomer out. And then there was Buddy Rich. On Sinatra's first one-nighter, he noticed that the bus seat next to the drummer was empty—not much of a surprise, given Rich's abrasive personality. (When Dorsey first introduced Sinatra to Rich, it was with these words: "I want you to meet another pain in the ass.") So Sinatra sat down. The two young men—Frank was twenty-four; Buddy, twenty-two—got to talking, and, lo and behold, they hit it off. After a few days on the road, Rich told Sinatra, "I like the way you sing." It was extravagant praise, coming from one of the biggest egomaniacs in the business—little did Sinatra realize how truly heartfelt the comment was. (In later life, Rich admitted he had had to turn his face to hide his tears when Sinatra sang "Star Dust.") The two became roommates. It sounds like a sweet story. It was doomed from the start.

Sinatra's days as an only child set the pattern: he had never been much for sharing a room—or much of anything, for that matter. (Traveling with the James band over most of the first year of his marriage, he had barely lived with his young wife.) The end to the Sinatra-Rich honeymoon came when Sinatra insisted on clipping his toenails in their hotel room at 2:00 a.m. Remarkably, Rich told his biographer Mel Tormé that the insomniac singer had also kept him awake by reading till all hours. Among all the big-band personnel crisscrossing the United States in the late 1940s, Sinatra and Artie Shaw may have been the only two men keeping late hours with, now and then anyway, a book.

But the real reason the singer and the drummer split was that each felt he was Dorsey's true star. (Tommy Dorsey knew he and he alone was the star, another problem altogether.)

Of course, Dorsey's name was printed in the biggest type on the band's posters, but the leader decided whose name would be featured under his, an honor with purely commercial underpinnings that depended on—and, in a circular way, determined—which band member was hottest. Often it was Bunny Berigan; lately, in early 1940, it had been the new star, Rich. But soon enough, it would be Sinatra all the way.

The Old Man shows 'em how. Frank with Tommy Dorsey and the orchestra, December 1, 1941. Connie Haines is front row far right, jitterbugging.

The life of a traveling band, even a highly successful band, wasn't for sissies. If the Music Makers had been a jaunty but slightly depressed boys' club, the Dorsey organization was like a well-disciplined Army platoon. They even wore uniforms—different suits depending on the venue. (College shows meant blue blazers, tan trousers, and brown and white saddle shoes.) Dorsey's musicians would play up to nine shows a day, then ride all night on their dilapidated former Greyhound bus, sometimes four hundred miles or more at a clip (at forty and fifty miles per hour, on two-lane blacktop), with infrequent rest stops, sleeping in their seats, the Old Man right up front, where he could keep an eye on everybody. "I can still see Tommy in the second seat on the right aisle with the hat on, riding through the night," Jo Stafford said.

Stafford recalled "lots and lots of laughs and good times together" on the Dorsey bus, but Sinatra's memories of those long rides are strikingly unpeopled: especially in later years, he would reminisce again and again about learning how to keep the crease in his suit while sitting in his seat, about falling asleep with his cheek pressed against the cold glass. "For maybe the first five months," he said, "I missed the James band. So I kept to myself, but then I've always been a loner—all my life."

He was naturally aloof, but he was also taking his cues from the man in charge. Tommy Dorsey was anything but hail-fellow-well-met: he was the model of a tough commander who kept his distance from his troops—except for occasional, fumbling attempts at intimacy. There was the time, during a long, cold drive across Pennsylvania ("a Greyhound bus is not the greatest place to spend winter in the East," Stafford noted drily), when Dorsey had the driver stop at a general store and bought the whole band scarves, earmuffs, and mittens. In warmer months, there were frequent band baseball games—though the Old Man seems always to have been mindful of his lofty status: Jean Bach, who was married to Dorsey's trumpeter Shorty Sherock, recalled one such game, at Dorsey's house in Bernardsville, in which the band members drank warm beer and sweated on the diamond while the leader relaxed in the shade of his porte cochere and sipped chilled champagne. Dorsey also loved practical jokes—a particularly sadistic form of amiability, usually involving liquid. He would leave wet sponges on his instrumentalists' seats, spray them with a fire hose from the wings, squirt seltzer down the cleavages of his girl singers. There were ambivalent smiles.

Sinatra watched and learned. And frequently rebelled. Curfews and deadlines were not for him. He also had a habit of letting a lock of his luxuriant hair droop over his forehead—a look that drove the girls wild, and made Dorsey furious. The bandleader kept his new pain in the ass in line through a combination of kindness and menace—much like a certain petite redhead from Hoboken. When the boy singer got too cocky (and it's hard to imagine Sinatra tamping down his natural style), Dorsey took to threatening to replace him with a smooth-voiced, and better-behaved, band singer named Bob Allen. "Once," Will Friedwald writes, "Sinatra walked into the band's dressing room . . . and discovered the other singer's tuxedo draped over his chair. After another session of pleading and shouting with Dorsey, Sinatra went on that night."

Ultimately, Sinatra took to cultivating Dorsey—though he insisted that it was a matter of compassion. "Tommy was a very lonely man," he said. "He was a strict disciplinarian with the band—we'd get fined if we were late—yet he craved company after the shows and never really got it . . . We all knew he was lonely, but we couldn't ask him to eat and drink with us because it looked too much like shining teacher's apple.

"Anyway," Sinatra recalled, "one night two of us decided to hell with it, we'd ask him out to dinner. He came along and really appreciated it. After that he became almost like a father to me . . . I'd sit up playing cards with Tommy till maybe five-thirty every morning. He couldn't sleep ever: he had less sleep than any man I've ever known."

If you detect a sneaking similarity to the ring-a-ding-ding Sinatra of the mid-1950s through the early 1960s, the infinitely lonely kingpin who couldn't bear to be alone, especially in the deep watches of the night, the man who would forcibly restrain (through force of personality, that is, which in Sinatra's case was every bit as powerful as physical force) his drinking buddies from going to sleep before he did—usually at or past the hour when Mr. and Mrs. America were waking up to go to work—then you understand. It's not enough to say that from the moment Sinatra joined the Dorsey organization he deliberately set about remaking himself in the bandleader's image: the process was both conscious and unconscious. Tommy Dorsey was the most power-ful male figure Sinatra had ever encountered—everything the younger man wanted to be, the strong father he had never had.

But in a certain way, Dorsey was also the mother he did have. To begin with, Dorsey was more feared than loved, and fear was a key part of Sinatra's makeup. The bandleader had a hot temper, as did Sinatra, but it stemmed from a different source: Dorsey's anger was black-Irish and bloody-minded; Sinatra's was the rage of a child who is terrified he will be slapped down—or worse, ignored. Sinatra once said that the only two people he was ever afraid of were his mother and Tommy Dorsey—a flip comment but also a sincere and deeply significant one.

With both the uncertainty was torturous, but in another way it must also have been thrilling, even sexually exciting. There's a psychological term for the attraction: identification with the aggressor. Rumors of sadomasochistic tendencies have always hovered around Sinatra, and it's not hard to see why. In many ways, Frank would become both Dolly and Dorsey, and the royal road to his fixation on the bandleader was his addiction to his mother.

Marty too was ingrained in Sinatra's psyche, but probably in a neg-ative way—by his absence rather than by his presence. In later years Sinatra would sometimes drop a comment about how his father had kept him in line, yet those comments had a way of feeling like a sop to the old man, a tacit admission that the non-reading, non-writing, non-speaking Marty should have been more of a dad than he really was. In post-Dorsey years, Sinatra would pick up several more father figures here and there, but Tommy was the first and the most powerful.

Still, there was one thing all the father substitutes had in common: Sinatra always left them before they had a chance to leave him.

In the beginning, Sinatra set out to learn everything he could from Dorsey, personally and musically. ("There's only one singer," the bandleader told Frank early on, "and his name is Crosby. The lyrics mean everything to him, and they should to you too.") Some of the personal lessons would take years, even decades, to achieve their full effect. The singer first experienced leadership himself amid his gradually expanding crew of cronies and gofers. His next subjects were musicians—but he only gained power with his players when, after Columbia Records dropped him, he was signed by Capitol and started to record in Los Angeles. (The producer George Avakian, who worked on both coasts, points out that California studio musicians were far more deferential to Sinatra than their New York counterparts, who were apt to be snooty classical artists.)

And it was only when rock 'n' roll killed his record sales and he started to tour heavily in the 1970s and 1980s that Sinatra became a true leader, in the more-or-less-benign-despot style of Dorsey. His musicians even gave him the same nickname: the Old Man. (Which, for most of the time he led a touring band, he actually was.) Frank even took up Dorsey's model-railroading obsession: in late middle age, the unabashedly nostalgic Sinatra devoted an entire building in his Palm Springs compound to an enormous electric-train setup.

What thrilled him at the outset was simply the way Dorsey carried himself, the way he handled his fame and power: his ramrod posture, his smooth patter on the bandstand and at radio microphones, his perfect wardrobe (he was once photographed, during a summertime stand in New York, wearing tailored Bermuda shorts with his jacket and tie). Not to mention his eye for the ladies and his heavy after-hours drinking. Sinatra, always an obsessive, even copied some of the tiniest details—Dorsey's Courtley cologne, his Dentist Prescribed toothpaste.

But of course the most important lessons the singer learned from the leader were musical. Sinatra was gigantically ambitious, virtually every move he made in his life had to do with the furtherance of his career, and in this respect he saw that Tommy Dorsey had a great deal to teach him. Much has been made of the magical breath control Sinatra supposedly learned at Dorsey's feet—or rather at his back, while he was playing his magical trombone. "I used to watch Tommy's back, his jacket, to see when he would breathe," he said. "I'd swear the son of a bitch was not breathing. I couldn't even see his jacket move . . . I thought, he's gotta be breathing some place—through the ears?"

Dorsey did indeed have spectacular breath control, through a combination of anatomical good fortune—he was extremely broad chested—and artful deception. His trick was to take an extra breath, when he needed one, through a pinhole he would form at the corner of his mouth and which he would shield from prying eyes with his left hand, which, in standard trombonist's form, was held close to the instrument's mouthpiece. Hence those sixteen-bar (or thirty-two-bar, depending on who's telling the story) legatos.

But his long trombone lines were more than trickery or showmanship: they were the melodic essence of his art. His band's numbers usually began with a solo by the lead trombonist, to (1) instantly announce the presence of TD, and (2) quickly *tell the story of the song.* Both things were crucial on the radio, which, as the main medium for mass communication of the day, had a tremendous imaginative force that all began with sound. Through long years of study, Dorsey had arrived at a method of proclaiming the artist, and his art, that was as aurally unmistakable as the call of some glorious mythological bird.

And his whole band—which, after all, was his true instrument, a sixteen-piece extension of his towering personality—needed to be up to the task. The saxophonist Arthur "Skeets" Herfurt recalled: "Tommy sometimes used to make the whole orchestra (not just the trombones) play from the top of a page clear down to the bottom without taking a breath. It was way too many bars! But I sure developed lung power . . . Everybody in the band would learn to play like Tommy did."

Clever as he was, Sinatra instantly realized he would have to raise his game vocally. Even if, as his first recordings with the band show, he began rather pallidly, trying to fit in and generally hold his own, he was watching and learning every second.[1] Tommy Dorsey was a superstar (even if that vulgar word hadn't yet been coined), and Sinatra was, by God, going to be one too. Even bigger. But copying Dorsey's breath control was a far more powerful statement than copying the cologne or toothpaste he used. Sinatra had heard other singers, even very good ones, take a breath in the middle of a phrase, and he thought it sounded lousy. It showed artifice, just like the hoked-up accents and stuffy styles of most vocalists in those days. It said, *This is a singer, singing a song.* Most of those guys—even the very good ones—never sounded as if they felt what they were singing, as if they really believed it. Singing the phrase straight through showed he really understood, and meant, the words.

A message that was not lost on his listeners. He saw the way the girls stared at him as he sang. He was telling them something, a story of love, and they were listening. (He could continue the story whenever he wanted, on or off the stage.) They didn't stare at Bing that way.

No one ever told the Sinatra story better than Sinatra himself. And one of the great chapters was the account of how he had developed powers of breath control even more legendary than those of the short-lived Dorsey (who—with horrible irony—died of asphyxiation, choking to death on his own vomit in his sleep after a heavy meal at age fifty-one, in 1956). After Dorsey mentioned offhandedly that he'd built up his lung capacity by swimming underwater, Sinatra decided that he too, by God, would swim laps underwater at the Stevens Institute's indoor pool—and let the world know about it. Not only that: he would also run laps on the Stevens track. It has the feeling of a Hollywood montage (and the Stevens theme must have been meaningful for a boy who had so gravely disappointed his father by failing to become an engineer). You can practically see the big varsity S on Sinatra's sweatshirt as he pounds the cinders of that Stevens quarter mile.

And yet, while Sinatra doubtless did some underwater swimming and ran some laps, it's hard to imagine an inveterate night owl and hedonist, fully engaged in the grueling existence of a touring swing band, taking on any sort of concentrated training regimen.

Jo Stafford insisted that all the mythic accounts of underwater swimming were just that: mythological. The true story, she said, was anatomical. "You can have a big enough rib cage to take a deep breath," she said. "And also, know how to let it out. You can sing a note and use half as much breath as most people do. I think that if you want to learn to do that, you can. Frank certainly could. I could. Tommy also."

Another chapter in the Sinatra-phrasing saga hinges on a Carnegie Hall classical concert that he attended, on a whim, in early 1940. The program consisted of Brahms, Debussy, Rachmaninoff, and Ravel; Jascha Heifetz was the soloist. "I was never a great fan of the classical music," Sinatra told Sidney Zion. "I enjoyed hearing the pretty parts of it; didn't understand most of it." This time, for some reason, he was ready to hear it. He was especially fascinated by Heifetz's violin technique. He could "get to the end of the bow and continue without a perceptible missing beat in the motion," Sinatra recalled. "I thought, 'Why can't I do that? If he's doing that with the bow, why can't I do it even better than I'm doing it now, as one who uses my breath?' I began to listen to his records. I couldn't afford many at the time, but I got some of them. I sat and listened to them and it worked. It really worked."

Soon he was listening to the above-mentioned composers as well as Ralph Vaughan Williams and Delius and Glazunov and Fauré. His ear expanded with his lung capacity.

Maybe Frank did have an extra-large rib cage; maybe, once the band came east from Chicago in February 1940 (to start a New York stand that would continue through the summer), he simply shifted into a new gear, swimming and running and listening to classical music. He was twenty-four, after all: starting to leave adolescence behind at last. As soon as he got back to New York, he returned to his old voice teacher Quinlan and practiced "calisthenics for the throat," resuming the "Let us wander by the bay" exercise that he would thenceforth practice for the rest of his career. He was gathering a huge new power, a kind of sexual supercharge. Sammy Cahn recalled watching Sinatra sing with Dorsey: "Frank can hold a tremendous phrase, until it takes him into a sort of paroxysm—he gasps, his whole person seems to explode, to release itself."

Zeke Zarchy could see it from the trumpet section. "The audience wouldn't let him off the stage," he recalled. "This scrawny kid had such appeal. I had never seen a vocalist with a band go over like that. He had a certain quality. Jack Leonard was a good singer, but a band singer . . . I could sense [Sinatra] knew that also."

Now, with the rocket booster of the Dorsey band behind him, Frank was going farther, faster—in fact, he was approaching escape velocity.

The rest of the band knew something was up, though they hadn't a clue how far it would really go. John Huddleston of the Pied Pipers (then Jo Stafford's husband) said, "He had something. He sure knew it. I could sense that he was going to do whatever he wanted." And Zarchy further observed, "When I say he was standoffish, it's not because he felt that he was better than anybody else. He knew that he was going to be a star because he wanted to be a star . . . And I didn't blame him one bit and neither did anybody else because we saw what his appeal was."

This last isn't entirely true. The band's first date after it returned from Chicago was at one of the biggest clubs in the East, Frank Dailey's Meadowbrook, on Route 23 in Cedar Grove, New Jersey. "It was at the Meadowbrook," Peter J. Levinson writes, "that Dorsey first gave Sinatra, rather than to Buddy Rich, featured billing. Buddy immediately expressed his anger to Tommy but to no avail. In retaliation, he speeded up the tempo on slow ballads behind Sinatra or played loudly behind him."

Things would escalate from there. But Rich was fighting a losing battle—and he knew it, which riled him up even more. He felt gypped: he had signed on with Dorsey to propel jazz, and now the ballads (totally boring to keep time to), and the ballad singer, were taking over. And no matter how blazing a drummer's solos, he sits at the back of the band; the singer stands in front. Literally and figuratively, Frank Sinatra was beginning to stand in front of everyone else.

Everyone.

Tommy Dorsey would have laughed in the face of anyone who told him that his boy singer, this pain-in-the-ass little guinea, was single-handedly bringing the primacy of the big band to an end and ushering in the age of the solo vocalist. The Dorsey empire was running smoothly, its ruler a superb businessman as well as a great bandleader. His band hit the ground running when it reached the Big Apple. Not only were they booked into the Paramount for four weeks in March and April, but they also began a blazing streak of New York recording sessions that would continue through August and result in almost forty of the eighty-three studio numbers that Sinatra eventually cut with Dorsey.

And Frank's confidence grew with every tune. He began a practice he would continue to the end of his career. "I take a sheet with just the lyrics. No music," he told the casino mogul Steve Wynn many years later. "At that point, I'm looking at a poem. I'm trying to understand the point of view of the person behind the words. I want to understand his emotions. Then I start speaking, not singing, the words so I can experiment and get the right inflections. When I get with the orchestra, I sing the words without a microphone first, so I can adjust the way I've been practicing to the arrangement. I'm looking to fit the emotion behind the song that I've come up with to the music. Then it all comes together. You sing the song. If the take is good, you're done."

The first number he recorded in New York was one that had been written by his old drinking buddy from the hungry years (just three years earlier), the brilliant former Remick and Company song plugger Jimmy Van Heusen. The number, co-written with the lyricist Eddie DeLange, was called "Shake Down the Stars."

Sinatra had a gift for seeing talent and allying himself with it. Both Sammy Cahn and Van Heusen were coming into their own in 1940, Van Heusen in a spectacular way: he would write sixty songs that year. Chester had already been wooed by Bing Crosby's lyricist Johnny Burke, and would move to Hollywood that summer (flying his own plane, a two-seat Luscombe-Silvaire, cross-country) to start collaborating with Burke on movie tunes for Bing.

But it was Sinatra—"Junior," as Crosby would soon refer to him—

who would make hits of two Burke–Van Heusen numbers that year. The first was "Polka Dots and Moonbeams," which he recorded on March 4, and which became Frank's very first charting song, reaching number 18 in *Billboard* for the week of April 28, 1940.

For the whole month of March he headlined at the Paramount, the crème de la crème of big-band venues. The girls were so gaga for him that they would line up hours ahead of time for the first show at 9:00 a.m. and then, when that show was over, refuse to leave, staying for five more. Sinatra came up with the brilliant publicity stunt of bringing out a big tray of food after the first show, to tide over his increasingly fanatical public. At the end of the day, he had to be escorted by the police to the Hotel Astor, just a block south on Broadway. The last time he had been escorted by police, they had escorted him to jail.

The band was putting up at the Astor; Nancy was staying with her parents in Jersey City. A big wide river lay in between. What with six shows a day followed by 9:00 p.m. rehearsals (crazy Dorsey felt that a band simply couldn't be too tight), plus recording sessions, Frank didn't have much time to get home. Nor was his ever-heavier wife much inclined to schlep over to the Paramount and listen to young girls scream for her husband.

Meanwhile, a little blast from the recent past arrived in the form of Connie Haines, whom Harry James had had to let go for financial reasons the previous August, but whom Tommy Dorsey could very much afford. Unlike the Pied Pipers, who, as splendidly as they sang, were strictly background, Haines was a star, a pint-sized nineteen-year-old with big eyes, a perky figure, a thick Savannah, Georgia, accent, and a big voice. She could really sing, and swing, and audiences ate her up (and Dorsey, a great showman, knew it). And Sinatra hated her thunder-stealing guts. *He* was the show. "Go ahead, do your thing, cornball," he would snarl at her as she jitterbugged, grinning, around the big stage.

But he would soon have the spotlight all to himself. Beginning in May, the band was booked to play the Astor's gloriously posh roof garden—it had a thousand-foot tree-lined promenade, with lights twinkling like stars among the branches. For New York's glitterati, the Dorsey stand was a much-anticipated event. Sinatra too was all aflutter. The Astor was Class with a capital C, and the singer, who from an early age craved class just about as much as he craved sex (but found it much more unattainable), was more nervous than he had ever been about a gig. It was one thing to play the Paramount, with its great sea of undifferentiated faces; it was quite something else to entertain the rich at close hand. He could depend on a certain number of swooning teenage girls (it was prom season), but the audience at the Astor would mainly consist of grown-ups—wealthy, arrogant, jaded grown-ups. With an exquisitely calibrated social sense born of deeply held feelings of inferiority—Italians had risen in the American public's estimation since Marconi and Toscanini, but not much—Sinatra felt an entirely reasonable fear of what he was up against.

Still, fear got him excited. And on opening night, Tuesday, May 21, 1940, he got the Astor excited. The band's first number featured Sinatra and the Pied Pipers, and—as was distinctly not the case when he shared the stage with Haines—his respect for his co-performers led him to vocalize selflessly and beautifully. It was yet another string to Sinatra's bow. "When you sing with a group, it takes a certain amount of discipline, and Frank was excellent at it," Jo Stafford said. "You can't wander off into your own phrasing. You've all got to do exactly the same thing at exactly the same time. Very few solo singers can do that. He could. When he sang with us, he was a Piper, and he liked it, and did it well. I don't know any other solo singer, solo male singer especially, that can do that."

Of course he wasn't like other singers. And on the next number, the hypnotically beautiful "Begin the Beguine," the stage, and the song, were all his. And, as the twenty-three-year-old pianist Joe Bushkin, who'd just joined the band in April, recalled: "He wound it up with a nice big finish, and the place went bananas!" The formerly jaded crowd, which had stopped dancing to listen, was screaming for an encore—but "Begin the Beguine" was the only solo feature Sinatra did with Dorsey at the time.

Canny showman that he was, Dorsey put his own ego on hold and stopped the band. If they wanted an encore, they'd get one. "Just call out the tunes," he told Sinatra, "and Joey will play 'em for you."

This went fine for three or four numbers, Bushkin said—until Sinatra turned around and said, "Smoke Gets in Your Eyes." The lovely Kern-Harbach tune has a notoriously tricky middle section, a chord modulation that looks great on paper but can be hell to pull from memory. Under pressure, Bushkin simply blanked. "Next thing I know," he said, "Frank was out there singing it all by himself . . . a capella. I was so embarrassed. I mean, Jesus, all the guys were looking at me, so I just turned around and walked away from the piano!"

The cream of New York society—gents in dinner jackets; dames in gowns; a few hundred fancy prom kids, all dressed to the nines— stood hushed, craning their necks to see, while the skinny boy with the greasy hair filled the big room with song, all by himself.

"And that is the night," Joe Bushkin said, "that Frank Sinatra happened."

———

Just two days later, Dorsey, and a stripped-down core unit that he called the Sentimentalists, went into the RCA recording studio in Rockefeller Center and took another stab at a number they had tried, without much success, a month earlier. The song, a mournful ballad written by a pianist named Ruth Lowe in memory of her late husband, was called "I'll Never Smile Again." The May 23 version moves at a dreamy-slow tempo. It begins with a piano intro, followed by the perfect five-part harmony of the four Pied Pipers, plus Sinatra, singing the first stanza and a half—"I'll never smile again, until I smile at you/I'll never laugh again"—and then Sinatra comes in alone: "What good would it do?" he sings, aspirating the initial "wh" of "what" with such plummy, Quinlan-esque precision that it comes out "hwat," a pronunciation that would not have sounded amiss to any of Cole Porter's society swells.

It sounded just great to America. When the record came out five weeks later, it quickly shot to number 1 on the *Billboard* chart—the first number 1 on the first *Billboard* chart—and stayed there for twelve weeks, turning Frank Sinatra into a national star. Meanwhile, on the strength of Frank's éclat, the Dorsey band's initial booking of three weeks at the Astor was extended to fourteen.

Did Tommy Dorsey come up with more solo ballads for Sinatra to sing? You bet he did. Just like that, the cart was pulling the horse.

Frank with Dorsey and the band in his first MGM musical, *Ship Ahoy*. Buddy Rich is on the drums, Tommy leads, Jo Stafford and her fellow Pied Pipers are behind the piano.

"Hey, Bing, old man. Move over. Here I come." Recording
with Dorsey's musicians, but, pointedly, no Dorsey. Frank is
the star on this session. Los Angeles, January 19, 1942.

Meanwhile. On a Saturday evening, June 8, Nancy Sandra Sinatra was born at the Margaret Hague Maternity Hospital in Jersey City. "Dad was in Hollywood with the band," Nancy Sinatra
writes in *Frank Sinatra: An American Legend*. In fact, Dad was not in
Hollywood with the band—he was at the Hotel Astor with the band,

Broadway and Forty-fourth Street, six miles as the crow flies from Jersey City, a million miles as the native son flies.

"I hated missing that," Sinatra told an interviewer years later, sounding as strangely cold-blooded—*that*—as if he were talking about missing a certain cocktail party. "It was just a taste of things to come, man. When I think of all the family affairs and events I would miss over the years because I was on the road."

If that last sentence looks incomplete, it's because Sinatra didn't finish the thought.[1]

Frank and Big Nancy, as she would now forever be known, named Tommy Dorsey as Baby Nancy's godfather. Of course, it was Frank's idea.

===

Four nights later, on an NBC radio broadcast from the Astor roof, Sinatra sang "I'll Never Smile Again" to another houseful of upper-crusters. The air check of the number reveals a small but striking difference from the recording: on the radio version's out-chorus (the last words sung in the song), as Sinatra sings "Within my heart, I know I will never start / To smile again, until I smile at you," he uses the vocal trick he'd discovered back at the Rustic Cabin, a breathy little catch in his voice, in this case before the initial *h* of "heart." It's a small thing, a showman-like touch that would have made no sense on a recording but all the sense in the world before a live crowd—a naked play for the hearts of the rich girls in the audience. Calculated, and thoroughly effective.

They watched him, and he watched them. Taking five during the fast numbers, standing by the piano, "Frank would tap me on the shoulder and say, 'Check the action out!'" Joe Bushkin recalled. "Some gal with a lot of booze in her would be shaking it up on the dance floor . . . Whenever he could take a shot at a woman he would."

In the beginning it had been both pretty ones and not-so-pretty ones. He didn't have to settle so much anymore. They were getting prettier all the time.

"It must have been sometime in 1940," Sammy Cahn wrote in his memoir. "He told me how unhappy he was being a married man. I gave him the George Raft syndrome. 'George Raft has been married all his life. Put it this way—you're on the road all the time, you at least can go home to clean sheets.' He kind of understood that."

═══

"Tommy Dorsey came up to see the baby," Ed Kessler remembered. "I thought my sister was gonna fall out the window."

Kessler was twelve in the summer of 1940. His family lived in a brown-brick apartment building at 12 Audubon Avenue in Jersey City; Frank and Nancy Sinatra, and now Baby Nancy, lived just upstairs. It was a nice, leafy neighborhood, around the corner from the State Teachers College and just across from Bergen Park.

"They were in a three-room apartment on the third floor," Kessler said. "We were upscale from them, five rooms on the second floor. My mother was very class-conscious—unless you were Jewish and lived within a certain area of Jersey City, you didn't count. She thought the Sinatras were low-class."

The kids disagreed. Kessler's sister, five years older than Ed, was agog when Sinatra moved in. And while young Eddie hadn't been entirely sure at first exactly who this singer was, he quickly took note of him. For one thing, there was his car. "About a quarter to a third of the tenants in our building owned automobiles," Kessler recalled. "Those who owned, owned Chevys, Fords, Plymouths, in black or gray. Sinatra had a two-toned blue-and-cream Buick convertible."

And then there was another impressive fact. "He didn't keep regular hours," Kessler said. "Most people in the apartment had jobs that were eight-to-five."

At first, Kessler's observations were simply those of a curious twelve-year-old. "But then," he said, "I got asked to baby-sit."

Suddenly he was in. What did he see? "I saw Nancy Sinatra naked!" Kessler laughed. (He was speaking, of course, of the baby.) Other than that, though, the household was depressingly ordinary: "reasonably neat, not very fancy," he recalled. "I can't remember any distinctive artwork or books—it was very working-class. They paid scale—twenty-five or fifty cents an hour."

And the young marrieds?

"Nancy was pleasant," Kessler said. "Very short, heavyset—what you might call a typical Italian-looking woman."

In all fairness, the heaviness was probably post-baby weight. What's most striking in Kessler's account, however, is the contrast in the nesting pair, between the brown-toned female and the gaudily feathered male. "I remember him sometimes in a yachting cap," Kessler said. "He also wore a blazer with an ascot. He looked very confident—he walked erect. He looked like he was ahead of the game all the time. He gave me an autographed picture of himself."

===

So now Frank had added a blazer and ascot to the yachting cap. Yet while his teenage dreams of stardom, as symbolized by the Crosby pipe and headgear, had come closer to reality, Sinatra wasn't quite there yet. He was suddenly well-known, but still not nearly on the level of Dorsey or Crosby. He was anything but rich. (He received a flat bonus of $25 for each recording session with the band, and—of course—no royalty for discs sold.) He was hovering on the doorstep of true fame, but still living in the third-floor walk-up, making payments on the Buick convertible. Yet *he was watching Dorsey*. He was learning from Tommy's example how to be a real star. Practicing.

And no matter his financial reality in the summer of 1940, Frank felt a yawning gulf between himself and the everyday, eight-to-five world of black or gray Chevys and Plymouths. Regular hours were for squares. He was the man that got away.

===

Dorsey loved Dolly, and Dolly loved Dorsey. They had more than one thing in common. Tommy used to take the band over to the Garden

Street house for big Sunday-night dinners, linguine and marinara sauce.

More often than not, Nancy was absent.

=====

The two strutting cocks of the Dorsey band couldn't get off each other's case. One muggy August night, backstage at the Astor, Buddy Rich decided he had finally had his fill of wielding the brushes, practically nodding off as he kept ultraslow time behind Sinatra's ballads. He called Sinatra a son-of-a-bitch wop bastard. And the next thing Jo Stafford knew (she was sitting at a table nearby, writing a letter to her mother), "they got at it."

Sinatra was standing near a waiter's table laden with pitchers of ice water. Furious, he picked up one of the pitchers and shied it at Rich's head. Rich ducked just in time. "If he hadn't," Stafford said, "he probably would have been killed or seriously hurt. The pitcher hit the wall so hard that pieces of glass were embedded in the plaster."

She laughed. "It splashed on my letter, which irked me pretty good. I left a few drops to show Mama what it was."

Stafford shook her head. "I don't even know what they were fighting about. I wasn't paying any attention to them."

They were fighting about the same thing they always fought about. This time, though, it was physical. Sinatra had never been much of a one for actual, as opposed to talked-about, fisticuffs, but these days, with his testosterone levels soaring, he was becoming fearless. The second after Rich ducked the flying pitcher, he flew at Sinatra, and the two bantamweights, Rich's biographer Mel Tormé writes, "went at each other . . . all the pent-up bad feelings exploding into curses and swinging fists. Luckily they were separated by members of the band before any real damage could be done. But it wasn't over."

After the dustup, Dorsey sent Sinatra home. "I can live without a singer tonight, but I need a drummer," he said. The bandleader had exacted a worse punishment than he could have imagined. It was humiliation, it was exile—it was *home*. Sinatra stewed, but not for long.

> A few nights later [Tormé continues], Buddy [went] over to Child's restaurant, just south of the Astor, for a bite between sets. As he was returning to the Astor, he felt a tap on his shoulder. He turned, and the night exploded.

The front page of *Down Beat*, September 1, 1940, trumpeted:

BUDDY RICH GETS FACE BASHED IN

> New York—Buddy Rich's face looked as if it had been smashed in with a shovel last week as Buddy sat behind the drums in the Tom Dorsey band at the Astor Hotel.
>
> No one was real sure what had happened except that Buddy had met up with someone who could use his dukes better than Rich. Members of the band—several of them "tickled" about the whole thing—said that Buddy "went out and asked for it."

Rich told Tormé he had been attacked by two men who took nothing from him, but rather administered a "coldly efficient and professional" beating. "He told me," Tormé writes, "that one night just before Sinatra left Dorsey (September 3, 1942) he quietly approached Frank and asked him point blank if the mugs who had flattened him two years before had done so at Frank's request. 'Hey, it's water under the bridge,' Buddy assured Frank. 'No hard feelings. I just want to know.' Sinatra hesitated and then admitted that he had asked a favor of a couple of Hoboken pals. Rich laughed, shook hands with Frank, and wished him good luck on his solo vocal career."

A singular relationship. But then, they were both singular men. When the band went west in October to open the new Palladium Ballroom in Hollywood, Jo Stafford and John Huddleston rode across the country with Rich and his father in Rich's new Lincoln Continental convertible. In these intimate circumstances, Stafford remembers, there was a good deal of talking, but she learned next to nothing about who Buddy actually was. "He was remote," she told Tormé.

As was Sinatra. The hottest, most accessible part of each man was his bottomless need, his seething ambition. The more people around, the better. As long as they didn't try to get too close.

I can live without a singer tonight, but I need a drummer. Ultimately, no matter how popular Sinatra got, he was dispensable. But then, that could work the other way, too.

For Dorsey, Frank was getting harder to take all the time. Sometimes he thought, *My God, I've created a monster.* Then he realized the monster was creating himself. As Sinatra's star rose, his ego, once mostly held in check, became rampant. The band (except for Rich), and even the bandleader, began to defer to him. "If Tommy Dorsey was late to a rehearsal," Sammy Cahn recalled, "Frank Sinatra acted as substitute orchestra leader. When Dorsey arrived, Sinatra would fix him with a glare of 'Where the fuck you been?' Dorsey would apologize that he'd been tied up in this and that and Sinatra'd say something quaint like 'bullshit.'"

No father, good or bad, goes unpunished.

Sinatra's third trip to the Coast was very different from his second. Just a year earlier, he had been traveling with Nancy and the destitute Music Makers, making the best of a bad situation after the Palomar burned down, then getting the hook while the caged canaries at Victor Hugo's looked on. Now he was free as a bird, a hot young up-and-comer with a number-one record, singing to all the stars of Hollywood, Bob Hope and Tyrone Power and Lana Turner and Errol Flynn and Mickey Rooney, at the Palladium, the million-dollar pink and chrome 1940s-Moderne palace (its twelve-thousand-square-foot oval dance floor could accommodate six thousand dancers) that had risen from the ashes of the Palomar, next door to Columbia Pictures on Sunset Boulevard.

What's more, he was in the movies. Sort of. During the Palladium stand, the Dorsey band got hired to perform four numbers in the new Paramount B musical *Las Vegas Nights*.[2] It was the kind of picture they called a "programmer"—the sort of lesser fare studios cranked out by the dozen in those pretelevision days, to fill out double and triple features. Hollywood was a funny place: Tommy Dorsey may have been a national figure, but in the magically self-enclosed kingdom of the movies, he was an outsider, a mere beginner. This would be his first film, and he was starting small—the bandleader was barely written into the action (such as it was). For the rest of the band—even for the nation's hottest young vocalist—it was strictly extra work, at $15 a day.

It didn't matter to Frank. Even if the band had to play the Palladium until two in the morning and be on the set at Paramount, in makeup, four hours later; even if moviemaking turned out to be a monumentally tedious affair, with long, long waits in between anything happening at all (the musicians mostly lay around the set sleeping)—even with all the exhausting boredom, appearing in his first real motion picture fit right into Frank Sinatra's master plan. And besides the obvious goal of getting his face on-screen, the enterprise contained a major side benefit.

He had seen, on his first trip to the Coast with the Major Bowes Number Five tour unit, that just about every spectacular girl in the country gravitated to Hollywood, hoping to get into pictures. Since only a small percentage succeeded, the town was ridiculously overstocked with ridiculously available young women, all of them working the angles, doing absolutely anything they could to get their moment in the klieg lights.

Alora Gooding's moment came when the director Ralph Murphy—who would go on to make such classics as *Sunbonnet Sue* and

Red Stallion in the Rockies—needed a pretty girl to stare adoringly at Frank Sinatra as he stood by a piano and sang the nation's number-one hit, "I'll Never Smile Again," along with the Pied Pipers. Murphy only had to glance around the set for a moment, tapping his megaphone against his hip, before he spotted the honey blonde with the long stems and big bright smile. He nodded at her. Okay, sweetheart. She beamed. The sequence required staging and setting up and lighting, all the painstaking and time-consuming effort stimulating the illusion, in the minds of Alora Gooding and Frank Sinatra, that the moment would be their Moment. In reality, the short segment of the number that made it to film happened in the background behind a close-up of the film's two stars, Constance Moore and Bert Wheeler. A moment in a sidelight in a B picture.

But there *she* was, staring adoringly, and, Christ, she was luscious, thought Frank—lissome, long legged, pert nosed, and smiling. So unlike Nancy, that vague, judgmental, faraway presence in Jersey City, all neighborhood-serious and heavy with the baby weight and fretting at him, clinging to him, even when, now and then, they indulged in the expensive, non-pleasurable luxury of a staticky long-distance call.

Looking at the honey blonde's big eyes and big bright mouth and perfect breasts and legs, he toppled. He had been with—where did the count now stand? a lot—a lot of women and girls, but something about this one, standing in glittering sunlight in front of the bougainvilleas and blue-blossomed jacarandas, something turned his brain to jelly, and he was gone.

Overseas, the Brits were fighting the Nazis in the skies over England. At home, Roosevelt had just announced a national draft. Hollywood on the cusp of the war was like a picnic on a cloudless day with thunder booming far in the distance.

The girl had a day job as a parking attendant at the Garden of Allah, a fancy, boisterous apartment complex on Sunset (Scott Fitzgerald had lived there in the late 1930s, and would die just around the corner, in Sheilah Graham's apartment on North Hayworth, that December).

Frank went to visit her. She wore a butt-twitching uniform and velvet gloves so she wouldn't get fingerprints on the chrome door handles of the nice cars that pulled up in front. Frank smiled that smile of his and took her picture with his new camera. He put the picture in his wallet, and forgot about it. (He should have remembered.)

It was the way she had of looking thrilled—thrilled just to be in his presence—that caught him. Innocent, but knowing just what to do. He couldn't get enough of her. The first time they woke up in his room at the Hollywood Plaza (on Vine, right across from the Brown Derby and just around the corner from the Palladium), he knew he wanted her there again that night. She moved in. Giggling when he carried her across the threshold. Nylons on the shower rod—it didn't matter. He loved her laugh.

Her real name was Dorothy, she told him. Like the girl with the ruby slippers. He nuzzled her neck, imagining she came from a farm someplace. Dorothy Gooding. It sounded like a girl who had milked cows.

In fact her name was Dorothy Bonucelli, and she was from a broken home on the wrong side of the tracks in Rockford, Illinois.

After her stepfather started paying her visits in the middle of the night, she'd fled west, winding up in Reno, a windblown high-desert town then, full of drunken cowboys reeling down the dusty streets looking for fun. She'd done what she had to. Working as a cocktail waitress, she met a man with a hard face and tight curly hair who became obsessed with her. She strung him along as long as was necessary, then fled again, this time to L.A. It was easier to disappear in those days. She was twenty-five, a few months older than Sinatra. She told him she was twenty-two.

They lived as husband and wife the whole time he was in Los Angeles. The whole band knew; it didn't matter. Tommy knew; it didn't matter.

When the band prepared to return east for another big stand at the Paramount, he kissed her tears away and gave her a ring with her birthstone, an amethyst. He whispered promises, promises to return, in her beautiful ear. He would be as good as his word, more or less.

—

One day, amid the interminable tedium that was a movie set, there was a stirring—like a rainstorm moving across an open lake. Hardened gaffers and propmen suddenly turned and smiled real smiles; sleeping musicians stirred awake. Ralph Murphy dropped his megaphone to his side and stared at an amazing sight: Bing Crosby, in a gorgeous tweed jacket, blooming pleated trousers, and no yachting cap (no toupee, either). Crosby himself, preparing to shoot *Road to Zanzibar* across the Paramount lot, was stopping by to pay a call on Dorsey. As it happened, Murphy was just about to start a take of the Constance Moore–Bert Wheeler scene with "I'll Never Smile Again" playing in the background. Crosby gave the director a nod and a wink and told him to go right ahead with what he was doing.

Murphy put the megaphone to his lips and called, "Action": the lovers spoke their witty lines, Tommy struck up the song in the background. Bing, putting his pipe to his lips and narrowing his eyes, watched Frank carefully. After it was over, he strolled over to Dorsey. The two cool Irishmen shook hands. Just to the side, Sinatra was saying something—he hardly knew what—to Jo Stafford as, his heart racing, he watched Crosby. *Crosby.* Who now was nodding in his direction.

"Very good, Tommy," Bing was saying. And, indicating Sinatra: "I think you've got something there."

Then Crosby came over to Sinatra and—as Jo Stafford stood back, her eyes lighting up—shook his hand. "Real nice, Frank," the older singer said. "You're going to go far." He said it with complete conviction. He didn't bullshit you, Bing. He didn't have to.

—

Going through his wallet after he returned, while he lay in bed snoring, Nancy found a snapshot of a beautiful blond girl. This girl, whoever she was, photographed well, and was smiling suggestively at whoever had taken her picture.

Nancy confronted Frank with the snapshot. He pretended to be seeing it for the first time. Her? She's nobody. A fan, that's all. Some kid who gave me her picture.

She stared straight into him with a look of terrible fury.

He repeated: She was nobody. Some girl who was hanging around the band.

Christmas came, and to make up for having to work over much of the holiday week—the Dorsey band was in the midst of its second big stand at the Paramount—he found ways to be extra-attentive. She wept again (she wept easily in the months after having the baby) and embraced him.

———

"Nothing meant anything to him except his career," Nick Sevano recalled long afterward. "He had a drive like I've never seen in any-body."

"I kept thinking to myself, 'I've got to climb a little higher in this next year,'" Sinatra told Sidney Zion, at Yale, forty-five years later. "I gave myself calendar times. What could I do in six months? How far could I go?"

Bullets Durgom was finding out how far. Durgom, Dorsey's short, roly-poly record promotion man (his real first name was George; he had acquired the Runyonesque handle by moving fast), had the job of visiting radio stations, in those palmy days before payola got a bad name, and doing whatever it took to drum up interest in the band's new sides. Drumming up interest might mean bestowing fancy meals, white-wall tires, expensive Scotch, even ladies. The marching orders, and the money, came straight from Tommy, the cagiest careerist around. But you couldn't flog a dead horse; what wouldn't sell, wouldn't sell. And what absolutely wouldn't sell to radio stations in 1941 were Tommy Dorsey instrumentals. Dead in the water. "All they wanted to hear about," Durgom told E. J. Kahn Jr. of the *New Yorker,* for a profile Kahn wrote around that time, "was Frank."

"Oh! Look at Me Now," Sinatra doing the vocal, a big hit. "Without a Song," with Sinatra, a big hit. "Alexander's Ragtime Band" and "Little Brown Jug," sans vocals: nowheresville.

"This boy's going to be big," Durgom told Kahn, "if Tommy doesn't kill him first. Tommy doesn't like people stealing the show—and he doesn't like people who are temperamental like himself."

In May, *Billboard* named Sinatra Male Vocalist of the Year. Over Crosby.

George T. Simon of *Metronome,* who less than two years earlier had thought the singer sounded like "a shy boy out on his first date," now found him "insufferably cocky."

He *was* insufferably cocky. (And insufferably charming.) He walked fast, talked fast, chewed gum fast, signed autographs fast . . . the only thing he did slowly (very slowly) was sing. He grinned, then stormed. He hurled out orders to his homeboys Sevano and Sanicola. "Match me," he'd command, and his cigarette would be lit, just like that. He wasn't a boy singer anymore. It was all coming true. The pipe, the yachting cap, the blazer and ascot . . . the costumes he'd tried on fit him perfectly. Bing himself had touched his shoulder. It was almost as if he had everything.

But he would never stop yearning, because he could never get what he truly wanted.

And he could never—ever—get it fast enough.

———

He was the one they came to see. Gradually at first, and then suddenly, a great national tide of girls surged up, their freshly sprouted breasts swelling with passion for *him*. Only a minute earlier, they'd been flat-chested kids, playing with their dollies in the dry dust of the Depression. Now they wore calf-length skirts and ankle-length white socks—bobby socks—with saddle shoes or Mary Janes, and they had a little bit of money in their purses: the Depression was over. Some newspaperman called them bobby-soxers, and it stuck.

And soon enough, the war would start, and the sad ballads he sang would hit them all the harder.

But he was the one they wanted. Kids still danced to Glenn Miller and Kay Kyser and Bob Crosby; they bounced to Benny Goodman's jazz. Artie Shaw could stir up the girls with his handsome face and clarinet wizardry, but then, he was never much for sentiment. And he had a strange relationship with his audiences: there had been the time, not so long before, when right in the middle of a concert, he'd decided the jitterbugs out on the floor were idiots, and said so, walking right off the bandstand and out of the business for a few months.

Yet right now the white-hot center of the business was the unlikely-looking Sinatra, his big Adam's apple bobbing over those floppy bow ties that Nancy, the good wife, made right at home.[3] When he sang the long, long lines of those slow ballads, sounding as though his heart might burst any second, why, those girls felt as though *their* hearts might burst, and they just had to cry out—

Frankiee!

Dorsey stood, ramrod straight and incredulous, the first time it happened. They were screaming, pretending to faint, *really* fainting, for Christ's sake, like Holy Rollers at a revival meeting. Tommy smiled indulgently (they were ticket buyers, after all), but actually felt a kind of genteel horror: What in the goddamn hell was the world coming to?

"I used to stand there on the bandstand so amazed I'd almost forget to take my solos," the bandleader remembered years later. "You could almost feel the excitement coming up out of the crowds when that kid stood up to sing. Remember, he was no matinee idol. He was a skinny kid with big ears. And yet what he did to women was something awful." (This last was a slip of the tongue, perhaps. In the spring of 1941, Dorsey's wife, Toots, walked out on him after she walked in on him doing something awful to sexy, redheaded Edythe Wright, right in their Bernardsville house. The bandleader's reputation as a prodigious cocksman was just another of the sources of Sinatra's admiration.)

Tommy smiled about it all—at first. At first, he even made fun of Sinatra. When the girls would start swooning, he would stop the band and have the musicians swoon right back at them. "This inspired the girls to go one better," Dorsey recalled, "and the madness kept growing until pretty soon it reached fantastic proportions."

In late August 1941, the band started its second run at the Paramount in New York, a three-week engagement that had sold out—unlike the previous year's stand—strictly on the basis of Sinatra. The theater's most spectacular feature was a gigantic moving stage that rose right up out of the orchestra pit when the show began and sank back down when it was over. One night, after the band closed with "I'll Never Smile Again," and the stage began to descend, a couple of bobby-soxers leaned over and grabbed the singer's bow tie, one on each end, and wouldn't let go. "He was hanging there," Connie Haines remembered. "I ran over and screamed and hit out at their hands. Tommy ran over too and joined in too, and we got him away!"

It was nice of Tommy. After all, he must have had conflicting impulses: the great trombonist was now officially second fiddle. Dorsey took it philosophically, furiously, humorously, incredulously—he took it all kinds of ways. He was a mercurial fellow, and in the summer and fall of 1941 his world was wobbling a little bit. His wife had left him. The IRS was after him for eighty grand in back taxes—big money anytime, but especially then. The combination would have undone almost any man, but Dorsey was made of iron. Still, he drank a lot. (He had stayed on the wagon for much of the 1930s, but fell off at the turn of the decade, as he climbed toward his greatest success.) And while he was in his cups, he couldn't help contemplating the perfidy of this kid who was like a son to him (Tommy loved Frank every bit as much as Frank loved Tommy, maybe even more), the treachery of this kid turning into a scornful adolescent and not just pulling away—that would have been bad enough—but actually overshadowing the Old Man.

And yet another father figure lurked in the wings.

In November, the band headed back to Los Angeles, to play a return engagement at the Palladium and shoot another movie. This time the picture was the real deal: an MGM musical. It was called *Ship Ahoy* (the original title, *I'll Take Manila,* was quickly changed soon after Manila fell to the Japanese two months later). It was a piece of froth, yet it starred the incomparable Eleanor Powell, a tap-dancing powerhouse and a class act. And Sinatra got to sing three numbers in close-up, not background, this time, two with the Pipers and one, "Poor You," more or less alone, though he had to alternate choruses with his silly old pal from Shea's Theatre in Buffalo, Red Skelton.

It wasn't quite a star turn, but that scarcely mattered: Sinatra was returning to Hollywood more and more frequently. One of these times he'd break through, he was absolutely certain of it. He was feeling his oats in a very big way. The big crowds at the Palladium had got the message: he was the show. He was also moving in sweller company in Los Angeles than the year before. This time he kept Alora at bay. He was back at the Hollywood Plaza, but told her Dorsey was making him double up with Joey Bushkin. It was a lie, of course. He had his eye peeled for bigger game. He had heard that none other than Lana Turner, who'd been married to Artie Shaw for ten minutes, was screwing Buddy Rich, and if Lana Turner was screwing Buddy Rich, anything was possible.

One cool morning—a rainstorm had swept through the night before; now the City of Angels sparkled like Eden itself—he was walking between soundstages in Culver City, carrying a cardboard cup of coffee, nodding to this glorious creature (dressed as a harem girl), then that glorious creature (a cowgirl), then *that* glorious creature (a secretary?)—they all smiled at him—when he ran into, of all people, an old pal of his from the Major Bowes days, a red-haired pianist who'd bounced around the Midwest in the 1930s, Lyle Henderson (Crosby would soon nickname him Skitch). Henderson was strolling with a creature much more glorious, if possible, than the three Sinatra had just encountered. She was tall, dark haired, with sleepy green eyes, killer cheekbones, and absurdly lush lips, lips he couldn't stop staring at.

Frankie! Henderson said, as they shook hands. His old chum was doing all right these days.

Sinatra smiled, not at Henderson. The glorious creature smiled back bashfully, but with a teasing hint of directness in her dark eyes. The pianist—he was doing rehearsal duty at the studio—then got to say the six words that someone had to say, sometime, but that he and he alone got to say for the first time in history on this sparkling morning: *Frank Sinatra, this is Ava Gardner.*

Ava Lavinia Gardner, to be exact. She was not quite nineteen, and she was from the picturesquely named hamlet of Grabtown, North Carolina, deep in tobacco-farming country. Her presence in Hollywood was a sheer fluke, the result of a mildly absurd chain of events set in motion by her traffic-stopping face. Visiting her older sister Bappie several months earlier in the big city, New York, Ava had been photographed by Bappie's boyfriend, who ran a photo portrait studio on Fifth Avenue. The boyfriend put one of the pictures of Ava in his store window as a sample of his work. Passing the window one day, a messenger from the New York legal department of Loew's, the parent company of Metro-Goldwyn-Mayer, was stopped in his tracks by the photograph. He decided he would like to go out with that beautiful girl. And so the messenger called the store and inquired about the girl, saying he worked for MGM and hinting he could get her into the movies, even though he could do nothing of the sort. Bappie's boyfriend told the messenger that the girl had gone back home to North Carolina; the messenger sighed and gave up his quest. But Bappie and her boyfriend, excited by MGM's "interest," and not wanting to let the matter drop, packed up the boyfriend's best shots of Ava and hand-delivered them to Metro's New York office. Things moved very swiftly from there.

Ava had just arrived in town that August with Bappie; the two were living together in a tiny efficiency apartment in a seamy hotel on Selma

Avenue. Every morning Ava took three buses to Culver City, then disembarked to spend her day taking lessons: in walking and talking and acting. The great studio machine was nudging and prodding and poking her, trying to mold her into someone as different as possible from the barefoot, sharp-tongued country girl she really was. Both she and the studio were having a rough time of it.

In the meantime, one of Metro's biggest stars was putting the full-court press on her. Mickey Rooney, only twenty-one but quite the rake, was crazy for Ava. In fact, Mickey Rooney wanted to marry her. *Marry* her. Why? Because Ava wouldn't sleep with him. That was the ridiculous 1941 long and short of it. And truthfully, Ava Gardner wasn't that interested in sleeping with or marrying Mickey Rooney—which made him even crazier with desire—but she had been watching him on the screen for years, and here he was, in person, right in front of her! And cute as a button, and so *persistent*.

Frank Sinatra knew none of this. All he knew as he shook her hand that morning—for just a second too long—was that he wanted to possess her. It was a familiar-enough feeling, and he was as confident as ever that he would. But as she released his hand, she gave him another look, slightly inquisitive this time, and something in his gut revolved a little bit. It was just the flicker of a sensation, and it confused him momentarily. He took a sip from his cardboard cup and smiled at her over the rim.

And then she turned and walked down the studio street and around a corner, and was gone.

———

Meanwhile, the big crowds kept coming to the Palladium, the movie stars in the VIP section watching with amusement as the teenage girls—the message had somehow traveled across the country, an unseen impulse of the kind that moves herds of reindeer or schools of fish—as the girls screamed Frankie's name and swooned. Out of the crowd one night, between sets, came a familiar face: a carved-out, acne-scarred countenance, on the young side of middle age, similar in some ways to his own, only Jewish where his was Italian, hesitant and thoughtful where his was mercurial and expressive.

His name was Emanuel Sacks—Manie (pronounced "Manny"), for short. He had been a talent agent with MCA, and he had come to the Rustic Cabin around the same time Harry had, and told Frank just what Buddy Rich had told Frank: *I like the way you sing.* Sinatra had instantly liked this serious, shyly smiling fellow—he ran across so many creeps and phonies, drunks and blowhards in nightclubs, and this guy was clearly none of that, he was clearly a smart Jew, a serious businessman, classy, and he'd given Sinatra his business card. Which Frank had put someplace and forgotten about.

Until tonight. He instantly remembered the guy, whose homely, sensitive features were totally out of place amid the beautiful, hysterical faces at the Hollywood Palladium. They shook hands, and after a moment of small talk Frank asked him what he was up to. Still with that agency?

Not anymore. He was manager of popular repertoire at Columbia Records.

Frank stared. At Columbia?

Sacks smiled, shy but proud.

Not shy, Sinatra looked Manie right in the eye and asked how he'd like to record him as a soloist.

Coming from almost anyone else short of Crosby, it would have been, in late 1941, an absurdly presumptuous suggestion. Singers sang with bands. Bands made singers. Where was the singer who could make it on his own?

Yet Sacks looked back at him with complete seriousness. And more—Sinatra felt it: respect. Sacks said he'd like nothing better in the world than to record Sinatra as a soloist. But wasn't he still with RCA, with Tommy?

Frank smiled. Things change.

Sacks smiled back. His teeth were crooked and stained. He was ready anytime Frank was. He took a small leather case out of his breast pocket, handed Sinatra a business card.

Sinatra took it and grinned: he would keep this card in a very safe place.

Two days later, *Down Beat,* in its annual poll, named Frank Sinatra Male Vocalist of the Year. The winner of the poll for the previous six years straight had been Bing Crosby.

Lion and cub. Bing and Frank, around 1940.

Newly married, and still in love. Frank and Nancy, circa 1940.

December 6 was a Saturday, the biggest night of the week at the Palladium. At about 2:00 a.m., after the band had left the stand and the musicians packed up their instruments and sheet music, a select crew, Tommy and Buddy and Frank among them, got into their big black cars and drove down Sunset to a large Tudor house on a quiet side street in Brentwood. No civilian could ever understand what it was like to finish a gig, your head still buzzing, your blood pumping. You could never just go to bed. You had to keep *going*—drink, smoke, drug, talk, get laid. Maybe all at once.

The Tudor house's owner, just twenty years old, had been in the star-studded crowd at the Palladium that night, hovered over by this square-jawed, tan-skinned actor and that, but she'd only had eyes for the bandstand. She was petite, bottle blond, and deliciously curvy, with a haughty, sultry, heart-shaped face that made her look older than her age. Lana Turner had been around enough—she was a veteran of four hard years in Hollywood—to know that actors were nice to look at, but she really loved musicians. Most actors were a hell of a lot more fascinating on-screen than in real life, and a lot of the handsomer ones were interested in other men. Musicians *did* something, besides speak someone else's lines. They were funny and profane, and the ones she'd met all seemed to like women a lot.

And they were young (many of them not that much older than Lana Turner) and wild and dangerous and brilliant—the rock stars of their day. Except that they could read music. (Well, except for Buddy and Frank.)

Buddy felt Lana was smiling at him and only him that night. A couple of the others felt the same way.

There was alcohol by the gallons at her house, and the sweet reek of reefer—especially around Joey Bushkin, giggling as he sat at her white grand piano, playing dirty songs and funny songs and beautiful songs. There were a few other girls, there were games and filthy jokes and hilarity, there was quite a bit of misbehavior, and then there was unconsciousness. Buddy ended up in Lana's bed (the sheets were still warm), but he had drunk too much to get it up, and you could have lit her breath with a match by that point anyway: he'd never found that very sexy.

The sun rose over Brentwood to the sound of snoring in the big Tudor. A few hours later, a black Plymouth coupe pulled up in front of the house, and Lana Turner's mother, Mildred, a rawboned Arkansas lady with a history of tragedy and pain, got out, a worried look on her long, plain features. She had been calling and calling, but nobody would pick up the phone. Now she opened the house's heavy front door with her own key, sniffed the pungent air, and frowned at the sight of snoring musicians draped every which way—over the couches and easy chairs and carpet. Her daughter was going to hell in a hand-basket, and so, apparently, was the world: she had come to bring the news that the country was at war.

> *Lucky Strike green has gone to war. Yes, Lucky Strike green has*
> *gone to war . . . Don't look for your Luckies in their familiar*
> *green package on the tobacco counters. No, your Luckies are*
> *wearing a different color now.*

Who the hell knew what was going to happen? The world was turning upside down, and Frank had to grab whatever he could. The word was buzzing along the musicians' grapevine: Bob Eberly, with Jimmy Dorsey's band, was thinking about going out on his own. Eberly was kind of a handsome lug, and he could really sing. He had a rich, supple baritone, and he and Helen O'Connell had just done a version of "Green Eyes" that sounded as if they were going to hop right into the sack the second they were through.

But if you listened closely, it was a trick. Eberly was just a voice—a terrific voice, it's true; a ballsy voice. He sounded like a man. But there was no ardor there, no yearning. There wasn't anybody around, with the exception of Crosby, who could put across a song, could make you feel it, the way Sinatra could. Bob Eberly wasn't half the singer Frank Sinatra was, and Sinatra knew it. But did the public? He didn't want to wait around to find out.

And so he began to pester Tommy relentlessly, always mentioning the *Down Beat* poll (and never Manie Sacks): Dorsey *had* to let him record a few on his own. Why not? They'd sell some records!

Dorsey finally said yes just to shut him up.

Frank rehearsed constantly for the next three weeks, afternoons at the Palladium before Tommy showed up, just he and Lyle Henderson or Joey Bushkin on the piano behind him, in the huge quiet stillness of the empty dance hall. He knew exactly which songs he wanted to cut. They were all ballads, of course, all dripping with romance: There was

"The Night We Called It a Day," by these new kids Matt Dennis and Tom Adair, who'd written "Let's Get Away from It All" and "Violets for Your Furs." There was a sweet Hoagy Carmichael number that hadn't been recorded much, "The Lamplighter's Serenade." And then two classics: Kern and Hammerstein's "The Song Is You" and Cole Porter's equally immortal "Night and Day," whose lyrics he'd blown in front of the great man himself.

He had told Dorsey that he wanted strings. Oh, how he wanted them. The last time he'd had the chance to sing with a string section had been at the end of 1938, right around the time of his arrest, when he'd jumped at the chance to do a once-a-week radio show at the WOR Bamberger station in Newark just because their orchestra had a few fiddles. The job paid all of thirty cents a week—the round-trip train fare between Hoboken and Newark. But they had strings. And he got to sing three songs with those strings behind him on every show. He loved the way they carried his voice, like a vase holding a bouquet of flowers. And now he would have strings again, and he knew just the man to make them sing.

Axel Stordahl was a first-generation Norwegian-American from Staten Island who had joined the Dorsey band as fourth trumpeter in the mid-1930s. He was a less than stellar horn player,[1] but it quickly became clear that he had a gift for arranging ballads. When Sinatra joined the band, it was as if he and Axel had each found his missing piece. Physically and temperamentally, the two couldn't have been more different: Stordahl, who was tall, bald, and pale lashed, looked like nothing so much as a Norwegian fisherman. He even wore a fisherman's cap and smoked a pipe. He was intensely calm, quietly humorous. Sinatra, who liked to nickname people he was fond of, called him Sibelius.

Frank Sinatra, of course, was the opposite of calm. Yet when he sang slow numbers, some sort of ethereal best self took over, and Stordahl's writing helped him attain it. The pattern had been set on the singer's first two recordings with Dorsey, "The Sky Fell Down" and "Too

Romantic," and it had continued on every ballad he'd done (and Buddy Rich had grimaced through) with the band.

The recording session, which took place at RCA's Los Angeles studios on Monday afternoon, January 19, 1942, went off perfectly. Stordahl conducted. There were fourteen players on the date: four saxes and a guitarist who were part of the Dorsey band, and an oboist, four violinists, a violist, a bass fiddler, a harpist, and a pianist—Skitch Henderson—who were not. Pointedly, there was no drummer. Nor did Dorsey attend the session—even though both of the two singles that resulted (released on RCA's discount Bluebird label) were labeled "Frank Sinatra with Tommy Dorsey and His Orchestra."

Sinatra had been a wreck in the weeks leading up to the session. Whenever he wasn't rehearsing, he was fretting about the huge implications of leaving Dorsey. No band singer had ever gone out on his own before (though Dick Haymes, who'd replaced Sinatra with Harry James, was trying some solo club dates in between his gigs as Benny Goodman's boy singer). Frank was "almost tubercular," Nick Sevano said. "He was seeing all kinds of doctors, but he was so nervous that he couldn't eat. He never finished a meal . . . He started talking a lot about death and dying . . . 'I get the feeling that I'm going to die soon,' he'd say."

Yet when he walked into the studio that Monday afternoon, it was with a swagger. Harry Meyerson, the Victor A&R man who ran the session, remembered: "Frank was not like a band vocalist at all. He came in self-assured, slugging. He knew exactly what he wanted. He knew he was good."

In fact, it was the bravado that was phony—half-phony, anyway. The fact of the matter was that Frank Sinatra was scared shitless. But (true to a pattern he would maintain for the rest of his life) when he was afraid, he liked to make others jump.

===

A few days later, when the first pressings of the recordings came in, his fear diminished considerably: they were terrific. Axel Stordahl later recalled sitting for an entire sunny afternoon in Sinatra's room at the Hollywood Plaza, listening to the four songs over and over on the singer's portable record player. "He was so excited you almost believed he had never recorded before," Stordahl said. "I think this was a turning point in his career."

Between the lines, Sibelius sounded a little distanced from the exultation, perhaps a bit regretful at not being able to get out and enjoy that glorious Los Angeles afternoon. That was the way it was, though, when you were close to the drama that was Sinatra: you stayed put in your orchestra seat until the performance was through.

Connie Haines remembered listening to Sinatra's "Night and Day" with some of the rest of the band, not long afterward: "Frank sat on a stool. He had on one of those hats Bing Crosby had made popular. It was slouched down over his head at just the right angle, and he had a pipe in his mouth . . . As the last note ended, we all knew it was a hit. The musicians rose to their feet as if one. They cheered. Then I heard him say, 'Hey, Bing, old man. Move over. Here I come.' "

Bing wasn't the only one who had to move over. Lana Turner, who Buddy Rich sweetly believed only had eyes for him ("Lana was the love of Buddy's life," said Rich's sister. "And he was the only one that didn't know about her"), was methodically sleeping her way up the band's hierarchy. First came a musician or two, then Dorsey himself, and then the man Turner was canny enough to realize now stood at the pinnacle. Tommy, the anti-sentimentalist, knew all about it: one night he bribed a waiter at the Hollywood Plaza to put his dirty dinner dishes, instead of the romantic supper Sinatra had ordered up for Lana and himself, under the food covers on the room-service cart.

So much for Alora Gooding.[2]

The story of Frank Sinatra's life is one of continual shedding, both of artistic identities and of associates and intimates who had out-

lived their usefulness. The saga of his disentanglement from one of
his most powerful relationships, his deep emotional and artistic bond
with Tommy Dorsey, is complex and bewildering. Out of forgetfulness,
self-protection, and self-mythification, Sinatra sowed no small amount
of the confusion himself. When a man he admired, Sidney Zion, was
bold enough to ask him, in front of an audience at Yale Law School,
about the fabled role of organized crime in the tale, Sinatra parried
with a genteel vagueness that befitted the surroundings—and that let
himself more or less completely off the hook.

"Now, in the story that is told in *The Godfather* . . . about how you
happened to get let out of the contract of Mr. Dorsey . . . , somebody
came there and put a gun at his head or whatever," Mr. Zion said.
"There's been a million stories. I heard one the other day from a guy who
said . . . , 'It wasn't the Italians, the Jews did it, and they put a trombone down Harry James's throat.' I said, 'Are you sure it was a trombone
or a trumpet down Harry James's throat?' So he had that a little wrong.
But there's been a lot of stories about this, made famous through the
years, and I think it would be interesting to set it straight."

Sinatra, seventy and dignified now, smiled in a distinguished way
and proceeded to set the record anything but straight. "Well, it's quite
simple, really," he said. (It was anything but.) "It got so blown out of
proportion that it took a long time to clarify it . . . I'll tell you here now,
for your edification, as to what happened with it—if it's important at
all. Really, it's passé, it's so old now."

Shut up, he explained.

"The reason I wanted to leave the orchestra," he continued, "was
because Crosby was number one, way up on top of the pile, and in
the field . . . were some awfully good singers with the orchestras. Bob
Eberly with Jimmy Dorsey's Orchestra was a fabulous vocalist. Mr.
Como was with Ted Weems, and he still is such a wonderful singer. I
thought if I don't make a move out of this band and try to do it on my
own soon, one of those guys will do it, and I'll have to fight all three
of them, from Crosby all the way down to the other two, to get a position. So I took a shot and I gave Mr. Dorsey one year's notice. It was in

September whatever year. I said, 'I'm going to leave the band one year from that day.' Beyond that year, I had another six months to do in the contract. He said, 'Sure.' That's all he said, was 'Sure.'"

Sure.

In fact, Mr. Sinatra gave Mr. Dorsey his notice in February 1942, with ten months left to run on the three-year contract he'd signed in January 1940, and he would continue to sing with the Dorsey band for just seven of those months, and it is quite unlikely that Tommy Dorsey responded to this highly unwelcome news with a simple "Sure."

We have this last from no less an authority than Art Linkletter—yes, the Art Linkletter of 1950s afternoon-television fame, who as a young reporter in February 1942 went backstage at San Francisco's Golden Gate Theatre to interview Tommy Dorsey, and found that Sinatra had just given notice, and that Dorsey was not happy. "He's such a damn fool," the bandleader vented to the kid journalist. "He's a great singer, but you know, you can't make it without a band . . . Does he think he can go out on his own, as good as he is? It upsets me because he's an important part of our band."

What Dorsey wouldn't say—or couldn't bring himself to say—was how betrayed he felt by Sinatra. This was a boy he had taught his deepest art, a boy he had elevated to national fame! A boy who had sat up till all hours playing cards with him . . . one who, despite the mere ten years' difference between their ages, had been like a son to him—and who had treated him, in many ways, like a father. And now, inevitably, the youth was leaving the nest. The bandleader was a tightly wound, thickly self-protected man, one who nursed his hurts deep in the sub-basement of his soul, and this was a wound that would stay with him till the end of his days.

Sinatra himself hadn't come to his decision lightly. Where his career was concerned, he never did anything lightly. He tormented Sevano and Sanicola—when he wasn't complaining of hypochondriacal symptoms, he was telling his minions, "I gotta do it, I gotta do it." Sevano recalled: "He kept telling me, 'I gotta do it before Bob Eberly does it.'"

"He was like a Mack truck going one hundred miles an hour without brakes," Sevano said. "He had me working around the clock. 'Call Frank Cooper [an agent at the management company General Amusement Corporation, recommended by Manie Sacks]. Do it now. Don't wait until tomorrow . . . Send my publicity photos to Walter Winchell. Get my records to the Lucky Strike *Hit Parade*.'"

Those he couldn't order around, he seduced. "I was sitting with Sinatra, and we were talking," Sammy Cahn remembered. "And he says, 'I'm going to be the world's greatest singer.' And I looked at him, and I'll never forget it, I said, 'There's no doubt in my mind. You are the world's greatest singer.' He said, 'Do you mean it?' I said, 'What do you mean, do I mean it? You're the best. You're the best. There's nobody better than you. You're the best.'"

This was a complicated moment, an intricate dance between two talented men. In part Cahn was being obsequious: as a lyricist, he had a career to further, and he correctly sensed that Sinatra could be an important part of it. But as a friend, he was also being utterly honest: Sinatra was the best.

Was Sinatra—*Do you mean it?*—being coy? Of course he was. He knew exactly how good he was.

But as always, the one who understood Frank Sinatra most deeply was his chief victim and champion, the girl who had known him when. "Tommy was a good teacher because he had a great band, and he had wonderful vocalists with him, and they were great together," Nancy Barbato Sinatra said. "But without Tommy I know it still would have happened . . . Frank had a master plan for himself, and he worked at getting there. I think he always had it in the back of his mind that this was a stepping stone."

As was she. As was almost everyone with whom Sinatra ever had a significant relationship. He would step on or over everyone in his path until he grasped the brass ring. The master plan for himself was exactly that: for himself. Alone.

His master plan now included Manie Sacks of Columbia, who had formally agreed to sign Sinatra the moment he was legally divorced from Dorsey and RCA.

═══

In the months after Sinatra gave notice, Tommy Dorsey went through the classic five stages of grief. There was denial, anger, bargaining, depression—and eventually acceptance, but only after ferocious resistance (on Dorsey's part), legal maneuvering (on both sides), and the possible introduction (by parties unknown) of a firearm.

In the meantime, Sinatra worked at a frenetic pace for Dorsey in the spring and summer of 1942. From California, the band one-nighted its way back east and opened a monthlong stand at the New York Paramount on April Fools' Day. Dorsey was at the peak of his powers and popularity: he wanted to milk it for all it was worth. (And with the IRS and his soon-to-be ex on his case, he badly needed the money.) If Sinatra stole the show, that was all right—it just meant more dough in Tommy's pocket. Moreover, if Sinatra really was going to leave, Dorsey wanted to squeeze as much work out of him as possible.

In advance of a rumored American Federation of Musicians strike over the summer, Dorsey also wanted to record as much as possible, to stockpile sides that could be released if there was a strike. Sinatra was happy to comply: he knew his freedom was imminent.

With the war raging in Europe and the Pacific (and not going well at first), millions of young men, including dozens of musicians, were joining up.[3] One of them was Artie Shaw, who'd enlisted with the Coast Guard in early 1942, and had promptly bequeathed his entire string section, eight players in all, to Dorsey. Buddy Rich was disgusted; Sinatra, delighted. The poignancy of string-backed ballads like "Just as Though You Were Here," "There Are Such Things," and "In the Blue of Evening" fit the country's anxious mood—and the singer's career plans—perfectly. It was as if Dorsey were rehearsing Frank for the next stage in his professional life.

Just as though you were here. ("I'll wake each morning, and I'll promise to laugh/I'll say good morning to your old photograph.") Now and then that spring, Frank popped up at home—new, nicer digs in a two-family house on Bergen Avenue in Jersey City—to pay a visit to two-year-old Nancy and Big Nancy, who was taking off the weight and looking at him hopefully. He tried to summon up some of the ardor he'd once felt, then gave her a good-bye peck on the cheek: he had places to go.

Many years later, Nancy junior would remember the civil-defense blackouts of 1942: "The curtains drawn. The lights turned off. And Mom and I sitting on the floor, holding each other in the darkness. Daddy was busy, I guess. He was, it seemed, a voice on the radio most of the time, or a picture in the newspaper . . . a figure composed of a bow tie and two black patent leather shoes, who was always going away."

After another eight-week run at the Astor roof in May and June (the prom girls wailing around the bandstand, a few getting lucky afterward), the band went back on the road. In Chicago, in July, Sinatra, feeling expansive, asked Dorsey if he wanted help finding a new singer. Frank mentioned as a possibility—poetic justice—his replacement with Harry James's Music Makers, Dick Haymes. Haymes was a good-looking blond guy who'd gone to Hollywood to try to break into pictures, and wound up singing instead. He had a romantic light baritone, and the girls loved him—but not the way they loved Sinatra. Haymes made them sigh; Sinatra made them nuts.

Despite the fact that he'd already given his notice, the suggestion did not go down well. "[Tommy] said, 'No no no, you're not going to leave this band,'" Sinatra recalled. " 'Not as easy as you think you are.' Well, words began to be back-and-forth, and finally he made it very difficult—and I left the band anyway."

Thus began the anger phase. Dorsey, who was drinking heavily that summer (he'd inaugurated the Astor roof engagement by getting into a boozy backstage fistfight with his brother Jimmy), promptly stopped speaking to Sinatra, and didn't start again until the end of August, when it became clear that the singer was going to leave no matter what. Acceptance had finally set in. "Let him go," Dorsey said with a shrug. "Might be the best thing for me."

What definitely wasn't the best thing for the bandleader was that Sinatra had yanked Axel Stordahl right out from under him, making the arranger an offer he couldn't possibly refuse: $650 a month, five times what Tommy was paying him. It was money Sinatra didn't have—yet—but it was a brilliant move: he knew old Sibelius could make him sound even better than he already did. Dorsey was furious, but there was nothing he could do: he had been thoroughly outflanked.

The bargaining then—if you could call it that. What happened next was a Mephistophelian sit-down between the singer and Dorsey and Dorsey's agent Leonard Vannerson, a meeting at which each side felt, not quite accurately, that it was holding a hand full of aces. In exchange for Sinatra's release, plus an advance of $17,000 (at least $225,000 today) to start his solo career, Dorsey and Vannerson had Frank sign a piece of paper—one can almost smell the sulfurous fumes rising from it—that made Dorsey his manager, and guaranteed not just a 10 percent agent's fee to Vannerson but also 33.3 percent of Sinatra's gross earnings to Tommy, either (by some accounts) in perpetuity or for the next ten years. The truth of the matter is that in those days, ten years might as well have been perpetuity. A singer going out on his own in 1942 might as well have been sailing over the edge of the earth in 1492. And there was a war on! God knew where anyone would be after all that time—ten years meant Frank Sinatra would still be performing in . . . *1952*. Who could imagine such a thing?

═══

Frank Cooper, the agent to whom Manie Sacks had sent Sinatra, took one look at that Faustian contract and blanched. Not only would the singer be forking over 43.3 percent to Dorsey and Vannerson, but he'd also have to pay *Cooper's* 10 percent. Plus income tax.

Sinatra smiled at the poor, sputtering mortal. "Don't worry," he told Cooper. "I'm not paying him a quarter." Meaning Dorsey.

Dolly's son had learned his lessons well.

———

Sinatra made his last radio broadcast with the Dorsey band on September 3, at the Circle Theater in Indianapolis. On the intro to "The Song Is You," you can sense the chaos under Tommy's steely-smooth, slickly cadenced patter. "After tonight," the bandleader told the Hoosier audience, "he's going to be strictly on his own. And Frank, I want to tell you that everyone in the band wishes you the best of luck."

"Thanks, Mac," Sinatra says, using the nickname Jimmy Dorsey had given his brother when the two were boys. The singer's voice sounds very young, very Hoboken, and—surprisingly—soft with emotion. "I'd like to say that I'm gonna miss all you guys after kickin' around for three years. And ladies and gentlemen, I'd like you to meet the boy who's gonna take my place as the vocalist with Tommy and the band— he's a fine guy, a wunnerful singer, and he was good enough for Harry James and Benny Goodman, and—that's really sayin' plenty. Folks, I'd like you to meet Dick Haymes."

After a nice round of applause, Haymes pipes up: "Well, Frank, I don't know if anyone can really take your place with this band. But I'm gonna be in there tryin'. You can bet on that. As for you, well, I know that you'll be knockin' 'em dead on your own hook."

Then it's almost as if Dick Haymes actually gets the hook—Dorsey jumps right back in, just about cutting him off: "I agree with you there, Dick, and thanks a lot, Dick Haymes—Frank, before you hit the road, how 'bout one more song just for—auld lang syne."

"That's all right with me, Tom," Sinatra says. "Gimme the beat on our arrangement of 'The Song Is You,' and I'll see what I can do with it."

It's all old-style showbiz corn, phony modesty an inch thick, but when Sinatra shifts from those Hoboken street tones to the first few bars of the Kern and Hammerstein masterpiece, you do a double take:

the Voice is that rich, gorgeous, and expressive.[4] *Look out world, here I come,* is the clear message—along with a quick *Good luck, kiddo* to Dick Haymes. And a quick thumb of the nose to Tommy Dorsey.

The way he ends the song—an ethereal falsetto high F—has an infinitely vulnerable sound: as always, his emotions were powerful and complicated. Dorsey told a magazine writer years later that at a party backstage after the show, Sinatra "was literally crying on my shoulder . . . depressed about what would happen to his career." Depressed? Good and scared was more like it. He had Tommy's seventeen grand in his pocket, but that would burn fast, especially with the way he spent. (He had just put down a payment on his first house, a wood-frame Cape with a front porch, in Hasbrouck Heights, New Jersey.) What he didn't have were bookings. Cooper had managed to land him a bit part singing one number, "Night and Day," in a Columbia B picture, *Reveille with Beverly,* and Sacks had wangled him a spot on a CBS radio show in New York. Period. Besides that, it was going to be strictly Sit and Wait.

He was terribly frightened. Excited, too—he believed in his luck. But some part of him always felt like that kid in bed in the dark on Garden Street, listening through the wall as his mother rattled on and on and his old man just lay there, grunting.

As for the Sentimental Gentleman of Swing, Tommy Dorsey drank a good bit backstage at the Circle Theater the night of that final broadcast, and liquor always put a fine edge on his cold Irish anger. When Sinatra cried on his shoulder, Dorsey had seven words for him.

"I hope you fall on your ass," the bandleader said.

———

At first it seemed that was exactly what was going to happen. After returning from Los Angeles (where Frank had stopped by the NBC radio studios, hat in hand, to ask for a job as staff singer that the network did not vouchsafe to give him), Frank got to spend a lot of time around the new house, helping Nancy paint and paper and fuss over their little girl, and she got to see what kind of good mood *that* put him in. Meanwhile, Frank Cooper was working hard to get his client a job, any job—against the opposition of many who felt that a solo singer, even Sinatra, couldn't draw an audience without a big band behind him.

It's hard to imagine in this age of instant information, but fame in those days was a far more parochial phenomenon than it is now. Frank Sinatra was a name to conjure with among the kids, the jitterbugs, the record-buying big-band fans; but to much of America, where singers were concerned, it was Crosby, period. Sinatra was really just catching on.

His own retrospective assessment of his situation in the fall of 1942 may have been a little bleaker than was actually the case—he always did like to buff his story a bit. "I was now free," he told Sidney Zion at the Yale Law School talk. "I had no ties with anybody. I didn't even have an agent to represent me. [Frank Cooper was very much alive when Sinatra—who in his later years would also sometimes claim never to have had a voice lesson—made this astounding statement.] I was living in Hasbrouck Heights at the time, and I found out that there was a theater [nearby] where they had vaudeville, and I went around, spoke to the manager, and I said, 'I'd like to play here for a couple of nights, maybe a weekend.' He said okay. So I played there for a week, Tuesday through Sunday. I found out later that each manager or booker from the theaters in New York—the Roxy, the Strand, the Loew's State, the Paramount, the Capitol Theater—sent their scouts over to see what all the noise was about."

In fact, Sinatra had not one but two agents working for him. Frank Cooper now joined forces with a man named Harry Romm—whose not inconsiderable claim to fame was having put together the Three Stooges—to try to browbeat Bob Weitman, the manager of the Paramount, into booking Sinatra. In a classic case of How Quickly They Forget, Weitman—who had seen the girls go ape for Frankie in his theater, had seen them camp out for five or six shows, refusing to go home—was skeptically disposed. It was one thing, he thought, when you had the matchless presence of Dorsey, the blazing drums of Buddy Rich, and the heavenly harmonies of the Pied Pipers all together on that gigantic elevator stage. But could bony little Sinatra, all by his lonesome, put four thousand asses in the seats?

Cooper and Romm finally hit on a clever ploy: they prevailed upon Weitman to attend an early-December Sinatra performance at the Mosque Theatre in Newark. What Weitman didn't realize was that Newark was Sinatra's backyard. If ever Frank owned an audience, this was it. The whole thing was strictly a setup. Years afterward, Weitman recalled sitting and watching in awe as "this skinny kid walks out on the stage. He was not much older than the kids in the seats. He looked like he still had milk on his chin. As soon as they saw him, the kids went crazy. And when he started to sing they stood up and yelled and moaned and carried on until I thought—excuse the expression—his pants had fallen down."

It was December 12, 1942: Sinatra's twenty-seventh birthday. An auspicious omen. Weitman phoned him at home that night. "He said, 'What are you doing New Year's Eve?'" Sinatra recalled. "I said, 'Not a thing. I can't even get booked anywhere.' Weitman said, 'I'd like you to open at the joint,' as he used to call it. He said, 'You've got Benny Goodman's Orchestra and a Crosby picture.' I fell right on my butt."

The Crosby picture was *Star Spangled Rhythm,* a patriotic musical starring not only Bing but also Bob Hope, Dorothy Lamour, Ray Milland, Paulette Goddard, and a few dozen other of the studio's stars, all playing themselves. And Benny Goodman was, of course, Benny Goodman: a godlike bandleader and instrumentalist at least on a par with Dorsey.[5]

"In those days," Sinatra said, "they called you an 'extra added attraction.' I went to rehearsal at seven-thirty in the morning, and I looked at the marquee, and it said, 'Extra added attraction, Frank Sinatra,' and I said, 'Wow! Wow!'"

Wow was not what Jack Benny (who was emceeing the show) said.

Such was the narrowness of Sinatra's renown at that point that the comedian had never heard of him. Benny recalled:

> I was in New York City doing a radio show, and Bob Weit-
> man . . . came to me and asked if just before I do my radio
> show, I could come over to the Paramount for the debut of
> Frank Sinatra. I said who? He said, "Frank Sinatra, and Benny
> Goodman's Orchestra is also playing and Benny Goodman
> will introduce you, and you will introduce Frank Sinatra . . ."
> I said, "Well, I'm sorry, but I never heard of him. But, Bob, I'll
> do this for you and Benny Goodman and Sinatra too if it is any
> help . . ."
>   Benny Goodman went on and did his act, and then he says,
> "Now, ladies and gentlemen, to introduce our honored guest,
> we have Jack Benny." So I walked out on a little ramp and got a
> very fine reception, you know, I thought it was nice. I certainly
> didn't think Sinatra would get much of anything 'cause I never
> heard of him. So, they introduce me and I did two or three
> jokes and they laughed and then I realized there were a lot of
> young people out there, probably waiting for Sinatra, so I intro-
> duced Frank Sinatra as if he were one of my closest friends—
> you know, I made a big thing of it and I had to make all of this
> up, 'cause I didn't know who he was—and then I said, "Well,
> anyway, ladies and gentlemen, here he is, Frank Sinatra"—and
> I thought the goddamned building was going to cave in. I never
> heard such a commotion with people running down to the
> stage, screaming and nearly knocking me off the ramp. All this
> for a fellow I never heard of.

Bob Weitman said, "There were about five thousand people in the theater at the time, and all five thousand were of one voice, 'F-R-A-N-K-I-E-E-E-E-E!' The young, the old—as one person—got up and danced in the aisles and jumped on the stage. The loge and the balcony swayed. One of the managers came over to me and said, 'The balcony is rocking—what do we do?' "

Standing on the stage, his back to the audience as he prepared to conduct his band, Benny Goodman had a different reaction as the huge sound burst forth.

"What the fuck was that?" he said.

Benny Goodman and Frank, Los Angeles, early forties.

Act Three

HIGHER AND HIGHER

"Good morning. My name is Frank Sinatra."
His first line in the movies, in the 1943 RKO Radio Pictures
feature *Higher and Higher*.

XTRA ADDED ATTRACTION" was indeed how the Paramount
first billed him: fourth on the program, beneath Benny Goodman
and His Famous Orchestra,[1] under a comedy trio called the Radio
Rogues and a comedy duo called Moke and Poke, and just above "DON
BAKER at the PARAMOUNT ORGAN." Frank Sinatra's name was, however, the only one besides Goodman's in boldface, and in type only
slightly smaller. And beneath the name, the slogan: "The Voice That
Has Thrilled Millions."

It was true enough. But the phrase itself sounded like something that would have rolled off the stentorian tongue of some radio announcer of the 1920s or 1930s. And here in January 1943—one of those hinges in time that come along periodically, a moment when everything simply *vaults forward*—Frank Sinatra, a radically new American product, needed drastic repackaging, and somebody new to do it.

The coiner of the slogan was another of Sinatra's agents at the time, a soon-to-be-forgotten figure named Harry Kilby. The publicist who convinced the powers that be at the Paramount to affix the tired-sounding strapline to the bottom of the marquee was one Milt Rubin, a Times Square hack and the willing slave of the Emperor Winchell—Walter, of course. Sinatra had hired Rubin in the fall of 1942, soon after leaving Dorsey, on a tip from the all-powerful columnist, and had quickly come to regret it. The PR man treated Frank like just another act, no more important than anyone else on his C-list roster of ventriloquists, acrobats, and female impersonators. Meanwhile, Rubin hovered around Winchell's table at Lindy's, laughing at the great man's jokes and begging for scraps. There were times Sinatra—admittedly a high-maintenance client—couldn't reach his $50-a-week publicist on the telephone. Nancy, who wrote the checks, began ignoring Rubin's bills. This got his attention, though not in a good way: the publicist initiated legal proceedings against his client.

Manie Sacks of Columbia, Sinatra's new rabbi, had the solution: George Evans was Frank's man. The best in the business—the best there ever was.

This was manifestly true. Between Rubin and Evans, there was simply no comparison. A glance into the former's fusty Times Square office would have made it clear: a cluttered couple of rooms behind a frosted-glass transom door, an old broad in a snood doing her nails at the reception desk while some sweaty guy with a Chihuahua cooled his heels. In George B. Evans's clean and modern Columbus Circle suite, on the other hand, there were three assistants fielding calls from clients like Mr. Glenn Miller, Mr. Duke Ellington, and Miss Lena Horne.

Evans was forty, in the prime of his life, and he was a dynamo, with a thrusting determined jaw and a ravening look in his piercing dark eyes. Lightly balding, bespectacled (tortoise-shell frames were his trademark), handsome in his way, he dressed well, spoke fast and crisply, came straight to the point. And he had a good opinion of himself, with reason: he lived for his clients, and his clients did well by him. Their joys were his joys; their sorrows were his, too. If they needed solace at 4:00 a.m., he picked up the phone, no questions asked. He was as expert at making trouble go away as he was at whipping up excitement.

In return he was choosy about whom he wanted to represent. Where this Sinatra boy was concerned, Evans was skeptical at first, Manie Sacks's laudatory call notwithstanding. Singers were a dime a dozen, and what was a singer, anyway, without a band? The bands made news; the bands brought the crowds. And the bandleaders were gods. Glenn, Duke: God, just the thought of these brilliant, elegant, authoritative men gave Evans chills. In some sense, representing them made him feel he was taking on their qualities.

But a boy singer! This one might even be different from the rest—from what he had heard on records and the radio, Evans was willing to grant that. It was a pleasant voice, nicely expressive. Still, George Evans didn't quite see what all the fuss was about.

Then he went, and he saw. Nick Sevano, Sinatra's Hoboken homeboy and soon-to-be ex-gofer (one too many tantrums about starch in the shirts; life was too short—except that Sevano would spend the rest of his very long life trading, like so many others, on his acquaintance with the singer), met the publicist in the Paramount lobby and whisked him down the aisle in the middle of the 2:30 show. Evans, not easily impressed, gaped at what he saw.

Actually, the sound and smell were what hit him at first. The place was absolutely packed with hysterical teenage girls, almost five thousand of them, fire laws be damned (a few hundred slipped into the right hands earned Bob Weitman a lot of extra money). They were jam-

ming the seats, the aisles, the balcony—all but hanging from the raf-
ters. And hanging raptly on the words to the song the starved-looking
kid in the spotlight at center stage was singing—

Be careful, it's my heart . . .

and going nuts when he hit that last word:

It's not my watch you're holding, it's my he-art.

The (by now very practiced) catch in his voice, the tousled spit curl on
his forehead (no Dorsey anymore to order him to comb it), the help-me
look in his bright blue eyes (always, pointedly, laser focused on one girl
or another in the audience)—it all set them off like dynamite. The air
in the great auditorium was vibrating, both with earsplitting screams
(FRANKIEEE!!! *FRANKIEEE!!!*) and with the heat and musk of female
lust. Evans could smell perfumes, BO, the faint acrid tang of urine
(the girls would come for the first show at 9:15 a.m. and stay for show
after show, determined never to relinquish a precious seat even if it
meant soaking it), and something else. They were like a great herd of
female beasts, he thought with wonderment, all in heat at once . . .

As Evans hovered close to the stage, openmouthed (Sevano just
behind him, grinning knowingly), a girl in an aisle seat stood and
tossed a single rose, its long stem wrapped in protective paper, up to
the singer. The flower hung for a second in the whirling beam of the
spotlight—and then, with a graceful movement, Sinatra caught it,
smiled at her, and closed his eyes as he sniffed the blossom, sending the whole theater into yet another paroxysm. The publicist's ears
picked out one sound above the din: a low moan, emanating from a
lanky black-haired girl standing next to the rose thrower. It was a sound
he had heard before—only in very different, much more private, circumstances.

Then and there George Evans decided he would represent Frank
Sinatra.

He had been in the business for ten years; he had represented Russ Columbo and Rudy Vallée at a time when such sappy crooners could capture the hearts of America's females—and when hearts were the only part of the female anatomy in play. Now the game had clearly advanced, and Sinatra was clearly the man responsible.

Evans knew at once he could take the game still further.

He stuck around for three more shows, taking careful note of what he saw and felt, his mind racing at the possibilities. This was something the publicist had never seen the likes of before. It was a great whirlwind, and he was being offered carte blanche to step in and harness it. But how?

He noticed—because each audience, after all, is a different animal—that not every show was successfully hysterical. Sometimes there were odd lulls in the tumult; sometimes the crowd got in its own way (and the singer's), just screaming, creating a massive wall of sound, preventing Sinatra from doing what he did best: singing. Pandemonium was all well and good if it served the purpose at hand— namely, making this boy a star like no other before him.

But Evans saw that Sinatra's visual appeal, while unique, was limited. What got to the girls was that voice—specifically, the unique blend of that personality and that voice. Other singers were better to look at. Others had winning personalities and terrific voices. But no one, absolutely no one, got his personality *into* the voice like this kid. He sold a song, and told a song, like nobody else. Especially, of course, if the song was a ballad. He yearned in front of thousands of females, making every girl in the place want to mother him or screw him—Sinatra had each and every one of them in a dither about which. But he had to be heard.

Then George B. Evans had his first great idea. "The Voice That Has Thrilled Millions"—the creakiness, the *sexlessness,* of that goddamn slogan made him cringe every time he thought of it. He could do so much better. What was it about Frankie Sinatra that got those girls' juices flowing? Evans closed his eyes and thought about what set them off. He saw those blue eyes focusing on one girl, then another;

and then he heard it: When, for just a half second, Sinatra stopped in the middle of a word, that was when the frenzy crescendoed. That was it! It was simple, really; all great human truths are. Evans didn't have to add a thing. All he had to do was subtract.

Frank was just . . . the Voice.

Simple. Instantly recognizable. You didn't have to ask whose. Accept no substitutes. This was it, now and for all time.

Evans lit a cigar; in the sweet cloud of blue smoke came the second idea. He would never admit to what inspired it. Like all Americans, he had listened with fascination to radio broadcasts of the era's great demagogues, orators who had a hypnotic effect on crowds: Roosevelt, Churchill, the evangelists Aimee Semple McPherson and Father Coughlin. But Evans was especially riveted by the Nazi broadcasts of Hitler whipping the German masses into a frenzy. The rallies were beautifully choreographed, the mass chanting swelled and fell precisely on cue. The dictator was never drowned out. Someone was behind this, Evans knew: someone very skillful.

George would have to be just as skillful in working his new client.

Evans had read how farmers would pay a pilot to go up and scatter certain chemicals on clouds to end a drought—seeding the clouds, they called it. Well, if clouds could be seeded, why not crowds? Rumor had it that Milt Rubin had handed out half-dollars in the Paramount lobby to girls who promised to make a racket during Sinatra's shows. It was the right idea, Evans felt, but unscientific in approach. In later years he would offer to donate $1,000 (he subsequently raised it to $5,000) to the favorite charity of anyone able to prove that "a kid was given a ticket, a pass, a gift, or a gratuity of any kind in any shape or manner at all to go in [to a Sinatra show] and screech." But Evans then went on to admit to E. J. Kahn Jr. that "certain things were done. It would be as wrong for me to divulge them as it would be for a doctor to discuss his work."

It was a self-aggrandizing comparison, but George Evans was in the aggrandizing business, and he was head and shoulders above his competition. "George was a *genius*," said Jerry Lewis, who, along with his partner, Dean Martin, was represented by Evans in the late 1940s. "He would audition girls for how loud they could scream! Then he would give each of them a five-dollar bill—no dirty money, just clean new bills; I learned that from him. The agreement was that they had to stay at least five shows. Then he spread them through the Paramount—seven sections. Evans would read the *scores* of the songs to see where the screaming should come in—the girls could only scream on the high, loud parts, never when it was low and sexy."

The publicist would even take groups of girls to the basement to rehearse them, giving them precise cues when to yell "Oh, Frankie! Oh, Frankie!"—not just during the loud parts, but whenever Sinatra let his voice catch. Evans also coached the singer. Picking up on Sinatra's intimate relationship with the microphone, Evans told him: Imagine that mike on its stand is a beautiful broad. Caress it. Make love to it. Hold on to it for dear life.

Sinatra looked impressed: the guy was good. Sanicola and Sevano bobbed their heads eagerly.

The publicist even trained both the singer and his claques in the art of call-and-response. When Sinatra sang "(I Got a Woman Crazy for Me) She's Funny That Way," with the lyric "I'm not much to look at, nothin' to see," Evans coached one of the girls to yell "Oh, Frankie, yes, you are!" On "Embraceable You," Evans told Frank to spread his arms beckoningly on the words "Come to papa, come to papa, do." The girls would then scream, "Oh, Daddy!" After which, Frank would murmur into the mike, "Gee, that's a lot of kids for one fellow." Evans trained some of the girls to faint in the aisles, others to moan loudly in unison. He hired an ambulance to park outside the theater and issued the ushers bottles of ammonia "in case a patron feels like swooning."

In the first two weeks of 1943, the hysteria at the Paramount built. At one show, thirty girls keeled over; only some of them had been prepped to do so. The crowds outside the theater were equally worked up. Times Square had become a twenty-four-hour Sinatra-thon. Wartime swing shifts abetted the overnight, around-the-block ticket lines for the 8:45 a.m. shows. The girls pushed and shoved, endangering each other and everything in sight. "I saw fans run under the horses of mounted policemen," recalled Sinatra's assistant road manager Richie Lisella. "I saw them turn over a car." Cordons of cops did their best to contain the hysteria. And George Evans did his best to fan it.

The publicist coined a whole new lingo, 1940s glib and gum-snappingly brash, to describe the phenomenon he was guiding. Winchell, Earl Wilson, and the other columnists could now refer to the singer as "Swoonatra," and to his bobby-soxed idolaters as "Sina-tratics." (Which was easier to read than to say.) The anguished pleasure they suffered in his presence was "Sinatrauma"; the specific physical reaction Dr. Evans had noted in one moaning female fan was, unsubtly enough, a "Sinatraism." ("Sinatrasm" might have been a little too on the money.)

George Evans was brilliant at leveraging publicity. No outlet was too insignificant—although it helped, in the case of high-school news-paper editors, if you could get a couple dozen of them in a room together to interview the star. Evans worked overtime planting Sinatra items — some of them lightly factual, most heavily laced with fancy—in the gossip columns and the news. Evans told reporters: Over a thousand Sinatra fan clubs have sprung up in the U.S.A.! (Who was counting? A thousand was a nice round number.) You had, among many, many oth-ers, your Sighing Society of Sinatra Swooners, your Slaves of Sinatra, your Flatbush Girls Who Would Lay Down Their Lives for Frank Sina-tra Fan Club. And let us not forget that glorious (and likely fictitious) gaggle of middle-aged aficionadas, the Frank Sinatra Fan and Mahjong Club.

Publicists have sown such corn since the Theodore Roosevelt administration, but this was a bolder variety, and the soil in which it took root was particularly fertile. The war was raging on two fronts, and America was hungry for upbeat stories. And it's always easier to make up good news than find it, and George Evans was delighted to oblige.

His greatest work of fiction was Sinatra's first publicity bio, a text that would have done Parson Weems (George Washington's early biographer and the inventor of the cherry-tree myth) proud. To establish greater solidarity with teenage fans, Evans first chopped a couple of years off the singer's age: Frank Sinatra had been born, it was now asserted, in 1917.[2] He had been raised poor but proud in the slums of Hoboken, narrowly avoiding mayhem at the hands of vicious street gangs. He had triumphantly graduated, rather than dropped out, from A. J. Demarest High, where he had not only lettered in football, basketball, and track but also sung in the glee club. The sports reporter's chair he had so hungered for at the *Jersey Observer* was now his. And in a truly inspired invention, Evans transformed Dolly from a cussing midwife-abortionist-political fixer into a former Red Cross nurse in World War I—from Mammy Yokum to Catherine Barkley in a single swoop.

And that was only the beginning. In Evans-world, the present-day Frank was a model suburban husband and dad, mowing the lawn, washing the car, patiently teaching Little Nancy chords on the family's upright piano. To document all this Potemkin domesticity, the publicist dispatched photographers to the Sinatras' new house, the cute Cape Cod at 220 Lawrence Avenue, Hasbrouck Heights, New Jersey. It was an upward-aspiring middle-class quarter of similarly cute houses, all set rather closely together. The Sinatra family doctor lived right next door. And down the block and around the corner—just a hop, skip, and jump away—lived the North Jersey crime boss Willie Moretti. Naturally, the publicity material did not mention this last fact, which may or may not have been sheerest coincidence.

It was also a crowded street, now that Swoonatra had moved in. There were all those publicity photographers, for one thing; for another, there was now a more or less nonstop procession of teenage girls tiptoeing up the driveway, hiding behind the bushes, swiping Frank's undershorts from the clothesline, writing love notes in lipstick on the garage door, or casting discretion to the winds and simply pressing their noses against the glass. "I'd look out my bedroom window and there would be somebody's face," Big Nancy recalled. "They'd sit out there on the lawn for hours. We tried asking them to go home, but they wouldn't leave. It scared me, but finally I'd feel so sorry for them I'd send out doughnuts and something for them to drink." As magnanimous as she was, it's hard to imagine Mrs. S. sending out those doughnuts and drinks more than once or twice before putting her foot down. Publicity, she was quickly learning, cut two ways.

So did fame, though if Sinatra had any regrets, he hid them well. The threadbare private life glimpsed by the twelve-year-old babysitter Ed Kessler in the Audubon Avenue apartment (a life in which, even then, Sinatra participated only sporadically) was now quite thoroughly a thing of the past. Private life for Frank Sinatra had simply winked out like a light, ceased to exist—or rather, he found what little privacy he could in his trysts, and in the wee hours with his pals. It was as though he had stepped out of his front door and into the basket of a hot-air balloon. As he ascended over the landscape of everyday reality, Mr. and Mrs. America got up early, went to work, punched a time clock, listened to the radio, worried about the bills. Far above, Frank Sinatra smiled amid the unimaginably sweet breezes of his new life.

It was a life that seemed somehow inevitable. He had done his share of hard scrabbling, and then some. "People call me an overnight success," he said. "Don't make me laugh." But when real success did come, it came fast. In early January, when RCA Victor released "There Are Such Things," one of the Dorsey-Sinatra recordings the bandleader had stockpiled in anticipation of the American Federation of Musicians strike (which had been in full swing since August), the record instantly went to number 2 on the *Billboard* chart. By the middle of the month, it had risen to number 1, knocking off Bing Crosby's "White Christmas." As a result, the Paramount held Sinatra over for another four-week run, a nearly unprecedented honor (only Rudy Vallée had accomplished it before). And on the strength of the Paramount run and the record sales, CBS, whose recording arm, Columbia, was about to sign the singer, named Sinatra the star of its flagship radio show, Lucky Strike's *Your Hit Parade*.

Your Hit Parade was based on a simple formula: bean counters somewhere would supposedly tabulate the week's top-selling songs,[3] and the studio orchestra and singers (Sinatra's female counterpart was the now-forgotten Joan Edwards) would perform the top dozen or so of them in reverse order, saving the biggest hit for last. Sandwiched in between were plenty of commercials for Lucky Strikes, with the brand's mystical, mellifluous slogan (L.S.M.F.T.—"Lucky Strike Means Fine Tobacco") and its catchphrase ("so round, so firm, so fully packed"): magic words that made you feel, if you happened to smoke the brand, part of an elect.

The show was hokey, and over Sinatra's two tenures there (1943–44 and 1947–49) many of the songs were dogs (not even Sinatra could do much with "Red Roses for a Blue Lady"). But radio was everything then, and Sinatra's selection as the star of *Your Hit Parade* was a direct weekly injection of his name into the American consciousness. Not everyone bought records. Certainly not everyone went to the Paramount Theater (although the cops in Times Square would have disagreed). But *everyone* listened to the radio.

And George Evans was succeeding beyond even his expectations—so much so that in early 1944 *Billboard* gave him an award for "Most Effective Promotion of a Single Personality," an occasion that inspired him to pronounce (a little indiscreetly) to the Chicago Tribune News Service, "Frankie is a product of crowd psychology . . . Understand, it was the Sinatra influence that provided the initial impetus. But it was I, Evans, who saw the possibilities in organized and regimented moaning . . . It's a big snowball now, and Frankie's riding to glory on it."

I, Evans. The publicist may have been a popinjay, yet he was a very successful one, and there is no evidence that Sinatra resented his ego—as long as that ego was doing good things for him. And Evans was more than just a publicist: he was a father figure, the third in a series of such figures in Frank Sinatra's life, after Tommy Dorsey and Manie

Sacks. While Sinatra invariably found a way to pry away the intimacies that complicated his life, with the father surrogates things were even more complex, and ultimately explosive. It was as if he had to kill the old man again and again. And each of the father substitutes was—as Sinatra's actual father of course was not—a considerable figure. Then again, to loom large in Sinatra's life at this point, a man had to be.

George Evans's genius went beyond mere publicity. He took a strong hand with his new client, the main issue being Sinatra's marriage, which was increasingly troubled. There was no deep psychological underpinning to this: it was simply that the more famous Frank Sinatra got, the more women there were who wanted to go to bed with him, and he saw no reason not to oblige as many of them as possible. Covering up the evidence was rarely his first priority. In the quaint era when there was still such a thing as bad publicity, this was one of the worst kinds: in 1940s America, a man—and especially a public exemplar—was nothing if he was not a family man. And if George Evans had anything to do with it, Frank Sinatra would, by God, be a family man—whatever the reality was.

Evans undertook a three-pronged offensive. The first was positioning, or what might today be called spin: the pictures of Frank mowing the lawn and dandling Baby Nancy.

The second was active interdiction. With Sinatra, the women gathered like flies, came in over the transom and through the emergency exit doors. Whenever possible, Evans headed them off, but he couldn't always be present to look out for his client's best interests. So whenever news of the singer's latest indiscretions reached him, the publicist started working the phones—to Sinatra, to the girl, to her folks in Oshkosh, if need be: anything to stamp out the brush fire. And there were a lot of brush fires.

Evans was earning his fat salary, and it was fine with Sinatra. He liked George, liked the fact that the older man was unafraid of him. He smiled when the publicist grabbed him by the elbow to steer him from trouble, smiled even when he stamped out another brush fire. There were always more fires to be lit.

The third prong of the offensive turned out, surprisingly, to be Nancy Sinatra herself. From the moment he met her, George Evans saw that she was a remarkable woman, direct and intelligent, with a quiet dignity and a real beauty behind a physically unconfident exterior. Her liquid brown eyes searched and questioned. And suffered. Evans immediately saw that Nancy was well on her way to becoming one of those Italian peasant ladies you saw sitting on apartment stoops—heavy, fiercely plain, all browns and blacks, coarse fabrics and unplucked hairs. As a married man himself, he understood how women battled with weight, and as Frank Sinatra's publicist he understood that Nancy was on the verge of giving in: there was simply too much competition.

For the longest time she had been grappling on her own with her position, and it was starting to wear on her. She made bargains with herself: She would lose the weight. (It wasn't easy.) She would look the other way as long as he came home to her. (He didn't come home very often.) What made it all so terribly difficult was that she still loved Frank, she was closer to him than to anyone else on earth: they were soul mates—except that the part of his soul that that bitch Dolly owned would never be satisfied. And not only did Nancy love him, but (and this made her furious sometimes) she had stuck by him since the beginning, since the days when they'd lived on spaghetti and meatless tomato sauce because meat simply cost too much. Now that he was really beginning to make some money, why should she share any part of his success with another woman?

But in George Evans, Nancy Sinatra found an ally. He looked at her appreciatively, he saw her as a woman, not just the suffering wifey. In truth, a great part of Evans's appreciation was professional: the woman had possibilities. Frank Sinatra had to be made to see those possibilities. Evans squinted at Nancy through his horn-rims, seeing the changes in his mind's eye. And then he went to work.

He took her to Bonwit Teller to shop for dresses—an unimaginable expense for a woman who had made her own clothes forever. He took her to Helena Rubinstein to have her hair done, and for a makeup consultation. He took her to a Park Avenue dentist to have her teeth capped. And then there was the matter of her generous Barbato nose: just a little thinning of the tip and she would be perfection itself. Louis Mayer would be testing her for the screen.

She gave him a level look. She had lived with this nose for twenty-five years, and it had worked just fine for her so far.

But she was a beautiful woman. Why not make the most of what she already had?

Was there a moment between them? He came to appreciate, more and more, the beauty that flowered under his ministrations. (Meanwhile, his own wife was sullen and resentful these days about the long hours he spent away from home.) And Nancy Barbato Sinatra longed—ached, really—to be looked at again *that way.* It had been such a long time. She melted a little when George called her beautiful, but at heart she was practical and decisive. As was he.

Then there came a day, in early April, when Frank looked at her with her new dress and her hair and her makeup and her teeth (and the five pounds she'd tortured herself to lose), and it was *that look* again. He took her into the city, to go dancing at El Morocco (Hank Sanicola, at a nearby table, shooed away the girls), and for a late supper at Le Pavillon, and they laughed together and looked in each other's eyes just the way they used to down the shore, down at Long Branch. Later they drove back to Hasbrouck Heights and paid the babysitter, and a month later she was pregnant again.

Warm Valley. Frank posts the sign he made himself on the front lawn of the
Hasbrouck Heights house, April 1943. Big and Little Nancy look on adoringly.

Frank at the Riobamba, February 1943. "You better push the walls
of this joint out. I'm gonna pack 'em in."

Even as Sinatra soared, he encountered occasional turbulence, not to
mention other highfliers. Handsome Dick Haymes (who was dogging Sinatra's trail, having followed him with both Harry James and
Tommy Dorsey) had now also gone out on his own, and was selling an
awful lot of records on Decca. A new kid named Perry Como was on
the rise. Nor was it clear, yet, that Frank Sinatra was anything more

than a national fad. He had the hysteria market locked up; the girls would buy his records. But would the grown-ups listen?

On this count, he failed at first. In February 1943, Sinatra's management moved heaven and earth to book him into the Copacabana, a big new club on East Sixtieth Street. These were the days when Manhattan was the center of the popular-culture universe, and nightclubs were the white-hot core of Manhattan sophistication. And the Copa was the hottest of the hot. The club was secretly owned by the top mobster (and Walter Winchell buddy) Frank Costello, but its majordomo was a pinkie-ring-wearing, frog-voiced thug named Jules Podell, who, where this kid Sinatra was concerned, was not buying.

Podell croaked his indignation. So the kid had had Times Square tied in knots for two months; so what. Fuck Times Square. Fuck all those little girls, and fuck Frankie Sinatra. Frankie Sinatra would not play the Copacabana. Sophie Tucker played the Copacabana. Jimmy Durante played the Copacabana. Fuck Frankie Sinatra!

A year later, Podell would be kissing Sinatra's pinkie ring. But for now, the singer's people, in a bind, had to do the best they could—which in this case was a Copa knockoff (right down to the Mob ownership), only smaller: a glitzy jewel box of a joint on East Fifty-seventh called the Riobamba. Unlike the Copacabana, however, the Riobamba was on its uppers, largely due to depressed wartime business. (There was also the minor detail that its proprietor, Louis "Lepke" Buchalter of Murder Inc., was in Leavenworth awaiting execution.) The club was delighted to book Sinatra—it needed a quick injection of whatever it could get—but the most it could pay was a cut-rate $750 a week, half of what he was earning at the Paramount.

Sinatra was angry, and scared. (The two usually went hand in hand with him.) He could make the bobby-soxers scream by raising an eyebrow; the Upper East Side snobs who frequented the Riobamba might not react so favorably, and he hadn't played a nightclub since his days with Dorsey. Moreover, the Riobamba was an intimate place—no stage, just a piano on a little dance floor. Sinatra would be out there on his own, the patrons at their tables close enough to see him sweat.

Typically, he turned fear into bluster. When the club's manager showed Sinatra the tiny setup, he said, "You better push the walls of this joint out. I'm gonna pack 'em in."

But then he got scared all over again. He really was going to have to prove himself. The club's ads for his appearance didn't even bill him first: he was listed as "SPECIALLY ADDED," under Walter O'Keefe (a monologist and comedian) and Sheila Barrett (a singer and comedian). On opening night, in honor of the sophisticated surroundings, Sinatra came out in a tuxedo instead of his Paramount uniform of suit and floppy bow tie. He had to make his entrance right across the nightclub floor, sidling among the tables, trying his best not to bump into anyone. Literally shaking with stage fright, he backed into the protective curve of Nat Brandwynne's baby grand and began to sing. That was when things started going his way.

"Frank was in a dinner jacket," Earl Wilson wrote, "and he was wearing a wedding band. He had a small curl that fell almost over his right eye. With trembling lips—I don't know how he made them tremble, but I saw it—he sang 'She's Funny That Way' and 'Night and Day' and succeeded in bringing down the house . . . It was a wondrous night for all of us who felt we had a share in Frankie . . . The *New York Post*'s pop-music critic, Danny Richman, leaned over to me and said, 'He sends me.'"

That night Frank didn't have to make his lips tremble: he was that terrified.[1] Many years later he would confess that he felt sick with fear every time he walked out onto a stage. The same is true of many other performers ("If you're not scared, it means you don't care," Jerry Lewis has said), but unlike most Sinatra never bothered to try to hide his vulnerability. Wide-eyed with trepidation and excitement, he gave an audience naked emotion. Dick Haymes or Perry Como or Bob Eberly would have made a very different presentation: a nightclub audience would have admired the handsome face and voice, the musical grace, the thoroughgoing professionalism. But what the swell crowd at the Riobamba got was a jolt of sheer electricity.

Life magazine wrote: "Three times an evening, Sinatra steps into the baby spotlight that splashes on to the dance floor. In a come-hither, breathless voice, he then sings such songs as 'You'd Be So Nice to Come Home To,' 'That Old Black Magic,' 'She's Funny That Way,' and 'Embraceable You.' As he whispers the lyrics, he fondles his wedding ring and his eyes grow misty. A hush hangs over the tables, and in the eyes of the women present there is soft contentment. The lights go up and Sinatra bows, slouches across the floor and is swallowed up by the shadows."

Suddenly, rather than having to try to hear him over screams, audiences—grown-up audiences—were hanging on the caress of his voice. He had made them come to him. Overnight, Frank Sinatra had become an adult phenomenon.

The word traveled like lightning around Manhattan, and within a week it was standing room only at the Riobamba, even for the 2:30 a.m. show. Just as Frank had predicted. Within a week, Sheila Barrett was history—the club had put her under Sinatra on the bill; she walked—and Walter O'Keefe followed quickly. "When I came to this place," O'Keefe told the audience on his final night, "I was the star and a kid named Sinatra, one of the acts. Then suddenly a steamroller came along and knocked me flat. Ladies and gentlemen, I give you the rightful star—Frank Sinatra!" Just like that, the joint was all Frank's. His pay was doubled, and his gig extended.

And no one was less surprised than Sinatra. To a young reporter, he said, "I'm flying high, kid. I've planned my career. From the first minute I walked on a stage I determined to get exactly where I am; like a guy who starts out being an office boy but has a vision of occupying the president's office."

Frank "was a sensation, doing extra shows," Sammy Cahn remembered, "and I went to the two-thirty a.m. show with a stop first in his dressing room. The moment he saw me he put his arms around me and said, 'Did I tell ya? Did I *tell* ya?'

"He had them in the grip of his hand," Cahn said. "One of my vivid memories is, while he was singing, some gorilla coughed. A giant guy, like two hundred fifty pounds. He turned and looked at this guy, and the guy didn't know what to do with himself. Do you understand what I'm trying to say? Frank had power, menace . . . It was an incredible experience."

Only a week or two earlier, he had been backed up trembling against the club's piano; now he was staring down tough guys. His bravado was a self-fulfilling prophecy: bluster away the terror; then, when victorious, strut and gloat and bully. It was unattractive, but Dolly's teaching had left him little middle ground. The triumphant present was maximum revenge on the past, on the days when the Flashes had used him as a punching bag. Suddenly he was the alpha-dog leader of a pack of hangers-on self-dubbed the Varsity.

The group was the first of its kind, the 1943 forerunner of a hip-hopper's posse, complete with camel-hair overcoats, golden bling, and nights at the fights. Among them were Sanicola and (for the time being) Sevano; Sammy Cahn and Jimmy Van Heusen when they were in from the Coast; Manie Sacks; the singer's music-publishing partner, Ben Barton; two pugilists (and crowd-control specialists) named Al Silvani and Tami Mauriello; and another Jimmy, Tarantino, a shady character who wrote for a boxing magazine picturesquely called *Knockout*. They would swagger around Manhattan, from watering hole to watering hole, the little man at the center of the group, protectively cordoned, the functionaries at the periphery greasing the way with crisp new bills. It was the beginning of a pattern that would continue for the next thirty-three years of Sinatra's life, until he slipped the wedding ring onto the finger of his fourth and final wife—who, in a self-preserving power play, proceeded, with ruthless efficiency, to force out the sycophants, cronies, and enablers, one by one.

In the meantime, for a long time to come, he was King, with all that that entailed. The oboist and conductor Mitch Miller, who would one day produce Sinatra's records at Columbia, recalled: "Jimmy Van

Heusen once canceled dinner with me by saying, 'I'm sorry, but I've got to eat with the Monster.' Everyone called Sinatra the Monster."

They called him that because he acted like that—not always, but too often for comfort. He gave free rein to the terrible impatience that had always plagued him; his temper too was sanctioned by his success. Anything could set him off: a bad review, a package of shirts mistakenly starched by the laundry. He felt too much: it was his burden, his gift.

———

And what did Manie Sacks think of all these macho goings-on? How did the quiet and Talmudic record executive blend in with the hearty extroverts of the Varsity? No doubt, like many reflective men, he took vicarious pleasure in the company of doers. We do know that by a complicated formula, Sinatra, who detested solitude and surrounded himself with loud talkers and backslappers, took great pleasure in Manie Sacks's company. And he trusted him. Sacks brought out (as no man ever had before) a better self in Sinatra, a contemplative side at his center that few, with the exception of Nancy, had ever seen. Manie calmed Frank down. It was a valuable skill, and a unique one. The arranger Stordahl was a serene character, yet when things went south during a recording session, he would quietly smoke his pipe (upside down, like the Norwegian sailor he actually was) as Hurricane Sinatra raged and threatened and finally blew itself out.

Manie Sacks was a different ball of wax. From their first meeting, Sinatra seems to have sensed that Manie didn't just have real business acumen, didn't just have something Sinatra wanted (a contract with Columbia, the Rolls-Royce of record labels); he also had—for lack of a better word—soul. Manie was honest to the core; he was incapable of disingenuousness. Sinatra, who could wear a half-dozen personalities in the course of a morning, was fascinated by the man's purity. Like George Evans, Sacks was in his early forties, old enough to feel like a father to Sinatra. But Evans was another extrovert, a man to whom words were verbs. Sacks was deep.

He was small and dark haired, with a long, thin, acne-scarred face and a sizable nose—not homely-handsome, really, but homely-memorable. When he began to spend time with Sinatra, the crazed fans would sometimes mistake the record executive for the recording artist. For a brief time the press, when it had nothing else to write about, would make much of the supposed resemblance between the two. In fact, though, only in the grossest possible details—stature, hair color, face shape—was there a correspondence. Sinatra, for all his facial imperfections, had a wild, Dionysian beauty. Manie Sacks looked like a rabbi.[2]

"He was a very unusual-looking man," George Avakian recalled. Avakian first met Sacks in the late 1930s, when, while still a student at Yale, he was starting to produce jazz albums for Columbia. "You got the feeling right away that this was a man who knew what he was doing. He could have a piercing gaze. I don't mean like Benny Goodman's famous ray. But he looked you in the eye, and he was very direct in his speech. He didn't waste a lot of time. He always looked as though he was on the point of doing something very intense. He looked very intense. And he was. Manie I think ended up getting ulcers."

And Sinatra would have been the one who gave them to him. But at first the relationship was a beautiful thing, even in a difficult time. The American Federation of Musicians strike against the record companies, which had begun in August 1942, was in full swing when Sinatra signed with Columbia Records. Indeed, the first time Frank stepped into a recording studio as a solo artist (Liederkranz Hall on East Fifty-eighth Street; Monday, June 7, 1943), beginning a commercial relationship with Columbia that would last for a tumultuous decade, he saw no musicians, only the eight-person vocal group that had recently accompanied him on the radio, the Bobby Tucker Singers. Sinatra hadn't made a record in eleven months. Manie Sacks was so desperate to get product out to Frank's female fan base that he had asked him to sing a cappella.

He was game at first. Listen to his maiden recording, of Hoffman, Lampl, and Livingston's "Close to You": You hear Sinatra in fine vocal form, backed by what sounds at first like a heavenly choir, trilling along in close harmony.[3] Unfortunately, the heavenliness quickly turns cloying. The effect is pretty, but . . . crowded. Too many voices in the room, when there should be only the Voice.

He would record nine of the instrumentless singles between June and November 1943, and the fans would dutifully buy them (five of the numbers hit the *Billboard* best-sellers chart), but none of the records had anything like the impact of a disc that Sinatra had cut an eon ago, with Harry James—and that Manie Sacks had the good sense to reissue on June 19. The song was "All or Nothing At All." Only eight thousand people had bought the record when it was first released in June 1940. This time it sold a million.[4]

Since Axel Stordahl was an orchestra arranger, and organizing the voices of a small chorus so they would sound something like a band of actual instruments was a highly specialized problem, Sacks brought in a new man to arrange and conduct Sinatra's Bobby Tucker sessions. His name was Alexander Lafayette Chew Wilder—Alec for short. He was an upstate New Yorker, thirty-six years old, and a genuine American eccentric: a self-taught composer who wrote both serious music and popular songs, Wilder lived alone in the Algonquin Hotel, passed his days doing crosswords and jigsaw puzzles, and spent his evenings drinking, smoking, drinking some more, and dazzling New York's best and brightest with his encyclopedic knowledge of more or less everything. "He is acutely aware of what is happening in the world and why it happens," read the liner notes to an album of Wilder's orchestral music released several years later—an album that would loom large in Sinatra's life. "He is passionately fond of living in hotels, riding on trains, and reading detective stories; he is equally enamored of sitting still in a small town, attending to a garden, and talking to children." Wilder was mustached and handsome in an old-money way, with a beetling brow and a distracted, kind of sideways, manner. The first time Sinatra laid eyes on him, he called him by the only possible nickname: the Professor.

Working with Sinatra would have been a big deal for Wilder, if

Wilder hadn't been above caring about such matters. But oddly enough, working with Alec did feel like a big deal to Frank. In Sacks and Wilder, Frank Sinatra was rubbing elbows with a new caliber of talent. Manie may have hung with the crew, have smiled at the hijinks, but ultimately he kept himself to himself. His integrity was inviolable. And as charmed as Alec Wilder was with Sinatra—and as bowled over by his musical gifts—he had absolutely no interest in joining the Varsity, or any fraternity at all. He might, out of anthropological curiosity, tag along to a Friday-night prizefight; he might, just as likely, spend the next evening drinking with Alexander Woollcott and Dottie Parker.

Both Sacks and Wilder had that ineffable quality that Frank Sinatra thought of as Class. He wanted the same thing of those who had it that those who lacked it wanted of him. Class didn't necessarily have anything to do with wealth: the rich stiffs who flocked to see him at the Riobamba mostly lacked the elusive quantity entirely, as far as he could see. (Though in later years, cleverer stiffs, primarily in Hollywood and Palm Springs, would gain access to Sinatra by assuring him that their money was no greener than his.) It was easy to feel superior to some jackass with dough; Sinatra never, for one second, felt superior to Manie or the Professor. If anything, it was quite the opposite. Which made things kind of complicated sometimes, but never stopped him from longing for just a little bit of what they had.

On August 11, 1943, Frank Sinatra made his grand entrance to Hollywood—except that it wasn't Hollywood. It was Pasadena. Nancy Sinatra writes, in *Frank Sinatra: An American Legend,* "Traveling by train to Los Angeles, Dad tried to avoid the waiting crowds by deboarding [*sic*] in Pasadena, but it was no use: A huge throng of bobby-soxers mobbed the station, and he was rushed by police to the safety of a nearby garage. 'They converged on our car and practically picked it up,' Dad recalls. 'There must have been 5,000 kids mashed against the car. It was exciting, but it scares the wits out of you, too.'"

This is disingenuous. In fact, Sinatra's true goal on that summer

Wednesday was not eluding the crowds but meeting them, and the waiting throng—probably closer to a few hundred than five thousand—had been lured by a radio "whisper" of the singer's arrival. As the Atchison, Topeka & Santa Fe Super Chief pulled in to the little Mission-style depot, a loudspeaker was blaring "All or Nothing At All." The whole event had been carefully orchestrated by the Evans office (Margaret Divan, Los Angeles representative), working in league with the West Coast Sinatra fan clubs and the RKO publicity department. Another photograph taken that day shows Sinatra standing on a ladder in the midst of an enthusiastic but notably restrained throng; a couple of female hands are proffering autograph books, but none are ripping at his clothing. The ladder is clearly stenciled "RKO GRIP DEP'T."

His fans weren't the only ones thrilled to see him. RKO executives were hoping Sinatra could help lift Radio-Keith-Orpheum Pictures out of the financial trough into which another young genius, Orson Welles, had sunk it with his brilliant but money-losing epics *Citizen Kane* and *The Magnificent Ambersons.*[5]

It was astonishing: Frank was about to sign a seven-year movie contract, and nobody really even knew whether he could act. He had appeared, very briefly, in three motion pictures to date: Paramount's *Las Vegas Nights* (1941), MGM's *Ship Ahoy* (1942), and—released earlier in 1943—a Columbia musical with the perky, patriotic title *Reveille with Beverly.* In *Las Vegas Nights* and *Ship Ahoy,* Sinatra had been a mere singing extra, the male vocalist for Tommy Dorsey and His Orchestra, and while he was featured in *Reveille,* it was only as the singer of one number, "Night and Day" (accompanied by six female pianists).

Still, whether he could play Hamlet was hardly the point. He had been playing one role, brilliantly, for almost ten years. He didn't have to act. He was *Frank Sinatra.*

===

The staid Chandler family's *Los Angeles Times* gave front-page treatment to the new star's arrival. SECRET OF LURE TOLD BY CROONER—IT'S LOVE, read the two-column headline. The story reported that Sinatra had come not only to start his movie career but also to play a concert with the Los Angeles Philharmonic at the Hollywood Bowl. L.A. classical music aficionados were outraged, the paper said, even though Sinatra's appearance promised to give the orchestra, and the bowl, a badly needed financial boost. One of the naysayers had been the *Times's* distinguished music critic, Isabel Morse Jones, a portly old-guard Angeleno who ventured bravely out to that besieged garage in Pasadena. It wasn't just the howling fans Ms. Jones was nervous about; it was Frank himself. "My objections to swooner-crooner singing in sacred precincts [had recently] hit the wires and reached him in New York," she wrote. But Sinatra smiled that smile at her, and practically from the moment she opened her reporter's notebook, Isabel Morse Jones was a goner. Frank knew just how to play the ladies, young and pretty or middle-aged and plump. And if the lady in question was a distinguished classical music critic, why, all the better. He spoke softly, and she listened carefully.

"I expect to get the thrill of my life Saturday night," he told Ms. Jones. "Oh, yes, I can be just as enthusiastic about classical music as those kids out there are about my kind. What do you suppose I have 500 albums of symphonies and so on for?"

Five hundred albums of symphonies . . . One can see the music critic's eyes widening, her features softening. . . "It's the words of a song that are important," Sinatra went on. "I pick my songs for the lyrics. The music is only a backdrop. I sing love songs and mean them. They're meant for two girls, both named Nancy. One is my wife, aged 24, and not jealous and the other is my three-year-old."[6]

"He is just naturally sensitive," Isabel Morse Jones wrote, her fingers flying over the typewriter keys, when she got back to the office. "He is a romanticist and a dreamer and a careful dresser and he loves beautiful words and music is his hobby. He makes no pretensions at all."

Another one bites the dust.

He handled his first meeting with Louella Parsons, a few days

later, with equal skill. Here was another small, pudgy female columnist, except that this one was a real dragon lady: a personal favorite of
her employer, William Randolph Hearst, and the most feared woman
in Hollywood. Her forty million readers gave her tremendous power.
Yet even Lolly Parsons's knees wobbled in Sinatra's presence. She
wrote that he had, "Noah Webster forgive me, humility. He was warm,
ingenuous, so anxious to please." He would grow less eager to please
as his own power grew. Parsons and Sinatra would have a love-hate
relationship over the years, until her clout waned and he decided he
didn't need her anymore. Long afterward, she would reflect: "Sinatra
couldn't have been so boyishly unspoiled, so natural and considerate.
But I have to admit he was. After I met him, I was enrolled in the Sinatra cheering squad. And I stayed in a long, long time."

Two days after Sinatra's arrival in Pasadena, a radio listener in San Jose
wrote a letter to the FBI:

Dear Sir:

The other day I turned on a Frank Sinatra program and I noted
the shrill whistling sound, created supposedly by a bunch of
girls cheering. Last night as I heard Lucky Strike produce
more of this same hysteria I thought: how easy it would be for
certain-minded manufacturers to create another Hitler here in
America through the influence of mass-hysteria! I believe that
those who are using this shrill whistling sound are aware that
it is similar to that which produced Hitler. That they intend to
get a Hitler in by first planting in the minds of the people that
men like Frank Sinatra are O.K. therefore this future Hitler
will be O.K. As you are well aware the future of some of these
manufacturers is rather shaky unless something is done like
that . . .

Crazy as it was, the letter was notable for one reason: it was the beginning of what would become a 1,275-page FBI dossier on Sinatra.

———

He rented a bungalow at the Garden of Allah, where the parties never stopped. Five years earlier, Sheilah Graham had moved Scott Fitzgerald out of the complex so he could get some work done. Sinatra, who had come to Hollywood not only to start a movie career but also to have some serious fun, had picked his new residence deliberately. He took some vocal coaching from his new neighbor Kay Thompson. And he commuted to Culver City to make *Higher and Higher*.

The picture was a trifle, the kind of silly B fluff the studios cranked out by the ton in the 1930s and 1940s. The upstairs-downstairs comedy, such as it is, is set in motion when the wealthy Drake family loses its money and Mr. Drake conspires with the servants to marry the scullery maid off to the rich boy next door . . . Who, in an unconsciously inspired bit of casting, is played by none other than the Hoboken Kid, as himself. His first line, ever, in the movies, to the maid who opens the Drakes' door: "Good morning. My name is Frank Sinatra." (The maid faints.)

The big surprise about Sinatra in *Higher and Higher* is not how well he can hold a big screen, but how beautiful he is. Not handsome—any Joe Blow can be handsome. The twenty-seven-year-old Frank Sinatra, shot in rich black and white by cinematographer Robert De Grasse, is resplendent. Lovingly lit, photographed in slightly soft focus (and largely from the camera's left, his right, to avoid the bad profile), he glows through his every scene, all cheekbones and wide, wide eyes. He's like Bambi with sex appeal.

As for his acting—it scarcely matters: you simply can't take your eyes off the guy. A great deal has to do with the undismissable fact that this is *Frank Sinatra*. Had he been killed in a plane crash in 1947, or had his career come to an end (as it almost did) in 1950 or thereabouts, maybe Sinatra wouldn't have glowed quite so luminously.

But Frank endured. He became, for better and worse, a kind of god, and it's particularly interesting to observe him in the celluloid guise of a bashful young swain. The role, of course, was just a slight variation of the role he played when he sang. Watching *Higher and Higher* (in which Sinatra also gets to perform five numbers[7]), you can understand why the girls went bonkers: the guy was gorgeous and magnetic and achingly vulnerable. Quite simply, he was phenomenal—way too much so for little RKO Radio Pictures, a fact of which Frank Sinatra, doubtless, was sharply aware. Surely he had his people working frenziedly on contingency plans to extricate him from the studio even as he wrapped his first film with them. After all, contracts, seven-year and otherwise, were only pieces of paper.

———

Another contract, one that grew progressively more irksome as Sinatra's earnings skyrocketed, was the onerous severance agreement he had signed with Tommy Dorsey. Having initially boasted he would simply stiff the steely-eyed bandleader, Frank now decided to toss Tommy a bone: reportedly, about $1,000 in commissions. Predictably, this was not an amount that made Dorsey happy—and he grew increasingly unhappy hearing Sinatra brag to the press how much he was raking in.

In response, Sinatra, under the brilliant aegis of Evans, was turning the dispute into a cause célèbre, having his radio writers inject comic jabs at the bandleader into his sketches (at the sound of a few out-of-tune bars of "I'm Getting Sentimental over You": "It's Dorsey, coming to collect his commission!") and paying bobby-soxers to carry picket signs ("Dorsey Unfair to Our Boy Frankie!") outside Tommy's show in Philadelphia, while eager newspaper photographers immortalized the event.

Battered in the public arena, Dorsey would have been down for the count—except for the fact that Tommy Dorsey took no shit from anyone. There was also the fact that Dorsey was represented by that rising giant, the Music Corporation of America (MCA), which was desperate to also represent Frank Sinatra. Despite the imaginative formulations of both Mario Puzo and Sinatra, the whole affair was resolved in the most Byzantine (and peaceful) way possible.

The Godfather, of course, was the vehicle that elevated the whole contretemps to the realm of myth. In the novel, Puzo relates how the fictional bandleader Les Halley pressures the fictional singer Johnny Fontane into an impossibly severe personal-services contract. When Fontane approaches his godfather, Don Corleone, and asks him to intervene on his behalf, the don goes to Halley and offers him $20,000 to release Fontane from the contract. Halley refuses to play ball. Even after Don Corleone ominously drops his offer to $10,000, the bandleader won't budge.

> The next day [Puzo writes] Don Corleone went to see the band leader personally. He brought with him his two best friends, Genco Abbandando, who was his *Consigliere,* and Luca Brasi. With no other witnesses Don Corleone persuaded Les Halley to sign a document giving up all rights to all services from Johnny Fontane upon payment of a certified check to the amount of ten thousand dollars. Don Corleone did this by putting a pistol to the forehead of the band leader and assuring him with the utmost seriousness that either his signature or his brains would rest on that document in exactly one minute. Les Halley signed. Don Corleone pocketed his pistol and handed over the certified check.

Still wincing from his portrayal as the sniveling Fontane, but loftily refusing to acknowledge it, Sinatra took the high road when Sidney Zion asked him in 1986 about the Dorsey contract. "The man who straightened it out was named Saul Jaffe," Sinatra told Zion. "He's a lawyer who now is retired. Mr. Jaffe was the secretary of the American Federation of Radio Artists, and Tommy Dorsey and his Orchestra would play from hotel [ball]rooms around the country on radio programs. I told [Jaffe] the whole story, and he went to Mr. Dorsey and he said to him, 'I represent Frank Sinatra in this case that you and he are involved in.' He said, 'I think we can come to a settlement quite simply.' Tom said, 'No no, I want one-third of his salary for the rest of his life.' So Jaffe said to him, 'Do you enjoy playing music in hotel [ball]rooms and having the nation hear you on the radio?' [Dorsey] said, 'Sure I do.' [Jaffe] said, 'Not anymore, you won't.'"

Whether other, darker forces were brought to bear—and if they were, whether Sinatra knew anything about it—are questions that will forever remain unresolved. The answers are tied up in Frank's relationship to the Mob, and mobsters, in 1943 and for the rest of his life: a teasing, conflicted, flirtatious dance on both sides.

Jerry Lewis had another version of the Dorsey-Sinatra brouhaha. He asserted that, based on the Mafia's early adoration for Sinatra, a summit consisting of Frank Costello, Albert Anastasia, Willie Moretti, and the Murder Inc. hit man Frankie Carbo got together and went to Dorsey to make him that offer he couldn't refuse. "Frank told me years later—laughing—how that talk went," Lewis remembered. "Carbo said, 'Mr. Dorsey, could you play your trombone if it had a dent in it? Could you play it if you didn't have the slide?' It was all just like that, and Dorsey got the idea."

One kernel of truth in this account would seem to be the participation of Sinatra's Hasbrouck Heights neighbor Willie Moretti, a.k.a. Willie Moore, the boss of North Jersey. Moretti was short, plump, bald, wisecracking, gregarious—and, as his job demanded, dangerous. He had his fingers in many pies, paid close attention to such profit centers as the Meadowbrook in Cedar Grove, the Riviera in Fort Lee, and the Rustic Cabin, and apparently took quite a shine to Sinatra. Still, whether that makes Moretti (who was about as different from the noble Don Corleone as it was possible to be) Sinatra's godfather, and whether Moretti interceded personally with Dorsey (who was, after all, a North Jersey resident himself), is another question.

Peter J. Levinson, in his Dorsey biography, tells us that the *"Bergen*

Record entertainment editor and syndicated writer Dan Lewis, [who] knew Moretti personally . . . once asked [the gangster] if there was any truth to these reports. Moretti smiled and, in a rare departure from *omertà,* answered, 'Well, Dan, let's just say we took very good care of Sinatra.' "

In fact, Moretti had a reputation for making frequent departures from *omertà.* He was an infamous blowhard whose garrulity—perhaps abetted by an advanced case of syphilis—would eventually lead to his elimination.

To complicate matters further, Dorsey's daughter, Levinson writes, "vividly remembers her father telling her about getting a threatening telephone call at dinnertime early in the Sinatra-Dorsey contretemps. The anonymous caller implied ominous consequences if Dorsey didn't 'cooperate' by letting Sinatra out of his contract. He was reminding Dorsey that he had two children, and that he wouldn't want anything to happen to them. That's when Dorsey responded by putting up barbed wire atop the wall surrounding [his house], installed sweeping search-lights that bathed the property on a nightly basis, and constructed an elaborate electric fence at the entrance to the property."

There is yet another story, told by an old Hoboken pal of Sinatra's, one Joey D'Orazio, that possesses a seriocomic ring of truth. D'Orazio asserted that Hank Sanicola sent two rough customers, "not real underworld characters but just some frightening fellows that he and Sinatra both knew," to threaten Dorsey if he didn't release the singer from the contract. Sanicola claimed that in order to protect Sinatra should things go wrong, he never told him about the two thugs.

But, according to D'Orazio, when the two threatened to break Dorsey's arms if he didn't sign legal papers to let the singer go, the bandleader "laughed in their faces. . . [saying] 'Oh, yeah, look how scared I am. Tell Frank . . . I said, "Go to hell for sending his goons to beat me up." ' "

Dorsey then told the men, "I'll sign the goddamn papers, that's how sick I am of Frank Sinatra, the no good bum. The hell with him."

"It wasn't much of an intimidation," D'Orazio said. "In fact, one of the guys was so excited about meeting Tommy Dorsey, he had to be talked out of going back and asking the guy for his autograph after they left his office."

The story seems just too charming not to be true.

There was little charm, however, once the lawyers and agents got involved. Saul Jaffe, who was indeed the secretary of the American Federation of Radio Artists, actually did threaten Tommy Dorsey with exclusion from the airwaves, and Dorsey—who perhaps had already been softened up by a threatening telephone call and a threatening visit—took his point. All that remained was the paperwork. MCA was able to snatch Sinatra away from his former agency, Rockwell-O'Keefe, by brokering the deal—which essentially just meant moving money around. Dorsey got $60,000 ($700,000 today) to finally cut Frank loose: $35,000 of it came from MCA itself, advanced to its new client; Columbia Records advanced the remaining $25,000 to its new recording artist.

Lawyers, agents, executives, goons, mobsters, gofers—all dancing attendance on the Golden Boy, who yawned, picked his teeth, and winked at the next beautiful girl at his dressing-room door, while his publicist pulled out what remained of his hair.

By the end of 1943, Frank Sinatra had ascended from mere teen idol to bona fide American superstar, one of only a handful of such creatures who had existed up to that point in history—think Caruso, Chaplin, Valentino, Crosby—but one who possessed unprecedented power and influence. Sinatra was a radio and recording star; he was soon to break through in the movies. He had smashed attendance records at the Paramount and wowed the snooty nightclub crowds at the Rio-bamba—and then, historically, in October, he knocked them dead at the Waldorf-Astoria's Wedgwood Room, a venue of such high tone that Cole Porter himself descended from his thirty-third-floor suite to take in the show (and, presumably, forgive the singer for blowing the lyrics to "Night and Day" back at the Rustic Cabin).[8] Sinatra had vocalized along with the Cleveland, Philadelphia, and Los Angeles philharmonics. Soon he would pay a call on the president of the United States— his idol Franklin Delano Roosevelt (who would ask Sinatra to clue him in on the winner of that week's *Your Hit Parade*). But he still had a big problem.

Along with sixteen million other young men, Sinatra had first registered for the draft in December 1940. As a new father, he had been granted an exemption from service, but now, in the fall of 1943, with the United States throwing every resource into the conflicts in Europe and the Pacific, the government was about to abolish deferments for married fathers. Meanwhile, Sinatra was already catching flak from resentful soldiers ("Hey, Wop. Why aren't you in uniform?"), and George Evans was doing plenty of scrambling to keep his prize client from looking like a slacker, making sure the press knew he was singing "God Bless America" at war-bond rallies (lots of them), and on American Forces Radio shows, and on unbreakable vinyl V-Discs to be sent to soldiers and sailors overseas.

But would *Frankie* be sent overseas? Plenty of entertainers were on their way: Buddy Rich had signed up, as had Joe Bushkin and Jack Leonard and Glenn Miller and Artie Shaw and Rudy Vallée, not to mention Gene Kelly and Mickey Rooney (with a heart murmur, yet) and Clark Gable (dentures and all) and Jimmy Stewart and Joe DiMaggio, though the only fighting John Wayne would do would be on celluloid.

At the end of October, Sinatra dutifully reported to the local board examining physician for the U.S. Army in Jersey City, where, in a preliminary examination, a Dr. Povalski declared the singer fit for service, classifying him 1-A. In early December, the Army, in the person of Captain Joseph Weintrob, M.D., examined Sinatra again, in Newark, and declared him 4-F. His Physical Examination and Induction form read, "Frank Albert Sinatra [note first name] is physically and/or mentally disqualified for military service by reason of: l. chronic perforation (left) tympanum; 2. chronic mastoiditis." The form noted the examinee's weight as 119 pounds (four pounds below the Army minimum for men of his stature) and his height as five feet seven and a half inches, and went on to say that he was further disqualified because of emotional instability.

There is every reason to believe that Weintrob's report was correct in every particular. Not only were Sinatra's height (sans elevators), weight, first name, and emotional state right on the money, but chronic left-ear infections would certainly account for the punctured left eardrum, and his mastoid operation would have further complicated matters.[9] Nevertheless, Sinatra's 4-F quickly became controversial big news. He was, after all, cocky, rich, famous, and Italian-American. Later that month, Walter Winchell received an anonymous letter at his New York *Daily Mirror* office:

> Dear Mr. Winchell:
>
> I don't dare give you my name because of my job but here is a bit of news you can check which I think is Front Page:
>
> The Federal Bureau of Investigation is said to be investigating a report that Frank Sinatra paid $40,000 to the doctors who examined him in Newark recently and presented him with a 4-F classification. The money is supposed to have been paid by Sinatra's Business Manager. One of the recipients is said to have talked too loud about the gift in a beer joint recently and a report was sent to the F.B.I.
>
> A former School mate of Sinatra's from Highland, N.J., said recently that Sinatra has no more ear drum trouble than Gen. MacArthur.
>
> If there is any truth to these reports I think that it should be made known. Mothers around this section who have sons in the service are planning a petition to Pres. Roosevelt asking for a re-examination of the singer by a neutral board of examiners.

You'll probably read about this in the papers within a few days unless you break the story first.

Winchell sent the letter on to his pal J. Edgar Hoover, and though it turned out the FBI had not been actively investigating Sinatra, it quickly set about doing so. Matters snowballed from there. Titillated to discover that the singer had two sex-related arrests on his record, the bureau looked closely into the dismissed cases, even though they had absolutely no bearing on the present matter. In the meantime, Dr. Weintrob wrote a letter to his superior officers amplifying his original physical assessment of Sinatra and adding, "The diagnosis of 'psychoneurosis, severe' was not added to the list. Notation of emotional instability was made instead. It was felt that this would avoid undue unpleasantness for both the selectee and the induction service."

Dr. Weintrob—his back to the wall—elaborated. "During the psychiatric interview," he wrote, "the patient stated that he was 'neurotic, afraid to be in crowds, afraid to go in elevator, makes him feel that he would want to run when surrounded by people. He had somatic ideas and headaches and has been very nervous for four or five years. Wakens tired in the A.M., is run down and undernourished.'"

The FBI report said that Weintrob "stated that no one had ever attempted to influence his opinion in this case and in fact no one had discussed the SINATRA case with him prior to the actual examination . . . Captain WEINTROB stated he was satisfied in his own mind that SINATRA should not have been inducted and was willing to stake his medical reputation on his findings."

The FBI closed the case. The press, the public, and the men of the armed forces did not.

=====

Was Frank Sinatra reluctant to serve his country? While his physical diagnosis alone would have been enough to disqualify him, the psychological interview is interesting. During his preliminary examination in

October, his response to the inquiry "What physical or mental defects or diseases have you had in the past, if any?" had been the single word "No." The answer didn't quite match up to the question, indicating a certain haste on his part. He was always impatient. In Newark in December, he was willing to take more time. Everything he said to Weintrob made perfect sense: He *was* neurotic, highly. Where crowds were concerned, the very real prospect of having his clothes ripped off or being choked by his own bow tie quite naturally made him afraid. He did suffer from claustrophobia, and elevators often terrified him (as they did Dean Martin). The somatic ideas and headaches would match up with Sinatra's occasional sinking feeling that he wasn't long for this world. Nervous for four or five years? Since the moment—just say— he'd first stepped on the bus with Harry James and His Music Makers . . . And anyone who had spent the previous day playing six shows at the Paramount, making public appearances, and doing three night-club shows (the last beginning at 2:30 in the morning), with plenty of gallivanting before, between, and after, would tend to wake up tired in the a.m. Or the p.m.

Sinatra was not the only star not to serve. Dick Haymes and Perry Como had not been drafted. And Crosby, at forty, was too old to join up (but would go to heroic lengths throughout the war to entertain the troops). There were a lot of singers out there, and Frank wasn't about to give those other guys a leg up by going away for the duration—or, God forbid, dying for his country.[10] It wasn't so much that he lacked physical courage; he simply had very legitimate fears about the fickleness of the American public.

And so he quashed his natural inclination to give a curt or rude answer to this square, this nosy medical officer, and instead sat back and responded at length: thoughtfully, feelingly. It could come in handy.

Frank's triumphant arrival in Hollywood—or Pasadena, anyway. August 1943.

Frank signs his induction papers at local draft board No. 19–160 in Jersey City, October 1943. He was classified 1-A. Two months later he was reexamined and exempted from military service due to a perforated eardrum and emotional instability.

Frank Sinatra had a knack for stirring people up. His draft reclassification did not go down well with the newspaper columnists, nor with the hundreds of thousands of men who were fighting overseas, or even just pulling mind-numbing Stateside duty, marching in the hot sun and eating creamed chipped beef on toast at Fort Ord or Fort Monmouth or Fort Benning. "Draft dodger" was an ugly epithet that people—mostly men—were starting to hang on Sinatra, for all his protestations to the press and even to friends that he was dying to serve, that the 4-F had been a crushing disappointment.

Part of him really did feel that way. And then there was the part that remembered what had happened to Jack Leonard: he had vanished, become just another serial number among the millions of Sad Sacks . . . Frank knew this was not his fate. His destiny was here, being Frank Sinatra.

His female fans were thrilled that their Frankie would be staying close to them. As for the servicemen, one old acquaintance gave it to Sinatra straight from the shoulder: Tommy Dorsey's former band manager Bobby Burns, the man who'd once slipped Sinatra a note telling him the Great Man himself would grant him an audience, was now a buck private at Camp Haan, in California. After Sinatra entertained at the base, Burns went up to him to say hi. "There's a lot of griping over your 4-F status," Burns told him. "The troops figure you're home living it up with the babes while they're away."

Frank grinned.

What other conclusion were the troops to draw? He *was* living it up, with every available babe, and he was sufficiently indiscreet that the whole world knew: not only his wife, but also millions of homesick, love-starved, generally disgruntled servicemen.[1] William Manchester wrote in *The Glory and the Dream,* his history of mid-twentieth-century America, "It is not too much to say that by the end of the war Sinatra had become the most hated man in the armed services."

George Evans was fighting a heroic public-relations battle, but he was bucking overwhelming odds. And his client wasn't helping matters. In the year since Sinatra had left Tommy Dorsey, he had become a spectacularly unrepentant hedonist, on the loose in a time of public piety and sacrifice. And as of January 1944, he was now on the loose in Hollywood, a continent away from Evans and Big Nancy.

On January 1, Sinatra legally became a California resident, a status he would maintain until the end of his life. On January 5, he began a new radio show on CBS, *The Frank Sinatra Program.* Unlike *Your Hit Parade*—on which the singer continued, but only as a glorified co-host—and the now defunct *Songs by Sinatra,* which had aired, unsponsored, for just fifteen minutes weekly, the new broadcast was a star vehicle, thirty minutes every Wednesday night, with a big-time backer, Vimms Vitamins. ("Take a minute! See what's in it! When you're buying a vitamin product, read the label! Make sure you get all the vitamins recommended by government experts! You do in Vimms! And three essential minerals also!")

In compliance with Sinatra's demands, the new show (with Stordahl conducting the orchestra, and the Bobby Tucker Singers back in service as the Vimms Vocalists) was broadcast from Hollywood.

He had come west to start shooting his second RKO feature, *Step Lively,* a musical version of the hit Broadway comedy *Room Service,* with songs written by his old pal Sammy Cahn and Cahn's partner Jule Styne. Radio could make a crooner an imaginary friend to the great American audience, but movies could make him larger than life: look at Bing.

First, though, came a minor distraction.

At 5:50 p.m. on Monday, January 10, Nancy Sinatra once again gave birth at the Margaret Hague Maternity Hospital in Jersey City, again unattended by her husband. During Little Nancy's delivery three and a half years earlier, Frank had been just across the Hudson River, singing with Dorsey at the Astor roof. For the birth of his only son, he managed to be all the way across the country. "Dad was on the air in the middle of a radio show broadcast live from Hollywood when Franklin Wayne Emmanuel [sic] Sinatra was born," writes Nancy junior, in *Frank Sinatra: An American Legend.* At 2:50 p.m. Pacific standard time on January 10, Frank Sinatra was certainly in the middle of something, but not a radio broadcast, since *Your Hit Parade* aired, live, on Saturday nights; the Vimms show, Wednesdays. And so Franklin Wayne Emanuel Sinatra came squalling into the world as he would remain in the world: fatherless, more or less.[2]

Evans immediately kicked into overdrive, slapping together a major photo op for the next day at Margaret Hague Maternity, arriving first thing in the morning to marshal the event. He first had Nancy don a pale blue quilted Best & Co. bed jacket, then brought in a cosmetologist and a beautician who made up, coiffed, and manicured her to the nines. Evans then handed Mom a framed photo of Dad and told her exactly what to do when the reporters trooped in: Smile. Hold up the baby. Hold up the photo.

Family was always an ambivalent matter with Sinatra. But the beautification of Nancy Sinatra was real. Once the nice ladies were done with her, she *was* beautiful—more so than any new mother had a right to be. When the reporters finally clumped in, clad in white coats for the occasion as if they were about to discover penicillin, brandishing their notebooks and giant flash cameras, Nancy was ready to answer their questions. Who was he named for? Which side of the family did he favor? Could he sing like his old man?

George stood behind them as they flashed away. He smiled at her, and she at him. And her smile was really beautiful.

Of course she wasn't just smiling at Evans. She was thrilled about this baby, and even loved the attention. She was, after all, *Mrs. Frank Sinatra*—a very important position in America, not so very different from being the First Lady. She was aware of the privileges and responsibilities.

To a great degree it was like a political marriage: the public had begun to overwhelm the private. The time they actually spent together, just the two of them, was almost nonexistent—especially with Frank so busy on the Coast. The phone calls were misery: with the three-hour difference, they always came at the wrong time, and since he hated being alone, there were usually other voices, even festive sounds, in the background, forcing her to imagine whom he was spending his evenings, not to mention his nights, with. Sometimes, when she was expecting his call, it wouldn't even be him, but that goddamn Hank Sanicola instead, going through his usual rigmarole about how long and hard Frank's days were, what with shooting the picture and broadcasting the radio shows and all. Frankie was dead tired, Hank would say; he never slept enough, couldn't keep any weight on—he made her husband sound like a candidate for Vimms himself . . .

It had been Frank who'd phoned the night of the birth—or rather, very early in the morning of the next day, most likely with the sounds of dishes and glasses and feminine laughter in the background.

How was she doing? How was their boy? Was he handsome? He missed her . . . He'd better go now—she needed her sleep . . . He missed her . . .

The hell of it was that she knew it was true—that he did miss her. In his fashion. And she missed him. With all her heart.

For the second Vimms show, on January 12, the fans began lining up at 6:45 a.m. outside the CBS Radio Playhouse at 1615 North Vine. By 5:00 p.m., an hour before broadcast time, more than a thousand of them—the vast majority girls, of course—queued around the block. The CBS studio seated 350. When Sanicola came in and told him most of the girls were about to be turned away, Sinatra saw red. How would 350 girls, as opposed to 1,500, sound to the American radio audience? Like a goddamn classical string recital, that was how.

He let the nervous-looking CBS executive hovering nearby have it. Then he turned to Hank. Was there a bigger studio?

Vine Street Playhouse seated fourteen hundred.

Sinatra pointed to the executive. Vine Street.

The man began to splutter. It would take hours to set up in another studio; they were scheduled to go on live in *one* hour. The sound levels were completely different in the other theater. The engineers . . .

The singer cocked his head and narrowed his lips.

Vine Street.

Dolly could have done no better.

The executive went to an office and stood by a telephone for a panicky moment before realizing he didn't have to put the impossible matter before his boss at all. A minute later, he leaned out the door, summoned Sanicola, and handed him the phone. It was not CBS but the chief of the local chapter of AFRA, the American Federation of Radio Artists, on the other end.

"Tell your boy either he goes on from the CBS studio or he's through as far as AFRA's jurisdiction is concerned," the stern voice said.

Sanicola went back to Sinatra, whispered to him behind his hand. Frank raised his eyebrows. Should he call Saul Jaffe? In a rare moment of forbearance—the exception proving the rule—Sinatra decided to pick his battles. He squared his shoulders and turned to Stordahl. Time to rehearse.

Back at Margaret Hague Maternity, the nurse turned on the radio just before nine. Now, as Nancy held the milky-warm little bundle close, Frank was talking to her: "I'd like to sing one of my favorite songs to my little son in New Jersey. So pull up a chair, Nancy, and bring the baby with you. I want him really to hear this."

It was hard having his tender voice so near and yet so very far away. That voice! Goddamn it, she knew it worked on a million other women, and it worked on her, too . . .

He sang his theme song, the schmaltzy number he'd written with Sanicola:

This love of mine goes on and on
Though life is empty since you have gone.

Goddamn *him*—he could sound closer when he was far away than when he was standing right next to her. Sometimes, when George called to see how she was doing—he was far more attentive than Frank—she would start to cry.

Lately, Evans had begun to tell her, in his calm, decisive way, that she must move out there.

She thought about it. It was the only thing that made sense—except that her whole family was here, in Jersey. Her sisters. Her parents. She didn't know a soul in Hollywood. She wouldn't fit in. She would die of homesickness.

She couldn't. Not yet.

But she knew it was the only way. She ached with loneliness. This wasn't a way for a married woman to live.

And Frank, of course, was almost never alone. Everyone wanted to be near him, to touch him; and it was so strange, he couldn't bear to be touched (especially by strangers) except on his own terms, but he needed someone near him, always, like a drug. Chance encounters arose at delightfully odd moments: in a janitor's closet off a soundstage, for example. But the constant was his entourage—the Western Varsity. Hank was here, naturally, and Sammy Cahn and now Jule Styne, and a couple of other funny Jews Frank kept running into at poker games and prizefights, Phil Silvers and a comedy writer named Harry Crane, né Kravitsky. Stordahl was rooming in a luxury suite in the Wilshire Tower with Jimmy Van Heusen, who was frequently absent for some shadowy reason . . .

———

In fact, three days a week, Jimmy was working as a test pilot at Lockheed's Burbank plant, flying P-38s and C-60s, under the name Edward Chester Babcock. The other four days, he was writing movie tunes at Paramount with Johnny Burke, under his professional name. No one at Lockheed knew about his other career, and nobody at the studios was wise, either. As Burke said, "Who wants to hire a guy to write a picture knowing he might get killed in a crash before he's finished it?"

And there were plenty of crashes: wartime production was so breakneck that quality control was haphazard. Test piloting was a dangerous business. "I was at Lockheed more than two and a half years and I was scared shitless all of the time," Jimmy later said. But he never told Sinatra.

It was Eat, Drink, and Be Merry time: the Wilshire Tower suite quickly became a twenty-four-hour free-for-all of poker, booze, and sex. The hookers paraded in and out while Cahn and Crane and Silvers sat around the card table, cracking wise, and Stordahl puffed serenely on his pipe. Once, all jaws at the table dropped when Frank walked in with his arm draped over the shoulder of none other than Marlene Dietrich. Forty-two years old, and dazzling as ever. Hello, boys, she said, in that German accent. And then, bold as brass, to Sinatra: Well, Frank? She took his hand, smiling, and they closed the bedroom door behind them. Just like that. The poker continued—but not before Sammy Cahn, ever the P.S. 147 wiseacre, stage-whispered what he'd heard about Dietrich's sexual specialty.

Phil Silvers gave him a look. Hearing was as close as Sammy was gonna get.

Soon afterward Sinatra brought another visitor, the dark, entrancingly beautiful starlet Skitch Henderson had introduced him to at MGM in 1941. As in one of those romantic comedies, Ava Gardner and Frank kept bumping into each other around town. The funny thing was that when he brought *her* up to the Tower, it turned out to be for a cup of coffee only. She was a smokingly sexy kid—but she *was* a kid, and she had a certain dignity to her; her heels weren't round. She appeared to be ambivalent at best about what every other girl in town was obsessed with: getting ahead at any cost. Therefore, there was no leverage, and in a funny way this was perfectly fine with Sinatra. He was content to stare at those cheekbones, those shy and haughty green eyes.

George Evans had his hands full in New York—he had other clients besides Sinatra, hard as that was to believe sometimes. So he deputized a West Coast pal, a firecracker of a young publicist named Jack Keller, to ride herd on Frank in Hollywood, a more than full-time job. The twenty-eight-year-old Keller was a character: a hard-drinking, chain-smoking, impeccably tailored former pro golfer who looked like Jackie Gleason. He had a fierce work ethic and a ferocious loyalty to his clients, both of which were good things where Frank Sinatra was concerned. After dropping by the Wilshire Tower suite once or twice,

Keller quickly realized he had his work cut out for him. Some whole-some diversion was called for, to throw Hollywood snoops like Hedda Hopper and Lolly Parsons off the trail of any potential scandal.

Sunshine and fresh air, Keller thought. And then . . . softball!

Some of the movie stars had an informal league that played Sun-day afternoons in a field behind the Hollywood Bowl. It was good for a few laughs and plenty of wholesome publicity photos—there were lots of nice shots of suntanned hunks and pretty girls in tight cheerleader shirts (real girls didn't play ball in those days).

Sinatra, Keller decided, would start a softball team. It would be called—but of course—the Swooners.

Evans agreed it was pure genius. He had hired the right man.

Keller had uniforms made up, and for a few Sundays, till Frank got bored (which never took very long), the Swooners took the field. Styne and Cahn and Sanicola and Crane played (Phil Silvers, not much of an athlete, preferred to kibitz from the sidelines), along with a couple of Frank's new movie pals, Anthony Quinn and Barry Sullivan. At 119 pounds, Sinatra didn't cut much of a figure in a baseball uniform—but the same couldn't be said of the Swooners cheerleaders in their official T-shirts: Lana Turner, Virginia Mayo, Marilyn Maxwell, and, oh yes, Miss Gardner.

Who was on deck? In play? You needed a scorecard to figure it all out.

———

Just a few days after his son was born, Frank performed at a benefit for the Jewish Home for the Aged, at the Roosevelt Hotel. It was an unusual cause for Sinatra: maybe he was thinking of his dear old baby-sitter Mrs. Golden—or maybe his new agents at MCA, Messrs. Fried-man and Wasserman, convinced him that the men who ran the town would eat it with a spoon.

After the interminable pious speeches, amid the red-velvet drapery and clink of coffee cups and crystal, Sinatra, stick thin in his monkey suit, stared out at the spotlight with moist eyes and gave them a giant ladleful: his version of "Ol' Man River," with a brilliant correction— Oscar Hammerstein's offensive phrase from the 1927 verse, "Niggers all work on de Mississippi," changed to the clunky, but patently uncontroversial, "*Here we all* work on the Mississippi."

Out in the audience, the emotional eyes of the most powerful man in Hollywood, the tiny, rectitudinous Louis B. Mayer, also grew moist. The former scrap-metal salvager from Minsk who had created a white-picket-fence vision of America (and had had amphetamine-laced chicken soup fed to Judy Garland to keep her thin and peppy) thrilled to what he was hearing. As Sinatra's magnificent voice soared to the final "just keeps rollin' along," Louie B. turned to an aide and stage-whispered, "*I want that boy.*"

He got him, of course. And it cost him, of course. In February— just as *Step Lively* was wrapping—Lew Wasserman and Harry Friedman sat down with Metro-Goldwyn-Mayer's lawyers and, over the next three months, hammered out one of the sweetest movie deals in history. The five-year, $260,000-per-annum contract would allow Sinatra to make one outside picture a year and sixteen guest appearances on the radio; it would give him the publishing rights to the music in every second film he made with the studio. As a final fillip, MCA got MGM to relax the terms of its famously strict morals clause.[3]

As for the seven-year contract he'd signed with RKO just six months earlier . . . well, thanks to MCA's iron fist, velvet glove, and fast-dancing legal tap shoes, it was more or less movie history. With the exception of one short subject (*The House I Live In,* 1945) and two loan-out features, one bad (*The Miracle of the Bells,* 1948) and the other worse (*Double Dynamite,* 1951), Sinatra wiped his hands of Radio-Keith-Orpheum. And, as with Dorsey, there was never any uncertainty about who wound up with the sweet end of the deal. True, RKO wouldn't languish without Sinatra: the studio rode out the 1940s on a spate of B pictures and star loan-outs from other studios. But *B* was the key initial for RKO Radio Pictures, Inc., and A plus was the only grade Frank Sinatra was interested in. MGM was the top of the heap, and now so was he.

———

Except—with Sinatra there was always an except—there was a fly in the ointment. His fame was still based on his records, and since July 1942 he hadn't cut a single side—V-Discs excepted—with an orchestra. As the American Federation of Musicians strike dragged on, vocal backgrounds were getting monotonous and annoying. Stordahl's arrangements for the radio orchestra were more beautiful every week: imagine the records he and Sibelius could cut together!

Even more annoying was the fact that other record labels, Bing Crosby's Decca in particular, had signed agreements with the AFM. Der Bingle was back in business—as were Eberly, Haymes, and Como. Sinatra was losing ground, artistically at any rate. He was nervous, and when he was nervous, he grew testy.

On February 10, 1944, Manie Sacks sent a letter to Frank:

I have just received word from Bill [Richards, Columbia's West Coast recording director] that you are not interested in making records with vocal backgrounds of tunes I sent. I've been hearing through many of your friends that you weren't going to make any more records with vocal backgrounds, but I always felt it was an over-exaggerated rumor and I took it with a grain of salt until Richards told me about it today. The thing that hurts me is the fact that you must have told others but never said a word to me. You don't think, do you, that I would tell you to do anything that would in any way impair your future? I feel badly that you would make a quick decision on such an important matter without even mentioning it to me first. I am not going to get into any long discussions, but I do want to go on record and point out a few things to you. If we were able to sell millions of Frank Sinatra records with vocal

backgrounds, I don't think now is the time to stop. I admit
they are not as good as instrumental backgrounds, but they are
acceptable to the public, and they're the ones that count.

Sinatra's typewritten reply to Manie, dated February 18, 1944, was
warm, almost conciliatory. Frank understood that Manie was upset. If
he had told anyone that he wasn't going to record anymore—and he
didn't quite admit that he had—"it was in complete innocence, believe
me!" If he had spoken, he had spoken impulsively, he insisted. He
would never hide an opinion from Manie.

On the other hand, Frank wrote, he was genuinely distressed
about having to use the vocal backgrounds. He understood record sales
had been good, "but, being very much an artist rather than a financial
genius or a cold businessman," didn't see why he had to be artistically
hamstrung just because Columbia couldn't strike a deal with the musicians. But, he said, he realized the situation was immutable, so he
would stay disgruntled.

Having lodged his complaint, Frank sent along his best to Columbia president Ted Wallerstein and vice-president Goddard Lieberson,
and signed—assertively, in blue fountain pen—with love and kisses.

It's a remarkable letter: articulate and affectionate and disingenuous and blunt, all at once. And exceedingly practical. Frank was wise
enough to vent his anger only indirectly at his esteemed friend the
warmhearted Manie.

While a truly cold businessman, the ice-blooded Wasserman, hammered away at RKO and MGM on his behalf, Sinatra traveled east
to attend his son's christening. It was a joyous occasion, but not a
happy trip. First the priest gave him a hard time about naming a Jew—
Manie, who else?—as little Frank's godfather. Sinatra simply stared
the watery-eyed old cleric down. Nancy was another matter.

His housebound wife, effectively a single mother, had built up a lot of unhappiness she couldn't express on a staticky and expensive transcontinental phone call (with God knows what starstruck operators listening in). The moment she saw her wandering husband, she let loose. Even though she knew she was on a tightrope, that they had had this baby to try to save what was left of their marriage, Nancy also knew that she was still Frank's wife, and still Mike Barbato's daughter. She would say whatever the hell she wanted to say. She did not intend to raise their children alone—what were his intentions?

At the same time, George Evans was on his case: Frank was a family man, and a family man lived with his family. If his life was in California now, that's where his family had to be.

So the hounds he'd been keeping a sweet three thousand miles away had caught up with him. As Frank looked around at the Sinatras and Garaventas and Barbatos (and little Chit-U, smiling at nobody) jammed into his living room for the christening party, he realized that Nancy and Evans were right. He was a family man. In the first flush of excitement at home ownership (it felt like a hundred years ago), he and Nancy had named the little Cape Cod at 220 Lawrence Avenue Warm Valley. (The sentimental Frank had even fashioned a plaque with the name on it, making the letters out of sticks he'd picked up in the park, gluing the sticks onto a varnished board. A fan stole the sign.) Now the house felt like a claustrophobe's nightmare. He needed a big place to match his big new life, and he knew his family had to be there with him.

He took Nancy aside while her mother cooed over the baby. The look in his wife's large expressive eyes was complex: full of love and distrust, anger and hope. He said he wanted them to live in a great big house in California. That was where the movies were, and that was where his family should be.

She stared at him. What about her family?

She could bring 'em out. Why not?

And what on earth was she going to do in California? She couldn't even drive a car.

He'd buy her the biggest goddamn Cadillac she'd ever seen. And driving lessons to go with it. She'd be the queen of Hollywood.

She shook her head: he was full of shit. But she didn't say no.

———

"Joe E. Lewis, the only comedian who doesn't do an impression of Frank Sinatra [the handwritten invitation reads], invites you to be a guest at a farewell cocktail party for the Voice on the eve of his departure for Hollywood, Friday, May 12th, at 4 p.m. in the cocktail lounge at Monte Proser's Copacabana, 10 East 60th Street.[4] Being quite a man with the ladies himself, Joe has induced the lovely Conover cover girls (and they really are beautiful) to take care of the charm department. They'll all be here, and Sinatra has promised to swoon for the girls just to confuse everybody. Drop in—but not without the card!"

Those Conover girls—they really were beautiful . . .

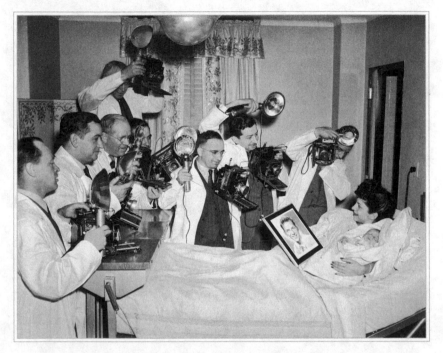

January 11, 1944: Franklin Wayne Emanuel Sinatra is one day old. Margaret Hague Maternity Hospital, Jersey City. Photographers dressed as doctors capture the blessed event. Frank is in Hollywood, otherwise engaged.

Rowdy sailors on shore leave throw tomatoes at Sinatra's image on the Paramount marquee, October 15, 1944. "It is not too much to say," historian William Manchester wrote, "that by the end of the war Sinatra had become the most hated man in the armed services."

He was at once the most loved and the most reviled man in the country: the line seemed to fall squarely between the sexes. SINATRA 1-A WITH US GIRLS, RATED 4-F BY ARMY DOCTORS, ran a typical headline. And men ran the newspapers. In the spring of 1944, as the Fifth Army fought inland from Anzio to Rome, much of America's civilian and military press mounted an offensive against Sinatra. And a columnist named Westbrook Pegler, flush from a 1941 Pulitzer for his exposés of racketeering in Hollywood's labor unions, and recently signed up by the FDR-hating Hearst Syndicate, began to make a special project of laying into the FDR-loving, "bugle-deaf Frankie-boy Sinatra."

Another newspaper writer named Lee Mortimer, the entertainment columnist for the Hearst-owned New York *Daily Mirror,* also got into the act. Mortimer, like his colleague Winchell a closeted Jew (né Mortimer Lieberman), was ambivalent about Sinatra at first—he'd apparently once tried, unsuccessfully, to sell Frank a song he'd written. His early columns about the singer accordingly seem strangely sycophantic. "Even I grow humble before the compelling force [of Sinatra's impact]," Mortimer wrote. "It is inexplicable, irrational but it has made him the most potent entertainer of the day . . . I'll go further. I think Frank is a showman without peer, he has a unique and pleasing personality plus talent of the first luster." Then this uncomfortable man found the stone in his shoe. "I love Sinatra but my stomach is revolted by squealing, shouting neurotic extremists who make a cult of the boy. As a friend [!], I call on the Hero of Hasbrouck to disown his fanatics. Neither they nor his projection onto the political scene can help his brilliant theatrical career."

Where his fans were concerned, Frank, who knew where his bread was buttered, didn't mind the idolatry a bit. He let everyone in show business know exactly what he thought of Lee Mortimer, and word got back fast. Spurned, the columnist used his platform to stick it to the singer at every opportunity. Sinatra, Mortimer wrote soon afterward, "found safety and $30,000 a week behind a mike" while Real Men were overseas fighting Krauts and Japs. And as for those fans, they were worse than neurotic extremists: they were nothing but "imbecilic, moronic, screaming-meemie autograph kids."

The columns weren't just personal. Much of Mortimer's and Pegler's invective was politically motivated: right-wing and intolerant at its core. Even amid the patriotism of the war, America was a deeply divided country. Great numbers of people, many of them moneyed, detested Franklin Roosevelt for the equalizing policies of the New Deal. To many—William Randolph Hearst significantly included— FDR's policies were leading the country straight toward Communism.

Sinatra had been a fervent Democrat since boyhood, when he'd helped ward boss Dolly stump for local Democratic candidates, and a Roosevelt lover since the early 1930s. The Democrats had established themselves at the beginning of the century as the defenders of America's minorities, and FDR, transformed by crippling polio from a shallow playboy to an avatar of noblesse oblige, was every bit as charismatic as Frank himself.

The situation was not without its complexities. For one thing, Hearst and Louis B. Mayer were extremely close. For another: not long after the beginning of World War II, Roosevelt ordered the FBI's director, J. Edgar Hoover, to compile a list of possible threats to national security, and one of the bureau's first responses was to round up some fifteen hundred Italian aliens. Dolly put the blame for this unpleasant act squarely on FDR, and took her son to task for his ardent support of the president.

Some have contended that Sinatra's crusade against racial and religious intolerance was opportunistic, a convenient publicity stunt. Some charged that the ardently pro-Roosevelt George Evans encouraged Frank's enthusiasm for FDR. And while it's true that it didn't hurt his image to support the president, it's also true that one of the singer's proudest possessions was a large autographed photo of Franklin D., which he hung prominently in the foyers of his residences at least until his politics veered sharply right in the late 1960s.

In fact, Sinatra was a convenient lightning rod for all kinds of antipathies. It's hard to imagine in this age of diversity what a strong hold white Anglo-Saxon Protestant males once had over America. Ethnics were an essential ingredient in the Great Melting Pot: they could be acknowledged sentimentally and smiled at condescendingly, but essentially were not to be trusted. (Of all the slurs against FDR, one of the strangest was that he was secretly a Jew named Rosenfeld.)

Frank Sinatra was definitely an ethnic; what's more, he was a small, rich, cocky, sexually potent ethnic. This didn't ingratiate him with much of the press. None of America's editorial writers were getting on John Wayne's case for not enlisting. But then Wayne wasn't Italian or liberal.

In May 1944, the Army newspaper *Stars and Stripes,* which had already waxed indignant about Sinatra's draft status, ran an article on the singer by one Sergeant Jack Foisie. It is a fascinating document, written in wisecracking forties slang, dripping with envy and contempt. Foisie strives for some sort of objectivity but at every turn battles, not very energetically, his own distaste for the singer:

Dateline New York. There is no denying, gentlemen, this guy Frankie Sinatra has something we ain't got. Most everyone is trying to discover what that something is, and the few who claim to know can't find the words to express themselves. So until a better explanation comes along, the homefront is simply calling this 26-year-old [sic] Hoboken-born crooner a national phenomenon. However, if one must get analytical, Sinatra, otherwise known as the Voice, has certain definite things which we ain't. For instance, he pulls down about ten-hundred thousand bucks a year, says press agent George B. Evans, carefully adding that about $930,000 goes back to the government in taxes . . .

Secondly, Evans estimates that The Voice has about 50 million bobby-sock followers and other less fanatical fans. The Sinatra fan mail averages 2,000 letters weekly, of which 40% are from other than young (14 to 18 years) girls. Of this 40%, a lot is from servicemen, but—Evans admits—very little is from servicemen overseas.

His bobbysock brigades are the most fantastic people. At

the very sight of 'The Voice' they break into screams . . . This
screaming has become Sinatra's trademark. At first encouraged,
if not suggested by Sinatra's press agents, the practice now is
very much frowned upon. Before each *Lucky Strike Hit Parade*
radio performance, the 5-foot-10 1/2-inch [*sic*], 140-pound
[*sic*] crooner pleads with his high school dumplings to please,
oh please, just be nice girls, and applaud, but don't scream.
He tells them that the War Department doesn't like them to
have screams show up on his program recordings for overseas
consumption. It is bad on the combat GI's morale, the WD
figures . . .

Now that I've seen Sinatra myself, I still can't imagine why
he does what he does to people, especially girls. Yet 50 million
Americans can't be wrong.

People will argue day and night over whether he has a
voice or not. The people who can hear him say he has, but the
people who can't hear him, especially when he has to compete
with the volume of Mark Warnow's band on the *Lucky Strike
Hit Parade,* say he hasn't.

On August 4, 1943, he appeared with the [Philadelphia]
Philharmonic Symphony Orchestra. The crowd, containing
a larger percentage of bobbysocks than ever before seen in a
concert hall, thought he was good, but the music critics almost
universally did not. They were not so much annoyed by his
voice as by his reference to the musicians of the Philharmonic
as "the boys in the band."

Sinatra is 4-F because of a punctured eardrum. As a civilian crooner, his friends point out, he is doing a lot more for the
country by packing them in at bond rallies and the like than he
could do in a uniform, an argument raised on behalf of many
entertainers, and seemingly a satisfactory one to the Selective
Service Boards.

In answer to my question whether he was planning any

overseas tours, Sinatra said: "I would like to if I can stand it physically . . ."

Frankie is now in Hollywood, fulfilling his RKO contract. Even in the city of movie stars, the fans single him out for special attention. That he is married and has two babies doesn't seem to matter.

This last is especially pointed—the military reader would have known at once exactly which fans were singling Sinatra out, and just what kind of special attention they were giving him. All in all, it was an article expressly designed to make soldiers' blood boil, and it was symptomatic of a spreading feeling about the singer. Despite George Evans's heroic efforts, the public was starting to sniff out things it didn't like about Frank Sinatra. He was a hedonist, in a nation under wartime restrictions. He was a man apart, in a time when men were supposed to be supporting their buddies. He was having the time of his life, while his countrymen were fighting and dying overseas.

———

And thanks to MCA, he was no longer working for the piddling RKO but starting his new contract with MGM, one that, according to Evans, helped make him the highest-paid entertainer in the world. This may have been close to the truth. By Sinatra's own later estimation, he earned $840,000 in 1944, the equivalent of over $10 million today.

Still, it wasn't just the money. He was now officially with the studio that had "more stars than in the heavens."[1] Back on the Coast in April from Frank junior's christening, he attended a party given by Mayer for the twenty-six-year-old Henry Ford II, freshly mustered out of the Navy and soon to take over the family business. (The record doesn't show whether young Ford agreed with his grandpa Henry's notorious anti-Semitic writings, but Mayer was never one to scruple where Americanism was concerned.) No doubt the event was a crashing bore except for the presence of several of the studio's loveliest, their morals clauses all atwitter at the sight of Frankie, and one other interesting party: a very handsome, quite funny, ever so slightly world-weary twenty-year-old English contract player named Peter Sydney Ernest Aylen Lawford.

Peter Lawford liked to give an impression of charming superficiality, but Sinatra was intuitive enough to see at once that like him, the young actor was a complex and layered personality and, also like him, carried scars both visible and unseen. For one thing, Lawford had a slightly deformed right arm, the result of a childhood collision with a glass door; ironically enough, the deformity was as much a source of his success as his good looks and suave manner, for it had kept him out of military service. Metro was currently keeping him very busy shooting war movies, in which he was a natural to play the sensitive young English pilot or Tommy Atkins, or even, in 1942's *A Yank at Eton,* a bullying young snob, opposite Ava Gardner's husband, Mickey Rooney. Mr. Mayer loved Lawford, though he was less fond of the young actor's eccentric stage mother, Lady May Bunny, who had a title but not a farthing, and who had tried (and failed) to prevail on Mayer to pay her a salary as her son's assistant. Lady May, young Lawford would reveal at the drop of a hat, had dressed him in girl's clothing until age eleven.[2]

On the surface, Sinatra and Lawford couldn't have been more different, but they had a natural affinity. Both had overbearing mothers; both had minor physical deformities. Both were beguiling and sexually voracious. Each had qualities the other envied.

Lawford—whose status consciousness as a Brit on the low end of the Hollywood pecking order was acute—was fully aware of Sinatra's status. And Sinatra seemed aware of *everything.* The singer's wide blue eyes surveyed the whole crowded room and took in everything at once—Greer Garson's lovely posterior (she was *forty,* for Christ's sake); the sonorous Louie B.'s awareness of same, even as he chatted up the moonfaced young Ford.

But the singer, for all his ability to snap his fingers and order up any woman in the room (the young Brit saw them gazing at him as if their knickers were already halfway down their thighs), saw that Lawford had something even Frank could never have—that six-foot height, those impossibly handsome good looks.

Frank regarded Lawford and shook his head. If he looked like *that,* he'd be—

Lawford's eyes crinkled. Dick Haymes?

The singer bent double at the waist, laughing hard. Then he straightened up and pointed at Lawford in a way that the young Englishman had always been taught was rude. Hey, Chauncey here was all right.

———

On the golf course I'm under par,
Metro-Goldwyn have asked me to star.

They arrived on June 1 at the Union Pacific station in Pasadena, Nancy and four-year-old Little Nancy and the baby, along with Nancy's twenty-one-year-old sister, Constante—known as Tina—whom she'd brought along for company, and also to fill in on official Frank Sinatra letter-writing duty while Nancy tended to the kids. Mike and Jennie Barbato, as well as their four other daughters, along with husbands, would soon follow. A whole cockeyed caravan, and they had to be put up somewhere while the new house was being prepared. With a sigh, Frank checked out of his private bachelor pad at the Art Deco Sunset Tower (where John Wayne and Bugsy Siegel also had suites) and into the Castle Argyle, a nice residential hotel conveniently located a stone's throw from the CBS Studios.

Sinatra had bought the new house at 1051 Valley Spring Lane sight unseen: a big pale pink Mediterranean-style stucco pile on Toluca Lake in the San Fernando Valley, ten miles from Hollywood—a posh suburb, orange-blossom-sweet, in those pre-freeway days. Bob and Dolores Hope lived just down the street. Bing and his brood weren't far away.[3] That spring, oddly enough, Sinatra's future arranger Gordon

Jenkins had written an upbeat, gospel-flavored hit called "San Fernando Valley," which Sinatra sang on the Vimms show:

> *I'll forget my sins*
> *I'll be makin' new friends . . .*

It was a lovely song, and one very much of its era: wholehearted, full of the American promise of rebirth through moving west. Crosby recorded it around the same time, and his version is a thing of beauty—the forty-year-old Old Groaner at the top of his game, playing with the number's spiritual flavor, then reaching down low to kick it home. Still, it's a middle-aged reading. Sinatra's version—lighter, more youthful, and genuinely optimistic—has that unique quality that Haymes and Eberly, for all their appealing masculinity, simply couldn't bring off: the quality of conversation. Frank had lasered in on the lyric and, as his old teacher Quinlan had taught him, understood its depths. As a result, the singer was able to tell the song as an irresistibly charming story.

It was an irresistible story to Frank himself. In his westward relocation, he was reinventing and expanding himself, moving onto a larger canvas. The new house was of a piece with the expansion. It was full of big rooms: an antidote to his claustrophobia. On the wall of his new den (his own den!) was a framed quotation from none other than Schopenhauer: "Music is the only form of Art which touches the Absolute."

The musician, however, did not himself wish to be touched: the house was surrounded by a high wall, to keep fans at bay. There were other lovely perks. Tied up at Sinatra's private dock was a new single-masted sailboat, a gift from Axel Stordahl. And whenever the phone's incessant ringing began to get to him, Frank could swim or sail out to a wooden raft and play poker with cronies. Hasbrouck Heights's Warm Valley, with its little rooms and lingering cooking smells and close-in neighbors, was a distant memory.

Frank and Nancy named the new place Warm Valley too, in hopes of importing some domestic good luck (not that that had been in high supply back in Hasbrouck Heights). But it might not have been a good omen that the house's previous owner was the bedroom-eyed actress Mary Astor, whose lurid private life had been a tabloid playground in the mid- and late 1930s.

Life remained complicated. Dolly was furious at being left in the dust of the Barbatos' mass westward exodus. Over each successive month in the last five years, less and less love had been lost between her and Nancy; now, to all appearances anyway, her snip of a daughter-in-law had triumphed. And gone Hollywood. The Sunday-afternoon long-distance phone calls between the dutiful son and the irrepressible Dolly grew increasingly tense. Her anti-Nancy vitriol cannot have failed to leach into her son's system. Even as he was making a game effort at reviving his domestic situation, Sinatra was increasingly skeptical about his marriage.

And rhapsodize as he might about reinventing himself, Frank knew the West was alien soil. "When I arrived at MGM, I was a nobody in movies," he later told his daughter Nancy. "What was I? Just a crooner. A guy who got up and hung on to a microphone in a bad tuxedo and brown shoes." Hollywood is traditionally inhospitable to presumptuous strangers, no matter how celebrated they may be elsewhere, until they have demonstrated both fealty and mastery.

Sinatra, of course, had demonstrated neither. He had done two features for RKO (only one of them released to date), and he had garnered some respectable reviews. He had wowed Old Man Mayer and entered the MGM stable. He hadn't really produced. He might be a national phenomenon, but he wasn't a Hollywood phenomenon. Then as now, Hollywood made its own rules.

And Sinatra broke them virtually from the get-go. He was due to start shooting his first MGM feature, a musical called *Anchors Aweigh*, in mid-June, but before he even began work, he insisted that the studio hire his pals Styne and Cahn to write the songs. Producer Joe Pasternak shook his head. Mack Gordon and Harry Warren, *they* were movie songwriters. Burke and Van Heusen, they were movie songwriters. But

Gordon and Warren and Burke and Van Heusen were all profitably engaged elsewhere, and Styne and Cahn's big movie credit was *Step Lively,* a little RKO picture that hadn't even been released, and MGM wasn't buying.

Sinatra, for whom business and friendship were inseparable, dug in his heels.

"It came to such an impasse," Sammy Cahn wrote in his autobiography, "that Lew Wasserman, head of MCA, came to me to plead, 'Unless Frank gives in, he'll lose the picture. Won't you talk with him?' I of course went to Frank and said, 'Frank, you've already done enough for me. Why don't you pass on this one? There'll be others.' He looked at me . . . and said: 'If you're not there Monday, I'm not there Monday.'

"I was there Monday. So was he."

Frank was there, but he wasn't happy. He was in over his head and he knew it. This wasn't RKO; he couldn't just float through a picture on charm and a few songs. He would get to sing in *Anchors Aweigh,* but he was also going to have to do something he had never done before: dance. And not just dance, but dance alongside Gene Kelly.

Kelly was three years older than Sinatra, and the same height, but forty pounds heavier. The forty pounds was all muscle, and there began the differences between Frank Albert Sinatra of Hoboken and Eugene Curran Kelly of Pittsburgh, who was unlike anybody Sinatra had met in Hollywood. Handsome, tough, cheerful, and athletically brilliant, Gene Kelly was a walking paradox: a blue-collar jock who happened to be a superlative dancer, the opposite of the slim, ethereally elegant Fred Astaire. (Even years later, when Sinatra and Astaire might have become friends, Frank remained intimidated by the dancer's aura. "Frank thought Fred was the class act of all time," said the director Bud Yorkin, who worked with both men at different times. "He said, 'I can't be Fred Astaire.'") Sinatra was intimidated by Kelly, too—not by his classiness, but by his sheer dancing ability. Very fortunately for him, though, Kelly shook the singer's hand, looked him in the eye, and decided to help him out.

Every meeting between two men, and especially between two men who might reasonably see themselves as competitors, is essentially an encounter between Robin Hood and Little John—a joust on a log over a stream, with one bound to wind up on his behind in the water. Kelly, who was both starring in *Anchors Aweigh* and directing its dance sequences, maturely decided that if he held Frank Sinatra's hand rather than kicked his ass, they would both come out the better for it.

What conditioned Kelly's decision was not just professional wisdom but confidence. He wasn't worried about yielding his position to Sinatra. (For one thing, though he had enlisted in the Navy early in the war, the Navy decided Kelly could best serve by making propaganda films, and allowed him to act in Hollywood on the side.) Sinatra saw his self-assurance, and respected it. And so it was settled in a split second: the two men decided to like each other.

The movie was directed by a boy wonder named George Sidney (who, four years earlier, had produced Ava Gardner's screen test—and would go on to direct *Annie Get Your Gun, Show Boat, Bye Bye Birdie,* and *Viva Las Vegas*). *Anchors Aweigh* was a standard MGM musical of the 1940s, built around the idea of two sailors on leave in Los Angeles—kind of a run-through for the much more successful *On the Town,* four years later. A tongue-in-cheek Kelly played the wolf of the fleet, and Frank was the goofily shy former church choirmaster Clarence Doolittle.

The ace MGM scenarist Isobel Lennart wrote the inspired characterization, which might as well have been cooked up by George Evans. Sinatra got to wear a uniform that at once flattered his slim physique and countered the draft-dodger image. (So flattering was that sailor suit that Frank would find it difficult to get out of it for the rest of his brief career at MGM.) And he got to act like a complete dunce around women. He was sweet and convincingly gentle.

The picture had several dance sequences, most notably a groundbreaking scene in which Kelly tripped the light fantastic with the Hanna-Barbera-animated mouse Jerry, of *Tom and Jerry* fame. But making Jerry Mouse move gracefully merely involved hand painting thousands of cels. Making Frank Sinatra dance was something else again.

Kelly did his heroic best. As Sinatra told his daughter Nancy:

> I was born with a couple of left feet, and I didn't even know how to walk, let alone dance. It was Gene who saw me through. We became a team only because he had the patience of Job, and the fortitude not to punch me in the mouth because I was so impatient. Moviemaking takes a lot of time, and I couldn't understand why. He managed to calm me when it was important to calm me, because we were doing something that we wanted to do. Apart from being a great artist, he's a born teacher, and he taught me how to move and how to dance. We worked hard and he was a taskmaster. Rehearsal for each routine took eight weeks every day. I couldn't dance exactly like he danced so he danced down to me. He taught me everything I know.

This is remarkably self-knowing. Frank *was* pathologically impatient, a characteristic that power and fame aggravated. (It was on *Anchors Aweigh* that his hatred of doing anything more than once, especially where the movies were concerned, earned him the nickname "One-Take Charlie.") Underneath was always a panicky uncertainty. He could be sweet when he was unsure: when he stepped on the actress Pamela Britton's toes during a dance number, he "quickly apologized," he recalled. Whereupon Britton "smiled bravely and said, 'Oh, that's all right. You're very light on my feet.'"

But more to the point was another confession: "Because I didn't think I was as talented as some of the people who worked [at MGM], I went through periods of depression and I'd get terribly embarrassed." When Frank felt humiliated, his first reaction was to bark commands. If others were humiliated in the process, all the better.

His hot-blooded reactions endeared him to no one, even the Job-like Kelly. "We used to play mean, nasty tricks on Frank Sinatra, because he was always a pain in the neck," Kelly's assistant on the film, the dancer Stanley Donen, told his, Donen's, biographer. "He didn't want to work and was very quixotic and quick to anger, so we used to take great pleasure in teasing him."

Kelly and Donen came up with a great practical joke, revolving around the MGM commissary, where they broke for lunch every day with Sinatra:

> The MGM commissary had square tables with blue plastic tops, pushed against the walls, like in a cafeteria. Every table was square, all but one, and that belonged to Gerry Mayer [Louis B.'s brother, who ran the studio's physical operations].
>
> So one day, mean bastards that we were, Gene and I said to Frank, "Wouldn't it be wonderful if we could have a round table? It's so much nicer that way, because then we could sit closer together." As soon as Frank heard us say that, he said, "You watch, I'll get us a round table."
>
> There was no way Frank was going to get us a round table. We knew that. Then, when he was told to forget it, he got into this huge argument. He steamed and he fumed and threw fits and said he was going to quit. All this for a round table.

Early in the shoot of *Anchors Aweigh,* Sinatra, insecure about how he was coming across in the movie (and probably worried about all those single takes), asked to see rushes. Pasternak told him that this wasn't done. When actors saw themselves on-screen, the producer said, they always asked for retakes, which cost time and money. Sinatra exploded; Pasternak relented. "Listen," he said, "I'm not supposed to do this, but I'll make an exception and let you see them. Just you, though, and nobody else."

Sinatra arrived for the secret screening with an entourage. This time Pasternak was the one who got furious. "I said just for you," he told Frank. "Not for half a dozen."

Frank announced, once again, that he was walking off the picture. Pasternak told him to go right ahead. Sinatra walked—then, not wanting to test his expendability, came back the next day.

But the pattern had been set. One afternoon, a United Press reporter who was on the set to interview the pianist José Iturbi got more than he bargained for: a choice outburst from a frustrated Sinatra. "Pictures stink and most of the people in them do too," he told the writer. "Hollywood won't believe I'm through, but they'll find out I mean it."

He had already pushed the limits by insisting on Cahn and Styne and upsetting the producer with his special needs. This blasphemous tantrum was the kind of thing that could get an actor, even a high-paid one, run out of town. Sinatra's team quickly went into damage control. "It was the hottest day of the year," his manager Al Levy told the press. "Naturally he was tired, but that crack was never intended for that fat fellow with the glasses [the reporter]." And Jack Keller quickly placed a statement by Sinatra (written by Keller) in the papers:

> It's easy for a guy to get hot under the collar, literally and figuratively, when he's dressed in a hot suit of Navy blues and the temperature is a hundred and four degrees and he's getting over a cold to boot.
>
> I think I might have spoken too broadly about quitting pictures and about my feeling toward Hollywood.

To say the least. And while it could certainly get hot under the klieg lights of a soundstage, especially in those pre-air-conditioned days, the summer of 1944 was in fact a typically temperate one in Culver City. In fact, as the war raged across Europe and the Pacific, it was a lovely summer in Los Angeles—a city of low white and pastel buildings, smogless in those days, full of fragrant blossoms and, for every working actor and screenwriter, five unemployed ones. Frank knew this, even as the black headlines blared of invasions and battles. Hollywood had its charms, and Sinatra was not about to lose them. Despite the aggravation of working at MGM, there were too many compensations: One day when the gaffers had taken around an hour too long to light the set, Frank simply got up and walked off the soundstage, into the studio alley. Turning right, down another alley to another soundstage, he went through another heavy door, with its sign saying QUIET PLEASE, past gaping extras, and up to a petite blonde deliciously filling out a tight WAC uniform. Her back was to him, but when she saw the reaction of the assistant director she'd been speaking to, she turned: it was Lana. She was in the midst of shooting another service comedy, this one about the Women's Army Corps and titled *Keep Your Powder Dry*. She was also in the midst of leaving her second husband for the second time (long story), and seeing Peter Lawford, Bob Stack, and the exotically handsome Turhan Bey. But her big grin at Sinatra said she wouldn't mind seeing a lot more of him, soon. And quite soon, she was, he was, they were.

＝＝＝

Even as he exhausted himself rehearsing dance sequences (and stepping out with Lana), Sinatra continued to do his radio shows that summer: it was important to maintain his multimedia presence. It was also expensive. Lucky Strike allowed him to broadcast his *Your Hit Parade* segments from the West Coast on the condition that the singer pay out of pocket for studio rental, Stordahl's orchestra, and the AT&T phone feed to New York. The total was $4,800 per show, $2,000 more than his weekly salary.

Even Sinatra couldn't be everywhere at once. In July, he had to cancel a scheduled return to the Riobamba in Manhattan; to replace him, MCA sent a kid whom the agency's man in Cleveland had spotted singing with the Sammy Watkins Orchestra. The tall, dark, athletically handsome twenty-seven-year-old, out of Steubenville, Ohio, had been christened Dino Crocetti, but naturally that wouldn't do for a stage name. Wrote the ever-perceptive Lee Mortimer in the *Daily Mirror,* "In Sinatra's singing spot is a chap by the name of Dean Martin, who sounds like him, uses the same arrangements of the same songs and almost looks like him." In a later blurb, Mortimer added a fillip: "Sings and looks like Sinatra—only healthier."

Frank and Gene Kelly play a couple of sailors on shore leave in MGM's *Anchors Aweigh,* 1945.

Sinatramania. The Paramount, October 12, 1944. Frank's publicist, George Evans, hired an ambulance to park outside the theater and issued the ushers bottles of ammonia "in case a patron feels like swooning."

In Hollywood, Sinatra was just one star in a galaxy (not to mention an official pain in the ass); in New York he was king. And, after finishing *Anchors Aweigh* in September, he came east to reclaim his crown. He was about to begin a new stand at the Paramount, the first in over a year. On the long train ride east, while Sanicola and Al Levy and Stordahl and his bodyguard Al Silvani played gin rummy, drank, and stared out the window, Frank read.

It was a habit he had picked up on the Dorsey bus, during the long rides through the night from city to city. He'd begun with dime novels, but quickly grew bored with the cheesy writing and flimsy plots. He wanted more than diversion; he wanted to improve himself. Now and then on the road he had been introduced to witty people who wanted to do more than gossip—they wanted to talk about the Depression and the New Deal and the labor movement. And while Sinatra had strong, inchoate emotions about the things they were discussing, to his embarrassment he lacked both the words and the hard knowledge to participate fully.

He began to read newspapers—not just the news, but the editorials and reviews. He was hungry for knowledge and the tools to express it. (He even began doing crossword puzzles, was pleased to find he was good at them.) When Frank thought about what moved him, he kept coming back to the times he had been made to feel small for who he was.

Everywhere he went, he felt revolted by the casual way Negroes were belittled and excluded. It helped to be white, but as soon as people found out he was Italian, things changed. If you were Italian, in fact, by many people's definition you weren't quite white anyway. When you had a name that ended with a vowel, it was easy to feel you weren't a full-fledged American.

Except that he knew he was. Just as he knew that Billie and Art Tatum and Teddy Wilson and Lester Young and all the other great musicians he met on Fifty-second Street and in Harlem were too.

Now Frank read to express these thoughts. He worked his way through thick books about prejudice: Gunnar Myrdal's *American Dilemma*, Gustavus Myers's *History of Bigotry in the United States*, Howard Fast's novel about Reconstruction, *Freedom Road*. When Sanicola and Levy saw him sitting in his train or plane seat with his nose in a tome, they'd shrug. "Frank," they'd say with a sigh, meaning that was just the way he was. He also washed his hands twenty-five times a day, for Christ's sake.

But when George Evans saw what his client was reading, he knew he had a gold mine on his hands. It wasn't just that Evans, a dyed-in-the-wool liberal himself, agreed with Sinatra; it was that a right-minded, crusading Sinatra would make people forget all about the Sinatra who had dodged the draft.

This time when he reached the city, Dolly demanded to see him the second he got off the train. Frankie winced ever so slightly as his mother reached up to pinch his thin cheek.

Jesus Christ! Didn't they fucking feed him anything out there?

After he saw his parents, he made another call, one that Dolly wouldn't be very happy with.

A good pal of Sinatra's, the frog-voiced, backslapping Times Square saloon keeper Toots Shor, badly wanted to meet the president. This wasn't just a wild dream—Shor was a world-class character, and his restaurant was a crossroads for manly men from many walks of life, the Democratic National Committee chairman, Robert Hannegan, among them. It was election season, the ailing FDR was running for a fourth term, and Hannegan knew that the weary Roosevelt was up for some diversion. He told Shor he was welcome to come to tea at the White House if he didn't mind a bit of a crowd—twenty people or so.

Tea at the White House! "Could I bring Sinatt?" Shor croaked, taking out his cigar and grinning. He pointed to the round table where Sinatra was holding court. "And could I bring Rags?"

Rags Ragland, a hulking former truck driver, boxer, and burlesque comic, was currently employed as a character actor in Hollywood. He had played a lovable cop in *Anchors Aweigh* and hit it off with Sinatra, who always liked having tough guys around. Now Rags was part of the entourage.

The motley little crew flew down from La Guardia the next day, and at 3:00 p.m. they were escorted into the White House's Red Room, where FDR himself sat, laughing that famous laugh at something a pretty lady was saying to him. Despite his gallantry, he looked like death warmed over. The war, the presidency itself, the polio—it all had desiccated him. The circles under his eyes were almost as dark as his suit. In fact he would live six months and two weeks from that day.

But Sinatra couldn't help himself: he had goose bumps just at the sight of the great man. Then Hannegan was introducing him, and FDR was staring up at Sinatra with those black-bagged eyes, grinning with his crooked gray teeth, shaking his hand. The two most famous men in America regarded each other.

The president turned to his secretary, Marvin McIntyre. "Mac, imagine this guy making them swoon. He would never have made them swoon in our day, right?"

Sinatra's smile tightened just a fraction. Implicit in the pleasantry was an ethnic dismissal: *this skinny little guinea* . . . Roosevelt was a democrat as well as a Democrat, but he was also a patrician, with ingrained prejudices. And Sinatra, beneath all his bravado and arrogance, was still a little guinea. This was the old order of things: the Founding Fathers were square-jawed white men, with noble heads and noble accents. Frank decided to love his president anyway.

———

On the flight home that night, Sinatra delved deeper into his Gustavus Myers. The next day, on Evans's recommendation, he made a substantial donation in his and Nancy's name to the Democratic campaign fund. (This was a far rarer act in those pre-media-saturated days than now. Most entertainers then, fearful of the effects political alignment might have on their careers, stayed studiously neutral. And the size of Sinatra's gift, $7,500—the equivalent of $90,000 today—was a surprise to Evans and especially to the purse-string-holding Nancy, who asked her husband on the telephone that night if he was out of his mind.)

With Evans's and Keller's encouragement, Sinatra accepted invitations to join the political action committee of the radical Congress of Industrial Organizations (CIO), and the Independent Voters Committee of the Arts and Sciences for Roosevelt (Fredric March, Bette

Davis, and Eddie Cantor were all members, as were John Dewey, Van Wyck Brooks, and Albert Einstein). Frank made radio broadcasts for FDR and spoke at rallies at Carnegie Hall and Madison Square Garden. But his largest audience by far would be in Times Square.

—————

When he opened at the Paramount it was as though a dam had burst. Sinatra had gone to California to become a movie star, but while he returned regularly, it was generally not to perform. The teenage girls who made up the first critical mass of his success knew that he had changed his base of operations, that he had gone Hollywood. They had waited faithfully by their radios, dreaming . . . But now he was back, and they came out in force, thousands upon thousands of them, lining up the night before to buy their tickets, packing Times Square, forcing the police department to send out reinforcements: detectives, traffic cops, and a dozen mounted men, 421 patrolmen and 20 patrolwomen in all.

Then came the first show, at ten o'clock in the morning on Wednesday, October 11, and Bob Weitman, the Paramount's manager, ignoring the fire laws, let almost five thousand fans (almost all of them girls) into a theater designed to seat thirty-five hundred. They brought sandwiches, apples, bananas, Cokes; they settled in and made themselves comfortable.

And ten thousand still waited restlessly outside.

The movie was *Our Hearts Were Young and Gay*—a Cornelia Otis Skinner biopic, of all things—with Charles Ruggles and Beulah Bondi in the starring roles. It might as well have been a documentary about wheat farming. The warm-up acts were *Hit Parade* singer Eileen Barton (Ben Barton's daughter), dancers Pops and Louie, impressionist Ollie O'Toole. They performed to the sound of coughs and rustling sandwich bags.

Then, with a soft hum and sleek hiss of silken pistons, up rose the great hydraulic platform bearing the forty-piece Raymond Paige Stage Door Canteen Radio Orchestra, and the screaming began.

Paige raised his baton, the orchestra struck up the first strains of "This Love of Mine," and the screams got louder.

Suddenly that unmistakable head—the face still bore the traces of a California suntan—poked through the curtain, and the screams reached a deafening crescendo. The curtain parted; the slim figure in a dark suit and floppy bow tie emerged and strode to center stage. Ten thousand feet stamped the floor in unison. The screaming was white noise. The few boys in the audience (their ratio was one to ten) grimaced and held their hands to their ears.

George Evans stood in the wings, awestruck at what he and his client had wrought.

Frank grinned and blew the crowd a kiss. The pandemonium continued for minute after minute, undiminishing. He held up his hands, trying to say something.

Finally the screaming quieted ever so slightly. "Please, please, please," Sinatra was saying. He glanced around the huge theater. In all the world, there were few gazes this intense.

"Oh, Frankiee!" one shrill voice among the many cried—and the tumult cranked up once more.

He raised his hands. And then, after a moment, just audibly: "Do you want me to leave the stage?"

"No, no, no!" they chanted. "No! No! No!"

"Then let's see—"

"No! No! No!"

"Let's see if we can't be quiet enough to hear a complete arrangement," Frank said forcefully.

They quieted down just a little, and he began to sing.

After an exhausting forty-five minutes of battling them, he sang his closing number, "Put Your Dreams Away," bowed, threw some more kisses, and walked off the stage. The great platform slowly descended into the pit as Paige and his orchestra continued to play.

Of the more than forty-five hundred in the theater, only a scattering stood up. In all, perhaps two hundred departed, a disproportionate number of them boys. The girls who filed out (no doubt having bowed to intense parental pressure) trudged with eyes downcast, as if they'd been expelled from paradise. Back in the seats, those who had stayed unwrapped more food, chatted with friends, filed their nails.

Outside, the huge line inched forward two hundred places and stopped. The crowds, slowly growing aware of the monstrous injustice, pressed against the stanchions. The cops looked nervous.

The theater doors closed.

The girls behind the police lines pushed, shouted, wept in disbelief. Several fainted and had to be passed through the crowd to waiting ambulances. In the jammed side streets leading to Times Square, cabbies got out of their stopped vehicles and scratched their heads.

There were six shows that day, and something like two full audiences got to see the show. But twenty, then twenty-five, then thirty thousand waited outside—screaming, shoving, crying hysterically, pissing their pants. During one of the shows, a cordon of cops suddenly burst from the theater, flanking a skinny, grinning eighteen-year-old boy in a double-breasted gray suit. His name was Alexander J. Dorogokupetz, and he had come to the Paramount to see what the big deal was about this little singer that the girl he was stuck on was stuck on. As the band had struck up "I Don't Know Why (I Just Do)," a tender Fred Ahlert and Roy Turk ballad (Frank exquisitely aspirated the *h*'s in "why," just as John Quinlan had taught him), Dorogokupetz had taken aim from third-row center and hurled an egg that hit the curtain and dropped on the stage. Sinatra barely saw it fly by. Then the second egg struck him smack in the face. The shell fragments stung like hell, the yolk and albumen dripped down his chin and onto his collar, but he managed to keep singing.

Then a third egg hit him smack in the eye. And a fourth landed on his bow tie. The music stopped. "I vowed to put an end to this monotony of two years of consecutive swooning," Dorogokupetz said later, sounding for all the world like an apprehended assassin. "I took aim and threw . . . it hit him . . . his mouth was open . . . I felt good."

SINATRA HIT BY EGGS, read a headline the next morning. THE VOICE SCRAMBLES SONG.

That afternoon, a gaggle of sailors on leave, inspired by the reports in the papers and more than a few Knickerbocker beers consumed in a Times Square bar, arrived in front of the Paramount with a bag of over-ripe tomatoes and began slinging them at the giant image of a standing Sinatra on the marquee. By the time they were through, the singer's face was streaming with red juice.

Backstage, Dolly was fielding reporters' questions. "He may be famous now, but he'll always be a baby to me," she told them, waiting till everybody had stopped writing before she began talking again. "And I always told him to be nice to people as he goes up the ladder, because they're the same people he'll pass coming down. So far," she said, looking around wryly, "he has followed my instructions."

Forty years later, a Long Island society girl named Mary Lou Watts, a special friend of Sinatra's since the Dorsey days, recalled the scene in his dressing room at the Paramount. "[It] was always jammed," she said, "especially when Frank's mother was there. She was a great big bossy lady and towered over her husband, who was about the size of a mushroom. He was as little as Frank, but that mother of his was huge and very domineering. Scare you to death."

Dolly had doubtless put on some extra padding since the days when she weighed ninety-odd pounds, but she still stood an inch under five feet zero. Her size was all in the eye of the beholder. Which didn't make her one bit less intimidating.

═══

The Paramount engagement was both a first and a last. Mass hysteria like this had never existed—not since the Children's Crusade, the newspapers noted. The events of October 11, 1944, came to be known, collectively, as the Paramount Riot, or the Columbus Day Riot. Little did anyone know at the time that in fact a template was being set: the scene would virtually repeat itself five years later when Dean Martin and Jerry Lewis played the Paramount, then would recur at successive intervals of seven years (for Elvis) and eight years (for the Beatles). Mass culture was inventing itself as youth came into power; only the avatars would change—until the explosions of the late 1960s burst the culture into a million glittering fragments.

For Sinatra, that stand at the Paramount was a kind of culmination, the final explosive orgy of his cult of youth. His fame would continue to grow until the inevitable backlash set in, but its character would change: several factors, including the war, the movies, even the musicians' strike, combined to broaden his appeal to a more adult audience. Whatever his official bio said, the singer himself was rapidly approaching thirty.

When Columbia Records finally struck a deal with the American Federation of Musicians in November, Sinatra and Stordahl rushed to Liederkranz Hall, orchestra in tow, as eager as honeymooners. Over the next month, they literally made beautiful music together, recording no fewer than seventeen new sides (with the 78-rpm phonograph record still the state of the art, a song was literally one side of the disc). Thanks to two years of prep work on the radio and on V-Discs, the Sinatra-Stordahl records were of an unprecedented splendor, the team's great ballad style fully formed. Compared with Frank's last orchestral record, Manie Sacks's rerelease of the Harry James "All or Nothing At All," the Sinatra of the fall of 1944 was not a boy any longer but a man. The Voice had changed.

To listen to his first recording from those sessions, "If You Are But a Dream," is to hear a Sinatra who, even amid the swelling strings and lush horns and soupy lyrics, is no longer yearning but relating the sad knowledge of maturity. That patented catch in his voice, the one that drove the little girls wild, now has a world-weary edge to it. And the vocal instrument itself is deeper, with a slight rasp to its low notes.

It was Frank's great artistic achievement, always, to give the world his best self in his music. Yet sounding more mature was by no means a guarantee of mature behavior. On election night, a week before he began laying down the fresh masterpieces with Stordahl, Sinatra went out on the town with a group of pals, including Orson Welles, and, at Toots Shor's, got loaded in celebration of FDR's landslide victory over Thomas Dewey. On their return to the Waldorf, Frank and the boys decided to give it to Westbrook Pegler, who was also staying at the hotel. "Let's go down and see if he's as tough as he writes," Frank is said to have said. The crew trooped to the conservative columnist's room, and Frank banged on the door.

At this point accounts diverge.

Sinatra later claimed that Pegler wasn't there, and that he and his pals left quietly. But in a 1957 *Look* magazine profile of Sinatra by Bill Davidson, a man claiming to have been an aide to Pegler recalled, "Peg was inside, and he kept needling Sinatra through the door with things like, 'Are you that little Italian boy from Hoboken who sings on the radio?' Sinatra became so frustrated that he went back to his suite and busted up his own furniture, throwing a chair out of the window."

Pegler reacted with outrage to the article, writing the editors of *Look:* "I was in my room at the Waldorf-Astoria continuously from about 11 p.m. until rising time the next morning. No person knocked on my door during that time, and your statement that I was inside and the implication that I was afraid to open the door and confront a drunkard who had come to see how 'tough' I might be is false, and no 'aide' of mine ever made that statement to your reporter."

Look stood by its story.

Frank never went mano a mano with Westbrook Pegler, but if he'd wanted a fight with the columnist, he got one. In the aftermath of the non-incident at the Waldorf, Pegler ramped up his anti-Sinatra campaign, making it political as well as personal. Frank's friendship with the arch-liberal and Hearst-kingdom Antichrist (see *Citizen Kane*) Welles was sheer serendipity. "In the company of Orson Welles and others," Pegler wrote, "Sinatra toured the circuit of expensive New York saloons known as the milk route and spent some time at the political headquarters of Sidney Hillman, which were the Communist headquarters too. He got shrieking drunk and kicked up such a row in the Waldorf that a house policeman was sent up to subdue him, and did."

The mention of the radical, Lithuanian-born Hillman, chair of the CIO's political action committee, was a red flag for the Hearst papers' Republican readers: Sinatra was not only a Commie but a Jew-lover to boot. The singer retaliated by having Pegler turned away at one of his performances at the Wedgwood Room, and the columnist fired back by writing about Sinatra's 1938 Bergen County morals arrest.

Alarmed at the escalation of hostilities, George Evans immediately picked up the phone and tried to make nice with Pegler. The publicist reminded the columnist that Frank had been young and foolish back in 1938, and that the charges had been dropped in any case. Evans asked Pegler, as nicely as he possibly could, to print a retraction. What he got instead (Evans, Pegler was sure, was a Jew who had changed his name; he was having it looked into) was this: "No indictment was found, and Sinatra was discharged. The incident would indicate a certain precocity, however, for it will be observed that the facts of the case never were tried and that this experience of the youth so soon to become the idol of American girlhood was by no means common to decent young American males, however poor."

Frank Sinatra had put a stick into a bee's nest and given it a good hard stir. Further results were to follow.

In December, Frank flew back to the Coast, reading all the way. He smiled when he stepped out of the shiny-skinned DC-3 into the bright kerosene-tinged air. The East had been fun and involving and politically passionate, but the East was *serious*. It was playtime again.

Back to the beautiful house by the lake, with its merrily splashing fountain on the terra-cotta-tiled front terrace and its big pots of blazing flowers and its sweet California smells. His well-spoken black butler, John, greeted him at the door, then came both Nancys, the little girl skipping with glee and leaping into his arms, his wife trailing behind and giving him that look.

He freed an arm and embraced both at the same time, but even after he had kissed Big Nancy's soft and not entirely yielding lips, she was still training the lie detector on him.

He gave her a look back. It was wonderful to see her too.

She smiled and shook her head at him. She always was a sucker for his nonsense.

A few days later, at the CBS recording studio in Hollywood, he sang the slightly weary-sounding "(I Got a Woman Crazy for Me) She's Funny That Way," which contained the line:

> *Though she'd love to work and slave for me every day,*
> *She'd be so much better off if I went away.*

He thought of her as he sang that—thought of Nancy even as he smiled at the gorgeous Marilyn Maxwell in her gorgeous sweater, staring steadily at him through the soundproof glass.

There was another song he'd recently sung in *Anchors Aweigh,* its emotionally didactic but all too telling lyric custom-written for him by his attentive hanger-on Sammy Cahn:

> *I fall in love too easily,*
> *I fall in love too fast.*

They had moved all their furniture from the East and they had bought more, but still the new house felt empty. The big rooms echoed. Nancy was doing her very best to make it nice with chintz curtains and pillows and flowers, but still the rooms echoed. The living room was enormous, with long white wooden beams across the ceiling, like a rec hall at a Catskills resort. It gave Frank an idea. They would give the new place a proper housewarming, with a New Year's Eve party. And not just any party—a show! He called his studio musicians; he called Sammy Cahn and told him to start writing special lyrics. He phoned the MGM properties department and ordered them to bring over some bolts of cloth that could be hung at the front of the room as stage curtains. (Bemused at Sinatra's curt directive, the head of the properties department kicked the request straight up the line to Mayer—who, fortuitously, had just received his invitation. *Of course! Nothing's too good for our boy!*) Dozens of folding chairs were rented; flowers were bought, and (of course) cases and cases of champagne. As always, no expense was spared. (Dizzying sums of money were coming in every week, and, as Nancy knew all too well, equally dizzying sums were going out. They had almost nothing in the bank.)

The big night was a Sunday, December 31, 1944. The war was winding down, but not easily. In the Pacific, Leyte had been secured, and the terrible fight for the islands was on. In France and Belgium, during the coldest winter in decades, the Battle of the Bulge raged; thousands of untested infantrymen, pressed into service to replace the dead and the wounded, died in the snow under withering German artillery fire. In Frank Sinatra's Toluca Lake living room, as Gene Kelly and Judy Garland and Phil Silvers and Sammy Cahn stood by, holding sheet music and grinning expectantly (Sammy a bit more expectantly than anyone else), Sinatra—wearing a tuxedo like the rest of the men—stepped to the microphone. He shielded his eyes from the light and peered out at the partygoers; he glanced a little nervously at his own sheet music and then at Cahn. Frank shook his head. Sam had outdone himself this time.

Oh boy, had he outdone himself.

A snickering from the crowded room.

Then Sammy cued the piano player, and Sinatra sang the special lyrics to the very familiar tune, a love song now transformed (as the stellar background singers harmonized behind him) into a satirical romp about the star who left the little studio and went to the big one, and the nice studio boss who had been smart enough—or was that gullible enough?—to sign him.

The lyrics were funny, biting, double-edged. The room was roaring with laughter. And as Mayer's long-suffering (but soon to be replaced) wife, Margaret, leaned over and whispered in her husband's ear that it was a joke, a funny song, the mogul gave a faint, thin-lipped smile.

Sinatra sings the National Anthem with Lower East Side kids at a UN Day ceremony, 1950. Frank's commitment to tolerance was genuine and profound.

Sinatra and Axel Stordahl, CBS radio broadcast, 1940s. Frank couldn't read
a note of music but knew precisely what he wanted at all times.

F rank began 1945 by ending his contract for Lucky Strike's *Your
Hit Parade*. The decision wasn't his. The show's producer, George
Washington Hill—the flinty-eyed old tobacco peddler whose grand
achievement in life had been the marketing of cigarettes to women—
had wiped his hands of Sinatra when the troublesome singer had the
temerity not only to ask for a raise but also to demand the show be
moved to the West Coast. In Frank's place, Hill hired the opera singer

Lawrence Tibbett—at $700 a week more than Sinatra had been earning. Still: no Mediterranean blood; much less trouble.

Sinatra too knew how to wipe his hands of someone. The big drawback of *Your Hit Parade* had been that he was only the show's co-star; the chief benefit had been to keep his voice and his name out there. He had plenty of other ways to do that, including his other radio show, *Frank Sinatra in Person,* which had now switched sponsors from Vimms to Max Factor and was based in Los Angeles.

Then, thank God, there were records again—with musicians. Sinatra spent much of the following year on a white-hot streak of recording for Columbia: an average of one session per month in Hollywood and New York, forty sides in all. The songs ranged from the timelessly sublime ("Where or When," "If I Loved You," "These Foolish Things," "You Go to My Head," "Why Shouldn't I?") to the schmaltzy and quickly dated ("Full Moon and Empty Arms," "Homesick, That's All," "The Moon Was Yellow") to the merely odd ("Jesus Is a Rock in a Weary Land," "My Shawl," "Old School Teacher"). Crosby, too, had experimented with offbeat material, Latin and gospel numbers. It was safe: the golden age of American popular songwriting was still alive. The vein, Frank believed, would never run out.

In August he cut—for the third time in a year!—a somewhat less than golden number, one whose lyrics, legend had it, Phil Silvers had dashed off in twenty minutes at a party and presented to Sinatra as a gift for Little Nancy's fourth birthday: "Nancy (with the Laughing Face)."

> *If I don't see her each day I miss her,*
> *Gee, what a thrill each time I kiss her.*

When the legend becomes fact, print the legend. In point of fact, Silvers did dash off just such a lyric at a party, and Jimmy Van Heusen—a great one for sitting down at the piano at parties—came up with a winsome tune to go along with it. But the song was originally titled "*Bessie* (with the Laughing Face)," in honor of Johnny Burke's wife, whom Silvers had reduced to giggles with one of his patented one-liners. Upon further consideration, though, Silvers and Van Heusen (who always had a sharp eye for ingratiating himself with the friend he would come to call the Monster) weighed the benefits of pleasing Bessie Burke against those of pleasing Frank Sinatra and wisely opted for the latter. The result was, even if saccharine, a big hit for Sinatra and a very nice birthday present for the little girl, to whom Chester, with superbly politic flair, assigned his songwriter royalties.

Some wonder why Frank recorded this number three times in the space of a year. He may have done it out of extreme love for his daughter and wife (for, after all, the song could be construed both paternally and amorously); he may have been trying to perfect it; or there might have been another reason. On that hot August afternoon in Hollywood, Sinatra might have been recording the song as an act of atonement, for he was behaving very badly that year and things were not going at all well at home.

He was in love. In fact, he was always in love. He could barely sing a song without feeling that giddy feeling for one girl or another. (In truth, the feeling itself counted far more than the girl.) This time, though, it was pretty serious. Sinatra had known Marilyn Maxwell since 1939, when he was with Harry James and she was an eighteen-year-old singer (alongside Perry Como) with the bandleader Ted Weems, using her real first name, Marvel. She and Frank ran into each other all over the map as their respective bands crisscrossed the country; she was one of the first people to advise him to go out on his own.

As for her given name, it was corny, but only slightly. She was a marvel: a stunning, corn-fed Iowa girl, bottle blond, with a body to kill for, a real brain in her head, and a truly sweet disposition. Marilyn was *nice,* and that was what made it so hard when she and Frank reconnected at Metro (where she had just wrapped *Lost in a Harem,* with Abbott and Costello). In Hollywood he picked up and threw away girls like Kleenex, and this one simply wasn't disposable, something about her genuineness got him where he lived.

At 1051 Valley Spring Lane, where various Barbato relatives were trooping in and out at all hours of the day, little romantic was happening. Nancy's sister Tina was still in residence, answering fan mail, and now the other sisters and their families had moved west, too, as had Mike and Jennie Barbato, who were in the process of building a house in Glendale. Somebody was always around, having a meal, a cup of coffee. It was all-Barbato, all the time, and Frank had had it. His wife had company, fine; but he had no wife. Between recording and seeing his agents and taking meetings at the studio and going out on the town, he barely appeared at the house. When he did, it was to stalk in at four or five or six in the morning, sleep till 1:00 p.m., have his breakfast served by the maid, then stalk out again. On the rare occasions when he and Nancy did have an extended conversation, it was either about his business (to which she paid close attention) or about her family (to which he objected strenuously). It seemed they were fighting all the time these days.

The hell of it was that she was still in love with him. She *knew* him: to her, he was still the boy with the ukulele who had courted her down the shore so long ago. Every once in a while, when the clouds lifted for a second and he smiled, she could see that boy. She knew about the other women, and she hated it, but what could she do? She had asked Frank to be discreet, but now they were in Hollywood, capital of indiscretion, where the night and the day had a thousand eyes. He was so cold lately: she knew exactly what was going on.

But what could she do about it?

It went without saying that when Frank went out, he went out without her. Once he left the house, he never wanted for company. Sanicola and Silvani were with him at all times, to fend off the riff-raff; and he could always summon the posse—Cahn, Stordahl, Styne, Silvers, Chester. Other stars might create a stir when they walked into a joint, but no one else walked in with such a retinue. One blossom-heavy night in May 1945, Sinatra and company stopped by Preston Sturges's restaurant, the Players, on Sunset across from the Garden of Allah. There, in a banquette near the front door, sat a man

Frank genuinely idolized, Humphrey Bogart, with his beautiful young bride, Betty Bacall.

Sinatra took immediate notice of Bacall: Bogart's fourth wife was just twenty, with lazily insinuating feline eyes, voluptuous lips, and perfect skin. She smiled at Sinatra, he smiled back at her, and Bogart took it all in. He was jealous—what man wouldn't be?—but he also wore an air of carefully maintained irony. He was a world-weary forty-five years old, with a rapidly receding hairline, bags under his eyes, and a perpetual cigarette between nicotine-stained fingers. Humphrey Bogart looked at Frank Sinatra and, smiling that wolfish smile, said, "They tell me you have a voice that makes girls faint. Make me faint."

Frank grinned. The world's toughest tough guy was giving him the full treatment. He accepted the compliment. "I'm taking the week off," he told Bogart.

Bogart liked his sand, asked him to sit down for a minute and have a drink.

But there were other nights when Sinatra was out with Marilyn— or, since she was, after all, married (for whatever that was worth in Hollywood), any one of a dozen other girls, at Ciro's, the Trocadero, Mocambo—and Hedda and Louella and their colleagues had to write *something*. "What blazing new swoon crooner has been seen night clubbing with a different starlet every night?" ran one blind item. Another: "Wonder if the wonder boy of hit records tells his wife where he goes after dark."

In a small town, a company town, Wonder Boy's wife was all too aware, and it was killing her inside, but what could she do?

═══

She did her best. In a land of extreme, overbearing beauty, Nancy Barbato Sinatra of Jersey City was mousy at worst, merely lovely at best. She did her best. She had more work done on her teeth, and, as much as she hated spending all that money (she could never forget the days when she'd slaved as a secretary at American Type Founders in Elizabeth), Nancy bought some Jean Louis gowns for those rare occasions when he took her out. She tried to look as good as she possibly could, but deep down she knew she was Jersey City and always would be. She was both ashamed of it and proud. She took care of her babies, she talked for hours with her mother and sisters, and—having taken the driving lessons but still unwilling to scratch the new Cadillac convertible—she tooled around town doing errands in the other new car he'd bought her, a big Chrysler station wagon. She was quite a sight in it. Petite as she was (a little taller than Dolly, but not much), Nancy could barely see over the steering wheel without sitting on a pillow.

She also took care of his business. In a handwritten letter to Manie Sacks, undated, on heavy white stationery with "FRANK SINATRA" embossed in blue across the top, she expressed concern for the record executive's health, noted that she was returning (for unexplained reasons) a check of his, passed along household news about the children's health and schooling (oddly, strikingly, referring to Frankie as Francis Emanuel'), and then came to the point. Frank was beginning a New York theater stand (probably the Paramount), and she asked Manie's help in seeing that he got his rest. "I am depending on you to watch him," she wrote, "for you know how Frank likes to make the spots . . . and stay out late talking."

It would take a heart of stone not to melt. *I am depending on you to watch him. Frank likes to make the spots and stay out late talking.* Talking. Poor Nancy! Poor Manie!

Frank Sinatra didn't have a heart of stone, but rather, one that was divided into a million chambers. He knew all too well how his wife felt, yet he could not change. Nancy was going thirty miles an hour; Frank was moving at the speed of sound. Even while he slept, his mind churned, calculating the possibilities: Metro. Columbia. Radio. Theater. Marilyn. Lana. Betty. Jean. Jane.

The possibilities were infinite, and he never stopped. He darted back and forth between the two coasts like a hummingbird. In February he reported, yet again, to his draft board in Jersey City, playing out the unfunny comedy a little further, getting reclassified yet again, to 2-A, which meant he was not only physically unfit to serve but also employed in an occupation "necessary to the national health, safety, and interest." IS CROONING ESSENTIAL? one headline asked. And then, on March 5, the draft board announced it had all been a mistake, that 4-F was the real classification. The headlines and editorials fulminated some more . . . but Sinatra was too fast for them. On March 6, he was back in the studio in Hollywood, recording four more numbers, including a Norman Rockwell poster of a tune Gordon Jenkins called "Homesick, That's All":

> *I miss the times I had to set the table,*
> *I miss the rolls my mother made when she was able.*

Sinatra gave the song his tenderest reading, pitching it shamelessly both to the audience that hated him most, the millions of men who were still far from home, and to the audience that adored him: the women who kept the home fires burning. Nancy, of course, heard it, too.

But she wouldn't get to see him: the moment he finished the session, he turned on a dime and headed right back east. There was a Western Union telegram, dated March 8, 1945, from Manie:

MR. FRANK SINATRA, 1051 VALLEY SPRING LANE, NORTH HOL-
LYWOOD, CALIFORNIA. JUST READ IN WINCHELL'S COLUMN
THAT YOU AND COLUMBIA RECORD EXECUTIVES ON THE OUTS.
WHAT IS IT ABOUT? THINK GOOD IDEA TO WIRE WINCHELL
TELLING HIM THAT SOMEONE IS GIVING HIM WRONG INFOR-
MATION. SEE YOU MONDAY. LOVE AND KISSES, MANIE.

But the next day, by return wire, Frank jokingly affirmed Winchell's position, telling Manie to look out for a punch in the nose when he got back to town. He, too, signed with love and kisses.

Frank's recording was going beautifully, the recording business, less so. Columbia was crimping him on studio charges, charging him for copying, arrangements, Axel's conducting fees. Crimping him, Sinatra!

Still, there is no evidence that he gave Sacks anything but a hug when they met in New York: Sinatra never was one for personal confrontation. Besides, even where Manie was concerned, Frank had someplace else to be—a radio show, a dinner at Toots's, a speaking engagement at the World Youth rally at Carnegie Hall. He was a blur of motion. Making the spots. Staying out late. Talking.

======

Strangely enough, one of the glamour girls Sinatra had claimed he could live without—in Phil Silvers's lyric at least—had started spending time at 1051 Valley Spring Lane, mostly when the man of the house wasn't there. Lana Turner had struck up a conversation with Nancy at the New Year's Eve party, and the odd couple had hit it off: the petite blonde from Idaho with the checkered past and the even more petite brunette from Jersey City with the practical turn of mind and an artist's hand in the kitchen. They had laughed together that night, at Lana's lightly scathing comment about the anatomical shortcomings of one of the handsomest men there. The remark let Nancy breathe easier about her own shortcomings, her new hometown's unrelenting tyranny of beauty.

Lana, of course, was almost impossibly beautiful, but something in her brown eyes spoke of pain and a restless sadness. Hollywood was nothing but a boiler factory as far as she was concerned, her privileged place in it notwithstanding. The men were all fairies or hounds, sometimes both. (Not Frank, of course. Nancy had a real man—maybe 'cause he didn't look like all those cookie-cutter hunks.) And the women were all out to slit each other's throats.

That was why Lana liked Nancy: she was someone she could really talk to. She played with a strand of Nancy's hair. And Lana loved the way she looked, too.

Nancy smiled, accepting the compliment. Finally she felt a little less lonely. And she was delighted to tell her family and her friends back in Jersey: At last she had a real friend in Hollywood, and they wouldn't believe who it was. *Lana Turner!*

———

Inconceivably—he had been president since Frank was seventeen— FDR died in April. Frank, in New York, went to light a candle at St. Patrick's Cathedral, then drove up to Hyde Park for a memorial service. He felt deeply sad, as though he had lost a beloved uncle; he felt sorrow with the rest of the country. You couldn't avoid it; it was in the air like the weather. But somehow the sadness didn't get Frank where he lived. He was young, in the vibrant prime of life; Roosevelt had been an old, sick man.

Still, Frank had shaken his hand, looked in his eyes . . . Death was such a strange thing: it gave him the creeps. Best not to think about it.

Less than a month later, with the nation still in mourning, the war in Europe was over, and grief turned to joy. It would still be months before the hundreds of thousands of troops came home, and George Evans and Jack Keller agreed that the time had come at last for Sinatra to go over and entertain them. It would quell the jingoistic newspapermen—not to mention the gossip columnists.

Frank's daughter Nancy has written that her father was unable to travel overseas before the end of the war because the FBI, suspicious of his left-wing activities, prevented him from getting a visa. In fact, J. Edgar Hoover didn't get really interested in Sinatra until after the war, and when he did, it wasn't just because of the singer's liberal sympathies.

The truth is that Sinatra hadn't gone abroad during the war because he'd been scared.

As he had every right to be. He read the papers. He had seen *Stars and Stripes,* even after Evans and Keller tried to keep it away from him. He had seen the tomatoes speckling his picture on the Paramount marquee, had heard the catcalls in the street, had felt it when he did

USO shows Stateside: not all of the servicemen hated him (he could win them over when he was in a room or a theater with them)—but an awful lot did. He was the ultimate cuckolder: He might not have actually screwed their women (still, who knew? rumor had it the guy really got around), but he was in their heads. Their wives and girlfriends wanted him, and that was bad enough.

For the troops overseas, it was much worse. Missing home and missing nooky most of all, they were convinced their women were stepping out on them—and in many instances, of course, they were right. Sinatra the draft dodger was the lightning rod for their insecurity. When Evans and Keller floated the idea of a post V-E Day Sinatra tour, the Hollywood Victory Committee, the group of Screen Actors Guild worthies who ran the Canteen, weighed right in. "There might be some unpleasantness," they said. Frank had heard rumors that the troops would throw eggs at him, maybe worse . . . These guys had *guns,* for God's sake.

Evans and Keller had a brilliant idea.

They'd seen Phil Silvers doing shtick with Sinatra at the Hollywood Canteen: making fun of Frank's skinniness, pinching his cheeks and pulling his ears, teaching him to sing. This last bit was particularly funny—the droopy-eyed comedian would go on and on about how Sinatra's tones weren't round enough, would play with his mouth to get his lips to form just the right shape . . . and no matter what Sinatra did, it was wrong. Silvers, who had come up through baggy-pants vaudeville, was brilliant, and the bit was hilarious.

Evans called Phil and asked him to oversee Sinatra's USO tour, introduce him at every stop. Do the same stuff he did with him at the Canteen. Make plenty of fun of him. Push him around a little. Silvers would be doing everything those GIs really wanted to do to him, and he'd be getting them on Frank's side in the process.

It worked like a charm. In June, Sinatra and Silvers flew to Casablanca on an Army C-47, along with the pianist Saul Chaplin, the actress and singer Fay McKenzie, and the dancer Betty Yeaton. At every dusty camp they played, Silvers slapped Sinatra's cheeks, and the soldiers roared. He ordered him offstage—"Go away, boy, you bother me. The Blood Bank's down the street"—and they guffawed. By the time the comedian was done with Frank, the GIs were begging to hear him sing. Not an egg was thrown. "The singer kidded himself throughout the program and had the audience on his side all the way," the *New York Times* reported. The troupe played bases in North Africa, then flew to Rome, where the singer had an audience with Pope Pius XII, who didn't know who Sinatra was ("Are you a tenor, my son? Which operas do you sing?"), though he had heard of Crosby. They played Rome and Caserta and Foggia and Venice. And then they flew home. They had done seventeen shows in ten days, entertained ninety-seven thousand servicemen and servicewomen.

The minute Sinatra stepped off the plane at La Guardia, he stuck his foot in his mouth. The USO and Army Special Services were incompetent, he told the crowd of reporters. "Shoemakers in uniform run the entertainment division," he said. "Most of them had no experience in show business. They didn't know what time it was."

What was his problem? Maybe the lighting cues had been off, or a few microphones hadn't worked. Maybe the dressing rooms had been insufficient; maybe he was still grouchy about the pope. (Or just the dirt. It couldn't have been easy for a true obsessive-compulsive, a man who was in the habit of showering and changing his underwear several times a day, to deal with military amenities in dirt-poor North Africa and Italy.)

He later defended himself by saying that GIs had asked him to complain about how poorly organized and presented most of the shows were. There was plenty to gripe about in a theater of war, even after the big show was over. But Sinatra, who could turn irritable if the wind shifted, was the wrong person to do the griping. His momentarily silenced critics got right back into gear. "Mice make women faint too," sneered the *Stars and Stripes*. "He is doing an injustice to a group of people who are for the most part talented, hardworking, and sincere.

There have been, of course, the usual prima donnas who have flown over, had their pictures taken with GIs, and got the hell home." And dependable Lee Mortimer jumped on the bandwagon, calling Sinatra's post V-E Day mini-tour a "joy ride," comparing him unfavorably to "aging, ailing men like Joe E. Brown and Al Jolson [who] subjected themselves to enemy action, jungle disease, and the dangers of traveling through hostile skies from the beginning of the war."

George Evans took it all with apparent calm. Even though his heedless client had innumerable ways of ratcheting up the publicist's blood pressure, even though Sinatra often seemed to work overtime at being his own worst enemy, the Sinatra machine looked unstoppable.

In mid-July, *Anchors Aweigh* came out, and it was a huge hit, with the critics and at the box office. Even the *Times*'s reliably crusty Bosley Crowther waxed grudgingly enthusiastic (after first giving well-deserved raves to Gene Kelly, "the Apollonian marvel of the piece"): "But bashful Frankie is a large-sized contributor to the general fun and youthful charm of the show."

The show made big money, and Louis B. Mayer's thin smile grew broader. He had been right about that boy.

Meanwhile, Evans and Keller plunged ahead with a new campaign. If the public was going to hear a lot of nonsense about the starlets Frankie was stepping out with in Hollywood and the ungracious remarks he persisted in making about worthy organizations like Metro-Goldwyn-Mayer and the U.S. Army, the public was also going to see another side of him: Frank Sinatra was going to be a humanitarian.

It wasn't phony. He was a humanitarian at heart. (Or at least in one of the many chambers of his heart.) He hated intolerance—first, of course, because it had smacked him personally in the face many times, but also because it attacked people he genuinely loved. Hadn't Mrs. Golden clasped him to her substantial breast and cooed to him in Yiddish? Didn't he love Manie like a brother? A couple of years earlier, when intimations of the Holocaust first started to emerge, Frank had

had dozens of medals made up with the cross of Saint Christopher on one side and the Star of David on the other (a daring gesture in those days). He had given them out left and right.

And where Negroes were concerned, anyone who was half a musician couldn't even begin to be prejudiced. Sinatra had encountered far too many black geniuses to feel anything but pity and contempt for the thickheaded smugness of racist America. He had kissed Billie Holiday the way she ought to be kissed one night outside a Los Angeles club; he had dreamed of doing much more. He would always have a thing for black women, though, in truth, this, like everything else about him, was complicated: by his misogyny, his own feelings of inferiority.

His feelings of compassion were purely emotional. But when he talked about them with George Evans, the publicist realized Frank was being honest. And those feelings were golden. Evans repped some of the greatest entertainers in the business, yet none had Sinatra's capacity to become a great *American*. Evans talked about it with Keller, and they agreed on a strategy: they would flood out the bad with the good. They sent their boy out to thirty speaking engagements in 1945, many of them at high schools in the throes of racial tension. In the fall, Frank went to Benjamin Franklin H.S. in Italian East Harlem, where there had been fistfights among the integrated student body. The future jazz giant Sonny Rollins, then a sophomore, recalled many years later, "Sinatra came down there and sang in our auditorium . . . after that things got better, and the rioting stopped."

He had less luck in early November in Gary, Indiana, where a thousand white students at Froebel High had walked out of school, smashing windows with bricks, after a new principal declared the school's 270 black students free to take classes, play in the orchestra, and share the swimming pool with everyone else. Sinatra, with Evans and Keller along for support, walked straight into a powder keg: a tough steel town where the white students' fathers feared that blacks had come to take away their jobs. The kids were their parents' outriders in hate; the whole city was united in toxic fury.

But of the five thousand Garyites who came to hear Sinatra sing—
and speak afterward—at the city's Memorial Auditorium, four thousand were women and girls. (He wore a bright blue bow tie—it went so
well with his eyes—and a chrysanthemum presented to him by one of
the students.) And while the overwhelmingly female audience assured
he would get a sympathetic hearing, the event made no guarantee of
strides toward racial tolerance in Gary, Indiana. Years afterward, Jack
Keller offered a stirring version of the scene:

> George and I were standing in the wings, and although we had
> told Frank what to say, we were skeptical and pretty damned
> frightened as to what might happen. Frank walked out onstage
> and stood dead center while all these rough, tough steel work-
> ers and their kids started catcalling and whistling and stamping
> their feet. Frank folded his arms, looked right down at them,
> and stared for a full two minutes, until there was a dead silence
> in the room. Evans and I were nervous wrecks wondering what
> in hell he was going to do.
>
> Without smiling, Frank . . . finally unfolded his arms and
> moved to the microphone. "I can lick any son of a bitch in this
> joint," he said. Pandemonium broke loose as the kids cheered
> him. They thought he was right down their street, and from
> then on, it was terrific.

According to Keller, Sinatra continued:

> "I implore you to return to school. This is a bad deal, kids. It's
> not good for you and it's not good for the city of Gary, which
> has done so much to help with the war for freedom the world
> over.
>
> "Believe me, I know something about the business of racial
> intolerance. At eleven I was called a 'dirty guinea' back home in
> New Jersey. We've all done it. We've all used the words 'nigger'

or 'kike' or 'mick' or 'Polack' or 'dago.' Cut it out, kids. Go back to school. You've got to go back because you don't want to be ashamed of your student body, your city, your country."

A contemporary newspaper account, under the headline GARY HIGH SCHOOL STUDENTS COOL ON SINATRA'S APPEAL, gave a more tempered view of the occasion. "The audience came to hear Sinatra sing and stayed to listen to what he had to say about the high school strike," reported Illinois's *Edwardsville Intelligencer*. "But at the soda fountain where some of the bobby sockers gathered after the meeting there was doubt that Sinatra's appeal had worked. The strike leaders had not attended the meeting, and few of the striking students who were there stayed even throughout the program."

This is somewhat at odds with the picture of the tough little singer facing down a roomful of hostile steelworkers. Maybe (it's a great story) Frank did offer to lick any son of a bitch in the joint; maybe the quote was a product of Keller's fertile imagination.[2] Nevertheless, Sinatra (perhaps emboldened by the warmer than expected response of the GIs in North Africa and Italy) must be given points for going to Gary at all. And in the weeks that followed—even though the Froebel strike continued after he left—he racked up even more points, collecting an honorary scroll from the Bureau of Intercultural Education in New York (Eleanor Roosevelt, with whom Frank would form a warm bond, was the keynote speaker); the Philadelphia Golden Slipper Square Club's annual unity award; the Newspaper Guild's Page One Award; a citation for "outstanding efforts and contribution to the cause of religious tolerance and unity among Americans" from the National Conference of Christians and Jews; et cetera, et cetera.

Evans and Keller were thrilled. All those awards washed out a lot of nasty gossip, given the public's short attention span. For the time being, anyway.

But it wasn't just the high-school visits that lent Sinatra new moral substance. Over the summer, at the suggestion of former MGM production chief Mervyn LeRoy ("You could reach a thousand times more people if you'd tell your story on the screen"), he'd made a fifteen-minute movie short called *The House I Live In*. Sinatra plays himself in the RKO featurette, appearing first in a recording studio, singing "If You Are But a Dream," and looking magnificent—slim, suntanned, and sleek (even shot from his bad side, though probably through gauze, by Robert De Grasse, who'd made him look so resplendent in *Higher and Higher* and *Step Lively*). His face, at this point in its development, is a long triangle beneath those sculpted cheekbones. He mugs shamelessly for the camera, acting the song, feeling the song, *being* the song—in short, dreaming. His eyebrows rise expressively, that beautiful mouth trembles passionately. Then he switches gears.

When he steps outside for a smoke, he encounters a gang of boys who have cornered another kid with dark hair and Semitic features.

"What's he got? Smallpox or somethin'?" Sinatra asks.

"We don't like his religion!" one of the gang responds.

"His *religion*?"

"Look, mister," another boy pipes up. "He's a dirty—"

"Now, hold on!" Sinatra interjects. He softens. "Look, fellas," he says. "Religion makes no difference. Except maybe to a Nazi, or somebody that's stupid. Why, people all over the world worship God in many different ways. God created everybody."

As he explains it to them, he's acting as passionately as he acted while he sang in the recording studio, only now it's in a slightly different key—now, rather than being romantic, Frank is being kind and thoughtful and gentle but strong: ultimately persuasive. You'd never guess in a million years that this is a man with a temper so violent and unpredictable that his best friends, including Sammy Cahn and Phil Silvers, are terrified of him. The man in *The House I Live In* is Sinatra's best self, twenty-nine years old and beautiful and solid and thoughtful. This self existed, not just on celluloid. Seeing him reasoning with the tough kids and persuading them, you just *want* to give this guy a prize of some sort.

Then, before long, he's breaking into song again, to the kids this time. It's the title number, a paean to tolerance. What was America to him?

> *All races and religions*
> *That's America to me.*

And it was dynamite. Looking at the film (and listening to the song) three generations later, you can't help thinking: Okay, this is corny in a lot of ways, but what's wrong with it? How far have we really come since then? It's that well done.

Mervyn LeRoy directed the short. The Hollywood leftist Albert Maltz wrote the script, and the New York leftist Abel Meeropol, under his pen name Lewis Allan, wrote the title song's lyrics. The little film had great impact. It got people talking about tolerance; the liberal press ate it up. Practically overnight, as Tom and Phil Kuntz write in *The Sinatra Files,* an analysis of the singer's huge FBI dossier, Sinatra became "a darling of the American left." LeRoy, the producer Frank Ross, Maltz, Meeropol, and Sinatra were all nominated for honorary Oscars, and they took them home in early 1946.

But the right-wing press, as powerful just after World War II as it is today, smelled a rat. Weren't Maltz and Meeropol, no matter what name he was hiding under, both not only leftists but also card-carrying Commies? (They were. And defiantly so: Maltz would become one of the Hollywood Ten; Meeropol, who'd also written Billie Holiday's great 1939 antilynching song, "Strange Fruit"—a number so hot Columbia Records wouldn't release it—would eventually adopt Julius and Ethel Rosenberg's two orphaned sons.) The tolerance Sinatra was preaching looked, to Hearst's Westbrook Pegler and the America First Party's Gerald L. K. Smith and the Knights of Columbus's Gerval T. Murphy, among others, like a newfangled cover for old-fashioned socialism. (In fact, much of the conservative criticism leveled at *The House I Live In* was a newfangled cover for old-fashioned anti-Semitism: virtually everybody involved in the short, not to mention almost everyone running Hollywood, was Jewish.)

It was directly in the wake of *The House I Live In* that FBI interest in Sinatra perked up again. On December 12, 1945, the special agent in charge of Philadelphia sent J. Edgar Hoover a memo advising the director that a confidential informant had identified "FRANK SINATRA, well known radio and movie star," as a member of the Communist Party. The informant, the memo continued,

> advised that the reason SINATRA was discussed was because of the recent article which appeared on him in "Life" magazine, setting forth his position on racial hatred and showing SINATRA talking before a Gary, Indiana, high school group.
>
> On November 25, 1945 a full page article appeared in the Sunday [Communist newspaper] "Worker" on FRANK SINATRA. This article was written by WALTER LOWENFELS, Philadelphia correspondent for the "Worker."
>
> In the Sunday "Worker" dated December 2, 1945 under "Pennsylvania News" the following item appeared: "FRANK SINATRA is going to get a gold medal and a silver plaque at the Broadwood Hotel, December 10. He will receive the first annual Golden Slipper Square Club Unity Award for his contribution to racial and religious tolerance."
>
> This information is being furnished for whatever action is deemed advisable.

The war was over, but the country was shell-shocked. The atrocities in Europe and the Pacific were emerging in their full horror. The U.S.A. focused on new enemies. In 1945, the House Un-American Activities Committee, having heretofore convened on an ad hoc basis, became a standing committee. And in January 1946, Gerald L. K. Smith—white supremacist, Jew hater, Holocaust denier—testified before HUAC that Frank Sinatra was acting "as a front" for Communist organizations. He spoke of "Hollywood's left-wing cabal" and called Sinatra "Mrs. Roosevelt in pants." It all would have almost been comical if much of America, at the moment, hadn't been taking Smith and the like so seriously. And Joseph McCarthy, campaigning for the Senate, was waiting in the wings.

At first Sinatra brushed off the right-wing rhetoricians like so many pesky flies. "You know," he told Walter Lowenfels, in the above-mentioned *Worker* interview, "they called [seventeen-year-old] Shirley Temple a Communist. Me and Shirley both, I guess." Yet soon he was tempering his cockiness. "I don't like Communists," he told another reporter, "and I have nothing to do with any organization except the Knights of Columbus."

═══

But there was another organization—to the extent that it actually was organized—that remained a constant in Frank's life. His connection to gangsters should be neither overemphasized nor underplayed. As many entertainers who came up in the great era of nightclubs (the 1930s through the early 1960s) have pointed out, it was impossible to play the clubs and not come into contact with the Mob. The Boys backed the clubs, often secretly owning them and hiring front men to present a legitimate face to the public. They operated the clubs as glamorous profit centers for many of the businesses in which they took a direct interest: entertainment and liquor and cigarettes and gambling and prostitution. Every enterprise touched on a dozen others. Organized crime during Frank Sinatra's early career, and prior to the U.S. government's tardy but assiduous attempts to break it up, was a vast, darkly shimmering American under-culture—an alternative economy so huge that the über-criminal Meyer Lansky was able to boast, famously, "We're bigger than General Motors." The problem with the remark being the small but crucial word "we." What was called organized crime was actually something far more complex—and less organized.

Unlike General Motors, organized crime was not publicly held;

it did not elect a board of directors or issue stockholders' reports. Unlike privately held businesses, it wasn't formally incorporated. It was ten thousand businesses, an enormous shape-shifting cluster of enterprises under the control of whoever happened to be in control until someone more powerful came along and took over, displacing or (often) eliminating the previous owner: an infinite chain of big fish eating smaller fish. It could be argued that while legitimate business operates under the nominal oversight of the law, it is actually subject to the survival of the fittest; illegitimate business merely eliminates the oversight. Yet organized crime, lacking any checks and balances or a structural superego, functions under brute power. This may seem glamorous to outsiders who have to live by (or at least contend with) society's rules. It seemed alluring to Frank, who in becoming a man sought stronger role models than his weak father. But to the men who live it, it is simply the Life. They swim like sharks: sometimes in pods or schools, sometimes alone, now and then turning to attack each other out of sheer bloodthirstiness.

Frank Sinatra's old Hasbrouck Heights neighbor Willie Moretti was one such. Another was Benjamin Siegel, who grew up on Manhattan's Lower East Side in the early twentieth century, a remarkably bold and clever and comely youth who quickly saw crime as the only chance he would ever have to get rich. Siegel turned thirteen—bar mitzvah age—exactly at the beginning of Prohibition and, around the same time, met seventeen-year-old Meyer Lansky, who was little and ugly and tough and brilliant: he could memorize and calculate great strings of numbers, useful skills. The two boys appreciated each other's qualities. Soon they were literally thick as thieves: running numbers and rum together, stealing cars, breaking heads. Lansky was fearless but not enamored of violence for its own sake; Siegel, whose pale blue eyes sometimes took on a crazed gleam, actually enjoyed bludgeoning, stabbing, and shooting. *Crazy as a bedbug,* they said. And so Benny Siegel acquired a nickname—Bug, or Bugs, or Bugsy.

Siegel and Lansky soon formed alliances with Charles "Lucky"

Luciano and Frank Costello. During the Castellammarese War among the New York gangs in the early 1930s, Siegel participated in the killing of the old-time Mob boss Salvatore Maranzano that elevated Luciano to supreme power. For this, Luciano was grateful. Having made an enormous amount of money from bootlegging, Siegel married, moved to Scarsdale, and began a family. For a while, he lived as a kind of commuter-gangster. But in 1937, when his partners asked if he might be interested in relocating to Los Angeles to set up a gambling operation, he jumped at the chance.

Most of the thugs connected to the various crime syndicates around the country were built along the lines of Lansky and Luciano: small, homely men, born in poor circumstances in the Old Country or in the teeming ghettos of the American cities to which their parents had immigrated. Undernourished as children, they were street fighters: short, big nosed, scar faced, fearsome. Benjamin Siegel was something else again, far more handsome and magnetic than anyone in his line of work had a right to be. He gravitated naturally to Los Angeles because Los Angeles meant Hollywood, and Siegel was good-looking enough to be a movie actor. He made show-business connections as soon as he got to town—most notably the tough-talking Harry Cohn, founder of Columbia Pictures, fellow Jew, and an inveterate racetrack gambler frequently in need of large sums of money. The two men were drawn to each other for symbiotic reasons. For Cohn it was the cash. For Siegel it was Cohn's ready access to actresses. Siegel had moved his wife and two young daughters west, but he was also happy to acquire a string of glamorous mistresses.

Even before Frank Sinatra come to California, Siegel's legend loomed large. He was a star in a town of stars, possessing something no movie actor had: an aura of real danger. Bogart and Cagney and Eddie Robinson were only tough on the screen. George Raft had shady connections, but he was a lover, not a fighter. Siegel looked as good as any of them, and—it was whispered—he really killed people. Then it was more than whispered. In 1939, he was tried for the murder of a fellow L.A. hoodlum (and childhood friend) named Harry Greenberg; the newspapers covered the trial extensively, and though he got off, Siegel, who had been attempting to pass as a legitimate racetrack operator, was revealed as an authentic mobster. The papers loved to throw around his nickname, which he had come to hate. The word "Bugsy" alone could trigger the madness that had engendered the name.

When Sinatra came to town, there he was, the handsome criminal with the killer temper and the long-lashed blue eyes and clean jawline and slicked-back hair and beautiful sports jacket, sitting right across the aisle at Chasen's, winking at *him*. The man who (Sinatra would have known from Willie Moretti) had personally pushed the button on Maranzano. Who had grown up with Luciano and Lansky. Who still ran the West Coast.

Which was better, to be loved or feared?

Both.

Hello, Frank.

Hello, Mr. Siegel.

Please—Benny.

Benny.

"Phil and Frank were enthralled by him," said Phil Silvers's first wife, Jo-Carroll, of Siegel. "They would brag about Bugsy and what he had done and how many people he had killed. Sometimes they'd argue about whether Bugsy preferred to shoot his victims or simply chop them up with axes, and although I forget which was his preference, I will always remember the awe Frank had in his voice when he talked about him. He wanted to emulate Bugsy."

In the case of a competitor named Louis "Pretty" Amberg, Siegel covered all bases, setting Amberg's car ablaze after shotgunning him and hacking him with an ax, not necessarily in that order.

Tough guy. Frank poses for a publicity shot in 1947, the same year
he allegedly knocked down the virulently anti-Sinatra columnist
Lee Mortimer with one punch.

17

Manie Sacks, Sinatra's rabbi at Columbia Records, with Frank in 1944.
The singer's high-handedness in business matters caused bitter divisions
between the two close friends. "Don't friendship and sincerity mean
anything to you?" Manie wrote to Frank in 1945. "Or is it that, when you
make up your mind to do something, that's the way it has to be?"

Throughout 1945, as Sinatra recorded up a storm in New York and Hollywood, he was building up a thunderhead of resentment against Columbia Records. Money was the ostensible cause—the singer was bearing costs, for music copying and arrangements and studio conducting, that he felt weren't his to bear. (On the other hand, once he bought the arrangements, he owned them forever—a fact that would aid him innumerable times over the span of his performing career.) But on the evidence of a remarkable correspondence between Frank and Manie Sacks in the late summer of that year, it seems as though something else, something deep and personal, was behind the fight.

The opening salvo was a relatively petty complaint: a late July telegram from Sinatra to Sacks, grousing that Columbia must not think much of him, since everybody except him, including Axel, was getting free records. "Oh, well," he concluded. "After taxes I still have a few bucks." He signed with a sarcastic thank you.

And then, an extraordinary reply, not from Manie, but from some suit:

AUGUST 1, 1945. MR. FRANK SINATRA, 1051 VALLEY SPRING LANE, NORTH HOLLYWOOD, CALIFORNIA. RE YOUR BRUTAL WIRE TO OUR MR. SACKS. THIS IS YOUR AUTHORITY, ON PRE-SENTATION OF THIS TELEGRAM TO ANDREW SCHRADE, TO DEMAND ONE EACH OF ANY COLUMBIA RECORDS YOU WANT FOR YOUR COLLECTION.

Brutal wire! A letter from Manie arrived a week or two later, attempting to clear the air:

Dear Frank. For the past six months, there seems to be a question in your mind about certain payments which I am at a loss to understand. I've discussed the matters with Nancy, Sol Jaffe, Al Levy, Eddie Trautman [sic; Sacks evidently means Sinatra's business manager, Edward Traubner: see below]— in fact, with everyone except yourself. For some reason or another, the opportunity never presented itself, although I'd much have preferred talking to you in person rather than writing to you . . .

I want to preface my remarks, though, by telling you (and

this really goes without saying) that your interests are very important to me, and I wouldn't permit anybody to take advantage of you. But in fairness to you, and also to Columbia, I want to point out and explain why we can't do certain things.

In the case of Axel: You will recall standing on the corner of 51st Street and Broadway after we had finished lunch at Lindy's, when we discussed what Axel should get [as a conducting fee]. The price of $300 [about $3,500 today] was agreed upon as being more than fair. At that time, I explained to you how it wouldn't cost you $300: I would arrange with Axel to return to you the amount that he got from Columbia for each session, which is Scale, and that you would pay him $300. For example, if we have a record date and he received $80, you would pay him $300, the $80 would be turned over to you and actually would be a net [cost] to you of $220. There was never any question at that time that we should pay the full amount for Axel. In fact, I wrote Nancy on January 31st explaining this setup and sending her some of Axel's recording checks.

Look, son, if anyone received compensation of that kind from Columbia, believe me, you would be the first to get it, but it's never been done and we couldn't start a precedent of that kind. It's not good business, and I'm sure, if you'll analyze it, you'll agree with me. I'm not trying to bargain or be cheap because you know I'm not built that way. I'm only trying to point out a principle and also tell you that there was never any question about who was to pay Axel's salary. To enlighten you, do you recall you asked me to speak to Axel regarding the money you were to pay him, and I told you the same evening that everything was okay and that he seemed very happy about it?

Now, regarding the second matter, which I don't understand. Lately, I've been getting bills from Joe Ross for copying. What is that all about? His work is your property . . . How could we set a precedent of paying for copying when we have nothing to do with it? . . .

Let's take a Sinatra date—say the one of March 6th. There were 37 men and the cost was $1,905. This we paid for. In other words, the cost of the orchestra is not deducted from royalties—it's a flat outlay by Columbia. You're the only artist who has such an arrangement . . . If you'll think about it for a minute, I'm sure you'll understand that the conductor's fee and the copying costs are not obligations of Columbia. If you want, I could go to Ted [Wallerstein, Columbia president] and ask him to advance these monies to you and charge them against royalties.

I don't have to tell you about the way I worry and look out for your interests. I am certainly not trying to take advantage of you . . .

I miss you—come home soon. Love and kisses, Manie.

P.S.—I just got a letter from Traubner charging us $2100 for Axel's services up to the last date, and $300 for the last date— ALSO $400 for *arrangements*! Are we supposed to be paying for arrangements, too? What's this all about?

A couple of weeks pass, then Sinatra lets Sacks—or rather Columbia—have it. He begins the telegram with a complaint that he can't reach Manie on the phone, then goes on to say that it's not personal, but he doesn't plan to pay *any* of the bills. Not one. If Columbia Recording doesn't agree, Frank says, he will have to request an immediate release. He signs with love.

Sacks writes back immediately, in a letter of August 24, 1945:

Dear Frank: I received your wire and to say that I was taken aback and surprised is putting it mildly. I'm sorry we aren't able to discuss this in person or on the 'phone, but since there is nothing else to do, I'll have to write you my thoughts on this matter.

You said, "Whatever decision I arrive at does not concern you personally." Well, *who else* does it concern? All the negotiations that had to do with records or anything else were worked out by the two of us. Why, ever since you walked into my office the first time, I have gone through everything with you. Your problems have been as much a part of my life as my own. No one, with perhaps the exception of George Evans, has lived Sinatra as I have. Many is the night I have gone sleepless thinking and worrying about your problems. I could write pages on how we sweated them out together. Everything of concern to you concerns me, too . . . So your unreasonable demands are actually a slap in the face to me . . . I explained in my last letter exactly what the situation was and why we can't pay for arrangements, copying, and the fees for Axel . . . If you are doubting me or questioning my sincerity, that really hurts.

Do you think for a minute that, as head of the department you work for at Columbia, I'd let anyone take advantage of you—or do so myself? You have a better deal today than anyone else at Columbia. We can't pay for the things you've requested—your demands are entirely out of proportion.

You've had pretty much your own way and have done the things you wanted to do. So far you've recorded 49 sides, and we've released 32 sides—more than any other artist. You've had the pick of songs, you've recorded anything you want to, you've had greater promotion than anyone else with Columbia. You told me yourself that our promotion was the most outstanding you'd ever seen. Every one of us here at Columbia, from Ted Wallerstein down, has gone out of his way to make you happy. What more do you want? Just because you've made up your mind that Columbia should pay for things that are strictly your obligations and I can't tell you Columbia can't pay for them, you become annoyed and try to convince me it doesn't concern me personally, and you want your contract back.

As long as you're talking bluntly, I will, too. We have no

intention of paying for all the abovementioned extras. Just
because you asked for your contract back, there's no reason
why you should get it. We don't do business that way. I
don't know who has been putting these ideas into your head
or where you're getting them from. They don't sound like
Sinatra . . . I had an operation, it took a lot out of me, I've had
family difficulties of which you're well aware. But nothing
has hurt me as much as the wire I received from you. Don't
friendship and sincerity mean anything to you? Or is it that,
when you make up your mind to do something, that's the way
it has to be? I'm telling you, I've seen it happen and so have
you. If this is the attitude you want to adopt, it's got to hit
you—you just can't get away with it; life itself won't permit it.
Love, Manie.

No doubt Frank was nervous. Both Crosby and Harry James were
outperforming him on the *Billboard* charts, and he was in a tight race
with Perry Como. Dick Haymes was nipping at his heels. Manie Sacks
was just learning some hard lessons about his protégé: First, friendship and sincerity weren't even on the same page with success where
Sinatra was concerned. Second, when Sinatra made up his mind to do
something (right or wrong, as witness the Frank Garrick clash), that
was precisely what he would do. And third, life would permit him to
get away with it for another full half century.

Columbia stood firm. Yet despite the label's refusal to change its
policy on paying for music copying, conducting, or arrangements, Sinatra would remain there for seven more years. Manie Sacks was another
story. Disillusioned and unwell, he would leave the company almost
three years before the man he'd once thought was his best friend.

———

On October 17, Ava Gardner, the gorgeous MGM B-film player Sinatra
kept running into all over town, married Artie Shaw in Beverly Hills.
Gardner was not quite twenty-three. It was her second marriage (she

had divorced Mickey Rooney two years before), and Shaw's fifth. Shaw kept company with artists and intellectuals and tried to get Ava to start reading. Instead, she began drinking. The marriage would be over by the following fall.

———

Frank would test Manie's patience even further that autumn. In November the singer returned east for a three-week stand at the Paramount, then another engagement at the Wedgwood Room, and, in between, further recording sessions at Liederkranz Hall. But that wouldn't be all: Frank would turn thirty on December 12, and he wanted to end the year in style.

Success had intensified his cravings for class. Playing the Wedgwood Room helped: Cole Porter once again rode the elevator down from his Waldorf Towers suite to catch Sinatra's act. All that was gratifying, but ultimately, as Porter had written, merely massage.

One of the first things Frank had discovered as a recording artist was the difference between New York and Los Angeles studio musicians: West Coast instrumentalists, though every bit as virtuosic as their eastern counterparts, were far more relaxed, accommodating, showbiz savvy. Most of them made a good living playing movie scores. They knew how to adapt, take orders, work well with others.

Their Big Apple brethren, on the other hand, tended to be temperamental and egotistic classical artistes. The record producer George Avakian, who worked at Columbia in the mid-1940s, said, "They were tough-minded, insular people who were protective of their own positions—even which chair you were going to sit in." Many of the musicians initially looked down their noses at Sinatra. And since the singer already had huge respect for musical virtuosity, and a fine sense for clubs that didn't want him as a member, he courted their admiration.

But one of their number, substantially more ambitious than the rest, sought Frank out. Mitchell William Miller—Mitch for short—was a short, chin-bearded, energetic careerist from upstate New York, a brilliant classical oboist who had a deep love for jazz and popular music. A child prodigy, Miller had graduated at twenty-one from the Eastman School of Music in Rochester, where he'd formed an abiding musical friendship with his fellow student Alec Wilder—a.k.a. the Professor, the very man who had arranged and conducted Sinatra's musicianless Columbia sessions with the Bobby Tucker Singers.

Sinatra had been intrigued by Wilder's effortless musical intelligence, his rumpled academic quality, his endlessly digressive sentences, and (most of all) by the fact that unlike virtually everybody else the Professor seemed to have zero interest in kissing up to him. That was classy. When Miller pushed forward to introduce himself to Sinatra after a recording session, he also pushed his friend Wilder. Alec wasn't just an arranger and a conductor, Mitch said, but also a composer in both the popular and the classical idioms.

"He's got a few things I think you should listen to," Miller told Sinatra. The singer liked the oboist's nerve, which went well with his sweet playing.

The first couple of things, it turned out, were songs, one by Wilder and one by a quirky writer of rustic Americana named Willard Robison. Both, tellingly, had the word "old" in the title: "Old School Teacher," by Robison, and Wilder's "Just an Old Stone House." The two numbers, similar tonally and thematically, couldn't have been more different from the love ballads Frank Sinatra was recording in the mid-1940s. They were art songs, with melodies that wandered and twined and landed in unexpected places. It was brave and imaginative of Sinatra to want to record them, and it was nervy, even for him, to push Manie for studio time and musicians, musicians to be conducted not by Stordahl but by Mitch Miller. But Frank pushed, and Manie yielded. Sinatra and Miller recorded the songs.

When it came to Sinatra's next high-art initiative, though, Sacks drew the line. Frank, whose ears were opening up to all kinds of classical music, listened raptly to an air-check disc Miller had given him, containing two of Wilder's serious orchestral compositions. Sinatra played the record three or four times, then picked up the phone and tracked down the Professor. "These should be recorded," he said. He called Manie first thing in the morning and told him the same thing.

Manie begged to differ. He pleaded wartime shortages: "We don't have enough shellac to even press the stuff from our own artists."

"Sinatra gave us the bad news," Miller recalled. "So I came up with an idea. I said, 'Why don't *you* conduct them? Then he can't refuse you—if your name is on it.' And Frank agreed, although he had never conducted."

Never conducted? He couldn't read a note of music! It was a crazy idea, but to his eternal credit Frank went at the project—which, as Miller had predicted, Manie was forced into okaying—with grace, dignity, and even a kind of humility.

"Listen," he told the studio full of tough New York musicians gathered to play Wilder's airs for oboe, bassoon, flute, and English horn, as well as two other pieces. "I don't know the first thing about conducting, but I know this music and I love it, and if you'll work with me, I think we can get it down."

"That was a very strange session," recalled George Avakian. "I thought to myself, 'My God, Sinatra isn't a musician; this will be a disaster.' But it wasn't. He really did conduct. Alec, of course, rehearsed the orchestra thoroughly, and they were also all crack musicians. In fact, I think Mitch Miller played oboe on that."

He did indeed, but Miller—never one to hide his light under a bushel—also claims to have been in charge of the whole show. "Sinatra was then at the Waldorf [Wedgwood Room]," Miller said, "and he would finish at one in the morning. All the top musicians were there with us at the old Liederkranz Hall on Fifty-eighth Street. And I rehearsed all the stuff and got it ready, and Frank came in and he waved the stick. And he didn't get in the way."

One of the musicians who played on the session, the flutist Julius Baker, was more charitable. "You know," he said long afterward, "Sinatra wasn't so bad as a conductor."

Frank Sinatra Conducts the Music of Alec Wilder, the cover of Columbia Masterworks Set M-637 declared, when it was released the following spring. Sinatra's name was in considerably larger type than Wilder's, a fact Frank protested, but Columbia, Manie explained, had to sell *something.* The album cover was a black-and-white photo of a skeletally thin Sinatra, on a field of yellow, tieless, his white shirt buttoned to the neck, a belt tightly cinching the twenty-eight-inch waist of his pleated pants. He was raising his arms, his mouth open, his eyes closed as if in transport. His head was highlighted in a white circle, like the halos on medieval icons.

Columbia Masterworks Set M-637 was an album in the old sense: a cover with contents. Heavy contents. Inside the album were three twelve-inch shellac 78-rpm records, green labeled, each with one Wilder composition per side, six in all: Air for Oboe, Air for Bassoon, Air for Flute, Air for English Horn, Slow Dance, and Theme and Variations. Goddard Lieberson wrote the delightfully forthright liner notes:

> If you don't know already, this album of records—if nothing else—will convince you that Mr. Frank Sinatra is a very versatile young man. I am sure that he has no pretentions [*sic*] as a conductor, but on the other hand his conducting these pieces of Wilder is not merely an exercise of a whim. Frank is an idealist and an energetic reformer . . .
>
> [He] had never conducted before, and because of his position in a different world of music, the orchestra players first looked upon him with an ill-disguised cynicism. But it did not last long. Frank knew this music by heart, knew what he wanted, told them in a straightforward way what he expected of them, made intelligent suggestions and, in short, really conducted the orchestra.
>
> The result was not only smooth, but artistic and expressive.
>
> If you are reading these notes, it will mean that Frank has

accomplished one of his prime objectives as a conductor,
which is to introduce you to this music in which he so thoroughly believes.

———

Frank finished up the second and final session for the Wilder album
late on the night of December 10, and the following Monday, after the
stand at the Wedgwood was over, flew back home. There was a New
Year's Eve party to prepare. And a girl he'd been missing a lot.

He had bought her a diamond bracelet at Tiffany while he was in
Manhattan, a ridiculous outlay, almost half a week's take from the Paramount, but he was a man in love. They'd talked on the phone almost
every day while he was away—not easy, between his work schedule,
her work schedule, and her husband. Not to mention the long-distance
operators: it had forced them to speak in a kind of code, which was
frustrating, but also kind of romantic.

They didn't dare write.

Sinatra had had John the butler leave the Cadillac convertible at
the airport, so he could drive himself home. He thought of the bracelet when he was a half mile from home. The robin's egg blue box was
under clothes in his suitcase, and Nancy always unpacked his bags. He
couldn't put it in his pocket; he was about to be hugged. He opened
the car's glove compartment and hid the box as best he could.

Nancy found it there a couple of days before Christmas. She'd
driven over to her beauty parlor in Beverly Hills and, absurdly enough,
wanted to comb her hair before she went in. She saw the robin's egg
blue box. Frank had been sweet, if a little distracted, since getting back
home: He'd missed her, he said. And it was sweet; it reminded her of
how it had been before the children.

She undid the ribbon and opened the box.

Sitting in the car on Cañon Drive, Nancy put her hand to her
chest. The bracelet sparkled in the brazen California light, the most
beautiful thing she'd ever seen—it must have cost a fortune. He spent

it as he made it, she thought. The gold engraved Cartier lighters and cigarette cases for all his pals, even useful acquaintances, tens of thousands of dollars' worth. Whatever else he was, he was hers.

———

On Christmas morning, with Little Nancy and the baby happy under the big tree with their dolls and toys, he handed her a Tiffany box. A small Tiffany box. She blinked in confusion as she opened it and saw the pearl earrings. Her smile as she hugged him was deeply confused.

———

The party that year was especially splendid: The war was over! And the show this year would be like no other. Harry Crane had written comedy sketches; Sammy and Jule had created a whole evening's worth of songs; Dickie Whorf, a young director at Metro, had personally painted a Parisian street scene on the backdrop curtain and supervised the rehearsals.

The men wore black tie; the women, gowns. Sinatra stood at the front door and greeted the guests himself. The songs and the comedy were hilarious. Frank sang "Mammy" in blackface, complete with Jolson voice and head-shaking shtick; Phil Silvers's dazzling new wife, Jo-Carroll, a former Miss America from Texas, sang a number called "I'm the Wife of the Life of the Party," enumerating Phil's many flaws, especially his habit of breaking into comedy routines whether they were asked for or not. A sketch in which Cahn, Crane, and Peter Lawford played three restaurant patrons served by Sinatra brought down the house: when Lawford, a notorious cheapskate, asked for the check, Frank dropped a whole trayful of dishes.

Nancy, struck by an attack of shyness, mostly hovered around the kitchen, seeing to it that the food was served properly. She felt comfortable around the servants. Now and then she stuck her head out to catch a song or a sketch. She watched the beautiful women watching Frank, watched their gleaming eyes and avid smiles, and felt sick with worry.

Then she shook her head in bewilderment at the sight of sweet-faced Marilyn Maxwell, sitting next to her handsome husband, John Conte, watching Frank sing with that *look* in her eyes. When Marilyn reached up to push aside a few strands of that perfect blond hair, the way women do when they're attracted to a man, there it was, glittering unmistakably, like the palest chips of ice. Her bracelet. And at that moment, Nancy literally had to hold on to the doorway for support: the earth had spun off its axis.

Frank clowns at a CBS rehearsal, circa 1944. Joking aside, however, the man who couldn't read music really could conduct.

Act Four

ICARUS

||||||||||||||||||||

"Let me welcome you to the MGM family."
"I'm proud to be in that family, sir."
—Louis B. Mayer and Frank Sinatra, on the radio show
Old Gold Presents Songs by Sinatra

===

Frank and the two Nancys, 1945. "Daddy was . . . a voice on the radio most of the time," Nancy junior wrote, years later. "A figure composed of a bow tie and two black patent leather shoes, who was always going away."

S he felt as if someone had smacked her in the face. Then she collected herself, straightening her shoulders, and walked across the room. She leaned over and took the woman's wrist—the wrist with the bracelet—and looked Marilyn Maxwell in the eyes.

She would have to leave. At once.

Marilyn just stared at her, saying nothing, admitting everything.

It was all done quickly, quietly, efficiently, so the all-important party could come to its triumphant conclusion. For all anyone knew, there had been a minor family emergency of some sort. The couple simply got up and left. Frank, trouper that he was, continued the song even as he watched what was going on in front of him. He got a big hand.

Afterward, in the bedroom (he wouldn't share it that night), he tried, as best he could, swearing she didn't mean anything to him.

His wife looked at him coldly.

It was a long, slow climb back toward civility, beginning with a week of silent penance and followed by a full floral offensive, bouquet after gigantic bouquet, all of which she loftily ignored. Frank stayed uncharacteristically close to home in the beginning of 1946, not even venturing into the recording studio until early February, then bringing Nancy, as tribute, a test pressing of one of the day's four cuts, a sappy something called "One Love" ("How sweet the way you play upon my heartstrings / How strange when you're away, you give my heart wings").

She ignored him, but she didn't smash the record.

═══

Maybe she should have. At this point in his career, Sinatra was doing what he would continue to do until the end of the line: look for hits. But this process was dicey, subject as the singer was to the whims of the marketplace and the tenor of the times. And in those days the times were tricky. The mid-1940s brought two paradoxical trends to American music: the rise of the singer at the expense of the big bands, and the decline of popular songwriting. Frank himself had much to do with the former,[1] but was powerless to change the latter. Times change; tastes change: the war's end had brought a kind of giddiness to the American zeitgeist, the result of post-traumatic stress and new fears. The longing wartime ballads that had made Sinatra's reputation were suddenly uncongenial to the national ear. Cheesy novelty numbers began to pop up like toadstools after a rainstorm. Kern and Gershwin were dead. Berlin and Porter were writing almost exclusively for Broadway, and while musicals continued to be a rich vein of material, the days of Tin Pan Alley cranking out lovely tunes that went straight to sheet music, records, and radio were swiftly coming to a close.

Astonishing as it may be to think about today, the idea of the standard—the great and lasting popular song, from the hands of one of the above-mentioned geniuses, or others such as Harold Arlen, Harry Warren, and Hoagy Carmichael—didn't really exist at the end of World War II. There was just a lot of music out there: great songs, good songs, fair songs, and poor songs, among which not even a great artist like Sinatra could always be depended on to navigate reliably.

He got an early leg up from a man who would become a romantic rival (and probably because of this, a Sinatra hater till the end of his life): Artie Shaw. Early in his career, the mercurial, intellectually arrogant clarinetist and bandleader hit on a simple but brilliant notion. "As Shaw put it," Will Friedwald writes, "the idea was to take the best possible songs and orchestrate them in the best possible way." With this guideline in mind, Shaw resurrected great (but incredibly enough, lightly dust-coated) tunes such as Porter's "Begin the Beguine," Kern's "All the Things You Are," and Gershwin's "The Man I Love" and made huge hit records of them.

Sinatra had ears, and he heard.

Also starting in the early 1940s, Sammy Cahn began scouting for him. "I take great pride in the fact that I introduced Frank to a lot of the great, great songs," he told Friedwald. He would continue to do so throughout their long professional relationship. But Frank was a lightning-fast learner, and the two geniuses behind his first album, which was issued in March 1946 and consisted almost entirely of what would come to be called standards, were Sinatra himself and the warm businessman Manie Sacks.

As previously noted, Frank recorded prodigiously in 1945. He committed to disc "Where or When" and "All the Things You Are" and "If I Loved You," and he also recorded "Mighty Lak' a Rose" and "Lily Belle" and "My Shawl," as well as a couple of dozen other mostly forgotten tunes. Yet in two sessions—one on July 30 in Hollywood, one on

December 7 in New York—he recorded eight numbers, six of which were masterpieces of songwriting, and these eight songs became the four discs of Columbia Set C-112, *The Voice of Frank Sinatra*. It was not only Frank's first album but also the first thematic album of popular music available to the American public.[2]

It was a time when Frank Sinatra's singing could be heard profusely, on the radio or in live performance or on shellac 78-rpm discs; yet it was also a time when the very notion of a Frank Sinatra album—indeed, of a phonograph album period—was new and exotic. An *album* was what you put stamps or family photos or butterflies in. Yet now you could buy a wide, flat, heavy box with four records inside, with Sinatra's curly-haired, red-bow-tied, grinning image on the 1940s-Moderne cover (dancing white, yellow, and black ellipses on a field of teal; a hint of Miró and Calder), selling for the not inconsiderable retail price of $2.50, the equivalent of $30 today. And the people bought it. By the tens of thousands. Canny businessman that he was, Sacks had paid attention to Frank's masterly (and unprecedented) notion of a musical self-portrait. He had put a new and irresistible product in a new and irresistible package, raising the price but also raising the game. In a very real way, Frank and Manie, together, had reinvented Sinatra.

The bobby-soxers could keep swooning over their fifty-cent discs of "One Love" or "I Dream of You"; but here was a box of music for grown-ups. The theme was adult love: J. Fred Coots and Haven Gillespie's "You Go to My Head"; George and Ira Gershwin's "Someone to Watch over Me"; Strachey, Link, and Marvell's "These Foolish Things"; Cole Porter's "Why Shouldn't I?"; Woods, Campbell, and Connelly's hymn to barefoot and pregnant, "Try a Little Tenderness"; Victor Young, Ned Washington, and Bing Crosby's "(I Don't Stand) A Ghost of a Chance."

The nod to Crosby was intentional. Bing had made hit recordings of "Ghost of a Chance" and "Tenderness" in the 1930s, and had also been first with "Paradise." He was still number 1 on the charts to Sinatra's number 2. Frank was paying tribute, but he was also throwing down the gauntlet. He was Picasso to the older singer's Matisse, coming on fast and strong.

And the market responded. Just over two weeks after *The Voice*'s release on March 4, it entered the *Billboard* Top 5 chart, and soon it hit number 1, a position it would hold for seven weeks. The album simply exploded onto the American consciousness, fixing Sinatra's reputation as not merely a crooner but a *singer*. "I was working in a record store," recalled the music publisher Frank Military, "and Dean Martin came in every day to see me. And one day *The Voice* album came in, and it sold like hotcakes. I didn't know Frank, and Dean didn't know Frank, but the two of us just sat there listening to all four 78s over and over."

They were something to hear. Sinatra had purposely chosen the July 30 and December 7 sessions not just because they contained great songs but because of their beautifully spare settings: in each case, a nine-piece string, woodwind, and rhythm ensemble highlighted his voice perfectly. These small-group tracks sounded brand-new and special. Even the two lesser numbers, "I Don't Know Why," of fateful Paramount memory—music to get egged by—and "Paradise," were quietly ravishing, in the former case because of George Van Eps's restrained and lyrical guitar work, and in the latter because of Mitch Miller's sublime oboe.

The singing was exquisitely tender and exact and assured and, most important, it was *Sinatra*. At thirty, he had cast off all influences and become, completely, himself. If he had ever sounded like Bing, he didn't anymore. If he had ever wanted to *be* Bing, he didn't anymore. And he wasn't Frankie anymore, either. Now he was just Frank.

═══

Three days after the release of *The Voice*, Sinatra, along with the producer Frank Ross and the co-producer and director Mervyn LeRoy, attended the Oscar ceremonies at Grauman's Chinese Theatre, where they received their special Academy Awards for *The House I Live In*. Nancy accompanied her husband. A photo taken of them afterward at Ciro's shows them together like the cutest couple in Hollywood. Frank is in black tie; Nancy is wearing a strapless evening gown. Her hair is up; she wears a pearl choker; her creamy décolletage is lovely to behold. She is a beautiful young woman; he is a handsome young man. Their shoulders are touching.

And yet it is a strange picture: The two of them seem both intimate and distant. Frank is ardently admiring his Oscar; Nancy is smiling at someone across the table. A real couple sitting this close would be holding hands, or at least touching fingers. Yet he holds the statuette in his left hand, and rests his right, with its big pinkie ring, on the table, almost willfully distant from her. Nancy's left hand, the one closest to Frank, also lies awkwardly on the table. And on her left wrist is what looks very much like a diamond bracelet.

———

What goes on behind any couple's bedroom door is one of the great mysteries, but history can say with some certainty that he was outside that door for several weeks after New Year's, and then, one night, he was back in again. There were conditions, there were strictures and continued reproaches, but he was back in again.

Did she believe him? Naturally she wanted to; at the same time, she wasn't a fool. She knew that their life as a couple was anything but simple. Yet she needed his promises, not merely to hear the words, but for the sake of her dignity. She needed Frank to remember that he had made this commitment—that whatever he did elsewhere, he would be thinking about her.

———

As spring lit Hollywood in a blaze of jacarandas and azaleas, Sinatra was making movies again, once more commuting to Culver City. First there was a cameo in a Jerome Kern biopic, *Till the Clouds Roll By*. At Mr. Mayer's behest, Frank sang "Ol' Man River" in a white suit, white bow tie, and white shoes, surrounded by a forty-piece (white) orchestra similarly attired. (The critics would justifiably kill him for it, but it really wasn't his fault. And the performance was magnificent.)

There was also a new picture, a musical called *It Happened in Brooklyn*. Frank was to play an Army vet (if the Duke could play soldier, so could he) named Danny Miller, returning from the war to find that the Brooklyn he'd lovingly obsessed about while overseas was not quite as he remembered. Jimmy Durante and Kathryn Grayson were to co-star, as well as—a nice surprise—his new pal Peter Lawford, portraying a sensitive young English composer named Jamie Shellgrove. (Of *course* he was a poofter. How could he not be a poofter with a name like Jamie Shellgrove?) Principal photography on the film began on the MGM back lot in March; in June, the company would travel to New York City for location work.

But in the meantime, there was the Metro lot, with its deeply shaded alleys between soundstages and sunstruck fake Main Streets and phony city blocks and its commissary and dressing rooms, and its many actresses—stars and supporting players and extras—every one of them beautiful, every one of them wanting him.

And he, of course, wanted them.

He saw *her*, Marvelous, on his first day back, walking across a knife-edge of shadow between buildings, her hair like the sun. They shook hands, just shook hands (passersby were watching them carefully, pretending not to). Frank suddenly remembered, just for a second, his promise that he would never speak to her again. But as his palm touched hers, her perfume, that perfume, made his brain turn over.

She smiled brightly and told him she was divorcing her husband. She would be free at last.

He smiled back. People were watching.

She didn't give a damn who was watching. She was going to be free at last. Did he want her?

He took a deep breath, inhaling her perfume.

More than anything.

Not three minutes later, turning a corner on his way to his dressing room, he came upon Lana, walking out of a soundstage in horn-rimmed sunglasses, dictating something to a secretary who followed her attentively. Lana saw him, and waved a dismissive hand to the secretary.

She looked at him and lowered her glasses, smiling.

And there were others, too, of course.

On March 7, 1946, United Press put a story on the wires about a forty-five-year-old New York construction-company executive, one Sven Ingildsen, who had filed a cross complaint in state supreme court to the separation action brought by his twenty-year-old wife, Josephine. "The day after our marriage, my wife told me she simply had to see Frank Sinatra, the singer, alone—both at the theater where he was appearing and in his apartment at the Waldorf-Astoria Hotel," Ingildsen's petition stated. "I objected emphatically. She replied that she knew him and his wife and that it would only be for a short visit and she would return in no time."

Frank Sinatra's wife was, of course, in Los Angeles. And newlywed Josephine Ingildsen (the report said) didn't return home to her husband until 5:00 a.m.

"If I had as many love affairs as you've given me credit for," Frank would tell reporters many years later, "I'd now be speaking to you from a jar in Harvard Medical School." It was a great quote, a true Sinatra quote, poetry down to the deliciously absurd image, the inner rhyme of "jar" and "Harvard"—except that it was an evasion. No, it was more than an evasion, it was the Big Lie. "Love affairs" was more than a euphemism, but less than the truth: Love was always what it was about, and never quite what it was really about. Love was the fleeting ideal, the thing to be sung about, to be dreamed of while he zipped his trousers on his way from one conquest to the next. In truth, there were probably even more affairs than the hundreds he'd been given credit for. For there always had to be someone. His loneliness was bottomless, but there was always someone to try to help him find the bottom.

At the end of March, Sinatra set out on a cross-country concert tour. He would play San Francisco, Philadelphia, Detroit, New York, and Chicago through June, then return to the Coast and perform at the Hollywood Bowl in August. Location work on *It Happened in Brooklyn* would proceed while he was in New York. Marilyn had planned a trip to Manhattan for early June, to clear her head and buy some clothes: they could spend days together, discussing the future.

Lana, as it turned out, was also going to be in New York, for the premiere of her big new picture, *The Postman Always Rings Twice*. In her career-defining role, she played a scheming adulteress to such sizzling perfection that MGM insisted her character dress all in white to mute the impression.

The concert tour was a huge success. Sinatra was at the zenith of his popularity. *Anchors Aweigh* had made him a major movie star; *The House I Live In* had made him the national voice of tolerance. In between concerts, he commuted back to Los Angeles for the weekly broadcast of his new radio show, *Old Gold Presents Songs by Sinatra*. Era-appropriate cigarette hawking aside ("Yes, light an Old Gold for cigarette comfort and pleasure! The comfort of extra protection against cigarette dryness, the pleasure of luxurious extra flavor!"), the show was classy—and all-Sinatra—from start to finish. He opened each program with a soulful version of "Night and Day," slightly slowed to make it more a concert piece than a dance number. The new tempo was a powerful statement, telling the world he'd now taken full ownership of the gorgeous song whose lyrics he'd fluffed before its composer just seven years earlier at the Rustic Cabin. Frank closed each broadcast with his lovely signature tune "Put Your Dreams Away." "Sinatra," Friedwald writes, "featured songs for the ages as often as he did the best new numbers and his own hits, and even devoted whole programs to the works of Jerome Kern, Johnny Mercer, Irving Berlin, and their peers."

The new album affirmed his dominance. The week he played the

Golden Gate Theatre in San Francisco (along with the Pied Pipers, who had left Dorsey and become a hit act on their own) was the same week *The Voice of Frank Sinatra* began its ascent to number 1 on the *Billboard* charts. The crowds swelled. In Philadelphia, he played to a house of ten thousand at the Convention Hall (the acoustics were beside the point). And in Detroit, the mass-steria was such that even his new friends at the Federal Bureau of Investigation took notice. When Sinatra arrived in the Motor City on May 8, no less a personage than Louis B. Nichols, one of J. Edgar Hoover's top aides, went to observe the goings-on. A few days later, the stunned G-man wrote a memo to the director:

> As a symptom of the state of mind of many young people
> I wish to call to your attention the following incident that
> occurred in Detroit on last Wednesday.
>   Frank Sinatra arrived in Detroit around midnight and a
> group of bobby soxers were waiting for him at the airfield.
> He eluded them and they then congregated at the stage
> door of the Downtown Theater where he was scheduled to
> give his first performance around 10:00 a.m. on Thursday
> morning. The line started forming at around 2:00 a.m. The
> police started challenging girls who appeared to be under 16
> and tried to send them home. However, I have been told,
> there was a long line of mere kids, many of whom carried
> their lunches, and they remained in line until the theater
> opened. Truant Officers started checking the lines early in the
> morning and were berated by the girls. There was widespread
> indignation on the part of numerous individuals that I came
> in contact with and a severe indictment [by] parents of the
> girls. One individual went so far as to state that Sinatra
> should be lynched.

Hoover was impressed. "Sinatra is as much to blame as the moronic bobby-soxers," he scrawled across the bottom of the memo.

At the Chicago Theatre later that month, the singer was paid $41,000—the equivalent of almost $450,000 now—for his week's work. And in New York, the Paramount wasn't big enough for him anymore. This time Sinatra was booked at Madison Square Garden, which could hold close to twenty-five thousand. The sight lines were miserable, especially from the cheap seats, and since smoking was allowed, a thick blue haze tended to gather in the balconies. In between coughing fits, the patrons in the upper rows would have barely been able to make out the tiny figure on the stage. The sound system was awful. But it was Sinatra!

He began location work for *It Happened in Brooklyn,* in Brooklyn. Dickie Whorf quickly discovered that it was one thing to direct a New Year's Eve show at Frank's house and quite another thing to direct him in a movie. Others were learning what Manie Sacks had learned, to his sorrow. Whorf, a darkly handsome, easygoing New Englander, was a man Frank liked, but the star tested the young director's patience to the limit. As Sinatra had discovered on *Anchors Aweigh,* being on a movie set made him anxious and panicky. He would leave at the slightest excuse—or simply not show up. "I got a break when we were starting this new picture in New York," he said later. "We were shooting on the Brooklyn Bridge. We'd get out there in the morning and there'd be fog, so I wouldn't have to work all day."

There were many distractions, but chiefly there was Marilyn Maxwell. All his cronies knew about Marvelous—in fact, most of New York knew. Certainly the staff at the Waldorf-Astoria were aware. She and Frank spent a lot of time in his suite, and when they went out, they were seen dining and dancing at all the right places. Marilyn visited him frequently on the set in Brooklyn, sometimes spiriting him away.

An MGM production memo for July 7:

Company had early call, stood by until 1:00 P.M., then called Sinatra to be ready at 3:15 P.M., sent car for him but could not locate him. Sinatra never came. Waited until 5:50 P.M. at doubletime on crew.

The crew rolled their eyes. His pals rolled their eyes. Sinatra was walking on air.

Toots Shor finally put his foot down when Frank said he'd be bringing Marilyn to the title bout between Billy Conn and Joe Louis at Yankee Stadium. For one thing, the fights were by definition masculine territory. When and if a lady came along, it was a big deal. All that pale flesh and perfume tended to attract attention around the ring. Especially if the lady happened to be the knockout date of a famous man with a wife.

Toots Shor was not amused at the prospect of seeing Marilyn Maxwell on Sinatra's arm smack in the middle of Yankee Stadium—not least because he planned on bringing Mrs. Toots to the fight. The presence of Frank's date would be insulting to the missus, to the institution of marriage itself. Not to mention the fact that the big rematch between Conn and Louis was to be televised, one of the first major sporting events ever to appear on the magic box. Thousands would be watching. But when Shor told Sinatra, in all gruff seriousness, that the only woman Sinatra could ever think about bringing was Mrs. Sinatra, the crumb bum looked at him and winked. Winked!

Toots shouldn't worry a bit—Marvelous would behave herself.

It was an impossible situation. So Toots called Manie, and Manie, having more or less given up on talking Frank out of irrational behavior, called Evans. Evans took a big gulp from the bottle of Maalox he kept handy in a desk drawer.

His client's life was rapidly heading for trouble. During the last year Sinatra had been Mr. Humanitarian, grabbing awards, neatly sidestepping the gossip. But Sinatra was Sinatra. There was just too much blatant misbehavior. Evans could only outflank the gossips for so long. The publicist had done his best and then hoped for the best, always a bad strategy. With Sinatra, the worst could always be counted on. "Frank was born to be a star," he once mused to a reporter. "But he was also born to be a controversial figure, and a star and controversial figure he will remain until the day he dies."

Evans knew about the production delays on *It Happened in Brooklyn*: the no-shows, the tantrums, the running battle with Jimmy Durante, the nicest man in the world. Sick of being stood up by Sinatra when the cameras were ready to roll, Durante had taken to disappearing himself. Whorf was looking gray faced. And Evans knew more than he wanted to know about Marilyn Maxwell.

Drastic measures were called for. The publicist phoned Maxwell at her hotel and came straight to the point. She had a morals clause in her MGM contract. Frank was a married man. Her own divorce was not yet final. Did he have to spell it all out for her?

She began to weep. He was being terrible.

Evans spoke gently but firmly. This was a terrible situation. A marriage was in jeopardy, and the emotional stability of two small children at stake. A little girl going into the first grade. A little boy waiting for his daddy to come home.

She wailed over the phone.

But she was the one who could make it all right. Marilyn could walk away and face the world with her head held high.

Frank called her an hour later and got the full waterworks. When he was finally able to make sense of what she was saying, he understood that they were not going to be able to see each other anymore. He didn't sound quite as devastated as she would have hoped. They'd figure it all out somehow. That was when she knew it was all over.

He went to the fight anyway on Wednesday night, with Mr. and Mrs. Toots and Marlene Dietrich and Joe DiMaggio. An odd couple indeed: Dietrich was thirteen years older than the Clipper and not his type at all (who was?), but there they were together, taking the evening toward its inevitable conclusion. (Later he would report, unchivalrously, that she had bad breath.) DiMag got the expected reaction at Yankee Stadium, a hero in his first season back from the war, rusty after the break but a hero anyway. Sinatra didn't mind a bit. (He was glad he hadn't had to take a break—he might've gotten worse than rusty. He might've gotten dead.) Nor did Frank mind being the fifth wheel: he was in oddly cheery spirits that night. He and Marlene exchanged wry looks while Joe, breathing through his mouth the way he did, gazed at the other Joe, the Brown Bomber, beating up Conn in the blinding white arc lights.

Later that night Frank called up Lana, who had stayed in town after the premiere of *Postman*. She was delighted to hear from him.

There were still other distractions that summer. Sinatra's quickly burgeoning FBI file reads: "The New York Office was advised by Frances Duffy, clerk of the Local Selective Service Board #180, New York City, that she resides at 424 Second Street, Brooklyn, New York, in a home owned by Mrs. Mary Fischetti. Miss Duffy stated that Sinatra, accompanied by Charles Fischetti, visited the home of [Fischetti's] mother and spent the evening there in about June of 1946."

The whole scene is sweetly absurd: Miss Duffy, the timid clerk at the Local Selective Service Board, renter of a small apartment (cat, crucifixes, lace doilies) in the brownstone of kindly widow Fischetti on quiet, tree-lined Second Street in Park Slope, had clearly seen Charles Fischetti before, and was clearly of a suspicious turn of mind. Though the silver-haired gent liked to pose as an art collector and sometimes introduced himself as Dr. Fisher, he was in fact a gangster, also known as Trigger Happy or, among friends, Prince Charlie. He was the oldest and most distinguished-looking of the crooked Fischetti brothers (the others were Rocco, three years younger, and Joe, the baby of the family). First cousins to Al Capone, the Fischettis had worked as Scarface's bodyguards during Prohibition and were now highly placed crooks in Chicago. They wintered in Miami, in a beautiful mansion in the exclusive enclave of Allison Island. There seemed no reason for Sinatra to have spent an evening with Charles Fischetti and Fischetti's mother in June 1946, when he was in the midst of shooting a movie.

As you might imagine, there is no dearth of speculation on the subject. Some sources mention darkly that the Sinatras had neighbors named Fischetti back in the cold-water-flat days, and that Frank was friends with one of the Fischetti children. In fact, census records tell us that there were Fischettis on Monroe Street in the 1920s, two large families of them, and that the heads of both households were in what was then called the junk business—waste management.

But a lot of Italian immigrants were in the junk business in the 1920s, and certainly not all of them were criminals. Moreover, Fischetti was a reasonably common surname (as, for that matter, was Sinatra). Maybe the Hoboken Fischettis were related to the Chicago Fischettis; maybe not.

Here's a wild hypothesis: What if Charlie Fischetti, having recently been introduced by his old pal Willie Moretti to Willie's pal Sinatra, was simply bringing Frank Sinatra over that night to impress his mom?

On the other hand, there is reason to believe that Prince Charlie had a small request to make of Sinatra that evening. And in truth, from here on, the Fischettis would begin to stick to Sinatra in increasingly disconcerting ways. In August 1946, according to the FBI, which was keeping a close eye on the brothers,[3] Charlie and Joe contacted Sinatra to ask him to get them hotel reservations in New York—probably at the Waldorf—so they could attend the Army–Notre Dame game at Yankee Stadium, a much-anticipated matchup between two football titans. (No doubt Charlie and Joe had a financial interest in the game; no doubt they were unpleasantly surprised by the final score: 0–0.) Sinatra got them deluxe suites. In gratitude, the boys sent him two dozen custom-made shirts.

The incident sounds innocuous, but it would have been remarkable if some of the table talk between Frank and Charlie that summer and fall hadn't concerned Benny Siegel. If, as seems likely, Sinatra had confessed his admiration for the Bug, Fischetti probably would have demurred.

That was a horse Frank might not want to bet on. Benny had been a naughty boy.

The specific complaint concerned funds forwarded to Siegel by

Meyer Lansky for the specific purpose of building the Flamingo Hotel and Casino in Las Vegas. The word filtering back to the Mob was that of every dollar Benny had received—and the sum now ran well into the millions—he was forwarding (via a courier, his girlfriend Virginia Hill) a significant portion to his private bank account in Switzerland. In casino terminology, this is known as the skim. In reality, Bugsy Siegel was nothing like the semi-saintly visionary Warren Beatty played in the movies: in reality, Siegel's gruesome slaughter of his fellow gangster Louis Amberg was just another day's work, and the dream of a great Hollywood-style hotel-casino in the desert was not even his. The true visionary was Billy Wilkerson, founder of the *Hollywood Reporter,* Ciro's, and Trocadero—not to mention the discoverer of Lana Turner. Soon after Wilkerson began erecting the Flamingo, he had made the mistake of running low on funds. Back east, Lansky, who missed nothing, saw an opportunity to muscle in. He called his old Lower East Side landsman Benny Siegel and asked if Benny might be interested in a major stake in a casino. It took some convincing—Benny was happy living the high life in Hollywood. Now he was not only racking

The Varsity—or a portion thereof. Frank rides on Toots Shor's back while Rags Ragland looks on adoringly. Jule Styne is directly to Shor's left. September 1944.

up enormous cost overruns with outlandish construction add-ons but also blatantly stealing from the heads of the Mob. He had come by his nickname rightly.

Hearing the inside story for the first time, Sinatra whistled softly and looked at the bankerly Fischetti with fresh admiration. Where the Boys were concerned, Frank was always admiring: he just couldn't help himself.

19
||||||||||

Serious trouble. Frank dances with Lana Turner,
with his very visible wedding ring giving the world
quite a mixed message. June 1946.

In the meantime, there was Lana. As much as Frank had loved Marilyn, it seemed to him in the late summer of 1946 that he was twice as crazy about Lana Turner. Later he would tell Hedda Hopper, "I haven't much to say in my defense except that I was in a terrible state of mental confusion." A nightclub photograph from the period confirms this. The picture shows Sinatra and Turner dancing close, Lana in a polka-dot blouse, her lush blond hair pulled up into elaborate whirls and topped with a kind of snood. She's smiling happily. Frank, in a gray suit with white pocket square, looks ecstatic. There are thousands of pictures of Sinatra smiling, but extremely few in which he's grinning with such complete lack of restraint. Eyes slit with pleasure, he looks like an eleven-year-old at his birthday party. His left hand is clasped tightly with Lana's right, and there on the fourth finger, for the photographer and all the rest of the world (including Nancy) to see, is his wedding band.

What was he thinking? Clearly, he wasn't thinking. He'd come back to L.A. in the middle of July and flown straight into Lana's arms. "Sinatra arrived from New York but reported he was ill and didn't work," the production memo of July 17 reported. On the other hand, perhaps he really was exhausted. Besides singing concerts, intermittently shooting a movie, making speeches, attending prizefights and ball games, rubbing elbows with mafiosi, and screwing around, Frank was recording at a blistering rate: five sessions and eighteen songs since February. After July he would pick up the pace. He was still in wonderful voice when he recorded "Begin the Beguine" and "How Deep Is the Ocean?" but, interestingly, the two versions he recorded of Rodgers and Hammerstein's great "Soliloquy" from *Carousel*, while pleasantly sung, don't really do justice to the material.

Maybe he just hadn't enough sense yet of what it meant to be a father. *When I think of all the family affairs and events I would miss over the years because I was on the road . . .*

Even when he was at home, he was on the road.

———

On August 20, Rags Ragland died. The cause was acute kidney failure, after, according to Earl Wilson, "an over-festive vacation in Mexico." Given the state of medicine in those days, who knows? In any case, the death was tragically premature: the hulking comic was three days shy of his forty-first birthday. His sudden demise came as a massive shock to Frank, who stood vigil at Ragland's hospital bedside along with Rags's old Minsky's Burlesque partner Phil Silvers. It was the first time Frank had witnessed the death of a close friend and near contemporary.

Among the deceased's possessions was a gold Cartier cigarette case, engraved TO RAGS FROM RICHES.

Sinatra sang at the funeral with tears in his eyes, as much for himself as for his friend: the absolute injustice and indignity of it all made him furious. With few exceptions after that, Frank resolutely avoided hospitals and funerals. Not only were illness and death unpleasant to witness, but they might also be contagious.[1]

> *You get word before the show has started*
> *That your favorite uncle died at dawn.*
> —Irving Berlin, "There's No Business Like Show Business"

Two days later, Frank was back in the CBS studio, recording four numbers, including "There's No Business Like Show Business." His rendition is game enough, but overall—quite understandably—shockingly dispirited: it sounds as though Stordahl's sprightly thirty-five-piece orchestra, plus the male chorus, is carrying all 127 pounds of the singer.

That was Thursday. On Monday morning, Frank was on the set at Culver City, but he was just phoning it in. It wasn't just the thought of Rags. Phil Silvers was calling every few hours, sounding desperate. Several weeks before, the comic had snagged a plum booking: the Copacabana, his first time. The problem was that the Copa had signed Silvers and Rags Ragland as a team.

Silvers telephoned Jules Podell the day after Rags's death to explain that he couldn't possibly make the booking, and—not entirely to the comic's surprise—Podell informed him, in terms both blunt and obscene, that Silvers would go on solo or he could forget about the Copacabana forever.

Playing the Copa was a career maker; banishment could have the opposite effect. But Silvers wasn't a solo. He was a top banana, and a top banana needed a stooge. Could Frank help him out? Phil didn't have to mention the beautiful music the two of them had made together playing exactly those roles on last year's USO tour—the tour that, thanks largely to Phil, had rescued Frank's reputation among thousands of GIs. On the other hand, you couldn't call in favors with Sinatra. When the comic pleaded, again and again, for the singer to step into the breach, Frank was glum. He hated being put on the spot; he hated not being able to be magnanimous. "I'd come in, but I can't leave the picture," he said.

It wasn't as if he hadn't left it plenty of times already, but that was just the problem. It was one thing to displease Dickie Whorf and Jimmy Durante and Kathryn Grayson; it was something else to displease L. B. Mayer. Now that Sinatra was back on the Coast, the Chief had called him in to his office, to discuss many things, including Frank's absences.

Going to Mayer's office was like being summoned by the principal, and then some. It could mean a lecture on any subject at all. First Frank had to face the boss's assistant Ida Koverman, a former secretary to Herbert Hoover and a formidable presence in her own right. Ida would welcome Sinatra briskly, send him into an antechamber, and close the door behind him. There was a moment of claustrophobic panic—then Ida pushed a button that opened the door to Mayer's office, revealing a long, long room, the little mogul behind his huge desk at the other end. The desk was on a platform, so that the Chief loomed above all visitors: from his side of the desk, Frank could see LB's feet, not quite reaching the ground.

His tone with Frank this time was warm and fatherly. But the message was clear: behave. *We are a family. Families pull together.*

Then Labor Day weekend came. The cast and crew were given both Monday and Tuesday off for the holiday. Frank paced, then decided.

MGM production memo for Wednesday, September 4, 1946:

Sinatra telephoned in to say he was ill but we were later informed that he had left for New York without permission.

Phil Silvers played the Copa dinner show solo on Thursday the fifth. He told jokes, made fun of the waiters, sang a few songs; the clink of tableware and the buzz of conversation were louder than the laughs. A waiter dropped a tray in the middle of a song. Silvers exited to polite applause. He sat in his dressing room, his bald dome still glistening with flop sweat. Like many comics, he was a gloomy, fearful man. This was what it came down to, he thought. You blew off the gig and got banned, or you just plain blew it and didn't get asked back.

Then there was a bustle outside, and the door popped open. It was Frank, grinning like a cat with a mouthful of canaries.

They sprang into action for the 10:00 p.m. show. Sinatra sat, as unobtrusively as possible, at a ringside table. Silvers marched out, reenergized, to the first few bars of "Fine and Dandy" and beamed at the audience.

"Good evening, ladies and gentlemen, and welcome to the world-famous Copacabana," he said. "And speaking of famous—turn on the house lights a minute, will ya? If there's anybody here tonight who's famous, I want to introduce them."

Up came the lights, the crowd clamoring at the sight of Sinatra. Silvers stared at the singer without comment. "Okay, turn down the lights," the comic said.

Full of confidence, he started his routine. Then he touched his tie and Frank rose and joined him. The place went nuts, the audience jumping to its feet. Silvers and Sinatra did the USO routine all over again: singing lessons for Frank, Phil pinching Sinatra's cheek, even a sharp slap or two when the stupid pupil just couldn't get it right.

The crowd ate it up. They stood again when Sinatra sat back down without bowing, yielding the floor to Silvers. At the end, Phil beckoned him back, and they took their bows together. Then the comic administered a killer.

"May I take a bow for Rags?" he said.

The place went dead quiet. Even Podell teared up. Sinatra stared at the floor. Fortunately, a *Variety* reporter was there to witness the whole thing. SINATRA'S STOOGERY FOR PHIL SILVERS NY NITERY PREEM AN INSPIRED EVENT, the headline read the next morning. The accompanying story said, "That appreciative gesture by Sinatra understandably sets him in a niche all his own in the big, sentimental heart of show business."

The reaction of the sentimental but businesslike Louis B. Mayer is unrecorded.

On Tuesday the tenth, Sinatra was back in L.A., wrung out by the trip. Whorf was doing his best to shoot the movie around him, but at a certain point the director could do nothing without his star. It turned out Whorf would have to wait a while longer. The studio's production memo for that day reads:

> Bobby Burns [now Sinatra's manager—another theft from
> Dorsey] phoned 9/10 and said Sinatra arrived from New York
> that morning, but was tired and would not report, that he
> would broadcast [his radio show] on Wednesday and report on
> Thursday.

A couple of days later even the production memos were beginning to sound exasperated:

> Called Sinatra for rehearsal but didn't report. He had
> an appointment to rehearse with [the choreographer]
> Jack Donohue at 10:30 a.m. but didn't come in. Publicity
> Department also had made appointment with him to shoot
> magazine cover still. He finally arrived on lot at 2:20 p.m., shot
> the poster still, and then went to Stage 10 and ran through
> number once with Mr. Donohue. Sinatra said it was a "cinch,"
> said he had an appointment and had to leave, which he did,
> without further rehearsing, at 2:45 p.m.

On the twenty-third, a Monday, Sinatra could barely pull himself out of bed:

Sinatra only worked part of day. He worked from 11:22 a.m.
to 12:05, when dismissed for lunch. He was called back to
rehearse at 1:05, but he did not report.

It wasn't just that he was ambivalent about filmmaking: there was
trouble at home. The ever-present low-level hostilities between Frank
and Nancy had escalated into open warfare. It didn't matter how much
he tried to justify that nightclub picture of him and Lana—yes, they
worked on the same lot; yes, Mayer liked his valuable properties to be
seen together, et cetera, et cetera. But there was no getting around that
giddy look on his face, his tight clasp of her hand. They looked like two
honeymooners. In apparent acknowledgment of her guilt, Turner had
curtailed her friendly visits to Nancy.

Nancy had other complaints. Frank had just bought Dolly and
Marty a new house in Weehawken for $22,000. Out of pocket, cash,
and without consulting Nancy, who tried hard to control the family
purse strings. Furious, Nancy opened her doors, wide, to her own family. At any given hour of the day, three generations of Barbatos were
present, nieces and nephews draped all over the place; aunts, uncles,
and cousins chatting in the kitchen. Frank, who had done his best to
look as though he lived there, now no longer saw the need. He and his
wife weren't speaking: What was the point?

On Saturday night, October 5, he went to a party hosted by Sonja
Henie: Lana was there. She and Frank danced together "many times,"
a subsequent newspaper account reported. He failed to go home that
night.

The next day he phoned Nancy and told her he wanted a separation. A divorce? she asked.

He wanted his freedom, he told her. He didn't want a divorce. He
was going to find an apartment. She slammed down the phone.

A half hour later, having done her best to compose herself, she
called Evans at home. Evans's wife answered, then handed the telephone to her husband. The moment Nancy heard George's voice, she
broke down sobbing.

As soon as he understood that the inevitable had finally happened, the publicist went into crisis mode. He could sit on the story for a little while, but just a little while. If he didn't shape the narrative, it would spill out raw or exaggerated into public. First, however, Evans attempted a desperation play: he called Frank and tried to talk some sense into him.

Frank, of course, wasn't having any. He had made up his mind.

So the press would have to be informed. The timing couldn't have been worse: the papers would be all over the story first thing Monday morning. Evans phoned the gatekeepers, Lolly Parsons and Hedda Hopper, and read them both the same script. "It's just a family squabble," he said. "The case of a Hollywood career, plus a man-and-wife fight. There's no talk of divorce. I think they'll make up in a few days. Frankie has a few days off so he's gone to a desert resort for a little privacy. This is the first public battle they've ever had, and I don't think it's serious. He will be back in three days to work on his current movie."

MGM production memo for Monday, October 7:

He did not report. He was called to rehearse but because
Durante was not available, Sinatra said he would not come
in as he didn't see any point in rehearsing by himself. Mr.
Donohue felt that he could have used Sinatra's services to good
advantage, but Sinatra said he would not be in.

The desert resort was Palm Springs.

═══

For centuries desert was all it was, home to the Agua Caliente band of the Cahuilla Indian tribe, a scattering of adobe buildings on the edge of the southern Mojave, in a bone-dry, sun-shattered valley surrounded by dead stony mountains. The springs themselves were hot— as though more heat were needed in the godforsaken place—and the palms around them not plentiful, but the waters were reputed to have healing properties. Crazy white people trickled out from the city looking for relief from their big-city ailments, and then the movie people began to come.

It was an ideal retreat from Hollywood: just 120 miles away, but in those days of two-lane blacktop, the drive took at least three hours. Tijuana was fun for whoring and horse racing; the Springs was for lying low, for basking like a lizard on a rock in the healing desert sun. Tan was good in those days. The big hotels, the Desert Inn and El Mirador, opened not long after World War I; the little resorts, with names like Wonder Palms and Lone Palm, cropped up in the 1920s and 1930s: clusters of Mission-style bungalows around crystalline blue pools, in the shade of the signature trees. Labor was cheap. People wouldn't bother you, the staffs were discreet, agents and publicists and columnists and spouses were far away, at the other end of a long-distance phone line.

Jimmy Van Heusen discovered the Springs in 1940, when he flew his shiny-skinned Luscombe-Silvaire to Los Angeles to go to work at Paramount, writing songs with Johnny Burke for Bing Crosby. Crossing the southwest desert as he entered California, he decided he'd better fuel up for his final approach—he wasn't quite sure where the Van Nuys airport was. He touched down at a primitive airstrip in the midst of the sand.

In the late summer of 1940 the Palm Springs airport was nothing but a couple of adobe huts and a few fuel drums, and the incredible heat shimmered off the tarmac, yet the minute Van Heusen stepped out of his plane, he was happy. He had suffered all his life from sinus trouble; suddenly he could really breathe. He fell in love with the desert and told all his friends, including Sinatra.

The place grew fashionable, as a secret shared among the rich and well-known. Fancy restaurants were a necessity, so a few opened up: the Palm House, the Doll House, Trav Rogers's Mink and Manure Club. You could get a superb steak for $2.50 or a lobster flown in on ice from Maine for $3. Then came the nightclubs. Even when you were lying low, entertainment was required. The first, and for a long time the best, was called Chi Chi. Dining, dancing, and big-time entertainment in the Starlite Room.

Frank thought the Springs was the perfect place to hide out: Lana had a little place down there. But Frank craved action and company, and so they went to Chi Chi.

During one fox-trot, Frank felt a tap on the shoulder. He turned and saw Howard Hughes, recently recovered from a near-fatal plane crash, dancing with his date, Ava Gardner, soon to divorce Artie Shaw. Sinatra and Hughes, who knew of each other only through their celebrity, nodded politely; Lana and Ava squealed and hugged. Until very recently Gardner had been a B player at Metro, best known for having been married to Mickey Rooney and Shaw. But in August, she'd finally had a breakthrough role, starring opposite Burt Lancaster in an adaptation of a Hemingway story called *The Killers*. The part put Ava on the map, and led to a friendship with Lana, who was nothing if not status conscious.

The two had much in common (besides very brief marriages to Artie Shaw), including hardscrabble backgrounds and fathers who'd died young. And an earthy sense of humor. They liked to drink cocktails and giggle together. Ava liked sex a good deal, as young ladies then, even young ladies who acted in the movies, were not supposed to. Lana, on the other hand, was a materialist. She quickly turned clinical while under the influence, comparing her lovers' respective endowments with the cold eye of a practiced anatomist.

Much information was conveyed in the mischievous glances the two actresses now exchanged.

Smiling obliviously, Hughes suggested to Sinatra that the two couples change partners. Lana's look suggested that Ava would be getting the better part of the bargain. Then Ava found herself in Frank's arms. The band struck up "Dancing in the Dark."

She had been drinking steadily over the course of the night—Hughes bored her—and she was in a saucy mood. Liquor, and success, and the desert emboldened her: she was considerably less demure than the young woman Frank had encountered before.

She looked straight into his eyes: she didn't usually dance with married men. He liked the challenge, and he liked the way she felt in his arms. In her heels she was as tall as he, maybe slightly taller, lean but curvy, fleshy in just the right places.

Except when she was married to them? The plural was pointed.

She smiled, sideways—with one plural pronoun he'd won the exchange—and put her head on his shoulder.

How about that, he thought.

Then the song was over, and she was back in Hughes's arms.

Frank and Lana were seen together, as they wanted to be. It was inevitable, a game of cat and mouse. He and Lana Turner had gone to Palm Springs and danced at Chi Chi, among other celebrities, and their presence had been duly noted and reported. Evans read about them within hours. As did Louis B. Mayer.

On Wednesday night, Frank was back in Hollywood to do his radio show, and Mayer was with him, to present Sinatra with an award from *Modern Screen* magazine as the Most Popular Star of 1946—along with a $10,000 bronze bust of the singer by the sculptor Jo Davidson. Before the mikes went on, however, the fatherly hand came down heavily on his shoulder.

Mayer glared at him. What was all this?

Frank shrugged. It was just a personal matter.

Mayer had to disagree. Where he and Lana were concerned, it was very much a professional matter. He must have Frank's word that he would sort this out quickly.

Frank nodded.

Then the mikes went on.

"Let me welcome you to the MGM family," Mayer told him. He didn't have to emphasize the last word.

"I'm proud to be in that family, sir," Sinatra said.

The studio chief gave him a look that would have done Benny Goodman proud.

The MGM conduct police went into overdrive, piling the pressure on Frank and especially on Lana, the more vulnerable of the pair. Turner's morals clause, unlike Sinatra's, was in full effect, and where Mayer was concerned, Lana Turner's morals were always suspect. "The only thing you're interested in," the studio chief had once told her in an office meeting, "is this." He pointed at his groin.

It would certainly have appeared that way. Turner was never a proponent of monogamy, serial or otherwise. Even as she was carrying on with Sinatra, she was also conducting a torrid affair with the also married Tyrone Power. Yet Turner appears not to have been a mere sex addict. In later, more contemplative years she wrote that sex itself had never been that interesting to her. What seems to have been much more compelling was company, and action, and drama. Turner was a deeply needy woman, in love with the idea of being a movie star. She was an actress playing herself, her daughter wrote in her memoir; she was unable to step out of character. Private life and public life were all of a piece.

The solemn injunctions of Louis B. Mayer held extraordinary power for her. And soon Lana was tearfully reading from a new script. "I am not in love with Frank, and he is not in love with me," she told Louella Parsons. "I have never in my life broken up a home . . . I just can't take these accusations."

Parsons played the good cop—"I think Frank has done his best to be a good family man and still remain the glamorous figure he's been in the public eye," she wrote in her column—and Hedda Hopper, the bad. Hopper took Sinatra to task in print and in person, warning him when she encountered him at a reception "that he was public property, and that part of that public property was Nancy and his children."

Sinatra didn't scare easily; normally, he would have shrugged off the admonition. But pressure was coming from all sides: after publicly (and somewhat contradictorily) musing, "You know, Frank has had a lot of career for one man, and he hasn't had much time for home life. I think they'll get it straightened out," the relentless Evans even sent Manie out to L.A. to try to reason with him.

And on October 23, Frank caved. The occasion was Phil Silvers's opening at Slapsie Maxie Rosenbloom's nightclub on Beverly Boulevard, and this time Sinatra's stooge act was in dead earnest.

He attended the opening as a friend, and also to contribute to Silvers's show in much the same way he had in New York. But this time the fix was in: Nancy was present, all dolled up and sitting at Jule Styne's table. Midway through the show, Rosenbloom—a former prizefighter who had turned to playing tough guys in the movies—asked Sinatra for a song.

Frank rose and asked the band to play "Going Home."

A very odd selection, given that the lugubrious spiritual was best known at the time for having been played at Franklin Roosevelt's funeral. But it was the title, not the song, that was the point: when Sinatra was through, Silvers—who after all had written the words to the song about Nancy—grabbed Frank in a bear hug and steered him over to his wife's table. Through tears, Frank asked Nancy (she was also crying) how the kids were. Fine, she told him. They missed their daddy. He had to clench his teeth to keep from bawling.

You could've heard a pin drop in Slapsie Maxie's. Then Frank asked his wife to dance, and the place went nuts.

———

Frank and Nancy didn't go home that night. She wanted to see his apartment, to feel its illicit thrill—and to make it her own. And so at the end of an evening of dancing at Slapsie Maxie's, they got in a cab and rode to Sunset Tower and went up to his penthouse and made a baby.

———

Despite the reconciliation, he continued to do exactly what he wanted. *It Happened in Brooklyn* was limping to a close amid further delays by the star; Sinatra and the director were barely speaking.

One of the problems was the rate at which Frank kept on recording that fall. He was privately gratified to hear that Dick Haymes's sales were beginning to drop. That was what happened, he thought, when you didn't keep pushing in all directions. There was a radio show Sinatra badly wanted to do in early November, George Burns and Gracie Allen's, and so he informed Whorf that he, Frank, needed to wrap up his work on the picture before then. Whorf refused. And so, as the MGM production memo for November 7 notes tersely, Sinatra "left at 2:30 to appear on Burns & Allen broadcast."

The camel's back was stressed to full curvature. Mayer called a conference with his production executives, then fired off a telegram to the recalcitrant star:

> NO CONSENT WAS GIVEN BY US TO SUCH A RADIO APPEARANCE AND YOUR PARTICIPATION IN SUCH BROADCAST WAS IN VIOLATION OF YOUR OBLIGATION AND AGREEMENT UNDER YOUR CONTRACT WITH US . . . THESE INCIDENTS ARE THE CULMINATION OF A LONG SERIES OF VIOLATIONS OF YOUR CONTRACTUAL OBLIGATIONS TO US.

The studio chief was sufficiently upset to have the story leaked to MGM's unofficial mouthpiece Louella Parsons, who wrote in her column of November 14:

> I won't be surprised if Frank Sinatra and MGM part company permanently. Frankie has been a very difficult boy on the lot, and I have a feeling MGM won't put up with it. Louis B. Mayer, who has a faculty for getting along with MGM actors, talked with Frankie, I hear, but that hasn't done very much good. The Voice's chief pout was caused when he was refused the rights to a song he sang in *It Happened in Brooklyn*. I have always liked Frankie, but I think right now he needs a good talking to.

The song—"Time After Time"—was just one of many issues. Sinatra didn't call Evans; he didn't call Keller. He called Western Union and fired off a wire to Parsons:

SUGGEST YOU READ THIS TELEGRAM WITH YOUR ARTICLE IN
YOUR OTHER HAND. I'LL BEGIN BY SAYING THAT IF YOU CARE
TO MAKE A BET I'LL BE GLAD TO TAKE YOUR MONEY THAT
M-G-M AND FRANK SINATRA DO NOT PART COMPANY, PERMA-
NENTLY OR OTHERWISE.

  SECONDLY, FRANKIE HAS NOT BEEN A VERY DIFFICULT BOY ·
ON THE LOT. FRANKIE HAS ONLY BEEN HEARD FROM WHEN
IT CONCERNS THE IMPROVEMENT OF THE PICTURE WHICH
YOU WILL FIND HAPPENS IN MOST PICTURES WHERE YOU USE
HUMAN BEINGS . . .

  LAST, BUT NOT LEAST, IN THE FUTURE I'LL APPRECIATE
YOUR NOT WASTING YOUR BREATH ON ANY LECTURES BECAUSE
WHEN I FEEL I NEED ONE I'LL SEEK ADVICE FROM SOMEONE
WHO EITHER WRITES OR TELLS THE TRUTH. YOU HAVE MY
PERMISSION TO PRINT THIS IF YOU SO DESIRE AND CLEAR UP
A GREAT INJUSTICE!

When the Los Angeles *Daily News* columnist Erskine Johnson had
the nerve to chide Sinatra for his temperamental behavior, he got a
telegram, too:

JUST CONTINUE TO PRINT LIES ABOUT ME, AND MY TEMPER —
NOT MY TEMPERAMENT — WILL SEE THAT YOU GET A BELT IN
YOUR VICIOUS AND STUPID MOUTH.

On hearing that Johnson weighed two hundred pounds and was eager
to mix it up with him, Sinatra decided not to press the issue any further.

Only a year earlier, Frank had been the press's hero, the humanitarian in chief, the noble and reasonable star of *The House I Live In*.
Now, much to the chagrin of his handlers, the Hollywood Women's
Press Club voted him Least Cooperative Star, in a landslide vote. Suddenly he was a bad boy again. And seemingly eager to prove it at every
opportunity.

First, however, there was a certain amount of penance to do. He was a married man: it appeared he was going to have to pay some attention to that part of his life. Frank was returning to the Wedgwood Room at the Waldorf after Thanksgiving, and so he decided to take Nancy and the children with him. It was his idea.

And that wasn't all. He bought Nancy a glorious pearl necklace, three strands, at Tiffany, and presented it to her before they went out for a family dinner at the Stork Club. She opened the big light blue box—bigger than the box the diamond bracelet had been in—with glistening eyes; she put the necklace on immediately. Evans made certain a photographer was at the restaurant to record the occasion: pretty mommy and handsome daddy, all dressed up, in between their adorable little boy and girl with identical fat cheeks and floppy bows at their necks.

Daddy was busy. He had rehearsals, business at Columbia and elsewhere, three packed shows a night at the Wedgwood (about which the joke was, If they could wedge any more paying customers in, they would). His schedule was so jammed that he barely got to see Nancy and the kids. Time was so tight that a recording session had to be scheduled for a Sunday, an unprecedented event.

George Avakian remembers the day well: December 15, 1946. Avakian, twenty-seven at the time, was a junior producer at Columbia; his boss, Manie Sacks, had asked him to come in to supervise the second half of the session, which would consist of two numbers Sinatra wanted to record with the Page Cavanaugh Trio, a jazz combo. Sacks himself supervised the first half, as he did with all Sinatra's important—that is, commercial—recording sessions. The first two songs were Irving Berlin's "Always" and something called "I Want to Thank Your Folks," a contemporary tune that Sacks felt had selling potential. Axel Stordahl arranged, and conducted the thirty-five-piece orchestra.

"Always" is fine: Sinatra is in good voice, and it would be hard for him not to do a good job on the great standard. At the same time, there's something slightly stilted and airless about his rendition: he's articulating beautifully, yet doesn't convey the song's passion. The problem is compounded on "I Want to Thank Your Folks," which, with its unexceptional tune and dreary lyrics ("I want to thank your folks for making you as sweet as you are / How else can I express how I feel, confess and reveal my love?"), against the sound of a sappily tinkling celeste, is the kind of schmaltz that gives 1940s music a bad name.

The recording session changes dramatically once the classical musicians have packed up their instruments, put on their scarves and overcoats, and bustled out of Liederkranz Hall. Axel and Manie have also left the building. Now that Frank is alone with the jazz guys (the trio's guitarist was the great Al Viola, who would continue playing for Sinatra for many years), the atmosphere shifts. With "Always" and "I Want to Thank Your Folks," Avakian recalls, Frank "was relatively tense because they were ballads. The other two songs were just pleasant throwaways. He's taking a drink and singing the song without worrying about it."

The results show. "That's How Much I Love You" and "You Can Take My Word for It, Baby" are hardly classics, but Sinatra's singing on the two jazz numbers is relaxed and good-humored and completely charming. He was especially relaxed at a one-off session he did two days later, a glorious recording of "Sweet Lorraine" with the Metronome All-Stars, including Johnny Hodges, Coleman Hawkins, Harry Carney, Charlie Shavers, Lawrence Brown, Nat "King" Cole, and, lo and behold, Buddy Rich. Many serious music commentators, George Avakian among them, have asserted that Sinatra never truly swings. They should redirect their attention to this "Sweet Lorraine." Maybe it all depended on the context.[2]

Avakian, who produced records for many musical giants, from Louis Armstrong and Duke Ellington to Miles Davis, disliked Sinatra from the moment he first saw the singer get off the elevator at Columbia's Seventh Avenue offices, flanked by four bodyguards.[3] "He used to call me 'kid' because he didn't know my name," Avakian said. "He gave off the feeling that, 'Listen, I'm a big man and you're unimportant,

and I'm putting up with your presence.'" On the first Sinatra recording sessions the producer witnessed, "everybody was sort of like, 'Oh,
Sinatra is very tough—you have to be careful. Don't cross him; don't
argue with him.'"

Yet to Avakian's surprise, Sinatra was loose and easy on the two trio
numbers the young producer supervised. "He did them very quickly,
two takes of each one," Avakian recalled. "I thought, 'Gee, if only he
could do this all the time, he's somebody I could enjoy working with.'"

Frank couldn't do it all the time, of course. He was simply too
important a personage to let his hair down (even while he still had
it in abundance). He knew exactly how miraculous a singer he was,
but he also knew how delicate his voice was—and how fickle public
regard. He was protecting his position as America's most important
ballad singer, and the effort made him tense.

Frank's entire life seemed to be based on the building and the
release of tension. When the release came in the form of singing, it
was gorgeous; when it took the form of fury, it was terrible. But release
was important and constantly needed. "Hard work and extended play,
I mean after hours, never hurt Frank," George Evans said, not entirely
accurately. "But emotional tension absolutely destroyed him. You could
always tell when he was troubled. He came down with a bad throat.
Germs were never the cause unless there are guilt germs."

To some degree, this was wishful thinking on Evans's part. Guilt,
with Sinatra, was as transitory as his other emotions. His mercurial
nature, as we have seen, was part of his finely tuned temperament.
And as his fame allowed ever-greater self-indulgence, there were times
he could simply shrug off guilt and go on to the next thing. He was
often in beautiful voice that late autumn in Manhattan. He was working hard and spending as much time with his family as he could. He
opened the Wedgwood gig with a smile, holding a cup of coffee and
singing "The Coffee Song," a cute Bob Hilliard and Dick Miles novelty
number he'd recorded in July.[4]

But then, unpredictably, the tension would return. He was less graceful with nightclub hecklers than he'd been before. "You must be glad the war is over—now you can get parts for your head!" he shouted at one. Another time he walked off the floor in the middle of a song. Something was eating him. In early December he issued an edict barring fans under twenty-one from his radio broadcasts. The public outcry was noisier than anything he'd had to endure in the studio. Frank quickly reversed his decision. He often seemed whipsawed at the end of that year. It wasn't just the rising pressures of fame: he was also secretly making time in his busy schedule for Lana Turner, whose similarly busy schedule, as fate would have it, had brought her to New York City.

=====

Bugsy Siegel, the jaunty sociopath, was uncharacteristically nervous. He was millions of dollars in the hole for cost overruns (and skimming) on the still-unfinished Flamingo Hotel, and the men who had fronted him the money, Meyer Lansky among them, were not patient people. These men already suspected Siegel of stealing from them, but if the Flamingo's opening, scheduled for the day after Christmas, was a success, promising rivers of revenue, all might be forgiven. The key to a big event, then as now, was stars. If major Hollywood talent came to the desert, the public would follow.

Bugsy knew everyone in Hollywood, and the week before Christmas he flew to L.A. to call in some chits. He had extended friendship, protection, and business help to some very important people, and now he needed their help back. He called on the biggest names in his address book: Sinatra, Lana Turner, Clark Gable, Katharine Hepburn, Spencer Tracy, Gary Cooper, Marlene Dietrich, and Jimmy Durante, among others. The response was not enthusiastic.

Worse, December 26 was cold and rainy and the airports in Los Angeles and Vegas were socked in. The Flamingo opening was a gloomy, under-attended event: the stars, to put it mildly, did not turn out. Gable, Hepburn, Tracy, Cooper, and Dietrich all came up with excuses—a mother was very sick, an ankle had been sprained, a cold had been caught. Durante and George Raft, always friendly where the Boys were concerned, somehow made their way to the desert, as did Lucille Ball and Desi Arnaz, Xavier Cugat, and George Jessel. It wasn't enough. "There can rarely have been a more cheerless scene," wrote Otto Friedrich in *City of Nets,* "than the newly opened casino at the half-empty and half-finished Flamingo, standing alone in the Nevada desert on the night after Christmas." Cheerless, and snakebit: though Raft compliantly lost $75,000 at the crap tables, the Flamingo's gaming coffers were $200,000 in the red after its first night of operation.

Maybe Siegel stole that, too. It didn't matter: his fate was sealed. The process had begun four days earlier, at the great conference of American mafiosi at the Hotel Nacional in Havana, organized by the plush hotel's co-owner Meyer Lansky (his silent partner, the Cuban president Fulgencio Batista) and presided over by Salvatore Lucania, a.k.a. Charles "Lucky" Luciano.[5] Luciano had been released from prison in return for protecting New York City's docks during World War II, but had had to accept permanent deportation to Italy; now he was back in the Western Hemisphere, hoping to set up a permanent base of operations just ninety miles from Florida. Lucky Luciano had a mesmerizingly cold face, with pitted cheeks, a piercing gaze, and a strangely beautiful mouth—up-curved at the corners, and with a sensual lower lip—that was virtually the double of Sinatra's. Every important gangster in the United States had convened in Havana to offer Luciano fealty and thick envelopes of cash—every important gangster except for Benny Siegel, who hadn't even been told about the conference. The message was clear. Meyer Lansky, who perhaps felt remiss at having urged Vegas on Siegel in the first place, argued with uncharacteristic passion that Benny should live, that he might still turn the Flamingo around and be of value, but few at the conference listened.

Sinatra was conspicuously absent from the Flamingo's opening ceremonies. Whatever Frank may have told Benny, the real reasons for his failure to show were complicated. As for the other absentees, maybe, as is so often the case with stars, the herd instinct had kicked in. And maybe, as has been rumored, William Randolph Hearst, who was so close to Louis B. Mayer, had put the kibosh on the event for MGM stars because Hearst suspected his mistress Marion Davies had slept with the handsome gangster. As for Frank: maybe Charlie Fischetti's warning about Ben Siegel still echoed in his head.

It was Frank's New Year's Eve party to welcome in 1947. There was a stirring in the big living room as a latecomer arrived: the twenty-three-year-old Peter Lawford, dashing in his well-tailored tux. Handsome as he was, though, it was his date who was drawing all the stares. Dark haired, with dazzlingly high cheekbones, a white fur stole on her wide shoulders, she walked with the easy grace of a tigress; Ava Gardner was on the prowl. Until recently a nobody in Hollywood, Ava entered the room with confidence born of success and buoyed by alcohol. *The Killers* had put her on the A-list; Mayer himself had told her the world was her oyster. She had just turned twenty-four the week before, and she was ready for adventure.

She was more tired than ever of Howard Hughes. She still grudgingly accepted his gifts—the fur she was wearing; a Cadillac convertible. What was harder to take were the spies sent to monitor her comings and goings. It would have been annoying enough if she'd been his only girlfriend, but she happened to know that Hughes was also keeping tabs on Linda Darnell, Jean Peters, and Jane Russell. The man was insufferable. Lawford, on the other hand, was fun, and charmingly irreverent, and a girl couldn't just sit at home on New Year's Eve.

It wasn't just that she didn't want to be alone, nor was it simply that this was *the* party that night. She had to admit that she was increasingly curious about the man she kept running into everywhere. She was intrigued by how persistently gentlemanly he was, unlike almost every other male she encountered—and unlike his reputation. And while she knew he was married, and the father of two small chil-

Durante, Lawford, Sinatra. February 1947.

dren, and she had a strict policy against seeing married men, she was intrigued. All the more so when Lawford took her over to introduce her (he thought) to Sinatra, and she and Frank exchanged an amused glance. Over his shoulder, a few yards away, stood the wife, mousy cute, smiling at another couple. Ava looked at her for a second, then back at Frank, who was still grinning at her. No contest. She felt like a thief inside a bank vault.

But the night was still young. From Sinatra's, she would have Lawford take her to a party at Mel Tormé's, and then home. By three-thirty the Englishman was done for the night, and she was still raring to go. She would wind up the evening gunning her dark green Cadillac convertible up the Coast Highway with the smitten twenty-one-year-old Tormé at her side, as her long hair blew in the wind and the sky turned baby pink in the East. She was quite sure it was going to be a spectacular year.

Louella Parsons and Frank sign autographs for servicemen at the Hollywood
Canteen, August 1943.

Well, Frankie and I have buried the hatchet deep," Louella Parsons
wrote in her column of January 27, 1947. "He promised me he
would not carry a gun, feed me poison, or otherwise harm a hair
of my defenseless head if I would have luncheon with him. So I went.
Frankie Sinatra, that is, and he will leave for Miami in two weeks.
He then will go on to Cuba and possibly to South America, and won't
return until MGM is ready to start *The Kissing Bandit,* his next picture."

Whether the part about carrying a gun was eerily prescient or merely a case of Louella's making it her business to know absolutely everything, three days later the *Los Angeles Times* photographed Frank being fingerprinted by Deputy Sheriff Robert Rogers as he applied for a permit to carry a pistol.

The gun may have been a Walther, as has sometimes been reported, or it may have been a Beretta. Sinatra later told Hedda Hopper he "wanted Nancy to have some protection in case of an emergency. So I bought a little gun for the house." (With what he was up to lately, Nancy would have been the last person in whose hands he'd want a gun.) Or maybe, as he told another reporter, he needed the sidearm "to protect personal funds."

Whose personal funds is another question. It seems unlikely Frank meant his own. He had already begun the habit of having someone in his retinue carry his wad of crisp new twenties and hundreds, but even if he kept the money in his own pocket, a couple of thousand bucks was scarcely worth protecting with a gun. Whatever he meant to use the weapon for, it was a symbol, and not a good one, of what Frank Sinatra was in the process of becoming.

———

Maybe Frank was frazzled and needed a vacation; maybe he was a man on a mission, however misbegotten. Maybe both were true. Or perhaps he simply needed to get out of town.

For Nancy had found out about his meetings with Lana in New York. News travels fast in Hollywood. If Lana Turner was under the illusion once more that Frank Sinatra was going to leave his wife for her, the story would travel even faster.

Nancy had other news for Frank: she was pregnant. Was Lana Turner going to give him babies? The bitch had one already, a three-year-old bastard daughter, by the nobody she'd married twice. Did Frank really want to be that child's stepfather? Did he really want to be Lana Turner's third husband (and fourth marriage)? Hollywood would laugh at him.

Nancy told Frank she was going to have an abortion.

He stared at her. In the mid-1940s, a time of enforced convention-ality, it was unspeakable. For a Catholic couple, it was unthinkable. And for this Catholic couple—Nancy knew it; Frank knew it—it was the stain that Dolly Sinatra had brought to their marriage.

The challenge was clear: if he left on this trip, whatever it was, anything could happen. She might do this unimaginable thing. He didn't believe it, even as part of him feared it. He repeated to her that he had obligations in New York and Miami—a radio show, a benefit concert—and that he was going to take a few days off in Florida and then Havana. Boys only.

He told her it was all over with Lana. He had been a fool, a great fool. It was his nature. He knew Nancy understood: she was the only one in the world who really knew him. There was a loneliness deep in his soul, and he was susceptible. Lana Turner was scheming, incon-stant (Frank knew about Tyrone Power), vain, and shallow. He real-ized she didn't love him, and—bending the truth—he certainly didn't love her.

He was exhausted, frayed out. He had been making bad decisions left and right, mistreating those who loved him best. He would make it up to her.

He had an inspiration: they would have a second honeymoon. In Mexico—Acapulco. Valentine's Day. Two weeks.

The car horn was blowing in the driveway. His suitcases sat in the hall. Frank tried to kiss her, but she evaded his lips. And then he was gone.

═══

He relaxed at the Fischetti mansion on Allison Island in Miami—cool tile floors, quiet servants, views of palm trees and the sparkling bay: a very nice place to be in February. The beautiful weather, luxurious surroundings, and pleasant company put Frank in such an expansive mood that on the night of the tenth he gave a free concert at the Colo-nial Inn, a gambling casino in Hallandale owned by Meyer Lansky and Joe Adonis.¹ The next morning at Miami International Airport, he climbed the steps to board a shiny-skinned TWA DC-3 to Havana.

A still frame from a newsreel taken when the plane landed in Cuba shows Sinatra, having just disembarked, in the midst of a small group of fellow passengers, all male. The faces all wear that distracted, just-got-off-the-plane look. Frank, seemingly unaware of being photographed (or simply inured to it at this point), is gazing off to the side, squinting in the tropical sun. He wears a snappy tweed sports jacket, a patterned necktie, a crisp white shirt. In his right hand is a large, squarish valise. From his posture—leaning to his left to support the valise's weight against his hip—the bag appears to be quite heavy. Behind him and over his right shoulder is a gray-templed man later identified as Rocco Fischetti. In the left foreground of the frame stands a dark-haired man in a gray suit, cigarette in his mouth, cuffs shot, his pinkie-ringed hand partially shielding his hunched head. The man looks patently like a gangster—more specifically, like the template for a 1940s gangster lovingly re-created in Francis Ford Coppola's movie of *The Godfather*. There is good reason for this—Joe Fischetti was a gangster. His big brother Prince Charlie, the man who had in all likelihood invited Sinatra on this trip in June at Mary Fischetti's Brooklyn house, luckily (or craftily) avoided the camera.

A vast amount of attention has been devoted to Frank Sinatra's four-day trip to Havana in February 1947, at the time in newspapers and magazines and over the years in the immense body of Sinatra literature. It wouldn't be an exaggeration to say that the sojourn achieved mythic status—which is not to say that much of what has been written about it isn't true. Even giving Frank the maximum benefit of the doubt, it would seem that he made some very bad decisions at a very sensitive time in his personal life and his career. This was his walk on the wild side with the Mob, with the men he had come to admire for all kinds of reasons, both inexcusable and understandable.

His Cuba trip wouldn't have become legendary had it not coincided with the Havana conference, but the coincidence was no accident. The many attendees had known for months that Frank would be coming; they had been looking forward to it. (One account has it that a Sinatra concert in Havana was, from the beginning, a cover story for the whole gathering.) Not only was the singer the biggest star in America; he was also an Italian-American. And no doubt due in part to efficient public-relations work by Sinatra's early supporter the affable and popular Willie Moretti, Frank was widely known to be friendly where the Boys were concerned, neither a pushover nor a pain in the ass.[2]

Most important, though, he was respectful.

But did respect translate to compliance—or, more pointedly, complicity? Was Sinatra's mere association with these men a form of guilt in itself? (Many have charged that it was.) Or did his sins run deeper?

It almost didn't matter. In the court of public opinion, Frank's goose was cooked—a predicament he owed, indirectly, to Ernest Hemingway.

In early 1947, a thirty-one-year-old Scripps-Howard columnist named Robert Ruark traveled to Cuba to visit the writer's haunts (Hemingway owned a villa a few miles outside of Havana) and, if possible, to meet the great man himself. While in the capital, young Ruark, who had quickly built a large readership with a lightly hard-boiled, humorous writing style that owed much to his literary idol, stumbled upon not Hemingway but the scoop of a lifetime. Fifteen years later, Ruark reminisced, in a column about the recently deceased Lucky Luciano:

> A freakish accident put me in Havana one time, just after the
> war, when I was a rookie in the cosmic column business, and I
> collided with Charlie, who was conducting a sort of hoodlum's
> summit with the big names of the mob . . .
>   I was young and brash and full of beans and when I ran
> into the aristocracy of gangland in Havana, said hoodlums
> being accompanied by Frank Sinatra, it seemed as newswor-
> thy as if I had come onto Bishop Cannon consorting with

[the famous madam] Polly Adler especially since Luciano
was supposed to be deported to Italy, and Sinatra was the
public-relations-invented leader of the nation's youth at that
particular period . . .

The young Ruark knew a great story when he saw one, and the
moment he finished his legwork, he immediately began cranking out
columns from Havana: three in the last week of February alone. They
were titled, none too subtly, "Shame, Sinatra!" " 'Lovable' Luciano,"
and "The Luciano Myth." In the first, dated February 20, he wrote:

Sinatra was here for four days last week and during that time
his companion in public and in private was Luciano, Luciano's
bodyguards and a rich collection of gamblers and highbinders.
The friendship was beautiful. They were seen together at the
race track, the gambling casino and at special parties . . .

Staying close to the action in a seventh-floor suite at the Nacional (the floor below Luciano's rooms), Frank rubbed a lot of elbows
that week. The conference was a veritable summit of crime, with all
the Jewish and Italian bosses from major and secondary American cities present. Naturally, New York and New Jersey were most heavily
represented: besides Lansky and Luciano, there were Frank Costello,
Vito Genovese, Joe Bonanno, Longy Zwillman, Joe Adonis, and Willie
Moretti. The Fischettis and Tony Accardo represented Chicago; Moe
Dalitz, Detroit; and Santo Trafficante and Carlos Marcello, Tampa and
New Orleans. There were closed-door conclaves on internal politics
and the divisive question of narcotics trafficking: even the Jews were
excluded from meetings that strictly concerned Cosa Nostra matters,
and Sinatra would probably not have been privy to any business discussions. He was there to provide a cover story and, in keeping with his
lifelong relationship to men like these, to admire and be admired. He
was, as Luciano later said, "a good kid and we was all proud of him."

Frank did what he was there to do, giving the attendees their promised concert in the hotel's banquet room. There is no record of the song list. Still, wouldn't it have been lovely to pan the house with an imaginary movie camera and watch those faces—fascinating faces, on the evidence of mug shots, but not inclined to be sensitive or reflective—while the Voice vocalized? There were probably more than a few moist eyes. "Luciano was very fond of Sinatra's singing," an associate later recalled.

Frank performed, he glad-handed, and he was rewarded, not just with fellowship, but with fun. Pre-Castro Havana was a twenty-four-hour fiesta of unapologetic pleasures. There was even allegedly an orgy in his suite—twelve naked women, a number of gangsters, plenty of alcohol. Improbably, a group of Cuban Girl Scouts, led by a nun, arrived in the midst of the festivities to present Sinatra with an official token of their esteem. He is said to have hustled the celebrants into another room and received the Scouts in a silk dressing gown and ascot.

It could be a slightly more ribald version of *Some Like It Hot,* set in the Batista Havana of *The Godfather: Part II.* The problem was that it was real life, and Frank's hero worship of tough guys had gotten him in way over his head. Danger made these men magnetic, and our fascination with gangsters suggests that few of us could have been in their presence without being, on some level, thrilled. But to the American public of 1947, the men were not faces and eyes and rough handshakes but names, names to be censured. And ethnic names at that. The court of public opinion would quickly take note of Sinatra's new friends, and would react violently.

Ruark wrote of Frank's wild going-away party on Valentine's Day (the day he was supposed to meet Nancy in Acapulco):

> In addition to Mr. Luciano, I am told that Ralph Capone
> [brother of Al] was present . . . and so was a rather large and
> well-matched assortment of the goons who find the south salu-
> brious in the winter, or grand-jury time . . .

The curious desire to cavort among the scum is possibly per-
missible among citizens who are not peddling sermons to the
nation's youth, and may even be allowed to a mealy-mouthed
celebrity, if he is smart enough to confine his social tolerance
to a hotel room. But Mr. Sinatra, the self-confessed savior of
the country's small fry, by virtue of his lectures on clean living
and love-thy-neighbor, his movie shorts on tolerance, and his
frequent dabblings into the do-good department of politics,
seems to be setting a most peculiar example for his hordes of
pimply, shrieking slaves.

In an era when Americans got their news almost exclusively from
newspapers, when every major city had at least two dailies and sometimes three or four, Ruark's columns, and the avalanche of follow-up
coverage they triggered, had huge impact. And long legs. "It was a
pretty story while it lasted, and it lasted quite a while," Ruark wrote,
in his best Hemingway-ese, in 1962. It was also George Evans's worst
nightmare: his star client, on ethnic thin ice under the best of circumstances, had done himself no favors by mingling his name with the
kinds of names many Americans reflexively associated with the darker
side of Italian identity. Sinatra's first response to the attacks was weak,
almost stunned—not to mention self-contradictory: "I was brought up
to shake a man's hand when I am introduced to him without first investigating his past. Any report that I fraternized with goons or racketeers
is a vicious lie."

Not long after the trip, Frank told Hedda Hopper what he insisted
was "the complete story":

> I dropped by a casino one night. One of the captains—a
> sort of boss—recognized me and asked if I'd mind meeting a
> few people . . . I couldn't refuse . . . So I went through some
> routine introductions, scarcely paying attention to the names
> of the people I was meeting. One happened to be Lucky
> Luciano. Even if I'd caught his name, I probably wouldn't have

associated it with the notorious underworld character . . . I sat down at a table for about fifteen minutes. Then I got up and went back to the hotel . . . When such innocent acts are so distorted, you can't win.

The tone of persecution would crop up more frequently over the next few years as Sinatra became ever more embattled; but it's hard to argue that Frank hadn't brought the controversy on himself. Hedonism was one thing; lawlessness was something else. Amiability could rapidly become complicity. Very soon after that week in February, attention focused on the picture of the heavy suitcase in Sinatra's hand. A story circulated that Frank had been acting as a courier for the Fischettis, carrying Luciano a large sum in business proceeds that had mounted up while Lucky was unavoidably out of the country. The story festered and swelled. Sinatra himself claimed, a bit absurdly, that the bag had contained painting and sketching supplies and his jewelry. (Spare pinkie rings?) In 1951 in the New York *Daily Mirror,* Lee Mortimer formally accused the singer of carrying $2 million in small bills to Cuba.

It was a compelling tale. Who wouldn't like to open up a suitcase and find that kind of money? But the idea of fitting $2 million in small bills into hand luggage was patently ridiculous, and Sinatra quickly set about bashing the straw man:

Picture me, skinny Frankie [he said, in a Sinatra-bylined magazine piece in 1952], lifting two million dollars in small bills. For the record, one thousand dollars in dollar bills weighs three pounds, which makes the load I am supposed to have carried six thousand pounds. Even assuming that the bills were twenties—the bag would still have required a couple of stevedores to carry it. This is probably the most ridiculous charge that has ever been leveled at me . . . I stepped off the plane in Havana with a small bag in which I carried my oils, sketching material, and personal jewelry, which I never send with my regular luggage.

But what if the bills were fifties? Or hundreds? By similar logic, since after all a $100 bill weighs the same as a single, a hundred thousand in Benjamins would weigh that same three pounds. Two million dollars in hundreds would therefore weigh sixty pounds. Which admittedly would make for one very heavy suitcase—one you'd have to lean against your hip while carrying it—but not one (even for skinny Frankie) that would require the assistance of baggage handlers.[3]

=====

There were other consequences. Frank's behavior at the end of 1946 and the beginning of 1947 had the effect of a giant electrical surge creating power outages in its wake. On February 14, the day an orgy unfortunately detained him in Havana, he sent a plaintive cable to Nancy, who was already cooling her heels in Acapulco:

WILL YOU BE MY VALENTINE?

When he finally arrived in Mexico for their romantic interlude, he made a shattering discovery: his wife, as good as her word, had aborted their third child. "She found a doctor in Los Angeles through a friend and had the procedure while my father was in Cuba," Tina Sinatra writes. "The doctor's prep was evident, 'and [Nancy told her daughter] he knew immediately what I'd done.'"

The horror—all too uncomfortably reminiscent of the scene in *Godfather II* when Kay tells Michael Corleone that she has not suffered a miscarriage but aborted their child ("An abortion, Michael. Just like our marriage is an abortion")—rings down the decades. Nancy Sinatra had exerted the only real power she had over her relentlessly wayward husband, and her single act of revenge had terrific impact.

Tina Sinatra tells us, strangely, that her father's reaction was to order his wife, "Don't you *ever* do that again." As though she had committed a nuisance. As though he had the upper hand. It seems more likely, given Frank's seismic temper and Nancy's by now steely resolve, that the result of his discovery was something more than a curt directive: that the two had a messy and furious scene soaked with tears.

Then, Tina writes, sunlight came after the storm:

> Dad made a dramatic turnaround. He kept his road trips
> briefer and threw himself into home life. By day he was
> absorbed in his children. By night he was courting Mom all
> over again, with dinner and dancing at Ciro's. He was really
> trying. He would make this marriage work in spite of himself.
>   Soon my mother was pregnant again, in the fall of 1947.

It's a romantic picture, but the real story is far more complicated: 1947 would be a long, hard year.

It seemed not to matter to him that his radio show, *Old Gold Presents Songs by Sinatra,* was a superb vehicle for his talents: Frank had made up his mind that the indignity of earning a mere $2,800 a week (for a half hour's work) was too much for him. In January he had publicly floated the notion of returning to *Your Hit Parade,* at almost three times the salary. *Variety* reported Sinatra's monetary musings, and Old Gold got upset, informing him that he still had a year to go on his three-year contract and that it would be very expensive to get out of it. Frank struck back as he often would in years to come, by announcing that he was sick and was taking three weeks off to rest up in Florida.

When it turned out that he had gone to Havana, his sponsor was unhappy, as were others. Afterward, while Frank hunkered down, throwing himself into family life and doing a little recording ("Stella by Starlight," "Mam'selle," "Almost Like Being in Love"), the newspapers raged, and Louis B. Mayer fumed. He never fumed long. Very quickly Frank was called to the principal's office to endure the tough squint from Ida, the panicky wait in the tiny antechamber, the long trudge to the big desk with the grim-faced little man behind it.

Mayer informed Frank that after his next movie, *The Kissing Bandit* (Frank had read the script, and looked forward to making it much as he would look forward to taking poison), in view of his recent deportment (Mayer cleared his throat), the studio would be loaning him out to his old employer, RKO, for a new picture called *The Miracle of the Bells.*

He would play a priest.

This last was pointed. Mayer studied him coldly through the rimless spectacles that rode his hawk nose. Frank's image must be rehabilitated.

In the middle of March, *It Happened in Brooklyn* premiered. It was a smaller movie than *Anchors Aweigh,* in black and white instead of Technicolor; this time Sinatra got to wear an Army uniform rather than a sailor suit. Kathryn Grayson was back as his love interest, trilling prettily and ringing new changes on haughty vulnerability. (And bringing as little chemistry to her side of the love equation as Frank did to his: if Grayson was ever on the fabled dressing-room checklist, she remained unchecked.) The great Durante was cute as the dickens in the thankless role of a sexless school janitor. Lawford, on the other hand, was a kind of black hole on-screen, too handsome for his own good, and much too pleased about it. The picture simply grinds to a halt every time he shows up. But Sinatra—for all his bad behavior on and off the set, for all the feuds with the Schnozzola—was every bit as good as Durante, once again getting great mileage out of playing another Clarence Doolittle character, a Bashful Frankie. Something about the black-and-white cinematography brought out the amazingly sculpturesque quality of his still-rawboned features and killer lower lip—a face that the sculptor Jo Davidson had compared to Lincoln's.

And when Frank sang . . . He had a self-conscious but bewitching way of stretching that lower lip over to the right at key moments (for emphasis? to sneak a breath? or just to look cute?), a habit he would retain to the end of his career. And the movie gave him great material to work with. After the success of *Anchors Aweigh*, MGM had welcomed Sammy Cahn and Jule Styne to the ranks of officially certified screen songwriters, and once again the team did itself proud. Their tunes fit Sinatra like a Savile Row suit. When he sang (to Durante!) a great number like "Time After Time," he not only sounded magnificent, but looked utterly at home. This was an exceedingly rare trick, requiring absolute confidence, consummate stage presence, and close work with gifted composers: only Crosby, singing the works of Burke and Van Heusen, could also bring it off on-screen.

The critics were impressed—with the notable exception of Lee Mortimer, who couldn't keep his mind off current events. "This excellent and well-produced picture . . . bogs down under the miscast Frank (Lucky) Sinatra, smirking and trying to play a leading man," he wrote.

It was wrong, and it was hitting below the belt. While Frank certainly deserved censure for the Havana escapade,[4] Mortimer (no doubt, in great part, to please his masters at Hearst) seemed to be on a special campaign to bring down the star who had rejected him. As an arts critic who had arrogated the right of sociopolitical commentary (he would be one of the first but far from the last), the *Daily Mirror* columnist was hammering at the wall between Sinatra's career and his private misbehavior. It was a wall George Evans had worked long and hard to build, and one that was now—thanks both to Frank's efforts and to his energetic detractors—crumbling into dust.

═══

Much as the Manson murders in the summer of 1969 killed the Age of Aquarius, the Black Dahlia murder in January 1947 symbolized the end of Hollywood's sunny image and the beginning of a much darker new era. It wasn't so much the crime itself—a fresh-faced young woman named Elizabeth Short had been stabbed to death and left nude and grotesquely mutilated in a downtown vacant lot—as what it said about Los Angeles: a city rife with decadence, moral ambiguity, drug use, racial tension, and police corruption, all playing out against a backdrop of national political paranoia. The vision of Hollywood as a place of wartime optimism—the world of *Anchors Aweigh*—had curdled; film noir flourished. And Frank Sinatra, now a certifiably dubious figure on the American landscape, seemed to be acting out a scene from one of these ominous movies when he and a male companion pulled the wrong way in to an exit driveway of Ciro's on Sunset Boulevard shortly after 11:00 p.m. on April 8.

Sinatra could have been trying to avoid the press by not giving his car to the nightclub's valet; on the other hand, his arrival, in retrospect, looks purposefully secretive.

Lee Mortimer was just finishing a late dinner with an Asian-American band singer named Kay Kino when Sinatra walked in. In the syndicated *New York Post* column he wrote a couple of days later, Earl Wilson, ever eager to excuse Frank for almost everything (in gratitude, Sinatra had given the columnist one of those gold cigarette cases, engraved: OIL, YOUSE A POIL), offered a somewhat incoherent account of the evening's events, citing Mortimer's choice of dinner companion itself as dubious. Mortimer, Wilson wrote, was "known in the cafés for liking all champagne (except domestic) and Chinese girls, the latter so much that he sometimes brought in practically their whole families. His preference for Chinese girls brought publicity which he never mentioned suing anybody about."

Frank had other grievances on his mind. After he and his companion—who was almost certainly Sam Weiss, a song plugger and old New York pal—had been inside the club for about fifteen minutes, Mortimer and Kino left. While Mortimer was standing on the steps outside the entrance to Ciro's, Sinatra suddenly emerged and blindsided him, hitting him behind the ear with his right fist and knocking him to the ground.

At this point, as is usually the case with stories of fistfights, the tale grows murky. Mortimer seems to have gotten up and asked Sinatra why he had hit him, upon which a large man with black hair and a blue pin-striped suit (probably Weiss) pushed the columnist—who was about the singer's height and weight, though ten years older—down again. Then Sinatra began to pound the columnist and scream at him (calling him, by one account, a "shit heel" and "a perverted bastard" and, by another, a "degenerate" and a "fucking homosexual") while either the original large man alone, or he and two others, held him. "I'll kill you the next time I see you!" Sinatra screamed in Mortimer's face. "I'll kill you!" A King Features photographer tried to intervene. And then the beating was over.

Frank, the only one who had done any punching, had not inflicted much damage. Mortimer stood up, went to the West Hollywood sheriff's substation to lodge a complaint against Sinatra, then stopped at a hospital to have his sore jaw seen to. After phoning his lawyer, he started calling the press. Sinatra, for his part, went back into Ciro's and ordered a double brandy.

As the phone wires began to buzz, the *Los Angeles Herald-Express* columnist Harrison Carroll hurried over and found Frank still at the bar, in an explanatory mood. Equipped with a reporter's notebook and a sympathetic, if tin, ear, Carroll quoted Sinatra on the Mortimer dustup:

> For two years he has been needling me. He has referred to
> my bobby-soxer fans as morons. I don't care if they do try
> to tear your clothes off. They are not morons. They are only
> kids fourteen and fifteen years old. I think I have had more
> experience with their tactics than any other star in the country,
> but I have never beefed. Honestly, I intended to say hello to
> Mortimer. But when I glanced in his direction, he gave me
> a look. I can't describe it. It was one of those contemptuous
> who-do-you-amount-to looks. I followed him outside and I saw
> red. I hit him. I'm all mixed up. I'm sorry that it happened, but
> I was raised in a tough neighborhood, where you had to fight at
> the drop of a hat and I couldn't help myself.

Frank may indeed have locked eyes with Mortimer inside Ciro's. His first sight of the columnist—whose cold eyes, puffy cheeks, and pouting lower lip gave him the look of a school-yard tattletale—would not have been a pleasant experience. Yet Sinatra could be a fearsome sight himself, and both men had certainly been building up a head of steam. ("Every time Frank read one of Mortimer's columns," Jack Keller later recalled, "he went into a towering rage and threatened that the next time he saw this guy he was going to wallop him.") What happened outside the club is Rashomon, although a reminiscence tape-recorded by Keller many years later gives a fascinating picture of spin control, 1947 style. The publicist recalled that Sinatra knocked on his door in the wee hours, saying, "Jeez, I think we're in trouble."

"You bet your ass we're in trouble and we better get out of here before the reporters start showing up," Keller said.

They drove over to Bobby Burns's house to hash the situation over. After much pacing, Keller came up with a solution:

There's only one thing to do. It's the only way to get out of this thing. Otherwise, you're going to have every newspaper in America against you, because regardless of what *they* think of this guy Mortimer, they resent any one of their number being manhandled by an actor. So Frank, you've got to pick up the phone and call all the papers and say, "This is Frank Sinatra" and listen to their questions. Then you've got to tell each one of them that when you walked out of Ciro's, Mortimer and this Chinese dame were standing there and you heard him say to her, "There's that little dago bastard now!"

This is a slur on your nationality, and no one in their right mind would expect you to take this in good grace. Knowing your temper, the press will go along with you and be more or less on your side. It's the only thing you can do to come out of this looking good.

Frank tried. He called all the reporters he knew and told them the fish tale. But when the papers ran it the next morning, Lee Mortimer went into a towering rage of his own, lodging a complaint of battery against Sinatra to the district attorney and announcing he would sue the singer for $25,000 in damages. On Wednesday afternoon, April 9, while Frank was in the CBS Vine Street studio rehearsing "Oh, What a Beautiful Mornin'" for the Old Gold broadcast, a deputy sheriff and two investigators from the district attorney's office marched in and told him he was under arrest.

He phoned his lawyer, then went along quietly to the Beverly Hills Justice Court. The press was already there. The *Los Angeles Times*'s account was jocular, treating the affair as the non-earthshaking event it clearly was:

SINATRA ARRESTED AND FREED ON BAIL
IN ROW WITH WRITER
Columnist Charges Singer Bopped Him;
Date of Trial Set

. . . Frankie was wearing a gray sports suit, regular necktie instead of his usual droopy bow tie, and a smile when he walked briskly into court.

"I plead not guilty," he announced in a firm voice, "and wish a jury trial—sometime late next month."

Judge Woodward set the trial for 10 a.m., May 28.

Then, there was the matter of bail—it was set at $500 on the warrant.

Frankie had $400 on him. His attorney, Albert Pearlson, had $300. But, the money would be tied up until the trial. They didn't want to part with it. So, there was a 30-minute wait until a bail bondsman showed up to post the bail.

Frankie's smile turned a bit sheepish during the bail episode and then it got practically sickly when a deputy sheriff gently informed him that his permit to carry a gun had been suspended . . .

Semiofficial weights for the "battle" were listed yesterday as: Sinatra, 130; Mortimer, 135.

Late that night, Frank flew to New York. He was going to receive yet another award for his good works—the Thomas Jefferson Award of the Council Against Intolerance in America. It also didn't seem like a bad moment to get out of town. He boarded a triple-tailed TWA Constellation—the state of commercial-aviation art in 1947—and caught a little sleep in first class before facing the public the next morning. Continuing its tongue-in-cheek coverage, the *L.A. Times* wrote:

> Frankie . . . was met by 500 screaming bobby-soxers and newspapermen who immediately changed his title from "The Voice" to "The Punch" . . . On his arrival in New York . . . "The Punch" told his version of the historic Hollywood "battle" to a roomful of newspapermen at La Guardia Field.
>
> One reporter wrote:
>
> " 'It was a right-hand punch,' Frankie said. He said it quietly, modestly, in the way of a man awed by his own strength."
>
> The crooner repeated for New York newsmen his assertion that he overheard Mortimer refer to him as "Dago ————— ———."
>
> "We all have human weaknesses," he was quoted as saying in New York, "and there is just so much a man can take."
>
> In Hollywood Albert Pearlson, Sinatra's attorney, said he is checking the law which makes calling a person a profane name in public a misdemeanor.
>
> "If my interpretation of the law is correct, I'm going to the District Attorney's office and demand a complaint against this fellow," Pearlson declared.

The counteroffensive was in full swing: always blame the victim. That evening, Frank ran into Mr. and Mrs. Earl Wilson at the Copacabana. "Frank came in and greeted both of us warmly," the compliant columnist recalled.

He wasn't objecting to my piece ["Frankie, you shouldn't-a," Wilson had gently written], but still said he'd done it because Mortimer had called him a name.

"Did you have to hit him?" I asked Frank.

"He was coming toward me. I thought he was going to hit me."

"He said you belted him from behind."

"I hit him on the chin! To hit him on the chin and hit him from behind, you got to be an acrobat." Frank's eyes lit up with excitement. "When he said what he did, I said to myself, 'Here goes,' and I let him have a good right hook. I felt very good about it afterwards. Somebody pinned my arms behind me—there was an awful tussle all at once, people coming out of walls."

What did he resent most in Mortimer's writings? That about his fans being moronic was one of the things—he'd always been loyal to them as they had been to him . . . And, curiously, he hated references to his being an overnight success.

"Don't make me laugh! All the cream cheese-and-nut sandwiches I ate when I was living on about thirty cents a day, working on those sustaining programs. Nancy was working in a department store and used to slip me a couple of bucks . . .

"The coldest nights I walked three miles because I didn't have bus fare. I wasn't getting anywhere, I was giving up, but after I got married, I got lucky."

Frank managed to mix lies and braggadocio and self-pity into one unattractive glop. Maybe he was starting to believe his own version of the Mortimer punch-up.

But the public wasn't. His second Columbia album, *Songs by Sinatra,* released not long after the Ciro's incident, wasn't selling so well. Granted, *Songs* didn't have the same novelty and artistic integrity as *The Voice,* but the avalanche of negative press that spring didn't help. The *L.A. Times,* which persistently treated the affair lightly, was the exception that proved the rule. The five hundred Hearst papers were, as *Time* noted, "[giving] the story headlines and space almost fit for an attempted political assassination. Mortimer suddenly attained the stature of Dreyfus."

And Hearst, as we have seen, mattered enormously to Louis B. Mayer. When Frank returned to the Coast, he was called, yet again, onto the studio chief's carpet. Mayer ordered Sinatra to apologize publicly to Mortimer and pay him a settlement of $9,000. On June 4, in Beverly Hills District Court, Frank read a statement saying that the whole incident had sprung from a misunderstanding, that Mortimer had never made any remark about him, and that he keenly regretted his actions. Mortimer read a statement saying that he had received satisfaction for his injuries, and was satisfied, also, at Sinatra's acknowledgment and apology. The columnist withdrew his charges and, Sinatra having paid $50 in court costs—and some $15,000 to his lawyers, plus the $9,000 to Lee Mortimer—the case was dismissed.

But within a week Old Gold had dropped Frank from his radio show and hired Buddy Clark as his replacement.

———

In early May, while the Hearst papers were inveighing against Frank and MGM lawyers were parsing the Ciro's case to see if their star had a leg to stand on, Mortimer requested an audience with none other than J. Edgar Hoover. He had information on Sinatra, he said, and he needed some questions answered. Tit for tat.

The bureau bit. On May 12, Hoover's aide Louis B. Nichols—the same man who had gone to Detroit the previous year to observe the bobby-soxer mob greeting the singer at the airport—wrote a lengthy memo to Clyde A. Tolson, Hoover's right-hand man, detailing talking points for Mortimer's meeting with the director the next day:

1. Mr. Mortimer said he had a picture of Sinatra getting off a plane in Havana with a tough-looking man whom he has been unable to identify. He believes he is a gangster from Chicago. [This picture, no doubt, was the still frame from the newsreel showing Frank with Rocco and Joe Fischetti.]

Observation: It is suggested that this picture be exhibited to Agents who have worked on the reactivation of the Capone gang in Chicago, as well as to Agents in the Newark Office who have been working on criminal work, in view of the known contacts that Sinatra has had with New York hoodlums. It is entirely possible that in this way the unidentified picture might be identified. If we identified the individual we could secure a picture of the person identified and furnish that to Mortimer and then in turn let him go out and verify the identification in such a way as to remove the Bureau from any responsibility of furnishing information.

2. Mortimer stated that Sinatra was backed when he first started by a gangster in New York named Willie Moretti, now known as Willie Moore.

Observation: It is well known that Willie Moretti of Hasbrouck Heights, New Jersey, controls gambling in Bergen County, New Jersey, and is a close friend of Frank Costello. According to Captain Matthew J. Donohue of the Bergen County Police, Moretti had a financial interest in Sinatra. In this connection, Sinatra resides in Hasbrouck Heights.

Observation: the actual place of Sinatra's current residence was far from the only key fact the FBI would get wrong in its lengthy dossier on the singer, a document that inspires scant confidence in the intelligence-gathering abilities and motives of the bureau. The memo went on to mention other juicy details that Mortimer wanted to discuss with the director, including Frank's relationships with Bugsy Siegel, the Los Angeles gangster Mickey Cohen, and the Fischettis; his "arrest on a sex offense"; and his draft record.

At the last minute, though, the bureau pulled a bait and switch on Mortimer. When the columnist walked into his May 13 meeting, he found not Hoover but Tolson waiting for him. Mortimer swallowed his disappointment and went on with the meeting, which turned out to be of not much consequence:

> I talked this afternoon [Tolson wrote in a memo to Hoover] to Mr. Lee Mortimer, of the New York Daily Mirror, who wanted to ask some questions concerning Frank Sinatra. I told Mr. Mortimer that, of course, he realized that we could not give him any official information or be identified in this matter in any manner, which he thoroughly understands.
>
> He left a photograph taken of Frank Sinatra in Cuba and asked whether we could identify one individual shown in the picture. Copies of this photograph are being made and an effort will be made to determine whether any of our Agents are acquainted with the person in question.
>
> Secondly, he was interested in the association between Sinatra and Willie Moretti of Hasbrouck Heights, New Jersey. I told Mr. Mortimer in this connection that his best bet would be to make appropriate contacts with the Bergen County Police and possibly with a Captain Donohue.
>
> Also, Mr. Mortimer was interested in Sinatra's arrest on a sex offense.

It's an unseemly image: the oily snitch (and secret Jew) meeting with the FBI director's boyfriend to discuss the Italian-American star's sex life. But then that was America in the late 1940s—ethnics were never to be entirely trusted; Communists and other subversive types were under every rock. And even though nothing of substance would come of all the bureau's scratching after Sinatra, for the moment both the FBI and Lee Mortimer could content themselves that they had met.

———

So what can be made of Frank's picaresque misadventures: the gun, the gangsters, the beating of the little columnist? There's something telling about his quiet, then not so quiet, swagger after the Ciro's incident: "It was a right-hand punch . . ." "I let him have a good right hook. I felt very good about it afterwards . . ." "There is just so much a man can take . . ." In a way, he was casting himself as a hero in a corrupt world, a little guy up against overwhelming forces, like the Hearst Syndicate.

Even when those forces were benign, they were white Anglo-Saxon Protestant. Certainly one unconscious purpose for Frank's Havana trip was to reclaim the power of his Italianness. On the other hand, even he wouldn't have painted his trip to Havana as heroic. Rebellious and defiant, yes; but not heroic. One common theme uniting all his exploits that bad year was manliness. There was something boyish and wistful about his need to carry that gun, to be accepted by those mostly Italian men of honor, even to claim bragging rights for taking care of Lee Mortimer. Macrophallus and all, Frank was a little guy (not a single record exists of his ever having prevailed in a real fight), and secretly he knew he was an artist, with an exquisite sensibility. How could such a person be a man among men? Even grunting, illiterate Marty—boilermaker, athlete, fireman—was that.

As Sinatra's fame grew and his hangers-on kowtowed and cowered, he came to believe in his own toughness. Yet there was always something artificial about it. He needed the bodyguards, needed not to risk his all-important life fighting somebody else's battles overseas. He had to protect his image; even more, he needed the hard shell that guarded the exquisite flower within.

———

Sammy Cahn, the least sexually adventurous member of the Varsity, had happily fallen into the tender trap in 1945, tying the knot with the young and beautiful Gloria Delson, a Goldwyn Girl (and a Jewess). Sixty years later, Gloria Delson Franks, long since divorced from Cahn, recalled an early weekend she and Sammy spent in the Springs with the Sinatras, at the Lone Palm. "Frank taught me to swim," she said. "He's the one who got me over my fear of water. I said, 'I don't like putting my face in the water, Frank; it scares me.' He said, 'Don't worry. You'll learn how to do it and you won't be afraid. I'm telling you.'

"He'd sit with me in the pool and hold me up, and he'd say, 'Okay, put your face in.' Like I was a baby. He treated me so gently, and he was so patient with me."

———

On Friday night, June 20, Benny Siegel ate a late dinner with friends at an Ocean Park seafood restaurant called Jack's. On the way out, he took a toothpick and a free copy of the next morning's *Los Angeles Times* stamped, "Good Night. Sleep Well. With the Compliments of Jack's." The party drove back to Beverly Hills, where Siegel let himself into the big Tudor at 810 North Linden Drive he was renting for Virginia Hill. (Hill herself was in Paris, perhaps on her way to or from Benny's Swiss bank—or perhaps keeping away from Beverly Hills.)

It was a warm night, the windows were open, and the ethereal fragrance of night-blooming jasmine suffused the living room, where Siegel sat at one end of a flowered chintz couch, his *Times* on his lap. He wore a beautifully tailored gray silk suit and handmade English shoes polished to a high sheen. At the other end of the couch sat his pal and business partner, a handsome, prematurely white-haired man who called himself Allen Smiley. The two men talked about the Flamingo, which had just turned the corner into profitability.

In the bushes outside the front window a man in dark clothing squatted with a .30-caliber carbine, listening to the ratchet of the katydids and the singsong of Benny and Smiley's conversation. When he

Pure hate. Lee Mortimer looks on as a Beverly Hills judge
sets bail for Frank. April 1947.

was sure Benny was speaking, the man rose and rested the carbine's
muzzle in the V of a trellis and took careful aim at Siegel's head. He
squeezed the trigger. There was a blast, a flash, and Benny's head
exploded. His right eye was blown across the room onto the Spanish
tiles of the dining-room floor. Smiley dove to the carpet. The man in
the bushes fired eight more shots—all redundant—then dropped the
rifle and fled into the soft night.

Sinatra heard the news late the next morning as he suited up for a
Saturday-afternoon Swooners softball game. The call came from Hank
Sanicola, who had heard from a friend of a friend of Mickey Cohen's.
Frank was shocked but not surprised. He felt sad at the death of his
beautiful and magnetic friend, and at its violence, but knew he must

suppress the feeling. He would soon hear that the hit had been engineered by Frankie Carbo—the same Frankie Carbo who was rumored to have helped persuade Tommy Dorsey to release Sinatra from his contract, and ironically, the same Frankie Carbo who had been implicated along with Siegel in the 1939 murder of Harry Greenberg. But it barely mattered who had done the planning, or who had pulled the trigger: Frank knew the order had come straight from the summit in Havana, and the manager of the project had been Charlie Fischetti.

He didn't want to put on a sailor suit anymore; MGM obliged. Frank wore fake
sideburns and a properly embarrassed expression in *The Kissing Bandit,* 1948.

―――

There is a weird light playing around Sinatra. Hitler affected many
Germans much the same way and madness has been rife in the world.
—Westbrook Pegler, in his syndicated Hearst column of
September 26, 1947

―――

As U.S. relations with the Soviet Union deteriorated, paranoia over
Communism mounted, particularly in Hollywood. The climate of
fear surrounding the 1946 congressional elections had put a Republican majority in both houses for the first time since 1932, including a
freshman senator from Wisconsin named Joseph McCarthy. The new

majority swung into action in 1947, moving the House Un-American Activities Committee to step up its inquisitions and pressuring Harry Truman into signing Executive Order 9835, the so-called Loyalty Order, which gave the FBI broad latitude to investigate citizens and suspected Communist-front organizations.

It was in this climate, in June, that Americans began spotting flying saucers: over Mount Rainier in Washington State; over Idaho, surrounding a United Airlines DC-3; over Roswell, New Mexico. And then all over the place. Every week, Norman Rockwell–covered *Saturday Evening Post*s were plunking into American mailboxes; every night, citizens were checking under the bed.

In its own intense way, Hollywood reflected the national anxiety. On the face of it, nothing had changed: swimming pools glittered in the sun; heavy black cars glided beneath the palm trees; carpenters banged on sets. But there was big trouble in the easily spooked company town—J. Parnell Thomas, the chairman of HUAC, was in Hollywood to brief studio executives on what the committee believed was Communist infiltration of movie content by the Screen Writers Guild.

At the same time, Frank Sinatra was reporting to Culver City every weekday morning to play Ricardo, the kissing bandit.

In his previous pictures, Frank had just had to put on a costume and a little Max Factor; his latest role required a more complex transformation. Every morning, the hair department glued a luxuriant toupee, complete with sideburns, over his already thinning locks; the makeup people spackled his mastoid and acne scars so that his left profile would photograph acceptably under the bright lights required for Technicolor. After the failure of the black-and-white *It Happened in Brooklyn,* MGM was reinvesting in the expensive film process, hoping *The Kissing Bandit* would duplicate the magic of *Anchors Aweigh.*

Once again, Sinatra's pal and fellow Hollywood leftist Isobel Lennart wrote the script;[1] once again, the haughty-faced coloratura Kathryn Grayson co-starred—and, once again, she and Frank enjoyed minimal affinity. "I couldn't stand kissing him," Grayson later confessed. "He was so skinny, so scrawny."

But chemistry was just one of the picture's problems. The story was a mixture common enough for the era: broad comedy, romance, and music. To write the songs, Metro (having jettisoned Sammy Cahn and Jule Styne, perhaps as the whipping boys for *It Happened in Brooklyn*) hired the dependable if less interesting Nacio Herb Brown, writer of "Singin' in the Rain" and Bing's classic groaner "Temptation." In this instance, though, Brown's tunes were strictly so-so; the romance wasn't quite believable; and the comedy was tragically bad.

You can practically see the wheels turning in the story department at MGM: The war's over; it's time to get Frank out of uniform. How about some laughs? How about a satire on Zorro? Sinatra plays Ricardo, a college boy who returns from Boston to Old California and takes over his father's spot as the titular bandit. The laughs are supposed to come from Ricardo's timidity—once again Frank is playing awkward and shy—and his physical clumsiness. (He falls off his horse a lot.) There's campy fun in the film, and the Technicolor is gorgeous, but from the first scene the star's discomfort is palpable. His ears and his Hoboken accent both stick out a mile. (In subsequent pictures, Frank's ears would be taped back; the movies would learn to live with the accent.) He tries hard to look adorable: he does that lower-lip twitch. But something has misfired badly. Sinatra is clearly not liking himself in this part, which makes it hard to like him.

He can hardly be blamed for his uneasiness. Each morning, while the hair and makeup people labored over him, studio lawyers were trying to figure out how to make the Lee Mortimer affair go away. Between anticipating the verdict of the Beverly Hills District Court and having to stay out of trouble, Frank was not in buoyant spirits that spring and summer.

Still, he always managed to find outlets. If he couldn't keep Lana Turner (he finally dropped her over the phone, sending her into a rage: *she* was the one who did the dropping), he was going to throw himself into his marriage. This meant keeping his hijinks low profile, but most important it meant making a grand gesture. In May, wearing a yachting cap and licking an ice-cream cone, he walked into the Palm Springs office of a young architect named E. Stewart Williams and said, as Williams later recalled, "I wanna house."

And not just any house. Frank wanted a Georgian mansion, he told Williams, and he wanted it pronto: by Christmas. Christmas was very important. Nancy was going to get a present she wouldn't forget.

Six days after Benny Siegel was gunned down, on June 26, Frank was in the studio recording Christmas songs. In 1947 he recorded as he never had before: a total of seventy sides in all. Let Old Gold drop him; let Lee Mortimer sue him; let the Hearst papers rake him over the coals: he would show them all.

=====

There was reality—complicated, thorny, less hospitable every minute—and there was Frank in a yachting cap with an ice-cream cone. He strutted; he kept up appearances; he would keep believing in himself till there was no other alternative. His agents had gone out and done battle for him and got him a new radio show, really a return to an old one: *Your Hit Parade,* still sponsored by Lucky Strike. The good news was that for the first time since the show's inception in 1935, a single star would be at its center, singing the tunes and doing many of the commercials himself.

The bad news was that—gradually, then all at once—it wasn't really Frank's show. He wouldn't get to sing his own songs, unless his songs happened to be on the hit parade, an occurrence that seemed less likely with every passing week. Even as Hearst kept snapping at his heels, the public's musical tastes were changing. Suddenly Sinatra's record sales were dropping; his concert and nightclub bookings had declined. His yearly income had dropped below $1 million for the first time since 1942. Nobody was feeling very sorry for him.

On the first broadcast of his second *Your Hit Parade* run, on Saturday, September 6, Frank introduced Axel Stordahl, who had replaced Mark Warnow as bandleader, and, as co-star for the show's first two months, Doris Day. From Sinatra's first song, it was clear that something was deeply wrong.

The song was called "Feudin' and Fightin'," a novelty number about life down in the holler, Hatfield-and-McCoy style. It was the kind of faux-folksy trifle Bing Crosby could bring off without breaking a sweat, but with Frank singing it, it felt as phony as a three-dollar bill. His heart wasn't in it. (And he certainly hadn't read these lyrics like a poem before singing them.) But it was on the hit parade, which meant the American public wanted to hear it. And more and more, Sinatra and the American public appeared to be going their separate ways.

The ground was sliding beneath Frank's feet. His singing was the one part of his life where he couldn't dissemble. His belief in a song was part of what made him great; when he lost conviction, his vocal quality became two-dimensional. *Metronome,* which only two years earlier had crowned Frank Act of the Year, and with whose All-Stars he'd recently recorded the sublime "Sweet Lorraine," was withering about the new edition of *Your Hit Parade:*

> The show is alternately dull, pompous and raucous. Frank
> sings without relaxation and often at tempos that don't suit
> him or the song. Axel plays murderous, rag-timey junk, that
> he, with his impeccable taste, must abhor. And poor Doris
> Day, making her first real start in commercial radio, is saddled
> with arrangements which sound as if they were written long
> before anybody ever thought of having a stylist like her on the
> show . . . Frank sounds worse on these Saturday nightmares
> than he ever has since he first became famous.

There may have been schadenfreude in this; even those who had been his biggest boosters probably weren't averse to the pleasures of piling on. But to listen to the show proves *Metronome* right. Westbrook

Pegler was another matter. The columnist, who had been otherwise engaged for a couple of years, now went at Sinatra with a fresh vengeance. Throughout September he hammered on Frank, trotting out all the sins for which the Hearst papers had lavishly been taking him to task, and now—his one new note—slamming Sinatra's defenders. "A campaign of propaganda has been running in some areas of our press, including magazines, and on the radio to rehabilitate the reputation of Frank Sinatra," his column of September 10 began, ominously. In this loaded time, such phraseology was guaranteed to raise a Red flag. In some papers this column ran side by side with one by Victor Riesel, which began:

> I insist the "Communist Party" is more of a plot than a party, and I say that for too long the Communist propaganda machine, directed by many Broadway and Hollywood publicists, writers and "wise-crack" specialists, has bullied government officials so that they fear to disclose evidence of this plot.

The message, to any right-thinking reader, was clear: subversive elements were trying to undermine America, and Frank Sinatra—with his Mafia connections, his draft-dodging and sex-offending past (not to mention his oily hair and Italian surname)—was their standard-bearer.

Pegler was clearly building a case, but for what? Frank had acted badly: this was not in dispute. He had acted very badly. In the matter of his Havana adventure, depending on the contents of that heavy valise, he may even have broken the law. Had he dodged the draft? Probably. So had John Wayne. Had he been convicted on those two 1938 sex arrests? He had not. But rhetorically speaking, Pegler (he portentously called the complainant a "girl") felt the arrests were worth mentioning again. As was the fact that somebody had been lying about Frank's age.

The rock-jawed columnist (a photo of his unimpeachably Waspy countenance ran with every installment) was throwing everything he had at Sinatra, building up to a bombshell of some kind.

The propaganda campaign, Pegler said, consisted

> of many writers, including night club, radio, and movie
> columnists of New York and Hollywood, who have minimized
> incidents of Sinatra's career which other persons might
> have viewed with severity. Dozens of these "interpreters"
> and propagandists purport to be authorities on the personal
> histories of all such "celebrities." Many of them draw
> outlandish salaries as "reporters." But not one of them has ever
> reported this episode [the 1938 arrests], the most dramatic in
> Sinatra's life.

So he was not only a crook, a bully, and a draft dodger; he was a pervert. And his apologists, Pegler said, were legion. Of all the supposed dozens, the columnist singled out two egregious offenders, the *Daily News*'s Ed Sullivan and the *New Yorker*'s E. J. Kahn Jr. Sullivan, still a year away from his television career, had, for whatever reason, early on adopted a Sinatra-right-or-wrong stance in his columns. The *News* columnist, Pegler thundered, had "impugned the professional integrity of legitimate journalists who had faithfully covered the 'Sinatra story' in the Havana and Hollywood [Mortimer] episodes. [Sullivan had insisted Mortimer's] motive was to punish Sinatra because he gave of his spare time and energy 'to persuade kids to be nice to minority groups.'"

Fair enough. Sullivan was more or less in the bag. (Maybe, as with Wilson, a gold cigarette case had sealed the deal.) But Kahn was scarcely another Broadway hack. On balance, the worst that can be said about his three-part *New Yorker* profile (subsequently expanded into the slight but charming book *The Voice*) is that it was written in the amused, breezy tone so common to that magazine in those days, the verbal equivalent of Eustace Tilley deigning to glance through his lorgnette at a butterfly. "Sinatra has several other friends who, while not precisely desperadoes, are fairly rough-and-tumble individuals," reads a typical sentence in Kahn's piece. The passage immediately following soft-pedals Sinatra's acquaintance with Joe Fischetti and his meeting with Lucky Luciano.

For whatever reasons—surely artistic rather than political—Kahn minimizes Sinatra's bad behavior. But the writer's worst offense, according to Westbrook Pegler, was this: "Kahn writes also that some of Sinatra's public earnestly believe that his birthday is second in importance to only that of Jesus Christ."

Pegler, who would become an increasingly rabid anti-Semite (he liked to refer to Eastern European Jews as "geese"), didn't have to state the obvious: Kahn was a Jew. And worse still, a Jew bowing down to an Antichrist. This is no exaggeration. In his column of September 26, Pegler wrote, "There is a weird light playing around Sinatra. Hitler affected many Germans much the same way and madness has been rife in the world."

This was not just some California kook writing the FBI about the nefarious possibilities of swooning bobby-soxers. This was a Pulitzer-winning columnist, with the broadest possible platform, the five hundred newspapers of the Hearst Syndicate, comparing a popular entertainer to the worst mass murderer in history.

And Pegler wasn't done yet.

On December 8, he went for the knockout punch, beginning with the magic triangulation: "From time to time, these dispatches have disclosed and commented on a strange liaison between our journalism and the underworld and Communist fronts of the amusement industry."

Communism never came up again in that column—in those days you only had to say it once. After dropping the word, Pegler segued right back into the familiar theme of Frank's nasty associations. First he took on the Varsity member Jimmy Tarantino, who had moved to California and started a scandal sheet called *Hollywood Nite Life,* a precursor of *Confidential.* Tarantino was a skanky character, one of the many who would stick a little too closely to Sinatra throughout the years.[2] In this case the glue was Hank Sanicola, Tarantino's partner on *Hollywood Nite Life*. (Mickey Cohen, quite the man about Tinseltown, might also have been involved.) Frank should have given Jimmy Tarantino—and a lot of other people throughout the years—a wide berth, but if a man was loyal and amusing, Frank never bothered to do a background check. He liked to laugh, and fun came first. If the price was the vitriol of Westbrook Pegler and Lee Mortimer, so be it. Yet there was another price to pay.

At the end of the column, Pegler returned to the reliable theme of sex: specifically, Sinatra's role as seducer of the nation's youth. But in a curious (and more than slightly kinky) twist, the columnist now blamed the seducees:

> There has been strident controversy as to Sinatra's real opinion of the nasty little chits who used to loiter late into the night around night clubs, theaters, and other inappropriate haunts for children, where Sinatra was earning his living or taking his ease with the Fischetti frcrcs of the Chicago underworld and Lucky Luciano, the exiled Sicilian prostitutioneer. Mortimer called them little morons. This was outlandish flattery in the reckless tabloid manner, and Sinatra caught him when his head was turned and slugged him . . .
>
> In a study of this matter at the time I wrote that Mr. Evans, the manager and press-agent, had expressed the same opinion of these sinister little tramps . . . It was . . . Mr. Evans, Sinatra's own manager and propagandist, the man who fomented the excitement over this exaggerated roadhouse moaner, who spoke to me of Frankie Boy's following as sexually excited jailbait, a million of them, squealing like animals.

Pegler is finally showing his true colors. The real surprise is George Evans's disaffection. No matter what he actually said to Westbrook

Pegler—and the lack of a direct quotation is suspicious—the fact that he spoke to him at all (and in all likelihood really did say something derogatory about Sinatra's fan base) hints at trouble in Frank's professional life. At the end of the column Pegler, in high poetic mode, wrote, "Sinatra laid an egg at the Capitol theater and the amorous cult had vanished away like the insect clouds that madly swarm and dissolve." There was certainly no love lost between Westbrook Pegler and Frank Sinatra, but where the Capitol Theater gig was concerned, the columnist was, for once, telling the straight story.

=====

Sinatra's stand at the Capitol, the site of his famous opening with the Hoboken Four, was meant to be a triumphant return. "FRANK SINATRA/M-G-M's Singing Star/IN PERSON," a poster trumpeted. But the tanking of *It Happened in Brooklyn*, along with the star's current publicity, hinted that triumph might not be in the cards. (And then, for anyone who cared to pay attention, there was the title of the movie that accompanied the Capitol show: *Her Husband's Affairs*, with Lucille Ball and Franchot Tone.) By the end of the second week of the three-week engagement, it was clear that something was very wrong. Lee Mortimer reported, gleefully but with the numbers to back him up: "The crooner, expected to pile up new highs, almost hits a new low. His second week . . . was a sickly $71,000, half of the advance estimate." And in a subsequent column: "Broadway whispers this will be Sinatra's last appearance here, and that didn't kill my appetite for the family turkey dinner."

It was no fluke: the wheel really had turned. The relentless bad publicity couldn't have helped; still, the cold fact was that Frank's core audience, those nasty little chits, that sexually excited jailbait, were growing up and moving on. Throughout the year, despite Sinatra's unprecedented number of studio sessions, his record sales had slipped badly: his discs spent just twenty-six weeks on the *Billboard* charts in 1947, as compared with ninety-seven the year before. He was putting more in and getting less out. On *Your Hit Parade,* he was almost always singing other people's songs: one of the first, in September, had been that old chestnut, "I Wonder Who's Kissing Her Now," a big hit for Perry Como—who, by the way, now stood one notch above Frank on *Billboard*'s annual performance chart.

Sinatra had been singing professionally for a dozen years; he had had an amazing run. Maybe his time was passing. He might have been The Voice, but there were other voices the public found pleasing. That nice Perry Como had a very pleasant tone (and a nice face too), and you didn't see him running around with gangsters or slugging people.

All but buried at the bottom of the poster for the Capitol Theater engagement, far beneath "SINATRA" and in significantly smaller type than the billings for Lorraine Rognan (Petite Comedienne) and Skitch Henderson (his Piano and his ORCH.), was the name of Frank's opening act: "WILL MASTIN TRIO with Sammy Davies Jr."

Misprint aside, the billing was deceptive: Sammy Davis Jr. was the one whose name should have been first, in big capital letters. He had been the star of the act since age three, in 1928, when his father, Sammy Davis Sr., and vaudeville partner Will Mastin first put the little boy on the stage. From childhood, Sammy had been a miraculous performer, a show-business prodigy who could instantly pick up complicated dance routines, sing like a natural, and learn to play any instrument that was put into his hands. About to turn twenty-two, having reached his adult height of just five feet three, he was a tiny whirlwind of singing and dancing genius: he not only had a beautifully rich baritone but could do tap routines of blinding speed and precision. He could play piano, saxophone, and drums. He did eerily accurate impersonations of Cary Grant, Boris Karloff, Edward G. Robinson—and of his idol Frank Sinatra.

He was also a desperately lonely young man. His parents had split when his father took him on the road; performing had been his whole life. Little Sammy spent his childhood running from truant officers, missing his mother, living for the charmed moments each day when he could win the love of an audience. The hours between those moments were long and empty. In his spare time he imagined the fame that would bring him true love at last. Fame, he knew, was everything.

Davis had been obsessed with Sinatra from the moment he first heard about him. That voice made his hair stand on end—as did the idolatry. As Sammy toured the unapologetically racist country, scrounging a living in flea-bitten vaudeville theaters, carrying the act named after the bitter and domineering old man who also loved him like an uncle, he thought constantly of Frank—bought his records and fan magazines, kept a scrapbook of articles about him, imitated his dress and mannerisms. And—since he was not just an entertainer but also a stargazing fan who haunted stage doors wherever he played, trying to get a glimpse of, and maybe an autograph from, stars like Milton Berle, Danny Thomas, Bob Hope—Sammy dreamed of the day he would meet his idol in person.

It came, unexpectedly, at Detroit's Michigan Theater in 1941, when the Mastin Trio filled in for Tommy Dorsey's warm-up act Tip, Tap, & Toe. There was a friendly backstage handshake between Sinatra and the awestruck sixteen-year-old, and then the road took them their separate ways. Over the next couple of years, as Frank's star rose and the Mastin Trio kept scrounging, Sammy dreamed of the reunion that would validate his existence. His chance came in the fall of 1945, in Los Angeles. Though he'd been discharged from the Army in June, he got out his uniform, had it pressed, and put it on so he could get a serviceman's ticket to Sinatra's radio show at CBS. Afterward, he recalled in his autobiography,

> I hurried around the corner to the stage door. There must
> have been five hundred kids ahead of me, waiting for a look at
> him. When he appeared, the crowd surged forward like one
> massive body ready to go right through the side of the building

if necessary. Girls were screaming, fainting, pushing, waving pencils and papers in the air. A girl next to me shouted, "I'd faint if I had room to fall down." She got her laugh and the crowd kept moving. I stood on tiptoe trying to see him. God, he looked like a star. He wasn't much older than a lot of us but he was so calm, like we were all silly kids and he was a man, sure of himself, completely in control. He acted as if he didn't know there were hundreds of papers being waved at him. He concentrated on one at a time, signing it, smiling, and going to the next. He got to me and took my paper. He used a solid gold pen to sign his name. I thanked him and he looked at me. "Don't I know you?"

The story rings true, solid-gold pen and all. Sinatra did have an amazing memory for names and faces, and Sammy Davis didn't look like anybody else. Frank invited him to come to his dressing room after the next week's show. Sammy remembered that once there, all he could do was stare at his idol and think, " 'I can speak to Frank Sinatra and he'll answer me.' But I couldn't think of anything clever enough to say so I just watched him, smiling and laughing at his every word."

It was a perfect relationship for both men.

By the time Frank got to the Capitol in November 1947, he had established a tradition. "Frank Sinatra," Will Mastin explained to the two Sammys after the fateful telegram came, "always has a colored act on the bill with him."

Even if George Evans had nothing but public relations in mind when he pushed his star client to accept all those tolerance awards, that didn't make Sinatra a phony liberal. And his sentiments about working with black entertainers ran deep: artistically speaking, he knew where his bread was buttered. He simply understood too much about the roots of American popular music to imagine that he didn't owe an important debt to the geniuses of Fifty-second Street, Billie Holiday first among them.

But aside from that, Frank genuinely liked black people. And, understanding this, most black people—who, by the fact of their existence in America, possessed an intricate radar for racism—liked him back.[3] He clearly understood what it was like to be discriminated against. He had great style. And that voice of his told the truth, no matter what color your ears were.

So he hired colored acts. Sinatra, in addition to being color-blind, was generous—and, once he had decided to help someone, tenacious. MGM could squawk all it wanted about taking on those unknowns Sammy Cahn and Jule Styne, but if they didn't, they didn't get Sinatra. The Capitol Theater could remind Frank until they were blue in the face that if he wanted a colored act, he could easily get the more famous Moke and Poke, or the Berry Brothers, or the Nicholas Brothers, who were even in a movie, for God's sake. Frank shook his head obstinately. "There's a kid who comes to my radio show when he's in town, he works with his family, his name is Sam something. Use him."

"All right, Frank, if you want 'em you got 'em. How much do you want to give them?"

"Make it $1,250."

"We can get the Nicholas Brothers for that kind of money and . . . they're hot."

"$1,250. That's it. I don't want the Nicholas Brothers. I want Sam and his family."

And once the Will Mastin Trio (which up to this point had been making $350 in a good week) was onstage at the Capitol, Frank would stroll out and throw his arm around Sammy's shoulder—in an era when such a gesture from a white man to a black man was a very rare sight indeed—and personally introduce him to the crowd.

Even if the crowd, especially by the second week, was no longer quite the size the crowds had been so very recently.

═══

During all this disappointment, Frank kept recording as though his life depended on it—which, in a very real way, it did. In October alone, he cut an amazing twenty sides at Liederkranz Hall, more than he had done in all of 1943. Committing to shellac such great standards as "All of Me," "Laura," "The Song Is You," and "What'll I Do?" was a kind of atonement for all the mediocre material he was being forced to sing on *Your Hit Parade*. On Friday, October 31—having spent the previous afternoon grinning through a cold rain as Hoboken celebrated Frank Sinatra Day—he recorded three beautiful songs, "Mean to Me," "Spring Is Here," and "Fools Rush In," and he sang them beautifully.

The only problem was, the public wasn't buying.

Dolly had stood close by Frank's side as the mayor of Hoboken presented him with a giant wooden key to the city. Wearing a big feathered hat and the mink stole Frank had bought her, she threw her head back as the photographers snapped away, a rapturous smile creasing her chubby cheeks. Rain or no rain, her moment in the sun had come at last. Frank Sinatra Day, Dolly Sinatra Day—same thing. At his son's other shoulder stood Marty, looking grim in his old-fashioned fire captain's uniform with its two rows of brass buttons. Firemen marched in parades; they didn't lead them.

Just out of range of the photographers stood Nancy, smiling despite the proximity of her mother-in-law. George Evans was holding an umbrella over her. She wore a wool coat, the Tiffany pearl earrings Frank had bought her, and, out of sight but cool against her breastbone, the triple strand of pearls. She was also carrying a very tangible token of her husband's recommitment to their marriage: she was pregnant again.

———

At the construction site on Alejo Road, out in the desert at the edge of Palm Springs, the bulldozers and cement mixers ran double shifts, working all day and then at night under floodlights as the builders hurried toward the Christmas deadline. E. Stewart Williams had shown Frank Sinatra two very different sets of drawings: one was of the Georgian mansion Frank had requested, and the other depicted Williams's far more modern concept, a low-lying concrete structure with tall picture windows and a shed roof. The young architect had literally held his breath as the singer scanned the drawings, a serious look on his tanned features. Sinatra's domineering reputation had preceded him, yet Williams, trying to forge a career, knew that building Georgian in the desert—impractical as well as retrograde—would make him a laughingstock in the field. He would be seen as a servant rather than an artist. Frank nodded, frowning, as he inspected the modern design, then, suddenly looking interested, nodded some more.

Williams exhaled.

The house wasn't quite a mansion—at forty-five hundred square feet, it was large but not gigantic, and there were only four bedrooms—but the rooms and the windows were big, and every window, as well as a sliding glass wall, looked out onto the swimming pool, which was shaped (Williams couldn't help smiling at this inspired touch) like a grand piano. A breezeway over one end of the pool was designed to shed shadows that would resemble piano keys. Bright sun and spar-

Twin Palms, Palm Springs. Architect E. Stewart Williams designed the desert retreat, complete with piano-shaped swimming pool, for his demanding client and his family; within weeks of its completion, Frank was courting Ava Gardner.

kling light off the pool filled the living room: if shade was needed, the flick of a switch closed a $7,000 motorized curtain. In the distance stony Mount San Jacinto shimmered white in the fierce sun; in the foreground, two palm trees waved in the desert wind. The house, made pleasant by air-conditioning in the summer and fireplaces in the winter, would be a shelter from the desert around it. Frank would call the place Twin Palms.

No one like her, before or since. "I just noticed the body,"
said Sammy Cahn's first wife. "It just moved like a willow.
She was built beautifully. She was a gorgeous creature."

As his wife grew great with child for the third time, Sinatra found
more and more reasons to be elsewhere. Pregnancy may be deemed
sexy by some cultures in some eras, but in late-1940s America it
was anything but. The women got fat and sick and peevish; the men
took increasing notice of the unbelievably slim waistlines of the young
women they passed. For Frank, the delectable bodies of the young
women all around him proved increasingly irresistible.

It was a time of challenge in general. A new American Federation of Musicians strike had begun on the first day of 1948: once again, there could be no recording with orchestras. The ban wouldn't end until early December. In the interim, Sinatra would go into the recording studio exactly twice, laying down just three sides—two that would be released later with overdubbed orchestral backing, and one with a choir ("Nature Boy," a version far inferior to the glorious one Nat Cole had recorded before the strike began).

Sinatra was not spending much time in movie studios, either. *The Kissing Bandit* had wrapped, thank God (though Frank's agony was to be prolonged: extra scenes had to be shot the following March); production on *The Miracle of the Bells* had finished at the end of September. He would start work on a new Metro musical with Gene Kelly, *Take Me Out to the Ball Game,* in July.

In the meantime, he was largely idle. On Saturday nights came *Your Hit Parade,* with its occasional pleasures but mostly its tribulations: in January, he sprinted through a version of "Too Fat Polka" ("I don't want her, you can have her, she's too fat for me") so dispiriting that to listen to it is to risk bursting into tears. Worse was to come. He did a couple of guest spots on Jack Benny's and Maurice Chevalier's radio shows. But mainly, he did a lot of drinking and poker playing with the Varsity.

Frank had officially moved out of his penthouse at the Sunset Tower apartments years before, but had held on to it—for the times he recorded late at night and had to be at the studio early the next morning; for business meetings; for other things. For a while, Axel and Sammy Cahn had roomed together in a suite a couple of floors below: now Sammy was married, but he still liked to stop by Frank's place now and then for a drink, a few hands of cards, some laughs.

One night, after some of each, Sammy and Frank were out on the terrace, looking down over the Sunset Strip. A violet evening, the little lights twinkling in the Hollywood hills. Sammy pointed, a little unsteadily, across the street. Did Frank know who lived down there?

Frank just shook his head at him.

"If you looked down from Frank's terrace," Cahn wrote in his auto-biography, "you'd see, across the street, a series of little houses, one of them owned by Tom Kelly, a noted interior decorator; the occupant of that house was Ava Gardner."

When Sammy told him this, Frank shook his head again, this time in wonderment. For a moment, he stared fiercely into the twilight. Then he cupped his hands to his mouth. "Ava!" he yelled. The big voice carried far into the quiet evening. "Ava Gardner!"

Sammy Cahn looked at his hero and grinned. Nobody like him. Now he cupped his hands to *his* mouth. "Can you hear me, Ava?" he called, in his high, hoarse tones. "We know you're down there, Ava!"

"Hello, Ava, hello!" Sinatra called. As if he were yelling down a wishing well.

The two men looked at each other and began to giggle. Giggling turned to laughing. Laughing became hysteria. Soon they were both clutching their sides painfully and bellowing into the night. Down on the sidewalk, one or two passersby—in those days there weren't many pedestrians on the Strip—stared up at the terrace.

And then a miracle: in the little house nestled into the trees on the north side of Sunset—torn down many years ago and replaced by a railroad-car restaurant—a curtain was drawn, a window opened.

Ava stuck her head out the window and looked up. She knew exactly who it was: the voice was unmistakable. She grinned, and waved back.

———

Was it an accident that they ran into each other just a few days later, in front of her place? And then again, a few days after that, near Sunset Tower? Frank wasn't much for walking, but suddenly there was some-thing compelling about those stretches of sidewalk. The third time, they both spotted each other a half block away; both began laughing as they converged.

He grinned as he said hello.

Ava's eyes searched his. Was he following her?

He met her gaze boldly. If he were following her, he'd be behind her.

She put a hand on her hip. Uh-huh.

"Ava, let's be friends. Why don't we have drinks and dinner tonight?"

"I looked at him," she wrote in her autobiography.

I damn well knew he was married, though the gossip columns always had him leaving Nancy for good, and married men were definitely not high on my hit parade. But he *was* handsome, with his thin, boyish face, the bright blue eyes, and this incredible grin. And he was so enthusiastic and invigorated, clearly pleased with life in general, himself in particular, and, at that moment, *me.*

She accepted his invitation, and they went to Mocambo, just up the Strip. There were a lot of drinks. She had taken up the habit soon after she married the tyrannical Artie Shaw, to quell the feelings of intellectual inferiority he so easily aroused in her. This night there were different feelings to quell. In any case, alcohol, in quantity, made her forget her deep self-doubt, made her feel like a different person— glamorous, intelligent, desirable, a person worthy of the attentions of Frank Sinatra. She had always had a thing for musicians: Shaw, with his Svengali act, had taken advantage of that. But Sinatra was in a category all his own. He was, she'd felt from the first time she heard him, "one of the greatest singers of this century. He had a thing in his voice I've only heard in two other people—Judy Garland and Maria Callas. A quality that makes me want to cry for happiness, like a beautiful sunset or a boys' choir singing Christmas carols."

And now here she was, sitting with him. She leaned her head on her hand tipsily and looked sideways at him. He was telling a story, animatedly. She could barely make out the words. It didn't matter. Could she be in love with this man? She shook her head, as if in wonderment at something he was saying, but really to herself: this wouldn't do.

Frank was not immune to guilt either, though alcohol and admiration could quickly make him feel that other rules applied in his case. He had told himself that with dozens of girls—but Ava was different. Marilyn Maxwell had been sweet and sincere and deliciously naughty; Lana was gorgeous and fiery but ultimately too self-protective and shallow: her deepest belief was in her own celebrity. This one stared at him—and stared at him and stared at him—and her green-gold eyes said that she knew all his secrets. The smile that curled one corner of those amazing lips confirmed it. And his deepest secret was this: she possessed him.

After a long time they realized they were hungry, and they ate a little something. But—there were more drinks with dinner—mostly they devoured each other with their eyes. And laughed, when the tension became unbearable. He lit both their cigarettes with a gold lighter, then paid the check. He took her hand (she kept stealing glances at his hands; they were beautiful) and led her to his car.

She resisted for a moment, then she didn't.

Just a little while.

As drunk as she was—and her head seemed to be floating a vast distance over her feet—she swore her deepest oath to herself: she would not sleep with him. Somehow, whether he knew it or not, he was testing her, and she was testing herself. If she crossed this line, he would categorize her. If she crossed this line, she would be back in the bad place she had been with Artie, adrift and uncertain, a poor fatherless girl from nowhere, and nothing.

They went someplace—she was never sure, later, just where. Not his place was all she knew. A beautiful apartment, someplace. With paintings, and big windows with a view of the city, and music—his— and a divine fragrance she couldn't get out of her mind for days afterward. He took her hand and led her to the bedroom, and she stopped in the doorway. He gave her the gentlest pull, but this time she stood firm. So they sat on the couch in the living room and kissed. Kissed and kissed. She had never kissed like this before. Kissing him, she thought, was in a different universe from fucking almost anyone else.

He reached around and began to unzip her dress. And though she loved her own body, and in most cases was out of her clothes in a second, at this moment she hesitated. She touched his arm.

Francis.

No one had ever called him this before.[1] He moved his hand back, and they kissed some more. For a long time.

He said her name, softly, after a while. Then he took her home.

Neither of them slept that night. It would be months before they saw each other again.

=====

The house in the desert was finished on time and, thanks to the round-the-clock construction schedule, phenomenally over budget. Twin Palms wound up costing $150,000, a huge sum in 1948, and five times the original estimate. But it was finished, and it was beautiful, and now Frank and Nancy and the children had an incomparable weekend refuge. Palm Springs looked like no place else. There were a couple of paved streets; the rest was just sand and stones and palms and orange groves and blazing flowers and crystalline air—it all made you feel you'd landed on a different planet. Frank felt freer there; the lines on his forehead smoothed out. He'd bought an Army-surplus jeep for fun, and he drove the kids over the sand (of course Nancy couldn't go in her condition), gunning the engine and beeping the horn and bouncing and whooping and laughing.

When they got back, Nancy was sitting by the pool in the sun, her belly rising like a hill in her maternity bathing suit. As the kids bounded into the water, Frank leaned down and kissed her on the top of the head; she patted his hand, pressing her lips together.

She knew almost everything, knew that this was the way it was going to be until—or unless—they weren't together anymore. She had fooled herself, till the pregnancy was too far along to change anything, that this time might be different. Tonight he would disappear once more: even in the desert, there were places to go. When he returned, deep in the night, she would smell the liquor and tobacco and perfume on him; when he patted her shoulder, she would turn and pretend to be asleep.

Many years later, Nancy Sandra remembered one of these weekends at Twin Palms: Her father had gone out there first, then the next day big Sam Weiss—the song plugger who had helped Frank out during the Mortimer encounter at Ciro's—drove Big Nancy and the children to the Springs. Three hours over two-lane blacktop, the warm wind shooting through the open windows, Nancy and Sam chatting in the front seat, then falling into long silences. "On this trip," Nancy Sandra writes in *Frank Sinatra: My Father,*

> the plan was . . . for us to see Daddy for a couple of days, and then for Sam to drive us home, leaving our parents alone. They didn't get to spend time alone very often. When I realized I was being sent away, I couldn't stand it. I cried and cried—not a tantrum, not angry, but afraid of leaving my mom; I had never been without her.
>
> I couldn't stop crying. Frankie, never lacking emotion, caught it, and we both cried and cried. Daddy, out of pity, or in a desperate attempt to save his sanity, eventually said to Mom, "I guess you'd better go with them." So Mom packed us up, put us in the car with Sam, and climbed in the back seat next to her spoiled brat of a daughter. When we were out of sight of the two skinny palm trees and Daddy, Mom started to cry softly. She tried to hide her tears behind dark glasses. Now, I had never seen my mother cry before—I mean, mothers don't cry, *children* cry. It's not a mother's job.
>
> I was shocked and frightened . . .

And Weiss, Nancy writes, was "disgusted" with both children—the three-hour drive back to Toluca Lake felt like twelve. When they got home, the children's new governess, Georgie Hardwick—until recently employed by the Bing Crosbys—came out to meet them:

> We'd had a few other governesses—Whitey, Kathleen, Dolores, Mamie—but Georgie was the toughest. She was great. And in this situation, expecting to see only two very small people walk through the door sans mother, she flashed me a look I'll never forget. From that day on, without lectures, without words, Georgie quietly, gently, transformed me into an unspoiled child.

The account is chilling—the gruff, ultimately unsympathetic body-guard; the frightened children; the distraught mother. The ever less present father. Frank himself is little more than a cipher in the epi-sode: *a voice on the radio . . . a picture in the newspaper,* as Nancy had recalled of her earliest childhood. Nothing had changed.

I guess you'd better go with them.

Why couldn't they all just have stayed? Was it pity that made him send them away, or impatience—or did he not really want them there in the first place?

What was the reason for Big Nancy's tears?

And what is it that makes a scared child a spoiled brat?

The trail leads straight to the governess with the Dickensian name, Georgie Hardwick. She had left the Crosby household for a very spe-cific reason. "When the Crosby kids talk about being punished and beaten, it was Georgie who did most of it, not Bing," Crosby's biogra-pher Gary Giddins said. Bing's son Gary Crosby wrote in his autobiog-raphy:

> I remember her as a short, stocky, fanatically devout Irish
> Catholic with a Boston accent, wiry hair and a grim face. She

was hired on as our nurse when I was about eight and quickly became the lord high executioner of all my mother's rules. The instant one was broken she went running off to Mom or, more and more frequently, took care of the punishment herself by going after us with wire coat hangers.

"When Bing realized what a monstrous thing she had made of the home," Giddins said, "he fired her, and Frank immediately hired her."

In the process of his research, Giddins tried to draw Nancy junior out about Hardwick: "She said, 'Well, yes, she worked for us. She was part of the family.' Long pauses. I finally said, 'Look, this is what I heard about her.' There was a long pause, and she said, 'All I'll say is, she was very, very—tough.' That was the end of the interview."

Without lectures, without words, Georgie . . . transformed me into an unspoiled child.

Leaving the "quietly, gently" open for discussion.

=====

In February, Frank sat down with *Metronome*'s George T. Simon—the very man who seven and a half years earlier had had to be sweet-talked into writing up the brand-new singer in the magazine—and did some serious venting about the state of American popular music.

"Right now certain conditions in the music business really have him down," Simon wrote. "Chances are that he can't stand *Your Hit Parade* any more than most of us can . . . But his biggest gripe of all right now is the terrible trash turned out by Tin Pan Alley."

In fact, Sinatra was more than down—he was hopping mad:

Frank was a pretty weary guy when he sounded off during a short break on a recording date . . . but it seems that when you're really pooped you relax more, you lose your inhibitions, and you say what you want to say. Some of the stuff Sinatra passed along was so libelous that it's not printable, but all the rest is something The Voice feels just as strongly about, even though the language may be more pianissimo.

"About the popular songs of the day," pet-peeves Frankie, "they've become so decadent, they're so bloodless. As a singer of popular songs, I've been looking for wonderful pieces of music in the popular vein—what they call Tin Pan Alley songs. You can not find any. Outside of production material, show tunes, you can't find a thing . . .

"I don't think the music business has progressed enough. There are a lot of people to blame for this. The songwriter in most cases finds he has to prostitute his talents if he wants to make a buck . . . The publisher is usually a fly-by-night guy anyway and so to make a few fast bucks he buys a very bad song, very badly written. And the recording companies are helping those guys by recording such songs. I don't think the few extra bucks in a song that becomes a fast hit make a dif-ference in the existence of a big recording company or a big publishing firm. *If they turned them down, it wouldn't do any harm and it would do music some good* [italics mine].

In a very short time, of course, Sinatra would be turning down very little himself.

The subject he was dancing around was the root causes of the change. Was the music business really leading the public, or was it the other way around? The one possibility the singer couldn't stand admit-ting, to the press or to himself, was that America's tastes had simply changed.

The novelist William Maxwell once told me, when I asked, starry-eyed, what it had been like to be alive during the Roaring Twen-ties, that it had been a terrible time, a time of giddiness, shallowness, escape. Much the same kind of mind-set was prevalent after World War II. The country wanted to forget the terrible near past and the deeply troubling present. America was jumpy. We wanted our pleasures quick, and we wanted them simple: they shouldn't trigger any problematic emotions. We got what we wanted.

———

The Miracle of the Bells premiered the day before St. Patrick's Day. RKO, having filled its coffers under the watchword of "Entertainment, not genius," was still saving money by cranking out B pictures. When it made the odd A feature, it borrowed stars from other studios. *Miracle,* with Sinatra on punishment leave from MGM and Fred MacMurray loaned out from Paramount, was an attempt, right down to its reverberating title, to cash in on the success of Bing Crosby's holy-Joe pictures *Going My Way* and *The Bells of St. Mary's.* The difference was that Crosby had Leo McCarey to direct him, and Sinatra had Irving Pichel. And then there was the fact that Bing, the sly old genius, could play quite a charming and credible priest. Frank, at this stage of his life, had too much sexual vanity and too many internal conflicts to believably act such a role. Maybe he could have pulled it off ten years later, when he was more manly and battle scarred and able to make fun of himself on-screen.

But the movie's problems didn't begin with its star. Ben Hecht, who co-wrote the screenplay with Quentin Reynolds, apparently took the job on the condition that he not be forced to read the sappy popular novel he would be adapting.[2] And then there was the picture's glum setting, a Pennsylvania mining town, and its generally dark tone. "Pompous and funereal," Bosley Crowther wrote of the finished product. And while Crowther was reliably stuffy, in this case he had a point. The story concerned a young actress who died—just like Camille, of a hacking cough—after starring in her first film. The cynical press agent (MacMurray) who lifted her from the burlesque house to movie stardom takes her body back to her Pennsylvania hometown for burial. Miracles occur.

The dark and dazzling Alida Valli played the actress: even *The Third Man,* the following year, would not be enough to resuscitate her career after this stinker. And as Father Paul, Sinatra, in his first drama, was subdued to the point of seeming depressed. ("Frank Sinatra, looking rather flea-bitten as the priest, acts properly humble or perhaps ashamed," *Time* wrote.) The best that can be said about him in this role is that, as would not be the case in *The Kissing Bandit,* he didn't sink the movie. It did that all by itself.

Sinatra was ashamed—not just of *The Miracle of the Bells,* but of the whole year. He was singing junk on the radio. He was losing his audience, his prestige, his hair. And with Sinatra, as we have seen, shame quickly changed to rage. When the movie's producer, the Hollywood institution Jesse Lasky, reminded the star that he was contractually obliged to attend the San Francisco premiere, Frank bullied the old man until Lasky was forced to plead for his presence. Sinatra went to San Francisco, but in full Monster mode. Ensconced in the biggest suite at the Fairmont hotel with Jack Keller, Bobby Burns, and Jimmy Van Heusen, Frank ordered eighty-eight Manhattans from room service. Up came several waiters pushing carts full of clinking glasses: Sinatra told them to leave the drinks in the entry hall, and there the eighty-eight Manhattans sat for three days, untouched. Unable to sleep at 4:00 a.m., he ordered a piano to be sent to his suite. A store manager had to be awakened, and a delivery-truck driver paid triple time to deliver the instrument. The next night Frank took twenty people out on the town, then brought them back to the suite for a party that didn't break up till 7:00 a.m. Two hours later, still revving, he took Keller, Burns, and Van Heusen to a swanky haberdasher and bought each man $1,200 worth of cashmere sweaters, ties, shirts, and socks— all of it charged to Sinatra's suite at the Fairmont, which of course was on the studio's dime.

Frank slept through the afternoon, then behaved perfectly at the premiere that night. The next morning, though, he decided he had to get to Palm Springs—instantly. Unfortunately, a thick fog had settled in over San Francisco during the night, and the airlines weren't flying. Sinatra ordered Van Heusen, the pilot, to charter a plane. No planes were to be had. In the end, Frank and Jimmy took a limousine from

San Francisco to Palm Springs—a five-hundred-mile trip—at a cost of over $1,100. Multiply all figures by nine to get the present-day equivalent. So much for cost cutting at RKO.

═══

Hedda Hopper summed up the feelings of pretty much every reviewer in the country when she called *The Miracle of the Bells* "a hunk of religious baloney." And then, more shame. In a wrap-up of the previous year's movies, *Life* chose Frank's cameo in the Metro musical *Till the Clouds Roll By* as "the worst single moment" in any picture: "MGM struck a high point in bad taste when Frank Sinatra stood on a fluted pillar and crooned 'Ol' Man River,' including the line 'You and me, we sweat and strain . . . ,' wearing an immaculate white suit."

With *The Kissing Bandit* in the can (and every bit as bad as he suspected it to be), and his recording career at a standstill, Sinatra didn't have much to look forward to in the middle of 1948—with one exception. In the early hours of June 20 (the anniversary of Bugsy's death), as Frank and Nancy played charades at Toluca Lake with the Jule Stynes and a few other couples, Nancy went into labor. Frank bundled her into the Cadillac convertible and—with great pleasure; just let them try to stop him—ran every red light between the Valley and Cedars of Lebanon Hospital. As it turned out, the haste was justified: Christina Sinatra (she would be called Tina, after Nancy's sister) was born just minutes after Nancy was brought into the maternity ward. Frank kissed his wife and new baby daughter and drove back to Toluca Lake and jumped right back into the charades, which were still going strong. He mimed an hourglass to signify it had been a girl and held up fingers to indicate her weight. It was early Sunday morning, Father's Day. It was the first time he had been in town for the birth of one of his children.

═══

On the next day, June 21, 1948, at a press conference at the Waldorf-Astoria, the Columbia Recording Corporation announced, with great fanfare, a startling technological innovation: the long-playing

33¹/₃-rpm phonograph record. At a simultaneous dealer conference in Atlantic City, a Columbia executive gave a speech lauding the new invention to the accompaniment of an entire movement of *The Nutcracker Suite*. The record played on a phonograph with a mirror mounted overhead so the audience could see there was no trickery. At the end of the eighteen-minute side—four times as long as one side of a 78-rpm disc—the assembled record dealers leaped to their feet applauding. The future had arrived.

The LP was the brainchild of Columbia's president, Ted Wallerstein, who had first conceived of it a decade earlier as the ideal medium for classical music. In addition to Tchaikovsky and Beethoven, one of the label's first pressings was a ten-inch LP reissue of 1946's *The Voice of Frank Sinatra*. The album sold well, but not nearly as well as the original: for one thing, few people had the equipment to play it. In October, Columbia brought out a Sinatra Christmas album that did a little better: it lasted a week on the charts, rising just to number 7.

His next hit album wouldn't come for five years—an eternity.

———

Four months after the Simon interview, one week after Tina's birth, Frank stood at the radio microphone at CBS and, with disbelief in his voice, introduced the latest addition to the hit parade: "The Woody Woodpecker Song." As the show's vocal group, the Hit Paraders, went into the supremely annoying number, which revolved around the cartoon character's supremely annoying laugh, Frank could be heard in the background, telling the studio audience: "I just couldn't do it!"

Meaning, he couldn't bring himself to sing it. That was June 26. On July 10, he no longer had any choice.

"Well, I guess I better keep my hat on, 'cause look who's here in spot number one," Sinatra told Mr. and Mrs. America—and then, as though he had lost a bet, unbelievably went into that Woody Woodpecker laugh: "Heh-heh-heh-*heh*-heh! Heh-heh-heh-*heh*-heh!"

It's a perfectly ghastly sound. To call it a desecration of Frank Sinatra's voice is no exaggeration. He got through the rest of the song as quickly as possible. He tossed the thing off, as it should have been tossed off, but also because he felt deeply humiliated. It was only the beginning.

———

Given the state of Sinatra's movie career, MGM decided the safest thing would be to put him back together with Gene Kelly. The new vehicle was to be a lighthearted turn-of-the-century musical called *Take Me Out to the Ball Game*. But much as Frank loved Gene, he had his own plans for resuscitating his film fortunes: he lobbied hard that summer to be loaned out to Columbia for a serious role in a Bogart picture, *Knock on Any Door*. If he got the role, Sinatra would not only get to act opposite Bogart; he would play a young Italian-American murder suspect, a street guy—a part he felt he could really bring to life. The producers took one look at Frank's hairline and hired twenty-two-year-old John Derek to play the role. Shooting on *Take Me Out to the Ball Game* began on July 28.

———

His memory for names and faces was phenomenal, as was his ability to hold on to grudges, slights, disappointments. Throughout the filming of *Take Me Out to the Ball Game*, as he danced and mugged for the camera, he couldn't get the disappointment of *Knock on Any Door* off his mind. Frank took it out on *Ball Game*'s veteran director, Busby Berkeley, showing up late, muffing lines and dance sequences, wasting hours. Berkeley, on what would be his last picture, consoled himself with the bottle. Kelly and his young assistant Stanley Donen wound up directing much of the movie.

One day during lunch on the set, Frank got a call from Mayer's office, saying his presence was requested. Expecting a rebuke, he was surprised to find the boss smiling thinly. He wanted to ask Frank a little favor.

The favor was to sing that evening at a Sacramento meeting of the National Conference of State Governors. Frank would be the only entertainer, the studio chief explained, and everything would be taken care of: Governor Warren would have Sinatra flown to and from the event on his private plane. The reward was implicit—at a moment when HUAC had established a Hollywood beachhead, doing this solid for Republicans Earl Warren and Louis B. Mayer would polish up Frank's tarnished image a good bit.

Sinatra smiled. Of course, Louis.

Later that afternoon Jack Keller and Frank's accompanist Dick Jones came to his dressing room to collect him. No Frank. The studio lot was searched: Frank's car was in his parking spot, but he himself was nowhere to be found. Heart sinking, Keller phoned Mayer's office and got the expected earful. Eventually, Mayer, furious and humiliated, had to wire the governor's office that Sinatra had fallen ill.

And where was Frank? Home—having sneaked off the MGM lot under a pile of boxes on the back of a pickup truck.

A few days later, Sinatra's agent Lew Wasserman got a message from Mayer's office: as per Frank's contract with MGM, the studio was once more exercising its yearly option to loan his services out to another studio. In November he would be reporting back to RKO, to film a quickie comedy called *It's Only Money* with Jane Russell and Groucho Marx.

═══

Sinatra's theme that fall was escape. He was going to Palm Springs more and more often, not so much as a retreat from hard work, of which there wasn't much in late 1948, as to get away from everyone and everything. One weekend in late September, batching it with Jimmy Van Heusen—his increasingly present Falstaff, pilot, pimp, and fixer—he stopped by a party at David O. Selznick's place. Sipping a dry martini, Sinatra looked across the room and got a jolt more powerful than any gin could've given him: it was Ava, smiling at the tall, homely producer.

She felt Frank's look, turned, and flashed him a dazzling smile. He raised his glass and walked over.

They greeted each other, and Ava introduced their host. Frank gave the man a curt nod—he knew that it had been Selznick who had landed John Derek, the producer's protégé, the plum role in *Knock on Any Door.* Knowing that Sinatra knew, and glancing back and forth between the two of them, Selznick excused himself.

"It's been a long time," Frank said, when they were alone.

"Sure has," Ava said.

"I suppose we were rushing things a little the last time we met."

"*You* were rushing things a little."

"Let's start again," Frank said. "What are you doing now?"

"Making pictures as usual." She had just finished shooting *The Bribe,* at Metro, with Bob Taylor. "How about you?"

"Trying to pick myself up off my ass."

She nodded sympathetically. "Though I knew all about Frank's problems," Ava wrote years later, "I wasn't about to ask him about them that night. And, honey, I didn't bring up Nancy, either. This night was too special for that."

They slipped easily back to their earlier, alcoholic mode. Both of them could hold a lot of liquor. After a couple of hours, they walked out in the crisp desert night, under an inky black sky strewn with more stars than either of them had ever seen.

He offered to take her home.

Ava smiled. It was very gallant of him, but she had to tell him that she wasn't staying alone—she was renting a little place with her big sister Bappie.

Frank shrugged. Did she feel like taking a drive?

Her smile grew broader. Sure she did.

After he went back into the house and gave the bartender a $100 bill for a fifth of Beefeater, they got in his Cadillac and set off. The top was down, despite the evening chill, and they rode under the river of stars, her hair flowing in the wind. She shivered and clutched her mink stole around her bare shoulders. He passed her the bottle; she took a long drink and passed it back.

Frank navigated out to a two-lane blacktop, Palm Canyon Drive, that led out of town, and they drove southeast, through sleepy villages separated by long black stretches of nothing: Cathedral City, Rancho Mirage, Palm Desert, Indian Wells. Each of the towns had a few streetlights, a couple of stores, a blinking traffic signal. Then it was black again. Once they passed a little graveyard whose gates fronted onto the highway. She shivered.

After a half hour, another pocket of light approached. A city-limits sign read: Indio. The two of them were singing, loudly, as they headed into the darkened town. She had a nice, tuneful voice; she could even do harmony. Frank looked impressed. She sang pretty good!

The gin bottle had gone back and forth a number of times, and the Cadillac was weaving when Frank pulled off the road and into a Texaco station. The car fishtailed as he put on the brakes. He cut the engine. A blinking traffic light hanging over the main drag swayed in the wind. It was two thirty in the morning, and Indio was out cold.

Ava looked around. It sure was a one-horse town. But where the hell was the horse?

He laughed, then kissed her. They kissed for a long time. She was still holding the bottle.

Then he got an idea: how about they liven the goddamn place up?

Frank reached across her, almost falling in her lap, and, after fumbling with the latch for a second, opened the glove compartment. He handed her a dark, heavy metal thing that smelled of machine oil. Ava cradled it in her hand, looked at it in wonderment. It was a snub-barreled Smith & Wesson .38 Chief's Special. Frank took out another pistol just like it and, squinting, aimed it at the traffic light.

——

An hour later, the phone rang in Jack Keller's bedroom. Though he had been deeply asleep, Keller knew exactly who was on the other end before he picked it up.

"Jack, we're in trouble," Sinatra said.

It was his one phone call. He and Ava were in the Indio police station, feeling much soberer than they had an hour before, when, whooping and hollering, they had both emptied their pistols, then reloaded and emptied them again, shattering streetlights and several store windows. Then there was the town's single unfortunate passerby, drunk as the shooters, whose shirtfront and belly had been creased by an errant .38 slug.

Keller shook his head. Sinatra always knew how to up the ante. Still, there was only one thing that concerned the publicist.

"Have you been booked? Do the papers know anything?"

Frank looked at the police chief, who was smiling expectantly at his famous guest, secure in the knowledge that for whatever unknown reason, the gods of chance had dealt him one hell of a payday. Sinatra told Keller that nobody knew nothin', but that Jack had better get down fast, with plenty of money.

And so, legend has it, Jack did just that. Gardner, in her memoir, denies the episode ever happened, but Keller taped a reminiscence of it before his untimely death—he was a four-pack-a-day smoker—at the age of fifty-nine in 1975; he also told the story to Peter Bogdanovich. In his account of that wild night in Indio, the publicist wakes up a pal, the manager of the Hollywood Knickerbocker hotel, who happens to have $30,000 in his safe. Keller borrows all of the money, charters a plane, flies to Indio, and papers the town with high-denomination currency to keep everybody quiet.

Everybody certainly kept quiet. Whatever happened that night in the desert, no one ever talked, and the dead tell no tales—unless they happen to leave a taped oral history.

"A lot of silly stories have been written about what happened to us in Palm Springs, but the truth is both more and less exciting," Ava Gardner wrote in her autobiography, which, while entertainingly blunt in its language, is unfortunately euphemistic when it comes to her many exploits.

> We drank, we laughed, we talked, and we fell in love. Frank
> gave me a lift back to our rented house. We did not kiss or

make dates, but we knew, and I think it must have frightened both of us. I went in to wake Bappie up, which didn't appeal to her much, but I had to tell someone how much I liked Frank Sinatra. I just wasn't prepared to say that what I really meant by like was love.

Perhaps Frank and Ava really were as chaste as junior-prom sweethearts that night. Yet Keller's story, while too good to be true, is too irresistibly crazy not to be. Sinatra certainly carried guns—once Lee Mortimer dropped his assault charges, the suspended pistol permit was reinstated—and he certainly drank heavily, as did Ava. There are copious records of wild, booze-fueled behavior on the part of Sinatra and Gardner once they became a bona fide couple. Why should the night they fell in love not have set the pattern?

===

Frank fell as fast as she did. In a blinding flash, all his self-discontent—a combustible amalgam of artistic failure and disgrace with fortune and men's eyes—alchemized into the most powerful feeling he had ever known. He was deeply in love with Ava Gardner. He phoned her, dead sober, when he got back to town, and asked her out.

> We met for dinner at a quiet place [Ava wrote], and we didn't do much drinking. This time I did ask him about Nancy. He said he'd left her physically, emotionally, and geographically years before, and there was no way he was going back. The kids, however, were something else; he was committed to them forever. I was to learn that that kind of deep loyalty—not faithfulness, but loyalty—was a critical part of his nature.
>
> We didn't say much more. Love is a wordless communion between two people. That night we went back to that little yellow house in Nichols Canyon and made love. And oh, God, it was magic. We became lovers forever—eternally. Big words, I

know. But I truly felt that no matter what happened we would always be in love. And God almighty, things did happen.

Not surprisingly, Frank's fabled confidence was starting to crack. That autumn, vocal problems cropped up for the first time. In October, when Sinatra made a guest appearance on the bandleader Spike Jones's *Spotlight Revue,* Jones, famous for cutting up, asked him seriously, "How you feeling tonight, Frank? Is your voice all right?"

Frank tried to make a joke out of it. "Well, I think so—lemme see," he said. He blew a pitch pipe and let out a big off-key bellow, much to the audience's amusement. "I am majestically in voice!" he crowed— and then, ominously, as the orchestra played the intro to "Everybody Loves Somebody,"[3] coughed. He then proceeded, on live national radio, to blow the first note of the song.

In November, three days after *The Kissing Bandit* opened to universal groans, mostly about its star ("Mr. Sinatra's performance . . . is not in that vein of skipping humor which more talented comics traverse," Bosley Crowther wrote, less unkindly than most), Frank started work on *It's Only Money* at RKO. It seemed curious, and somehow ominous, that the studio's new chief, Howard Hughes, whose anti-Communist witch hunts had purged more than half of RKO's workforce, had decided to hire Sinatra. Remembering the time in Palm Springs when Ava had come to Chi Chi with Hughes, Frank wondered if the studio head simply wanted to humiliate him by sticking him in this silly piece of crap.

Since Frank could behave badly among movie collaborators he respected, it's easy to imagine how he conducted himself on a quickie comedy (the shooting schedule was just three weeks) at the off-brand studio he thought he'd outgrown, alongside the remote and distrustful Groucho Marx and the menacingly protuberant Jane Russell (whom the delighted boob man Hughes had discovered a few years earlier— not working at his dentist's office, as the myth has it, but through his casting department). "Frank and my father did not get along at all,"

Groucho's son, Arthur, recalled. "Sinatra always showed up on the set like a real star, like two hours late, and my father would be fuming because he already knew his lines, which Sinatra usually did not know. So they weren't too compatible and the movie wasn't too good either."

Yet Frank got along swimmingly with Jane Russell, who, like him, was not especially happy to be working on *It's Only Money*. "It was nothing," she said. "It was not a very good picture. Frank and I certainly knew it." And he was a perfect gentleman with Russell. "Frank was always very polite and very sweet," she remembered. "There was no funny business at all."

For good reason. "Ava was sitting up in the sound booth most of the time while we made the picture," Russell said. "She certainly was a character. A raving character."

It's Only Money—such a stinker that RKO wouldn't release it until 1951 under the hokily lecherous new title *Double Dynamite*—was the least of Frank's problems. His life was coming unmoored. His recording career was dead in the water; his one performing outlet, besides the occasional radio guest spot, was the reliably lousy *Your Hit Parade*. In December, a headline in the industry journal *Modern Television & Radio* read, IS SINATRA FINISHED? Around that time Frank told Manie Sacks, according to Nancy junior, that "so many things were going wrong that he felt like he was washed up. Sacks replied that life is cyclical, and that he was too talented not to bounce back. 'In a few years,' he said, 'you'll be on top again.'"

In the meantime, though, he had fallen off the mountain. *Down Beat's* end-of-the-year poll for Best Male Singer, which Sinatra had easily topped since 1943, found him in the number-four spot, beneath Billy Eckstine, the leather-lunged Frankie Laine ("Mule Train"), and Bob—not Bing—Crosby.

Frank was still making big money—MGM paid him $325,833 that year—but as always, he spent it faster than it came in. Taxes were for chumps. The IRS respectfully disagreed. In her year-end wrap-up for *Silver Screen*, the columnist Sheilah Graham estimated that Sinatra had made $11 million in the last six years, yet he "not only can't save anything but . . . is behind with his income tax."

Frank's solution was to buy a new house.

Holmby Hills, just north of Sunset and to the east of Beverly Glen, was a pricey enclave whose denizens included Loretta Young, Walt Disney, and Humphrey Bogart. Three-twenty North Carolwood Drive was a sprawling redbrick Mediterranean on three acres. There was no lake, but the summer heat didn't settle in the way it did in the Valley, and the drive to MGM was just fifteen minutes instead of forty-five. The house cost a fortune—a quarter of a million in 1948 dollars—but then, that's what movie stars had to pay for a house in those days.

Why the Sinatras moved just then is something of a mystery. They had paid a huge sum for the Palm Springs place not a year before, and Frank's career was on the downswing. What's more, he was in love. But as always, no matter his circumstances, he liked to have the best of everything. Still, however nice the new digs, the uprooting must have been difficult. Nancy junior, eight at the time of the move, writes that her father bought 320 North Carolwood "to be nearer his work so that he could spend more time at home." This sounds more hopeful than realistic. A photograph from the period shows Sinatra sitting in an armchair holding baby Tina as his adoring family surrounds him: Big Nancy at one shoulder; Little Nancy at the other, gazing at her sister; little Frank is resting his elbow on Dad's knee. Frank himself is directing a ghastly fake smile at his young son (maybe the needy Frankie was already starting to get on his nerves). He looks as if he can't wait to get the hell out of there.

Tina, always more clear-eyed than her sister about her father's character, has a different take on the move to Holmby Hills: it was, she writes, a move "up in the world." This rings truer. If Frank couldn't act with Bogart, at least he could live across the street from him.

Yet he was restless and discontent. He was recording again, but not well. The yearlong layoff during the AFM strike, in combination with the weekly travesty of *Your Hit Parade,* had eroded not just his artis-

And this was what he was leaving. The Sinatras at home, 1948.

tic confidence but his relationship with Axel Stordahl. The two men weren't making magic anymore; they were just making music, much of it not very good. The week before Christmas, in his first post-strike recording with Sibelius, the all too appropriately titled "Comme Ci Comme Ça," Sinatra's voice seems utterly without conviction:

> *It seems my friends have been complaining,*
> *They say that I've been acting rude.*

At this moment, unfortunately, the lyrics—filled with petulant world-weariness, the ennui that sets in when a grand passion is absent—fit him like a glove.

"It wasn't a very happy Christmas in 1948," Big Nancy recalled, "but it was the cutest card I'd ever seen." Cute, yes: the card was a cheery cartoon of a Christmas tree, with photos of the family members printed inside globe ornaments. Little Nancy and Frankie each occupied one of the upper globes; underneath, Big Nancy and baby Tina cuddled cozily inside one ornament, and Frank—all alone—grinned from another.

Jimmy Van Heusen with Ava and Frank, early 1950s.

Look at him! Who you got waitin' for ya in New York? Ava Gardner?
—Jules Munshin, as Ozzie, to Gene Kelly's character, Gabey,
in *On the Town*

It hadn't been a very happy Christmas thanks to Frank's extreme emotional distance—an air of distraction that drifted in more and more often, like a fog bank, at which point he would simply walk out of the house to God knew where. Nancy finally admitted to herself that whatever he promised, whatever he bought her, he was never going to change. Out in the world, Sheilah and Hedda and Louella were stepping up the drumbeat about his affairs. Years later, Nancy junior wrote:

> One day while I was playing dress-up in Mom's dressing room, I climbed up on a chair to get a shoe box off a shelf and knocked to the floor a stack of magazines that Mom had hidden in her closet. I sat down in the midst of the pile. They were movie magazines like *Photoplay* and *Modern Screen,* and they were filled with pictures of Dad and . . . Mom and Frankie and Baby Tina and me. There were also pictures of Dad with other ladies. I remember Marilyn Maxwell and Lana Turner. I was devastated.

For a long time Frank's wife had shielded herself from the extent of his infidelities, but more and more she realized, with a sorrowful but hardened resignation, that just about everything she'd heard or imagined was true. He came and went as he pleased and did exactly what he wanted, with whomever he wanted. Nancy tried to busy herself with fixing up 320 North Carolwood, but there were times when she couldn't take it anymore. At those times she would phone George Evans and complain; Evans would listen sympathetically and tell her he'd talk to Frank. And he did talk to Frank, for all the good it did.

At a January engagement party for Mel Tormé and the Columbia starlet Candy Toxton, Frank and Jimmy Van Heusen showed up uninvited (and in Frank's case, loaded). Sinatra was carrying a magnum of champagne wrapped in ribbon. "Here ya go, Mel. Happy Birthday," he said, handing the bottle to the younger singer—whose birthday had been in September—and calling loudly for the bride-to-be, on whom he apparently had a crush. "The moment Candy saw him walk in," Tormé recalled, "she rushed up the stairs to my bedroom and locked herself in." Tormé ran up the stairs, on the heels of Sinatra, who announced that he wanted to "wash up." He went into my bathroom, tried the door to my bedroom, found it locked, and began to bang on the door. Invited or not, he was a guest in my home, so I tried to reason with him . . .

He tossed an expletive at me and continued to pound on the door. I heard Candy, inside my bedroom, say, in a small, rather sad voice, "Go away, Frank, please." Van Heusen, a true gent, shamefacedly came up the stairs and pried Frank away from the bedroom door.

"Come on, Frank. Let's go," he pleaded.

"No," Sinatra said sullenly. "Wanna see Candy."

I gritted my teeth. I could now hear Candy crying in the bedroom. "Frank, I think you'd better get out of here," I said.

Van Heusen tugged at his arm. "Yeah, he's right, pal. Let's go." Frank hesitated at the top of the stairs and gave me one hard look. Buddy Rich told me that Sinatra was able to handle himself pretty well, and I sure as hell did not want to tangle with him.

Frank stormed out of the house.

When he was drunk, which was more and more often these days, he was a law unto himself. Evans saw it happening and despaired, then he too grew resigned. Around this time, Earl Wilson ran into the publicist at the Copacabana:

I found [him] in a grave mood. "I make a prediction," Evans said across the table in the lounge. "Frank is through. A year from now you won't hear anything about him."

"Come on," I protested to the man who'd done more than anybody to make him famous.

"He'll be dead professionally," Evans said. "I've been around the country, looking and listening. They're not going to see his pictures. They're not buying his records. They don't care for Frank Sinatra anymore!"

"But you're the fellow that's supposed to whet up that yearning for him, aren't you?" I asked.

"I can't do it anymore," Evans said. "You know how much I've talked to him about the girls. The public knows about the trouble with Nancy, and the other dames, and it doesn't like him anymore."

"I can't believe that," I said.

"In a year," Evans reiterated, "he'll be through."

In January, MGM celebrated its Silver Jubilee by gathering fifty-seven of its biggest stars, including Lassie, for a historic group photograph. There they sat (except for Lassie, who stood in front), in chairs arranged on bleachers on a soundstage, row on row of them, Tracy and Hepburn and Gable and Astaire and Garland and Durante and Errol Flynn, living proof that the great studio had, if not quite more stars than in the heavens, then at least more than anyone else. Wearing an unflattering light gray suit and looking oddly pallid (and distinctly balding), Sinatra sat at the far right in the second-to-last row, in between Ginger Rogers and Red Skelton (who had broken everyone up when he walked in, calling out, "Okay, kids, the part's taken, you can go home now"). Ava sat front and center in the second row, between Clark Gable and Judy Garland, strangely sedate in her blue suit and pearls and bright red lipstick. Her hands, clutching a pair of red gloves, lay demurely folded in her lap.

Appearances—as was always the case where the movies were concerned—were deceiving. As was the distance that separated Ava and Frank in the bleachers.

When she drove onto the studio lot that day, Gardner recalled, "a car sped past me, swung in front, and slowed down so much I had to pass it myself. The car overtook me again and repeated the process.

Having done this about three times, the car finally pulled alongside me, the grinning driver raised his hat and sped away to the same photo session. That was Frank. He could even flirt in a car."

======

The first weeks of February saw an escalating series of transcontinental shouting matches between Sinatra and George Evans, who was increasingly exasperated with his most famous client. Evans, who had eyes and ears everywhere, knew about Ava. And by early 1949, the publicist was at his wits' end. When Frank wasn't yelling at him over the phone, Nancy was. She wanted George to do the impossible: Make him change. Bring him back.

Evans had worked wonders before, but in Ava Gardner he saw real trouble. He was sure she didn't care whose life she destroyed, whose home she wrecked. Evans had gotten a whiff of her heedlessness. "Do you suck?" she liked to ask strangers, when shaking hands for the first time. Lana Turner had been a different story: At least she cared about her career. There was leverage. Gardner cared about nothing except having a good time. She was that most dangerous of creatures, a gorgeous nihilist.

Frank, for his part, had made up his mind about her years before when he saw her on the cover of a movie magazine. "I'm going to marry that girl," he remarked to a friend—forgetting, for the moment, that he already was married. Now when Evans told him, over and over, that he couldn't have her, that she was bad news, that she would drag him and his career down, Sinatra reacted much as he had when Manie Sacks had informed him that he had to pay for his own arrangements—with complete outrage and absolute assurance.

Despite Jack Keller's heroic efforts on Sinatra's behalf, Frank demanded that Evans fire his West Coast counterpart. The main problem was that while Keller was an energetic publicist, he lacked subservience. Jerry Lewis, who employed Keller for many years, laughed when he recalled the press agent's insolence: "I'd say, 'How come you didn't get my name in the paper this week?' And Jack would say, 'I kept it out, you putz.' " Keller's first reaction when Sinatra phoned from Indio at 3:00 a.m. to say "We're in trouble" had been: "How can I be in trouble when all night I've just been lying here in bed?"

Yet Evans steadfastly resisted firing Keller, who was really just the whipping boy: Frank's real beef was with George Evans. At the end of February, Sinatra finally called it quits with the man who, in many ways, had made him Sinatra.

=====

In March, *Take Me Out to the Ball Game* came out, to tepid reviews. "Don't be surprised," Crowther wrote, "if you see people getting up for a seventh-inning stretch." The movies were providing diminishing returns for Sinatra, but with not much else going on in his career, he needed that MGM paycheck. At the end of the month he got back into a sailor suit and began shooting *On the Town,* with Gene Kelly, who was co-directing the film with Stanley Donen. For the first time on one of his movies with Sinatra, Kelly would get first billing. Not only were Frank's fortunes falling, but he was thirty-three, not so young in those days. The thinness that had once seemed so cute was now something more like gauntness: with age and trouble, his face was growing harder. "He just didn't seem comfortable with his looks," said Betty Garrett, who co-starred with him on both *Ball Game* and *On the Town.* MGM cosmeticians had to do extensive work on him every morning, augmenting his hairline, filling in his facial scars, even padding the posterior of his sailor pants to give a more pleasing contour to Sinatra's totally flat fanny.

Frank's discontent went well beyond the physical: The rift with Evans gnawed at him. He would impulsively reach for the phone to call George for advice, only to realize he had burned that bridge. The IRS was dunning him, big time, for back taxes, and Dolly was hitting him up for money every time they talked. He was nervous, self-doubting, and cranky—sometimes his skin felt too tight. At a party in Palm Springs, he sucker punched a retired businessman named Jack Wintermeyer after Wintermeyer, who was acting as bartender, couldn't figure out how to make the drink Sinatra wanted.[1] Frank only avoided a lawsuit by agreeing to say he was sorry—then reneged at the last moment by shaking hands without a word. "He just can't bear to apologize," wrote the *Los Angeles Examiner* sports columnist Vincent X. Flaherty, who was present. "No matter what the cost—career, money, anything."

Sinatra didn't like himself very much, and the world seemed to agree with him. In March, *Down Beat* wrote, of a group of sides Frank had done with the Phil Moore Four, a jazz quartet, "They don't quite get the intimate between-you-and-me feel that was attempted and Frankie hits a few off-pitch ones to boot." He wasn't about to explain to *Down Beat* what kind of mood he was in these days. They could all go screw themselves.

At the end of May, he told *Your Hit Parade* to take a hike, issuing a statement decrying the material he had been forced to sing and the style in which he had been compelled to sing it. Yet Lucky Strike swallowed the insult and immediately went into negotiations with Frank's people to create a new broadcast. The new show, unambiguously titled *Light Up Time,* would debut in September. One thing about that Sinatra: he certainly sold cigarettes.

But not records. His latest album, *Frankly Sentimental,* released in June, completely failed to chart: a bad first. And while Sinatra's singles did far better than in the annus horribilis of 1948—they spent a total of fifty-nine weeks on the charts in 1949—not one record rose above number 6. Other singers, some of them on Columbia, were charting higher with the same songs Frank was recording. The big seller of 1949, on RCA Victor, was the soothing but insipid Perry Como song "A—You're Adorable" ("M, N, O, P, I could go on all day/Q, R, S, T, alphabetically speaking, you're OK"). It was perfect pabulum for the masses in a nervous year: in August, the Soviet Union would confirm Americans' worst fears by testing its first A-bomb.

Frank was striving after an ideal impossible at that point in history: to succeed commercially and satisfy himself artistically. When he merely went for hits, he produced abominations like the pseudo-country "Sunflower" (whose melody would later reappear, unimproved, as "Hello, Dolly"). When he let himself go, as he did in the three up-tempo numbers he recorded in a remarkable July session orchestrated by George Siravo and the great Sy Oliver ("It All Depends on You," "Bye Bye Baby," and "Don't Cry Joe"), the results were thrilling. Lacquer-disc safety copies of the Sunday-evening session (Sinatra always preferred recording at night—"The voice is better at night," he was fond of saying), transcribed and analyzed by the Sinatra musicologist Charles L. Granata, have preserved Frank's obsessive pursuit of artistic perfection in exquisite detail:

> The recording date is July 10, 1949. As the evening session gets underway at Columbia's cavernous 30th Street Studio, Sinatra, arranger Sy Oliver, and conductor Hugo Winterhalter are auditioning a second instrumental run-through of George Siravo's arrangement of "It All Depends on You." Tonight's date will be jazz-flavored, the orchestra really a big "band"—no strings. Amid the chatter and bustle on the studio floor, the vocalist, listening intently to a passage by the brass section, feels that something is amiss . . .
>
> "I'd like to hear the introduction, with the muted brass," he instructs the conductor. The musicians comply, and the brief section is played for his approval. After hearing the passage, Sinatra carefully instructs both the musicians and the engineers: "I'd like to get that as tight as we can. Trombones: you may have to turn around and face the microphone or something. I'd like to hear the six of you, as a unit," he says. The engineer brings down a microphone with two sides, to help capture the precise tonal quality that Sinatra desires. The section played through again, the singer continues. "Just once more, Hugo, and would you use less volume in the reeds, with

the clarinet lead? And would you play it lightly, trumpets and trombones, if you don't mind? I mean *softly*," he emphasizes.

The trombone problem rectified, Sinatra, now in the booth, turns his attention to the rhythm section. He inquires of drummer Terry Snyder: "You got enough pad on the bass drum? It booms a little bit." Then, without the slightest hesitation, he turns to the studio prop men. "Would you put in a small piece of carpet, enough to cover the entire bottom of the drum?" Satisfied, he addresses the pianist. "Say, Johnny Guarneri, would you play something, a figure or something, and have the rhythm fall in? We'd like to get a small balance on it." Guarneri begins an impromptu riff on the melody, as bassist Herman "Trigger" Alpert, drummer Snyder, and guitarist Al Caiola join in. After a few moments, Sinatra's directions continue. "Bass and guitar: Trig, can you move in about a foot or so, or you can pull the mike out if you wish. And the guitar—also move in a little closer. Just a shade—uh, uh, uh—that's enough."

This was no mere voice: this was a great artist in full command of his powers and the means required to convey his art.

And yet the public mostly failed to pay attention.

The malaise seemed to be catching: as Sinatra flatlined, Columbia sputtered. Dinah Shore and the producer and arranger Mitchell Ayres defected to Como's label, Victor, which had come out with a record format to compete with the LP, the 45-rpm microgroove single. The two formats, and their labels, dueled for a couple of years, and at first things didn't look good for Columbia Recording Company.

On Labor Day, September 5—exactly a week after the Russian A-test—Sinatra began *Light Up Time*. The NBC program, broadcast from Hollywood, aired every weeknight at 7:00 p.m. (on the East Coast) for just fifteen minutes: its format and time slot were copied directly from another NBC show, *Chesterfield Supper Club*. As a sign of Sinatra's still existing but rapidly waning power, the Chesterfield show—hosted by Perry Como on Mondays, Wednesdays, and Fridays, and by Jo Stafford and Peggy Lee on Tuesdays and Thursdays, respectively—was bumped to 10:00 p.m. in the East. Frank's co-star on the new broadcast was the Metropolitan Opera soprano (and fellow New Jerseyan) Dorothy Kirsten. The jam-packed format featured two solos by Sinatra, one by Kirsten, and one duet wedged between commercials. Every show began—it seems impossible to imagine in these days of fifteen-second TV ads—with a *two-minute* commercial for Luckies.

Frank was earning $10,000 a week for the show. *Newsweek* wrote, "The sometimes unruly crooner, whose exuberance over rapid fame has left him in staggering financial debt, could look to the show as a good boost back up the money trail." Could—but didn't. Ten thousand a week was a grand salary for the era, but it was a per-broadcast comedown from *Your Hit Parade,* and a drop in the bucket as far as his fiscal woes were concerned.

He was on a treadmill. With the breakneck pace of arranging for a five-day-a-week show, Stordahl was unable to conduct the *Light Up Time* orchestra: a further erosion of his relationship with Frank. His replacement, the choral director Jeff Alexander, went into the recording studio with Sinatra in mid-September in Sibelius's stead, arranging and conducting three numbers, including an Italianate piece, lush with mandolins, accordion, and Stordahl-esque strings, called "Stromboli":

> *On the island of Stromboli*
> *Recklessly I gave my heart.*

The too-apt tune was the title song for a romantic movie of the same name, directed by Roberto Rossellini and starring Ingrid Bergman. The film had just wrapped in Italy. In the course of making the picture, Rossellini and Bergman, who was married and the mother of a ten-year-old daughter, had fallen in love and conceived a child. The affair became a monumental scandal—unimaginable in the present era of casual celebrity couplings. Soon after Bergman gave birth, she would be denounced on the floor of the U.S. Senate and effectively driven out of the country.

But that night in September, Frank Sinatra was just recording a pretty song.

=====

The next day, he sat down and typed yet another letter of complaint to Sacks. He began by giving his old friend the benefit of the doubt: Maybe Manie didn't know about it, Frank wrote, but other Columbia artists were recording the same songs he was. The charge was more serious than it sounds. Sinatra pointed out that he had put in many hours poring over standards to find the best songs to record. It was part of his genius to know which numbers worked for him, which tunes he could move into and make his own. And when his own label let its other singers record songs like "That Old Feeling" and "You Go to My Head" after he had already put his stamp on them, it hit Frank where it hurt the most: the pocketbook. He wanted to hear from Manie, he wrote, with stiff, furious formality, "advising me why you permit this policy and if you intend to pursue it in the future." This time he signed not with love but best regards.

The letter, typed on Sinatra's stationery ("FRANK SINATRA" and "BEVERLY HILLS, CALIFORNIA" embossed across the top), is signed assertively in blue fountain pen, with the singer's first and last names. Sacks annotated it in pencil. "Check this," he wrote, next to "You Go to My Head." And then, underneath, "Doris Day's album."

It was treacherous, and it was true: Day, whose name Sinatra hadn't been able to bring himself to mention, had recorded both songs. The late-summer correspondence between Frank and Manie reflects a growing tension between the two, a tension that in some ways was symptomatic of the singer's troubles at Columbia. On September 20, Manie fessed up:

Dear Frank:
I must admit that recording with another vocalist standards you have already recorded should not be done. Frankly, I must also accept the blame in this instance because, without

enough thought, I selected the songs, and not until I received your letter and checked the list did I realize you had recorded the same songs.

In the future, I assure you I'll pay closer attention so that it won't happen again. I am the guilty culprit and I'm sorry.

Kindest regards. Sincerely, Manie

The tone of this exchange is markedly different from the Sinatra-Sacks letters of 1945. In those days, the two men had closed their missives with "Love"—even "Love and kisses." Now it was "Best regards" from Frank, and from Manie—who apparently didn't want to be outdone in the coolness department—"Kindest regards," immediately followed, with sublime passive aggressiveness, by "Sincerely."

Sacks also sent his reply to Sinatra's office and not to his home address, as he had done previously. Maybe this was just a bureaucratic detail; more likely, it meant Manie's friendship with Frank was slipping.

All that summer and fall, Frank visited the little stucco house high over Nichols Canyon. Ava had worked hard to make the place her own, hanging the walls with Degas prints, lining the den with massive antique bookcases containing all the volumes Artie Shaw had bullied her into reading: *The Magic Mountain* and *Buddenbrooks* and *The Interpretation of Dreams* and *Babbitt*. She really had read them, mostly—and also, under Artie's dictatorship, learned to play chess well enough to beat him. All this despite what she once told an interviewer: "Deep down, I'm pretty superficial." In truth, she was anything but. Still, her lack of intellectual confidence never left her. On the other hand, when it came to her beauty, she had no doubts.

The house was surrounded by a picket fence covered with yellow roses, a trellis with petunias and honeysuckle, drying laundry snapping in the breeze. Inside was heaven.

But beware, her friend Lana told her:

We met in the ladies' room during a party [Ava wrote], and she told me her story. She had been deeply in love with Frank and, so she thought, Frank with her. Though he was shuttling backward and forward between her bedroom and Nancy's, trying to equate obedience to Catholic doctrines with indulgence in his natural inclinations, divorce plans were all set up and wedding plans had been made.

Then Lana woke up one morning, picked up the newspaper, and read that Frank had changed his mind and gone back to Nancy for good. It was the old Catholic arrangement: wife and family come first. Nancy had almost made a theme song out of it: "Frank always comes back to me."

I really liked Lana. She was a nice girl, and she felt neither anger nor malice toward Frank and me. She just thought I ought to know. I told Lana gently that Frank and I were in love, and that this time he really was going to leave Nancy for good. If I'm in love, I want to get married: that's my fundamentalist Protestant background. If he wanted me, there could be no compromise on that issue.

That cataclysm, along with a number of others, was close at hand.

━━━

The roster of Sinatra's activities that autumn was strikingly sparse. His daughter Nancy, usually the most assiduous (and relentlessly upbeat) of chroniclers, can come up with only two events between the summer and December. "October 30, 1949: Dad returned once again to *The Jack Benny Show*," she notes. And, "November 6, 1949: He performed on *Guest Star*, a radio show for the U.S. Treasury Department." (Trying to butter up the IRS? Or the FBI?) Frank wasn't shooting a movie, and he was barely recording: between September and the end of the year, he cut just eight songs, in three sessions. (In all of 1949, despite the end of the musicians' strike, he laid down only twenty-seven sides, compared with seventy in the pre-strike year of 1947.) He did *Light Up Time* every weekday afternoon, but the quarter-hour show was rushed and frequently superficial. Stordahl's absence didn't help, nor, due to NBC budgetary constraints, did the absence of a string section.

As Frank had noted in his pained September letter to Manie, others—even at Columbia—were recording the same songs he was. And selling better. There was a new Italian boy on the scene, with a husky tenor voice so dramatic that some listeners thought he was black. To add insult to injury, he also called himself Frankie—Frankie Laine. (He had been born Francesco Paolo LoVecchio.) He could sing torch songs, spirituals, and up-tempo rip-roarers, and he could crank out gold records ("That's My Desire"; "Mule Train"). Laine's career was being shepherded by a brilliant, fiercely ambitious A&R man at Mercury named Mitch Miller—the same Mitch Miller who had turned Sinatra on to the classical compositions of Alec Wilder.

But the king that year was Perry Como. "Anodyne," with its dual meanings of pain relief and insipidness, applied perfectly to the smooth-voiced, smooth-faced former barber from Canonsburg, Pennsylvania. Times change; the culture shifts. Yearning was out of fashion, and Sinatra was now just part of a big pack of popular singers. *Billboard* ranked him number 13 at the end of the year; the *Down Beat* poll put him at number 5. He was officially yesterday's news. Lee Mortimer all but jumped up and down with glee. "The Swoon is real gone (and not in jive talk)," he wrote, in his *Daily Mirror* column, noting that all the hysteria over Sinatra had merely been "an unhealthy wartime phenomenon."

Emotionally, Frank was as busy as it is possible for a human being to be: he was in love. And not sweetly and contentedly in love, but in the throes of a grand passion, one whose DNA was stamped with wildness, violence, contradiction, pain. In Ava Gardner he had literally met his match. In a woman of spectacularly sensuous beauty he had found a soul whose turbulence equaled his own. Like Frank, Ava knew herself to be a kind of royalty, but still harbored profound feelings of worthlessness. In each, this duality fueled volcanic furies. "Both Frank and I," Ava wrote in her memoir, "were high-strung people, possessive and jealous and liable to explode fast. When I lose my temper, honey, you can't find it anyplace. I've just got to let off steam, and he's the same way."

Frank had found a true partner in the opera that was his life. All his other women had been supporting players; Ava was a diva. Like Frank, she was infinitely restless and easily bored. In both, this tendency could lead to casual cruelty to others—and sometimes to each other. Both had titanic appetites, for food, drink, cigarettes, diversion, companionship, and sex. Both loved jazz, and the men and women, black and white, who made it. Both were politically liberal. Both were fascinated with prostitution and perversity. Both knew the bottomless loneliness that stalks the deep watches of the night: both distrusted sleep—feared it, perhaps, as death's mirror. Both hated being alone.

And behind every move each of them made lay a fine and regal contempt for the banal established order of the world.

It was around then, Ava wrote, that Frank told her, "All my life, being a singer was the most important thing in the world. Now you're all I want."

For a man whose ambition had always preceded all else, this was an astonishing statement, even if he felt differently a few hours later. To the extent that he meant it (and to a great extent he did), it was as if his towering ambition had suddenly gone up in smoke. But their love was like a fire that flamed up and consumed them both. And since both were performers, exhibitionism was part of the kick—even at the very outset, there were amazed onlookers. Among them were Sinatra's manager Bobby Burns and his wife, Betty, who tried to help the adulterous couple early in the affair. Betty Burns remembered:

> Bobby and I had a house on the beach, and so Frank and Ava
> would be there all the time. We would be sitting in the living
> room and hear them upstairs in the bedroom quarreling and

arguing. Ava would scream at Frank and he would slam the door and storm downstairs. Minutes later we'd smell a very sweet fragrance coming from the stairs. Ava had decided she wasn't mad anymore, and so she sprayed the stairwell with her perfume. Frank would smell it and race back up to the bedroom. Then it would be hours before he'd come back down.

It's like something out of *Wild Kingdom*.

"She was like a Svengali to him," Skitch Henderson said. "She was an enigma. A mysterious presence. You didn't quite know how she had done it to him, and I'm not sure I wanted to know. She was ruthless with him. And it used to affect his mood a great deal. It could be horrible to be with him then. Her acid tongue and her ability to just put you away. If ever I knew a tiger, or a panther . . . I'm trying to think of an animal that would describe her . . . To be honest—I didn't let anyone on to this—but I did what I could to stay out of her way. I was scared to death of her."

She was a pisser. She scared the shit outta me. Never knew what she'd hate that I'd do. Frank must have found the similarity to the first woman in his life unspeakably exciting. Some part of him was still that little boy, not knowing if he'd get a hug or a rap with the nightstick.

For all Ava's autobiographical professions of eternal love, she had trouble with intimacy. When she got it—and she'd got plenty since she'd first arrived in Hollywood—she didn't feel she was worthy of it. And so when a man fell in love with her, she reciprocated for a little while, then she began to torment him.

Jealousy was their emotional ammunition. They both understood it. Frank could trigger it in her literally with the blink of an eye, so conditioned was he to scanning any crowded restaurant or nightclub or party and possessing any beauty he saw.

His suspicions about Ava were better founded. She had it all worked out: if he wouldn't leave his wife, she told him, she was free to do whatever she wanted. She toyed with her old flame Howard Duff, who was desperate for her. She teased Howard Hughes, who continued to have her followed. She stepped out with a minor gangster named Johnny Stompanato (who would meet his sad end, years later, at the hands of Lana Turner's daughter). She had a little fling with her co-star in *My Forbidden Past*, Robert Mitchum. He went back to his wife, whose secret was: she always took him back.

The infidelities—if you could call them that—diverted her momentarily and had their desired effect on Sinatra, stoking his passions. And she had to hand it to him: his fury made the anger of her other lovers pale in comparison. As did his wandering eye. They screamed at each other, they chased each other from room to room, breaking things, and then, their bodies still abuzz with anger, they had the most amazing makeup sex that (they were quite sure) anyone had ever had.

Set against all this, what were the demands of marital duty and family life? Background noise. This was a passion that not only scorched everything in its path but demanded absolute and constant attention. When Frank went to New York City in early December for the premiere of *On the Town,* Ava went too. Strikingly, Manie Sacks, cool and correct toward Sinatra just three months before, let the lovebirds stay in his suite at the Hampshire House: maybe he was feeling guilty. Big changes were afoot in his professional life, changes that would affect Frank profoundly.

On December 8, Frank and Ava attended the Broadway premiere of *Gentlemen Prefer Blondes:* book by Joseph Fields and Anita Loos, songs (including the suddenly all too appropriate "Bye Bye Baby") by Leo Robin and Jule Styne. The pair, with the protective coloration of another couple (Manie and a date), tried their best to blend in with the first-night crowd at the Ziegfeld Theatre. Inside, Sinatra and Gardner laughed and held hands as they listened to the newcomer Carol Channing cooing "Diamonds Are a Girl's Best Friend." Afterward, along with Manie and his lady friend, they ducked into a car and disappeared. The photographers and gossip columnists waiting outside the Ziegfeld (New York had a half-dozen daily papers, only one of which, the *Times,* refused to stoop to scandalmongering) shook their heads and stared at each other. Was this what it looked like? Remarkably, the papers held off. For the time being. The next morning, in the "Celebs About Town" section of his column, Walter Winchell, after taking note of "Quentin Reynolds and Heywood Broun's widder having a lobby confab at the Algonquin," mentioned "Ava Gardner Period."

It was as if the columnist were biting his tongue, waiting to see what developed.

Nancy Sinatra, wired in as she was to the Hollywood gossip network, already knew. In fact, she had known about Ava for months: almost since the beginning. What was most hurtful to her was the fact that soon everyone else would know, too. That was the hardest thing about being married to Frank Sinatra—whatever he did, everybody seemed to find out about it pretty quickly.

This time Nancy made her decision: the comedy of endless breaches, hollow promises, and public reconciliations was over. She loved Frank, but finally, whether she admitted it to herself or not, she hated him, too. He was ultimately impossible. Her faith told her that Frank Sinatra was her cross to bear, forever, whether they were together or apart. Her faith also didn't allow divorce. But from here on they would no longer live as husband and wife. It was as simple as that: she had her pride, and her children, to consider.

Dolly Sinatra, who met Ava at the *On the Town* movie premicre, was delighted. She had never liked Nancy much to begin with, and over the last half-dozen years Frank's wife, with her new teeth and her new gowns and her abiding sense of holier-than-thou, had earned her outright enmity. This Ava Gardner, though, was something else. Three nights later at the Copa, at the thirty-fourth-birthday party the nightclub manager Jack Entratter threw for Frank, the two women got to talk for a few minutes. And Dolly loved every bit of it. Ava drank and swore like a sailor, and Dolly Sinatra could keep right up with her. At the same time—this was the amazing thing—the girl was just stupefyingly beautiful. In Dolly's travels around Hudson County, she had run across plenty of dirty girls with dirty mouths, yet with the pretty ones, and especially the beauties, butter mostly wouldn't melt. But this one! Dolly, like everyone else in the Copa, couldn't take her eyes off her. And Ava wore her gorgeousness so lightly, smoked her cigarettes so off-handedly, swore so fluently, and laughed so raucously that Dolly fell as hard as her son had. She pinched his skinny cheek and congratulated him on the great fuckin' girl he'd landed.

Frank smiled at Dolly, too happy to be angry with her (Dolly's demands for money had stepped up as his bank account dwindled). His every waking hour—there weren't many sleeping ones—was occupied with thinking of her, seeing her, making love with her, fighting with her, making up with her.

In truth, he was running ragged. In between obsessive bouts with Ava, there were very bad fights with Nancy. Work—what little there was of it—was going badly too. Back in California, on *Light Up Time*, two days after Christmas, he sailed into an up-tempo, jazz-combo arrangement of Brown, DeSylva, and Henderson's "You're the Cream in My Coffee" ("You're the salt in my stew") like a ship without a rudder, fast and out of tune and not seeming to care much. Then, in the second chorus, he simply blew the lyric. "You're the starch in my collar," he repeated, like a man sleepwalking. "I said that, didn't I," he remarked with a laugh, then tossed off the rest of the song, more of a walk-through than a performance.

Frank arrives at the CBS Playhouse to rehearse for a radio show, mid 1940s. George Evans, in hat, flanks him; Manie Sacks is to the right, in dark coat.

F inally there was good news. *On the Town* got splendid reviews and, more important for MGM, did big business. Betty Comden and Adolph Green's adaptation of their Broadway musical (originally a ballet by Jerome Robbins and Leonard Bernstein called *Fancy Free*) made for a wonderful picture, a perfect piece of postwar exuberance. The story of three sailors on leave in the big city sparkled, especially in its spectacular opening sequence, shot in Technicolor-glorious locales around New York. The performances by Kelly, Sinatra, Jules Munshin, Ann Miller, Betty Garrett, and Vera-Ellen were buoyant. But in the end the picture was Gene Kelly's: Frank was really just along for the ride. Kelly got top billing. He not only co-directed and choreographed; he (along with Donen) had insisted, brilliantly, that they shoot on location in New York instead of on an MGM soundstage.[1] It had cost a lot more, but the results were worth it. *On the Town* set box-office records at Radio City. "Never before has any motion picture grossed as much in one day in any theater anywhere," exclaimed *Motion Picture Daily*.

Frank Sinatra wasn't celebrating. He didn't like being outshone by Kelly, and he hadn't gotten to sing any important ballads in the film (he'd especially coveted the beautiful "Lonely Town," but it had been jettisoned by the studio, along with most of the rest of Leonard Bernstein's great score, and replaced with chirpier songs by the less than great Roger Edens). But mostly he was tired of putting on a sailor suit. He said so loudly, and Louis B. Mayer had big ears. There was another big problem: Ava Gardner. Mayer's stars misbehaved all the time, and, LB knew, often with each other, but most of them had the good sense to keep it hidden from the public. These two simply didn't give a damn. It got under Mayer's skin. It was a direct challenge to his power, and with the rise of television and the fall of MGM's profits, power was something that Louis B. Mayer was fretting about constantly.

And so—much given to saber rattling these days—Mayer had warned months earlier that Sinatra's contract was in jeopardy, as was Ava's, if the two didn't stop their carryings-on.

Frank at least had the good sense to take stock of his career at the beginning of 1950, and everything he saw worried him. In the middle of January he flew to New York and, after taking in Lena Horne's show at the Copacabana, sat down for a 4:00 a.m. cup of coffee with George Evans.

Evans represented both the Copa and Horne, who was making $60,000 a week there. Lena Horne's career was booming; Sinatra's, not. He told Evans all about Ava; he laid his cards on the table. There had been many women, but he had never felt this way before. He was going to marry this girl. Evans stared at him through the tortoise-rimmed glasses, speechless for a change. He let Sinatra talk it out. Finally Frank put down his coffee cup, looked Evans in the eye, and said he needed his help.

It was a very tall order, one that both Sinatra and Evans knew only Evans could handle. The publicist extended his hand, and Frank took it.

———

Nancy had first confronted Frank at Christmas. He denied nothing, but told his wife angrily that she was blowing the whole Ava business out of proportion. When she pursued the matter, he insisted he didn't want to talk about it—and Nancy, for the sake of Christmas, let it go. She stewed through the holiday, though, and when Frank got back from New York in January (she suspected he had gone for another assignation), she let him have it.

Technically on solid ground—Ava had been in Los Angeles while he visited Evans—Frank defended himself angrily, but Nancy's anger was white-hot: she opened his closet, grabbed a handful of his sports jackets, opened their bedroom window, and threw them out. By this time the noise had awakened the children and Little Nancy was pounding on the door. Frank's wife stared at him in fury. Did he see what he was doing to the children? Did he *see*?

Frank opened the bedroom door, kissed his terrified daughter on the head, and, without looking back, walked out. The next morning, Sanicola and Al Silvani came and—apologizing fervently to Nancy— removed a carload of Frank's clothing, shoes, and toiletries and took it to his office on South Robertson, where he had spent the night.

———

To put some money in the bank (so he could send it right out to the IRS), Sinatra was doing live appearances again, for the first time in two years. In December he had surprised himself and his agents by break- ing records at the State Theater in Hartford, grossing $18,000 for two nights; now MCA had signed him for a similarly plush gig at a gigantic, brand-new hotel in Houston, the Shamrock. The place had been built by a legendary wildcatter named Glenn McCarthy, the model for the James Dean character in *Giant:* those were the days when Texas oilmen strode the earth, making big things happen. On Thursday the twenty-sixth, Frank and Van Heusen set out from Van Nuys Airport in Chester's plane. When they landed to refuel in El Paso, an airport manager in a leather jacket ran out onto the tarmac and handed Frank a piece of paper bearing an urgent message: he must call George Evans's office in New York at once.

A secretary answered the phone, her voice trembling. Evans was dead. He had stepped out of the shower that morning in his Bronx apartment, said he didn't feel well, and collapsed of a heart attack. He was forty-eight. The rumor emerged that he had gotten into a loud argument with a reporter the night before, about Sinatra. It was easy to get into arguments about Sinatra, especially when you had to stick up for him relentlessly. Evans had had a long career of it—seven years, not counting their brief separation. But sticking up for Sinatra and Ava Gardner was another matter.

Devastated, Frank let the Shamrock know he was canceling and had Van Heusen fly him to New York for the funeral, even though he loathed funerals. Evans had meant more to Frank than any other man except Manie; he had been a friend and tireless champion, the architect of his career. "I'm quite sure that when Frank learned of his death, the first thought that swept through [his] mind was: 'Thank God, we made up,'" Ed Sullivan wrote in his Little Old New York column, a few days later.

It's pretty to think so. What feels more plausible is that Frank's first thought was: *My God, I killed him.* Sinatra may have been incapable of apology, but guilt was a key part of his makeup. Money was usually the solution. The day after the funeral, Frank sent Evans's widow the $14,000 that he owed the press agent. In the weeks to come, he would put Evans's son Philip, who had recently made George a proud grandfather, on the Sinatra payroll for life.

======

The same issue of *Billboard* that announced George Evans's death bore the news that Manie Sacks was leaving Columbia Records for RCA. Victor had been pursuing Sacks for months, and given the cataclysmic changes at Columbia—Dinah Shore and Mitchell Ayres both gone to the rival label; Buddy Clark dead;[2] Sinatra a walking shadow—Sacks must have felt the timing was right. He was forty-seven years old, getting on, and RCA, in red-hot competition with Columbia, was offering real money.

Sacks would have no official replacement as manager of popular repertoire at Columbia, but in February the label brought in a new head for its pop-singles division: Mitch Miller.

George was gone, Manie was gone, but business was business: Frank rescheduled the Shamrock gig for the first week of February. On the sixth, he and Van Heusen flew from New York to Houston—and unbeknownst to Frank, Ava, in Hollywood, decided impulsively to go meet him. Following MGM protocol, she put in a request to the studio to make the trip. Mayer sent down the word: no. She went anyway. Gardner biographer Lee Server wrote:

> She arrived late for his performance, the house lights down,
> but even in the dark she caught every eye and provoked a stir
> of excited whispers across the entire room. When he saw her
> Sinatra beamed as if he had been hit with a hot red spotlight.
> If the audience wondered about a possible relationship
> between the two stars, Sinatra did little to disconnect the dots,
> compulsively directing each song directly to Ava as if everyone
> else in the room had gone home.

After the show, the mayor of Houston, Oscar Holcombe, took Frank, Ava, Van Heusen, and several others to dinner at an Italian restaurant, Vincent's Sorrento. It wasn't a spontaneous decision: Holcombe's office had made a reservation—and the restaurant's owner, delighted at the prospect of such spectacular glamour descending on his establishment, had tipped off the *Houston Post,* which dispatched a photographer. The next morning the wires reported:

> Frank Sinatra squired Siren Ava Gardner to dinner last night and almost got a chance to show off his fancy footwork in the art of fisticuffs . . . In the middle of his spaghetti Houston Press Photographer Eddie Schisser approached the table to ask Sinatra to pose for a quick shot.
>
> "I'd like to take your picture eating spaghetti," Schisser said.
>
> Unsmilingly, the bantam singer said he wasn't having his picture taken, with or without spaghetti.
>
> Schisser reminded him that it would "take only 30 seconds," and Sinatra shoved back his chair, as if about to rise.
>
> Nobody heard exactly what was said, but a few uncomplimentary phrases allegedly were passed by both sides as the management moved in to maintain equilibrium.
>
> Miss Gardner tried to cover her face with her hands.

George Evans, freshly laid in his grave, was already spinning in it.

It was the first in what would be a lifelong series of such conflagrations with the press, and in a very real way the subtraction of Evans (and even the departure of Manie) made it all possible. The requisite accelerants were present: the interrupted meal; Sinatra's powerful but scarcely admitted guilt (he would later call going out publicly with Ava "a major mistake," then said, "But I was so in love I didn't care"); his generally battered self-esteem. And then there was (again relevantly) the casual, barely understood ethnic insensitivity of the times: an Italian-American *should* be photographed eating spaghetti, the same way an African-American, in 1950, would be photographed eating watermelon. Sinatra didn't like it a bit, nor should he have.

But far more damaging than the flare-up itself was the national publicity. For Nancy Sinatra, who had held a scrap of hope that her husband might come to his senses and return to his home, this was her final humiliation. That afternoon she called a hardware store and had the locks changed at 320 North Carolwood.

Their eleventh wedding anniversary had been two days earlier.

=====

The affair, previously just whispered about (though in Hollywood it was the worst-kept secret in town), was officially public. Reading about it over his morning coffee, moving his lips as he read, Frank's champion and old Hasbrouck Heights neighbor Willie Moretti shook his head, frowning. Never one to keep his opinion to himself (and now, in the grips of secondary syphilis, more disinhibited than ever), Moretti phoned Western Union and, in his high, hoarse voice, dictated a telegram: "I am very much surprised what I have been reading in the newspapers between you and your darling wife," he said. "Remember you have a decent wife and children. You should be very happy. Regards to all. Willie Moore."

=====

Still. Now Frank could—God help him—do precisely as he pleased.

On February 10, Sheilah Graham wrote: "Ava Gardner's current travels with Frank Sinatra include a stop-over in San Francisco. Ava is telling her friends that she wants to get married. She did not say to whom."

=====

The day after Valentine's Day, Hedda Hopper's piece ran in the *Los Angeles Times*:

FRANK SINATRA'S WIFE DECIDES ON SEPARATION

Nancy Sinatra has finally decided to separate from her husband Frank, claiming that her married life with the crooner has become "unhappy and almost unbearable."

"But I do not see a divorce in the foreseeable future," she said yesterday.

First a property settlement will be worked out, and Nancy will ask for custody of their three children, Nancy, 9; Frank, 6; and Christina, 2. Her attorney is Arnold M. Grant.

This is the third separation for the Sinatras, who were married Feb. 4, 1939. Frank left home in October, 1946, but reconciled with his wife two weeks later.

In January, 1950, he again left home, but that time Nancy said, "He's done it before and I suppose he'll do it again, but I'm not calling this a marital breakup."

With Nancy taking the initiative this time, it looks like the real thing.

The next day, as Gardner wrote in her autobiography,

the shit really hit the fan. In the next few weeks, I was receiving scores of letters accusing me of being a scarlet woman, a home wrecker, and worse. One correspondent addressed me as "Bitch-Jezebel-Gardner," the Legion of Decency threatened to ban my movies, and Catholic priests found the time to write me accusatory letters. I even read where the Sisters of Mary and Joseph asked their students at St. Paul the Apostle School in Los Angeles to pray for Frank's poor wife.

Louella Parsons had apparently heard the good Sisters' plea. She wrote:

I am very glad Nancy Sinatra will not divorce Frankie—that she will ask for a legal separation, because somehow I believe these two will go back together.

Frankie is planning a trip to Europe this spring, just about the time Ava Gardner leaves to make *Pandora and the Flying Dutchman* with James Mason in England.

But I've seen Frankie get these crushes before, and I'm not for a minute taking his friendship with Ava as anything serious. Ava, too, gets crushes, and gets over them. But the one I really feel sorry for is little Nancy, who is such a fine woman.

And hate mail was only the beginning of Ava's problems. Soon Dorothy Kilgallen was reporting in her column that, as if Ava weren't in enough trouble with the country at large, her "romantic episode with Frank Sinatra has put her in the MGM doghouse. She has been warned to avoid further 'entanglements.'"

===

Earlier that month, in Wheeling, West Virginia, Senator Joseph McCarthy held up a piece of paper and said, "I have here in my hand a list of names that were made known to the Secretary of State as being members of the Communist Party and who nevertheless are still working and shaping policy in the State Department."

The effect of the so-called Wheeling speech on a country already in the throes of Communist paranoia was electric. McCarthy, heretofore a marginal and intensely unpopular legislator, instantly shot to prominence.

Frank Sinatra, suspected by many of having Communist sympathies and now a certified moral reprobate, was ripe for the pillory. As was Ava. Erskine Johnson's March 10 column noted: "Ava Gardner's lines as a husband-snatching hussy in *East Side, West Side* drew snickers at a preview."

There was a satisfying symmetry in the equally squalid Ingrid Bergman affair. On March 15, another senator from the heartland, Edwin C. Johnson of Colorado, mysteriously decided that the Bergman and Rossellini affair was the nation's business. On the Senate floor he called Ingrid Bergman an "apostle of degradation" and declared that the Committee on Interstate and Foreign Commerce, of which he was chairman, would begin hearings on "the serious moral questions raised by movieland's lurid headlines."

Bergman or Sinatra? Newspapers could hardly decide which scandal to run with on any given day. The March 17 edition of the Lebanon, Pennsylvania, *Daily News* carried a page-one story headlined HUSBAND WILL FIGHT BERGMAN IN COURT and, inside, a United Press dispatch that read as if it had been written by Lee Mortimer himself:

> Crooner boy Frankie Sinatra's charm seems to have gone afleeting.
>
> His bobby sox brigades are conspicuous—by their absence.
>
> Frankie currently is sequestered in a 33rd-floor duplex suite at Hampshire House, on Central Park, where reportedly he is paying a little bagatelle of $100 a day.
>
> By a coincidence, actress Ava Gardner occupies a suite in the same diggings . . .
>
> And—horrible thought—the crooner's once-faithful squealing teen-age admirers aren't bothering him a bit. Only two fans showed up yesterday at Hampshire House to get a look at their idol.
>
> One was a youngster of about 13. The other, a patient middle-aged matron, hid behind a potted evergreen in the lobby.
>
> But the irked Frankie avoided them like the plague.
>
> Nor was there any word from Miss Gardner.
>
> Times, it seems, have changed. Maybe the bobby soxers are getting more absorbed in such little matters as the H-bomb.

Sinatra was in New York to begin an eight-week stand at the Copacabana,[3] his first New York nightclub appearance since he'd played the Riobamba five years earlier. He was scared. He had avoided the Copa, worried that its grinding three-show-a-night format would strain his vocal cords. And these days, he had plenty of reason to worry about his instrument: those guilt germs George Evans used to talk about were in the air.

=====

Walter Winchell, March 19: "Items-We-Doubt: That F. Sinatra's parting from his wife is a gimmick to attract the attention he used to get by crooning."

=====

It was the phone calls that got to him, Little Nancy calling every day and asking when he was coming home, that little voice sounding so far away on the scratchy cross-country connection, the voice of Judgment itself. Frank had the shakes. "I found myself needing pills to sleep, pills to get started in the morning and pills to relax during the day," he would recall. And it wasn't just pills. Ava remembered: "Every single night we would have three or four martinis, big ones in big champagne glasses, then wine with dinner, then go to a nightclub and start drinking Scotch or bourbon. I don't know how we did it."

They were both on edge. She was on her way to England to start shooting her movie; the steady barrage of angry letters and bad press was tempting her to get out of the country early. But she stayed for Frank's big opening on Tuesday, March 28.

It didn't help that Nancy's birthday, her thirty-third, was on the twenty-sixth. He sent her a mink coat: no reply. Ten grand and no reply. For days he pestered everyone around him (except Ava, naturally), agonizing: Should he call her? Should he?

Sanicola and Van Heusen, who sensed that he really did want to call his wife, advised him to do so.

So he called her—and reached the maid, who told him that Missy Sinatra was in Palm Springs. Frank phoned there, too: no answer. He found out later that night that her friends had thrown her a big party, that Nancy had made a grand entrance in the mink coat.

Frank knew he needed help. You couldn't open at the Copa without special material. Sammy Cahn was the world master of special material—but Cahn had been on Sinatra's shit list for over a year for some minor infraction. That was the way it went with Frank. ("Someone told Sinatra that at a dinner party at my house his name was, as I believe they say, taken in vain," Sammy recalled. "He thought I should have slapped the offending person's face.")

Another man might have called and mended fences; Frank just called. Out of the blue, after a year and a half.

"Sam, Frank."

"Hey, Frank."

"Sam, you got a moment? I'm opening at the Copa."

"Hey, not only did I know that you were opening at the Copa, but I've been thinking, if we were speaking, what would I have written?"

"Will you come to New York?"

"Yes, I will."

So Sammy took the Super Chief to Chicago and the Twentieth Century Limited from Chicago to Grand Central—three thousand miles, two and a half days; writing the whole way.

The night of the opening, Sinatra paced his tiny dressing room, unable to stop sweating. He had to shower and change his shirt twice. Ava was sitting with him, her brow wrinkled with concern. She could be awful, but when he was really in trouble, she could be wonderful.

She stroked his hand and looked into his eyes. She hated to see him this way. She would call the doctor and get Frank something for his nerves.

While she dialed, he stared at Nancy's good-luck telegram on the mirror.

When the doctor arrived, Ava went out to the table at ringside—there was a stir when the other customers spotted her, incandescent in a black off-the-shoulder dress—and sat down with Dolly and Marty, Sammy Cahn, Phil Silvers, Manie Sacks, Joe Fischetti, and Willie Moretti. The house was packed, the place vibrating with excitement. Then Frank bounded out and went into his opening number, Cole Porter's "I Am Loved":

I'm adored, I'm adored,
By the one who first led my heart astray.

The crowd went nuts. They ate it up when he did Sammy's special material, putting on a coonskin cap, snapping a whip, and blowing a duck call as he sang bawdy new lyrics to Frankie Laine's "Mule Train" and "The Cry of the Wild Goose." They roared when he ripped the press: "My voice was so low the other night singing 'Ol Man River' that I got down in the dirt, and who do you think I found throwing mud down there? Two Hollywood commentators! They got a great racket. All day long they lie in the sun, and when the sun goes down, they lie some more!"

He was a smash hit. "After the opening, he got great reviews," Sammy Cahn recalled. "I was so proud, I was so happy."

But Cahn's memory was rose-colored: the show-business crowds loved Frank; the critics weren't so sure. "Whether temporarily or otherwise, the music that used to hypnotize the bobbysoxers—whatever happened to them anyway, thank goodness?—is gone from the throat," the *Herald Tribune*'s reviewer wrote. "Vocally, there isn't quite the same old black magic there used to be when Mr. Sinatra wrenched 'Night and Day' from his sapling frame and thousands swooned."

Sammy wasn't the only one with a forgiving memory. "Frank was nervous before he went on, which was unlike him," Ava Gardner wrote in her autobiography, "but he sang like an angel, especially 'Nancy with the Laughing Face,' a song written about his daughter, not his wife. I've always thought it was a beautiful song, and contrary to what everyone seems to believe, it was never the reason for a single quarrel between us."

Another account has it somewhat differently. "Did you have to sing that fucking song?" Ava is said to have asked Frank, after the Copa audience snickered during the number. "It made me feel like a real fool."

That wasn't the only thing she was unhappy about. As she loyally stayed for night after night of the Copa stand, MGM pelted her with telegrams reminding her she was overdue to start filming in England. And night after night she found herself in the company of some of Frank's less classy friends, including the Fischetti brothers and Frank Costello. She was bored, feigning smiles. She and Sinatra were starting to squabble.

Meanwhile, Artie Shaw was in town.

Her own Svengali was back from one of his periodic sabbaticals from the music business, playing a gig at Bop City on Fifty-second Street. Shaw had a beautiful apartment on Central Park West. He was getting some interesting people together: Would Ava and Frank like to come up to his place for cocktails?

Frank wouldn't like to. Over the years, he would go considerably out of his way to forge bonds with people he considered classy. He just hated Artie Shaw.

The feeling was mutual. In the early 1940s, Frank had wanted to sing with Shaw's band, then the hottest in the land: Shaw had turned him down. Over the course of his long life, the pedantic bandleader, always eager to flaunt his intellect, would go to great lengths to deprecate the singer, with subtle rationalizations or faint praise. "We took a plain, ordinary singer, who was a good singer—there was nothing wrong with that; he was able to sing—and we made him into an icon," Shaw told an interviewer many years later.

Frank knew that Ava still called Shaw up for advice sometimes. ("Artie solved other people's problems in a couple of sentences," she would write years later, with barely disguised irony.) Frank also knew that Artie Shaw was very smart, very talented, and a devil with the ladies, and he had a gnawing fear that Shaw was going to lure Ava back into the sack.

And after a couple of nights of listening to the Fischettis' deses, dems, and dirty jokes, she was feeling not just bored—always a dangerous mode for her—but rebellious. Who the hell was *he* to tell her what she should or shouldn't do? And worse, what did it say about him that he *liked* those goons?

She finally went to see Shaw.

Accounts of the evening differ. One version says that Ava rebelled and decided to attend one of Shaw's high-toned gatherings alone. Ava herself—not necessarily the most reliable of narrators—says she and Frank had a fight, ostensibly about his wandering eye:

> Restaurants were frequently where our quarrels began, and I
> have to confess I started a lot of them, sometimes before the
> appetizer arrived. A pretty girl would pass and recognize Frank.
> She'd smile. He'd nod and smile back. It would happen again.
> Frank would feel the temperature rising across the table and
> try to escape with a sort of sickly look. I'd say something sweet
> and ladylike, such as, "I suppose you're sleeping with all these
> broads," and we'd be off to the races.

She says she stomped out that night and took a taxi back to the Hampshire House. After stewing awhile, she phoned Shaw, who told her his girlfriend was with him but she was welcome to come over and talk. Another account has Ava leaving the Copa, ostensibly to wait for Frank back at their suite, but actually to go nightclubbing with a writer friend, Richard Condon,[4] and Condon's girl. According to this story, the three wound up at Bop City, seated at Shaw's table, and when Ava phoned Frank, ostensibly to ease his mind about her whereabouts, Frank shouted that he was going to kill himself.

In Ava's version, Sinatra shows up at Shaw's apartment, loaded for bear—or, rather, Frank's version of being loaded for bear, which meant bringing along Hank Sanicola. This is where Artie Shaw's side of the Rashomon tale comes into play. Since he told the story frequently, he occasionally liked to freshen it with piquant new details:

> She called at two a.m. and said she had been with Sinatra
> and the Fischetti boys. One of the guys had thrown a glass of
> whiskey in the face of one of her girlfriends, and she had to get

away. She said she wanted to see me. I explained that I wasn't alone. But she came anyway, dressed to the nines and saying she wanted to ask me some questions. I asked my girlfriend to go back to bed so Ava and I could talk.

Ava complained to Artie about Frank and his mobsters, but then, according to Shaw, she got down to the nitty-gritty:

> "When you and I were, you know, doing it"—that was her way of saying it—"was it good?" I said, "If everything else had been anywhere near as good, we'd have been together forever and I'd never have let you out of my sight." She gave a sigh of relief. I asked why. She said, "With him it's impossible." I said I thought he was a big stud. She said, "No, it's like being in bed with a woman. He's so gentle. It's as though he thinks I'll break, as though I'm a piece of Dresden china and he's gonna hurt me."

Then, as if the sexual self-aggrandizement weren't enough, Shaw declares Ava left and Frank entered, along with "the heavyweight fellow." All that's missing are the slamming doors.

It's all very entertaining. And ultimately, what truly happened is unknowable. But on this score everyone seems to agree: After Ava got back to the Hampshire House, where she and her sister Bappie were sharing one bedroom and Frank was staying in another, her phone rang. "It was Frank, and I'll never forget his voice," Ava recalled. "He said, 'I can't stand it any longer. I'm going to kill myself—now!'"

> Then there was this tremendous bang in my ear, and I knew it was a revolver shot. My whole mind sort of exploded in a great wave of panic, terror, and shocked disbelief. Oh, God! Oh, God! I threw the phone down and raced across the living room and into Frank's room. I didn't know what I expected to find—a body? And there was a body lying on the bed. Oh, God, was he

dead? I threw myself on it saying, "Frank, Frank . . ." And the face, with a rather pale little smile, turned toward me, and the voice said, "Oh, hello."

The goddamn revolver was still smoking in his hand. He had fired a single shot through a pillow and into the mattress.

She wasn't mad at him, only relieved. "He was alive, thank God, he was alive," she wrote. "I held him tightly to me."

At this point—since a gunshot in the middle of the night in a luxury hotel suite will not go unnoticed, even in New York City—the farce continues: the desk clerk phones, Sinatra professes innocence, good

Frank on the edge. The Copacabana, spring 1950, just before his voice gave out. He wears a coonskin cap and snaps a whip to lampoon Frankie Laine; meanwhile, he's taking "pills to sleep, pills to get started in the morning, and pills to relax during the day."

old Sanicola is summoned to spirit away the incriminating mattress (in one version he's helped by, of all people, David O. Selznick, who's staying down the hall). The NYPD arrives, and different versions of the story hit the papers.

Whatever really happened that night, the episode speaks to Frank Sinatra's deeply divided nature. He is a thirty-four-year-old man, famous and brilliant and deep voiced and well-endowed and sexually voracious, certainly by many measures the big stud Artie Shaw makes him out to be. Yet his behavior throughout this singular evening is oddly childlike, especially when it comes to the faked suicide. That pale little smile when Ava—on top—finally gives him his sought-after, maternally consoling embrace; that cartoonish "Oh, hello." It's like the climax of a game of hide-and-seek.

Artie Shaw's story about Ava's sexual confession ("It's like being in bed with a woman") may be half-true; it certainly shows Shaw to best advantage, and Sinatra to worst. But it chimes oddly with the incident at the Hampshire House. Sinatra certainly had a hysterical side, and was nothing if not hypersensitive. And Ava was all things to him, siren and drinking buddy and mother surrogate, and great artists have polymorphous souls. Even her private name for him, Francis, sounded (perhaps purposely) androgynous. Picasso, who was every bit as macho as Frank, said, "Every artist is a woman and ought to be *une gouine* [a dyke]." In any case, if Ava was looking for a man who would dominate her, she was, as would become increasingly evident, betting on the wrong horse.

Frank and Mitch Miller rehearse in Columbia recording studio, circa 1951. The tension between the domineering singer and the domineering producer is palpable.

Now that Manie had left the picture, Columbia, too, was starting to wonder about Sinatra. From virtually carrying the company, he had become a major liability. (As soon as Sacks arrived at RCA, he tried to sell his colleagues on signing Sinatra: no one was interested.) On March 30, 1950, Columbia Records' president, Ted Wallerstein, sent a memo to his next in command, Vice President Goddard Lieberson:

As you know, we got rid of a very bad Sinatra deal some six months ago by a new agreement under which we advanced him $50,000 and agreed, at the same time, to pay the income tax on this original $50,000 the following year, and the tax on the tax the third year.

The total of this is going to run to about $120,000. This, as accompaniment costs, with certain limitations, are advances against royalties; therefore, practically the biggest problem we have in the pop field is to get some big-selling records out of Sinatra . . .

Please push this continuously while I am away.

Manie, Frank's ultimate protector, had been the one behind the big advances. With Manie gone, and RCA surging, a cold wind was blowing at Columbia. Wallerstein had already given Mitch Miller the same message he'd sent Lieberson: "Mitch, we've got to make this money back."

The head of the pop-singles department knew exactly what he had to do. Before this, Frank's ratio of rhythm numbers to ballads had been about one to ten; Mitch Miller decided to try the reverse. The producer's exquisite ear and classical background never got in the way when it came to commercial matters. "What makes you want to dig in your pocket and buy a record?" he mused many years later. "It's got to be something you want to play over and over again. You look for qualities to make somebody buy it. I was trying to put stuff in records that would tighten the picture for the listener."

For Miller's first collaboration with Sinatra, the producer brought the singer an up-tempo Arthur Altman, Hal David, and Redd Evans tune, "American Beauty Rose":

Daisy is darling, Iris is sweet,
Lily is lovely, Blossom's a treat.

With a bouncy Dixieland-style arrangement by Norman Leyden, who'd pepped up Glenn Miller's and Tex Beneke's bands, "American Beauty

Rose" bounds out of the gate at a breakneck tempo and never lets up.
(Miller himself conducted.) The astute Will Friedwald calls the number "irresistible," and Sinatra's rendition "joyous," but to my ears the
song just sounds fast and mechanical, a vapid counterpart to Como's
"A—You're Adorable." Frank is in great voice, but there's no smile in
his voice. He sounds as if he's just watching Mitch's relentlessly waving baton and going through the motions.

The heartbreaking thing is that Miller knew exactly what he was
doing: America *wanted* vapid novelty numbers in 1950. It just didn't
want Sinatra very much—"American Beauty Rose" charted, but only
made it to number 26, and only for two weeks. At this point, Frank's
name was plastered all over the newspapers every day of the week as a
family deserter and a has-been. You didn't have to be officially declared
persona non grata on the Senate floor, the way Ingrid Bergman had
been, to be counted out by the American public.

But Mitch Miller had set the new tempo, and Frank had to keep
dancing faster and faster. Not only was he playing three shows a night
at the Copa and broadcasting the frenetic *Light Up Time* five evenings a week from the NBC studios at Rockefeller Center, but he was
cranking out new records at a brisk new clip in hopes of generating the
hits that would pay back Columbia (not to mention the IRS). In April
alone, he did three recording sessions and eight new songs—almost
a third as many as he'd recorded in the entire previous year. All eight
were up-tempo numbers.

Almost all the new songs were arranged by George Siravo, the same
man who'd been arranging fast-paced numbers for Frank throughout
the 1940s and who had collaborated with Sy Oliver on the July 1949
session that produced the joyous versions of "It All Depends on You"
and "Bye Bye Baby." But the differences between July 1949 and April
1950 in Sinatra's life and spirit were profound. The previous July, he'd
been in the first flush of his grand affair with Ava. Now the affair had
entered a complex second phase. Siravo's new arrangements were
lively and inventive, but Sinatra was subtly dragging them down. As
with "American Beauty Rose," he was singing well enough, but joy-

lessly. On "You Do Something to Me," he hit some outright clams, flat notes that seemed to mirror his mood.

None of the new sides charted.

In the meantime, Ava had finally heeded MGM's importuning and flown with Bappie to London. For all the sweet sorrow of parting with Frank—they wept as they embraced—she felt nothing but relief as she boarded the BOAC Stratocruiser. She would be going to Europe for four months—four months without hate mail, American newspapers, the Legion of Decency. Whether she and Frank would be seeing each other during that time was left up in the air.

"Oh, God," Ava wrote in her autobiography, "Frank Sinatra could be the sweetest, most charming man in the world when he was in the mood."

But being with him, she thought, was what it must be like to have a particularly demanding child.

In addition to three shows a night at the Copa, five radio broadcasts a week, recording sessions, and the usual fun and games with the Varsity, toward the end of April Frank opened a one-week stand at the Capitol Theater, where he had drawn less than sensationally in 1947. This time there were even more empty seats. He had been in show business half his life, and he was tired: his eyes bloodshot, his face drawn and thin. The rumors that he was having voice problems persisted—he had a cold that wouldn't go away. And now there was new gossip: Ava, shooting in Spain, had taken up with a bullfighter. Frank's stomach hurt at the thought, but he knew just where to look for consolation: sweet Marilyn Maxwell was in town, glad to listen to his troubles and not as worried about being sloppy seconds as, perhaps, she should have been. Then there were the Copa Girls, four of them—imagine the possibilities. The long nights melted into blue dawns, then he slept a little and woke to the brazen light of Manhattan afternoons . . .

Coughing. He would light a cigarette before he got out of bed, and when he was through shaving, he would light another. Then whoever had shared his bed would have to get the hell out of there, because he had to get ready for the show.

Meanwhile, in Santa Monica on April 26, Nancy filed a suit for separate maintenance. Her lawyer was Gregson Edward Bautzer— Greg to his friends, of which he had many, mainly female. The dashing, hard-drinking Bautzer was renowned in Hollywood for having taken Lana Turner's virginity (she didn't seem to have enjoyed the experience very much), and his specialty was representing beautiful women in their divorce cases: Turner; Ginger Rogers; Ingrid Bergman. These days he was seeing Rogers, when he wasn't seeing Joan Crawford. Maybe he was also seeing Nancy?

Her suit alleged that Frank had treated her with "extreme cruelty" and caused her "grievous mental suffering" without provocation on her part. "She estimated the crooner's 1949 income at $934,740," said the Associated Press, "and the value of their community property at $750,000." She also asked for custody of their three children.

There was a crowd of reporters outside the courthouse: they wanted to know if the couple were getting a divorce. Nancy, dignified in a gray dress and the three-strand pearl necklace Frank had given her, said quietly that no divorce action was contemplated. Both she and her husband were Catholics, she said, and "neither of us wants one."

Two days later, Frank was in the news again: MGM had let him go.

Frank Sinatra, cast loose romantically when sued for separate maintenance by his wife, Nancy, last week, was a free lance in his profession as well today.

Breaking another tie of years of standing, the singer asked for and was given a release from his $5,000-a-week contract with Metro-Goldwyn-Mayer Saturday.

The parting, effective immediately, was described as friendly.

A joint statement by the studio and Sinatra's agent, Music Corporation of America, pointed out:

"As a free lance artist, Sinatra is now free to accept unlimited important personal appearances, radio and TV offers that
have been made to him."

His contract with MGM restricted him in all of those
respects and particularly with regard to television. The studio
does not permit its stars to work in that medium.

While it was true that Sinatra wanted to work in television, and equally
true that in 1950 the movie studios were increasingly paranoid about
the hot new medium, Frank's separation from Metro came at the studio's request, not his—and in particular at the request of Louis B.
Mayer, who had a very specific grievance. A couple of months earlier,
after a horseback-riding accident, the boss had been pushed into work
in a wheelchair, a cast on his leg. While Sinatra sat with some pals
at lunch in the MGM commissary, someone said, "Hey, did you hear
about L. B.'s accident?" And Frank said instantly: "Yeah, he fell off of
Ginny Simms."

Ginny Simms, a former band singer with Kay Kyser and now a
wannabe movie star, was Mayer's mistress.

Frank's remark got a big laugh at the table. He could be funny
when he wasn't trying too hard, though, as with Dolly, his jokes usually
had a stiletto concealed—or not concealed—about them. In this case,
the blade was double-edged: Simms, while vivacious and appealing,
was no beauty. To put a finer point on it, she was a bit horse faced.

The remark got back to Mayer.

Frank made the long trudge into the inner sanctum. The old man
was ominously calm. He was even smiling a little.

"So," he said. "I hear you been making jokes about my lady friend."

Frank winced. "I wish I could take that back, Louis. I'm so sorry. I
wish I'd never said anything so stupid."

"That's not a very nice thing to do," Mayer said. "I want you to
leave, and I don't ever want you to come back again."

That had been in February. Mayer had been genuinely offended by Frank's remark, but he was also a businessman. The gaffe had given him a perfect pretext to unload damaged goods. By the end of April, MCA was finished working out the severance: Sinatra would receive a final payment of $85,000. Greg Bautzer instantly called MGM and slapped a restraining order on the check until Nancy and Frank settled the separate-maintenance suit.

Meanwhile, Frank was doing big business at the Copa, thanks to the cognoscenti, who, heedless of his troubles, continued to roll in night after night. But every dime he made, and then some, was going straight out the door. He went to MCA's chairman, Jules Stein, for a loan; Stein all but laughed in his face. Those "unlimited important personal appearances, radio and TV offers" mentioned in the press release were in fact extremely limited: Frank Sinatra was a drug on the market.

Not to mention a king-sized pain in the ass. He treated everyone at the agency like a servant, including his chief representatives, Lew Wasserman in Hollywood and Sonny Werblin in New York. MCA might have stood for this behavior if he'd been bringing in money. As it was, Sinatra's agents had effectively cut him loose: by 1950, they were no longer working actively on his behalf.

Worse, he was losing what was most precious to him: his voice. Many years later, Mitch Miller recalled:

> Listen, Sinatra had a marvelous voice, but it was very fragile.
> There were certain guys like Gordon MacRae who could stay
> up all night and drink and sing the next day—he could sing
> underwater. But if Frank didn't get enough sleep or if he drank
> a lot the night before, it would show up. And Frank was a
> guy—call it ego or what you want—he liked to suffer out loud,
> to be dramatic. There were plenty of people, big entertainers,
> who had a wild life or had big problems, but they kept it quiet.
> Frank had to do his suffering in public, so everyone could see
> it. And this was a time he was having trouble with Ava, she
> was in Spain, and it showed in his work. He would come in to

record, and he couldn't get through a number without his voice cracking.

Every time Frank's voice went, Miller would have to start the session over again, racking up studio fees and musicians' overtime. (Which, as per Sinatra's unique contract with Columbia, were the label's responsibility.) But thanks to the new technology of tape recording, Miller was able to come up with a simple fix:

I can say this now: I could have been kicked out of the musicians' union because tracking was not allowed. There were a lot of musicians involved. So what I did, to save the session, I just shut off his mike and got good background tracks. Didn't even tell him.

Then after it was over, I said, "When your voice is back . . ." We'd come in crazy hours, in a locked building, so no union representative could come in. Then when Frank came in, say, at midnight, we would play the disc. He would put earphones on and he would sing, just the way they do now. And we would remix it. He did them very well after that, and the whole orchestra was perfect on it.

It sounds simple, but it couldn't have been. Sinatra, who revered musicians and always insisted on doing right by them, knew he was taking money out of his musicians' pockets, not to mention depriving himself of the pleasure of working directly with them. The pleasure of *being with* the musicians was central to Sinatra as an artist, and it infused all his best recordings. Indeed, even as recording technology advanced and tracking (today known as overdubbing) became almost universal, Sinatra did not like to record separately—and when he did, the music was always the worse for it. The renowned sound engineer Lee Herschberg, who supervised most of Frank's Reprise sessions in the 1960s, noted that unlike most other singers, Sinatra couldn't bear to sing behind sound-absorbing isolation panels—gobos. "You couldn't do that with him, because he wanted to hear the piano, number one," Herschberg said. "He'd stand right behind Bill Miller, or whomever."

Frank wanted the intimacy. He'd stand right behind Miller and tease him, and Miller, or whoever, would joke back, and the studio would start to take on a kind of glow. "Sinatra wasn't like some of the other people you would record," Herschberg recalled. "When he walked in, it was special. Because there was an air in the studio that something special was going to happen. He always had the best arrangers and he had the best players, and everybody was having such a good time and was so happy to be there, and it really made him give what he had to give."

That was in the 1960s. In 1950 it was a very different story: good times were in short supply; Sinatra was sinking fast. During the day he was stripping the gears—and obsessing over Ava. "Every day," writes Gardner's biographer Lee Server, "he would send off a heartfelt cable and then telephone her in the early evening in New York, late night in Spain, and try again sometime after midnight, early morning [at the location] in Tossa de Mar."

> But long-distance telecommunication in Catalonia was still erratic at best. Sometimes hours of transatlantic operator assistance were necessary only to be told again that the lines were down or that no one was answering. When at last he would reach her, the connection was often filled with static and her voice a maddeningly faint and broken echo. Conversations would end with his frantic declaration of love and anguished hope that he had correctly heard Ava declare the same.

I don't think it's an exaggeration to say that you can hear the disconnect in the records he made during that grueling April: As Mitch Miller triumphantly noted, the orchestra was perfect. Frank, however, was merely good. And the main thing was that he and the orchestra didn't sound good *together*.

Then, at the Copa dinner show on May 2, Sinatra reached for

a high note on *South Pacific*'s "Bali H'ai." The note wasn't there. He somehow managed to finish the show—then rushed back to his bed at the Hampshire House, where he sat in his pajamas, weakly calling for hot tea and honey. As Frank rested, feeling deeply sorry for himself, Hank Sanicola let slip a rumor that had been making the rounds in midtown: Lee Mortimer had bet Jack Entratter $100 that Sinatra would never finish out the Copa engagement.

That was all he needed. At 2:00 a.m., strictly against Dr. Goldman's orders, Frank was back at the club, dressed and ready for the last show of the evening. He cleared his throat and dedicated "I Have But One Heart" to Ava. He sang it all the way through. Then Skitch Henderson kicked the band into gear for "It All Depends on You." What happened next "was tragic and terrifying," Henderson recalled:

> He opened his mouth to sing after the band introduction and nothing came out. Not a sound. I thought for a fleeting moment that the unexpected pantomime was a joke. But then he caught my eye. I guess the color drained out of my face as I saw the panic in his. It became so quiet, so intensely quiet in the club—they were like watching a man walk off a cliff. His face chalk white, Frank gasped something that sounded like "Good Night" into the mike and raced off the floor, leaving the audience stunned.

It may have been tragic and terrifying to Skitch and Frank, but to the newspapers it was a source for gloating:

BALI TOO H'AI;
VOICE VOICELESS

Frank Sinatra's voice deserted him Tuesday and his doctor said it was because the crooner tried to make it do the impossible— hit a soprano note.

Dr. Irving Goldman explained that Sinatra's normal range is two octaves in the baritone-tenor class. When Frank tried to hit too high a note in the song "Bali H'ai," the physician said, his left vocal chord [*sic*] dissented.

In medical terms, Sinatra suffered what the doctor called a "submucosal hemorrhage."

Doctor Goldman ordered ten days of silence for "The Voice," who has been appearing at New York's Copacabana night club. Sinatra is due to open an engagement in Chicago May 12, and if he is to make it, said the doctor, he must keep mum until then—no talking or singing.

Sinatra's friends said that to keep the ban of silence, Frank will go to a vacation hideaway.

The hideaway was Charlie Fischetti's mansion on Allison Island in Miami, an establishment where hoarse monosyllables would not be at all out of place.

=====

On May 12, Sinatra was tanned and rested, his voice much improved. But instead of heading to the Chez Paree in chilly Chicago, he was waving to reporters, pointing to his throat, and boarding a flight to sunny Spain with Van Heusen. "Yes, I'll probably see Ava," he croaked to the reporters. "But we'll be as well chaperoned as at a high-school dance."

"Even if he has to hire sixteen duennas," Chester piped up.

Frank was, of course, bearing gifts: Ava had said she was missing her gum and her favorite soft drink, so he carried along a carton of Wrigley's Spearmint and a six-pack of Coke. And a $10,000 diamond-and-emerald necklace.

The suits at MCA were grim faced at the news that he had blithely canceled the Chicago engagement (though the owners of Chez Paree, where the Fischettis had a special table, were quite understanding).

But Frank had to reestablish contact with Ava. She had been gone for over a month now—anything could have happened. Knowing her, plenty probably had.

If he was pining for her, the reverse did not seem to be true, as a production assistant on *Pandora and the Flying Dutchman,* Jeanie Sims, recalled. "I remember one time we were shooting a scene of Ava by herself," Sims told Lee Server.

> She was supposed to be lost in some deep thought about the man she was in love with. And she couldn't sort of get it right for [the director, Albert Lewin] . . . Al finally went over and said to her, "Ava, is there some one person in your life who you love or have loved more than anyone else on earth?" And she answered him so quietly I could not hear her. And he told her to think of that person and it was just the impetus she needed, and she got it perfect on the next shot. And afterward I was a bit curious, and I asked Al what she had said, who she had loved more than anyone, and Al said, "The clarinet player— Artie Shaw."

Ava, though, was living for the present. She took her pleasures as she found them, and she found them everywhere. With a kind of beauty that comes along once in a hundred years—not just in her lush and haughty face but also in her long-limbed body, her smoky voice, her feline walk—she transfixed men and women alike. She had never been out of the States before, and Europe, still depressed after the war, was stunned at the sight of her.

"A very, very wild spirit," recalled her *Pandora* co-star Sheila Sim. On a quick sightseeing and shopping jaunt to Paris before filming began, Ava and Bappie had ditched their MGM driver and sneaked off to see the *real* sights. Soon, completely by accident—or so Ava swears in her memoir—they were shocked, shocked, to find themselves in a bar full of men who weren't really men. Well, Bappie was shocked.

As her little sister wrote: " 'Ava,' Bappie said in her dark-brown North Carolina Baptist Belt voice that fortunately nobody understood except me, 'we are in a *House of Lesbians!*' " From Ava's point of view, however, "All the girls [were] welcoming, and charming."

Everyone was smitten with her. Albert Lewin, recalled the cinematographer Jack Cardiff, "thought she was the most beautiful woman in the world, and he used to just gaze and gaze at her. And we would shoot her, and he would say, 'I want to do another close-up. Closer.' And we would do that. And then he would say, 'Let's do another one. Different angle.' Then one more, '*Closer.*' And on and on like that."

But her biggest admirer was the bullfighter: the rumors were true, kind of. His name was Mario Cabré, he was thirty-five years old, and he was a second-rate torero but a first-rate self-promoter. He was playing a bullfighter in the film, one of Ava's suitors, and so he figured, why should fact not mirror fiction? He was instantly bewitched by her, but also saw her as his ticket out of Palookaville. To complicate matters, the MGM unit publicists were eager to promote a romance in order to distract the world from the grand opera of Gardner and Sinatra.

And then there was Ava herself, incessantly complicated. In her autobiography she is at great pains to dismiss Cabré as a mere nuisance:

> Someone had passed on to him the concept that there is no
> such thing as bad publicity: if you want to be famous you've got
> to get into the headlines. And what greater opportunity could
> he have than an attempt to replace Frank in my affections? His
> motivation was cynical self-interest. His declamatory rhetoric
> about this great passion in his life, his love for me and mine for
> him, made headlines in Spain, America, all over the world, and
> that's all he cared about. He gave interviews saying I was "the
> woman I love with all the strength in my soul," wrote the most
> idiotic love poems imaginable, and then marched off to recite
> them at the American embassy in Madrid.

Initially, I suppose I thought this was vaguely amusing, and since we played lovers in the same film, no one was exactly encouraging me to come out and publicly say he was a nuisance and a jerk. But when he started to involve Frank in his shenanigans, saying he would not leave Spain alive if he came on that visit, Mario became a major pest.

It must be remembered, however, that Gardner dictated her memoir (to not one but three successive ghostwriters) toward the end of her life, when she was sick and the beneficiary of numerous gestures of goodwill, including money, from Frank Sinatra. In the spring of 1950, by the testimony of her colleagues on *Pandora and the Flying Dutchman*, it was a different story: she was initially resistant, but then not so resistant, to the charms of the handsome torero. At first he was just a very good-looking Spaniard. But when he fought that bull, "it just got into her blood right away," recalled the set dresser John Hawkesworth. "The excitement and the color and the drama of the thing, she loved it."

Sinatra's arrival, on the other hand—he landed in Barcelona on May 11—was an unwelcome surprise. Maybe he wanted to test her. If so, he found the true Ava: When he arrived in Tossa de Mar, she was off someplace with Cabré, and the crew had to distract Frank with a poker game until she could be found. Then she waltzed in, all smiles and wreathed in that perfume, and all his questions—Where had she been? What had she been doing?—evaporated.

"Oh, what a lovely surprise!" Ava exclaimed, at the sight of him. "Darling! How great!"

The next few days were a combination of melodrama and low comedy. Upon hearing of Sinatra's arrival, the torero swore that he would kill the singer. Director Lewin had the good sense to take Cabré at his word and have him sent to a remote location to prepare for his bull-fighting scenes. In the meantime, off went Sinatra and Gardner, with the Spanish press in hot pursuit. It rained; shooting was halted. The lovers spent the day in her villa; the reporters camped outside. Inside,

Frank and Ava were at each other like wasps in a bottle, fighting about the bullfighter (she denied everything). Then they made up.

The sun came out. Shooting resumed. The sun hurt Sinatra's eyes. As Chester sat by solicitously, Frank sulked and drank champagne and out of sheer boredom tossed a few bones to the reporters. ("Of course, I knew what people would say when I flew here. I am not a youth any-more," he said, sounding oddly Spanish. "I expected this curiosity.")

"Don't you have anything else to say, Frank?" a reporter asked.

"Yes," he said. "Bing Crosby is the best singer in the world."

On Sunday, the lovers and Van Heusen went out tuna fishing. The sea sparkled; the Americans laughed and drank more champagne and caught a couple of big fish. The reporters were far away.

On Monday she had to go back to work. The reporters were clustering again. One of them handed Sinatra an American newspaper carrying a story about Nancy. She had spent Mother's Day without Frank for the first time ever, the report read. She had received gifts from the children, but nothing from her husband, who had spent the weekend in Spain with Ava Gardner. The story mentioned the diamond-and-emerald necklace.

"They can't make this one of those things," Frank growled. He denied the existence of the necklace. "We have been chaperoned every minute we have been together," he said. He was referring, in all seri-ousness, to Van Heusen. "We know now that because of this publicity, it was a mistake for me to have come here," he said, and announced he was leaving twenty-four hours early.

There was another tearful parting, then he and Van Heusen flew to Paris to console themselves with whores.

Earl Wilson tracked Frank down at the Café Lido, a lively night-club featuring bare-breasted chorus girls. Frank shouted over the phone—partly because he had to, due to the faint transatlantic con-nection, but mostly because he was upset:

"This bullfighter is nothing to her. NOTHING! This girl is very upset because she's had nothing to do with this boy," Frank went on. He was screaming a little; him with not too good a throat, either!

"What did you and Ava do in Spain?" I innocently inquired. A reporter on this kind of story has got to ask a lot of foolish questions.

"We were sunning ourselves all day and we went out for a ride when she wasn't working," Frank shouted.

"She and I took a lot of drives. We took a lot of looks at the countryside. We caught a couple of tuna fish."

And that reminded Frank of something he had been wanting to get across to the whole world and, though that beautiful Lido show with the creamy-skinned beauties was waiting, he took time to explain.

"We've kept this clean as anybody could," he exclaimed. "Just so nobody could hit below the belt, we were well chaperoned all the time. We were chaperoned like a high school dance. ALL THE TIME!"

"And did you talk about getting a divorce so you can get married?"

"I've never said a word about it. NOT A WORD," he fiercely insisted, "and here's something you can use. Everybody's talking about Ava and me getting married . . . EVERYBODY . . . except Ava and me!"

The trip to Spain had been a fiasco. He wasn't working (while Ava was): he hadn't sung in a month. On the way home—and where exactly was home? in his office on South Robertson?—squadrons of reporters met him at every stop along the way, in London and in New York and finally in Los Angeles, all asking the same stupid questions: Was Ava in love with the bullfighter? Was Frank running away from the bullfighter? And by the way, were Frank and Ava planning to get married?

He stopped at his office just long enough to shower and change clothes, then drove out to Holmby Hills bearing gifts: dolls and toys from Paris for the kids, a gold charm bracelet for Nancy, engraved: "Eiffel Tower and stuff." Not so romantic. It wasn't meant to be. What note was he supposed to strike? She gave him a look that would have broken his heart if he'd had the courage to hold her gaze.

Instead of an apology, he tried for a molecule of levity, at his own expense: he wished her happy Mother's Day.

She just stared at him. He averted his eyes again.

He had gone over in the early evening so the kids would still be awake, wanting to see them but also knowing that his wife wouldn't make a scene in front of them. He was disappointed to find Tina, the baby (she was about to turn two), asleep.

He offered to come back in the morning.

She considered it. Then nodded.

Sinatra and Bob Hope. Hope gave Frank a guest spot on his TV show—Sinatra's first television appearance—soon after his voice came back, when no one else wanted to employ him.

He returned the next morning—two visits in twenty-four hours! Little Nancy, thinking this might mean Daddy was home for good, ran and jumped into his arms; Frankie hung back and stared. Tina clung to her mother's leg. Frank picked the baby up with his other arm, held both his girls at once. The little one didn't seem quite sure who he was. In the years to come she would have no memory of this visit, nor of many others.

That night he flew back to New York with Bob Hope, who, miraculously enough, had given him a job.

The Frank Sinatra Show. "Bad pacing, bad scripting, bad tempo, poor camera work and an overall jerky presentation," *Variety* said. The broadcast limped along from late 1950 to early 1952, often sponsorless, until CBS pulled the plug.

Sinatra's savior at this juncture was his hardworking lawyer Henry Jaffe, who—since MCA was sitting on its hands where Frank was concerned—had been pestering Hope's people for months to hire his client for the comedian's new television variety show. TV was new and scary territory for Bob Hope, but he had to try: his NBC radio show, a mainstay of his career since 1937, was rapidly losing listeners to Crosby, Jack Benny, and Arthur Godfrey. Accordingly, when General

Motors offered Hope a five-show contract (at $150,000) for a television broadcast to be sponsored by Frigidaire, Ski Nose jumped at it.

The medium was barely out of its infancy: programmers were making it up as they went along. Sid Caesar's frenetic, wildly inventive *Your Show of Shows,* which had premiered on NBC in February, was doing brilliantly. Bob Hope's *Star Spangled Revue* (the title was the frightened era's equivalent of a flag lapel pin) debuted on NBC on Easter Sunday, and did not fare as well. Hope, who had to share the stage with refrigerators, seemed to think it sufficient to put on a vaudeville show in front of the camera. Douglas Fairbanks Jr. and Dinah Shore played along gamely, but the music-hall pacing, in the given context of early TV—live and uncut—was less than galvanizing, and reviews were less than ecstatic. The second show had to be better.

Hope's choice of guests for that broadcast was interesting. Beatrice Lillie, an old pal from his London music-hall days, was funny and eccentric; Peggy Lee was ascendant, and sexy; but the best you could say about Frank Sinatra (besides the fact that until a couple of months earlier he could sing) was that he certainly was in the papers a lot.

One place Frank had never been, though, was in front of a TV camera. Acknowledging the fact, Hope introduced him a little nervously: "It takes real courage to get your feet wet in television. I'm really glad this chap decided to take the plunge. I'm thrilled to introduce Mr. Frank Sinatra."

Yet if Bob Hope was tentative, his first guest was anything but. "Sinatra, astoundingly thin, balletic in his movements, and dazzling with his smile, showed no nerves about appearing on the tube," writes Peggy Lee's biographer Peter Richmond. "He nailed 'Come Rain or Come Shine' with a suggestion of cockiness that was in equal parts annoying and appealing. His absolute composure, performing live in front of an audience whose size he couldn't begin to guess at, made it instantly obvious that he would have no problem climbing back to the top."

Obvious to whom? Frank's absolute composure was—now more

than ever—mostly an artful illusion. And television was not to be his medium. The whiff of arrogance, whether contrived or real, made him a hot presence on the cool tube: the contrast jangled. Nor did he have much of a gift for comedy, the lifeblood of television variety. He was too angry, too edgy. In a sketch on the Hope show he played—of all people—Bing Crosby, the avatar of cool. The results were less than impressive, counteracting the magic Frank had spun with his singing. "If TV is his oyster, Sinatra hasn't broken out of his shell," *Variety* noted.

The day after his television debut, Frank went back to radio—for one more week. His contract for *Light Up Time* had expired, and Lucky Strike wasn't hustling to renew. Yet another company had cut him loose. On Monday, June 5, he was officially at liberty.

In the meantime, Jaffe was in talks with CBS, which was laboring mightily to squeeze some value out of its rapidly diminishing asset, to create a pair of vehicles for Sinatra that fall: another radio program and, against all better judgment, a TV show. Frank was also booked at London's Palladium in early July; until then, he was facing an empty month, and a vacation was the last thing he needed. His voice was back; he wanted to sing.

———

In late May and early June, while Sinatra's first collaboration with Mitch Miller, the dreadful "American Beauty Rose," was having its brief moment at the bottom of the charts, it became clear to Miller that none of the other eight up-tempo numbers Frank had recorded that spring were tickling the public's fancy. Accordingly, the producer decided to take a stronger hand with his star. If the public didn't want to hear Sinatra swing, then maybe he should sing something else.

Miller had been instrumental in the decision to move Sinatra up-tempo, but it had been Frank and George Siravo who'd made all the creative decisions in April. For the session on June 28, Miller had a new concept, one he controlled completely. The songs, "Goodnight Irene" and "Dear Little Boy of Mine," had an earnest, folksy quality

("Irene" had recently been a big hit for the Weavers), and to heighten that quality, background voices were used—the Mitch Miller Singers. Miller himself, naturally, arranged and conducted. And Frank Sinatra just sang along with Mitch.

If he hated it, it didn't show. Sinatra was in excellent voice on both numbers—utterly unsuited to his character and personality though they were. Listen to them, and even with the corny background chorus they almost make sense. In fact, "Goodnight Irene" went straight to number 5 on the *Billboard* charts, Sinatra's biggest hit in over three years.

Ava had finished all her location shooting for *Pandora*. All that remained were some interiors, to be filmed at Shepperton Studios outside of London. With a fond farewell to Spain and an *hasta la vista* to Mario Cabré, she moved into a luxury flat near Hyde Park, and a corps of reporters and photographers promptly set up camp at her doorstep. She greeted them with husky-voiced, affectionate ribaldries when she went out in the morning and returned at night, and they, like everyone else, fell in love with her.

On July 5, Sinatra flew to England, in high spirits: Henry Jaffe had arm wrestled Bill Paley into giving Frank a five-year contract for a TV variety show, to commence in October. (CBS also threw in a new radio show, *Meet Frank Sinatra*, to start concurrently.) At $200,000 per annum, the deal was potentially worth $1 million, and while it was subject to all sorts of provisos, escape clauses, and caveats, it theoretically gave Sinatra the edge over Bing Crosby as the highest-paid singer in show business.

Landing in London was like stepping out of a time machine. In the States, it was a new, bad decade: President Truman had just sent U.S. troops to Korea; Joe McCarthy was rapping pieces of paper and barking threats. In England, where bombed-out buildings were still much in evidence, it felt like the early 1940s, a time that had been very good to Frank Sinatra. London, a town desperate for some cheering up, greeted him with the kind of hysterical acclaim he'd been missing badly lately—especially from teenage girls, who once again came out in screaming droves.

When he reunited with Ava, it was as a man who'd gotten his mojo back. He was a cock of the walk again, and she liked him that way.

He in turn devoured the adulation. One night, Ava's co-star Sheila Sim and her husband, Richard Attenborough, picked up Ava and Frank to take them to the premiere of a new Noël Coward musical. Crowds were gathered outside Ava's flat, and when she emerged, she whisked right through them and hopped into Sim and Attenborough's car. Frank came out a moment later, a huge grin on his face, and signed every autograph book thrust at him. When he finally got in the car, Ava was furious: they had agreed ahead of time that they would skip all that. Frank just shrugged.

He may have been One-Take Charlie for the movies, but when it came to his music, he was a man possessed. The Palladium was at least the equivalent of the Paramount, and he rehearsed all day, every day, until the opening.

And he didn't disappoint. Backed by England's biggest big band, Woolf Phillips and the Skyrockets, Frank knocked them dead. Nancy junior writes:

> Sipping tea on stage between songs, he began with
> "Bewitched," "Embraceable You," and "I Fall in Love Too
> Easily." When he started singing "I've Got a Crush on You," the
> screaming started. Saying "Steady now," he changed the mood
> with "Ol' Man River," followed by a parody, "Old Man Crosby,
> He Just Keeps Singing Along," that brought down the house.

The critics loved him too. "I watched mass hysteria," wrote the *New Musical Express*'s reviewer. "Was it wonderful? Decidedly so, for this man Sinatra is a superb performer and a great artiste. He had his audience spellbound." The *Sunday Chronicle*'s man mustered even less English reserve: "Bless me, he's GOOD! He is as satisfying a one-man performance as the Palladium has ever seen."

The deeper thinkers of Fleet Street tried, hard, to analyze Sinatra's appeal. Most of the results reflected the eternal cultural divide between the two great countries separated by a common language. But the London *Sunday Times*'s distinguished drama critic, Harold Hobson—later to be a prescient champion of Harold Pinter, John Osborne, and Tom Stoppard—was far ahead of the rest of the world in his penetrating assessment of Sinatra:

> People who simply put Frank down as "the Voice" are missing the point. It is not the voice but the smile that does such enormous, such legendary execution . . . the shy deprecating smile, with a quiver at the corner of the mouth. Here is an artist who, hailing from the most rowdy and self-confident community the world has ever known, has elected to express the timidity that can never be wholly driven out of the boastfullest heart. To a people whose ideal of manhood is husky, full-blooded and self-reliant, he has dared to suggest that under the crashing self-assertion, man is still a child, frightened and whimpering in the dark.

Kissing Ava good-bye—no tears this time; she'd be returning to the States soon—Frank flew back to New York and, on August 2, walked into the Columbia studios to record a number from an upcoming Bing Crosby picture (there was no escaping Crosby!), *Mr. Music*. The song, written by Bing's personal tunesmiths Johnny Burke and Jimmy Van Heusen (Chester may have traveled with Sinatra, but he was still earning his money from Crosby), was called "Life Is So Peculiar."

The arranger and conductor was the Canadian-born Percy Faith, who, long before "Theme from *A Summer Place*" and "Love Theme from *Romeo and Juliet*," knew how to swing. Sinatra, backed by a superb small band (including his old pal Matty Golizio on guitar and the great Johnny Blowers on drums) and accompanied by singer Helen Carroll and the vocal group the Swantones, was in a fine mood, and it showed. The number is a trifle, to be sure, but it's a charming, exuberant trifle—and something more.

In an earlier context, the producer George Avakian spoke of a contrast he observed at a 1946 Sinatra recording session: when Frank sang a couple of heavily orchestrated ballads, Avakian said, he seemed tense; yet late in the session, when laying down a couple of "pleasant throwaways" with a jazz trio, the singer was utterly relaxed.

So it was on the "Life Is So Peculiar" session. Even though this band was fourteen pieces rather than three, Sinatra was clearly comfortable with the jazz context and, even more important, with the triviality of the tune itself, which he would soon refer to, in an interview, as "a cute little novelty song." But he sounds (if a bit husky around the edges) just great, easy and swinging. And most remarkably, his voice, imbued with a new maturity, actually harks *ahead* to the great Capitol sessions he will do two and a half years later, in a new, unimaginable lifetime.

And further: there's a positively eerie moment at the end of the second chorus as Frank sings:

> *Life is so peculiar, but as everybody says,*
> *That's life!*

The rascally lilt he gives to those two very familiar last words harks ahead *two* lifetimes, across the Capitol years and deep into the Reprise era, to the turbulent year in which Sinatra's wedding to the twenty-one-year-old Mia Farrow would be bookended by two disastrous physical altercations, signaling the singer's deeply disquieted state of mind. Frank was angry when he recorded "That's Life" in October 1966, angry at a world that was starting to pass him by and angry at a record producer who'd just told him that his previous take of the song had been . . . well, not so interesting. (His audible anger made the final take very interesting.) In August 1950, of course, he was simply having fun.

———

In the middle of the month Ava returned to Los Angeles, and Frank was there to meet her. Then she vanished. "There's no sign of life around [Gardner's] pink stucco house on a mountain top behind Hollywood," a wire-service report noted, a little plaintively.

> Her trunks are in the garage, but the shades are drawn and telegrams are piling up unopened on the doorstep.
> She's cut off her private telephone. And she's cancelled the messenger service that used to take her calls.
> Reports have her hiding away in a tiny cottage in Laguna beach . . . staying with friends . . . dining with Sinatra in a secluded beach café . . . and staging a roaring battle with him at Charley Foy's nightclub in San Fernando valley.

She wasn't in Laguna Beach, or staying with friends. In fact, Frank had quietly rented a house on the beach in Pacific Palisades, and she had moved in with him. For the briefest of moments, they had eluded the press.

But not their problems. As soon as Frank and Ava set up housekeeping, he began having his children over on weekends. She didn't like it, and said so. Often. In front of the kids or not; she didn't give a good goddamn. The one true piece of the wire-service report was that roaring battle at Charley Foy's.

———

Over Labor Day weekend Frank returned to the Steel Pier in Atlantic City, where he had sung as a fresh-faced young pup with Harry James and His Music Makers. He could still draw a crowd, but this time what the people wanted to hear was "Goodnight Irene." "I don't think Frank liked it too much, but it was a big hit for him," Johnny Blowers recalled. "I used to think to myself, How in the world did Mitch ever get him to do this? But anyway, he did it and it was big. It went over."

Later, though, doing a radio interview with a local disc jockey, Ben Heller (who'd played guitar with Harry James way back when), Sinatra tried pushing the "jazz things" he'd recorded with George Siravo in April: "Bright, with good jump tempos, both to listen to as a vocal and to dance to." Heller, though, wanted to know what was *new*.

"We've got a new one now that is moving pretty good called, if you'll excuse the expression, 'Goodnight Irene,'" Frank said.

"Hey, that's a nice tune," said Heller.

"You wanna bet?" Frank replied.

After a beat, he realized he might have gone too far, even for him. "Nah, it's pretty good," he added.

"You should sing a lot of songs like that," Heller told him.

"Don't hold your breath," Sinatra said.

———

Life was getting more and more peculiar for Frank Sinatra. Later that week he dispatched an intermediary to the New York office of the Federal Bureau of Investigation with an extremely unusual offer. An FBI memo reveals:

DATE: SEPTEMBER 7, 1950
TO: MR. TOLSON
FROM: J. P. MOHR
SUBJECT: FRANK SINATRA

_____ [name deleted] called at my office today after having endeavored to arrange an appointment to see the Director. I explained to _____ that the Director was extremely busy, that he was fully committed and would be unable to see him. _____ stated that he had been requested by Frank Sinatra to contact the Director with . . . a proposition that Sinatra had in mind. _____ said he was a friend of Sinatra, that he considered him to be a sincere individual and that he has known him for six years. _____ described Sinatra as a "Dago who came up the hard way" and said he is a conscientious fellow who is very desirous of doing something for his country. _____ stated that Sinatra feels he can do some good for his country under the direction of the FBI.

_____ stated that Sinatra is sensitive about the allegations which have been made concerning his subversive activities and also his draft status during the last war. Sinatra feels that the publicity which he has received has identified him with subversive elements and that such subversive elements are not sure of his position and Sinatra consequently feels that he can be of help as a result by going anywhere the Bureau desires and contacting any of the people from whom he might be able to obtain information. Sinatra feels as a result of his publicity he can operate without suspicion . . .

_____ stated that Sinatra's principal contacts are in the entertainment field in Hollywood and New York City. _____ further advised that he didn't know whether Sinatra has any current information with respect to subversives. He said that Sinatra understands that if he worked for the Bureau in connection with such activities it might reflect on his status and his standing in the entertainment field but he is willing to do anything even if it affects his livelihood and costs him his job.

_____ said that Sinatra is willing to go "the whole way."

. . . I told _____ that I wasn't aware of Sinatra's

activities other than what I had read in the papers. I told him
further that I wasn't aware of Sinatra's possibilities and that
that was something we would have to analyze and determine.
I further told _____ that we would not ask Sinatra
or any other individual to engage in any activities that would
reflect on the individual and that any action taken by the
individual would have to be a voluntary decision on his part.
_____ was also informed that I was not aware of the
fact that Sinatra could be of use to us but that I would call to
the Director's attention _____'s visit to me and that
we would consider Sinatra's request and that if he could be
utilized we would communicate with him.

On the bottom of the letter is a handwritten notation by Tolson: "We
want nothing to do with him. C."
Then one by Hoover: "I agree. H."[1]

———

What had possessed him? The Communist witch hunts were in full
swing; guilt by association was guilt presumed. Sinatra knew the FBI
was sniffing around him—in June he'd requested permission to go
abroad to entertain U.S. troops, but had been denied a security clear-
ance because of "subversive activities": namely his mid-1940s idealism,
reconsidered in the hard light of 1950. The bureau was even watching his Manhattan dentist, Dr. Abraham Weinstein. In a typical screed
that May, Westbrook Pegler managed to lump Sinatra, George Raft,
Leo Durocher, Frank Costello, "the Hollywood–Los Angeles underworld," and President Truman's supposedly lax Department of Justice
into one subversive-smelling ball.

However hopeful Frank may have been about his upcoming TV
show, he was scared: his career had sprung a leak. "Sinatra's decline,"
Pegler wrote, "has been just a matter of fair wear and tear . . . plus the
natural waning of a hopped-up reputation." Many others were saying

the same. Was he really "willing to do anything" for the FBI, "even if it affect[ed] his livelihood and [cost] him his job"? His job was on the line in any case.

———

Ava blew through town on her way back to California to prepare for her new movie, *Show Boat*. Frank was starting his CBS television and radio shows, and was looking for a Manhattan apartment. In the meantime, he was once again borrowing Manie's suite at the Hampshire House. A temporary—very temporary—love nest. Work was about to separate the lovebirds again, and the tension, as always, was erotic. But Ava wanted to get married, and while Frank told her he wanted that too, she could sense his ambivalence. When she called him on it, he'd shake his head. He didn't know if Nancy would ever give him a divorce. It was the Church—she was just a better Catholic than he was.

Ava, her biographer Lee Server writes, "heard the whispered scuttlebutt from others: 'She thinks she can wait you out, you two will blow over and she'll have him back one day. That's all she wants.'" Server continues:

> To Ava, it was an infuriating irony: There they were, wanting to do the right thing and get married, and there was this woman using her religion as an excuse to keep them "living in sin" . . . The affair and the scandal had provoked the first serious rift in her relationship with Bappie, who disliked Sinatra and believed he was harming her career. "You hang on to him, Ava," Bappie told her, "and he's going to ruin you like he's ruined himself."

So there was more fighting, more makeup sex; they stayed in and they went out. Going out was always important. On Wednesday night, September 27, the two of them attended the Joe Louis–Ezzard Charles fight at Yankee Stadium: the news photographers snapped them sitting cozily close, Sinatra with his thinning hair and love-struck grin, Ava with a fur coat, thick red lipstick, and a cigarette between her fingers. Charles outpointed the former champ Louis in fifteen rounds to become the world heavyweight champion.

The next day, Nancy Sinatra outpointed Frank in Santa Monica Superior Court, winning her separate-maintenance suit and custody of their three children. The *Los Angeles Times* ran a large photograph of her above the photo of Frank and Ava at the prizefight, and she won this contest, too, hands down, looking every inch the wronged woman in her demure checked suit, white blouse with Peter Pan collar, and brown leather gloves. Her chin is held high, her hair attractively (and no doubt freshly) coiffed in soft waves, her expression neither triumphant nor stricken but distant and philosophical. To glance back and forth between the pictures of her and Ava—who looks frankly vulgar— is to wonder what the hell Frank was thinking about.

Nancy (who had lived in Hollywood long enough to know the value of images) surely had all of it in mind when she dressed for her court appearance.

She dabbed away "a tear or so," the *Times* reported, as Judge Orlando H. Rhodes awarded her "the Holmby Hills home, its furnishings and effects, a 1950 Cadillac, 34 shares of stock in the Sinatra Music Corp. and one-third of Sinatra's annual gross earnings on the first $150,000 and 10% of the next $150,000." For his part, Frank got a 1949 Cadillac, a jeep, the Palm Springs house, rights to some oil property in Texas, and "any phonograph records or radio transcriptions he may desire." He was also given "all money in bank accounts"—not much at that point.

At the hearing, the *Times* account continued,

Mrs. Sinatra testified that on numerous occasions her husband would go to Palm Springs for week ends without her and that he would "stay away for days at a time."

On other occasions, she said, when they were alone or had

company he would go into another room, ignoring her and the guests.

Accompanying this particular testimony were tears edging down her cheeks. She dabbed them with a dainty handkerchief.

Summing up, she said her husband's conduct "made me terribly nervous and upset and humiliated me."

Mrs. Sinatra's sister, Miss Julie Barbato, was her corroborating witness.

She testified that she knew from her own knowledge that Sinatra embarrassed his wife by staying away from home and by rudely refusing to assist in the entertainment of guests.

Frank didn't contest the action.

As Nancy left the courthouse, the photographers called out to her, asking for a smile. "I don't feel much like smiling," she told them.

She had won, but it was a Pyrrhic victory. "I would see her faint into her plate at dinner from the stress," Nancy junior wrote.

Sometimes it was heart palpitations, sometimes a cold, sometimes fatigue. Until then, she had never been sick. I used to think it was the food. Maybe she wasn't eating right. She was in pain. And though I wasn't aware of it, her pain was exacerbated by the scandal. She was deeply in love and terribly hurt. I would hear her crying quietly at night while I was going to sleep. She would never show it in front of us, never, but my room was next to hers and I would tiptoe out and I'd listen at her door and she'd be crying. Sometimes I would go in to her and just put my arms around her. And sometimes I would just go away, thinking, "Mind your own business. Daddy's just on the road again," and cry myself to sleep.

The picture of Frank painted in court by Nancy and her sister is not a pretty one, and while it was certainly tinged by rancor—no doubt many of the guests he snubbed were Barbatos—it feels all too true. Sinatra certainly used Twin Palms as a bachelor pad, and would continue to do so for as long as he owned the place. And though his remoteness was exacerbated by his obsession with Ava, it was also deeply ingrained in his character. He was, and always would be, the loneliest son of a bitch he knew.

———

It therefore made perfect sense, in Frank's world, that the Varsity was still up and running: Sanicola, Ben Barton, Toots Shor, Jackie Gleason, Al Silvani, Tami Mauriello, Manie Sacks, and whoever else might be lighting his cigarettes and laughing at his jokes. Ava hated the whole thing, hated the sycophancy and the boys'-club exclusivity, but there was little she could do about it. Frank—much like Picasso, with the group of hangers-on he called his *tertulia*—was a king who required a court.

And he needed all the support he could get on October 7, at 9:00 p.m., when *The Frank Sinatra Show* made its debut on CBS television, opposite the smash hit *Your Show of Shows* on NBC. Continuing Bob Hope's swimming-pool metaphor, the *New York Times*'s Jack Gould wrote, "Frank Sinatra walked off the television high dive on Saturday night, but unfortunately fell into the shallow end of the pool." Gould went on to call the show "a drab mixture of radio, routine vaudeville and pallid pantomime." John Crosby, of the *Herald Tribune,* called Sinatra "a surprisingly good actor but a rather bad emcee." And *Variety* cited "bad pacing, bad scripting, bad tempo, poor camera work and an overall jerky presentation."

And the $41,500 the episode cost was money straight out the window for CBS, which hadn't been able to attract a sponsor.

Clearly the occasion called for a big celebration.

Toots Shor's (of course) was the venue, and Sinatra's new publicist, Nat Shapiro, invited 150 of the singer's closest friends. Three hundred showed up, along with a writer and a photographer from *Look* magazine, which ran a feature on the bash.

But no amount of publicity could slap much life into *The Frank Sinatra Show*. The broadcast would limp along for the rest of the season at forty grand per episode (though in November, Bulova signed on to sponsor the first half hour), as the critics continued to snipe and the viewing public mostly tuned to Sid Caesar. Things might have been different if Sinatra had devoted himself to the program, but he appeared to have other fish to fry. "Frank was always late, sometimes two and three hours late," recalled Irving Mansfield, whom the network brought in to produce after the first show bombed.

> He hated to rehearse and refused to discuss the weekly format. Usually, he ignored the guest shots entirely. Once he wanted to book Jackie Gleason, who was very hot at the time, but Frank would not rehearse. Even though he and Jackie were pals, Jackie refused to go on the air without a rehearsal, and we ended up having to pay him $7,500 [almost $70,000 today] plus expenses for being the guest star who did not do Frank's show. Another time I came to work and was told by [Sinatra's entourage] that Brian Aherne was the guest star for the following week. "Frank wants to class up the show," they said. What could I do? Aherne was a B actor with a mustache and no flair for television. He was a disaster, and Frank was furious afterwards. "Why'd you put that bum on my show?" he screamed. "It wasn't my idea," I said. "It was yours." He refused to talk to me again for days.

As was so often the case, Frank was furious because he felt out of control. His movie career was DOA; his concert and nightclub bookings were flatlining. The one place where he felt most dominant, the recording studio, was increasingly dominated by another. His response was not only disengagement and petty tyranny but also a spike in his obsessive-compulsive symptoms. "Frank was always washing his hands, constantly washing, washing, washing, as if he was trying to wash his life away or something," Mansfield said. "When he wasn't washing his hands, he was changing his shorts. He would drop his pants to the floor, take off his drawers, and kick them up in the air with his foot. Some flunky would chase those dirty shorts around the room while Frank put on a clean pair. He must've changed his shorts every twenty minutes. I've never seen anything like it in my life."

He felt unclean. Unworthy.

He also grew obsessed with the idea that Ava was cheating on him. Three thousand miles away, who knew what she might be up to? The main suspect was Artie Shaw. According to Mansfield, "Frank was insanely jealous of Shaw. Whenever he couldn't get her on the phone he'd start screaming on the set that she was having an affair with Artie. 'I know she's with that goddamn Artie Shaw,' he'd yell. 'I know she's with that bastard. I'll kill her. I'll kill her. I'll kill her.'"

He was in a dangerous state of mind: the world seemed to conspire against his every move. The condition is all the worse for its circularity. Jackie Gleason, riding high, understood that rehearsal brought polish, which brought success, which brought more confidence. Sinatra, feeling like a failure, was ensuring nothing but more failure for himself.

The new radio show, on Sunday afternoons, was a blip. Some programming genius at CBS had come up with a weird formula for *Meet Frank Sinatra*: Frank wouldn't just sing, he would engage in repartee with his studio audience and guests. The talk felt scripted, forced. The singing was another matter: he was backed by a five-piece rhythm combo, a format that always made him feel comfortable and spontaneous. The only problem was, nobody was listening.

That same month, Columbia released *Sing and Dance with Frank Sinatra,* his first album specifically conceived as a ten-inch LP—and, as it turned out, his last for the label. The record consisted entirely of George Siravo–arranged, up-tempo numbers, seven of them from the overdubbed April sessions, and even if there was a slight disconnect between Frank and the Frank-less musicians, the album was—and still is—joyous, swinging Sinatra.

But *Sing and Dance* failed to even graze the *Billboard* charts.

He flew to Los Angeles for Christmas, to bring his kids presents and remind them who he was, but mainly to see Ava. It had been over three months, yet the reunion was ambivalent. She was thrilled at her gift: he'd bought her a puppy, a Pembroke Welsh corgi; they named it Rags. And she was thrilled with *Show Boat*, which was close to wrapping at Metro, the studio that had fired him. Frank's smile slowly chilled. He had scant patience for listening to Ava enthuse about her director, George Sidney—who had directed Frank in *Anchors Aweigh*—and her co-star Kathryn Grayson, who had co-starred with Frank not once but three times. Not to mention the wonderful Howard Keel.

Was she banging him?

She was never one to flinch, not even for a second. How about Marilyn Maxwell—was he still screwing her?

His voice rose. What about Artie Shaw?

She gave as good as she got. What about his wife? Was he ever going to leave her, or was that going to go on forever?

The puppy cowered. Then came more screaming, and breaking dishes, and slamming doors—followed, of course, by the absolutely stupendous making up. After which she nestled sweetly in his arms, and they swore never to fight again.

Then he was back off to New York again.

September 1950: Nancy, beautiful in distress, wins her separate-
maintenance suit in Santa Monica Superior Court. She dabbed
away "a tear or so," the *Los Angeles Times* reported, as Judge
Orlando H. Rhodes awarded her "the Holmby Hills home, its
furnishings and effects, a 1950 Cadillac, 34 shares of stock in
the Sinatra Music Corp. and one-third of Sinatra's annual gross
earnings on the first $150,000 and 10% of the next $150,000."

Frank and Ava with Dolly and Marty at the premiere of *Meet Danny Wilson,* November 1951. Dolly, who constantly clashed with Nancy, was crazy about Ava.

One night in January, as Frank walked into the Columbia recording studios, he passed a group of teenage girls, who noticed him at once. They giggled. As he smiled expectantly, they called out in unison: "We like Eddie Fisher!"

Frank shrugged, chastened. "I do, too," was all he could come up with.

Edwin Jack Fisher was a nice Jewish boy from Philadelphia with a handsome face, a thick head of dark hair, a soaringly confident tenor voice, and no sense of musical tempo whatsoever. "You had to tell him when to start," said the record producer Alan Livingston. "It was amazing." Fisher had started singing on the radio in high school, had been discovered by Eddie Cantor, and had signed with RCA Victor in 1949, at twenty-one. And in June 1950, an appearance on Milton Berle's *Texaco Star Theater,* the biggest show on television, had turned Eddie into a national sensation.

Fisher was the first popular singing idol created by the new medium, which was growing by the month beyond anyone's ability to calculate. The new stars of TV—Berle, Sid Caesar, Jackie Gleason, Martin and Lewis—were riding the crest of a tremendous wave, and by 1950 Eddie Fisher was riding along too. Days after the *Texaco* appearance, his agent booked him into Ben Miller's Riviera, an elegant nightspot atop the Palisades in Fort Lee, New Jersey, and over the span of a two-week gig Fisher came into his own not just as a pop phenomenon but as an important American entertainer—the clubs were still a key cultural component in those days. It was a feat akin to the one Sinatra had pulled off at the Astor roof ten years earlier. Earl Wilson wrote, "Singer Eddie Fisher . . . is merely wonderful. There's no reason he shouldn't become a big star." And in the *Daily Mirror,* Frank's old nemesis Lee Mortimer raved, "The cash customers cheer and beg for more, indicating the lad is the song find of the year." *Variety, Time,* and the *New York Times* printed similar plaudits.

"I became the hottest act in show business," Fisher recalled many years later. He was twenty-two.

> Within weeks I was performing before sold-out audiences at
> the best clubs in the country . . . Every variety show on televi-
> sion wanted me as a guest . . . By the end of the year I had
> been named America's Most Promising New Male Vocalist in
> *Billboard*'s annual disc-jockey poll, as well as Discovery of the
> Year and Male Singer of the Year.
>
> All the major motion-picture studios begged me to take a

screen test. I began receiving thousands of pieces of fan mail every day, and fan clubs were organized around the country.

Then, in February 1951, Fisher played the Paramount:

> Few entertainers have ever experienced the kind of adulation
> I received when I opened at the Paramount. There is no way
> to describe accurately the feeling of being at the center of that
> kind of frenzy . . . I was the new Sinatra, the *Jewish* Sinatra.

Eddie Fisher was writing his memoirs at the end of the 1990s, at a moment when the world had all but forgotten him. There is a poignant odor of insistence about his recollections: *Remember me. I used to be huge.*

Yet in February 1951, Frank Sinatra had no way of knowing that Eddie Fisher would be forgotten and he himself would be immortal.

One night Frank was walking through Times Square when he saw the giant crowds of girls beneath the Paramount marquee. The sight was like a vision at once of his past and his death. He hurried back to Manie Sacks's suite at the Hampshire House, went into the kitchen, closed the door, laid his head on the stove, and turned on the gas. Manie happened to return not long afterward, smelled the odor, and went into the kitchen, where he found Frank lying on the floor, sobbing, a failure even at suicide.

———

In December 1950, the Tennessee senator Estes Kefauver, a Democrat possessed of a crusading temperament and presidential aspirations, convened the Special Committee on Organized Crime in Interstate Commerce. In reality, the committee's investigations had less to do with commerce than with an organization of which few Americans were aware in that more innocent time: the Mafia. The country got a crash course. The hearings ran for ninety-two days in fourteen cities, including New York, Chicago, Detroit, and New Orleans, with a cast of witnesses who became instantly infamous: the likes of Giuseppe Doto (Joe Adonis), Albert Anastasia, Frank Costello, Jake Guzik, Virginia Hill, Willie Moretti, and Longy Zwillman. The committee's sessions were televised, quickly becoming America's most popular show. Appliance stores tuned the TV sets in their display windows to the Kefauver hearings as an inducement to buy. The nation was mesmerized by the raspy-voiced testimony of the Copacabana owner, Costello, who had refused to allow his face to be shown on camera. Instead, viewers saw a dramatic close-up of the gangster's well-manicured hands, which he wrung constantly as he spoke.

At a committee meeting during the investigation, Kefauver handed one of his lawyers, Joseph Nellis, an envelope containing eight eight-by-ten glossy photographs. The pictures were all of Frank Sinatra. "I almost fell off my chair," Nellis recalled many years later. "I opened the envelope and saw a picture of Sinatra with his arm around Lucky Luciano on the balcony of the Hotel Nacional in Havana; another picture showed Sinatra and Luciano sitting at a nightclub in the Nacional with lots of bottles having a hell of a time with some good-looking girls. One picture showed Frank getting off a plane carrying a suitcase, and then there were a couple pictures of him with the Fischetti brothers, Lucky Luciano . . . Kefauver wanted to know more about Sinatra's relationship with Luciano, who was running an international narcotics cartel in exile. So I called Frank's attorney and arranged a meeting."

Nellis didn't just want to talk to Frank's attorney—he wanted Frank to testify, on camera. This, of course, would have been the final nail in Sinatra's coffin: a TV show to end all TV shows, a big broadcast that would have blown the singer's career right out of the water. Kefauver and Nellis were entirely serious about this: the senator had ordered his lawyer to bulldoze Sinatra with the full power of the U.S. Senate. What Nellis hadn't reckoned on was his adversary.

Frank (or in all likelihood, Henry Jaffe) had chosen his attorney well. Sol Gelb was a former assistant to New York's governor, Thomas

Dewey, and the Manhattan district attorney Frank Hogan, now in private practice. Ironically—or appropriately, depending on your point of view—he had worked for Dewey when the crime-busting governor convicted Lucky Luciano of running a prostitution ring. He had also helped Hogan bring Lepke Buchalter of Murder Inc. to justice. Gelb was a tough lawyer who knew organized crime inside and out, and he had no fear of Kefauver. He argued strenuously to Nellis that if Sinatra had to testify alongside the likes of Costello, Moretti, and Adonis, the singer's public image and career would be permanently ruined. Nellis argued back no less strenuously, citing the incriminating photographs. Finally, the two lawyers reached a compromise.

Frank would testify in absolute secrecy. Gelb chose a law office on an upper floor of Rockefeller Center, at four o'clock in the morning on March 1, 1951.

At 4:00 a.m. on the dot—no being two hours late for this one—Sinatra and Gelb stepped off the elevator to find Nellis and a court reporter, stenotype machine in hand, already waiting. Frank's famous bluster was nowhere in sight: the Kefauver Committee, with its implicit threat of fatal publicity, had thrown the fear of God into him. He looked "like a lost kitten, drawn, frightened to death," Nellis recalled. "He kept shooting his cuffs, straightening his tie, and he smoked constantly." His right hand shook so badly each time he tried to light a fresh cigarette that he had to hold it with his left.

"He knew that I was going to ask him about Willie Moretti and Lucky Luciano," Nellis said, "but he didn't know about all the photographs that I had. He also didn't know that I had a report about a rape he had allegedly been involved in and the blackmail that had reportedly been paid to keep that story from ever being published."

The rape story was the first of many such Sinatra rumors that would pop up, like malodorous bubbles in a swamp, over the years. The venue was usually Las Vegas or Palm Springs. Usually prostitutes were involved; so, usually, was Jimmy Van Heusen. For all his vaunted courtliness where ladies were concerned, Van Heusen—a self-confessed sex addict—was obsessed with prostitutes, and allegedly had some outré tastes. Sinatra allegedly shared some of these tastes. "Van Heusen was a wild man, they said—a crazy man as far as women were concerned," said Gloria Delson Franks, Sammy Cahn's first wife. "Sometimes not in a nice way, too; he abused a lot of women, apparently. Pushing them around. Whatever. I think there was a time when Nancy felt he was a bad influence on Frank. Not that Frank was a choir boy before."

And Sinatra's association with Jimmy Tarantino was coming back to haunt him. Tarantino was the former Varsity member whom Frank had helped set up in business with a scandal sheet called *Hollywood Nite Life*. No good deed goes unpunished. Maybe Frank knew at the outset that Tarantino's modus operandi was blackmail: that celebrities had to pay for good publicity in the rag or get the bad kind. Maybe the $15,000 he invested was really protection money; or perhaps he was just being kind to a compadre. In any case, the minute Tarantino got wind of squalid doings in Vegas involving Sinatra, he tried to shake Frank down. This was complicated, given that Tarantino had Hank Sanicola and Mickey Cohen as business partners, and maybe Willie Moretti, too. Furious, Frank told Sanicola to tell Bobby Burns to write Tarantino another sizable check, ostensibly as a business loan, and to deliver the following proviso: this was the end of the line for Tarantino as far as Sinatra was concerned. The whole thing stank, but it was the kind of nonsense that happened all the time on the fringes of show business.

Now here was this Washington lawyer with his eyeglasses and narrow stare, getting in Frank's business.

"We have information," Nellis intoned, as the stenographer clicked away, "to the effect that you paid Tarantino quite a large sum of money to keep him from writing a quite uncomplimentary story about you."

"Well, you know how it is in Hollywood," Sinatra said—as if this prick had any idea. "Jimmy called up and said he had an eyewitness account of a party that was supposed to have been held down in Vegas in which some broads had been raped or something like that. I told Jimmy if he printed anything like that, he would be in for a lot of trouble."

"Did he ask you for money?" Nellis asked.

"Well, I asked Hank Sanicola, my manager, to talk to him and that's the last I heard of it until [the columnist and crime reporter Florabel] Muir printed a story about it in the *Los Angeles Herald*."

"Did Hank tell you he paid Tarantino?"

"Well," Frank said, "I understand Tarantino was indicted and I don't know the rest of the story, but the *Hollywood* [*Nite Life*] quit publishing this crap afterwards."

Nellis produced the photographs of Sinatra with Luciano in Havana, and proceeded to ask a series of questions about Frank's February 1947 trip to Cuba. First, though, he wanted to know how Frank had met the Fischetti brothers. Frank said he had first met Joe while performing in Chicago in 1946. "He had a little speedboat on the lake, and one afternoon he took me for a ride," Sinatra recalled nostalgically. "Having dinner with him, going to the theater." Joe introduced him to Charlie and Rocco in Chicago, Frank said, and now and then over the following year he encountered the three casually.

"Did you ever have any business with any of the Fischettis?" Nellis asked.

"Not an ounce," Sinatra replied.

"Where were you staying at Miami when you met them?"

"I had a little cottage."

"How did you happen to bump into the Fischettis?"

"I went to either the Beachcomber or one of the clubs downtown in the entertainment center, and I saw Joe, and then later that evening I met Rocco," Frank said. "He came in with some friends, and I said hello and met his friends, and that was it."

But that was not it: a series of what seemed to be escalating coincidences kept bringing Sinatra and the brothers together. The same night he encountered Rocco, as Frank recalled, "I said to Joe, it is too cold, I think I am going to get out of here and go where it is warm. I said I think I will go down to Havana, said if I went down I would stay a couple of days because I promised my wife I would meet my wife in Mexico around February 14. It was St. Valentine's Day; that comes back to my mind."

As well it should.

Frank continued: "Then that is when [Joe] told me they had also contemplated going to Cuba. I think the next day he called me on the phone and wanted to know when I was going down to Cuba. Apparently, at that time I probably did say what morning I was going, either the following morning or the morning after he called me, and when I got out to the airport, they were checking the baggage through; that is when I saw them on the plane."

Nellis gave Sinatra a hard stare. "And you had given him your phone number where you were staying?"

"Yes, he asked me for the phone number, and I gave it to him."

"Now, you rode over together on the same plane?"

"Yes."

"When you got off the plane, you got off with them together?"

"No, actually I didn't know. As a matter of fact, I suspect, now that we discuss it, that when the plane landed, they may have seen the guys with the cameras. They may have seen somebody with a camera because why should they fall behind. I found myself alone . . ."

"Were you carrying any baggage off the plane?" Nellis asked.

"Yes."

"What was it?"

"A tan piece of hand luggage, a briefcase like," Frank said.

"Could you have had a paper-wrapped bundle?" Nellis asked.

"No, I don't remember actually, but I don't think so. I think I had a topcoat and a bag."

"What was in the bag?"

"Sketching materials, crayons, shaving equipment, general toiletry."

"Did you habitually carry that bag?"

"All the time, constantly," Sinatra said. "I am now. I also use it for papers."

"How large a bag is it?"

"It is about the size of a briefcase with a handle on it. Instead of carrying under your arms, like a little overnight bag."

"Did either of the Fischettis give you anything to carry into Cuba?"

"No, sir."

"Did anybody else give you anything else to carry into Cuba?"

"No, sir."

The lawyer made a sour face. "Will you go ahead with the rest of your story," he said.

In his lengthy account Frank described leaving his room at the Hotel Nacional (in the company of a Chicago columnist he had encountered, Nate Gross of the *Herald American*) and proceeding to have a series of accidental meetings with a group of gangsters who kept showing up wherever he went—the bar of the Nacional, the hotel dining room, an "American show" downtown. One of the gangsters was Lucky Luciano.

"I remarked to Nate, I said that name is familiar," Frank recalled. "Yes, he said, that's the guy you think it is. He started to tell me something of the history of this man. I was a boy and remember when his trial was on and remember reading about it . . ."

That night, according to Sinatra, was the last time he ever saw Luciano.

Nellis shook his head. "There has been stated certain information to the effect that you took a sum of money well in excess of $100,000 into Cuba," he said.

"That is not true."

"Did you give any money to Lucky Luciano?"

"No, sir."

"Did you ever learn what business they were in?"

"No," Frank said. "Actually not."

"Where did you get started in the entertainment business?" Nellis asked.

"In a small club in Hoboken; I must have been around seventeen."

"What's your attraction to all these underworld characters?"

"I don't have any attraction for them," Frank said. "Some of them were kind to me when I started out, and I have sort of casually seen them or spoken to them at different places, in nightclubs where I worked, or out in Vegas or California."

"Do you know Frank Costello?"

"Just to say hello. I've seen him at the Copa and at the Madison, and once we had a drink at the Drake where I stay when I'm in New York."

"What about Joe Doto?"

"I've met him," Sinatra said. "He's the one they call 'Adonis,' right?"

"Right. How well do you know him?"

"No business," Frank said. "Just 'hello' and 'goodbye.'"

"Well, what about the Jersey guys you met when you first got started?" Nellis asked.

"Let me tell you something, those guys were okay," Frank replied. "They never bothered me or anyone else as far as I know." He was wringing his hands now—almost as though he were washing them. "Now," Frank said, "you're not going to put me on television and ruin me just because I know a lot of people, are you?" His famous voice was wavering a little. Nellis couldn't help feeling a little thrill of power.

"Nobody wants to ruin you, Mr. Sinatra," the lawyer said waspishly. "I assure you I would not be here at five in the morning at your lawyer's request so that no newsmen could find out we're talking to you if we intended to make some kind of public spectacle of any appearance before the committee."

Frank wasn't placated. His voice rose and tightened. "Well, look," he said. "How in hell is it going to help your investigation to put me on television just because I know some of these guys?"

Nellis shook his head impatiently. "That will be up to Senator Kefauver and the committee," he said. Then he softened ever so slightly. "Right now, if you're not too tired, I want to continue so we can see whether there's any basis for calling you in public session. Let's get back to what I was asking you about. And I will ask you specifically: Have you ever, at any time, been associated in business with Moretti, Zwillman—"

"Who?" Frank asked.

"Abner Zwillman of Newark," Nellis said. "They call him 'Longy.' Or Catena, Lansky, or Siegel?"

"Well, Moore, I mean Moretti, made some band dates for me when I first got started, but I have never had any business dealings with any of those men."

"But you know Luciano, the Fischettis, and all those I have named?"

"Just like I said; just in that way."

The sky outside the dirty windows was still black. "What is your attraction to these people?" Nellis repeated.

"Well, hell, you go into show business, you meet a lot of people," Frank said. "And you don't know who they are or what they do."

The lawyer's eyes flashed behind the circular lenses. "Do you want me to believe that you don't know the people we have been talking about are hoodlums and gangsters who have committed many crimes and are probably members of a secret criminal club?"

Sinatra had to stifle a smile. *Club.* That was rich. Like the Turk's Palace, with secret handshakes and orange and black silk jackets. Well, it was a little like that, actually. Except for the silk jackets.

"No, of course not," Frank said. "I heard about the Mafia."

"Well, what did you hear about it?"

Frank shook his head, elaborately disingenuous. "That it's some kind of shakedown operation," he said. "I don't know."

"Like the one you were involved with in the case of Tarantino?"

Finally, Sinatra allowed himself a half smile. It was almost six in the morning; the torment was almost over. Out over the East River, the sky was beginning to lighten. "I'm not sure that one was anybody's idea but Jimmy's," he told Nellis.

———

What's your attraction to these people? The question was by no means a simple one: no wonder Joseph Nellis asked it not just once but twice during the session. However much revulsion or incredulity the government lawyer may have felt at Sinatra's associations, he also understood the Mafia's mystique. His boss, after all, was scoring the biggest success in the brief history of television by putting these people on the air. Something about the Mob got—and still gets—to everyone. To a great degree the American fascination with gangsters stems from the pleasant fantasy that they have razored away the troublesome complexities of life by sheer, brutal acts of will. Sinatra sometimes fantasized that his celebrity had accomplished the same end. It was an illusion he would entertain until the end of his life, but the chickens always came home to roost. Life's troubling messiness won out in the end. So it went, too, with gangsters: there was no escaping the condition of being a human being.

And yet every time Frank shook the hand of one of these powerful, magnetic men, the man on either end of the handshake enjoyed the same fantasy about the other: *This fucker has got it knocked.* The smiles broadened; the handclasp grew firmer as the warm thought took hold.

———

Gelb assured his client that it had gone reasonably well, but Nellis had handed Frank a subpoena before he left, and Frank didn't see much assurance in his lawyer's eyes. Sinatra thanked Gelb, dismissed Sanicola, went back to the Hampshire House. He took two Seconals, chased with three fingers of Jack Daniel's, and paced. A fucking subpoena. If they called him in to testify, he was well and truly fucked. He got in the shower and ran the hot water for twenty minutes; he couldn't stop yawning. He sat on the side of his bed, towel around his waist, and drank another glass of whiskey. Gelb had assured him he was unlikely to be recalled. How unlikely? The lawyer met his eyes with a hard gaze. Unlikely, he repeated. Frank swished the whiskey in the glass. A crazy thought intruded: He was standing on the bar at Marty O'Brien's, naked, trying to sing, unable to make a sound. The old men stared at him; Dolly tapped her stick on her palm. When he opened his eyes again, it was after five thirty, and the sun was setting over the Hudson.

=====

Later that morning Nellis reported to Kefauver. Sinatra had been lying, the lawyer said; he was certain of it. On the other hand, "He's not going to admit any complicity concerning Luciano or the Fischettis in terms of being a 'bagman' or courier for them or anybody else," Nellis said. "If we take him into public session, his career will really be jolted—possibly beyond repair. He may even balk at the TV cameras and raise a lot of hell without saying anything."

Kefauver accepted Nellis's recommendation not to call Sinatra to testify. The senator was less concerned about Frank's career than his own: people were already calling the hearings a show; there was no sense turning them into a circus.

=====

They were rowdy at Toots Shor's that night, making pleasantly filthy jokes about Kefauver, and Frank felt braver. The next evening, trailed by Sanicola, Silvani, and Ben Barton, he strode into the Columbia studio at Third and Thirtieth to record two numbers from the new Rodgers and Hammerstein show, *The King and I.* It didn't get any better than Rodgers and Hammerstein. Axel was there to conduct his arrangements of "Hello Young Lovers" and "We Kiss in a Shadow," and it didn't get any better than Sibelius. Frank joshed with the violinists; he joked with the drummer Johnny Blowers about the miniature Zildjian cymbals Axel had brought to give the music a Siamese sound. Then the engineers turned the tape on; Stordahl brought down his baton. Sinatra put up his hand.

His voice wasn't right. He sipped hot tea, he joked with Sibelius and the musicians, he tried to keep smiling, but all of it—the late nights on the phone with Ava, the bad calls at odd hours from Little

Nancy, the cigarettes and whiskey and the fucking subpoena—all of it was starting to get to him, scratching away at his confidence and at his instrument itself.

Yet even though "Hello Young Lovers" took not three or four or even ten but twenty-two takes, Frank smiled; he sipped his tea, happy to keep going however long it took. It was Rodgers and Hammerstein; it was Stordahl. He was, for the moment anyway, in the best possible hands.

===

Of course the mood couldn't last. While MCA was busy attending to its important clients—in a groundbreaking precedent, Lew Wasserman had recently secured Jimmy Stewart profit participation in his pictures—Sinatra was screaming at Henry Jaffe to get him a goddamn movie, fast.

Offers were not pouring in. But then the screenwriter and Sinatra drinking buddy Don McGuire came up with a hard-hitting scenario he thought might be right up Frank's alley, a story about a hot-tempered saloon singer who gets a career boost from a mobster and regrets the consequences. It was a little close to the bone, but Frank liked it anyway. Here was a chance to put Clarence Doolittle and all those sailor suits behind him, to do the kind of gritty movie he could have done with *Knock on Any Door*, if they'd let him do it. To be, at last, a man on-screen. As for the subject matter: Let the goddamn public think whatever they wanted, he thought; they were already thinking it anyway. The screenplay was called *Meet Danny Wilson*.

Jaffe managed to sell the script, and Frank as the star, to Universal International, a studio that was making its big money from Abbott and Costello and Ma and Pa Kettle and Francis the Talking Mule. Universal offered Sinatra a flat fee of $25,000 to do the picture. It was almost an insult, but things being what they were, he jumped at it.

In the meantime, Ava's fortunes were skyrocketing. MGM was thrilled with her performance in *Show Boat*, convinced it had a major new star on its hands. Her contract was soon up for renewal, and there was serious talk of a big increase, something in the neighborhood of $1 million a year. She soft-pedaled the money when she spoke with Frank on the phone, but he could hear the excitement in her voice. Some part of him was happy for her—he did love her—but naturally enough, he also felt belittled. He knew all about career trajectories. There were times, at four and five o'clock in the morning (and who could he tell about this?), when he felt like the lowest of the low.

═══

He and Axel and many of the same musicians were back in the Thirtieth Street studio to record three more songs on the night of March 27. The first was another number from *The King and I*: a cute thing called "I Whistle a Happy Tune," with a typically inspirational Hammerstein lyric about coping with fear by pretending not to be afraid. And Mitch Miller, who was in the control room that evening, had come up with a cute idea—Frank himself would do the whistling parts. Sinatra gave the tune a charming, convincing performance, which made the next number he recorded all the more shattering.

The song, composed by Joel Herron, the former musical director of the Copacabana, and the lyricist Jack Wolf, was called "I'm a Fool to Want You." It was a big, melodramatic ballad, much in the style of "Take My Love," another melodramatic ballad Herron and Wolf had previously sold to Ben Barton, who ran Sinatra's publishing company, Barton Music Corporation. Frank's recording of "Take My Love," which turned a perfectly honest theme from Brahms's Third Symphony into an outright weeper, sold like the dog it was. "I'm a Fool to Want You," however, was something else. Yes, it was sappy, but the vaguely Slavic, minor-key melody felt original rather than canned, and when Frank sang it that night, something amazing happened.

Herron and Wolf had given him a lyric sheet, and Sinatra, as always, had studied it carefully, trying to absorb the words into his bloodstream. But when the orchestra started to play, Frank sang lyrics that were subtly but emphatically different from those that Wolf had written. Joel Herron, still alive in the mid-1990s, when Will Friedwald interviewed him, confirmed that Frank had changed the words but, enigmatically, refused to be drawn out on exactly how. "I asked him specifically, and he evaded the question," Friedwald recalls.

Sinatra sang just one take—a take for the ages—and then, as the legend has it, fled the recording studio, unable to go on. In this case the legend rings absolutely true. "I'm a Fool" may not be a great song, but Sinatra's shattering performance of it transcends the material. His emotion is so naked that we're at once embarrassed and compelled: we literally feel for him.

"That's a heartbreaking performance," said George Avakian, not ordinarily a fan. "And the lyric, which I understand Sinatra contributed largely to, is very powerful. Psychologically, it's very much a part of Sinatra. The fact that it's a song that reflected his life at the time always intrigued me. There aren't too many occasions when a record comes out of a person's life so directly."

Mitch Miller disagreed sharply on the autobiographical interpretation. "That's bullshit!" he said. "Because what he's drawing is the emotion from *your* personal life. He's saying it for you."

But then, Miller was always an ornery cuss—especially in later years, when critics constantly assailed him for supposedly ruining Sinatra's career. In this case, his irritability probably trumped his better judgment: never before or again would Frank sing so transparently from the heart.

The change from Wolf's original lyric was marked enough that "when they played us the side, I freaked out," Herron recalled. "When the session was over, we were with Ben Barton and Hank Sanicola, and Jack and I went off by ourselves and said, 'He's gotta be on this song!' We invited him in as a co-writer." There are clues to what Sinatra created. Lyric writing, in the great era of American popular song, was an extremely precise art, marked by concision and consistency of style. And at two junctures in this lyric, the style veers ever so slightly, first in the expressively awkward "A love that's there for others too" and then in the metrically inconsistent "Pity me, I need you," with its incorrect use of a word—"pity"—whose first syllable must be emphasized, throwing off the rhythm.

Bolstering the case for making these two lines the culprits is their emotional relevance: Frank did indeed worry constantly—and justifiably—about the "others" in Ava's life. And pity was something he sought constantly throughout his life, but never more so than during the near death of his career in the late 1940s and early 1950s: a period that coincided more or less precisely with his Ava years.

———

MGM had started test screening *Show Boat,* and the response cards were coming back with almost unanimous raves for Ava Gardner. She had entered that rarefied realm where she could do no wrong. Accordingly, when she asked Dore Schary if she could take some time off to go to New York, the production chief told her to enjoy herself.

With Frank, as always, everything at first was sweetness and light. Ava was feeling grand. She prevailed on him to take her to visit Dolly and Marty in Hoboken, even though Frank, driven to distraction by Dolly's incessant demands for money, hadn't spoken to his mother in nearly two years. Dolly answered the door and greeted Ava like a long-lost daughter, reaching up to embrace her, then giving her wayward son a Look. He was *still* too fucking thin.

Great to see you too, Ma.

The house smelled delicious—Dolly had prepared a tremendous meal: antipasto with cold cuts (especially Genoa salami, Frank's favorite); veal piccata; homemade ravioli with meat and spinach. And Ava was charmed:

> Dolly showed me the house, every inch of it, and was it clean?
> Oh, my God. I mean Frank was the cleanest man I ever
> knew . . . If I'd caught him washing the soap it wouldn't have
> surprised me, and he inherited it all from his ma . . . And of

course Dolly had to tell me all about Frank, with Frank squirm-
ing at every word . . . getting more and more furious as Dolly
dragged out album after album of cute pictures of Frank as a
child, dressed up in all kinds of little outfits . . .

It was all so welcoming, such a great warm Italian household
with no holding back. They even had an old uncle, either her
brother or Marty's, living with them.

No holding back, except for the fact that Marty ("quieter, withdrawn,
with a nice smile") said barely anything, and poor Chit-U, not a single
word. Dolly was the one who didn't hold back; Ava followed her lead,
growing less inhibited with every glass of Chianti. And Frank, Ava
recalled, "[looked] at me very carefully, trying to sense how it was going,
whether I was approving or not, his face reflecting that slight worry you
have when you want someone *you* love to love what *you* love."

Also that more than slight worry he felt every second he spent with
his mother.

Of course the visit was more than casual. And once Ava saw how
thoroughly her prospective mother-in-law approved of her, she applied
the screws even more tightly to Frank. When was he going to get a
divorce?

They were riding back to the city. Frank stared out the car window, drawing on his cigarette. He had no answer: it was all in Nancy's
hands.

Ava, who had heard it once too many times, told the driver to pull
over as soon as they emerged from the tunnel. She gathered her stole
around her, loosing a cloud of that mind-numbing perfume, opened
the car door, and got out.

===

A few days earlier, Frank had taken Ava along to watch the live broadcast of his television show. She was unimpressed. "Stagehands running
in and out," she recalled. "You never knew what camera was on you. I
got a nervous breakdown just watching."

The production values of a TV variety show in the early days certainly couldn't bear comparison to those of a gold-standard movie studio like MGM, but *The Frank Sinatra Show* had—technically and artistically—an especially flea-bitten air about it. The rudimentary comedy sketches submerged the talents even of bright lights such as Phil Silvers and Don Ameche. And then there were lesser lights, such as one Virginia Ruth Egnor, known professionally as Dagmar.

Dagmar was *Li'l Abner*'s Daisy Mae incarnate: a tall, eye-poppingly buxom West Virginia blonde with a big wide smile and a pleasant, unaggressive personality. She could act a little, but mostly all she needed to do was stand there. She was so well-known to the national TV audience that all Sinatra had to do to draw big laughs was raise an eyebrow.

She was therefore a natural to join the troupe when Frank began his first live engagement in six months, a two-week stand at the Paramount starting on April 25. He introduced her by saying, "Please nobody sit in the front row—if she takes a bow you'll get crushed." The comedy stayed on that level, though the musical portion of the show was solid: Sinatra was backed by a band led by his old Dorsey pal Joey Bushkin. But the bobby-soxers were gone; there were empty seats in the orchestra. "The only autographs I'm being asked for now," Sinatra told Bushkin, "are from process servers." And the movie on the bill was, all too poignantly, *My Forbidden Past,* starring Ava and her old flame Mitchum.

The only notice the *New York Times* took of Frank's Paramount show was in a single sentence at the bottom of a two-column review of the movie: "Featured on the stage of the Paramount are Frank Sinatra, Dagmar, Eileen Barton, Joe Bushkin and his orchestra, Tim Herbert and Don Saxon."

Not a single Sinatra side had charted since "Nevertheless (I'm in Love with You)" notched a pallid number 14 the previous December. Ballads weren't working; up-tempo numbers weren't working; folk tunes were last year's news. Mitch Miller felt stumped. Then two things happened in quick succession: Miller saw Frank and Dagmar do comedy together at the Paramount, and a songwriter named Dick Manning brought Mitch a cute new novelty number called "Mama Will Bark."

A great mythology has gathered around this song.[1] The deliciously awful title alone has become a shorthand for the downfall of Sinatra's career, a collapse that—according to myth—was all but engineered by the nefarious Miller. Sinatra himself liked to reinforce this impression. "I growled and barked on the record," he told his daughter Nancy. "The only good business it did was with dogs." Nor did Miller, an irascible and self-promoting character, do much to help his own reputation.

In fact, Mitch Miller was doing everything he could to jump-start Sinatra's dying recording career in the spring of 1951: the goateed hit maker was up for trying anything—anything—that might work, and so, for that matter, was Frank Sinatra. A novelty number? Why not? It was a crapshoot, but plenty of them had succeeded: look at Frankie Laine's "Mule Train"; look at Rosemary Clooney's "Come On-a My House" (both produced by Miller).

Frank Sinatra loved recording great songs, but even more he loved recording hit records,[2] and he desperately needed a hit that spring. Moreover, unlike, say, Clooney and Jo Stafford, both of whom were under constant contractual pressure by Miller and Columbia to record songs they didn't like (and pay for the recording sessions),[3] Sinatra had, through the good offices of Manie Sacks, grandfathered final approval over material into his contract with the label. In other words, Mitch Miller wasn't foisting anything on Frank Sinatra. Miller brought "Mama Will Bark" to Sinatra, and Sinatra said yes.

However, Frank had been able to be considerably choosier just twelve months earlier. Returning from his disastrous visit to Ava in Spain, Frank had stepped off the plane at La Guardia to find his new producer brimming with excitement over two new songs he'd found. "Great stuff, Frank!" According to Sinatra archivist Ed O'Brien, Sinatra and Miller drove directly to the Columbia recording studio, where Miller had an orchestra waiting. Sinatra looked at the sheet music for the numbers, "The Roving Kind" and "My Heart Cries for You." He gave the producer a look, but gamely enough ran through both songs with the musicians. The first was a bouncy, faux-folksy sea chantey ("She had a dark and roving eye-yyy, and her hair hung down in ring-a-lets"); the second, a swooner with a polka-esque chorus ("My heart *cries* for you, *sighs* for you, *dies* for you"). Hearing these atrocities actually set to music was all Sinatra needed. "Frank looks at Miller and says, 'I'm not recording this fucking shit,'" O'Brien said. "He throws the sheet music on the floor and says, 'You get yourself some other boy—I'm not doing this in a million years.' And he walks out.

"Here we are, we're all set up, we've got the music, we've got the musicians, the session is that night, we're paying everybody—'What the hell am I going to do?'" Miller told O'Brien. "So Miller jumps on the phone and calls Guy Mitchell."

Guy Mitchell—born Albert George Cernik—was a twenty-three-year-old former child movie actor and radio singer recently signed to a Columbia recording contract by Miller (who came up with Cernik's new name thusly: "You're a nice guy, and my name is Mitchell—we'll call you Guy Mitchell"). On the phone, according to O'Brien, Miller asked Mitchell, "'Guy, would you like to come in and do a couple of quick songs for me?' And Mitchell comes in and does the songs, and they both go right to the top of the charts. One was Number 1, the other made Number 2."

By May 1951, Guy Mitchell was an important recording star, and no one knew this better than Frank. And so, when Miller—filled with certainty and energy, the main ingredients of persuasiveness—asked him to record "Mama Will Bark," Sinatra said yes.

And on May 10, Frank and Mitch and Axel, along with a horn section, a rhythm ensemble including the reliable Johnny Blowers and Matty Golizio, a radio and cartoon voice artist named Donald Bain, and—yes—Dagmar, went into the Columbia Thirtieth Street studio and perpetrated the song.

Yet the truth is that Sinatra made many—many—recordings in his career just as bad as, if not worse than, "Mama Will Bark." In the late 1940s and early 1950s alone he did a substantial number of true dogs, the likes of "Chattanoogie Shoe Shine Boy," "One Finger Melody," "The Hucklebuck," and, in a July 1951 reunion with his old boss Harry James (who was also under Miller's thrall at Columbia), "Castle Rock," which James called "the worst thing that either one of us ever recorded."

"Mama Will Bark" isn't that. It's kind of cute and kind of sweet, and even if it's ultimately regrettable, it's also pretty harmless. It is, quite simply, a cartoon of a song—a dream-duet between a boy dog (Frank) and a girl dog (Dagmar)—and Frank, whether to his credit or his shame, is wholeheartedly into it. He sings along to the mambo beat in good voice and with good humor, neither taking the thing too seriously nor (sorry) dogging it. Between Frank's wooing choruses ("You look so lovely in the moonlight . . . Your eyes are shining like the starlight"), Dagmar delivers her recitativo interjections ("Mama will bark . . . Papa will spank") in absurdly flat, Appalachian-accented tones—she was clearly a lot better to look at than to listen to. And despite what Frank said about growling and barking, Bain handles almost all the heavy lifting in that department: all Sinatra has to do is give out with a couple of yips and a single "woof" at the end.

But he hated himself in the morning.

Friedwald points out he might not have had any regrets if the record had simply died, but it didn't—it charted. The canny Miller released "I'm a Fool to Want You" and "Mama Will Bark" as the A and B sides of a 45-rpm disc on June 23, and (based on number of jukebox plays) "Fool" reached number 14 and "Mama," number 21. It was ironic, to say the least: the apex and the nadir of his art on two sides of one thin disc. And the public, at this point anyway, liked them both just about the same.

28

Frank and Ava at the Desert Inn, September 1951. He would
try facial hair from time to time over the years: It was not a
good look for him.

A week after woofing that woof, Frank flew west with serious business in mind. Ava was taking his calls, but barely: she was curt and
wouldn't see him. When he went to 320 North Carolwood to try to
talk Nancy into giving him a divorce at last, it was with hat in hand.
And Nancy, who couldn't help herself when it came to Frank, was genuinely worried about him. All at once, his sadness (which she knew so
well) had a quality of desperation. "If I can't get a divorce," he begged
her, "where is there for me to go and what is there for me to do?"

They talked, and agreed to talk again. He greeted the children sadly and left. He came back twice more—it was the most the kids had seen of him in a long time. As always, Little Nancy had the fantasy that he might be coming home to stay. Husband and wife went into the living room and closed the door; the nanny shooed the children away. Nancy Barbato Sinatra looked into the eyes of the man who had occupied the center of her life for almost fifteen years and asked him if this was what he really wanted.

He quietly told her that it was.

On May 29, Nancy informed the press that she and Frank had come to a decision. "This is what Frank wants," she said, "and I've said yes. I have told the attorneys to work out the details."

A few days later, she told Louella Parsons: "I don't think a woman can be blamed for trying to hold her home together, especially when there are children. I held out a long time because I love Frank and I thought he would come back. But, when I saw there was absolutely no chance, and that he really wanted to marry someone else, I had my lawyer get in touch with his lawyer." Then she said, "I am now convinced that a divorce is the only way for my happiness as well as Frank's."

Yes was one thing; lawyers were another. Happiness would be a quantity in short supply all around.

=====

As soon as he left the gloomy confines of the Holmby Hills house (which, without telling him, Nancy had already put on the market, priced to move fast at $200,000), Frank's mood lifted. His spirits soared as he drove the winding roads up to Nichols Canyon.

He was still walking on air when he returned to New York. "Frank Sinatra was the happiest I've seen him in years—and also in wonderful voice—when he opened a one-week engagement at the Latin Quarter," Earl Wilson wrote.

> Nancy's decision to give him a divorce so he can marry Ava
> Gardner had seemingly put fresh bounce in his songs—espe-

cially some of the love songs that some of us romanticists thought might have reminded him of Ava.

Frank—who was bending those notes beautifully—told a friend, rather proudly, that when Ava's next picture, "Showboat" [sic], is released, she'll be one of the outstanding movie actresses of the world.

And as for his movie career? *Meet Danny Wilson,* which he spent July shooting at Universal, would show him how transient happiness was. The problems began with Frank's co-star, the formidable Shelley Winters. Winters, whom the studio was wrongheadedly trying to build up as a blond bombshell, was a Jewish girl out of St. Louis and Brooklyn (née Shirley Schrift): an actress of unconventional looks, high intelligence, and strong opinions. Like Sinatra, she was a committed liberal, though, if anything, her sympathies lay even further to the left. Prickly and vulnerable, Winters usually liked her leading men—but she hated Frank.

The enmity was inevitable, and mutual. Winters, determined to become a serious actress, was hardworking and insecure. She was scared of him; he was irritable and distracted. When he sent a note suggesting they rehearse together in his dressing room, she saw only one possible interpretation. She fired a self-righteous note back saying they would rehearse, as planned, on the soundstage. It wasn't that she found him unattractive. "I too had sat in the orchestra at the Paramount Theater when I was a teenager and screamed every time he opened his mouth," Winters wrote in her autobiography. "But he was married to Nancy, whom I knew and liked from various charity committees, and there were the children. I was determined to keep my association with Mr. Sinatra as professional as possible. In retrospect, I suspect he wanted the same thing."

That was in retrospect. In the near term, her rebuff sat less than well with him. They began on a footing of edgy hostility, which made their romantic scenes tricky. When it came to their big duet together (as the titular nightclub entertainer, Sinatra performed a half-dozen songs in the movie), Winters was so intimidated that she could barely open her mouth. Her nerves seem to have inspired Frank to his only charitable moments of the shoot—he helped her through.

The rest, though, was debacle. As the lawyers hammered out the details of the divorce, Sinatra realized just how complicated winning his freedom was going to be. "His children were quite young and there were always psychiatrists and priests and his kids visiting him on the set," Winters recalled.

> Sometimes the children would come to the commissary and I would join them. A priest from the Catholic Family Counseling Service would sometimes be with them. The priest was a very nice man, but the afternoons he visited Frank on the set we all might as well have gone home. Frank was truly impossible and so disturbed that he couldn't hear anything that anyone said to him, including the other actors, the crew, and the director, Joe Pevney.[1]

Halfway through the shoot, Sinatra attended the premiere of *Show Boat* with Ava, all of Hollywood falling at her feet. A few days after that, his radio show *Meet Frank Sinatra* (which he'd been broadcasting from L.A.) came to the end of its sputtering run. Neither of these events could have improved his mood.

He was achingly thin ("Frank was losing about a pound a week, which made me look heavier in the rushes," Winters recalled). He was discontent with the cut-rate movie studio and the small change they were paying him. Winters, on the other hand—she already had a career-changing performance in *A Place in the Sun* in the can—was on her way up.

And on the night they shot *Danny Wilson*'s penultimate scene, outdoors at Burbank Airport, the storm finally broke. "I can't remember what started our vicious argument," Winters recalled, "but the mildest things we called each other were 'bow-legged bitch of a Brooklyn blonde,' and 'skinny, no-talent, stupid Hoboken bastard.'"

> At about three in the morning Frank flew into a terrible rage at me, and despite my gorgeous hat and white gloves and beautiful elegant navy dress and stone martens, I screamed like a fishwife and I think I slugged him. For a second I thought Frank's makeup man/bodyguard—who I suspected carried a gun—was going to shoot me. Contrary to other Italians I have known since, he didn't hit me back—I guess I was lucky—he just slammed into his limousine and roared away. Maybe he went home and hit Ava Gardner.

The production head Leo Spitz pleaded with Winters to feel some empathy. "Mr. Sinatra is going through a terrible and troubled period of his life and career," he told her. "He's going against all his religious training and has periods when he loses his voice, and it terrifies him. And he is not famous as an actor but a singer . . . That's no excuse for him behaving so outrageously, but you're both liberals, and maybe with your ideals of brotherhood you can bring yourself to understand the reasons that are making him behave the way he did."

Grumbling, Winters returned to the set—to endure Frank's revenge. They rehearsed the final scene, in which, as Winters's character lay in a hospital bed, Sinatra was to say to his romantic rival (Alex Nicol), "I'll have a cup of coffee and leave you two lovebirds alone." Once the camera was rolling, however, what Frank said was "I'll go have a cup of Jack Daniel's or I'm going to pull that blond broad's hair out by its black roots."

Winters hit him over the head with a bedpan, raged off the set, and went home. She stayed there for two days—until she got a tearful phone call from Nancy Sinatra. "Shelley, if Frank doesn't get the twenty-five thousand dollars for the picture, the bank might foreclose the mortgage on the house," Nancy said. "My children are going to be out in the street. Please finish the picture."

Shelley finished the picture. When *Meet Danny Wilson* wrapped on July 31, all concerned breathed a huge sigh of relief. The film would go on to do just so-so box office. Yet considering the disastrous course of the production, the *New York Times* review is surprisingly positive, calling the film "pleasantly tune-filled and amiable," and going on to praise the battling co-stars: "Frank Sinatra is charming, natural and casual as he breezily portrays the cocky Danny Wilson . . . Miss Winters is equally slick as that desired dame and she neatly adds to the performance in a snappy duet with Sinatra on 'A Good Man Is Hard to Find.'"

So much for the artistic benefits of peace and harmony. In truth, Frank was improving as a film actor, if anyone cared to pay attention.

═══

The day after shooting ended on *Meet Danny Wilson,* Sinatra and Ava took off on what was meant to be a secret jaunt to Acapulco. From the beginning, the trip was snakebit: crowds of reporters and photographers turned out to see the pair off at the L.A. airport, taking note of the ungodly number of suitcases they had with them. Was this something more than a quick vacation? You could get a fast divorce in Mexico. You could get married there too.

The photographers clustered on the stairs that were pulled up to the plane, snapping away; the pilot was helpless to start the engines until they were cleared. Sinatra leaned out the door and gave it to them with both barrels: "GET THE FUCK OFF THE STEPS!"

"You shouldn't act that way, Frankie," one of the lensmen piped up. "The press made you what you are!"

"The press didn't make me, it was my singing! You miserable crumbs!"

Reporters were alerted all down the line. They showed up in swarms at the flight's layover in El Paso and at the airport in Mexico City. From there, a wire-service story went out:

> Crooner Frankie Sinatra said angrily tonight he has "no intention" of eloping with Movie Queen Ava Gardner.

The surly singer said "there's not a bit of truth to these rumors" that he came to Mexico for a quickie divorce and marriage.

The couple would not talk to newsmen about their romantic plans, but the bobby-sox idol telephoned friends here that they plan to return to Hollywood without being married.

"We're really just on a vacation," he said. "I'm in no position for a divorce just now."

Their attempt to slip quietly into Mexico by air last night turned into the most publicized romantic goings-on since Rita Hayworth's trip here with Prince Aly Khan before their marriage.

Their host, a Mexican millionaire named Jorge Pasquel (newspapers liked to call him a "wealthy sportsman"), flew the couple from Mexico City to Acapulco in his converted B-17, *El Fantasma,* and put them up in his palatial digs. Rumors swirled that Sinatra had gotten his quickie divorce and secretly married Ava in Cuernavaca. Officials denied it. Another wire-service dispatch, on August 4, reported the big news that Ava had been snubbed by Hedy Lamarr in Acapulco:

The two movie queens eyed each other coldly at a night club owned by Miss Lamarr's new husband, but the older actress didn't even nod to the hand-holding pair who are Hollywood's most torrid new romance.

One night just after midnight, Frank and Ava adjourned to a club called the Beachcomber. An American photographer who had stationed himself outside asked if he could snap their picture. Frank told him to fuck himself. The flashbulb went off anyway. A Mexican bodyguard—another contribution from Pasquel—went for the camera, but the photographer held on to it. "If you don't give me that camera," the bodyguard said, "I'll put a bullet into you." Somebody called the police, who listened to Sinatra's complaint, took the camera, and handed it to Frank, who opened it and yanked out the film, raining a blue torrent of obscenities on the photographer while Ava dabbed at her eyes.

Surely somewhere on the Baja California in 1951 there was a deserted beach town, minus wealthy sportsmen, former movie queens, and Eurotrash, to which Frank and Ava might have managed to spirit themselves for a few days of solitary relaxation. Surely Sinatra with all his resources could have found a way to ditch the paparazzi. But it was the same as with his bachelor jaunts to Palm Springs: he wanted to get away from it all, but not too far away. Solitude, unglamorous surroundings, were anathema. So he went to the usual places, with the usual suspects, and got into the usual situations. With the usual resultant attention. Attention was very important. What was he, who was he, without it? The idea that he could manage it completely, that the press of the world would fall in at his heels like Earl Wilson, was a fond illusion.

Look at me. Leave me alone. The tension between the couple's need for publicity (Ava's was more ambivalent) and their need for privacy was killing the relationship as it was struggling to get started. When the two of them were alone—it was far too seldom—she cried to him about the scenes. She was a tough girl, with a thick skin, and she liked showing off as much as any actress, but she was sensitive too. He tried to console her; in reality there was little he could do. His power was diminishing every minute.

After three less-eventful days (though the United Press had done some digging and discovered that the Mexican bodyguard had a long murder record), Frank and Ava flew back home. "It was dark when we arrived, but a horde of photographers were gathered anyway, eager to pounce, and flashbulbs were popping as we scrambled into the waiting car," Ava recalled.

The horde of photographers consisted of about a half-dozen members of the press, but one of them, a cameraman for KTTV, shone a spotlight at the Cadillac. This infuriated Sinatra, who kept screaming,

"Kill the light! Kill the light!" According to the testimony of a news photographer named William Eccles, Sinatra swerved the car directly toward him and struck him with the fender, screaming, "Next time I'll kill you! I'll kill you!"

Eccles filed a criminal complaint against Sinatra, but withdrew it when he received a letter of apology allegedly written by Frank.

———

Some good news after he got home put Frank in a better mood: Nancy announced she would permit him to file for a divorce in Nevada, where the complainant had only to satisfy a six-week residency requirement. Broker than ever, Sinatra had his people get him what work they could: two weeks at the Riverside Hotel in Reno, followed by another couple of weeks at the Desert Inn in Las Vegas.

He arrived in Reno on August 9 in fine spirits—and determined not to let any bad press scuttle his plans. Frank smiled at the reporters and said, "I hope I'm going to get along with you fellows." Then he shook hands with each, and invited them all to his hotel suite to ask him whatever they wanted. The men glanced at each other in disbelief.

Soon they were cozily swilling free booze and noshing on canapés in Sinatra's suite at the Riverside. They got out their notebooks.

"Frank," one of them piped up, "I'm sorry to have to ask you this, but some people are saying you're too broke to file for divorce."

Frank looked at the ceiling, exhaled a plume of smoke, and leaned back in his chair like a man without a care in the world. Outside the picture windows, the snowcapped Sierra Nevada stretched gloriously across the horizon. He grinned at the reporters. Was that what they were saying? Well, the gentlemen of the press would all be getting their bill for the drinks and snacks in a few minutes.

Everyone laughed. Frank turned serious. He didn't like to brag, but this joint was paying him twenty-five grand for two weeks, which wasn't too shabby, plus he had another engagement in Vegas after that, and his television show—Saturday evenings from eight to nine on

CBS—would start its second season in October. Frank guessed he had a couple of nickels to rub together.

Someone piped up: Was he going to marry Miss Gardner?

Frank looked at his fingernails. "I presume I will."

Another voice called out. What about all that trouble down in Mexico?

Sinatra shook his head. "Grossly exaggerated," he said. "I got sore because I got some pretty rough handling from a couple of guys. They were the exception to the rule, though, for the press has done a lot for me."

Frank gave a small, sincere smile. Butter wouldn't have melted in his mouth.

Ten days later Ava flew up to Reno. Continuing the charm offensive, Frank escorted her into another roomful of reporters, grinning like the cat that ate the canary. For reasons of his own, he had spent the last week and a half growing a sparse mustache. He would try facial hair from time to time over the years. It was not a good look for him.

But his skin was tan, his eyes were the blue of the high-desert sky, and he and the press were still romancing each other. He didn't even flinch when somebody asked if he knew what Nancy's plans were.

"I honestly don't know what she'll do," Sinatra said. He looked meltingly at Ava. "But I think you can safely say that Miss Gardner and I will be married."

Over dinner one night—they were relaxing at the Cal Neva Lodge, on the glorious shore of Lake Tahoe—he asked her to tell him about the bullfighter. Had they done it? She artfully changed the subject, smiling brightly; he smiled back at her, then asked again over coffee. She gave him a cross look and asked him why he was trying to fuck everything up. They fought; they made up. Later, they lay together quietly in the bedroom of his cabin: with the wind swishing through the pines, it seemed they could hear the earth turning. And he asked her again.

She got up on one elbow and looked down at him, her hair falling over one eye. Didn't they have better things to discuss than this?

It was no big deal, he swore; he just wanted to know.

She shook a cigarette out of the pack on the nightstand and lit it. She smoked for a minute, saying nothing.

"Ava, honey," Frank said. "It doesn't really matter to me. We've all fallen into the wrong bed at one time or another. Just tell me the truth and we'll forget all about it."

She thought for a moment. She tapped the cigarette on the ashtray, though she didn't need to.

All right, she said, since he wouldn't leave it alone. Once. One mindless night. She'd been drunk—she didn't really even remember it.

Once, Frank repeated, dully.

The next day Sanicola rented them a gleaming new Chris-Craft so Frank and Ava could go for a picnic cruise on the lake. Hank came along to steer the boat; Ava's maid, Reenie, brought sandwiches and champagne. It was perfect early-September weather, crisp and sparkling, a light wind blowing across the steel blue water. Frank and Ava sat on the back deck drinking champagne while Hank drove. The big engine thrummed as Sanicola steered into a quiet inlet. Ava lifted her face to the sun, her eyes closed.

"I suppose you wish you were out here with Howard Hughes," Frank suddenly said.

Reenie cleared her throat and slowly shook her head.

"Why the fuck should I wish I were out here with Howard Hughes?" Ava said.

"I bet he's got a bigger boat than this, doesn't he? That guy's got enough bucks to buy ten boats the size of this one."

Up on the bridge, Sanicola looked back at them.

"I don't care if he owns the fucking *Queen Mary*," Ava said. "I'm not sorry I'm not with him. So shut up."

"Don't tell me to shut up."

Sanicola looked pleadingly at Reenie. She shrugged.

"Then don't tell me I'm thinking about Howard Hughes when I'm not thinking about Howard Hughes."

"I'll t——" Frank stopped in mid-utterance as the boat jerked and shuddered to a halt with a terrible grinding noise. They all were nearly knocked out of their seats. The boat had struck a large, mostly submerged rock in shallow water about a hundred feet out from the shore. They were already beginning to list to starboard.

The water was only around four feet deep. Hank helped Reenie climb down the ladder, then descended himself. They both splashed toward shore. Frank was next. Ava stayed put.

"Get off that fucking boat while there's still time, you fucking fool," Frank called from the water.

"Go fuck yourself," she said. "I'm staying here."

And there she sat, sipping champagne.

"It was about that time that I discovered that this fancy boat was stocked with a monstrous amount of toilet paper," Ava recalled.

Why in the name of God the owners had decided to store so much on one boat I'll never know. But all the champagne I'd drunk convinced me that this wealth must be shared with the world. So I unwrapped roll after roll and floated them all off in the general direction of Frank. His rage was now off the charts, and he screamed a variety of curses in my direction that even I found impressive, but nothing he said deterred me from my appointed rounds.

Eventually, the boat began to sink in earnest, and I carefully joined Frank on the shore, carrying with me, with perfect survivor's instincts, the last bottle of champagne and two glasses. We managed to get the bottle open and sat down to regard the scene. What was a little rumpus between lovers, anyway? We clinked glasses, laughed and made up.

This is breezy and funny, a memoir written to amuse when the reality cannot have been so amusing. Both Frank and Ava had become serious drinkers by this point: in his case, he needed more and more alcohol to blur his worsening career and family problems; Ava just liked to drink. During the recent shoot of *Lone Star,* a dog of a Western that Metro had forced her to make, she had been loaded much of the time. And when the two of them were together, alcohol was as apt to loosen their tongues as their libidos. "Just a few nights later, when we both had drunk so much, Frank made an offhanded remark that hurt me so deeply that I didn't stop to argue or shout back, I just left," Ava wrote.

> I ran out into the darkness, my bare feet heading toward the
> lake . . . Then I heard someone running behind me, trying to
> catch up. It was Reenie.
>   I stopped and we both sat there in the darkness . . . Finally,
> Reenie said in a quiet, resigned voice, "Come on, Miss G.,
> knock it off. Why don't we just go home."

So they did. It was dawn when they reached Pacific Palisades. They walked into the house to find the phone ringing. It was Hank Sanicola, and he sounded desperate.

"Oh my God, Ava—hurry back!" he said. "Frank's taken an overdose!"

She hurried back.

> A car had rushed us to the L.A. airport. A car had rushed us
> from the Nevada airport to the house at Lake Tahoe. Hank
> Sanicola met me at the door. He looked as tired out and worn
> as I felt. I had difficulty speaking.
>   "How is he?" I said.
>   "He's okay," said Hank.
>   I thought, Thank God! I ran through into the bedroom. I
> looked down at Frank and he turned his sad blue eyes to look
> at me.

"I thought you'd gone," he said weakly.

I wanted to punch him, I really did. I wanted to punch him as much as I'd ever wanted to punch anybody. Frank had tricked both Reenie and me back to his bedside.

The difference with this suicide attempt was that this time the authorities were involved. Sanicola had called a doctor, and though he had tried to divert suspicion by identifying the patient as himself, the doctor had been obliged to file a police report. By Labor Day weekend, the newspapers had a juicy new Sinatra story.

Frank and Ava sat down, hand in hand, to meet the press once more.

"I did not try to commit suicide," Frank said. "I just had a bellyache. What will you guys think of next to write about me?"

"So what really happened, Frank?" a reporter called.

Sinatra looked around the room, making a visible effort to hold his temper. "Tuesday night, Miss Gardner, my manager Hank Sanicola and Mrs. Sanicola dined at the Christmas Tree Inn on Lake Tahoe," he said. "Ava was returning to Hollywood that night. We came back to the Lake and I didn't feel so good. So I took two sleeping pills. Miss Gardner left . . . I guess I wasn't thinking because I am very allergic to sleeping pills. Also, I had drunk two or three brandies. I broke out in a rash. The pills felt kind of stuck in my chest. I got worried and called a friend who runs the steak house here. He sent a doctor who gave me a glass of warm water with salt in it. It made me throw up and I was all right. That's all there was to it—honest."

Honest.

Nevada Route 91, the Arrowhead Highway, was a two-lane blacktop snaking southwest across a vast expanse of sand, mesquite, and sage. The road didn't look much less desolate in Las Vegas than it did anywhere else in the Silver State, even along the four-mile stretch known optimistically as Las Vegas Boulevard or, more popularly, the Strip.

Sand blew across the macadam; scorpions scuttled among the desert weeds. In the early 1940s, the first casino-hotels began to pop up in this unpromising landscape: El Rancho Vegas opened in 1941; the Hotel Last Frontier debuted the following year. The Flamingo came to its problematic completion in 1946; the Thunderbird opened in 1948; and the fifth gambling resort on the Strip, opening in 1950, was the Desert Inn.

The DI was the brainchild of one Wilbur Clark, a onetime San Diego bellhop and Reno craps dealer who, much like the Flamingo's Billy Wilkerson, found himself strapped mid-project for the cash necessary to bring his dream to fruition. As with Wilkerson, the Mob—this time in the person of the Cleveland syndicate boss Moe Dalitz—stepped into the breach. Dalitz's good friends at the Teamsters Union's Central States Pension Fund provided the cash—unbeknownst to most of the teamsters. The Cleveland gangster, who had run gambling operations throughout Ohio, Kentucky, Indiana, and Michigan, had western ambitions. Unlike Bugsy Siegel, however, the businesslike Dalitz chose not to muscle out the casino's originator but to retain him as an agreeable front man. "Wilbur Clark," after all, had a more congenial ring to it than "Moe Dalitz" out in these parts. And so Dalitz, a big-nosed, six-foot tough Jew, graciously allowed the place to be christened Wilbur Clark's Desert Inn. Clark's name, in mock-signature script, adorned the giant electric sign, with its Joshua-tree-cactus logo.

The groundbreaking architect Wayne McAllister had designed the place to a 1950s-modern fare-thee-well, with pink stucco walls, fieldstone pilasters, jutting roofs, and, around back, the first kidney-shaped pool in town. The inn's crowning glory was a three-story, glass-cupolaed structure, the tallest in Vegas in 1951, built to look like an airport control tower. Behind the picture windows, the Skyroom lounge, with little lights faired into the ceiling to simulate desert stars, offered dining, dancing, and an unobstructed vista of the Las Vegas valley in all its sand-and-sagebrush splendor. The entertainment might have been Hollywood, but the clientele was strictly string tie: southwestern oilmen, cattle ranchers, and their ladies. Even if the DI's 450-seat Painted Desert Room could draw some top acts, nobody mistook it for the Copa.

Sinatra was the top of the bill: after him came the comedian-magician Jay Marshall, also known as "The Funny Bunny Man"; Ruby Ring, "Dancer Extra-Ordinary"; and the Arden-Fletcher Dancers. The Singing MC was Gene Griffin, and the orchestra was led by Carlton Hayes.

If Frank closed his eyes, he could remember the Major Bowes Number Five tour unit.

Sinatra's shows sold out. He ran Carlton Hayes and his musicians through their paces, belting out "My Blue Heaven," "Come Rain or Come Shine," and "That Old Black Magic," singing his heart out and working hard to make his audience—never mind that they weren't café society—feel he was singing to them alone. He worked a little too hard for Ava's taste. Sitting ringside with Axel Stordahl and his new wife, June Hutton, "Ava was chatting away happily," Stordahl recalled, "and then suddenly she said, 'Let's get out of this trap.' She thought Frank was looking at a girl in the audience a little longer than necessary. They ended up throwing books and lamps at each other after the show, and Frank walked out in the middle of the night."

Jealousy, of course, was their aphrodisiac. Rosemary Clooney, who was working at the Thunderbird while Sinatra played the Desert Inn, remembered how Ava would come in to catch part of her act (perhaps having just walked out on Frank), telling Clooney afterward how much she loved the singer's rendition of the Gershwins' "They Can't Take That Away from Me": "Every time I get a chance, I'm going to come down here and listen to you sing it, even though the old man doesn't like it much." Clooney finally figured out why: Artie Shaw had had a hit with it.[2]

Jimmy Van Heusen flew up from L.A. for the whole Desert Inn stand—because Frank expected him, and because he loved to fly, loved the desert, and loved the whores who, even in Vegas's early days, could be found there in such great numbers and variety. In between shows,

Chester took to wandering the inn's halls, looking for fresh talent. One night he was drawn into the Skyroom by the sound of a tasty jazz trio playing his own "Polka Dots and Moonbeams."

It wasn't just his own music that Chester was admiring but the way it was being played. The man at the baby grand—cadaverously pale and thin, with a thick head of straight greasy hair, pointed shoulders, and long, spidery fingers darting over the keys—had a hauntingly spare technique, with rich sonorities tossed off like afterthoughts. And, amazingly, he swung.

During the break, Chester went up and introduced himself: "I like the way you play."

"I like the way you write," the piano player replied.

His name was Bill Miller, and as Van Heusen squinted in vague recognition, Miller reminded him that he had worked the big bands for a long time, playing for Red Norvo and Charlie Barnet until the mid-1940s.

"Sinatra's my pal, God help me," Van Heusen said. "I'm in Vegas to cheerlead—and get laid, of course."

Frank with his greatest accompanist, Bill Miller, early fifties.

Miller grew animated—for him. "Speaking of getting laid," he said. "In the summer of 1940 I was working with Barnet at the New York World's Fair, and I was dating a showgirl." He gave that crooked smile. "One night we were driving back into the city, and the car radio was on, and Harry James was playing 'All or Nothing At All,' behind this boy singer. And my girlfriend said, 'Hey, listen, doesn't that sound good? That's Dick Haymes.' I said, 'No, it's not Dick Haymes. Dick Haymes doesn't sing that good.' Turned out the singer was someone named Frank Sinatra. I'd never heard of him before, but I thought he was great."

"He still is," Chester said. "He's still a pain in the ass, too. He doesn't deserve the shit he's been getting, though." He paused for a second. "He's also looking for a piano player."

"Well, hell, now that you've built him up."

"Listen—he's still the best singer there is. And he's only a pain in the ass to his friends. He likes musicians. Especially good musicians."

"Then why doesn't he have a piano player?"

"Why the hell do you think? He's broke!"

Miller grinned. "Now I'm really interested."

"He's got a television show, though. And CBS isn't broke."

Later that night, having been sold on Miller by Chester, Sinatra accompanied the songwriter up to the Skyroom. The pianist struck up a solo version of "Polka Dots and Moonbeams," lightly swinging, with sparse tasty chords—the dancers on the floor barely had to break stride—and both Frank and Jimmy couldn't help smiling.

After a short medley of other Sinatra hits, each played so perfectly that Frank's vocal cords twitched sympathetically as he listened, Miller took a break and Sinatra walked over to the piano.

"How'd you like to work with me, kid?" he asked.

Miller, who was almost a year older than Sinatra, pursed his lips, then nodded. "Okay," he said.

Wedding day, November 7, 1951. Their bliss was short-lived,
as bliss always was for Frank.

Frank hadn't recorded since July, the same month the sponsors pulled the plug on his radio show. (He would go into the recording studio only once more that year, in mid-October, to wax a studio version of his *Meet Danny Wilson* duet with Shelley Winters, "A Good Man Is Hard to Find." Due to lack of interest, the record was never released.) There were no future bookings. His six-week Nevada residence was up on September 19, but as he prepared to file for divorce, his attorney got word from Nancy's attorney that to better protect the children, she planned to contest Frank's action and secure a prior California divorce. The property settlement in the separate-maintenance agreement was no longer acceptable, Nancy and her lawyer said: Frank owed her back alimony—$40,805, to be exact.

With the checks from the Riverside and the Desert Inn going straight to Nancy, Frank barely had $400, let alone forty thousand. Knowing this, she sent her lawyer to court to obtain a levy against Frank's office building at 177 South Robertson.

Frank and Nancy were at a standoff: he didn't want to pay her all he owed her until she gave him his freedom; she didn't want to give him his freedom until he paid all he owed her.

He flew to New York to rehearse for the TV show, but even as he stood in CBS Studio 50, a cardboard cup of coffee in one hand and a Camel in the other, he got word that the L.A. law firm that had been representing him in the divorce proceedings was suing him for $12,250 in unpaid legal fees. The firm had slapped a lien on the already-levied 177 South Robertson building and, for good measure, on Twin Palms as well.

He drew on the cigarette and exhaled. Fuck 'em.

There was more bad news. Bulova had pulled out of *The Frank Sinatra Show*. The only sponsor the network was able to attract was Ekco, the housewares company, for just the first fifteen minutes of the sixty. And CBS had moved the show from Saturday night to Tuesday, opposite another TV behemoth, Mr. Television himself, Milton Berle, on *Texaco Star Theater*.

Fuck 'em.

On October 3, at the Polo Grounds, the New York Giants' Bobby Thomson hit the most famous home run in baseball history to win the National League play-offs against the Brooklyn Dodgers. The game was all the more dramatic because play-offs were the exception rather than the rule in those days: the Giants, after trailing the Dodgers by thirteen and a half games in mid-August, had surged back and tied Brooklyn on the final day of the season. The teams had split the first two games of the play-offs, and betting was heavy on the rubber match. One of the biggest bettors was Sinatra's friend Willie Moretti, who laid thousands on the Dodgers.

Willie discovered later that day what it took the rest of the world decades to find out: The Giants had stationed a coach with a telescope and a buzzer in their centerfield clubhouse. With the telescope, the coach was able to pick up the Dodgers catcher Rube Walker's signs to the pitcher Ralph Branca; with the buzzer, the spy sent a signal to the Giants dugout, whence a hand signal to Thomson told him to expect a fastball.

Willie Moretti decided that all bets were off.

The next day, Moretti went to lunch at his favorite restaurant, Joe's Elbow Room, a block from the Hudson in Cliffside Park, New Jersey. He left his cream-colored Packard coupe at the curb, walked in, and found four friends waiting for him at a table. The men chatted amiably for a few minutes, and then, when the waitress on duty went into the kitchen, the man on Moretti's right leaned over and in a low voice began to tell him a dirty story. As Willie smiled expectantly, the man on his left took out a .38 revolver and shot him twice in the head.

The four men departed in such haste that two of them left their hats on the table (and $2,000 in Moretti's pants pocket). The image of Willie's body on the white-tile floor in a widening pool of blood, snapped by a news photographer, quickly gained wide circulation. In death, Willie became as celebrated as he had recently been in life, the short, fat, jolly mobster who had wisecracked his way through the televised Kefauver hearings. "Everything is a racket today," Moretti had told the amused senators. "Why not make everything legal?" When Kefauver himself asked Willie how he operated politically, Moretti said, "I don't—if I did, I'd be sitting where you are now."

It was funny to everyone except Moretti's partners in crime, who hated Kefauver, hated loose talk under any circumstances, let alone on national television, and knew that Willie, in the grips of syphilis, couldn't help himself. But blabbing was one thing; welshing on sports bets, another matter entirely. Though Moretti had been a marked man for months, he had fast-tracked his own elimination, and Sinatra lost yet another father figure at a time when he needed all the friends he could get.

———

The second-season premiere of *The Frank Sinatra Show*, on October 9, co-starred Perry Como, Frankie Laine, and the Andrews Sisters. The reviews were slightly better than they'd been the year before: *Variety* said the show was "spotty, taking full advantage of its all-star talent lineup to sparkle in some spots and settling down to a slow walk in others." And the *New York Times*'s Jack Gould allowed that Frank had "a very real degree of stage presence and a certain likeable charm," but also sounded an ominous note: "The evening's honors were captured effortlessly and smoothly by another gentleman, Perry Como."

Como was a perfect character for 1950s television: attractive, bland, comforting. Who knew who Perry Como really was? Who cared? He seemed to be a solid citizen with a good marriage; he was good-looking, friendly, with a sweet voice and a nice sense of humor about himself.

Sinatra, on the other hand, could sing wonderfully, but that miraculous audience connection he created in person was diminished by the TV camera's cold eye. Though he could do comedy serviceably, his real skills were elsewhere, and his self-mockery was never entirely convincing: his ego was too palpably gigantic. He was also all too apt to wear his anger on his sleeve, in a not especially funny way.[1] By 1951, audiences felt they knew all too well who Frank Sinatra was, and they weren't buying.

Of course Uncle Miltie murdered him in the ratings.

The miracle was that amid all his travails, Sinatra kept doing the show week after week, and actually got somewhat better at it. Berle's ratings even started to erode slightly.

Still, Frank's sponsor, never fully committed in the first place, grew more and more disaffected. The columnists continued to inveigh against Sinatra; priests advised their congregations to avoid buying his records and attending his movies. He was the anti-Crosby.[2]

Frank couldn't bear the thought of losing Twin Palms. He borrowed the twelve grand he owed his lawyers from Ava—though since she didn't have that kind of cash lying around, she borrowed it from her agent Charlie Feldman. It was a hell of a way to start a marriage, but what else could he do? She smiled sadly and handed him the check. Her dowry. His big grin assured her she'd done the right thing: he was unencumbered at last. He signed a new property settlement, increasing Nancy's separate maintenance to the tune of one-third of his gross income up to $150,000 a year, plus 10 percent of earnings above that. On October 15, his soon-to-be ex-wife filed for her California divorce.

Two weeks later, Nancy appeared once more in the Santa Monica courthouse, this time to receive her interlocutory decree of divorce. One photographer, presumably a municipal employee, took several shots as she sat in a courtroom.

They are extraordinary images. Wearing a checked suit, white gloves, the triple-strand pearl necklace and pearl earrings Frank had given her, and a small black hat with a face net, Nancy Rose Barbato Sinatra looks radiant. It is a face without mean-spiritedness. In two of the pictures she's grinning delightedly right at the photographer, but two others, both with eyes averted, are far more arresting. In one Nancy appears lost in thought, and whatever she may be thinking seems of the greatest possible interest. And in the other, smiling slightly and looking up to the left, she looks, quite simply, transcendently beautiful.

———

Two days later, in a five-minute closed session in a Las Vegas courtroom, Frank was awarded an uncontested divorce. That night he flew east, and on November 2 he and Ava applied for a marriage license in Philadelphia, where they hoped to avoid publicity.

It was all a circus, of course. How could it have been anything else? The newspapers were watching their every move. When Frank and Ava went to the judge's chambers to apply for their license, they were accompanied by Manie Sacks and another Philadelphian, CBS co-founder and board member Isaac Levy. Levy, who was enormously wealthy, had a mansion on the Main Line in Germantown. It stood to reason that the wedding was going to be held at his house. And since the couple had applied for their license on Friday the second, and Pennsylvania had a seventy-two-hour waiting period, clearly the date would be Monday the fifth.

Then the pair returned to New York for the weekend, and the wedding nearly fell through. On Saturday they went out for a celebratory dinner at the Colony with the James Masons. Afterward, the two couples went nightclubbing in Harlem, and then Frank and Ava returned to the Hampshire House. In the suite Ava was sharing with Bappie, there was a knock at the door. It was a bellman, with a letter. Ava made him wait while she found fifty cents in her purse.

She opened the envelope and unfolded the sheets inside. The letter was handwritten in a looping feminine scrawl, slightly childish, its forward thrust suggesting urgency. It was full of misspellings. As Ava's eyes traversed the page, her heart began to thud.

The letter described several trysts the writer claimed to have had with Frank. So far, so bad. But as Ava read on (putting her hand to her chest and sitting in a wing chair without even realizing she was doing so), it came to her that the woman had to be telling the truth. There were details, shameless and horrible details about Frank and his anatomy and his proclivities, that only a lover could know.

Except that this woman wasn't a lover. She was a pro, cold and precise and crude and impertinent, even going so far as to congratulate Ava on attracting a man of Frank's prodigious endowment—then pitying her because her husband-to-be needed to pay for sex.

The writer of this letter, Ava realized, wanted to reduce her to nothing.

Like an automaton, she walked over to the window and with some effort pulled up the heavy sash. The cold November night wind, ripe with the tang of burning trash, swirled in. Bappie stood in the doorway. Her first horrified thought was that her sister was going to jump.

"Ava—" Bappie moved toward her.

But self-destruction was the furthest thing from Ava's mind. Gritting her teeth, she pulled Frank's engagement ring—a six-carat emerald set in platinum, flanked with pear-cut diamonds—from her finger and threw it out into dark space.

She turned to her sister, not registering the look of fear on her face. "The wedding is off," Ava said. "Finished. Forget it!" She ran to her bedroom and slammed the door behind her. The lock clicked.

"Now the bedlam began," Ava recalled.

> Frank was going crazy, Bappie and Manie Sachs [*sic*],[3] Hank Sanicola, and [the former Dorsey arranger and Varsity member] Dick Jones were all rushing backward and forward between Frank's room and mine arguing, wheedling, yelling, protesting. They told me no one could cancel a wedding at this late date. It had all been prepared: the cars, the catering, the minister, the flowers, the elegant house. I said I was an important part of that wedding and I could damn well cancel it.
>
> I think it took most of that night with a lot of back and forth before I agreed to change my mind. Thinking about it now, and wondering who could be so malevolent as to arrange for that letter to arrive at such a critical moment and drive me almost out of my mind, the finger points in only one direction.

The diabolical rival Gardner had in mind was none other than Howard Hughes. When the dashing aviation tycoon and movie mogul wasn't busy crashing experimental aircraft and running RKO into the ground, he was keeping obsessive tabs on a whole harem of real and imagined lady friends, including Jane Russell, Katharine Hepburn, Lana Turner, the sisters Olivia de Havilland and Joan Fontaine, Gene

Tierney, Jean Peters, and Ava. For the handsome but strangely sexless Hughes, the chief pleasure of romance seemed to lie in the pursuit, even (if not especially) if the object of his desire had told him in no uncertain terms to beat it. This Ava had done any number of times, but then his lavish gifts would soften her a little, again and again. The cycle continued until Frank came along, but Hughes kept having her watched anyway, waiting for something to give—or trying to make something give.

The singer and the tycoon had infinite contempt for each other. For Sinatra, Hughes was a right-winger and a creep, in all likelihood a pervert of some kind. For Hughes, with his ultraconservative Texas oilman's mentality, Sinatra was a greaseball pinko, bent on undermining American family values. As for the fact that RKO had a soon-to-be-released Sinatra film in the can—well, the studio head would deal with that shortly.

In the meantime, his attempted sabotage failed. On the rainy morning of Wednesday, November 7, Frank and Ava emerged from the Hampshire House holding hands. "They were giggly, obviously very much in love and sober," recalled Earl Wilson.

> I congratulated them and wished them eternal happiness.
> Frank threw his arm around me; Ava gave me a kiss. They
> slid quickly into the backseat of a limousine with two friends
> [Frank's best man, Axel Stordahl, and Stordahl's wife, June
> Hutton, the matron of honor] in the frontseat, and waved
> to me. Some photographers who had been waiting for them
> were unable to move quickly enough to get pictures, and that
> delighted both.

Just before he got into the car, though, Sinatra barked out, "No questions, no questions!" and clamped his hand over the lens of a Movietone newsreel camera. Then the car door slammed behind him and the flotilla of Cadillacs headed off to what the wedding party fervently hoped were parts unknown. To throw off the press, the nuptials had been switched to a top-secret new location, in less palatial but still elegant digs—the West Germantown home of Manie's brother Lester Sacks, a well-to-do garment manufacturer.

The press was waiting for them anyway. Frank stared incredulously as his car rolled up in front of Sacks's big fieldstone house. He jumped out of the car while it was still rolling. "How did those creeps know where we were?" he asked nobody in particular as the photographers snapped. It was dusk; a cold drizzle was falling. "I don't want no circus here!" he called to the press. "I'll knock the first guy who attempts to get inside on his ass—and I mean it!"

While he sputtered, Ava grabbed his hand and dragged him indoors. But even the company of friends couldn't cool his rage. "Frank was so angry, poor baby," Ava remembered. "He spent the whole time at the window upstairs screaming at the press, 'You lousy parasites, fuck off!' at the top of his lungs. He was tempted—we had to hold him—to go out and fight with them. But we finally got him downstairs, got him in front of the preacher."

It was a very small wedding, just twenty guests in all. Frank had his crew—Sanicola and Ben Barton and Stordahl and Jones and Manie (Van Heusen, who would remain allergic to marriage, except for writing songs about it, until his own at age fifty-six, was conspicuously absent)—but Ava only had Bappie, who was hoping that after Mickey and Artie (she'd attended both those weddings, too) the third time might be the charm.

But the portents weren't favorable. When Dick Jones sat down at the grand piano in Lester Sacks's living room and began to play Mendelssohn's Wedding March, he discovered that like so many pianos in prosperous homes, this one hadn't been tuned in ages. Jones tried a simpler number, "Here Comes the Bride." It didn't sound much better. Then, as Manie escorted Ava down the stairs, he tripped and they slipped three steps before regaining their balance.

The bride wore a slinky mauve cocktail dress by Howard Greer

("Wonderful designer," Ava recalled, "but you couldn't wear a stitch underneath"); the groom, a dark blue suit and a gray silk tie. The ceremony, conducted by the police court judge Joseph Sloane, was brief: the couple spoke their vows, slipped thin platinum rings on each other's fingers. Then Frank turned to the guests, grinning, and said, "Well, we finally made it! We finally made it!"

As Stordahl filmed the proceedings with a home-movie camera, the guests toasted the couple with champagne; Ava embraced Dolly, who burst into tears and patted her new daughter-in-law lovingly on the arm, unable for the moment to think of a word to say. Then the bride cut into the seven-tiered cake and, to laughter and applause, messily fed Frank a piece. Dolly came up and pinched her son's cheek. "This marriage is blessed with good luck," she told the couple. "You got married at the seventh hour on the seventh day of the eleventh month. Seven, seven, eleven. You can't miss." Marty smiled.

There was a bustle in the foyer. A butler approached Frank and handed him a note—it was a formal request, from the photographers outside in the rain: Could the newlyweds possibly come to the front door for a picture?

Sinatra went to the door and threw it open. "Who sent this? Who sent this?" he called, pointing to the press corps. "Who? You? You? You're not getting any pictures, understand? You'll get shots from our photographer when he gets around to it."

"My editor wants *my* pictures," one of them called back.

"I'll bet you fifty dollars you don't get a picture," Sinatra told him, "and another fifty dollars that if you even point your camera at me, I'll knock you on your ear."

He slammed the door and returned to the party, summoning back his smile.

———

After a while Ava went upstairs and changed into a brown Christian Dior travel suit and the mink stole Frank had given her as a wedding present. When she came back down, Manie took her aside, peering at her with his dark emotional eyes.

"Look after him, Ava. He's had some hard knocks and he's very fragile. It isn't going to be easy living with a man whose career is in a slump."

"I'll do anything to make him happy," Ava said.

"Then help him get back his self-confidence," Manie told her.

This time they went out the back door. Before the newsmen out front knew what was happening, the couple ran to a waiting car and sped to the airport, where they boarded a chartered twin-engine Beechcraft—a fantastic extravagance; Frank's idea, naturally—which would take them to Miami, where they planned to stay for a night before going on to honeymoon at the Hotel Nacional in Havana. As Ava stepped onto the plane, she realized that in the flurry of escape she had left the suitcases containing her honeymoon trousseau at Lester Sacks's house. "All I had with me was my handbag!" she recalled.

> Well, there was no point in having a fit; it would rejoin me
> sometime or other. But hell, I didn't even have the beautiful
> little nightie I'd saved for our wedding night. I didn't have a
> bathing suit. I didn't have anything to go to the beach in—
> nothing! So I slept in Frank's pajamas, at least the top half of
> them, and the next day we walked along the empty beach, me
> in the bottom half of my travel suit and Frank's jacket.

To throw reporters off the trail, they had chosen an out-of-the-way hotel, the Green Heron, on the beach in the Sunny Isles district north of town. "It was a chilly day for the beach resort and a brisk wind dotted the ocean with whitecaps," wrote the early Sinatra biographer Arnold Shaw. "As they strolled along the deserted beach in the afternoon, a lone photographer shot one of the most appealing pictures ever made of them. Their backs to the camera, they walk barefoot, hand-in-hand. Frank's trousers are rolled up above his thin ankles. And Ava is wearing Frank's jacket over an old blouse and sports skirt."

It is an appealing picture, and an iconic one, but Ava Gardner had a different view of the moment. "Naturally a photographer was lying in wait and snapped a shot of us, barefoot, holding hands," she remembered.

> I've always thought it was a sad little photograph, a sad little
> commentary on our lives then. We were simply two young
> people so much in love, and the world wouldn't leave us alone
> for a second. It seemed that everyone and everything was
> against us, and all we asked for was a bit of peace and privacy.

Just two kids in love . . . not exactly. Publicity was not something that could be turned on and off like a spigot. Ava seems to be setting up the argument that the world came between them, but what possessed him to book their honeymoon at the Nacional, the site of his Mafia disgrace? It only fed the stories in the press.

From the beginning, there was a third party in the marriage: the fourth estate.

In Ava's autobiography, she recalls their Havana sojourn as idyllic. "We drank a lot of Cuba libres and went out to the nightclubs and the gambling joints," she writes.

> Fortunately, most of the paparazzi seemed to have other things
> to do, so we were pretty much left alone. I don't even know
> if I would have noticed if we weren't; I was finally on my
> honeymoon with the man I loved. On one of our last nights,
> I climbed up on one of the hotel's high archways, convincing
> Frank that I was going to throw myself off. But I was just
> being mischievous, swinging along on rum and Coke with no
> intention of ending it all. I was having far too much fun.

Yet in a taped interview that didn't make it into the book, she remembered things a little differently. "Frank and I didn't start very good," Ava said.

> We went to Havana, in Cuba, and had a fight the first night.
> Who knows what we fought about? . . . I remember standing
> up, pissed drunk, on the balcony of the hotel, on the edge.
> Standing there, balancing. Frank was afraid to go near me. He
> thought I was going to jump . . . God, I was crazy!

Back in New York there was further unpleasantness with the press
the moment they stepped off the plane.

Where were the couple staying?

Frank scowled. None of their damn business.

Ava grinned and shook her head. The reporters followed the couple to the curb, where a black Cadillac stood waiting. Couldn't Frank
give them *anything*?

He'd give them something. He gestured with his fist as he opened
the car door for Ava. Then he got in the backseat and slammed the
door in their faces.

SNARLING FRANK, GIGGLING AVA BACK, the *Daily News* headline ran, over an unflattering photo of the newlyweds (unflattering,
mostly, of him: it was hard for her to take a bad picture).

His surliness was getting old, fast. As another tabloid headline
around the same time put it, pointedly: WHAT A BORE IS FRANKIE.

"Frank Sinatra evidently craves privacy," the Hearst columnist
George Sokolsky wrote.

> When these theatrical folk are on the make, they curry favor
> and seek notices and hire publicity men to spread interesting
> and exciting tales about them, true or untrue. Then they try
> the gag of seeking privacy, which some believe is of human
> interest. If it is privacy that Frank Sinatra wants he should be
> kept out of the public eye permanently. Perhaps the day might
> come when he would like to be remembered.

Soon enough, though, the press would have another tidbit to play
with: Frank had had the very sizable bill for the chartered Beechcraft,

along with the tab for the rest of the honeymoon, sent to Ava's financial manager in Los Angeles. Nancy had cleaned him out.

=====

Not only was Frank without bookings, but the press was knocking his new records. *Down Beat* wrote: "By every ordinary standard, 'London by Night' and 'April in Paris' are poorly sung. Frank sounds tired, bored, and in poor voice, to boot."

Sinatra is slightly rough around the edges in those recordings, which had been made the previous fall, but in truth the writers were just kicking him when he was down. He was an easy target in the autumn of 1951.

And he fired back, laying the blame squarely on Mitch Miller. While playing the Desert Inn in September, Frank had gone into another one of his diatribes about the generally downward trend in popular song, singling out Rosemary Clooney's recently released Columbia single, "Come On-a My House." It was a zany, fast-moving novelty number with a goofily lecherous lyric by, of all people, William Saroyan ("Come on-a my house, my house/I'm gonna give-a you candy"), set to, of all things, a hard-swinging harpsichord obbligato that presaged rock 'n' roll. Miller had been proudly responsible for the whole concept, and the record—which Clooney made under protest—sold like hotcakes.[4]

Frank had nothing bad to say about Clooney. He reserved his venom for Mitch. Word got back and Miller exploded. In November, *Billboard* noted a "long smoldering feud" between the singer and the producer, continuing: "Chief beef hinges on Sinatra claim that he isn't getting a fair shake on song material." The report quoted Frank as saying he was in talks with RCA and Capitol Records.

In fact, this was sheer invention on his part, a ploy to try to stir up some action where there was none at all. Manie Sacks had already informed Frank, with great regret, that he couldn't work up any enthusiasm for him at Victor. And as for Capitol (the only West Coast–based label), it was doing just fine with Nat "King" Cole, Dean Martin, and Peggy Lee. Who needed Sinatra?

On the November 13 broadcast of *The Frank Sinatra Show* the guests were Jack Benny and ten-year-old violinist Charles Castleman. Benny's presence helped Sinatra to garner a good review for a change. "Kidding each other's known idiosyncrasies for laughs," *Variety* wrote, Jack and Frank "sparked the show into one of the better ones [Sinatra has] done this season."

But it was faint praise: the show was sinking fast, and everyone involved knew it. When the host requested that the broadcast be relocated to Los Angeles, CBS agreed, perhaps feeling that a change of venue might slap some life into the enterprise.

Frank's return to Hollywood didn't stir up much excitement—his only real currency in that toughest of company towns was as the husband ("Mr. Gardner," the latest mean joke had it) of its hottest female star. As far as the movies were concerned, he was all but DOA: a two-picture deal with Universal, at a pathetically low fee, was the closest thing to unemployment.

Meanwhile, the newlyweds made a nod at nesting at Twin Palms. "We're going to redecorate Frank's home," Ava gushed. "I'm going to learn to make all of Frank's favorite dishes. Mama Sinatra has promised to send the recipes. Oh, it's all so thrilling and wonderful! And Mrs. Sinatra—you know, I'm not used to my new name and it takes a second before it clicks—Mrs. Frank Sinatra is the happiest girl in the world!"

And she was, sometimes. Then, in December, Frank and Ava flew to London, where Frank was to give a charity command performance before Princess Elizabeth and Prince Philip. While he was rehearsing—and yelling at his British horn section for playing too loud during the tender passages—a burglar climbed up to the Sinatras' third-floor suite at the Hotel Washington and stole $17,000 worth of jewelry, including the diamond-and-emerald necklace Frank had taken to Ava in Spain. As if that weren't trouble enough, after Ava reconsidered her plan to sing a duet with Frank (stage fright), the press reported they'd quarreled about it. Sinatra, furious at everything and everybody, gave a lackluster performance. The newspapers reported yawns among the star-studded audience.

======

Soon after Frank and Ava relocated to Hollywood, they sat down with Sinatra's new West Coast press agent, Mack Millar, to figure out how to rehabilitate the singer's image.

Millar, an old Hollywood hand, looked his client in the eye and gave him the bad news: Frank was going to have to end his feud with the press and woo the newspapers. Aggressively. Millar told his client that a writer at the *New York Post,* Fern Marja, was writing a six-part series on him. Why not call her and use that fabled charm and that fabled voice of his and woo the pants off of her? Sorry, Ava.

Sinatra thought about it: Maybe humility would work. Anything was worth a try at this point. He phoned Marja and, on his nickel, gave her an hour's worth of honey. He explained, carefully and undefensively, how often he felt he'd been misquoted and mistreated by the press—but then, in the next breath, allowed that he'd sometimes mistreated them back. "I lost control of my temper and said things," he told the young reporter. "They were said under great stress and pressure. I'm honestly sorry."

While he spoke the last sentence, he made a hideous face, a face like a medieval gargoyle, for nobody's benefit but his own.

Marja asked, over the scratchy connection, how Frank was feeling.

He was much better. Better all the time.

And his voice?

It had been a little rocky there for a while, but it was improving, too.

And he and Ava—?

They were extremely happy.

The articles appeared in the *Post.* Fern Marja, young but nobody's fool, acknowledged her initial skepticism about Sinatra's insistent niceness, but then admitted he had won her over. The *Post* called the series "The Angry Voice."

Double Dynamite, with Frank billed third after Jane Russell and Groucho Marx, opened on Christmas Day. The movie had been sitting in the can for three full years while Howard Hughes tried to figure out what to do with it. There was nothing much to do with it—the picture was an out-and-out dog. But in December 1951, as RKO was divesting its theater chains and hemorrhaging money, it was time to get the thing out there and try to make a couple of dollars back.

Nobody was buying. "Even the most ardent devotees of Frank Sinatra, Jane Russell and Groucho Marx," wrote Bosley Crowther in the *New York Times,* "will find meager Christmas cheer in 'Double Dynamite,' yesterday's arrival at the Paramount. Whatever that sizzling title is supposed to mean, this thin little comedy is strictly a wet firecracker."

That sizzling title, to the puzzlement of nobody except Bosley Crowther, referred to Jane Russell's size 38D breasts, a subject of endless fascination to Howard Hughes—and, to paraphrase Bob Hope, the two and only marketing gimmicks the sinking studio had for this crummy picture. (So low had Sinatra's reputation sunk, and so complete was Hughes's detestation of him, that Frank didn't even appear on the poster, which—it was a simpler time—showed Groucho's eyes popping after he got a load of Jane's chest.)

The story, such as it was, concerned a meek bank clerk, Johnny Dalton—Sinatra, in his last Bashful Frankie role ever—who saves a gangster from being beaten up by rival thugs, thus earning the crook's deepest gratitude. The crook, who runs a bookie joint, gives Johnny a thousand-dollar reward—and then, with a few phone calls, parlays Johnny's thousand into sixty grand. Voilà—the timid little clerk now has enough money to marry his ladylove and fellow bank wage slave, the pneumatic, perpetually sneering, helium-voiced Russell. Except that his sudden wealth arouses everyone's suspicions. Groucho, as the philosophical waiter in the couple's favorite luncheonette, hijacks the picture.

It's all kind of low-grade fun for a little while. Frank is charming and natural, despite the tiresomeness of the milquetoast act, and his scenes with Groucho are pretty good, their on-set enmity notwithstanding. The most surreally delightful touch is Nestor Paiva's energetic turn as the sunglasses-wearing bookie: with his bald dome and dark round lenses, he bears an eerie resemblance to 1960s photos of Sinatra's great and good friend Sam Giancana.

Then comes the world's cheesiest process shot (even Robert De Grasse couldn't make this dog look good) as Frank and Groucho skip down a soundstage sidewalk with a street scene shakily projected behind them, singing "It's Only Money," the lousy would-be title song (one of the two mediocre tunes Sammy Cahn and Jule Styne dashed off for the occasion), and your heart sinks for just how bad movies can be sometimes.

Double Dynamite fizzled, like the dud it was.

———

Frank kept reading. His nose was always in some tome or other, especially when he was flying (which was often). And there were a lot of good books to read in late 1951. There was John Hersey's *Hiroshima* and *The Diary of Anne Frank* and John Gunther's big book about the United States and Churchill's and Eisenhower's memoirs and *Kon-Tiki* by Thor Heyerdahl and *The Caine Mutiny*. Then somebody gave him a great big doorstop of a novel called *From Here to Eternity*, James Jones's scathing postwar portrait of the prewar U.S. Army. Once Frank started reading it, he couldn't put it down.

Early in the novel, there was a character Frank couldn't stop thinking about. His name was Angelo Maggio, and he was a buck private from Atlantic Avenue, Brooklyn, "a tiny curly-headed Italian with narrow bony shoulders jutting from his undershirt." A fast-talking, wisecracking, no-shit street guy who liked to drink and play cards and craps and pool and cared little about Army discipline. Frank read all the Maggio parts raptly, speaking his dialogue along with him. He knew this guy. More than that. He was this guy.

The book had come out in February and immediately shot to the top of the best-seller lists. In March, Harry Cohn of Columbia Pictures bought the screen rights for $85,000—a fortune in those days, especially for a novel that was critical of the Army in an era of fear and conformity. Soon cynics were calling the project "Cohn's Folly."

But from the moment Frank laid his eyes on Maggio, he was obsessed with wanting to play him. Fuck *Double Dynamite*. It was forgotten anyway. All he needed to turn his career around, Frank began to tell everyone around him over and over and over, was one good role. This was that role. (And it was better than good. As Tom Santopietro wrote in *Sinatra in Hollywood:* "No wonder Sinatra felt desperate to play Maggio—the character is ingratiating, complex, a bit dim-witted, vulnerable, and ultimately doomed. It was a role that had Oscar written all over it.") That he was the last person on anyone's mind to play Maggio was a mere technicality.

The Empress Club, London, December 1951. When nothing else got in the way—
which was seldom—they cared deeply for each other.

Ava Gardner writes in her autobiography that Frank was once again having voice troubles soon after their marriage, but she doesn't say why. It doesn't take much imagination to figure out why. In early 1952, Sinatra's matchless instrument was undergoing unusual physical and emotional stress, for a whole gamut of reasons. One of the new ones was his marriage itself.

Sammy Cahn's then wife, Gloria Franks, recalled a dinner she and Cahn had early on with Frank and Ava and the Axel Stordahls. "It was like we were sitting on cracked eggs," Franks said. "You never quite knew if it was going to be pleasant or there were going to be verbal daggers, or if she was not in a good mood. And Frank was so subservient to her. He was *insane* about that woman. I thought, 'My God, look at him.' He'd hold the door, pull the chair out, that kind of thing. I used to think, 'God, I don't remember seeing him do that with Nancy.' It was a whole other Frank. He was a different person around Ava. And she was . . . Ava."

It was hard work being married to Ava Gardner. It was hard work being married to Frank Sinatra, too, but there is evidence that he did the heavy lifting in the relationship. "Neither gave an inch, though I must say Frank worked harder on the marriage than she did," a friend of Ava's once said. "She's a very selfish girl."

Well, she was a movie star. And classically, show-business marriages involve one high-maintenance partner, usually the better-known spouse, and one maintainer. Frank was being pushed into the latter role. God knows he could be high-handed with friends and lovers and underlings, but Ava had a unique power over him—and all the more so as his own power waned. As a foulmouthed and dominant facsimile of Dolly (certified by Dolly), she wielded the metaphorical baton. (Jimmy Van Heusen, who when out of Frank's earshot could be scathing about all things Sinatra, took to calling her "The Man.") As a sexual volcano, she ruled him in bed. And to top it all off, she was paying the bills.

The combination was corrosive. Sinatra's voice was delicate in the best of circumstances, and now he was spending sleepless nights worrying about his career, taking downers and uppers, reading obsessively at *From Here to Eternity*, dog-earing pages, marking up the Maggio sections. He was ragged and irritable during the day, and when he snapped at Ava, she snapped right back. At a point when even getting to make love with his wife involved a lot of preliminary yelling, it was a wonder he could sing a note at all.

Yet just a week into the new year, he went into Columbia's Hollywood studio and recorded three songs in gorgeous voice and high style.

Axel Stordahl arranged and conducted, and for the first time Bill Miller was sitting at the piano. The first number, Rodgers and Hart's "I Could Write a Book," marked a new artistic peak. Singing with beautiful simplicity and perfect diction, Frank sounded like the artist he was fated to become after he had crossed the valley of the shadow of death. He made a great song sound so believably brand-new (it had debuted on Broadway in *Pal Joey* in 1940) it practically glistened with dew. Then, after the forgettable "I Hear a Rhapsody" (schmaltzily written, beautifully sung), he belted out the utterly charming (and little-known) "Walkin' in the Sunshine," a romping, brassy, bluesy jump, growling and winking his way through in a wham-bam style that looks ahead to the best of his late-1950s collaborations with Billy May:

> *Just so you know, dear, I'm gonna tell ya*
> *Your smile's my golden umbrella.*

Unfortunately, the world outside the studio wasn't listening. Frank urgently needed to get something going. He was, according to his old pal, the Paramount Theater manager Bob Weitman, "knockin' on doors."

It was February; Weitman was down in Miami, getting a tan. Someone handed him a poolside phone. The voice on the line was unmistakable. Frank wanted to know when Bob was coming back. He was in trouble.

Meet Danny Wilson, which had premiered in L.A. and San Francisco in early February, was to open in New York in late March, Sinatra told Weitman; maybe it could premiere at the joint, with him singing onstage?

Weitman shook his head. It wasn't a Paramount picture.

Frank knew, but couldn't Bob make an exception this one time? It was a nice movie—it had a lot of nice songs and a pretty good story. And it'd been getting pretty good write-ups. Frank thought it, and he, could do business.

Weitman put the question to Paramount's chairman, Barney Balaban. A long silence on the phone line. Then old Balaban growled: "What are you starting up with that guy again for?"

Weitman mulled it over and decided to go ahead anyway. "Frank was a friend and we knew he had talent," he told Earl Wilson years later. "We took a chance on him for two weeks with Frank Fontaine, June Hutton and Buddy Rich."

Ava, though, had plans of her own.

———

Metro had loaned her to 20th Century Fox for one picture,¹ an adaptation of the Hemingway short story "The Snows of Kilimanjaro." "Adaptation" is putting it extremely loosely. The script, as conceived by the producer Darryl F. Zanuck and the screenwriter Casey Robinson, took the downbeat, stream-of-consciousness tale of a writer dying of an infected wound in the shadow of the African mountain and turned it into a Hemingway extravaganza, replete with grafted-on characters and story elements from *The Sun Also Rises, A Farewell to Arms, For Whom the Bell Tolls,* and "The Short Happy Life of Francis Macomber." ("I sold Fox a short story, not my complete works," the author later complained.) In addition, the movie's writer-hero and Hemingway surrogate, Harry Street, played by Gregory Peck, would live, rather than die, at the end of the story. But then, that was big-studio moviemaking in the 1950s.

Legend has it that Papa Hemingway himself, who apparently had seen Ava in *The Killers* and liked what he'd seen, nominated her to play the love of Harry's life, "Cynthia, from Montparnasse, a model with green-gray eyes and legs like a colt, who lit a fire in Harry Street that could only be quenched by . . . *The Snows of Kilimanjaro,*" as the hard-breathing ad copy put it. The whole Technicolor mess was shot on the Fox back lot—a gigantic cyclorama painting of snowcapped Kilimanjaro was erected on Stage 8—and not in Kenya, as some Sinatra books have reported. However, it might as well have been Africa as far as Frank was concerned: production on the movie was scheduled to run from mid-February through the third week in April, and he badly wanted his wife with him for his Paramount premiere on March 26, about which he was much more nervous than he was letting on.

At first Frank refused, explosively, to let Ava do the movie at all. She told him to fuck himself. Complicated negotiations ensued. In the end, Zanuck, Robinson, and the director, Henry King, worked out a formula by which all her scenes could be shot in ten days, freeing her to get to New York in time for Frank's big show.

It didn't work out. On her tenth day of shooting, technical problems developed during a big Spanish civil war scene, outdoors, involving hundreds of extras. Rather than go into costly overtime, King approached Ava, hat in hand, and asked: Could she possibly give him one more day of work?

Ava burst into tears. Frank had been phoning her every day from New York, worrying that she wouldn't finish shooting in time. She'd kept reassuring him: Everything was going fine. What was she supposed to tell him now? Finally she worked up the courage to call Frank—who promptly blew up at her. She blew up right back. Three thousand miles apart, they couldn't even make up properly.

———

Later that week, in a report headlined SINATRA SCRAMBLES TO RECOVER FRIENDLY PUBLIC HE ONCE HAD, the old Hollywood hand Wood Soanes wrote that *Danny Wilson* had flopped so badly at its San Francisco premiere that exhibitors had demoted it to the second half of a double-feature bill in Oakland. Frank's troubles were beginning to snowball. Universal International elected not to proceed with the second film in Sinatra's two-picture deal. "And the crowning blow," Soanes wrote, "came in a decision of Music Corporation of America to withdraw as his agent."

Jules Stein and Lew Wasserman, long irritated at Sinatra in general, and long embroiled with him in a dispute over $40,000 in back commissions the agency said he owed, finally decided to cut their losses. And not quietly: MCA took out full-page ads in *Variety* and the *Hollywood Reporter* to trumpet the divorce.

Frank was devastated. (He wouldn't speak to Wasserman for years.) On the advice of his publicists, he had gone to New York ten days in advance of the Paramount premiere to try to mend fences with the press. But by this point he couldn't even manage a good entrance. Stepping off the plane, he obligingly offered to pose for pictures—and then, when Joan Blondell came down the stairs right after him, the photographers ditched him en masse. Two of them, though, paused for a moment in front of Sinatra. "Fuck you," they told him in unison.

On the advice of his New York PR men, Frank agreed to suck it up. He sent a note to the National Press Photographers Association. "I'll always be made up and ready in case you want to take any pictures of me," he wrote, rather pathetically. He got no takers. He even lowered himself to a practice he had abandoned long ago, dropping in on disc jockeys to sweet-talk them into spinning his latest record—in this case, "I Hear a Rhapsody," with "I Could Write a Book" on the flip side, from the January session.

In Sinatra's new upside-down world, all journalists were welcome. When the jazz columnist George Frazier, freelancing for *Cosmopolitan,* interviewed him backstage during rehearsals at the Paramount, the writer had the nerve—and the leverage at that point—to inform Frank that he might not write a completely complimentary piece. Frank's first reaction came straight from the heart: he winced, then gave Frazier a long, angry stare. Then he remembered the fix he was in. "Nodding, he became amiable again," Frazier wrote.

> "Look," he said, "I won't mind if it pans me just as long as it helps me correct the things I've been doing wrong" . . . It was the first time I ever heard him concede that Sinatra is only human. For the first time, he seems skeptical of his own infallibility . . . He no longer takes the view that he is a law unto

himself. His sullenness has given way to an authentic eager-
ness to be pleasant and cooperative.

———

Earl Wilson did all he could, up to and including papering the house,
to try to ensure a successful Paramount premiere for Frank. "As one of
his surviving and loyal friends in the press, I tried to create excitement
for him," Wilson recalled.

> The Paramount gave me a couple of rows of seats for VIPs
> whom I got out for the opening on March 26, 1952. Jackie
> Gleason, Phil Silvers, Ted Lewis, Jimmy Durante and the
> columnists stood up in the audience and sang out greetings to
> Frankie, and I reported it in the papers: "Jule Styne reached for
> his handkerchief when Frank sang 'The Birth of the Blues.'"

Maybe he was blowing his nose. After all, a claque was just a claque, no
matter how high the star wattage. The rest of the crowd, while enthusiastic, were dry-eyed. After the *Times* reviewer gave his kind word about
Meet Danny Wilson, he reflected on the "somewhat subdued" crowd,
noting: "Perhaps it is the beginning of the end of an era."

A feature article in the *New York World-Telegram and Sun* was
far less genteel. GONE ON FRANKIE IN '42; GONE IN '52, read the
three-column headline. And to put a finer point on it, the subhead:
"What a Difference a Decade Makes—Empty Balcony." The article
was cast in the form of an open letter from the reporter Muriel Fischer.
Fischer was young and ambitious, and her tone was snarky. "I saw you
last night. But I didn't get 'that old feeling,'" she wrote.

> I sat in the balcony. And I felt kind of lonely. It was so
> empty. The usher said there were 750 seats in the second
> balcony—and 749 were unfilled . . . Later I stood outside the
> stage entrance. About a dozen people were waiting around.

Three girls were saying "Frankie" soft and swoonlike. I asked, "How do you like Frankie?" They said, "Frankie Laine, he's wonderful." I heard a girl sighing, "I'm mad about him," so I asked her who. "Johnnie Ray," she cried. All of a sudden, Mr. Sinatra, I felt sort of old!

Johnnie Ray wasn't just that season's sensation but a game changer: a skinny, androgynous, half-deaf, sob-singing white soul singer who pounded the piano and writhed on the bench—even sometimes on the floor—while he performed. Elvis and Jerry Lee Lewis were in the wings. Just four months earlier, Ray had been all but unknown, but then along came "Cry," his million-selling 45 on the Columbia subsidiary Okeh. The lyrics, by the one-hit-wonder composer Churchill Kohlman, were sheer schmaltz:

If your sweetheart sends a letter of goodbye
It's no secret you'll feel better if you cry

and Ray's vocalizing was appropriately sappy. He had a theatrical way of hanging on to syllables ("but it's on-lyy fal-se ee-motions-uh that you feel-l-l"), and something about his whole sound—that Great Plains accent (he was an Oregonian, half Native American) and keening voice, that big echo behind him—chimed with the era's taste for emotional bombast (Mario Lanza; Laine) and pointed toward a growing American predilection for countrified songs and singers such as Brenda Lee, Teresa Brewer, Patti Page, and, of course, the great Hank Williams himself. We were still a spread-out, lonely nation in those blue-highway days, and something about those high, lonesome sounds struck home in ten thousand back-roads burgs—and, maybe, served as welcome counterpoint to such urban (and ethnic) sensations as Uncle Miltie, *Your Show of Shows,* and Martin and Lewis, not to mention Sinatra himself.

Under the headline JOHNNIE'S GOLDEN RAYS DAZZLE MUSIC

BUSINESS, *Down Beat* wrote that Ray had "most certainly established himself as the phenom of the music-record business of the second half of the century." Big words—there were many phenoms still to come. But the point was made: Bing and Frank, those sensations of the century's *first* half, were old news. Even Earl Wilson succumbed. "Do you folks suffer, too, from juke box jitters, or Johnny [*sic*] Rayitis?" the columnist wrote in March. "Well, you will. They call Johnny Ray 'the Heat Ray' and he's the wildest, craziest, looniest, goofiest, weirdest singer since Frankie Swoonatra . . . He has this broken-hearted voice and . . . when he opens soon at the Copacabana, we expect to hear crying all over town, especially at the other night clubs."

With Ava in tow (she'd finally come to New York, so the fighting and making up could commence afresh), Frank attended Ray's Copa premiere in early April—more on his wife's say-so (and of course to be seen) than because he really wanted to be there. When Earl Wilson asked him what he thought of the new sensation, Frank said, "I'd like to tell you, but my girl won't let me."

His girl was behaving as singularly as ever. One night at the Paramount, Johnnie Ray returned the favor and came backstage to meet Sinatra, entourage in tow. According to eyewitnesses, Frank was gracious, introducing Ava to one and all and making amiable chitchat. Then he was called out of the room on a business matter. While he was gone, Ava climbed onto Ray's lap and began stroking his hair and cooing to him. Frank returned while she was still at it. After an awkward moment, he grabbed his unrepentant wife's arm, yanked her off the fruity upstart's lap, and hustled her out of the room.

=====

On April 1, CBS finally pulled the plug on Sinatra's TV show. Ratings had continued to erode (introducing an act on *Texaco Star Theater,* Berle smirked, "These people have never been seen on TV before—they were on the Sinatra show last week"). Ekco had dropped its sponsorship in early January. Since then, except for fifteen minutes of the

Valentine's Day broadcast underwritten by Elgin watches, *The Frank Sinatra Show* had been entirely sustaining, a straight cash drain to the network of $41,500 a week. Word around the industry was that CBS had taken a million-dollar hit on the program.

———

Frank was now reduced to booking himself, and the only engagements he could scrape up were a couple of concerts in Hawaii. He mulled it over for about a half minute, and agreed to go. The weather in New York was cold and rainy; he could use a change of scene. He had nothing else happening.

Ava, on the other hand, had been summoned by MGM to Mexico, to shoot something called *Sombrero*—a frothy confection about three pairs of lovers, complete with cockfights and bullfights and beauty contests.

It sounded like *The Kissing Bandit* warmed over, Frank told her. Why not come to Hawaii? He could do a little work, then they could relax.

She smiled mischievously.

Ava (who these days was signing autographs "Ava Sinatra") wired MGM's vice president Eddie Mannix that a vacation trip with her husband unfortunately prevented her from being able to report, et cetera—and Mannix wired her right back, expressly forbidding her to go to Hawaii.

Three days later, in Honolulu, Ava got another wire from Mannix's office, informing her that Metro-Goldwyn-Mayer had sent Yvonne De Carlo to Mexico in her stead, and that Miss Gardner was now officially on suspension. Stop. All further salary and benefits were to be withheld. Stop.

She flipped the telegram into the wastebasket. They would come crawling back, she knew it.

Frank winked at her. But in truth, he was afraid. He was broke—and now she had nothing coming in, either. The chicken feed he was getting paid in Hawaii wouldn't take them very far.

The weather on Kauai mirrored his mood: heavy rain on a Sunday afternoon. Ava was back at the hotel in Honolulu, and Frank was playing a county fair in a tent. A leaky tent.

He pulled aside a flap and peered out at the audience. It was just a couple hundred red-faced tourists and hicks in aloha shirts and jeans and muumuus. Jesus Christ. The rain was drumming on the canvas, dripping on the ground. There was no orchestra, just an upright piano on a wooden platform. He closed the flap and looked at Bill Miller sitting on a folding chair, lean as a spider and pale as death—in Hawaii!—and sipping a cup of tea. Miller raised his eyebrows. Sinatra shook his head. Soon he'd be playing revival meetings.

Miller's thin lips formed into something like a smile.

Suddenly two brown-skinned girls in grass skirts came in, carrying flowered garlands, beaming. They dropped the leis over Frank's head, one by one, giggling, covering his cheeks with little kisses, and even as he grinned, his eyes grew moist.

Frank turned to Miller. Should they do it?

Miller nodded and rose. Frank pulled the canvas aside and walked out onto the little stage, the garlands around his neck. The small crowd went nuts the second they saw him, clapping over their heads, whistling, stamping the ground. For a minute you couldn't even hear the rain on the tent. Sinatra was still smiling, the first time he'd been happy in weeks. He sat on the edge of the stage, dangling his legs, and said: "What do you want to hear?"

———

On the plane back from Hawaii (he and Ava had quarreled, and she'd flown back ahead of him) he sat with his dog-eared copy of *From Here to Eternity* on his lap, rereading for the tenth time all the Maggio sections—the scenes with the bugler Prewitt, whorehouse scenes, drunk scenes, the fatal fight with Fatso—and marking them up in pencil. After he landed, he began sending telegrams: to Harry Cohn; to the director the Columbia chief had chosen for *Eternity*, Fred Zinnemann; to the producer, Buddy Adler; to the screenwriter, Daniel Taradash.

One wire a week per man, every week, beseeching, cajoling, joking, but always coming straight to the point: he was the only man who could play this role. He signed every telegram "Maggio."

═══

One night in early June, Sinatra recorded five songs at the Columbia studios in Hollywood. (Three songs per session, the maximum before the musicians went into overtime, was the norm.) It was Frank's third recording date of only four that year, and the last on the West Coast that he would do for the label. Mitch Miller had flown out for the occasion.

Columbia was about to announce that it was not going to renew Frank's contract. He hadn't come close to making back the more than $100,000 Manie Sacks had advanced him to pay his taxes. Miller was looking for just one last hit from Sinatra to slow the flow of red ink, and he and Sinatra were on the coolest possible terms.

There were any number of bones of contention, not least of them the fact that Frank didn't want Mitch around when he was recording. The headstrong executive, as brilliant and domineering in his own way as Sinatra, tended to march in and take over all aspects of a session, even the recording engineer's role of manning the dials in the control room. "Frank didn't want you turning dials," recalled the drummer Johnny Blowers.

> But Mitch did [turn them], and then all of a sudden one day Frank had as much as he could stand. Quietly, he looked in the control room, pointed his finger, and said, "Mitch—out." When Mitch didn't move, Sinatra turned to Hank Sanicola. "Henry, move him." To Mitch, he said, "Don't you ever come in the studio when I'm recording again."

Now Mitch was back. And while Frank had decided to make the best of a bad situation and go ahead with the session, Miller was bent on showing him who was boss. Columbia's West Coast A&R man Paul Weston, who was nominally producing, stood aside and let Miller take over.

One of the songs Mitch had high hopes for—and let us remember that Sinatra had the right of refusal—was a twangy piece of nonsense called "Tennessee Newsboy." To give the tune the right country-and-western-flavored sound, Miller had hired a steel guitar player named Wesley "Speedy" West, who, as Weston recalled, "was known for making the guitar sound like a chicken. Frank sang the vocal, and Mitch rushed out into the studio, and everybody thought he was going to congratulate Frank for getting through, because he did it well. Instead, he rushed right past Frank, and embraced Speedy West, because he'd made a good chicken noise on the guitar. Frank was disgusted."

Nothing Frank recorded that night became a hit, but "The Birth of the Blues," orchestrated by the clarinetist, saxophonist, and arranger Heinie Beau, was every bit as brassy as January's "Walkin' in the Sunshine," and much tougher. Sinatra's singing had a forward-looking, microphone-cord-snapping authority, the same kind of authority he would wield in Vegas ten years later. And his little vocal snarl at the end was certainly directed at the goateed tormentor behind the control-room glass.

———

He was still booking himself, scrounging whatever gigs he could, running around the map. Meanwhile, Ava was sitting at home, nursing a grudge. "Today is our seventh anniversary," she told *Modern Screen* that spring. "Seven *months*. You want to see your husband, and where is he? Playing the Chez Paree in Chicago! Then he's hitting St. Louis . . . it's rough."

In late May, despite feeling lousy, she'd done her noble-wife bit by attending Frank's opening at the Cocoanut Grove in L.A.—and then he went and ignited their usual tinderbox by winking at some broad in the audience. Afterward, having drunk too much for a change, they started going at it, then he gave her a hard slap that sent her reeling. She tripped over a table and landed on the floor, and suddenly she was bleeding.

An ambulance rushed her to Cedars of Lebanon Hospital, where Dr. Leon Krohn, a gynecologist and friend of Frank's, discovered that Ava had suffered a miscarriage. She honestly hadn't known she was pregnant—or perhaps she'd just tried to pretend she didn't know.

When the Hollywood columnist Harrison Carroll interviewed her a week later, she was still hurting—and still mad. Would Ava accompany Frank to his engagement at the Chez Paree in Chicago? "I don't know," she replied coldly. "It will depend on how I feel."

It wasn't just Frank's anger, and the lost pregnancy, that ate at her; there was also her continued tenancy in MGM purgatory.

This she tried to brazen out. Carroll wrote:

> Under present conditions, Ava isn't anxious to get off suspension. "I believe," she says, "that the studio has given me a series of bad parts and has showed a lack of interest in my career."

The truth was that she was as undecided about her own career as she was about having children, or about her marriage to Sinatra. "She is unwilling to admit she cares about what she is doing," noted Stanley Kramer, who would direct her in *On the Beach* several years later. "She regards such an admission as weakness of some kind, with the result that she will not give of herself as fully or as effectively as she can."

"Ava had a reckless look about her," Nancy junior wrote, remembering her first rapt impressions, as a twelve-year-old, of her father's new wife:

> She didn't bother with her hair or makeup—it was sort of haphazard. No matter. Her hair was naturally curly. On my first

weekend with them in Palm Springs she was wearing her hair short. She would dive into the pool, looking like a goddess on the diving board, swim a few lengths, throw on a terry robe, come inside, kneel down in front of the wall heater, turn on the fan, dry her hair with a shake and a few rubs with her fingers, and be a goddess again. No makeup, perfect skin, and a wonderful voice . . .

She had the magnetism that few stars possess . . . At last, in my preteenage wisdom, I had some understanding of why Daddy had left us.

This was what MGM was attempting to deal with. It was the quicksilver essence of stardom, all the more potent for its ambivalence.[2] As for the studio's lack of interest in her career, to a certain extent it was simply repaying her in kind. She had turned down work, disobeyed directives, been generally careless. And the movies were a tough business. In theory, MGM had every interest in furthering her career, but in those studio days, as now, good parts came along when they came along, and actors kept working if they wanted to keep getting paid. Metro had given her *Show Boat*—then it had given her *Lone Star*. With nothing else lying around, the studio had loaned her to Fox. What else was new? Bette Davis, whom Ava idolized, followed *All About Eve* with . . . *Payment on Demand*. An actor *worked*. And just then, Ava wasn't working.

Frank was—barely. At the Chez Paree, which could seat 1,200, one night he drew 150 customers. At the Desert Inn, he sang to half-full houses of wildcatters and cattle ranchers, and suffered from Vegas Throat. Ava flew up on the weekends, and complained the whole time.

But then, as she'd predicted, Metro came crawling back. In truth, her agent Benton Cole saved her bacon, reasoning with Eddie Mannix: She was a big star. Metro was a big studio. They needed each other. For its part, the studio agreed to halt the suspension and reinstate her salary, effective immediately—she would even get back what she'd been docked. Furthermore, it was contract time, so MGM offered her a new seven-year, multipicture deal, with compensation graduating from $90,000 to $130,000 a film.

Her agent was happy. Ava wasn't.

She wanted (or Frank wanted) a clause written into her contract stipulating that she and her husband could work together. The project they had in mind was an adaptation of a 1946 musical called *St. Louis Woman,* with a book co-written by Countee Cullen, music by Harold Arlen, and lyrics by Johnny Mercer. The show had been a middling success on Broadway, but it had a great pedigree, and MGM wasn't averse to it per se.

What it was averse to was Frank Sinatra.

The studio lawyers stroked their chins for a minute, and came back with a codicil titled "Services of Frank Sinatra"—or, as it came to be known around Metro, the Frank Sinatra Clause. It read:

a) Should we buy the rights to and produce a photoplay based on "St. Louis Woman," we agree that she will be assigned to do this picture and we further agree that we will employ Frank Sinatra to appear in the photoplay.

b) Should we not acquire the rights to "St. Louis Woman" or produce a photoplay based on this property, then we agree that at some time prior to the expiration of her contract, we will do a picture with her in which Frank Sinatra will also appear.

The clause wasn't worth the paper it was written on. It didn't oblige MGM to make *St. Louis Woman,* and as for hiring Sinatra somewhere down the line, well—seven years was a long time.

But the addition satisfied Ava, and, even more important at that sensitive moment, it satisfied Frank. She signed.

In return, Metro sent her to hell.

She was to report to work immediately on *Ride, Vaquero!* yet another dog of a Western, to be shot largely on location in Kanab, Utah, in the

hottest part of the summer. It was the foothills of the Rockies, a hundred dusty miles from civilization of any kind: "the asshole of creation,"
recalled her co-star Howard Keel. "Beautiful territory, but we were out
there for about, oh, Christ, a month, and there was nothing there and
nothing to do there. Nothing."

Nothing, that is, except drink and fuck. Ava did a lot of the former
and some of the latter with the stuntmen, and a little of both with the
director, John Farrow, a cold-eyed drunk who came on to her so relentlessly that she finally gave in out of sheer boredom, hating herself for
it afterward and hating Farrow, too, who was even mean to the horses.[3]

———

When Sinatra wasn't being ignored, he was being attacked. His old
nemesis Lee Mortimer still wasn't through with him. The columnist
went at Frank hard in 1952 with an *American Mercury* piece called
"Frank Sinatra Confidential/Gangsters in the Night Clubs" that
pinned Mafia control of show business squarely on the singer's skinny
shoulders. Mortimer extended the theme in a book called *U.S.A. Confidential,* which he co-authored with his uncle and *Daily Mirror* boss,
Jack Lait.

In a time of ringing public piety, a season when Dwight Eisenhower was making common cause with Joseph McCarthy to further his
presidential campaign, Sinatra decided to wax confessional. He hired
a publicist named Irving Fein (whose main client was Jack Benny) to
ghostwrite a long apologia—and to place the piece with Hearst. The
two-part article, titled "Frankly Speaking," ran under Sinatra's name
in two July issues of *American Weekly,* the syndicate's Sunday sup-
plement. Fein's version of Frank was lavishly contrite. "Most of my
troubles with the press were my own fault," the piece began. It then
tried to milk sympathy by playing up Frank's supposedly rough childhood in those purported Hoboken slums. His poor parents, Fein wrote,
"needed whatever money I could bring into the house"—thus young
Frankie had had to resort to "hooking candy from the corner store, then

little things from the five-and-dime, then change from cash registers, and finally, we were up to stealing bicycles."

It was an odd foundation on which to lay his denial of any associations with organized crime.

And then there was the failure of his marriage to Nancy, for which he knew America blamed him. Yet in fact, the Frank of the article pointed out, he had been not blameworthy but heroic. Having realized a year into his first marriage that he had mistaken friendship for love, he'd strived, out of family mindedness, to make it work anyway. Should he have been less public about his pursuit of Ava? He should have— but when you're so in love (Fein wrote), it's hard to think about things like that. Besides, he insisted, he and Ava had never dated until after his separation from Nancy.

Any reader who bought all that would love the windup. "Well, there it is," Fein-as-Frank wrote, inflated with phony piety. "That's my side of the story, and I must say I feel better for having gotten it off my chest. I know that I never meaningly hurt anyone, and for any wrongs I may have done through emotional acts or spur-of-the-moment decisions, I humbly apologize."

"That should have told you right there that Frank didn't write that thing," his former gofer Nick Sevano said years later. "He's never apologized to anyone in his life."

Decades afterward, the memory of the piece still stung. "When I recently asked Dad whether he wrote it," his daughter Nancy wrote in 1995, "he said succinctly, 'It's C-R-A-P. They made the whole thing up.'"

Yes, and he paid them to do it.

Landing in El Paso en route to Mexico City, August 1951.
They oscillated constantly between hot intimacy and cold
distance. And the press ate it up.

I t would be a very busy fall. "Ava Gardner, upon finishing 'Vaquero,'
goes directly to New York for the opening of 'Snows of Kilimanjaro'
Sept. 17," Hedda Hopper wrote from Hollywood, soon after Labor
Day.

She then returns here to prepare for her journey to Africa and
wait for Frank Sinatra to finish his night club engagements.

They both will leave for location around Oct. 9, and Ava hopes they'll have time to visit North Carolina so she can introduce Frank to her family.

Frank not only goes to Africa with her, but will remain on location there unless business calls him elsewhere.

Ava was going to shoot *Mogambo,* a remake of the 1932 Clark Gable–Jean Harlow sizzler *Red Dust. Mogambo* would be a considerable step up from *Ride, Vaquero!*—Gable would be starring again (and the newcomer Grace Kelly co-starring), and the great John Ford, as opposed to the considerably less than great John Farrow, would be directing. Ava was excited. "After all," she recalled, "I still remembered sneaking into the theater balcony in Smithfield, Virginia in 1932 and swooning as my hero Clark Gable tried to decide between Jean Harlow and Mary Astor in *Red Dust.*"

As for Frank, his new agent, Abe Lastfogel of William Morris, was making the best of the hand he'd been dealt. The first gig was at Bill Miller's (formerly Ben Marden's) Riviera,[1] in Fort Lee, New Jersey, the place that had helped launch Eddie Fisher. (Sinatra might have gotten in with a little help from the wiseguys who ran the club's clandestine casino, Angelo "Gyp" DeCarlo and Longy Zwillman.) Frank opened there on Friday the fifth. The reviews were good, if a little backhanded. "Whatever Sinatra ever had for the bobbysoxers, he now has for the café mob," *Variety* wrote, going on to commend him "for self-assurance and a knowing way with a crowd, whatever the misadventures of his personal life and career."

Ava flew in on Wednesday the tenth. That night, before the first show in Fort Lee, she accompanied him to the Firemen's Ball at the Union Club in Hoboken.

It was a favor for Marty Sinatra, and it was a disaster for Frank. Maybe his confidence was down; maybe, after his recent run of bad luck, the local crowd smelled blood. Their boy had made good and gotten too big for his britches, then the world had cut him down to size;

now it was Hoboken's turn. "He sang onstage that night and hit some clinkers, and so people booed him and threw fruit and stuff, kidding around," recalled his boyhood friend Tony "Mac" Macagnano. "Oh, did he get mad."

And when Sinatra got mad, he stayed mad. On his way out of the club, he told a cop he knew, "I'll never come back and do another thing for the people of Hoboken as long as I live." He would be as good as his word, not returning to the Square Mile City for decades. Once, flying over his hometown years later, he spat at the plane window.

═══

The premiere of *Snows of Kilimanjaro* was September 17 at the Rivoli. Ava's nephew Billy Grimes, a North Carolina college student in town to visit his famous aunt, remembered: "There were twenty thousand people there. Police barricades were up, and spotlights and flashbulbs were everywhere. There were at least fifty Pinkerton guards trying to control the crowd."

The fuss was all for Ava. (Sammy Davis Jr., who was in town at the same time, recalled spotting Sinatra walking in Times Square one afternoon, alone and unrecognized.) After the movie, Frank proceeded to the Thirtieth Street studio for his final Columbia recording session. Mitch Miller was present to seal the fade-out. Percy Faith, rather than Stordahl, conducted the orchestra. The one and only song Sinatra would wax that night, written by a twenty-three-year-old wunderkind named Cy Coleman, was a perfect valedictory to both the label and Miller. It was called "Why Try to Change Me Now." Frank sang it exquisitely:

Don't you remember, I was always your clown,
Why try to change me now?

After the musicians faded to silence, Miller turned on the studio intercom.

"That's it, Frank," he said, in a flat voice.

And that was it. Sinatra's association with Columbia was over. He was now officially adrift, on a cold, dark sea.

Billy Grimes, who had gone to the opera after the *Kilimanjaro* premiere, had come afterward to the recording session at Frank's invitation. When it was over, they rode back to the Hampshire House in silence. Ava met them at the door.

"Well! What whorehouse have you two been to?" she said.

"Whorehouse?" Billy said. "I've been to an opera house!"

"That's the worst excuse I've ever heard!" Ava told him.

Earl Wilson stopped by the Hampshire House the next day to interview the couple. "Breakfast with the Sinatras is . . . well . . . sort of different," he wrote.

> It was . . . about 2 p.m. Ava was in white silk pajamas and housecoat. Frank was dressed. Both were waiting for room service to bring the food . . . Ava meanwhile sucking a lollypop.
>
> "How long've you been married now?" I asked Ava.
>
> "Ten months in about a week," she said. "Twelve months on Nov. 7. A whole fat year! Anybody want a lollypop?"
>
> "It's true about you wanting a family?" I asked later.
>
> "Well, sure, anytime. I'm ready," Ava answered. "Maybe in Africa . . ."
>
> Frank was by now in the next room listening to a ball game.
>
> "He's going with me. He's going to do some theaters around Nairobi. God, I look sick, don't I?" She was looking at herself in a mirror.
>
> She referred to chest pains she suffered from a fall in Hollywood.

Lollipops and silk pajamas aside, there was a lot of psychodrama packed into this little meeting. *Maybe in Africa . . . He's going with me.*

He's going to do some theaters around Nairobi. (Really?) *God, I look sick, don't I?*

Their volatility was at its peak. "The battles between Ava Gardner and Frank Sinatra are getting louder and longer," Erskine Johnson had noted in a recent column. Now things were about to blow.

That night she accompanied him to the Riviera and, in the packed house, spotted a head of blond hair glowing softly at ringside: Marilyn Maxwell. As Frank softly sang

You're all that I desire,
Love me

his lower lip gave that patented quiver. Ava looked at her husband, who at that moment was singing in Miss Maxwell's general direction. It was all she needed.

She stood up in the middle of the song. *Fuck this shit.* She stomped toward the exit.

She went back to the Hampshire House, took off her platinum wedding ring, scrawled a bitter note on hotel stationery, sealed the note and the ring in an envelope, and left the envelope on the bed. Then she packed her bags and caught the early-morning flight to Los Angeles.

The hotel bill would be sent to her.

Billy Grimes recalled many years later that when he left New York to return to North Carolina, Sinatra asked him if he needed cab fare. Billy, who had $40 in his pocket—decent money in that year—told Frank that he was fine. But then Frank, who, as Billy and the rest of the world knew, was "nearly broke and unsure of his future," pressed a $100 bill into his hand.

Sinatra badly needed the next booking Lastfogel had secured for him, a week at the Chase Hotel in St. Louis—and badly wanted to break the date. He was climbing the walls with anxiety: once more Ava wouldn't take his calls, wouldn't even talk to Sanicola. Lastfogel insisted Sinatra go to St. Louis: candidly speaking, his career was teetering. In the meantime, Hank had to ply his boss, who was by turns agitated and despondent, with uppers to get him started in the morning, downers to try to give him some rest at night. Frank would sometimes sit on the edge of the bed, talking in a monotone about the futility of life. Hank was keeping careful track of the .38, making sure it was unloaded at all times, the bullets inaccessible.

Somewhere during the trip from New York to St. Louis, Ava's wedding ring vanished. Frank had a duplicate made, at no small expense (the money advanced by William Morris against his next paycheck), and sent by overnight courier to the Chase Hotel.

On October 7, the wire services quoted Earl Wilson as saying Frank and Ava were desperately trying to avert "a crackup of their marriage."

"We're having oral battles and I'm trying to fix it all up," Sinatra told the columnist. When Wilson phoned Ava, she blamed the marital problems on "conflict in commitments requiring separation for weeks at a time."

The conflict in commitments had nothing to do with it. Ava could easily have gone to St. Louis for a week. Instead, she was back in Hollywood, doing the few things she had to do to prepare for *Mogambo,* but mostly going to parties, like Marion Davies's giant soiree for Johnnie Ray, where Fernando Lamas looked deeply into her green eyes and she didn't mind a bit . . .

———

Sinatra had been continuing his telegram barrage of the *From Here to Eternity* principals, but now that he was back in town, he decided to pursue the matter directly. He phoned Harry Cohn and invited him out to lunch.

It was important. Cohn wouldn't be sorry.

Cohn, a petty tyrant who until World War II kept an autographed picture of Benito Mussolini on his desk (like the Italian dictator he had a firm jaw, a bald pate, and bulging emotional eyes), had started

Columbia Pictures in the 1920s on a shoestring (and a Mob loan) and built it into a major studio. He was proud of his friendships with gangsters, proud of his reputation as a tough character. His actors jumped when he yelled; the riding crop he wieled to emphasize his points got their attention. He loved money, he loved the ladies, he loved horse racing, and he loved making movies. Cohn had first met Sinatra when Frank was still big and Columbia still smacked of Poverty Row. Even as late as 1949, Frank had been in a position to do Cohn a favor: at the studio chief's request, Sinatra had arranged for a minor Columbia comedy, *Miss Grant Takes Richmond,* to premiere at the Capitol, where the singer was making a personal appearance. The picture did good business on the strength of Frank's box office.

Now Columbia was one of the Big Five and Sinatra was on the skids. Tough luck. What could the singer possibly have to talk about that would be of interest? The studio chief accepted the invitation out of nostalgia and mild curiosity.

Once the waiter had taken their menus, Sinatra hunched down and fixed Cohn with those searchlight blue eyes. "Harry, I want to play Maggio."

Cohn shook his head in exasperation. This was what was so important? He had read the first telegram, thrown the rest away. "You must be out of your fuckin' mind," he told Frank. "This is an actor's part, not a crooner's."

"Harry, you've known me for a long time. This part was written about a guy like me. I'm an actor, Harry. Give me a chance to act."

Cohn buttered a roll and munched on it, staring out the window.

Desperate to get Cohn's attention back, Frank went to the one subject he knew would grab him. "About the money—" he began.

"Who's talking money?" Cohn said. "But what about the money?"

"I've been getting a hundred fifty thousand a picture—"

"You *used* to get a hundred fifty thousand a picture."

"I'll do it for expenses," Sinatra said. "You cover my expenses, you got your Maggio."

"What are we talking about?"

"A grand a week. Seven-fifty. Come on, Harry—that's nothin'."

"You want it that much, Frank?"

"I told you, it was written for me. It *is* me."

"Well, we'll see, Frank. We'll see. Let me think it over."

Frank sat up straight, eyes wide. "You're not turning me down, then?"

"I was, but let's see, let's see. It's a pretty crazy idea."

"You won't regret this, Harry."

In the afterglow of the lunch he went to Ava on bended knee, with flowers, and gifts he couldn't afford, and they made up as they always did, and remembered.

———

Joan Cohn was staring at Ava Gardner's feet. Ava, who loved to go barefoot, and removed her shoes at every possible opportunity, was resting her legs on the coffee table in the living room of Harry Cohn's house, and Joan Cohn couldn't get over how small and beautifully formed the actress's feet were. Harry Cohn's second wife had been a model before they met; she had a clinical eye for beauty, and was therefore all the more able to appreciate exactly how astounding a creature Ava Gardner was.

It was a slightly surreal moment. Joan Cohn had the flu. She had been lying in bed feeling mildly hallucinatory when Ava Gardner had phoned and asked if she could come over and speak to her about a matter of great importance. Now Harry Cohn's wife was sitting in her living room in her dressing gown looking at Ava's beautiful feet and wondering why the actress had called. She prayed it wasn't something about Harry. She knew about her husband's habits; they had been married for over ten years, and her hope now after three children, one of whom had died in infancy, was that he would keep his affairs minor and private.

She asked Ava if she would like something to drink. Ava asked for vodka.

"God, Ava," Joan Cohn said, when the maid had brought the vodka, "you're going to ruin your skin."

"What the hell," Ava said, and took a long pull from the glass.

The two women looked at each other, the studio chief's wife aware that Ava seemed on edge. Finally, the actress lit a cigarette and said, "Joan, I've come to ask you a big favor."

Ava seemed to gather her courage.

"I want you to get Harry to give Frank the Maggio role in *From Here to Eternity*," she finally said.

Joan Cohn lit a cigarette herself. She stared at Ava, who continued in a nervous rush of words. "He wants that part more than anything in the world, and he's got to have it, otherwise I'm afraid he'll kill himself. Please, promise me that you'll help. Just get him a test. Please, Joan. Just a test."

Harry Cohn's wife blinked at the spectacle of this haughtily gorgeous woman, this major star, pleading with her, almost stammering. Harry had mentioned Sinatra's telegrams, had told her about the lunch where Frank begged Cohn to let him work for nothing. It had touched the studio chief in a strange way, but, he admitted to his wife, it had also made him feel a certain contempt for the singer. That, Cohn had told his wife, was all Sinatra was: a fucking crooner. What possessed this schmuck to think he could do anything on a movie screen besides sing and dance and smile? The balls on him!

Still, Cohn's wife told him about the visit, and Harry Cohn found himself intrigued by the notion of Ava Gardner as a supplicant. He conceived an idea. The studio chief and his wife had a tenant living in the guesthouse on their property, a painter named Paul Clemens. Clemens, a former WPA artist, had moved to California in the late 1930s and now made a good living doing portraits of movie stars. He was an amusing fellow, tall and bespectacled and distracted-looking, slightly cynical but good company, and it pleased Cohn to feel he was supporting the arts by housing him. Cohn, who prided himself on knowing everything about everybody in Hollywood, knew that Clemens and Ava were pals—he'd painted her picture, probably gotten a lay out of the deal. And so one morning on his way to work, Harry tapped on his tenant's door and suggested—as landlord to tenant—that the artist invite his pal Miss Gardner over to the Cohns' for dinner sometime.

It was a pleasant evening, and Ava got loaded right away. She knew all about Cohn's reputation as a bully, but wouldn't have been scared of him in any case. She looked him in the eye. "You know who's right for that part of Maggio, don't you?" she said. "That son of a bitch of a husband of mine."

Cohn stared at her with that bulldog-terrier face. Christ, she was gorgeous.

"For God's sake, Harry," Ava suddenly said. "I'll give you a free picture if you'll just test him."

The studio chief smiled as he looked her up and down. What else, he wondered, might she give him for free?

———

"We bumped into Frank and Ava at Frascati's restaurant in Beverly Hills, and whatever trouble they might have had is evidently over," Hedda Hopper wrote.

> We've never seen a more loving couple. They were extremely
> considerate and attentive to one another. Ava, a brunette again
> with a "little boy bob" haircut, looked wonderful. While Ava
> is doing "Mogambo" in Africa, Frank will stay as closely as
> possible to her. He told us that there were 60 theaters in Africa
> in which he could play. When the company goes to England,
> it'll be easy for Frank to be on hand, as he has a standing offer
> from the Palladium. He also wants to tour the provinces.

Touring the provinces . . . it had such an air of noblesse oblige about it. And it was all talk, of course: if Frank was going to tour any provinces, it would be the provinces of Missouri or Pennsylvania, or wherever else he could dig up a gig or two. The humble act that had gone over so well with Ava was all too real, and the flip side of it was that he felt lousy about himself. All that stuff about staying as close as possible to her in Africa was her idea: that, and a visit to her family in North Carolina, were her price for reconciliation. A family visit he could take; Africa was another matter. In truth, he dreaded the trip—dreaded John Ford with his sharp tongue and his three Academy Awards, even dreaded Gable, the King, with his phony teeth and his easy insouciance (and, perhaps, his assumptions about the leading man's prerogatives when it came to Ava). What would Frank say to them?

He had heard nothing from Cohn. A day went by, and another day, then a week, and soon Sinatra began to believe that Cohn had just been humoring him. In fact, Columbia was dickering with the stage actor Eli Wallach, whom everybody, Cohn and Zinnemann and Buddy Adler, wanted for Maggio. But Wallach's agents were being a pain in the ass, insisting that the thespian be paid $20,000 for the role when the studio had budgeted $16,000, tops.

Frank, knowing nothing of all this, was as nervous as a cat. Three nights after Hedda spied him in Frascati's, he made a guest appearance on Jimmy Durante's *All-Star Revue*—a bone tossed to him by his old *It Happened in Brooklyn* sidekick. Afterward, Frank and Ava went out to dinner with friends in the Valley, and they got drunk, and Frank said something awful. It was all too predictable. "By the time we'd gotten home to Pacific Palisades, my mood had taken on an icy, remote, to-hell-with-all-men tinge," Ava recalled.

> To emphasize the remoteness I felt, I retired to the solitude of my bathroom. So there I was, lying in my tub, soothing myself under the bubbles, when Frank came breezing in, picking up the argument where it had left off.
>
> I was furious. I hate intrusions when I have my clothes off. It's a bred-in-the-bone shyness, some sort of deep insecurity which I guess comes from my childhood. As I've said, with

each of my three husbands it took me several drinks and a lot of courage to appear disrobed in front of them.

I reacted instinctively. "Get out of here!" I yelled.

Naturally, that gave my husband the feeling that he was not truly loved.

Frank exploded. He yelled back, "For Christ's sake, aren't I married to you?"

That cut no ice with me. I was still outraged.

"Go away!" I screamed.

Which paved the way for what I have to admit was a truly memorable exit line. "Okay! Okay! If that's the way you want it, I'm leaving. And if you want to know where I am, I'm in Palm Springs, fucking Lana Turner."

How to get your wife's attention . . . Thus began a Hollywood operetta that would become the subject of heated fascination for years to come. History swirls with conflicting accounts of the next twenty-four hours, which commenced with Frank slamming doors, jumping into his car, and screeching off into the night, ostensibly in search of Lana Turner, who was indeed in Palm Springs—a fact of which Frank was well aware because she was staying in his goddamn house. Ava had lent her the goddamn house.

Frank's old flame was hiding out in Twin Palms under the protection of her (and Ava's) business manager Benton Cole, because Turner's boyfriend, Fernando Lamas, had recently beaten her up in a jealous rage. Lana, who possessed an infallible trouble-seeking radar when it came to men, had provoked Lamas's ire by dancing with the movie Tarzan Lex Barker at the very party (Marion Davies's) at which Lamas had stared deeply into Ava's eyes . . .

In fact, Hollywood in the early 1950s was a slick and dark fantasy world in many ways like the climactic house-of-mirrors scene in Orson Welles's recent *Lady from Shanghai*—self-reflective to the point of disorientation. Lamas, a hotheaded Argentinean who was about to co-star with Turner in MGM's *Latin Lovers,* had recently slapped her on-screen in *The Merry Widow*—which, he apparently felt, now gave him license to do the job for real. First, though, he turned his perfect profile to gaze soulfully at Ava precisely as a newspaper photographer snapped the scene—and as Lana sat at his side, looking appropriately humiliated.

All this at a party Marion Davies had thrown for over a thousand guests, including the press, because, said Davies, "I want to have some fun before I die."

Benton Cole had come to Lana's aid before. The previous September, in the wake of marital woes and a couple of box-office flops, Lana had (not unperceptively) declared her career "a hollow success, a tissue of fantasies on film," and slit her wrists in the bathroom of her Beverly Hills house. Cole broke down the door and took her to the hospital.

Now, with her career on the upswing but her personal life a familiar shambles,[2] the movie queen Frank Sinatra had once promised to marry was sitting with her manager-protector, smoking and drinking and bruised, in the love nest on Alejo Road as Frank and Ava converged separately on Palm Springs.

Despite his shouted declaration, Frank had absolutely no desire to fuck Lana Turner. He had just been angry. (Not to mention the fact that in her early thirties, she was already starting to look middle-aged.) He had passed over Lana and married Ava for a reason, and it was more than just that the sex was great. Lana Turner was, as witness her long, sad stumble through life, an empty shell of a human being, devoid of intellectual or spiritual resources of any sort. Ava Gardner, on the other hand, was a woman of enormous mettle and variety and spirit, one who would, after Frank, go on to fascinate Hemingway and Robert Graves, and not just because of the beauty of her person.

Frank knew all this (and the sex was great). Ava knew it only intermittently. She wasn't sure she could act, she wasn't sure she could think, but she did know she was a physical phenomenon. It was her one piece of certainty, and she gloried in it and suffered from it like any other star—if not more so, because of the depth of her sensibility. Her perpetual state of insecurity often made her feel that at bottom, nothing was really worth anything. The ground was constantly shifting beneath her feet—and beneath the feet of anyone who stood close to her. It made her at once fascinating and impossible.

Some of this may have occurred to Frank as he drove toward the desert in the pre-sunrise twilight, but what he was mainly thinking about was his own problems. He was feeling extremely sorry for himself, and he just wanted to take solace in the one place that gave him any comfort. And he wanted to be there alone. First, though, he wanted to pay a call on Jimmy Van Heusen—who loved the desert as much as Frank did, and had a place out in Yucca Valley—and talk it all out.

The first thing Ava did after Frank's dramatic exit was call Bappie and ask her to drive with her to Palm Springs. She wanted, against all logic, "to catch Frank in the act." When the sisters reached Twin Palms, Ava climbed over the chain-link fence in back and tried to peer in the windows, but the curtains were all drawn. Then the door opened. Benton Cole had heard her poking around; now he let her in—and Frank was nowhere in sight. Just Lana, "looking lovely as ever," Ava remembered.

> I knew that at one time she felt like she'd been on the verge
> of marrying Frank, which certainly gave some impetus to my
> suspicions, but we'd always been good, if not close, friends.
> And I'd always admired her as a great movie star. I remembered
> when I first arrived in Hollywood, a starlet green as a spring
> tobacco leaf. I'd glimpsed Lana on a set one day, and I'd
> thought, Now, there's the real thing. She had a canvas-backed
> chair inscribed with her name and a stool next to it holding her
> things. What struck me was that among them was a gleaming
> *gold* cigarette case and a *gold* lighter. Without envy I'd thought,
> Now that's what a *real* film star should look like. That's style.

To say that she was style without substance is perhaps shining too harsh a light on Turner: stardom is a real phenomenon. But the remoteness that combines with physical presence in the peculiar chemical reaction that produces stardom is usually a measure of distance from self. "Everybody wants to be Cary Grant," Grant once said. "Even I want to be Cary Grant." "It is true," Earl Wilson wrote, "that movie stars get to believe their own publicity." It is actually half-true. Stardom is a seductive idea, easier to believe in if the self doesn't get muddled up in it. Stars find it easier to believe in other stars' publicity. *Now, there's the real thing.* To Ava, Frank's angry talk had all the power he'd intended: he was, after all, talking about *Lana Turner.*

On the other hand, in the morning light that filtered in around the edges of the heavy drapes, Ava couldn't help taking note of the tired-looking woman who sat across from her in Frank's living room—the tired-looking woman with bruises on her face who kept tapping her cigarette on the ashtray as she drank glass after glass of vodka. Ava and Bappie and Ben Cole and Lana had decided to make a regular party of it, getting pie-eyed and telling scandalous Hollywood stories, hooting with laughter.

That was when Frank burst in, furious.

Chester had not been home. And so Sinatra had headed down to his place, seen the cars parked outside, driven around Palm Springs awhile as the sun rose, building up a head of steam. When the light began to hurt his eyes—he loved the blue just before sunrise, hated the full morning light—he went back to Alejo Road, walked up to the front door, and heard the loud laughter inside. In his goddamn house.

At first the sight of them all sitting there having a gay old time rendered him speechless. Then Ava piped up. "Ah, Frank! I thought you were going to be down here fucking Lana!"

He blinked, looking flustered for a second. "I wouldn't touch that broad if you paid me," he said.

Lana jerked upright as if Fernando had slapped her again. It was the truth, and the truth hurt. No one was more sharply aware than she of the new lines on her face and the puffiness under her eyes, not to mention the contusions on her cheek.

For his part, Frank could only think of his own hurt. "I bet you two broads have really been cutting me up," he said.

Lana was shaking her head, her eyes brimming at the injustice.

"Frank—" Ava warned.

At this point, accounts diverge. Frank either ordered Ava into the bedroom or commanded everyone to get out of his house. Ben Cole and Lana may have left immediately or somewhat later. In her memoir, Lana recalled that Ava shrugged and went to the bedroom, followed by Frank, and that soon the sounds of a terrific battle, complete with crashing furniture, could be heard. According to Turner, Bappie later brought a "battered" Ava to stay with her and Cole. "We did what we could to make Ava comfortable," she recalled.

> Poor Ava. She was badly shaken, and after my own grim
> experience, I could sympathize with her humiliation. But alone
> in my room I was surprised that I also felt sorry for Frank. It
> was a bad time for him. His career had slipped badly, and he
> was losing Ava.

This has a self-serving sound to it—as though Turner merely wanted a sister in suffering. In her own reminiscences, Ava mentions nothing about a beating, even though her fights with Frank always seemed to devolve into physical mayhem as a prelude to sex. Instead, she claims she gave as good as she got, informing her husband haughtily that it was her house too, and proceeding to pull all her books and phonograph records from the shelves. "Frank seemed to approve of this idea," she remembered.

> Furiously he scooped up everything I'd thrown on the floor
> and heaved it all out the still-open front door . . . and onto
> the pitch-dark driveway. Not to be outdone, I stalked across

to the bedroom and bathroom and started to pile my clothes, cosmetics, and every other goddamn odd and end I had in a heap on the floor. And Frank grabbed those as well, raced to the door, and tossed them out into the night to join the ever-growing mess in the driveway.

Soon, according to Ava, Frank had seized her by the waist and was trying to toss her out too, while she clung for dear life to a doorknob. In the meantime, the forty-nine-year-old Bappie—conceivably with a martini in one hand and a cigarette in the other—was attempting to make peace between the two. "For God's sake, kids, will you please knock it off?" she said. "This is *disgraceful!*"

At last somebody, either Frank or the neighbors, or both, called the police, who arrived, in the form of the genial former football star August "Gus" Kettmann—Palm Springs PD chief and, according to Ava, a friend of Frank's. Kettmann looked at the mess, looked at Mr. and Mrs. Sinatra's flushed faces, looked at the mess again. He pushed his hat back and scratched his head. There had been a lot of noise but no criminal activity, and the whole episode had taken place on private property. He could book the couple for disturbing the peace, but what would be the point? He told everyone to simmer down and left.

Naturally, word got out. Word always got out.

Two days later the *Los Angeles Times* put the story, what they had of it, right on page one, under the headline NOT CONFIRMED, and the subhead "Sinatra-Ava Boudoir Row Story Buzzes."

At that point it was all sizzle and no steak. The *Times* quoted Chief Kettmann as saying he knew nothing about anything. "I was off duty and there's nothing on the record about a disturbance," he claimed, not very convincingly.

The reporter then tried to goad the chief into more of a response by citing "Palm Springs rumors": namely, "that Sinatra ordered his beautiful film actress wife out of their desert mansion."

"Well," harrumphed Kettmann, "after all, if John Smith and his wife had a fight at their house I wouldn't feel privileged to tell you of any discussion that went on in their bedroom between Mr. and Mrs. Smith and our officers. I know nothing about it."

Kettmann may not have been telling the press much, but according to Earl Wilson "the Palm Springs police were talking"—their tongues perhaps loosened by some folding money. It was the peak of a big presidential election season—a tight race between Adlai Stevenson and Dwight D. Eisenhower—but the Frank and Ava Show was vying for America's attention. In the October 21 *Fresno Bee,* at the top of a page filled with headlines like NIXON SAYS ADLAI HAS RING IN NOSE, BARKLEY PREDICTS SWEEP IN SOUTH, STEVENSON OPENS LAST BIG WHISTLE STOP CAMPAIGN, and MRS. FDR PICKS ADLAI AS HER CHOICE IN RACE, there appeared the following news flash:

COLUMNIST SAYS SINATRA BOOTS AVA
OUT OF HOME

NEW YORK—AP—Columnist Earl Wilson reported today in the New York Post Frank Sinatra and Ava Gardner have separated after a spectacular quarrel.

When Wilson phoned Van Heusen and asked to speak to Sinatra, Chester said, "Frank's in the bathroom throwing up."

In the absence of hard information, rumors sprouted and flourished. Soon the kinds of salacious tales that Ava and Lana had been bandying over vodkas in the living room of Twin Palms were flashing around Hollywood: Ava had walked in on Lana and Frank having sex. Frank had walked in on Lana and Ava having sex. A more elaborate version even found its way into a subsequent FBI report on Sinatra: Frank had walked in on Lana and Ava having a three way with another man. Why not throw in poor Bappie too?

The fact was, Frank Sinatra and Ava Gardner were a permanently unstable compound, and no amount of sexual intercourse, no matter how spectacular, was sufficient to keep them bonded. Or as Ava later confided to the singer Bricktop: "The problems were never in bed. The problems would start on the way to the bidet."

———

Then they were back together again. Fittingly, since they belonged to the public, the reconciliation proceeded largely through public channels. Phase one was brokered by their hovering chronicler Earl Wilson, who leaned on Frank to admit how miserable he was, then ran a column in the *New York Post* headlined FRANKIE READY TO SURRENDER; WANTS AVA BACK, ANY TERMS. After friends and colleagues alerted her to the piece, she let it be known that she would accept her husband's call.

He called.

After the obligatory private phase two, phase three took place onstage at the Hollywood Palladium in front of four thousand people, at a rally for Adlai Stevenson on October 27. Then as now, many of the stars came out for the Democrats, Frank and Ava prominent among them. The couple had been slated to appear together for weeks, but of course in the wake of the previous weekend's events no one had any idea if they would actually show up.

Then Ava walked out onto center stage, wearing a black-satin strapless dress and a mink jacket, and smiled dazzlingly into the spotlight. The audience, filled with her peers, smiled back at her, knowing a great show when it saw one. She stepped to the microphone and waited for the applause to fade. "I can't do anything myself," Ava said, "but I can introduce a wonderful, wonderful man. I'm a great fan of his myself. Ladies and gentlemen, my husband, Frank Sinatra!"

The roar that followed was more about them than about him and he knew it, but he smiled anyway as he stepped into the spotlight and put his arm around his wife's shoulder. Frank looked like hell. He wore a big ADLAI button on the lapel of his dark suit, and as he stood with Ava, he spoke a few words about the candidate they both admired, but he might as well have been moving his lips soundlessly for all the audience cared. Here was a couple whose magnetism trumped that of all Hollywood couples before or since.

Then Frank was kissing Ava, she was waving and stepping out of the spotlight, and the band struck up and he sang—first hard and swingingly, on "The Birth of the Blues"; then soft and feelingly, on "The House I Live In"—and the hushed crowd remembered, for a few minutes, just how great he had been.

———

She stood in the wings staring at him as he sang, head over heels all over again. He was just fucking magic, she thought. The reporters gathered backstage kept tossing questions at her as she watched and listened, but Ava just gazed at Frank, smiling.

Some guy from a Chicago paper, greasy hair and thick glasses, tried to cut through the clutter. "Hey, Ava—come on!" he called. "What do you see in this guy? He's just a hundred-and-nineteen-pound has-been!"

Not even blinking, she said, "Well, I'll tell you—nineteen pounds is cock."

The reporter stood frozen, his mouth open, his pencil poised over his notebook amid heavy masculine laughter. Ava smiled serenely and kept watching the audience held spellbound by the memory of Sinatra.

———

Frank and Ava and Bappie landed at Idlewild and found the usual wall of reporters, hoping for a fight, a cross word—anything. Seeing the couple apparently happy, the men of the press did their best to get something going.

"So, Frank—are they going to try and find you a role in *Mogambo*?"

He gave the guy a look. "Yeah, I'm gonna play a native, in blackface."

Another reporter: "What'll Frank be doing while you're making the movie, Ava?"

"Oh, he'll do his act in some African nightclubs."

"Who's opening for him, Tarzan?" a guy in the back called out.

After braving it as best they could, they had sandwiches and a few drinks, then got on another plane for Winston-Salem. This was Frank's end of the bargain, or the first half of it at any rate: they had spent plenty of time with his family; now it was time for him to meet hers. It was her first trip back home in three years.

He was not in a good frame of mind. A month had gone by since his lunch with Cohn: no word. Frank now knew Columbia was testing other actors, real actors, for the role of Maggio. He had sent more telegrams signed with the character's name, trying to be cute, trying not to show how desperate he felt. Silence. Ava, of course, had mentioned nothing of her meeting with Harry's wife: she understood her husband's complex Italian pride. She looked at him, worried; she tried to keep his spirits up. The best he could manage was gallows humor. Most of the time he was uncharacteristically silent. He read and reread his rumpled copy of *Eternity*.

This was his life for now. They would go to North Carolina, then they would go to Africa, where she would work and he would sit. Just before Thanksgiving he would fly back to do two weeks at the French Casino, a club in the Paramount Hotel on Forty-sixth Street, at ten grand a week. It would have been half-decent money if Frank were actually getting any of it. (By comparison, Martin and Lewis, who were all over television, radio, the movies, theaters, and clubs, were then earning a guaranteed ten thousand *a night* for live performance.) It wasn't much of a booking, but it was a booking. He had no television or radio show, no movie deal, no record label, no concerts, no nothing. Lastfogel was working on all of it for him, making heroic efforts. "Sinatra smelled like a loser in those days," the agent would say years later.

So, reeking of failure, Frank went to Winston-Salem. There, at least, he was *Frank Sinatra*. There, the locals blushed and tripped over themselves at the mere sight of him—or rather, him and Ava. He and his wife and Bappie went to Ava's sister Myra's house: a little house, filled with relatives and the smells of delicious cooking. It all took Frank back to Hasbrouck Heights: the smells were different, the voices were different, but the mixed tides of love and claustrophobia were much the same.

Ava gleamed and glittered, too big and bright for the small rooms, her gorgeousness burnished by her success and the proud love of her family. Frank did his best. Myra's husband, Bronnie Pearce, ran a laundry in Winston-Salem, with a pick-up-and-drop-off diaper service. Frank's interest in the laundry business was limited . . . But they were good people, the Pearces and the Grimeses and the Creeches and the Gardners, so he made an effort, answering every question no matter how dumb, making conversation while he held a plate heaped with country food, glancing out at the gray trees and wondering when he could escape.

"Frank was very nice—a little quiet and shy," Billy Grimes's sister Mary Edna remembered many years later. A stray moment stayed with her: seeing Sinatra in the living room, sitting on the piano stool and talking with her ten-year-old brother about his clarinet lessons at school. "I heard him tell Michael how he'd learned to play the flute when he was young," she said. She was struck by Frank's serious respectfulness with the boy.

He was also depressed. Under the circumstances, one day in North Carolina was about all he could stand. He told Ava he had to get back to Manhattan; he was desperate to recharge his batteries. She wasn't happy, but she understood. She told him she needed another day with her family. Things were cool between them now: she was rising, rising, like a runaway balloon, and there was nothing Frank could do to stop her. Nor anything she could do to stop him—Ava went to see him off at the airport. Reporters were present, of course: they groaned with disappointment when Frank gave her a farewell peck on the cheek. Once more with feeling, please, for the cameras . . . And then he was dashing across the tarmac, turning for a second to say one more thing to his wife as he ran to the plane. The men of the press listened carefully, pencils poised.

"Goodbye, Dolly," Frank yelled, over the engine noise. "I'll call you."

Arriving in Nairobi as Ava heads to work on *Mogambo*,
November 1952.

They celebrated their first anniversary on board another plane, this time en route to Nairobi, opening a warmish bottle of champagne and exchanging gifts that she had paid for: a diamond-studded ring from him, a platinum watch from her. "It was quite an occasion for me," Ava recalled. "I had been married twice but never for a whole year."

Clark Gable came to meet their flight at Eastleigh Airport in Nairobi. "Hiya, Clark!" Ava called, when she spotted him. They embraced. Gable growled hello: she looked as ravishing as always. He looked magnificent in his khakis and bush hat. Frank, standing by in his rumpled airplane suit, his tie loosened, his thin hair flying in the breeze, faked a smile. In fact he needn't have worried. Though Ava and Gable were old drinking buddies from their co-starring stint in the miserable *Lone Star*—and had had the obligatory on-location fling—she'd quickly come to see the gulf between image and reality. "Clark's the kind of guy that if you say, 'Hiya, Clark, how are you?' he's stuck for an answer," she told friends. She loved him like an uncle—and kept sacrosanct the steamy black-and-white memory of his commanding eyes in *Red Dust*.

But while the 1932 *Red Dust* had been shot in its entirety on Stage 6 at MGM, the Technicolor 1950s required greater verisimilitude. *Mogambo* would be filmed, as Metro's ad copy trumpeted, "on safari in Africa amid authentic scenes of unrivaled savagery and awe-inspiring splendor." The savagery was a little too real for comfort: the Mau Mau Uprising had recently begun in Kenya, and Kikuyu rebels had killed dozens of whites. "The movie company had its own thirty-man police force," Ava remembered, "and when we got to what was then British East Africa, we were under the protection of both the Lancashire Fusiliers and the Queen's African Rifles . . . Everyone in the cast was issued a weapon." There is no record of whether Frank brought his own.

East Africa had never seen a safari quite like this: a cast and crew of almost six hundred, including bearers, guides, chefs, nurses, servants, native extras, and no fewer than eight big-game hunters, chief among them a rakish English expat named Frank "Bunny" Allen. The whole contingent moved from location to location in a convoy of fifty trucks, and, Ava recalled,

> once we settled our encampment was three hundred tents
> strong. And if you think those tents were just for sleeping,
> think again. My God, we had tents for every little thing you

could think of: dining tents, wardrobe tents with electric irons, a rec room tent with darts for the Brits and table tennis for the Yanks, even a hospital tent complete with X-ray machine, and a jail tent in case anybody got a tiny bit too rowdy.

Along the Kagera River on the Tanganyika-Uganda border, the stars (twenty-three-year-old Grace Kelly played Gable's other love interest) lived in Abercrombie & Fitch–like safari splendor: fancy flown-in French food (Sinatra brought a supply of pasta and tomato sauce), fine wines and liquors, even heated water for baths and showers. It might as well have been a penal colony as far as Frank was concerned. The temperatures rose well into the hundreds during the day; dust blew into every crevice. One shower a day didn't begin to suffice . . . But mainly, he was a fifth wheel. Ford liked throwing orders at him, with a broad wink to the others: "Make the spaghetti, Frank." The malicious old Irishman constantly tested everyone around him for weakness, prodding and needling: one of the first things he told Ava was that he'd really wanted Maureen O'Hara to play her role.

For Frank, all of *Mogambo* boiled down to one object—a camp chair. While Ford took the cast and crew out into the bush every morning to shoot, Frank parked his ass in that damn chair, rereading that goddamn book for the umpteenth time, thinking about all the other actors who were testing for Maggio, and wondering if Harry Cohn was ever going to call him back.

It didn't make him especially good company. By the time the movie people returned in the evening, he was two or three drinks ahead of them, grumbling into his glass about the dirt and the flies and Columbia Pictures.

Out in the bush at night, there was little to do but drink, and behind thin tent walls there were few secrets. The show people and crew engaged in the usual location mischief—Gable and Kelly had a hot affair; Bunny Allen had quite a few—but Frank and Ava mainly battled. The situation wasn't helped by the fact that she was feeling lousy. Maybe it was dysentery—a lot of people, including Ford, were sick—but by the time Frank had complained for the thousandth time about his troubles, she had had it. "Why don't you just get on with your fucking life?" she screamed at him one night. Many heard her.

Every morning, the company's DC-3 would bump down in the clearing the crew had bulldozed, bringing supplies and mail from Nairobi. And one morning, a long week after Frank and Ava had arrived, there was a cable for him in the morning mail.

Some say it was from Buddy Adler; some say it came from Bert Allenberg, one of Sinatra's new agents at William Morris. In any case, the cable was short and to the point: Frank was to report to Culver City to be screen-tested for the role of Maggio.

He read it over and over again. There was no mention of exactly how he was supposed to get to Culver City from the middle of the goddamn jungle, and he didn't have the price of a ticket.

Frank hated asking Ava for money, but she didn't hesitate for a second. She had an MGM account: all she had to do to charge airfare was say the word. It was the best she had liked her husband in weeks— because it was the best he had liked himself in weeks. Go knock 'em dead, she told him.

With the New York gig coming up, he might as well stay through, he said. It meant he wouldn't be back for almost a month.

She agreed with him, the faintest hint of coolness in her voice. He picked it up, but there was no time to investigate.

He threw his things together in record time, kissed her, and clambered aboard the DC-3, strapping himself into a jump seat behind the pilot and waving out the window as the plane started to bump down the runway. Then he was gone.

=====

He left the location on Friday, November 14, took a long overnight flight from Nairobi to London, and arrived the next day. He stayed at the Savoy, and when he departed on Sunday for New York, he left a brown-paper-wrapped package he'd brought with him in the hotel's safe-deposit box. Ava had asked him to take the package, containing her diamond earrings and a diamond bracelet, so the Mau Maus wouldn't get them.

Frank landed at Idlewild on Monday morning. He had handed his declaration sheet to the customs agent and walked blearily through the checkpoint when another agent waved him aside. Suddenly two cops appeared and escorted him to an office. Frank asked what was going on, but nobody said anything. Soon the office was filled with cops and U.S. customs agents. The agents asked if they could open his suitcases, then told him they had the authority to do so whether he agreed or not.

Frank asked once more what the hell was happening. No one answered.

He stomped around a side office for almost two hours, fuming, while the agents inspected his bags minutely. He was going to miss his goddamn flight to Los Angeles. He was going to call a lawyer. He phoned Sol Gelb, who said he would look into it, but that in the meantime Frank should try to be cooperative. Frank phoned Sanicola, who drove out to Idlewild and butted heads with the customs people, who were very polite but very firm. No one would say what was going on. Finally, when it was clear that Frank had indeed missed his flight, customs let him go. Cursing, he got into Hank's car, rode into the city, checked in at the Regency, and phoned Buddy Adler—who told him that tomorrow would be fine for his screen test.

The next morning he went to Idlewild to catch another flight, and the plane was delayed for three hours by mechanical problems. Frank turned around, went back to the Regency, and opened a fifth of Jack Daniel's. Buddy Adler was understanding. Sanicola said that Sol Gelb had spoken to customs—which informed the lawyer that someone had sent in a crank letter saying that Sinatra was going to smuggle diamonds into the country.

On Wednesday the nineteenth Frank finally made it to Los Ange-

les. It was after five when he landed, and Adler's office said Frank
could come in the next day. He spent the evening drinking, rereading
the Maggio passages for the thousandth time, and wondering if he had
a snowball's chance in hell of getting the role.

═══

Ava had suspected it for a while, and by Tuesday of that week she
knew she was pregnant. It was definitely Frank's (she'd been good for a
while), but she didn't want it. "I had the strongest feelings about bringing a child into the world," she would recall years later.

> I felt that unless you were prepared to devote practically all
> your time to your child in its early years it was unfair to the
> baby . . .
>   Not to mention the fact that MGM had all sorts of penalty
> clauses about their stars having babies. If I had one, my salary
> would be cut off. So how would I make a living? Frank was
> absolutely broke and would probably continue to be (or so I
> thought) for a long time . . . [T]he fact that I was pregnant
> would be showing quite plainly long before [*Mogambo*] was
> finished, so Jack Ford had to be told for starters. I felt the
> time just wasn't right for me to have a child.

The time would never be right. She was at best ambivalent and
at worst terrified; the prospect of motherhood held no charms for her.
As the adored and magically splendid baby of the Gardner family, *she*
was the world's child; there was no room in her life for others. (For
all Nancy junior's starry awe about her, Ava wasn't always particularly
friendly to Frank's children.) And having a baby would change her
body, and she knew where her bread was buttered. "I often felt," Ava
wrote, "that if only I could act, everything about my life and career
would have been different. But I was never an actress—none of us kids
at Metro were. We were just good to look at."

It wasn't just that she felt she couldn't act. Usually she didn't want to, much. "The truth is that the only time I'm happy is when I'm doing absolutely nothing," she wrote in her memoir. "I don't understand people who like to work and talk about it like it was some sort of god-damned duty. Doing nothing feels like floating on warm water to me. Delightful, perfect."

Nice work if you can get it. "Let's put it this way," Ava told Hedda Hopper before leaving for Africa. "I was going to be a secretary. But I'd rather be a star than a secretary . . . I'll go along with acting so long as it gives me financial security."

Oddly enough, though, she was having more fun making *Mogambo* than she'd ever had on a picture before. Ford was a great director, despite his surliness—or maybe because of it. He was a strange cat: a self-invented character and natural storyteller, obsessed with manliness (and perhaps a closeted homosexual), prone to the most outrageous verbal cruelties . . . It was said he was the only man who could make John Wayne cry. Ava was made of sterner stuff. She brought the director around, after he'd zinged her early on, by telling him to take that handkerchief he was always chewing—nervous habit—and shove it up his ass.[1] That did the trick with John Ford. He put his arm around her shoulder, took her aside, and said, "You're damn good. Just take it easy."

Besides, the part she was playing, the tough and careless sexual firecracker pioneered by Harlow in *Red Dust,* was made-to-order for Gardner. "For someone with my naturally irreverent temperament," she recalled,

> playing a sassy, tough-talking playgirl who whistles at men,
> drinks whiskey straight from the bottle, and says about wine,
> "Any year, any model, they all bring out my better nature," was
> a gift from the gods. I never felt looser or more comfortable in a
> part before or since, and I was even allowed to improvise some
> of my dialogue.

Ava sparkled in *Mogambo*. At the peak of her charm and beauty and wry elusiveness, she seemed, for the first time in her movie career, like the best possible version of herself on-screen. Even by her own account, she would never again be quite as good. No doubt the slightly sadomasochistic waltz she did with Ford—tension and release—helped her achieve that ease. It also didn't hurt that the director was more than a little in love with her.

She was well aware of Ford's devotion. But that didn't make it any easier to tell him she wanted to leave the shoot after less than three weeks and have an abortion. He was a devout, if highly conflicted, Catholic; and this was, after all, the early 1950s. "Jack Ford tried quite desperately to talk me out of it," she wrote.

> "Ava," he said, "you are married to a Catholic, and this is going to hurt Frank tremendously when he finds out about it."
>
> "He isn't going to find out about it, and if he does, it's my decision."
>
> "Ava, you're giving yourself too hard a time. I'll protect you if the fact that you're having a baby starts to show. I'll arrange the scenes, I'll arrange the shots. We'll wrap your part up as quickly as we can. Nothing will show. Please go ahead and have the child."
>
> I said, "No, this is not the time, and I'm not ready."

What she couldn't tell Ford—and couldn't tell the world when it came time to write her memoirs—was that she was no longer certain that she loved Frank, and that throughout the fall she had often detested him. Even now, when his heart's desire seemed within reach, when he might actually be able to turn things around for himself, he had to leave her for a month, and she knew what that meant. He hated being alone every bit as much as she hated it, and he would find company. He always did.

Frank had to cool his heels for most of Thursday the twentieth while Columbia ran other screen tests on Stage 16 of the Sunset-Gower lot: not all were for *Eternity,* but one was of the actor and comedian Harvey Lembeck, who was also trying out for Maggio (and had already acted in a service role in *Stalag 17*—and would wind up in Sergeant Bilko's squad on *The Phil Silvers Show*). When Sinatra finally walked into Buddy Adler's office, he was in a state. The handsome, prematurely silver-haired producer handed him a script, and Frank waved it aside. "I don't need this," he said. "I've read it many times."

"I didn't think he had a chance, anyway," Adler recalled. "So I said, 'Well, okay.'"

For his test, Frank was to play two drunk scenes: In the first, Maggio interrupts a heart-to-heart talk in a bar between the bugler Prewitt and the prostitute Lorene (to be played by Montgomery Clift and Donna Reed in the movie), amusing them by pretending to shoot craps with cocktail olives. In the second, drunker still, he goads a pair of MPs outside the Royal Hawaiian Hotel into beating him up. Both scenes embody perfectly what Prewitt says of Maggio: "He's such a comical little guy and yet somehow he makes me always want to cry while I'm laughin' at him."

The role, in other words, was an actor's dream—a softball teed up to be knocked out of the park. Yet as Sinatra walked onto the soundstage, it wasn't quite as an actor. "Frank had never been that crazy about acting," Ava said. "[B]ut he knew he *was* Maggio and besides, he was dying to do a straight dramatic part and escape from the typecasting he'd been subjected to in musicals."

Maggio would be redemption; Maggio would be vindication. After all, the typecasting of the 1940s was based on unquestioned American stereotypes: an Italian's role (much like a black's) was to sing and entertain. Even the downturn in Sinatra's career could be tied to the country's accumulated indignation at his hubris—the nerve of the little wop, trying to stand on the national stage! Small wonder that, as Frank remembered, he was "scared to death" when the camera started rolling. Thirteen thousand miles and endless delays, all for one chance, ten minutes of film . . .

Reports on the result conflict. "The [screen] test was all right but not great," said the *Eternity* screenwriter, Daniel Taradash. "We'd tested Eli Wallach, and in terms of acting his test was much better. We'd all settled on Wallach."

But the man who would direct the movie—and who was conducting Sinatra's screen test—felt differently. At forty-five, Fred Zinnemann was a filmmaking veteran of more than twenty years' experience, a Viennese Jew who'd come to Hollywood from Europe as a young man, and now, as the director of *The Member of the Wedding* and *High Noon,* had gained a reputation as a meticulous, thoughtful craftsman for whom a film's moral vision meant as much as the box-office receipts. Zinnemann gravitated to stories that set underdogs against overwhelming forces: *High Noon,* in which Gary Cooper's sheriff had to face down a vengeful ex-con without the help of the fearful townsfolk, was seen by many as a parable for the McCarthy era.

Angelo Maggio is nothing if not an underdog, a cog in the great machine of the U.S. Army, in rebellion—much like his friend Prewitt—against that institution's many strictures and inequities, as well as its bullies. Prewitt has his ethnicity, his white Americanness, on his side. But Maggio is a little man, an Italian, with no weapons except his Brooklyn chutzpah and his wits. His physical delicacy is part of his charm. Zinnemann had seen Eli Wallach's screen test and been bowled over by his acting, but he had misgivings. Wallach was a physically powerful man. The minute the director saw Sinatra's small frame and narrow shoulders and haunted eyes, he was intrigued. When Frank condensed all the pain of the last two years into ten minutes of screen test, Zinnemann was floored.

In his office, Buddy Adler was getting ready to go home. "Since [Sinatra's] was the last test of the day, I didn't intend going down on the stage," the producer recalled.

But I got a call from Fred Zinnemann, "You'd better come down here. You'll see something unbelievable. I already have it in the camera. I'm not using film this time. But I want you to see it."

Frank thought he was making another take—and he was terrific. I thought to myself, if he's like that in the movie, it's a sure Academy Award. But we had to have Harry Cohn's okay on casting and he was out of town. So Frank went back to Africa.

Adler's recollection conveniently foreshadows Sinatra's Oscar and elides all the complications surrounding Eli Wallach—leave it to a producer to spin a good yarn. Cohn was out of town, in New York talking to his moneymen. But it would be almost two months before final casting for *Eternity* was set, including Maggio. And Frank would not go back to Africa for three long weeks.

One thing he knew, though: he had nailed it, no matter what Harry Cohn wound up deciding.

=====

Meanwhile, Ava's pregnancy threw Metro-Goldwyn-Mayer into a tizzy. Once she had notified her MGM publicist and her agent of her intention to have an abortion, the front office fired off a vehement, if euphemistic, cable to John Ford:

CONFIDENTIAL: UNDERSTAND GARDNER CABLED AGENT SHE UNSETTLED AND NOT WELL AND PLANNING BRIEF TRIP TO LONDON FEEL THIS VERY UNWISE FOR MANY OBVIOUS REASONS UNLESS YOU DECIDE IT NECESSARY OTHERWISE SUGGEST YOU USE YOUR PERSUASIVENESS AND HAVE LADY STAY PUT.

But by this time, Ava and Ford were as thick as thieves. The director cabled back:

GARDNER GIVING SUPERB PERFORMANCE VERY CHARM-
ING COOPERATIVE STOP HOWEVER REALLY QUITE ILL SINCE
ARRIVAL AFRICA DEEM IT IMPERATIVE LONDON CONSULTA-
TION OTHERWISE TRAGIC RESULTS STOP SHOULD NOT AFFECT
SCHEDULE WEATHER HERE MISERABLE BUT WE'RE TRYING NO
MOZEL BUT HARD WORK REPEAT BELIEVE TRIP IMPERATIVE.

Ford's cable was a remarkable performance itself. In forty-three words, he established his faith in his star, the integrity of his shoot, and his winking solidarity with his Jewish corporate masters. A masterpiece of persuasion, and an undeniable call to action.

MGM made all the arrangements. Ava Gardner was an extremely valuable asset, and MGM was very good at making arrangements. Transportation had to be set up, a clinic in London contacted—abortion was legal in England—and publicity spun. The cover story was a tropical disease, painful but not too serious, although the *Los Angeles Times*'s page-one lead was attention-grabbingly dramatic:

AVA GARDNER STRICKEN ON SET IN AFRICA

LONDON, Nov. 24 (AP)—Doctors pumped powerful shots of antibiotics into Actress Ava Gardner tonight to beat down a tropical infection picked up while movie-making in Africa.

The Hollywood beauty—who made the mistake of drinking the local water in Kenya's native country—lay in pain with stomach troubles.

But her doctors said it is not serious and promised to have her back on her feet again in a couple of days.

She was whisked to London by plane and rested this afternoon at the Savoy Hotel. Then, said a Metro-Goldwyn-Mayer official, she went quietly to a nursing home tonight for treatment.

Strict privacy was ordered for the actress, wife of Crooner

Frank Sinatra. There are neither visitors nor phone calls. Only
a doctor saw her.

Filming continues in Kenya by shooting scenes in which
Miss Gardner does not appear.

Frank got the news along with everyone else, and, at length,
reached her by phone in London.

Her voice was weak. There was an echo on the line. God only
knew who was listening in.

He'd been worried sick about her. Was she okay? What had happened?

What had happened was that like a moron, she'd eaten some fucking lettuce, which any sane white person in Africa knew you should
never do in a million years . . . More important, though—what about
his screen test?

He told her, and she was happy for him. Genuinely happy, even
though she had just aborted their child . . . But she was so tired—
would he understand if she slept a little?

Of course he would understand. She should get her rest, and he
would call her when he got to New York.

The first thing he did when he hung up was drive to Billy Ruser's
jewelry store in Beverly Hills and pick out a present, for her birthday
and Christmas—a pair of earrings, emeralds to go with her eyes. Ruser,
an old pal, helped Frank himself.

They were gorgeous. "How much?"

"Twenty-two thousand."

Frank exhaled and looked out the window, his eyes suddenly moist.

"Frank, give the earrings to Ava."

"Billy, I can't afford these."

Ruser put them in a box and pushed it across the counter. "You pay
me when you have it."

Then he bought Christmas presents for the kids and Nancy—he
would be far away at Christmas. Frank borrowed a couple of grand

from Van Heusen, who was swimming in dough, still cranking out movie songs for Crosby. He and Chester made plans for later, a couple of girls, one black and one white . . .

He drove over to Holmby Hills. Nancy was holding the fort with the money he sent her, though the big house was still on the market. She simply didn't need all that space, and she could bank a nice sum if she sized down.

She was practical. But Frank was also surprised to see, when she opened the front door, just how good she looked—as though, without him, she would have withered up and blown away, grown old overnight. She was wearing his pearls, and the smell of something delicious cooking in the kitchen somehow added to her allure. Ava couldn't—wouldn't—boil water . . . He kissed his ex-wife. On the mouth. She kissed back just a tiny bit, as if she'd momentarily forgotten everything—but then she was tapping him on the chest. Asking him what he was doing.

Then Nancy junior was there, in a sweater and blue jeans and saddle shoes. He noticed the little swellings underneath the sweater.

Tina, four, edged up under her mother's arm, staring up at him; behind them, eight-year-old Frankie sat silently on the steps, his hair combed neatly, a scab from a playground accident on his forehead, his dark eyes suspicious.

Frank picked up the bags he'd brought. Christmas was early this year!

Nancy Sandra cheered. Her little sister smiled shyly; the boy raised his eyebrows. Frank's ex-wife gave him a knowing look, but seemed pleased anyway.

He asked if he could come in. She nodded.

Her dignity was indestructible; she had begun to make a life without him. She cultivated the gossip columnists, many of them women; they naturally took her side. Hedda Hopper wrote in early November:

When I was on my lecture tour, a Nancy Sinatra fan wanted to know if she'd take Frank back. So I asked her.

"The idea is ridiculous," she said. "Frank's a married man now. He sees our children all the time, and he loves them. But as for anything else, it never enters my head." Her friend Jim Henaghan brought an oil man to see her house, so maybe one of these days she'll sell it and buy a smaller place. Nancy's quite a gal.

Romances were hinted at, but her most steadfast companion outside the Barbato circle seemed to be the similarly single Barbara "Missy" Stanwyck. Mostly, though, the former Mrs. Sinatra took great care to stay busy. The columnist Edith Gwynn wrote (on the very day of Ava's abortion): "Spent a pleasant evening at Nancy Sinatra's where a dozen or so dined on fancy Italian dishes the gal herself cooked up, and looked at some movies later. Nancy is proud of her three kids— and well she might be. They're dolls—and talented like crazy!"

———

Frank opened at the French Casino on Wednesday night, November 26, and though it wasn't the Copa, the house was full and he was in good voice—and good spirits, even when a heckler called out, "Where's your wife?"

"Where's *your* wife?" Frank shot back.

After the show, he strolled over to his favorite Manhattan restaurant, Patsy's, on West Fifty-sixth Street, for a late dinner. It was a cozy Italian joint run by the Scognamillo family, unpretentious and fiercely loyal to Sinatra. "At the end of the meal," the *New York Times* reported in 2003, "Sinatra asked the owner what he was serving for Thanksgiving, which was the next day. Aware that Sinatra had not seen the 'closed for Thanksgiving' sign on the door, the elder Mr. Scognamillo replied, 'Whatever you like.' After Sinatra left, the owner took down the sign and announced to the staff: 'Tomorrow we are open. Everyone, please come, and bring your family. I don't want Mr. Sinatra to eat alone.'"

That night Frank went straight back to work at the Casino. Between songs he schmoozed the audience, turning his ordeal at customs into an amusing anecdote ("A funny thing happened to me on the way here from Africa . . .") and even essaying a couple of slightly nervous *Mogambo* jokes. On Gable's marksmanship: "Is he good! In one week, he shot six natives!" And on Ava: "It's pretty lonesome here without my wife. After all, you know the dangers she'll face making a movie in Africa—lions, tigers, crocodiles; Clark Gable . . ."

Gable wasn't the danger. In early December, Ava returned to the *Mogambo* camp and, as always, managed to stir up some action right away. When she wanted to go out into the bush and get up close to some wild animals, the handsome white hunter Bunny Allen was happy to oblige her. They soon found themselves in the midst of a herd of elephants, where Ava, suddenly startled by a fire-hose-like splashing very close at hand, grabbed Allen's arm. "It's all right," the hunter whispered coolly. "Elephant's just gone to the bathroom." Ava's loud laughter sent the herd thundering off—but there she was, still holding on to Bunny . . .

It wasn't a grand affair, just a couple of nights, then sweet, dry-eyed good-byes. They were alike, the two of them: good-looking and easily bored.

"Ava couldn't be alone," the production coordinator Eva Monley said. "That was, I think, why she had so many affairs. She'd say, 'Hey, come on, have a drink with me, I'm bored all by myself,' and she'd bring back a prop man or whoever [to her tent]."

Back in New York, the French Casino was asking Frank to extend his stay, but, Earl Wilson wrote, "he has a prior commitment—Ava." On Friday the twelfth, his thirty-seventh birthday (not his thirty-fifth, as he still led the world to believe, and as Wilson dutifully reported), he "was given a birthday cake by lady fans . . . [who] squealed just like they did at the Riobamba almost 10 years ago."

Ten years . . . The girls were ladies now, and Frankie was verging on middle age. Many of the ladies were still willing to go to bed with him—and a few did—but road romance wasn't the same as it had once been.

He really did miss his wife.

Frank arrived back on location the following week, bearing gifts for Ava's big birthday, from himself and her family. Some accounts say he brought a diamond ring and a mink, the latter of which seems unlikely in darkest Africa, but then Sinatra and sensible gift giving never did go together. Ava is said to have made a scornful remark about who really paid for the gifts—but what of Billy Ruser's layaway earrings? Reports are inconsistent. Ava insists it was a charmed period. "Frank came back to Africa in time for Christmas—and my thirtieth birthday—full of enthusiasm and joy," she recalled.

But Frank wouldn't know for weeks if he had clinched the *Eternity* role: Cohn was still horse-trading with Eli Wallach's people, and Frank was on pins and needles, which wouldn't have made him delightful company. "Then came the death wait," he told Hedda Hopper in 1954, of his return to the *Mogambo* shoot.

> I thought I'd collapse waiting for reaction to that test. My agent sent word that Columbia was testing six other fellows, among them some fine stage actors. My chin hit my knees and I gave up. Ava was wonderful at cheering me up, and said, "I wish you wouldn't quit just because you got one stinking telegram." Clark Gable . . . kept saying, "Relax, skipper. Have a little drink and everything will be all right."

Drinking rarely made things all right where Frank and Ava were concerned. Given his tendency to prettify the past, his stark language ("thought I'd collapse . . . I gave up") is striking. Then sometime while he was waiting to hear from Columbia, the alcohol loosened Ava's tongue, and she told him about the abortion. The revelation could only have been devastating to him.

Frank's first thought would have been the terrible memory of

Nancy's abortion. His second would have been the big family he had proclaimed he and Ava would have. His Italian procreative pride had finally collided with his wife's skittishness about childbearing—not to mention her own physical and professional pride.

The two of them had much in common, but too much of it was negative. And in each, the capacity for intimacy was stunted. The story Ava told on herself about her fury at Frank for interrupting her in her bath, and her general shyness about appearing naked in front of her husbands, clashes tellingly with all the accounts about her fascination with prostitution and anonymous sex, the dalliances with propmen, the naked parading in front of native bearers on *Mogambo*. If she could see a man as an inferior, her own shaky self-worth wasn't challenged. She was drawn to strong men but ultimately threatened by them.

For his part, Frank had briefly known, and quickly fled, the confinements of conventional marriage. Jersey City, Hasbrouck Heights—he could still remember that tight feeling in his chest . . . Nancy had ruled those small households and, during the couple's tenure in them, ruled him as well. And the big households in Toluca Lake and Holmby Hills cohered around Nancy, not him. He was gone.

He would keep returning for the rest of his life, would be an inveterate dropper-in. He would always be wedded to Nancy; she knew him as no one else did. He craved this intimacy as he craved all intimacy, but with Nancy, as with almost everyone else, the rules were the same: he must be able to leave the second he got bored. And he was too intelligent not to realize that almost nobody in the world defined intimacy his way. The one exception was Ava, who played by the same rules he did. Which made it impossible for them to stay together. The contradictions would torment him till the end of his days.

———

"Fred Zinnemann . . . has gone to New York to test stage players for 'From Here to Eternity,'" Hedda Hopper wrote in her syndicated column on December 3, 1952.

The picture will have seven top roles; but Columbia figures with that set-up a Broadway actor or actress can be built into a movie star and put under contract as was Judy Holliday in "Born Yesterday." Seems that every rugged actor in town, including Humphrey Bogart, wants to play the part of Sgt. Warden. Bogie is due to go to Europe for "Beat the Devil" with John Huston. But I hear that picture may be postponed if he lands "Eternity." Frank Sinatra has already tested for the role of Maggio. From the reports I've been getting from those who've seen the test I'd wager he's in.

"Frank's still in there pitching for the magic [sic] role in 'From Here to Eternity'; and I think he's just right for the part," the columnist noted a week later.

His manager assured me that, despite the printed report, Sinatra was not gumming up the deal by holding out for too much do-re-mi. When he wants a part badly, as he does this one, Frank considers money of secondary importance. If memory serves me correctly, he gave at least a bulk of his salary for playing the priest in "The Miracle of the Bells" to charity. And, besides, the "Eternity" role could open up a completely new phase to Sinatra's acting career.

Nobody knew this better than Sinatra, but casting for *Eternity* was in flux, as casting frequently is for big movies. As were Frank's nerves. He distracted himself by organizing a Christmas show for the *Mogambo* company: he sang carols, native choirs performed, Ford recited "A Visit from St. Nicholas." Christmas passed, then New Year's, and there was still no word from Columbia. He could exert only so much influence on Harry Cohn, and being thirteen thousand miles removed from the action didn't boost his confidence. Since Frank was currently without a press agent—he could no longer afford the weekly retainer he'd been paying Nat Shapiro, and had precious little to publicize anyway—he did what he could. He worked the phones from Nairobi, kept Sanicola jumping, spun the columnists. At least one of those positive reports about Frank's screen test came straight from Frank himself. And it was sheer genius to convert his desperation—his offer to Cohn to play Maggio for next to nothing—into largesse. (Who was keeping exact track of how much of his *Miracle of the Bells* pay he'd tithed? It had to have been "at least a bulk," whatever that meant.)

To a certain extent, a publicist was unnecessary. To an extent, by sheer virtue of his continued notoriety and his connection to Ava, Sinatra's name stayed in the news. This cut two ways, though. Ava was now the star; Frank, the consort. Those who knew something about the pathetic but plucky character of Maggio from the novel (as Hedda Hopper clearly did) appreciated the delicious appropriateness of Sina-

Ava and John Ford on the set of *Mogambo*, early 1953. Two tough characters who clashed at first, then grew deeply fond of each other.

tra's seeking the role, but they were in the minority. Most of the world had had it with him. Even Earl Wilson. "When Frank Sinatra was flying to Africa and then back to play a nightclub date in Boston, nobody in the press was interested," the columnist recalled. "Even I wasn't much interested. I noted that when he arrived at the airport, Frank needed a haircut."

Act Five

THE PHOENIX

Montgomery Clift and Frank shoot *From Here to Eternity,* Hawaii, April 1953.
Sinatra, ordinarily a prima donna on movie shoots, "was very, very good—all
the time," director Fred Zinnemann recalled. "No histrionics, no bad behavior."
He knew the film was his last best chance.

The second week of 1953 brought a welcome distraction—welcome
to Frank, at any rate: Ava was pregnant again. For her part, Ava felt
doubly miserable, for she was sick as a dog and she knew the baby
wasn't his.

It might have been Bunny Allen's; it might have belonged to any
one of two or three different propmen, she wasn't sure. Once she tied
one on after work, anything could happen, and frequently did. But she
knew it wasn't Frank's: the numbers didn't add up. Conception would

have occurred in early December, right around the time he was playing the French Casino. Maybe even as late as the tenth or twelfth. Happy Birthday, Frank.

She couldn't bear to tell him that she would have to get rid of this one too, and he mistook her misery for mere physical discomfort. "He was delighted," she recalled.

> I remember bumping across the African plain with him one day in a jeep, feeling sick as the devil. Right on the spot, for the first and only time in our relationship, Frank decided to sing to me. I know people must think that he did that sort of thing all the time, but the man was a professional and the voice was saved for the right occasions. This must have been one of them, because he sang to me, oh so beautifully, that lovely song, "When You Awake." It didn't stop me from feeling sick, but I've always remembered that moment.

> A week later he was gone again.

Had his plane gone down on this trip—as, for example, would the plane of the great young classical pianist William Kapell, later that year—Frank Sinatra's legend would no doubt have grown over the decades to come. He would not have been forgotten like the two-dimensional Russ Columbo or Buddy Clark; rather, he would have left a large, tragic, stunted legacy, that of a great talent cut short at a low ebb (like Hank Williams, who had died of an overdose that New Year's Day). The grand and troubled relationship with Ava, never resolved, would have been remembered and romanticized; the dozens of great recordings he had already made would have grown in stature. Even the few slight but charming movies would have taken on a nostalgic glow. His career decline near the end would have given the saga an extra fillip. Sinatra would have been recalled not only as an important figure of the mid-twentieth century but also as a great should-have-been. Who knew what he might have become?

But his plane didn't go down (nor, for all his abject fear of heights and flying, would any of the thousands of flights he would take over six decades). Instead, he arrived, unheralded, at Idlewild on a chilly afternoon in late January 1953.

"Frank Sinatra, needing a haircut, got into town from Africa and Ava and headed for Boston . . ." This was the full extent of Earl Wilson's item on Sinatra, final ellipses and all, in his column of Friday, January 23. In fact, Frank had landed in New York on Monday the nineteenth, but he was such old news at this point that Wilson could wait awhile to take note of his arrival. All but incognito, Sinatra was on his way to do two weeks at Lou Walters's Latin Quarter (where Lou's daughter Barbara, aged twenty-three, was director of publicity). From there he would fly to Canada and play a week at the Chez Paree in Montreal. As promised, he was touring the provinces. The gigs were all he could get, and he was glad for them.

The next day—it was Eisenhower's inauguration—Frank got that haircut, flew to Boston, checked in at the Ritz-Carlton, and went over to the Latin Quarter to rehearse. Young Barbara Walters greeted him eagerly, telling him proudly of the newspaper interviews she had lined up. Frank smiled wearily, imagining the line of bullshit he would have to spin for the gentlemen of the press. He took the band through its paces, liked what he heard, and went back to the hotel alone. A little bit after eight, the phone rang. It was Bert Allenberg, calling from the Morris office in L.A. Was Frank sitting down?

Sinatra poured himself a tumblerful of Jack Daniel's after he hung up. He drank the whiskey, refilled the glass, and drank that one off too. He paced the living room of his suite, fast, talking to himself. "I wanted to tell somebody but there was nobody around to tell it to!" he later recalled. "I thought I'd go off my rocker."

The shock of finally getting what he had wanted so badly was so great that at first he wasn't sure how to feel. One of his first emotions, irrationally enough, was sharp regret at having agreed to work for so little. A thousand dollars a week . . . It was not only less than pocket change;[1] it could brand him for life as cut-rate. A couple of nights after opening at the Quarter, he went over to George Wein's Storyville club in the Hotel Buckminster to hear Duke Ellington, and got to talking with Pearl Bailey, who was also on the bill.

She asked Frank what he was up to. Another movie? Bailey turned to her husband, Ellington's drummer, Louie Bellson, and gave him a wink. She just loved to see Frankie in those sailor suits. Bellson gave her a mock scowl.

Frank shook his head. No more sailor suits. "Pearl, they've offered me a movie called *From Here to Eternity*. They're paying me a thousand bucks a week, which is nothing."

Bailey looked impressed. *From Here to Eternity*? That big book?

That was the one.

"Take it and don't look back," Bailey told him.

———

He took it. And he'd brought it off without having to put a horse's head in Harry Cohn's bed. Mario Puzo was the one who did that, fifteen years later. The famous scene in *The Godfather* has a Sinatra-like singer named Johnny Fontane beg his padrone Don Corleone to help him land a career-changing movie role in the face of strong opposition from a Cohn-like studio chief named Jack Woltz. The novelist knew that Sicilian criminals frequently used dead animals as warning signs to their enemies, and he knew that Harry Cohn was an avid horseplayer (though he never owned a racehorse). Puzo was also aware that Cohn had had close gangland ties since the beginning of his career, that he fancied himself a tough guy—he even wore a gold-and-ruby friendship ring given to him by a smooth mafioso named Johnny Rosselli, Frank Costello's West Coast representative.

Puzo, who was of southern-Italian ancestry, was steeped in his subject. Yet he was also a writer of considerable imagination, a novelist, not a journalist. And while the lecherous and tyrannical Woltz bore a strong similarity to Harry Cohn, comparisons could also be drawn to other studio heads and producers.

But strong narratives seduce us: we want them to be true. And while *The Godfather* was a powerful novel, the movie version (whose screenplay Puzo also wrote) was even stronger. The sum of the film's parts—the dark and haunting beauty of Gordon Willis's cinematography, Nino Rota's score, and Dean Tavoularis's production design; the majesty of Francis Ford Coppola's direction and the actors' performances—all the components, taken together, had a great and somber force that made the world feel absolute faith in its truth, whatever the messy and ambiguous facts of real life.

Numerous writers and would-be authorities have put considerable effort into cobbling up a case that the Mob really was behind Frank Sinatra's getting the role of Maggio. Various commentators have constructed elaborate scenarios based on the second- and third- and fourth-hand testimony of unreliable witnesses, many of them definitively unreliable career crooks. And all the mass of speculation rests on two simple assumptions, as neatly expressed in *All American Mafioso: The Johnny Rosselli Story,* a work taken as gospel by many in the Mob-conspiracy-hunting business: "Cohn hated Sinatra, and felt he was wrong for the part to boot."

Or, as fictionally expressed by Jack Woltz (as played by John Marley) to Don Corleone's consigliere Tom Hagen (Robert Duvall) in *The Godfather*: "Now listen to me, you smooth-talking son-of-a-bitch! Let me lay it on the line for you and your boss, whoever he is. Johnny Fontane will never get that movie! I don't care how many dago guinea wop greaseball gumbahs come out of the woodwork!"[2]

Harry Cohn, no shrinking violet, was certainly capable of such an explosion. But Jack Woltz is a fictional character and Harry Cohn was not. And Harry Cohn did not hate Sinatra. In fact, as Cohn's biographer Bob Thomas wrote, "Frank Sinatra and Harry Cohn became good friends during the years when Sinatra was enjoying his initial burst of fame in Hollywood." And the friendship had legs. In the fall of 1949, after Frank allowed the premiere of *Miss Grant Takes Richmond* to occur during his stint at the Capitol, Sinatra came down with strep throat so severe that an oxygen tent had to be set up in Manie Sacks's apartment. "It was the first time since his rise to fame that he had been seriously ill, and he was surprised to learn how few of his so-called friends responded with offers of sympathy and aid," Thomas writes.

> A singular exception was Harry Cohn. Cohn flew to New York and spent the morning with Sinatra from 10 o'clock to 1:30. Cohn went off to business appointments and returned at 5 in the afternoon. He remained with Sinatra until his time for sleep at 9:30. Cohn read to the patient, reminisced of his early days in films, told jokes, and delivered numbers recalled from his early days as a song plugger. Cohn continued the daily routine until Sinatra recovered.
>
> Cohn's parting remark was in character: "You tell anybody about this, you son of a bitch, and I'll kill you!"

Cohn was a businessman with a soft heart and a hard head. He had flown to New York on business, and gone to Frank's bedside less out of love than gratitude: Sinatra's box office at the Capitol had buoyed the take of Columbia's minor comedy to such an extent that Cohn was able to take out an ad in the trade papers bragging about it. He certainly didn't hate Sinatra—quite the opposite. But in 1949 and now in 1953, the studio chief was nothing if not a pragmatist. *From Here to Eternity* was a big-budget production, to be shot on location with a star-heavy cast. The budget was creeping up. All the parts had been set except Maggio, and Eli Wallach's agent was digging in his heels on the actor's high fee.

Harry Cohn had agonized over the decision. He had met with Wallach, had even provoked him in order to test his mettle. ("He doesn't look like an Italian—he looks like a Hebe," Cohn said when the actor entered his office. Understandably, Wallach exploded, and Cohn was impressed: the man had fire and presence.) What's more, Wallach had done a terrific screen test—as had Frank. Cohn kept running the two back-to-back, feeling uncustomarily indecisive. Finally he asked his wife's advice. Joan Cohn watched the two tests and said of Wallach, "He's a brilliant actor, no question about it. But he looks too good. He's not skinny and he's not pathetic and he's not Italian. Frank is just Maggio to me."

Cohn nodded. He had to admit it: the little putz really could act. And (just as important) Sinatra could save the studio some serious money. But there was one more practical consideration. If Frank's name went above the title along with the other stars', would people assume *Eternity* was a musical?

Fuck it. Time was wasting. Leave it to the lawyers to hash out the billing. Cohn told Adler to call Sinatra's agent, then patted himself on the back.

"Frank Sinatra has been notified to report to Columbia in ten days to start 'From Here to Eternity,' " Louella Parsons noted in her February 2 column. Two days later, Parsons elaborated: "Talked to Frank Sinatra, who arrived in New York from Boston. He told me Ava Gardner has been in Rome and goes on to London to make another picture.

" 'This separation,' he said, 'is difficult for both of us. I go to California in ten days for 'From Here to Eternity,' so I won't be able to see Ava for at least two months.' "

Frank had been ordered to report to Columbia in ten days; opportunity of a lifetime or not, however, he would take a good deal longer to get there. He was booked in Montreal from February 6 to 15; rehearsals for *Eternity* were set to start on the twenty-third. During the intervening week, a nervous Harry Cohn wanted his least experienced and most temperamental star doing everything necessary to prepare—but mostly showing he was ready to be a good soldier. Frank had every intention of complying. Then he received an even more urgent summons.

Louella had been wrong about Ava's new picture. That movie, a

Robert Taylor historical clunker called *Knights of the Round Table,* wouldn't start shooting till June. In fact, *Mogambo* was still in process: location work had wound up at the end of January, but there were still interiors to film, at MGM's Boreham Wood Studios northwest of London. Before that, however, she had some crucial personal business to attend to.

After closing in Montreal, Frank made a flying visit to London, a trip so abrupt that he had to phone in a last-minute cancellation of an appearance on Martha Raye's TV show, infuriating the writers and producers, who had to rip up the script and start from scratch. Some of the columns snickered that Sinatra was up to his old high-handed tricks, but Dorothy Kilgallen seemed to understand that this trip was necessary. "Chums say Frankie flew to London," Kilgallen wrote on the twentieth, "because he hadn't heard from Ava for a week."

He'd finally tracked her down in Rome, screwing Clark Gable, for all Frank knew.[3] In truth, Ava being Ava, she was brothel-crawling with her new gal pal Grace Kelly. When Frank asked anxiously how she was feeling, her voice was husky from fatigue and edgy. It was a bad conversation. Just when he needed her by his side to share in his good fortune, she was a million miles away physically and emotionally.

Then she'd gone off the radar screen.

She had checked out of the Grand in Rome; Reenie Jordan and Benton Cole were vague about her whereabouts. Frank had Sanicola phone Metro's production department in Culver City and extract her drop-dead date for arriving at Boreham Wood.

But she still sounded remote when he reached her at the Savoy—all she would say was that there was some kind of medical problem. That was when he got on a plane.

The newspaper accounts tell how Ava met Frank at Heathrow, minus her customary sunglasses, and didn't recognize him at first because he was wearing a hat. The man whose icon status in the 1950s would be synonymous with a fedora clearly hadn't worn one up to this point. The simple reason for the change was that his baldness was accelerating. And while Frank had begun wearing a hairpiece on film at least as early as 1948's *The Kissing Bandit,* he wasn't yet solvent (or shameless) enough to sport a toup in civilian life.

If his wife didn't recognize him, the public wouldn't either: Sinatra's trip to London was not only abrupt but furtive. He told one of the few reporters who tracked him down that he had come to make arrangements for a European tour he'd be doing in the late spring and early summer. This might have been true, but what he was mainly there for (he finally discovered after he landed) was to try to talk Ava out of having another abortion.

Unsurprisingly, her memoir glosses the episode over. "I didn't think that big expensive clinic [where she'd had the first abortion in November] was prepared for a second round of someone responding to their ever-so-correct questions with my incorrect answers," she wrote,

> so I was checked into a small nursing home near Wimbledon
> where they didn't ask any questions at all. I knew Frank
> was coming across to London to start a singing tour through
> Europe, but I wasn't sure exactly when. But clearly someone
> told him about what I was doing, because as long as I live I'll
> never forget waking up after the operation and seeing Frank
> sitting next to the bed with tears in his eyes.

She'd probably avoided the big expensive clinic for secrecy's sake—and because she could scarcely ask MGM, which had picked up the tab for the first procedure, to pay for another one three months later.

And the procedure was in February, not in May as some accounts have it, and as Ava's red herring about Frank's coming over to start his European tour would indicate. A May abortion could have made the baby Frank's for sure, but she can't have it both ways. If her tender story about his singing to her as they bumped across the African plain in a jeep is true—and her memory in this instance has a solid ring of truth—then that second (or third[4]) pregnancy had commenced while she was still on location, which means no later than January, and specifically no later than mid-January, because that's when Sinatra left for his Latin Quarter gig. (Nor could the jeep-bumping-over-the-plain story refer to the first African pregnancy: Frank had departed for his screen test in November before he knew she was with child.)

She meets him at Heathrow; the next thing we know, he's sitting by her bedside in tears after the procedure. Sometime after he took off his hat, Ava told him where she was going and what she was going for. He can't have been happy about it. To put it mildly. Coming so soon after the November abortion, this one would have been unacceptable, unimaginable. And yet she was adamant—and of course could never, ever tell him the real reason: not only did she not want a child—not now, not ever—but she also wasn't sure whose baby this was. (If one dalliance with a bullfighter had driven Frank crazy, an out-of-wedlock child would have ended the marriage for good.) The collision between them, irresistible force and immovable object, must have been terrible. And the tears on his face were surely from fury as much as sadness. Starting with Nancy's 1947 abortion, this would have been (by his reckoning, anyway) the fourth child he had lost. "He never got over it, he never discussed it," Hank Sanicola recalled. "The only thing he ever said to me about it was, 'I shoulda beaten her fuckin' brains out for what she did to me and the baby, but I loved her too much.' "

Amid the angry bluster, he couldn't admit to Sanicola that there had been two babies.

———

Frank and Ava made it up somehow—it can't have been the usual way—and flew to Paris for a few gloomy days. The cable from Harry Cohn, even with its where-the-hell-are-you subtext, could only have come as a relief:

MONTGOMERY CLIFT ALREADY PROFICIENT IN ARMY DRILL
STOP SINCE YOU MUST DO SAME ROUTINE, SUGGEST YOU GET
BACK FEW DAYS EARLY STOP HARRY.

Excited now, Frank dashed off an answer:

DEAR HARRY, WILL COMPLY WITH REQUEST STOP DRILLING
WITH FRENCH ARMY OVER WEEKEND STOP EVERYTHING OK
STOP MAGGIO.

Then, with the best possible excuse, he dashed off, period. They
had spent a little over a week together, most of it fighting or in an abortion clinic. The marriage had become a travesty.

═══

Army drill was just the beginning of Montgomery Clift's proficiency.
Like Sinatra, he had been galvanized by *From Here to Eternity* from
the moment the novel came out, knowing at once that he was born to
play the role of Robert E. Lee Prewitt, Angelo Maggio's best friend in
G Company. It was almost as if James Jones had been thinking specifically of the actor when he described Prewitt: "a kind of intensity in the
face . . . a sort of deep tragic fire in the eyes." Also like Sinatra, Clift
was not the first choice for his role: Harry Cohn wanted the Columbia
contract player Aldo Ray—a raspy-voiced, muscle-bound former Navy
frogman, whose slight air of vulnerability stemmed mainly from his
inexperience as an actor. Ray hadn't worked for a couple of months, his
salary was mounting up, and as far as Cohn was concerned, that was
that. But Fred Zinnemann, to his great credit, was firm on Clift—so
firm that the director threatened to quit unless Clift was cast. Taken
aback by the soft-voiced Austrian's vehemence, the studio chief asked
him why.

"Because I want to make a good picture, and Montgomery Clift is
the only actor who can play Prewitt," Zinnemann said.

He knew what he was talking about. Zinnemann had directed Clift
in the actor's second movie, *The Search,* in 1948, and was well aware of
his gifts. The two had collaborated closely, the director even allowing
the actor to rewrite his lines, much to the chagrin of the film's producer.
"His scenes bristled with life," Zinnemann remembered. "And he filled

the screen with reverberations above and beyond the movie itself." The role of Prewitt—a sensitive outsider, a boxer who quit fighting because he accidentally blinded a friend in an Army boxing match—required an actor of depth and mystery, one who was himself a sensitive outsider. Montgomery Clift, a tortured homosexual and alcoholic, filled the bill in every respect.

Clift was a brilliantly intuitive, groundbreaking actor, with a gift for vanishing into his roles. He believed in the souls of his characters more than the words they spoke. "Good dialogue simply isn't enough to explain all the infinite gradations of a character," he said. "It's behavior—it's what's going on behind the lines." And as one who instinctively looked beyond surface appearances, he understood Frank Sinatra's potential. As early as the fall of 1952, when Sinatra was still a dark horse, Clift told a friend that Frank would be perfect to play Maggio.

Sinatra hit the ground running from the moment he landed in California. First came the week of rehearsals at the end of February, then five weeks of shooting interiors at Columbia. And remarkably, during this intense month and a half, the company and crew of *From Here to Eternity* saw not a trace of One-Take Charlie, the movie-set prima donna. Frank was thoroughly in gear, heeding Zinnemann and, especially, Clift as though his life depended on it. Which, in a real way, it did.

The two actors hit it off instantly. Each man stared into the other's remarkable blue eyes, recognizing not just the other's brilliance but also the wounds. "We had a mutual admiration thing going on," Frank said later, deflecting with characteristically tough talk his attraction to Clift's looks and obvious classiness (the actor was related to Abraham Lincoln's postmaster general and a secretary of the Treasury under Andrew Jackson)—not to mention the instant meeting of minds and sensibilities between Sinatra, the secretly sensitive genius, and Clift, the equally brilliant artist with the troubling sexuality. On the set of Clift's first movie, *Red River,* John Wayne had ostracized the young actor, and burst into laughter when the director, Howard Hawks, first tried to rehearse the climactic fistfight between the two men. But remarkably, despite all Sinatra's swaggering, no evidence exists that, even in the hypermasculine atmosphere of his coterie, he ever made a belittling remark about Clift. Rather, Frank seems to have understood at once that as deeply as he understood Maggio, he would need acting instruction from Clift on the order of the dancing instruction he'd received from Gene Kelly.

"Monty really coached Sinatra in the part of Maggio," said Clift's close friend Jack Larson. "He spelled out every beat, every moment, and Sinatra was grateful." The process began during rehearsals and continued throughout the shoot. After work was over for the day, the two men often went to the Naples Restaurant up the block, continuing their shoptalk over dinner.

"By his intensity," Zinnemann recalled, "[Clift] forced the other actors to come up to his standard of performance." And he forced Sinatra to raise his game as an actor. As Frank later explained:

> As a singer . . . I rehearse and plan exactly where I'm going.
> But as an actor, no, I can't do that. To me, acting is reacting.
> If you set it up right, you can almost go without knowing
> every line . . . If I rehearse to death, I lose the spontaneity I
> think works for me . . . With Montgomery, though, I had to
> be patient because I knew that if I watched this guy, I'd learn
> something.

In his singing career Frank had gotten huge mileage out of communicating vulnerability, and in Montgomery Clift he recognized a fellow artist. Screen acting, though, involved considerably more than looking soulful and putting a catch in your voice. There was an intense subtlety to it, a poetry of minute gestures. It was Sinatra's brilliance to understand this, and to observe, minutely, every move Clift made.

As Tom Santopietro wrote:

Sinatra here took on Clift's hunched posture, allowing it to emphasize his own vulnerable, frail physique. It's a physical approach that aided Sinatra immensely in conveying Maggio's "doomed gaiety." Maggio may have been a supporting role, but it made Frank Sinatra a top-drawer movie star. By blending small parts of Cagney's toughness with Bogart's jaded but vulnerable wiseguy, and overlaying the mix with his own distinctly Italian-American physicality—a lovable underdog with a chip on his shoulder—Sinatra arrived at an entirely original screen persona.

The rhythms of Maggio's Brooklynese were music to Frank's ears: when Sinatra spoke Maggio's lines, he might as well have been talking himself. He moved into the dialogue just as he inhabited the lyrics of a song, only in this case the words fit like a glove:

This outfit they can give back to Custer.

Or:

Man, what I would not give to have this character in the corner poolroom in my hometown.

That's "would not," not "wouldn't." The difference is tiny but crucial: it instantly and sharply denotes the wised-up street-corner character, circa early-to-mid-twentieth-century Greater New York–New Jersey area, that Damon Runyon immortalized, James Jones humanized, and Frank Sinatra was and would ever more publicly show himself to be. There's a poetry to this breaking up of contractions into their constituent parts that Sinatra would carry to the end of his life.[5] Maggio freed him to become himself.

As a singer, Frank seemed to have understood from the beginning that he could be nobody but himself. As awed as he might have been by Bing Crosby and Billie Holiday, he was remarkably free from influences. His voice, and the personality behind it, were unique. With acting it was a different story—he'd come to the art late. Singing is a form of acting, but a limited one. And the only persona Sinatra could come up with in his first films was a version of his early stage persona, which emphasized only his better angels—boyish charm, shy modesty.

Now he wasn't a boy anymore. The world had gotten more complicated, and so had he. His face and hair had thinned; his spirit had darkened. Wanting to update his image in 1948, he'd tried for the delinquent role in *Knock on Any Door,* but he was clearly too old to play a juvenile. Three years later, he'd attempted to bring somber tones to his performance in *Meet Danny Wilson,* but the movie came and went too fast for anyone to notice.

From Here to Eternity was his big chance, in every possible way: not only because of the distinguished material and company and the huge conspicuousness of the project, but also because of where Frank was in his life. His first legitimate shot at a big dramatic role had arrived at a moment when he was truly old enough, and experienced enough, to give a complicated performance. The paradox was that he had come to dramatic acting late enough in the game that he needed to get up to speed very quickly. "He was scared," said Ernest Borgnine, who played Fatso. "He had to prove himself again because he was right down to nothing." But he was also canny enough (and humbled enough) to realize his great good fortune at playing opposite a master.

An immediate bond between Frank and Monty was alcohol, though both were punctilious about not drinking during working hours. After hours was a different story. The author of *From Here to Eternity,* James Jones, a constant, starstruck presence on the shoot, was the third leg of the triangle. A little man with a big head and a tough scowl, Jones, like Sinatra and Clift, and like the author's fictional surrogate, Prewitt, was a sufferer: a hypersensitive former boxer and combat soldier battling his own demons of conflicted sexuality and alcoholism. Jones was strongly attracted to Clift, and though the feeling wasn't mutual, the actor, who was obsessed with dragging every possible bit of information about the military and his character out of the writer, stayed close. Frank, for his part, was awed to meet the author of a great book, and charmed to hear Jones's stories about the real Maggio.

"The three of them became inseparable during the filming of *From Here to Eternity,*" wrote Clift's biographer Patricia Bosworth.

"They were a motley trio," a press agent said. "Jones looked like a nightclub bouncer with his thick neck and broken face. And there's this edgy cocky little wop Sinatra always spoilin' for a fight, and then Monty who managed to radiate class and high standards even when pissing in the gutter . . ."

"We would get very, very loaded," Jones said. "After dinner and a lot more drinks we would weave outside into the night and all sit down on the curb next to a lamppost. It became our lamppost and we'd mumble more nonsense to each other. We felt very close."

While Burt Lancaster rolled in the surf (and, off camera, the hay) with Deborah Kerr, and other company members engaged in the usual occupational amours, Sinatra, Clift, and Jones behaved like a trio of moony frat boys on spring break—the worst thing any of them got accused of was dropping beer cans out the windows of the Roosevelt Hotel. Lancaster, wrote his biographer Kate Buford, "got so used to carrying Sinatra and Clift, dead drunk, to their rooms each night, undressing them, and putting them to bed, that on his birthday for years afterward he would get a telegram from Sinatra with the message 'Happy Birthday, Mom.'"

Frank was also apparently being faithful. (Or just careful. "After we filmed the knife fight between Montgomery Clift and myself," Ernest Borgnine recalled, "he said, 'Oh, hell, you guys are going to get through early. Maybe I'll come by and we'll have a couple of drinks, and then some broads, and who knows?' And he never showed up.") The gossipmongers of the era must have felt keenly disappointed. They were watching him carefully for slipups—something with Lana Turner would have been nice, but Lana had gone to Spain on vacation. Marilyn Maxwell had finally given up on him. The only real piece of dirt that spring was his continuing tax problems, which were all over the newspapers, the IRS having just slapped a lien on his income. Never had that measly *Eternity* salary looked so good. The most striking item that March reveals is that sometime during the week of the ninth, while the company temporarily closed down so that Burt Lancaster (who'd been detained wrapping *South Sea Woman* at Warner's) could rehearse, Frank slipped off to New York—and shopped for matching nutria trench coats for himself and Ava. The height of devotion, if not fiscal responsibility.

———

The role of Maggio may have had Oscar written all over it, but Sinatra was going to have to work very hard to bring it off—and to convince the world he could. Frank felt defensive enough that March that he went even further into hock to buy full-page ads in the trade papers proclaiming himself "box office insurance." The ads trumpeted that he'd been "a smash success at Riviera, Fort Lee; Chez Paree, Chicago; French Casino, N.Y.; Latin Quarter, Boston; and Chez Paree, Montreal," and urged the public to "watch for him as Maggio in Columbia Pictures' forthcoming production, 'From Here to Eternity.'"

Sinatra was talking not just to Hedda and Louella but also to such second-stringers of the Hollywood press as Frank Morriss, who had less than earthshaking business in mind. "We concocted a little joke, which I hope will work," Morriss wrote in his column.

Next week, Frank Sinatra will be working in the picture, and I'm going to visit the set. We're going to show Frankie boy the Match the Stars pictures, including the one of Ava as a child. We'll just see if Frankie can recognize his own wife. If not there'll be an awful lot of razzing.

Frank and the papers were virtually collaborators at this point: he was working hard to try to convince them (and by extension the public) that he was behaving himself and up to the task of playing Maggio, and the press seems to have been trying to persuade itself. "Crooner Frank Sinatra Tuesday joined the ranks of film greats who have switched from song and dance roles to straight drama," proclaimed a wire-service report, mentioning Joan Crawford, Ginger Rogers, Dick Powell, and Jane Wyman.

> Frankie flew 10,000 miles from Africa to Hollywood to try out for the role he coveted and finally won. His highest hope now is that his new impersonation will be well received by the public.
> "I know how I feel about it, but how the public will feel is another thing," he said.

It sounded rather plaintive. In a way Frank was raising expectations, putting huge pressure on himself; at the same time, though, he was asking for what the public had always been reluctant to extend him: tolerance. It was a brilliant job of public relations, one that he couldn't possibly have brought off himself, and in fact he hadn't: *Eternity's* unit publicist, Walter Shenson (who would go on to produce *A Hard Day's Night* and *Help!*), had taken over the latest Sinatra charm offensive and was stage-managing it in grand style. "I told him that I could do a lot for him if he'd just behave himself with the press," Shenson recalled.

> He was a pussycat. "Whatever you say, kid, whatever you say," he said. So I started bringing around news people to interview him. A couple of times he said, "I won't talk to that one. He was rude to Ava." Then I'd remind him of his promise to cooperate, and he'd be a charmer.
> One day I got a call from a press guy saying that the govern-

ment had just released a statement that Frank owed $109,000 in back taxes. He wanted a comment from Sinatra, so I went to his trailer and told him. He looked at me very calmly and said, "You don't think this is news, do you? If you owe $109,000, you know about it." I explained that I was getting phone calls from the press wanting a statement. He said to tell them anything I wanted. If I do, I said, it will have to be a quote from you. "Go ahead," he said. "Tell them whatever you want."

"Surely your lawyers and accountants are working with the government, aren't they?" I asked. Frank said they were, so I went back and called all the reporters. "Mr. Sinatra asked me to tell you the following: 'My lawyers and my accountants are

Frank and Monty. The two men had enormous respect for each other. By example and through the advice Sinatra eagerly sought from him, Clift raised Frank's acting to a new level.

working with the government lawyers and accountants, and if
it takes *From Here to Eternity*, I'm going to pay it all back.'" I
later told Frank that I *had* to publicize the picture first and him
second, but he thought that was brilliant.

Tax troubles and Ava troubles weren't his only distractions that
month. "Isn't Frank Sinatra switching soon from Columbia records
to RCA-Victor?" Earl Wilson wrote in early March. Not exactly, as it
turned out.

Nelson Riddle and Frank. The genius arranger and the genius singer
had much in common: a New Jersey background, domineering mothers,
solitary natures, restless sexual drives.

Of course, since Columbia had dropped him months earlier, Frank
couldn't "switch" to any record label. And he especially wasn't
switching to RCA Victor, where Manie Sacks, despite all his power
and influence as head of A&R, had tried more than once, with no success, to sell the washed-up singer to his sales force.

William Morris, too, was trying to peddle Sinatra: What good was a
singer who didn't record? (And what good was a client earning a mere

thousand a week?) Sam Weisbord, the president of the agency and the man who'd sewn up the *From Here to Eternity* deal for Frank, rang every record company's phone off the hook until he finally reached Alan Livingston.

Livingston, Capitol's vice president in charge of creative operations, had started at the fledgling label at the end of the war, fresh out of the Army and wet behind the ears. As low man on the totem pole, the boyish-looking ex-GI had been given the theoretically unenviable assignment of creating a children's record library: he responded by inventing Bozo the Clown. Together with Livingston's other brainstorm, the read-along record, Bozo sold millions of units and brought in huge merchandising revenues. Almost overnight, Alan Livingston achieved boy-wonder status. Seven years later, still just in his mid-thirties, he was hungry for a grown-up coup.

"Alan, we've just taken on representation of Sinatra," Weisbord told him.

"Really?" Livingston said. The response was more than polite; the record man was actually intrigued by what sounded, at that point, like a contrarian notion.

"Yes," the agent said. "Would you be interested in signing him?"

"Yes," Livingston said at once.

"You would?" Weisbord said.

It had popped out involuntarily: not an attitude that laid the foundation for a strong bargaining position. But bargaining wasn't the point at this stage of Sinatra's career; getting him a foothold was.

Capitol was more of a natural for Frank than Weisbord had imagined. The label had recently signed Axel Stordahl, who'd been telling everybody who would listen, "Frank's singing great again." A house producer named Dave Dexter, formerly a critic for *Down Beat*, was similarly vocal about his enthusiasm for Sinatra.

Weisbord took Frank in to meet with Livingston. Livingston recalled:

> He was meek, a pussycat, humble. He had been through terrible times. He was broke, he was in debt . . . I was told he had

tried to kill himself on occasion. He was at the lowest ebb of
his life . . . Everybody knew it.

Frank and I talked, and I signed him to a seven-year contract, one year with six options, which is as long as you can
sign anybody. I gave him a standard royalty of five percent and
gave him a scale advance. He was glad to have a place to make
records. And that's how I signed Sinatra.

Maybe Frank's humility was genuine; maybe he was employing
some of the acting skills he was learning from Monty Clift. He knew
that Capitol was hot, that Livingston was largely responsible, that the
label had recently made a superstar out of Nat "King" Cole. No matter
that the deal Livingston was offering was the kind that new artists, not
superstars, got (the advance was in the low three figures). No matter
that for the first time in his life, Sinatra would have to cover his own
recording costs. He was glad to have a place to make records.

If he was superstitious, he wasn't thinking about it when he agreed
to meet Livingston for lunch on Friday, March 13, 1953, at Lucey's,[1] a
celebrity watering hole on Melrose, right across the street from the
Paramount gate and Capitol's recording studios. The food smelled delicious, and Frank was in great good spirits—he felt hungry again. As
his witness, Livingston had brought along his girlfriend, the actress
Betty Hutton, a square-jawed blonde who liked to laugh: there were
plenty of laughs. Sinatra had brought Sanicola and Frank Military, a
music-publishing pal who screened songs for him. Livingston waited
till the drinks had arrived before unsnapping his briefcase and taking
out the papers. He raised his glass to a great association.

The toast was seconded by all. Frank clinked his glass with the
executive's, then took a long pull of Jack Daniel's. Livingston handed
him a fountain pen; Frank regarded the papers on the table. He knew
well what Capitol's option clause specified: the label could drop him in
a year if things didn't work out. March 1954. Who knew where anybody
would be in March 1954? But things would work out, if he had anything to do with it. He scratched his signature on the contract.

It was a long, pleasant lunch, yet the proceedings were of little note to the outside world. The next morning, a tiny wire-service item on page two in many of the nation's papers carried the news, buried beneath articles about a UFO sighting over New Mexico's Kirtland Air Force Base and the illness of the president of Czechoslovakia. "Frank Sinatra was signed to a Capital [*sic*] recording contract today, terminating his long association with Columbia records," it read, not quite accurately.

The next week, Alan Livingston flew to Capitol's annual sales convention in Estes Park, Colorado. "We had every salesman in our distributing company there, every branch manager, every district manager, every promotion man," he recalled. "There must have been a couple of hundred people. And I got up and talked about future artists and recordings, and I announced that we had just signed Frank Sinatra."

Everyone in the room groaned.

Livingston raised his hands to quiet them. "Look," he told his sales force, "I can only judge on talent. I can't judge what people did in the past. I only know talent, and Frank is the best singer in the world. There's nobody who can touch him."

Still, that groan stayed with him. The past was exactly what Sinatra had to get away from.

"Hey, do me one favor and do yourself a favor," Livingston told Frank when he got back to town. The executive said he had a great young arranger he wanted to team Frank with. But Sinatra shook his head practically before the executive had finished speaking.

"I've worked with Axel for practically my whole career," he said. "I can't leave Axel."

Livingston asked Frank just to hear him out. The arranger was amazingly talented. His name was Nelson Riddle.

Frank shrugged—never heard of him. Practically nobody had. Riddle, a former trombonist and arranger with Tommy Dorsey in the post-Sinatra period, seemed to specialize in working anonymously. When Livingston told Sinatra about all the sides Riddle had arranged for Bing Crosby, Nat Cole, Mel Tormé, and Billy Eckstine, Sinatra shook his head again. Why hadn't he heard of this guy?

They hit on an agreement: Frank would do a session with Stordahl, Capitol would put out the record, and they would see what ensued. If the cash registers rang, fine. If not, Frank would give what's-his-name a shot.

———

"All hair restorers having failed," Erskine Johnson confirmed on March 16, "Frank Sinatra has now taken to wearing hats."

———

A week or so later, Sinatra had yet another on-set visitor at Columbia: the syndicated columnist Harold Heffernan, whose prose style was as clunky as his byline. "Salient factors that keep the pugnacious Frank Sinatra's career from wallowing are a dogged tenacity and an enthusiasm about whatever he attempts," Heffernan thesaurused, in his April 2 column.

> No one could be more hopeful about a movie role than the bean-pole singer is over his non-warbling, unromantic part in Columbia's "From Here to Eternity."
>
> "I play Montgomery Clift's pal," explained Frank on the set. "No girls for me. I just adore this fellow, and eventually give up my life, indirectly, for him. It's a complete change from anything I have ever done."

It would have occurred to nearly anyone who read Heffernan's piece that Thursday that Sinatra hadn't done much warbling in a while. This day was to be different. All morning and afternoon Frank worked hard on his scenes at the Columbia-Gower studios, then he showered and put on a dark suit and grabbed a quick bite with Monty at the Naples. At about 8:30 p.m., Sanicola picked him up, and they took the short drive over to Capitol's recording facility, KHJ studios, a former radio station next to Paramount.

Excited, Frank walked into Studio C, where Stordahl, Livingston, and a putty-faced, high-pantsed producer named Voyle Gilmore were waiting for him. Record producers ran the gamut from control freaks like Mitch Miller to mere knob turners: the soft-spoken Gilmore fell somewhere in the middle. He knew how to get a good sound from a session, but also knew that Sinatra had a thorough understanding of what did and didn't work for him. Gilmore was also aware that Alan Livingston had originally picked Dave Dexter to run the control room that night, and that Frank had vetoed him. In fact, at the mention of Dexter's name, Frank had frozen, his phenomenal memory for slights and insults having instantly clicked onto a mildly critical review in *Down Beat* that Dexter had written years before.[2]

Gilmore was an amiable and gentle man, as quiet and thoughtful as Stordahl. Frank saw other friendly faces there: the reedman Skeets Herfurt and the trumpeter Zeke Zarchy, old pals from the Dorsey days; Bill Miller at the piano. In fact, he knew almost every musician in the room, since most of them had worked on Hollywood sessions for Columbia. Total pros, all of them. He was in good hands.

Frank sang happily that night, recording four songs: "Lean Baby," an infectiously jivey Billy May blues about a skinny girlfriend; a sappy ballad called "I'm Walking Behind You" and an equally sappy waltz, "Don't Make a Beggar of Me"; and one standard, Johnny Mercer and Rube Bloom's great "Day In, Day Out."

It was an odd session. Sinatra was in excellent voice, but the material didn't quite rise to the occasion. True, "Lean Baby"—arranged not by Stordahl but by his (and the bandleader May's) musical deputy Heinie Beau, in the bright and brassy Billy May style—was thoroughly charming. And "Day In, Day Out" was magnificent, if somewhat sedate—but Sinatra, for reasons of his own, would eventually decide not to release it. Of greatest concern were the middle two numbers, "Walking" and "Beggar," both of them outright dogs.

But he was recording again, and he was pleased. After the session, Livingston took Sinatra across the street to Lucey's for a celebratory drink. Sanicola lagged a few paces behind. The record executive noticed that Frank was walking taller, looking more alert, smiling. "It was late and we were sitting in the bar having a drink," Livingston recalled.

> Nobody else was in the place except for a man who was sitting across the bar. Frank and I were talking. I said, "Why don't you take it easy? Get a better image." He said, "Alan, I don't do anything." All of a sudden, the man says [to Livingston], "What are you doing, buying a drink for your leech friend?"
>
> Frank said, "Knock it off." The guy said, "Knock it off, knock it off . . ." And Frank didn't do a thing, but his kind of a bodyguard went up and grabbed this guy—I thought he was going to kill him—and threw him out of the restaurant. Frank said, "See? That's the trouble I get in. It's not my fault."

Sometimes, miraculously enough, it wasn't. But the image of Sinatra as an aggrieved innocent to whom trouble came unbidden was no truer, then or later, than the image of him as a thug. He was more complicated than that, even if the world didn't know it yet.

=====

Astonishing to think that only a couple of months before, he'd been languishing in Africa, cooking spaghetti and sweating bullets. Now he was back in action—not quite clicking on all cylinders, but busy. Hedda Hopper spotted him dining with Judy Garland and Sid Luft. "Could they have been talking about getting Frank to play opposite Judy in the musical version of 'A Star Is Born'?" the columnist wondered. (If indeed that's what they were discussing, Frank might have found the role of the alcoholic fading movie star Norman Maine a little too close for comfort.) The television columnist Hal Humphrey noted that "Sinatra appears to be almost set to star in a TV series to be produced by Lucille Ball and Desi Arnaz. The story would deal with the trials and tribulations of a musician and is called 'Blue in the Night.' "

Also a little too close to the bone.

Frank was talking to all kinds of people. Amazingly, given the state of his finances, not to mention his situation with the IRS, it was reported in March that he was seeking a Nevada gambling license and a 2 percent share in the brand-new Sands Hotel & Casino, in Las Vegas, at a price of $54,000. Where did a man who barely had a pot to make pasta in intend to get $54,000? A lot of people, including the Nevada Tax Commission, were interested in that one. "The singer said in his application that the money would come from his own assets and that he has no liabilities," reported the Associated Press. "But the tax commission said it wants to investigate, among other subjects, Sinatra's federal tax status."

The seventh casino on the Strip, which had opened on Frank's thirty-seventh birthday, December 12, 1952, was a natural foothold for Sinatra. With its ultramodern Googie-style architecture by the Desert Inn designer Wayne McAllister, its seventeen-story main tower looming in lonely splendor over Route 91, the Sands was a signpost of the new Vegas, a spaceship that would transport the town from its spurs-and-tumbleweed past into a neon-bright future. A big-time Houston gambler named Jakie Freedman had founded the place, but unlike the Flamingo's Billy Wilkerson and the DI's Wilbur Clark, who had run out of money while constructing their dream palaces and had to let the Mob muscle in, Freedman came to town loaded (after it got too hot for the quasi-legal casino he owned in his native Houston) and stayed loaded. Freedman was also connected. He had important friends in Vegas, and in New York and Miami, friends who were eager to tap into the cash cascades that were flowing from the Sands, but shy about seeing their names in cold type in the newspapers and on legal documents.

Sinatra and Freedman had friends—or, as the expression went, friends of friends—in common. Possibly some of the men who had looked kindly on Frank from the beginning were now extending him a favor, fronting him the money to buy into a dream? Or was he being asked to return a favor, by putting his name to a contract in their stead?

Suffice it to say that Frank had nothing like $54,000 lying around, that the money he wasn't sending straight to Nancy's lawyers he was paying to William Morris, and that Las Vegas—and the Sands in particular—had suddenly become a very friendly place. Jakie Freedman had even persuaded the guy who'd been running the Copacabana for its real owner to bring a little New York west and run the Sands for him. Jack Entratter was the guy's name: a former bouncer—a big, heavyset fellow with dark slick hair and a ready grin on his tough moon face. In honor of Jack (and of Frank Costello, too), Jakie decided to name the main showroom at the Sands after the Copa. It was a room Sinatra would soon own a piece of, then more than a piece.

═══

On the evening of Monday, April 6, Fred Zinnemann and the stars of *From Here to Eternity* flew to Hawaii for two weeks of location shooting. Burt Lancaster recalled the flight:

> Deborah Kerr and me and Frank and Monty are sitting up in the front of the plane. And he and Monty are drunk. Monty, poor Monty, was this kind of a drinker—he'd chug-a-lug one martini and conk out. And Frank was, I believe, having a few problems, and so, when we arrived, these two bums were unconscious. They were gone! Deborah and I had to wake them up.

Harry Cohn, who had already taken up residence at the Royal Hawaiian Hotel in Honolulu, met them at the airport, all but tapping his wristwatch. Perhaps, he told Zinnemann, one of the night scenes could be shot right away—maybe that thing with Burt and Deborah on the beach? Zinnemann took Cohn aside and told him gently that there were tides and other logistics involved; it wasn't a scene that could just be dashed off. Besides, he asked (as Lancaster discreetly helped his two groggy co-stars into a car), mightn't everyone do better with a day to get acclimated? Cohn grumbled. Zinnemann gave him a Viennese smile. Production began on Wednesday morning the eighth.

The work went fast and mostly smoothly. Frank was still completely engaged, but Zinnemann had stumbled upon an unusual challenge in shooting the scenes between Maggio and Prewitt:

> Sinatra was at his best in the first or second take of a scene: in later takes he was apt to lose spontaneity, whereas Clift would use each take as a rehearsal to add more detail so that the scenes gained in depth as we went on. It was an interesting problem when they did a scene together: how to get the best performance from them both in the same take.

As the actor Robert Wagner recalled, "Frank was very conscious of his lack of [acting] training; he was never sure that he would be able to reproduce an effect more than once or twice because he had to rely on emotion more than craft." But Zinnemann's account shows that it wasn't just about temperament: Sinatra knew what really worked for him.

He and Monty labored diligently during the day, but as had been the case the previous month, the evenings were another story. "Every night, after work, we would meet in Frank's room," Lancaster recalled.

> He had a refrigerator and he would open it and there would be these iced glasses. He would prepare the martinis with some snacks while we were getting ready to go to an eight o'clock dinner. We'd sit and chat about the day's work and he would try his nightly call to Ava, who was in Spain. In those days in Spain, if you lived *next door* to your friends you couldn't get

them on the telephone, let alone try to get them on the phone from Hawaii. He never got through. Not one night. When you finished your martini, he would take your glass from you, open up the icebox and get a fresh cold glass, and by eight o'clock he and Monty would be unconscious. I mean really unconscious. Every night. So Deborah and I would take Frank's clothes off and put him to bed. Then I would take Monty on my shoulders and we would carry him down to his room, take *his* clothes off and dump *him* in bed. And then she and I and the Zinnemanns would go out and have dinner.

Ava was in Spain on vacation, after recuperating from the abortion and finally wrapping *Mogambo,* but she wouldn't be coming back anytime soon: she had become an expatriate. She would remain one, more or less, for the rest of her life, having learned—Frank wasn't the only one worried about taxes—that she could keep the bulk of her income out of the clutches of the goddamn IRS if she lived overseas. And Europe, with its wine and its siestas, its depressed economy and its relaxed attitudes about all kinds of things that upset puritanical, work-obsessed, Red-obsessed America, was more to her liking anyway.

She was investigating the many advantages of her new turf. Frank wouldn't have been consoled to know that, as was her habit when he was far, far away, Ava was kicking up her heels. And not alone. As Dorothy Kilgallen noted provocatively in her column: "Frank Sinatra, who tossed Lana Turner out of his Palm Springs house when he found her visiting his wife a few months ago, may make more blow-top headlines before long. Despite his disapproval—to put it mildly—of their friendship, Lana and Ava have plans to do some vacation chumming in Europe."

Then, in Ava's case, there was another bullfighter.

This was a very different one, and this time she was the pursuer rather than the pursued. Mario Cabré had been a clown, a puffed-up poetaster, but Luis Miguel Domínguin was the real deal: the greatest matador in Spain, after the tragic death of Manolete. Tall, coolly humorous, devastatingly handsome, Dominguín was a great favorite of Ernest Hemingway, who would later write about him—calling him "a combination Don Juan and Hamlet"—in *The Dangerous Summer*. At twenty-six, he was also four years younger than Ava; he also had a gorgeous Portuguese-Thai girlfriend, which made him all the more intriguing. The movie star and the torero smiled, they flirted; he spoke no English. It was three glorious weeks of sun and fiestas, then Lana had to go home and Ava had to return to London to work on *Knights of the Round Table*.

Frank was luckier. In photos from the set, he was all business in his regulation khakis and Smokey the Bear campaign hat, looking as neat and trim as the soldier he never was, eyes wide with interest as he listened respectfully to Zinnemann. For weeks on end Sinatra channeled all his intensity into the role. "He was very, very good—all the time," Zinnemann said years later. "No histrionics, no bad behavior . . . He played Maggio so spontaneously we almost never had to reshoot a scene." Yet during the shooting of a climactic scene, he finally exploded. Zinnemann recalled:

> One of the last location scenes to be shot in Hawaii was a night exterior—Maggio's arrest by the military police. Maggio, blind drunk along with Prewitt in a Honolulu park, feels harassed beyond endurance; his rage boils over, he *jumps up,* berating the policemen, who are twice his size, and attacks them.
>
> The afternoon's rehearsal was excellent, but Cohn had heard about it and thought that we would be in trouble with the Army—Sinatra was just too provocative. He wanted us to tone things down; the actors and I disagreed with this view, although I felt the objection had come from someone outside, above Cohn.
>
> For a few mad hours I believed that I could get away with shooting the scene as rehearsed and presenting Cohn with an accomplished fact. Night fell; lights and camera were ready.

Cohn was not present, but his informers were. At the last moment, he roared up to the set, together with the garrison's top echelon of officers. They had come ostensibly to watch us at work but it soon became clear that a confrontation could develop and lead to closing down the picture. We were, after all, on army territory. I knew that we could be jeopardizing the whole film; it was a situation I could not win. To quit was out of the question as far as I was concerned.

In Kitty Kelley's rendition of the incident, "Frank and Monty had rehearsed the scene standing up, but, just before shooting, Frank decided that he wanted to do it sitting down. Zinnemann objected, but Frank insisted—loudly and profanely. Monty backed Zinnemann and remained standing to follow the script. This so angered Sinatra that he slapped Monty hard. The director tried to placate Sinatra by agreeing to film the scene with Frank sitting if he would also do one take standing. Frank refused and became extremely abusive."

Zinnemann, Harry Cohn's wife, Joan, and the unit publicist, Walter Shenson, each gave a different account, but none of them jibe with Kelley's version, which feels off. Why would the kinetic and impatient Sinatra want to do any scene sitting rather than standing? What seems more likely is that Zinnemann rehearsed the scene as written, and that when Cohn came roaring up (memorably, in a military limousine, still dressed in the white dinner jacket he'd been wearing while dining with the general in command of U.S. Army forces in the Pacific), a Situation developed. Zinnemann chose the better part of valor, and Frank, who had believed passionately in the film from the beginning, but even more so now that he'd put in six weeks' worth of hard work, simply blew. "His fervor, his anger, his bitterness had something to do with the character of Maggio," Burt Lancaster said,

but also with what he had gone through in the last number of years: a sense of defeat, and the whole world crashing in on him, his marriage to Ava going to pieces—all of those things caused this ferment in him, and they all came out in that performance. You knew this was a raging little man who was, at the same time, a good human being. Monty watched the filming of one of Frank's close-ups and said, "He's going to win the Academy Award."

And now they—whoever they were—wanted to neuter his big scene. No wonder he lost it.

"I was on the sidelines watching but not hearing anything," Shenson recalled.

I could just see the pantomime of Harry Cohn running up in his white dinner jacket, striding into the middle of the set and making some pronouncement. Then he turned around and walked out and got back into the limousine. The next morning was Sunday, and I was on the beach with the rest of the crew. Cohn spotted me and asked if I had been there last night.

"Did you see that son of a bitch, Sinatra?" he asked.

"Yeah, I saw him but I don't know what was happening."

"Well, that bastard guinea was trying to tell us what to do. You know where he is now? He's on an airplane going back to the studio."

"How could you send him back without seeing the rushes?" I asked.

"I don't care," said Cohn. "That dirty little dago is not going to tell me how to make my movies."

In fact, he hadn't. In the end, as Zinnemann said, "Sinatra delivered his speech while *seated.*" Frank had caved, not triumphed, and the resulting scene isn't nearly as powerful as it would've been had Zinnemann been able to follow the script, and Sinatra, his artistic instincts. Remarkably, though, during the course of this long day Frank had both rehearsed and capitulated, two courtesies he would be less and less willing to grant his directors as his star began to rise again.

All too predictably, though, Sinatra blamed Zinnemann. (And in all likelihood, kept blaming him. In the seventy-plus linear feet of Fred Zinnemann's papers in the Margaret Herrick Library of the Academy of Motion Picture Arts and Sciences, there is not a single piece of correspondence from Sinatra.) "I can't blame him for being upset," Zinnemann recalled, years after tempers had cooled—or his had, any-way—"but I wonder whether he ever understood what was at stake."

In the director's estimation, the movie itself had been at stake. *Eternity* was made with the cooperation of an all-powerful U.S. Army, not so long after that army had done nothing less than save the free world, and just three months after General Dwight D. Eisenhower had been elected president. It was not a time for tweaking authority. Dur-ing the filming of *From Here to Eternity*, the accused atomic spies Julius and Ethel Rosenberg sat on death row; Senator Joseph McCarthy was continuing to conduct hearings of accused subversives, many of them in the movie industry. Fred Zinnemann was a European Jew, with an acute sense of the unpredictability of power. Harry Cohn was a tough American Jew who, as the maker of a movie determinedly friendly to Army interests, could break bread with the commander of U.S. forces in the Pacific.

And Frank Sinatra didn't care about any of it. They had messed with his scene, and they could all screw themselves.

=====

He'd had another reason to be tense. The afternoon before shooting that last scene, Frank had phoned Axel Stordahl. They had a record-ing date at Capitol set up for the Thursday after he got back from Hawaii, and Sinatra wanted to discuss the song list. But after a couple of moments of chitchat, the arranger fell silent. Frank asked him if anything was wrong.

Axel said he couldn't be at the session. He was leaving for New York tomorrow.

He was what?

He was beginning a TV show. With Eddie Fisher.

The last three words might as well have been a carving knife plunged into Sinatra's chest. There was a long silence.

Apparently, Axel hadn't heard what Frank had said. They had a recording session at Capitol on Thursday night.

Stordahl said he couldn't be there. He had a contract.

Another deep silence.

The arranger began to elaborate, but then he realized the line had gone dead.

Frank called Alan Livingston and let him have it. Livingston was ready for him. He listened patiently, counted to five, and then almost instantly defused Sinatra's anger by telling him he'd secured Billy May to lead the session. May was a top-drawer bandleader, one of the hippest arrangers and conductors around (and also an old Livingston cohort who'd done the music for the Bozo the Clown records). A big, hearty guy, tough but cheerful. Livingston knew Frank couldn't object, and he didn't.

In fact, though, the executive was playing a shell game with the singer. Livingston had known for a while that Stordahl was leaving—he'd encouraged it. It was time for Sinatra to move on. Axel was wonderful, but those somnolent strings of his were a relic of Frank's Columbia past. Livingston had made big hits with Nelson Riddle and Nat "King" Cole, and now he wanted to make more big hits with Riddle and Sinatra. Riddle wanted in, too, but Riddle was an arranger's arranger, a studio man who'd never led a band or made a splash. Livingston would have to work a minor subterfuge.

The morning after his climactic scene, Frank was on an airplane back to Los Angeles. His movie work was done, his fate was in the hands of a thousand imponderables—Hollywood, in other words—and it was time to get back to what had made him great in the first place. To what he could, to a great degree, control.

Just after 8:00 p.m. on Thursday, April 30, an unseasonably cool and rainy day, Frank got out of his car, flicked his cigarette into the gutter, and strode into Capitol's KHJ studios at 5515 Melrose Avenue. Studio C, down the hall on the first floor, was warm and pleasantly crowded, once again full of familiar faces—Skeets, Zarchy, Miller, Alvin Stoller, Conrad Gozzo—and a couple of unfamiliar ones. One was a sad-eyed trombonist with a jutting lower lip: his name was Milt Bernhart. Frank, who had specifically requested Bernhart after hearing his beautiful solo on a Stan Kenton number called "Salute," looked right through the newcomer, more concerned with another stranger standing on the podium, right where Billy May should have been. Sinatra turned to a producer he knew, Alan Dell, and with a sideways jerk of his head indicated the serious-looking, chubby-cheeked, V-hairline character with the baton in his hand.

"Who's this?" he said.

"He's just conducting the band," Dell said quickly. "We've got Billy's arrangements."

May, Dell explained (Livingston had prepped him), had had to leave town unexpectedly to do a gig in Florida. But his arrangements were golden, and what's-his-name on the stand—Sinatra didn't catch the name—was very capable.

Frank reviewed the song list: Ted Koehler and Harold Arlen's "I've Got the World on a String," Koehler and Rube Bloom's "Don't Worry 'Bout Me," a bouncy old Harlan Thompson–Harry Archer tune, "I Love You" (not to be confused with the Grieg-inspired "I Love You" he'd recorded for Columbia, or the Cole Porter "I Love You" he wouldn't get around to recording for a few more years), and his Dorsey standby "South of the Border." He'd been singing the last one since he was a kid, and the second two for years. As for "String," he'd only put it on his repertoire for club dates during the past year, partly in ironic tribute to his troubles, also from a sincere wish that things might actually go his way again, soon. In any case, it was a great song. He liked to perform it at medium tempo, a semi-ballad cadence: ballads were still his home base.

From the moment the nervous-faced guy on the podium signaled the downbeat, Frank knew something was up. Stoller clashed a pair of cymbals; the horns swirled a downward-spiraling cadenza; and then the second Frank sang, "got the string around my fin-ger," the brass *kicked*—BANG!—and the band was cooking. Frank was smiling as he sang, as the seventeen musicians swung along behind him—he even had a smile for the unsmiling guy on the stand, who was waving his arms for all he was worth.

It sure didn't sound like Billy to Frank. It didn't sound like any-body. He loved it.

They did a take, and then another, got it just right. It was golden—but it wasn't Billy May. "Who wrote that arrangement?" Frank asked Alan Dell.

"This guy," Dell said, indicating Mr. Serious, who was distractedly leafing through pages of sheet music. "Nelson Riddle."

The name registered for the first time. Sinatra made a surprised face. "Beautiful," he said.

It was a serious compliment. Frank was generous with gifts and money but extremely stingy when it came to praise. If he said it, he meant it; if he didn't mean it, he didn't say anything.

He looked at Riddle and said it again. "Beautiful." And Mr. Serious managed a quick, almost undetectable smile: more like a wince, really.

═══

Nelson Smock Riddle (the unfortunate middle name was Dutch) may have been the most important man in Frank Sinatra's life whom Sinatra never even tried to befriend. Unlike so many men in the popular-music business, the arranger never pretended to be a hail-fellow-well-met; rather, he was intimacy averse, a dour, caustic, buttoned-up Lutheran who happened—like the man he was meeting for the first time that Thursday evening in April 1953—to be a musical genius.

Like Sinatra, Nelson Riddle was a New Jersey–born only child of a domineering mother and a weak father, a man with powerful sex-ual urges and a fondness for alcohol. Like Sinatra, he was awash in

conflicts; unlike Sinatra, Riddle buried his conflicts rather than acting them out. He was a solitary drinker, and he either sublimated
his obsessions with women into his work or hid them in clandestine
affairs. Although he would become moderately famous, his introverted
nature and his preference for the more intellectual art of arranging
over composition threw him into the shade. Later Riddle would feel
desperate envy for the fame and wealth of such big-name show-offs
as Henry Mancini and André Previn, men who could compose and
arrange and smile for the television cameras. He would chew himself
up inside as he created masterpieces for others.

He was a middling professional trombone player, skillful enough
to play for the Charlie Spivak and Tommy Dorsey big bands at a young
age (he joined Dorsey at twenty-three, in 1944, and held the third chair
in the trombone section), but more valued for his skills as an arranger.
When Nelson Riddle set pencil to paper, magic happened.

It is extraordinarily difficult, in the post–rock 'n' roll, post-singer-
songwriter, digitized world of modern popular music, to convey just
how important a figure the arranger used to be. Of course orchestration
was always essential to classical music, but in the early twentieth century jazz and jazz-based popular music began in improvisation. Yet as
the Jazz Age turned into the Swing Era, as the bands got bigger and the
dance numbers got more elaborate, arrangements became ever more
essential. And writing the tempi and harmonies and counterpoints in
such a way as to match—or even deepen—the heart-quickening rush
of improvised jazz was an art few men could master. Many of the early
white big bands—like Paul Whiteman's—were tootling, anodyne versions of more dynamic and artistically complex black organizations
such as Duke Ellington's and Jimmie Lunceford's. This had less to do
with the players—there was no shortage of great white instrumentalists—than with the men who were writing the charts. Tommy Dorsey's
band got a rocket boost in 1939 when Dorsey stole Lunceford's great
arranger Sy Oliver. And Oliver was still writing for Dorsey when Nelson Riddle joined Dorsey's band five years later.

Riddle had great ears—classically trained ears—and he paid close attention. According to Peter J. Levinson, "He couldn't help but notice the inherent charm in Oliver's writing—his strong sense of the beat, the basic swinging effects, staccato phrases with an element of humor; a brilliant sense of continuity and climax—which was combined with his superlative use of dynamics. (As Oliver once told Dorsey's close friend Eddie Collins, 'Dynamics, that's the secret.')"

Nelson Riddle had all kinds of secrets. While the other players in Dorsey's band were staying up to all hours, getting pie-eyed, chasing skirts, snoring through the morning, then staggering blearily to the next gig, Riddle was listening to his records of Debussy and Ravel and Delius. He too loved liquor and women and the pounding beat of great jazz. He loved Sy Oliver's arrangement of Lunceford's "Stomp It Off"— and he loved Jacques Ibert's "Ports of Call." His writing flowered in the territory between.

Riddle spent a year in the Army at the end of the war, then, fatefully, decided against returning to being a cog in Dorsey's trombone section. He wanted to write. As the big-band era gave way to the age of the singer in the mid- and late 1940s, he found himself in Los Angeles, arranging for anyone who would hire him. Up to the time when he first met Sinatra, Riddle's strongest suit had been ghostwriting. He was so musically adept—and so naturally self-effacing—that he could arrange in anybody's style. He also frequently subcontracted: he first connected with Nat "King" Cole when an overtaxed arranger named Les Baxter threw Riddle a couple of tunes to orchestrate for a Cole recording date. One of the songs was 1950's "Mona Lisa." It turned into a monster hit.

By late 1951, Riddle had become Nat Cole's musical director, a job that led to freelance arranging gigs for a wide variety of singers: Billy Eckstine, Kate Smith, and Mel Tormé, among others. Yet, according to Will Friedwald, "Riddle was still considered a newcomer when [Alan] Livingston and [Voyle] Gilmore brought him to the attention of Frank Sinatra in 1953."

Hence all Alan Dell's prefatory disclaimers about Billy May at the

April 30 session—and hence Riddle's extreme seriousness. The state of Sinatra's career didn't matter a hill of beans to Nelson Riddle: he knew a fellow genius when he heard one. And he wanted very badly to work with Frank Sinatra—as himself. His grave demeanor on the podium hid the fact that he was quaking inside.

He was able to show what he had on the first two numbers, "I've Got the World on a String," then "Don't Worry 'Bout Me." Then he waxed chameleonic. "Now we have to make like Billy May," he announced, in businesslike tones, as he led Frank and the band into "I Love You" and

Frank recording at Capitol Studio C, West Hollywood, April 1953.

"South of the Border." The arrangements sounded exactly like May, and the players swung precisely as they would have under his baton. Fifty years later, Ted Nash, a sax player on the session who'd also worked with May, declared, " 'South of the Border'—I thought that was Billy's arrangement—it's so typically Billy. I can't picture that Nelson would have done that in Billy's style—Nelson was *so* ultra-serious! All Billy's arrangements were written out for us. Billy was known for his special slides and slurps. There would be special coding on the paper, so the notes to slide on were known. We all knew how he worked and the sounds to aim for."

Riddle had written every slide and slurp. And not only the latter two May-esque cuts, but the first two also, would be released under the label "Frank Sinatra with Billy May and His Orchestra."

Frank loved Billy May; he would do important work with him in the years to come. But as Sinatra listened to the gloriously exuberant playback of "I've Got the World on a String" late that Thursday night, he knew that something very new, and very big, was up, something rich and strange and quite extraordinary. It was as if he had awakened from a long winter into a spring unlike any he had ever imagined. And more: the words of the song had come true at last.

"Jesus Christ," he breathed, almost prayerfully, his eyes wide and blazing. "I'm back! I'm back, baby, I'm back!"

Frank and Ava in Italy, May 1953. He knew he was back, but the world would take a while to find out. His European tour went from bad to worse.

Yet the rest of 1953 was to be a period of hard work and only momentary triumphs, of dazzling new artistic landscapes glimpsed teasingly, then fogged in. The day after Frank recorded "I've Got the World on a String," he had another session at Capitol, with the same players as the day before, a tight jazz ensemble—reeds, brass, rhythm, no strings. Riddle was once again on the podium. This time it was his session, with his arrangements exclusively, and it went terribly wrong on the first run-through. The first number was Koehler, Barris, and Moll's "Wrap Your Troubles in Dreams." "Sinatra was at his lead sheet—I don't think we'd even made a take yet," the trombonist Milt Bernhart recalled.

> He was running the song over, and suddenly stopped—cold. And the band stopped. Frank said, "Give them a break." He crooked his finger at Nelson, and they walked out of the studio. I recognized that the arrangement hadn't gone over at all. Most of the guys began to play poker; I don't know why, but I followed [Sinatra and Riddle], and watched them in the smaller studio, from the hallway.

Bernhart could see the singer and the arranger behind the soundproof glass, but couldn't hear what they were saying. "Nelson was standing frozen, and Frank was doing all the talking," Bernhart said.

> His hands were moving, but he was not angry . . . he seemed to be telling [Riddle] something of great importance. He was gesticulating, his hands going up and down and sideways. He was describing music, and singing! When we came back, the date was over. And I was positive that I knew what Frank was telling him—it was about the arrangement! I could tell it was very busy. Too busy. There was no room for the singer. If they had taken away the singer, it would have made a great instru- mental . . . At that point, Nelson had a lot of technique as an arranger, but he had to be told to take it easy when writing for a singer. And he was told! Frank was giving him a lesson: a lesson in writing for a singer. A lesson in writing for Frank Sinatra . . .
>
> Sinatra could have dumped him. Other singers would have said, "Well, get another guy," if they were as important as Frank Sinatra. But he didn't. Which means that he recognized some- thing in Nelson that a lot of people wouldn't.

Namely, that Nelson was brilliant, and he was trying too hard. He had already passed the audition. Sinatra addressed him as one craftsman to another, and with a note of gentle respect. Frank chose four new numbers, Riddle worked feverishly through the night, then they reconvened the next day, this time with a full orchestra and strings, for a rare Saturday session.

Frank and Nelson shelved "Dreams" and tried four ballads: "Anytime, Anywhere," "My One and Only Love," "I Can Read Between the Lines," and, of all things, the theme to *From Here to Eternity*, onto which lyrics had hastily been slapped to capitalize on the film's summer release. Sinatra was in wonderful, mature voice that Saturday, but the material was mainly unremarkable, with the mixed exception of Robert Mellin and Guy Wood's "My One and Only Love." It's a beautiful melody, but Frank can't quite find his way into the stilted lyric— and to make a song great, he always needed to live inside the words. (Oddly enough, two versions of the tune that have held up better are the glorious Johnny Hartman–John Coltrane collaboration and Chet Baker's cracked and whispery rendition: in each of these cases, however, the singer is more instrument than interpreter.)

What's most notable about the four tracks Sinatra and Riddle laid down is that they *worked*. The recordings weren't ecstatic, but the strings supported Sinatra's voice warmly and solidly—and never (as Stordahl's strings always threatened) soporifically. At times Riddle's fiddles lilted ever so slyly, giving promise of glories to come. The session was a noble effort and a good place holder. Nelson had labored heroically to make it simple and beautiful, but for the time being, simple and pretty would have to do.

=====

Crooner Frank Sinatra arrived at London airport today and greeted his wife, Ava Gardner, in the privacy of the customs hall [the Associated Press reported on Monday, May 4]. "It is two months since we have seen each other—much too long," Sinatra said.

They will leave this week end for Milan, where Sinatra will
begin a three months' singing tour of the continent and Britain.

It sounded romantic and glamorous: Frank had told Ava it could be
their second honeymoon, but the tour was also desperately practical.
Working for over two months on *From Here to Eternity* for a sum total
variously reported as $10,000, $8,000, or $5,000 (he didn't get a dime
for the weeks of preparation and rehearsal) had put him in deeper
hock than ever. His first Capitol single, "I'm Walking Behind You," with
"Lean Baby" on the flip side, had come out on April 27; a week later it
had reached the nether regions of the *Billboard* chart—but troublingly,
RCA Victor had released Eddie Fisher's version of "Walking" just a few
days after Sinatra's, and by the time Frank left the country, Fisher's
record was already starting to pull ahead.

Lacking a radio or television show, domestic bookings, or any record
royalties from Capitol, Sinatra was trying to drum up whatever cash he
could. That spring, quietly, he had put his beloved Palm Springs house
on the market. A wealthy widow, one Mrs. George Machris, scooped
it up at a fire-sale price of $85,000—just a bit more than half of what
it had cost Frank. The proceeds went straight to Nancy, who was still
hanging on in the Holmby Hills house. The place was too big, too
expensive to maintain, she worried; she and the children really should
move someplace smaller (but this didn't happen until Nancy junior
and Frankie left home, years later).

In the meantime, Nancy entertained regularly, giving her best
impression of a merry divorcée. On slow news days, the columns liked
linking her to one suitor or another. "Nancy Sinatra's steadfast date is
Tom Drake . . . Barbara Stanwyck's is George Nader," wrote Winchell.
In fact, it was Stanwyck—whose marriage to Robert Taylor had been
broken up by Ava Gardner—who was Nancy's steadfast companion.
"Sob sisters," the two women sometimes liked to joke, clinking their
cocktail glasses. The truth was that finding another man was the last
thing on Nancy's mind. Between the children, the church, the Barbatos, and her various causes, she had more than enough to occupy

her. According to Frank's longtime valet, George Jacobs, "There was no way she would ever get remarried, or even go on a date." Nancy had her own explanation for this. "When you've been married to Frank Sinatra . . . ," she liked to say in later years. *You stay married to him.* She even kept some of her wandering ex-husband's clothes in the closet and welcomed, in a complicated way, his periodic visits.[1]

———

At Heathrow, Ava fondled her husband's cheek, amazed all over again at his face. She was amazed, too, at how much she wanted him. She hadn't been especially good over the long weeks since she'd last seen him, but then, she hadn't been too bad, either. They stayed in each other's arms in the back of the big car that took them to her flat in Regent's Park; they stayed in bed for three days, until it was time to leave for Italy. And then, since the dreadful piece of trash in which she was currently acting wasn't in need of her services for a couple of weeks (Metro had tried but failed to argue her into taking horseback-riding lessons so she could more convincingly portray Guinevere), she and Frank—along with many pieces of luggage—got back in the car and headed for Heathrow.

The car blew a tire on the way to the airport (Frank gritted his teeth and drummed his fingers while the liveried chauffeur, apologizing constantly, put on the spare). When they finally arrived, their plane was taxiing out to the runway. A BEA gate agent patiently explained, as the couple goggled at him in disbelief, that Mr. and Mrs. Sinatra were simply too late.

Frank's face was dangerously flushed. "Too *late*?"

Ava looked over the top of her sunglasses. "*What*?"

The agent explained that the next flight to Milan wasn't leaving until tomorrow, but there was a flight to Rome leaving very shortly, if the lady and gentleman were willing to alter their plans.

Frank stared at the mild-mannered young man until he had to look away. Then he put his hands to his mouth; his big voice echoed through the waiting room. "This is the last time I'll ever fly BEA!" he called.

"I'd rather swim the Channel!" Ava shouted.

They and their seventeen bags got on the flight to Rome.

The term "paparazzo" wouldn't exist until Federico Fellini gave the name to a character in *La Dolce Vita* years later, but Rome was Rome, and the photographers were all over the famous couple as they walked across the tarmac. One in particular wouldn't let up, kept demanding Frank and Ava kiss for the camera. Just like that, Frank hauled off and socked the guy in the face. The photographer shook it off and went straight back at Frank. The carabinieri swiftly intervened. But the tone of the tour had been set.

The concert halls were only part full. England would always have a soft spot for him after the war, but his appeal hadn't completely translated to the rest of Europe. Ava Gardner, though, was another matter. Ava was a goddess, her dark beauty making perfect sense to Continental tastes, and Europe couldn't get enough of her. At the next stop, Naples, the promoter put Ava's name right on the bill with Frank's. This, of course, was a terrible mistake. Frank Sinatra had no intention of sharing the stage with anyone else, even his wife, and Ava had no intention of stepping out on a stage with Frank. She'd come close to trying that just once, for charity in London, and wisely changed her mind.

But when Sinatra got up onstage for a matinee in Naples without that gorgeous wife of his, the spotlight picked her out in the crowd, who booed and whistled and threw seat cushions. They had paid up to 3,000 to 4,500 lire each—the equivalent of $5 to $7, a fortune in postwar Italy—to see this goddess. They chanted her name—"*Ah-va! Ah-va! Ah-va!*"—and Frank stomped off the stage. Ava fled.

The crowd threatened to riot. The carabinieri cleared the theater. For the evening show the house was half-full. Ava had stayed at the hotel. Sinatra sang one number, looked at the empty seats, then shook his head and walked off once more. The audience began to stamp the floor. After much fevered back-and-forth between Frank, the promoter, and the chief of the Naples riot police, who had fifteen officers waiting in the hall, Sinatra understood he had two choices: he could go on with the evening show and collect two-thirds of his $2,400 fee ($800 had been slotted for Ava), or he could walk and get nothing. He went on with the show.

The worse Frank felt, the worse he sang. The concerts didn't improve. Naturally, he hadn't been able to afford to fly a full complement of musicians over from the States, so he'd brought Bill Miller along as an accompanist and musical director. They hired pickup bands for each leg of the tour, but the quality varied from fair to poor. Sometimes Frank thought bitterly, longingly, of Studio C at Capitol on the night of April 30. The combination of Sinatra, a Dutch band called the Skyliners, and an English conductor named Harold Collins was a disaster in Scandinavia. "Sinatra has been a flop in Denmark and Sweden," said the *New Musical Express,* the English counterpart of *Billboard.* On May 31 the Associated Press wrote that Frank had drawn boos during two concerts in southern Sweden. "Agence France Presse reported that Sinatra received an unenthusiastic reception from small audiences in Malmoe and Helsingborg," the dispatch continued.

AFP said the manager of the Helsingborg theater refused to pay Sinatra, claiming the singer spent more time backstage checking his boat schedule than entertaining the public.

The manager also charged that Sinatra stopped his program after 32 minutes when the agreement called for 50 minutes.

Frank was looking for the exit. From performing, from Ava, from everything. Then he pulled the plug.

FRANK SINATRA
HAS COLLAPSE

STOCKHOLM, Sweden, June 1, UP—Crooner Frank Sinatra today was reported suffering from a severe case of "exhaustion" and/or bad press.

His manager, John Harding, said Sinatra probably will call off his Swedish tour because he is "completely exhausted" and "needs going over very thoroughly."

Harding admitted that the criticism in Sweden has been rough, but said Sinatra's real trouble is "complete exhaustion."

Ava was due back in England on June 7 to start shooting *Knights of the Round Table,* at $17,500 a week. Frank's wallet was all but empty. It didn't improve matters between them.

======

On May 16, precisely as the Naples audience was stamping, booing, and yelling for Ava, "I'm Walking Behind You" hit number 7 on the *Billboard* chart. It was Frank's first hit since "The Birth of the Blues" had charted at number 19 the previous November—his longest drought in ten years. The problem was that Eddie Fisher's version of "I'm Walking Behind You" was number 1.

It was not to be a great year for Sinatra sales. Paradoxically, "Walking" would be Frank's biggest hit for 1953, though Alan Livingston knew in his bones that the Stordahl-arranged song represented the singer's past, not his future. But even the present looked iffy. When "I've Got the World on a String" hit the charts on the Fourth of July, it was only at number 14, and it stayed there for just two weeks.[2] Nineteen fifty-three was a year for Fisher and Perry Como (who had two number-one hits) and Patti Page, with her monster Columbia hit "Doggie in the Window," conducted and arranged—complete with barking—by Mitch Miller.

In many ways it seemed as though 1953 might not be Sinatra's year at all. He had little to show but bruises for his Continental tour. He could dimly remember having thrown heart and soul into *From Here to Eternity;* but back in England (where Ava had rented a big flat in St. John's Wood), in the days when overseas really was overseas, he'd only heard second- and thirdhand about the excited rumors—about both the film and his performance—flying around Hollywood. He was cast up on foreign shores, with little to back up his confidence, least of all his wife's esteem. "We came back to London under a terrible cloud," Ava recalled. In truth, she was sick of him. In a photograph of the two of them at a prizefight in early June, their bodies aren't quite touching. (At one point, during a lull in the action, Frank called out, "Why don't ya fight, ya bums, ya!" Ava rolled her eyes.)

Still, his manager had been able at the last minute to throw together a tour of Great Britain: from June till early August, Sinatra would scramble from London to Bristol back to London up to Birmingham and back to London, then up to Glasgow and Dundee and Edinburgh and Ayr, then down to Leicester and Manchester and Blackpool and Liverpool, then back to London. Ava, busy playing Guinevere (and perhaps also busy with her co-star and old flame, Robert Taylor), would not accompany him.

Then a successful June show on the BBC buoyed Frank's morale. The Brits, having just crowned a new young queen, were in correspondingly good spirits. They didn't come out in huge throngs to hear Frank, but the crowds who did come applauded appreciatively as he sang old songs ("Night and Day," "Sweet Lorraine," "You Go to My Head") and new ones ("The Birth of the Blues" and "I've Got the World on a String") and sipped tea between numbers. His voice gained strength with every stop. "Sinatra is still the greatest male singer in pop music," the *New Musical Express* said. "His range and power seem greater than ever." And his cheekiness ("Good evening, ladies and gentlemen, and welcome to the Odeon or whatever this joint's called," he said at the Blackpool Opera House) rubbed the Brits the right way. They knew all about bloody-mindedness.

———

Harry Cohn used to say that he could tell whether a movie was any good depending on whether his fanny squirmed or not. "Imagine," said the screenwriter Herman Mankiewicz. "The whole world wired to Harry Cohn's ass!"

And strangely enough, when Columbia Pictures ran its first

preview of *From Here to Eternity,* "Cohn had decided to use a new electronic system of recording audience reactions," Fred Zinnemann recalled. The screening took place over the summer: a few weeks, pointedly enough, after the Rosenbergs were electrocuted.

> About two hundred people were, literally, wired to their seats in a large projection room. There were small levers each could push—to the right if they liked the scene, to the left if they didn't. At first this seemed a ridiculous enterprise, especially discouraging because there was absolutely no reaction from the audience. They sat there like wax figures at Madame Tussaud's, busy concentrating on those levers. I was convinced we had a disaster on our hands.
> Then Harry Cohn came tearing in, carrying a roll of paper twenty-five feet long, with the combined graph of those two hundred people plotted on it, and he said excitedly that the curve indicated Columbia was going to have its biggest-ever hit.

He was so certain of his film's success that he conceived a crazily inspired plan for the premiere. "We all thought Cohn had gone mad when he decreed that 'this picture will open in the Capitol Theater on Broadway in New York in August,'" Zinnemann wrote.[3]

> There was no air-conditioning then, and in August New York was a sweatbox. No one had ever heard of releasing a major film in mid-summer. We were convinced that his gambler's instinct was leading to certain suicide. More was to come: Cohn declared that there would be no publicity, except for one full-page ad in the *Times* which *he* would sign as president of Columbia, urging people to see it.

Wednesday, August 5, was a reliably miserable summer day in Manhattan, the temperature a humid eighty-eight degrees. The smart money, of course, was at the beach; those unlucky enough to have to stay in town walked around fanning themselves and complaining. "I was in Los Angeles when the picture opened on Broadway, on a sweltering August night," Zinnemann recalled.

> No premiere, no limousines, nothing. At 9:00 p.m., Marlene Dietrich (whom I hardly knew) called from New York and said that it was midnight there but the Capitol Theater was bulging, people were still standing around the block and there was an extra performance starting at one in the morning! I said, "How is that possible? There has been no publicity." "They smell it," she said.

William Morris cabled the good news to Frank: *From Here to Eternity* looked like a huge hit, and his performance was a big part of the equation. His mood, already up from a successful week at the Empire in Liverpool, soared. Suddenly Frank was grinning and strutting, and Ava's eyes were narrowing. But the two of them pulled it together on August 6, when they paid a call on Mr. and Mrs. Earl Wilson at the Savoy. The columnist and his Beautiful Wife were beginning a round-the-world tour, Mrs. Wilson was celebrating her birthday, and the mood was festive. Frank and Ava "came up from the lobby and were in a merry mood," Wilson recalled.

> "He doesn't know whether to believe all the talk," Ava said when Frank went to the bathroom . . . Frank was torn about what attitude to take about all the buildup. Should he be humble or, as one of his realist friends said, "should he start getting that old shitty feeling toward everybody who'd helped him?"

Including his wife, who after all had been instrumental in getting him the role in the first place?

"There was a series of senseless quarrels with Ava," Wilson wrote.

She wanted him to stay in London until she was finished shooting her picture; he had no intention of playing the prince consort. "I've got a career too, you know," he said coldly. A couple of nights after they made nice for the Wilsons, the Sinatras had such a violent battle in the St. John's Wood flat, replete with flying furniture and broken crockery, that their landlord lost his English composure and, red faced, threatened them with eviction. It didn't matter: Frank was already gone.

"Dialogue between Ava and hubby Frankie Sinatra as actually heard in London's swank Ambassador hotel dining room," Frank Morriss wrote in his August 12 column:

Frankie-Boy: What time is it? Ava: How do I know?
Frankie-Boy: I'll be seeing you . . . Whereupon he exits . . .

That night he packed his bags and flew home. Alone.

═══

When he landed at Idlewild, it was as if he'd gone through the looking glass—from drab, still war-ravaged England, cool and clammy even in August, to hot, pulsating New York City, where everyone—*everyone,* from baggage handlers to cabbies to cops—was congratulating him on his brilliant performance.

Hey, Frankie! Hey, Frankie! Hey, Maggio!

He couldn't stop grinning. Suddenly everybody wanted to be his friend. The phone in his suite at the Waldorf Towers was ringing off the hook, with more congratulations, and with offers. NBC, which had been interested in him in 1952 but had faded fast when CBS canceled his TV show, was back, talking about an exclusive contract for radio and television. Milton Berle, the guy who used to make fun of his low ratings, wanted Frank to appear on his show for $6,000. Six thousand dollars, for one night—almost as much as he'd made for all twelve weeks of *From Here to Eternity;* more than three times as much as they'd paid him for that night in Naples.

Offers kept flooding in. Skinny D'Amato's 500 Club in Atlantic City wanted Frank as soon as he could get there; so did Bill Miller's Riviera in Fort Lee. He was called for television and films: an Army movie with Dan Dailey; a Fox musical with Marilyn Monroe, *Pink Tights*. And most interesting of all, a waterfront picture with Elia Kazan, set in Hoboken . . .

In the meantime, MGM was planning to rerelease *The Kissing Bandit*—a backhanded compliment if there ever was one. His agents at William Morris were suddenly all smiles: he could hear it in their voices over the phone.

Frank distrusted every last glad-hander. He preferred to believe the grudging noises his former detractors were making. "Looking through my Frank Sinatra file today, I discovered that I have been about evenly divided in my praise and my criticism of Frankie-boy," the Hollywood gossip Jimmie Fidler wrote in mid-August.

> Of late, the file is heavily critical, so it pleases me at this time to add something to the good side of the Sinatra ledger.
>
> I am referring to the strong comeback Frank has made, just when everybody figured he was washed up . . .
>
> About his performance in "From Here to Eternity" a number of columnists are predicting that Sinatra has next year's Academy Award in his hip pocket.

His performance had thrown everybody for a loop. The toughest reviewers were melting. "For the first time," the *New York Post*'s Richard Watts wrote, "I find myself in the ranks of his ardent admirers. Instead of exploiting a personality, he proves he is an actor by playing the luckless Maggio with a kind of doomed gaiety that is both real and immensely touching."

"Doomed gaiety"—that was good. For the past three years doomed gaiety had been the only kind he'd had. But it was the death scene that got them, he knew it. He and Monty had talked about that scene a dozen times. The trick, according to Clift, was not overplaying it. Dying was like snow falling.

But now he was living—livin' in a great big way, as the old Dorothy Fields lyric had it. Again he could stroll into Toots Shor's like the conquering hero ("You crumb bum!" Toots sang out happily at the sight of him); again he could wink at the Copa Girls and decide which would be on the menu first.

Atlantic City was golden in the late-August sun. Frank flared his nostrils and inhaled the salty air. Skinny spread his well-tailored arms to hug him, then indicated a short, sour-looking man in sunglasses and a fedora. Surely Frank remembered their good friend Sam Giancana?

The boardwalk crowds surged into the club to get a glimpse of Frank; the sunburned honeymooners held each other close as he sang to them, better than ever. Dolly came down and pinched his cheeks some more. Skinny wouldn't let her touch her purse. He was having to put on extra shows at 2:00 a.m. to accommodate the overflow.

Eternity was breaking box-office records in New York and Chicago, the only two cities where it was playing so far: canny Cohn had decided to build the fire slowly. And the Oscar talk was gathering steam. ACADEMY AWARD RACE BEGINS, read an August 30 headline in Lubbock, Texas, where *From Here to Eternity* couldn't even be seen yet. "Biggest surprise of the film is the reportedly fine straight acting of Song-and-Dance Man Sinatra," the accompanying story read, a little wistfully.

Naturally, his good fortune couldn't go uncontested. "Frank Sinatra has been receiving a merciless needling," Jimmie Fidler noted, "from a New York columnist—one with whom Frank swapped punches in front of a night club a year or so back. Some of the newspaperman's cracks have been so ugly that even people who admit they have no great admiration for Sinatra are beginning to take offense."

In fact, Frank's assisted mugging of Lee Mortimer at Ciro's had taken place not a year or so before, but in April 1947—ancient history in newspaper terms. Mortimer had long since had the opportunity to mug Sinatra back, and to savor his downfall. And Frank had fallen and fallen, but—maddeningly—never quite hit bottom. Now, just as the singer was starting to enjoy an improbable resurgence, the columnist was gently fading into obscurity. Throughout the summer, filling in for the vacationing Walter Winchell, Mortimer snapped at Sinatra's heels. On August 31, he wrote: "Those dark cheaters Frank Sinatra is sporting on Lexington Ave. are not to hide him from the autograph hunters. He's got a beautiful shiner."

Whether Frank had received an actual black eye from a romantic rival or a metaphorical one from the envious columnist was never answered. It was Mortimer's last shot at the singer.

=====

Frank called his wife almost every day, even after he'd sent another conquest home in a cab. Ava, after all, was the one he couldn't conquer. He tried everything on the transatlantic phone that August: at times, knowing that she took pleasure in his success (and disdained him for his failures), he spoke with pride of his growing triumph; but the second he began to sound cocky, he could hear her glancing at her watch. Then there were the bad moments, when she made him crazy enough to try to bully her.

The hell with *St. Louis Woman*. He'd rather work with Marilyn Monroe.

Click.

At last, they made a provisional agreement to make up. The minute Ava's work on the dumb costume epic was completed, she and Reenie threw all her things into her bags. She was bored with England anyway. Clark Gable, who'd stayed in London after *Mogambo* wrapped, came over for a farewell drink—and reminded her that she'd completed only half of the eighteen months' foreign residence the IRS required for a massive tax break.

"Ava, honey, you do know what you're doing, don't you? You're packing up and throwing away a hundred fifty thousand dollars in those suitcases."

She didn't give a flying fuck. She wanted to see her husband.

Gable smiled, squinty eyed, over his highball glass. Lucky husband.

But at the last minute, Ava decided to stop over in Madrid: Spain made her happy, and she had new friends there, not the least of whom was Luis Miguel Dominguín.

═══

As always, the press took note of her every movement, and since Frank read the papers like everyone else, he got wind of her layover. As far as he was concerned, she had stood him up, but he wasn't about to tell the reporters that. No comment, was what he said instead. He was booked at the 500 Club through Labor Day—the very day Ava arrived in New York. Frank stayed put.

Ava walked off the plane at Idlewild, her big sunglasses hiding the circles under her eyes, and ran smack into a crowd of eager reporters.

Where was Frankie? Were she and he not getting along?

She adjusted the shades and walked coolly through the pack. "I have nothing to say about it," she said. She believed he had a singing engagement in Atlantic City.

Did she plan to see him?

"Not today," she said. "I have no definite plans." She pulled off her gloves—every man watching her hands with widening eyes—and put them in her bag. "I don't want to discuss it."

The reporters crowded closer. One suggested that her answers strongly implied there was some kind of rift.

"It doesn't imply anything," she said, getting into a waiting car. The driver closed the door, and then she was gone.

Frank came to New York the next day and checked into the Waldorf. Ava was in the Hampshire House.

The press smelled blood. "A close friend said the couple had been squabbling and that things might be patched up with a telephone call or 'blow sky high in 24 hours,'" the United Press reported on September 9. And, the next day:

FRANKIE AND AVA FEUDING

NEW YORK (UP)—Ava and Frankie are feuding in frosty silence today just 12 city blocks apart . . .

Sinatra . . . told his friends he was completely mystified over Ava's unannounced return three days ago and her anger. He refused to say why he didn't pick up the phone and ask Ava.

"I hope to see Frank before I leave next week," Ava said. "That's what I came home for." She wouldn't say why she neglected to phone him or where she intended to go from here.

"I don't care to talk about it further," she said pleasantly, leaning back on the couch and exposing her bare legs. The question of hemlines arose.

"If women follow that very short skirt fad they're fools," Ava said. She paused and smiled. "But then, we're fools."

It sounded like a high-school quarrel. Speaking to another reporter, Sinatra was the soul of disingenuousness. "I saw a picture of Ava at the airport," he said, "and that's the first inkling I had that she was in town. I don't understand it. We'd had no trouble. I can't make a statement because I don't know what she is planning. It's a crying shame, because everything was going so well with us. Something may work out, but I don't know."

Ava replied (to another reporter): "You start with love, or what you think is love, and then comes the work. I guess you have to be mature and grown up to know how to work at it. But I was the youngest of seven kids and was always treated like the baby, and I liked it, and played the baby. Now I'm having a hell of a time growing up."

While Frank opened at the Riviera, she went with a girlfriend to a Broadway show—as it happened, the premiere of *Carnival in Flanders*, book by Preston Sturges, music and lyrics by Jimmy Van Heusen and Johnny Burke. Despite the brilliant creative team, the critics murdered the show, which ran for only six performances. The failure hastened

Burke's decline into alcoholism and steeled Chester's resolve to stick to writing for the movies. (But as Ava sat there that night, she got to hear John Raitt debut Van Heusen's greatest song, "Here's That Rainy Day"—of which Sinatra would record the greatest version six years thence.)

Meanwhile, across the river, Frank was knocking them dead. "Every big star—except Ava Gardner—was at Frank Sinatra's big, spectacular opening at Bill Miller's Riviera," Earl Wilson wrote. "(Martin & Lewis couldn't get a table!)"

It was true: Dean Martin and Jerry Lewis, virtual protégés of Frank's, and now arguably the biggest stars in the world, were refused the ringside table they demanded. It was a maître d's dream and nightmare: the place was simply too jammed with celebrities to admit any more. The duo walked off in a huff. It was a subtle changing of the guard.

Dean and Jerry missed a hell of a show. "Electrifying," said Eddie Fisher, who had been more prudent about getting a reservation. "Frank let loose a vocal tour de force, accompanied by Bill Miller at the piano and a seven-piece band," *Variety*'s critic wrote.

> He held the floor a solid 60 minutes and while he might and should cut 10 minutes there was no gainsaying the consistency of his socko. He's in for $10,000 a week, for two weeks, and both he and [club owner] Bill Miller owe a lot to Harry Cohn for what the Columbia picture did for all concerned. Oh yes, he also sang "From Here to Eternity" and wisely sh-sh'd some exuberant bobby-soxers who squealed an occasional "Oh Frankie."

Frank was in great voice and delighted to be performing for an American audience, and a hip one at that. He could even make fun of his marital troubles: when he sang Cole Porter's "I Get a Kick Out of You," he mimed getting booted in the butt, as if by you-know-who, to gales of laughter. "Frank Sinatra's intimates say he hasn't been as happy in years, despite the rift with Ava," Dorothy Kilgallen wrote early in the second week of the stand. "The success of his dramatic effort in 'From Here to Eternity' plus his great hit as a ballad singer at the Riviera have lifted him out of the bitter depression that was beginning to worry all his associates. In the long run, his career seems to be more important to him than any luscious female."

While this was true in the long run, Sinatra was paying a bitter price. Friends like Van Heusen and Sanicola and Jule Styne, friends he made stay up with him every night until dawn, took the true measure of his misery. And no matter how many laughs he enjoyed with his buddies, Ava made him miserable. He couldn't dominate her; he couldn't understand her. The more inconstant she was, the more he needed her.

On September 12, Earl Wilson, who fancied himself a friend, devoted almost his entire column to a jocular account of his failed attempt to bring Frank and Ava back together. "As a Cupid, I'm stupid, for I just made a gallant effort to melt the deep freeze between Ava Gardner and Frank Sinatra . . . and fixed everything up so good that the freeze is now twice as deep," he wrote.

> Ava and I met in a large eatery run by a large eater. After talking about her next picture, "Mogambo," in which she is a real sexpot, I happened to mention her Herculean husband whom she considers has neglected her, which—if it's true—makes him this century's man of iron.
>
> "You still haven't seen him or talked to him?" I asked.
>
> "No." She sipped her tea . . . She was wearing, I noticed, Frank's wedding ring, also a large frosty smile of independence . . .
>
> "Can I be an intermediary?" I asked. "I know a lot about patching up quarrels with wives. First the husband says it was all his fault and after that everything's easy."
>
> "Nobody can help us but ourselves," she answered. "You

must talk, you must understand each other. Listen to me. Lady psychiatrist!"

"I still think you should have been [at the Riviera]," I said.

"I don't have to defend myself," she said, "as long as I'm sure in my heart that I was right."

Dolly sailed into the breach. Talking to her son on the phone, she instantly heard the sadness in his voice.

He went on and on about the crowds at the Riviera. He was doing great.

Dolly grunted. Bullshit.

She phoned Ava at the Hampshire House. Ava asked her please to come right over. "She kissed me, and after a few minutes she began to cry," Dolly recalled.

> She had been tired, she said, when the plane came in, and when she didn't see Frank, she felt bad. Then she found out he was in Atlantic City with me and said, "Mama, I don't know how to explain this, but I know how little you get to see him. I thought for once you're together, just the two of you, and I didn't want to spoil it."

"Frankie is so upset," Dolly said. "It's drivin' him nuts you two not speakin'." He was drinking; he was taking pills to sleep. Ava's mother-in-law looked her up and down.

"Jesus Christ! You know you two kids love each other! So quit all this fuckin' shit, for God's sake!"

And so Dolly hatched her grand plan. She invited Ava to Weehawken for a big Italian dinner the next night, then she phoned Frank and invited *him*.

"Who's gonna be there?" he asked suspiciously.

"Never mind—you just come." Seven sharp. If he was late, she would feed his dinner to the dog.

Ava came at six thirty; Frank, at seven. They stood in the hall and stared at each other, smiling a little bit. "Hey," Dolly told her son and daughter-in-law. "Come into the kitchen and see what I'm making for you tonight."

They followed like obedient children. "We walked to the stove," Dolly recalled, "and I took the big spoon I use for stirring the gravy and I made them both taste it. Then they both began to laugh and talk and before you knew it they were hugging each other and then they grabbed me and the three of us stood there just hugging and laughing and I think we all felt like crying a little bit too."

After dinner, Dolly and Marty and Ava and Frank drove to Fort Lee for Frank's late show. He forgot all about the boot-in-the-ass shtick from "I Get a Kick Out of You"—now he sang the song right to her. Her eyes gleamed. "The Voice unleashed a torrent of sound at the sultry Ava," the *New York Journal American*'s reviewer wrote. "Emotion poured from him like molten lava."

The next day, Frank moved out of the Waldorf and into Ava's suite at the Hampshire House.

Ava at the Los Angeles premiere of *Mogambo,* October 8, 1953. Alone.
She and Frank were headed inexorably toward separation.

It couldn't last, of course: it never had, and it never would. In the end, Dolly's Cupid act was to prove no more effective than Earl Wilson's. Cupid didn't have enough arrows in his quiver for this pair.

A couple of nights after Frank moved back in with Ava, he told her he'd be home by 2:00 a.m.—and stayed out till 5:00, getting congratulated for everything by his pals. He could take a lot of congratulation.

"Isn't it a little late to be coming home?" she asked him.

His lips tightened. "Don't cut the corners too close on me, baby," he said. "This is the way my life is going to be from now on."

That night Ava's reserved table at the Riviera was empty. His concentration shot, Frank gave a dud of a show.

"When he was down and out," Ava said, "he was so sweet. But now that he's successful again, he's become his old arrogant self. We were happier when he was on the skids."

There was a grain of truth to it, but just a grain. The reality was that their relationship was impossible by definition. They were competitors as well as lovers. And now the only glue that held them together was loosening: Ava confided to friends that Frank could no longer satisfy her sexually.

"Almost since their marriage, the Ava Gardner–Frank Sinatra situation has been what the military experts call 'fluid,' " Dorothy Kilgallen wrote on September 30.

So anyone who writes a newsnote about them does so in the full knowledge that it may be one hundred per cent wrong by the time the paper is on the stands.

However, the latest bulletin from their chums has them apart again. As evidence, the pals point to the fact that Frank dined alone at the Villanova and later turned up at the Marciano-LaStarza fight without his glamorous bride. True, they say she might not like fights (especially after all the ones she's had in her own private life) but what has she got against spaghetti?

It wasn't the meals she disliked; it was his choice of dining companions. At Joe E. Lewis's Copacabana opening, Frank sat ringside with a group including Frank Costello and a comely young thing who reportedly found Sinatra "devastating." Ava read the report, and blew up. Ava's old ally, the quiet but effective MGM publicity chief, Howard Strickling, got wind of the umpteenth domestic disturbance, and gently reminded her that the studio was still paying her sizable salary. Could she and Strickling figure out a way, just for a moment, to divert the public's attention from her marriage and redirect it to *Mogambo*? It would be nice if Ava could attend the premiere with her husband; it would also be nice if they managed to look like a happy couple.

Somehow they brought it off. On October 1, at Radio City, an Associated Press photographer got a shot of the pair standing close together and grinning real grins. "Together again," the caption read. "The situation may change greatly before press time, but Frank Sinatra and his actress wife, Ava Gardner, were together Thursday night and here's a picture to prove it."

The next morning, the papers were full of rave reviews for her performance as Honey Bear Kelly. But when a reporter phoned and read her some of the notices, she told him, "Don't believe a word of it—I don't."

She might as well have been talking about her marriage.

That night, she and Frank took a TWA Constellation to Los Angeles—she had an L.A. premiere for *Mogambo*; he was booked for a week at the Sands—and, somewhere over Nebraska, they reached an accommodation. A reporter called one of Strickling's minions (the studio employed a publicity staff of fifty) and wondered aloud about the dissonance between the cozy images and the continuing reports of marital unrest. "They're together—and that's the main thing," the MGM rep said.

Ava did her best to defend the united front. "If Frankie goes to New York to do 'Waterfront' for Elia Kazan, I'll accompany him," she told a columnist. "Meanwhile, we are sort of up in the air. We don't have a house or even a car."

It was all a ruse. The moment the press wasn't looking, they put on their sunglasses and went their separate ways—Frank to 20th Century Fox to discuss *Pink Tights*, Ava to Culver City to see what fresh outrage Metro had in mind for her. But it seemed there was a live possibility outside the studio: Joseph L. Mankiewicz, Herman's younger brother and currently the hottest writer-director in Hollywood (he'd won Oscars in both categories in 1950 and 1951, for *A Letter to Three Wives* and *All About Eve*), had written a script called *The Barefoot Contessa*, and would be shooting it in Rome in January. Mankiewicz would also be producing. He had already signed Humphrey Bogart, and he wanted Ava, badly. He was bargaining with the studio chairman, Nicholas Schenck, in Metro's New York office, for her services.

Ava sat up and took notice. Bogart . . . Rome . . . a barefoot contessa . . . She didn't know what the hell the movie was about, but it sounded just right for her. She decided she wanted it.

Meanwhile, an odd item appeared in Jimmie Fidler's column:

> Two intimates of Frank Sinatra are the source of my information that the singer is becoming daily more upset over the constant bickering between himself and his wife, Ava Gardner. They don't think Sinatra will put up with it much longer, because (they swear to this) Frank is a changed man since his career went on the zoom and he wants to settle down to a quiet, secure future . . . One of the two mused into my willing ear: "Wouldn't it be ironic if Sinatra, now apparently desirous of a peaceful life, should return to the person with whom he had it, his ex-wife?"

Most likely the leak was an attempted warning, on Frank's part, to Ava; but it only steeled her resolve to get out of town—without Frank. On October 5, she officially asked MGM for a temporary release from her contract in order to do *The Barefoot Contessa*.

And Frank went on the radio. He didn't want to do another television series—it was too hard, and the screen was too small. His future, he felt, would be about making records and movies. In the meantime, though, he could keep his profile high, and his wallet full, with comparatively little effort. On October 6, at Radio City West on Sunset and Vine, Sinatra taped the first episode of a detective-themed new series titled, a little too poignantly, *Rocky Fortune*.

Frank played the title character, "a footloose and fancy-free young man"—out of work, in other words—who got a different job assignment every week from the Gridley Employment Agency. Over the show's twenty-five-week run, Rocky would labor as a process server, museum tour guide, cabbie, bodyguard (to a professional football player—the magic of radio!), truck driver, and social director for a Catskills resort, among other things.

On the premier episode, he took script in hand and read into the mike: "Hi, I don't know what it is about me and employment—we start out together but sooner or later, usually sooner, we reach the fork in the road. You take last week: the employment agency sent me out on a job as an oyster shucker, but someone tried to serve me up on a half shell, with a real crazy cocktail sauce—blood."

It was the radio equivalent of a B movie—unapologetically cheesy, though perhaps there should have been some apologies. Among the writers who produced this claptrap were Ernest Kinoy and George Lefferts, both of whom would go on to win Emmy Awards for dramatic television—but Sinatra really should have known better. Still, he imparted a certain tongue-in-cheek verve to the enterprise, and he collected that paycheck.

———

Of all the numerous characters who'd been buttering Frank up in the last two months, the most insistent was a movie producer named Sam Spiegel. Spiegel was an operator straight out of a Saul Bellow novel: heavy jawed, prow nosed, and pinkie ringed, he had an indefinable Eastern European accent, a looming, slightly menacing stare, and a murky past, complete with at least one deportation and jail time for kiting checks. "He was always surrounded with beautiful women, whom he graciously dispatched to his friends, or whomever he wanted to sell something to," recalled George Jacobs. "He seemed like a joke. Yet he was the real deal."

Spiegel began his producing career in Berlin and fled Germany upon the rise of the Nazis. His path to America was circuitous, and likely illegal: when he finally made it to Hollywood in the late 1930s, he adopted the alias S. P. Eagle in an attempt to throw off the blood-hounds. Over the next decade he bootstrapped himself into a Hollywood career, forming important alliances with two equally colorful characters, Orson Welles and John Huston. In 1951, Spiegel produced *The African Queen,* with Huston directing and Katharine Hepburn and Humphrey Bogart in the starring roles: Bogart won an Oscar for Best Actor.

Sam Spiegel began pursuing Sinatra relentlessly. According to Spiegel, the role of the longshoreman and ex-prizefighter Terry Malloy in Budd Schulberg's script for *On the Waterfront* had practically been written for Frank. The film was even going to be shot in Hoboken: it was perfect. "For Chrissakes, you *are* Hoboken!" the producer told Sinatra.

But in Hollywood's eyes, Frank was still not a star. He had given one terrific performance, but in the cold-eyed view of the movie business he might still be a flash in the pan. He had dazzled in an ensemble, but could he actually carry a dramatic picture? Was Sam Spiegel, gambler though he was, willing to make that bet?

In fact, with Sinatra, Spiegel was hedging his bets.

The actor Spiegel really wanted to play Terry Malloy was Marlon Brando. Marlon Brando could carry a dramatic picture; Marlon Brando was It. Not yet thirty—eight years younger than Sinatra—Brando had already redefined the art of movie acting. When he was on a screen, even just scratching himself, you couldn't take your eyes off him. He had already been nominated for two Academy Awards, once as the oaf Stanley Kowalski in *A Streetcar Named Desire,* and then—utterly transforming himself—as the titular Mexican revolutionary in *Viva Zapata!* He had transformed himself again and again—into Mark Antony in *Julius Caesar,* into a motorcycle hood in *The Wild One.*

Marlon Brando could do anything, especially put asses in movie seats. But Brando didn't want to join the cast of *On the Waterfront,* because both Elia Kazan and Budd Schulberg had named names in front of the House Un-American Activities Committee.

For months, the actor refused even to read Schulberg's script, yet

Spiegel, even as he wooed Sinatra, kept after Brando. "Politics has nothing to do with this," the producer told him. "It's about your talent, it's about your career."

Finally, Brando read the script, and saw Spiegel's point. It was an extremely powerful story, a metaphor for important themes of the era: political corruption, the perils of silence. None of the roles the actor had played so far embodied an inner torment anything like that which Budd Schulberg had written into Terry Malloy. As with Maggio, there was a Christlike quality to Malloy. It was another story about a common man facing down brute authority, and it would have been right up Sinatra's alley.

Elia Kazan almost agreed. "Frank Sinatra would have been wonderful, but Marlon was more vulnerable," the director said. "He had this great range of violent emotions to draw from. He had more schism, more pain, and so much shame—the actor who played Terry had to have a lot of shame."

An interesting point. Frank was filled with vulnerability, but shame wasn't quite part of his artistic palette. Not that it was a foreign emotion—he would feel deep shame at crucial moments throughout his life—but it wasn't one he was fond of showing. Vulnerability was useful: vulnerability could get you laid. Showing shame, by Frank's lights anyway (and maybe even by the code of the streets of Hoboken), could get you nothing but contempt.

Kazan was right: Brando was the better choice for Terry Malloy. And when Spiegel had to break the news to Sinatra, he found it convenient to blame the decision on the director. It was a rotten business, the producer cooed; a terrible thing—might Frank be interested in the role of Father Barry, the waterfront priest?

Frank swallowed the urge to tell Sam Spiegel that he and Elia Kazan could go fuck themselves. Instead, what he said was that he had already played a priest once, in *The Miracle of the Bells,* and it hadn't worked out. He was going to leave the turned-around-collar business to Crosby.

With all due respect, Spiegel said, *The Miracle of the Bells* was pap. And that had been years ago, before Frank showed the world what he could really do as an actor. Father Barry was a great part, an important part in a hard-hitting script, Spiegel said. Would he consider it?

He considered it. "Frank Sinatra's now practically sure to play the labor priest in S. P. Eagle's waterfront picture," Earl Wilson wrote on October 2.

Then, on October 10, Louella Parsons wrote, "Frank Sinatra has decided against doing 'Waterfront' with Elia Kazan in New York. 'I love the role of the priest,' he said, 'but I only had two scenes.'"

But what had really happened in the week between Wilson's column and Parsons's was that Spiegel and Kazan had given the key role of Father Barry—who was in many more than two scenes in *On the Waterfront*—to Karl Malden, who'd co-starred with Brando in *A Streetcar Named Desire* and had won an Academy Award for the role. Frank had been quite thoroughly shut out.

———

George Jacobs, Frank Sinatra's valet for almost twenty years, recalled in his memoir that in the fall of 1953, his boss was even more preoccupied with work than with matters of the heart. "In what would become a continual aspect of my working for Sinatra, we'd sit and play cards late into the night, and he'd drink 'Jack' (Daniel's) and obsess about his career," Jacobs wrote.

> He was on the comeback trail, though he didn't feel he was home free again by any means. As far as he was concerned, his career was still up in the air. Although *Eternity* was doing big box office, Oscar nominations had not been tallied, and Mr. S still did not have his next film job . . .
>
> The first (of many) people I would see Frank Sinatra hate was the man who went on to be considered one of the grandest of all Hollywood producers, Sam Spiegel. One day I

arrived to see the living room half destroyed. Two lamps had been knocked over, broken glass was covering the floor. At first I thought there had been a burglary, until I began cleaning up and found the remnants of several drafts of a script entitled *On the Waterfront* by Budd Schulberg . . . I found Mr. S in bed nursing several bad paper cuts on his hands, which he got ripping up the script. He apologized for flipping out and told me he had just been fucked over by the worst real Sammy Glick in the business, Sammy Spiegel . . . Then he went into a tirade against Sam Spiegel that lasted for the next couple of weeks.

Mysteries abound in Jacobs's beautifully candid, thoroughly believable autobiography, *Mr. S.* For one thing, the Sinatra he presents us with is far more human and complex and vulnerable than the two-dimensional images—Sinatra the Thug; Sinatra the Genius; Ring-a-Ding-Ding Sinatra; Sinatra the Wonderful Dad; Greathearted Sinatra the Secret Philanthropist—put forth by so many books and remembrances. Of course Frank could be all these things at various times, but he was also much more: at his center was the compound enigma of which George Jacobs enjoyed a uniquely close-up view. "I slept in the same *room* with that man," he told me in 2009.

Other paradoxes crop up when Jacobs's account appears to contradict the smooth chronology of Sinatra's life. Why, for example, would Frank even *have* a valet in 1953, when he was rarely in the same place for more than a week at a time, and in any case was pretty much broke?

Sinatra appears to have first met George Jacobs sometime in the summer of 1951, when the singer's career was plummeting. The scene was a Hollywood party. Jacobs was standing outside, next to the Rolls-Royce he drove for the agent Irving "Swifty" Lazar.[1] Lazar was indoors. Jacobs badly wanted a cigarette, and decided he would cadge one from the first person who came up the street. That person was Frank Sinatra. Sinatra told Jacobs he didn't have a cigarette—oddly enough—but a few minutes later emerged from the party holding a gold bowl full of them. Jacobs took one, but Frank insisted he keep the whole bowl. He patted Jacobs's arm and went back into the house.

Sometime in early 1952, Sinatra realized he needed a Los Angeles base of operations. Hotels were too expensive, and Ava's Pacific Palisades love nest was often a little too hot for comfort. Accordingly, Frank rented a five-room apartment in a Spanish Mission–style garden complex at the corner of Wilshire Boulevard and Beverly Glen—the same complex, it turned out, where Irving Lazar lived.[2] According to George Jacobs, Lazar spoke witheringly about Sinatra's career slump. "He's a dead man," the agent would say. "Even Jesus couldn't get resurrected in this town."

Now and then, after Frank moved into the new place, Jacobs would spot him taking a walk down Beverly Glen to Holmby Park, "head down, all alone," as Jacobs remembered.

> Where were all those screaming teenagers now that he needed them, I'd think to myself . . . If I ever made eye contact, I'd smile at him, and no matter how down he looked, he'd always pull it together and smile back. I'm not sure he remembered the cigarette incident. He was just a naturally nice guy. "Everybody's nice when they're down and desperate," was Lazar's take on the situation. "Losers have the *time* to be nice."

By the fall of 1953, things had changed substantially. Frank's marriage was disintegrating: he didn't just need a place to camp out; he needed a permanent residence. At the same time, counter to everyone's expectations (especially Swifty Lazar's), his career was on the upswing—there was enough new action that he had to hire a secretary, a mousy-looking lady in spectacles named Gloria Lovell, and install her in an office at the Goldwyn Studios. One day, while Jacobs was doing an errand there for Lazar, he ran into Frank, who greeted him with great friendliness and directed him to go see Lovell at once. She handed him an envelope that turned out to contain keys to Frank's apartment. "Welcome aboard," Lovell said. Sinatra, who always enjoyed giving Swifty the needle, had simply hired Jacobs away.[3]

This was the apartment where Frank retreated from the chaos with Ava; this was where he ripped up the script for *On the Waterfront*. Everything about the place spoke eloquently of its unique and obsessive-compulsive tenant. "When I opened his apartment door, I was surprised he needed a valet at all, the place was so immaculately neat," Jacobs recalled.

> The five-room, two-bedroom unit was a shrine to Ava Gardner. There were pictures of her everywhere, in the bathrooms, in the closet, on the refrigerator. There were a couple of framed photographs of his children and of his parents but none of his ex-wife Nancy. Aside from one bookcase, almost all biographies (Washington, Lincoln, both Roosevelts, Booker T. Washington, and a lot of Italians—Columbus, da Vinci, Machiavelli, Garibaldi, Mussolini), most of his possessions were records and clothes. There was a whole wall of sound, though it wasn't all jazz as I would have guessed, but albums and albums of classical music.
>
> The closets were in perfect order, with all the clothes organized by color, fabric, and style. Most of the colors were orange (his favorite) or black. I figured the guy wanted to come off like a tiger. There were more sweaters than I'd ever seen, cashmere, mohair, lamb's wool, alpaca, you name it. And as for shoes, Imelda Marcos had nothing on Frank Sinatra. He had a whole closet just for shoes, dozens of wingtips predominating, with a good number of elevators. No wonder he seemed taller than his given five seven. There were also a lot of hats, which seemed odd for casual Los Angeles, but because of a receding hairline, hats had become his thing, just as they were Hum-

phrey Bogart's. It was clear from his wardrobe that he had been
keeping his eye on Bogart, because a lot of Sinatra's clothes
were identical to Bogart's. The biggest surprise in the apartment was the industrial supply of Wrigley's Spearmint Gum. I
had no idea the man was a gum chewer, like his original teenage fans, but he was.

Frank chewed a stick of Wrigley's Spearmint as he drove Jacobs
(rather than the other way around; he insisted) up Beverly Glen in his
black and silver Cadillac Brougham Coupe. He was taking his new
valet to meet his family.

It was odd, Jacobs recalled, being introduced to his new boss's
ex-wife, "who didn't seem ex at all." On the other hand, the valet
thought, "Mr. S was like a little boy who had just gotten out of camp
coming home for a home-cooked dinner . . . Big Nancy was so mater-
nal to Frank, she seemed like his mother rather than his wife."

Jacobs was struck by 320 North Carolwood's "rococo New Jersey
style" furniture, its "bright orange and black color scheme, and count-
less family pictures everywhere, with Mr. S in all of them." The place
looked, he thought, exactly as though Frank still lived there.

After dinner, while her ex horsed around with the kids, Nancy gave
George a crash tutorial on how to cook for Frank:

> The correct way to prepare the paper-thin steaks and pork
> chops, the scrambled-egg sandwiches, the bread to be sautéed
> in Italian, never Spanish, olive oil, the soft, never crisp, bacon
> he wanted for breakfast. She emphasized his disinterest in
> most vegetables, except for eggplant parmigiana and roasted
> peppers, and precisely which brands of pasta were acceptable,
> how many minutes to cook each, and how much salt to put
> in the water. Finally, of course, that marinara sauce, with the
> Italian plum tomatoes, crushed just so, and the prescribed
> balance of garlic, parsley, and oil.

When they left,

[t]he kids never begged him to stay, but their longing
expressions conveyed the powerful message, and it hurt.
Driving back to the apartment, Mr. S looked down. I told him
how much I liked his family, and all he could say was, "I know,
I know." He would call them every single day, wherever he
might be, at six o'clock just before their dinner, and be the best
telephone father there ever was.

And in the meantime, the woman for whom he had sacrificed it all
wasn't speaking to him.

———

While Frank opened at the Sands, Ava attended the Los Angeles premiere of *Mogambo* on the arm of her business manager Benton Cole,
looking spectacular in a décolleté silver-spangled gown and a white
mink stole, throwing her head back and laughing as the flashbulbs
popped. "There's nothing like the premiere of a girl's new picture to lift
her spirits," read a newspaper caption.

"Everything is fine, for the moment at least, between Frankie and
Ava," Louella Parsons wrote a few days later, "in spite of the rumors of
a new rift that popped up when she failed to attend his opening at the
Sands in Las Vegas."

Of course everything was far from fine. On opening night at the
Copa Room, in front of a capacity crowd, Frank cursed out his musicians when somebody hit a clam; a couple of days later he was crying
on Parsons's shoulder over Ava: "I can't eat, I can't sleep, I love her."

He certainly wasn't sleeping. Not even in the Sands's Presidential
Suite, with its three huge bedrooms and its own swimming pool. After
finishing the last show of the evening toward 5:00 a.m., Frank, in his
silk dressing gown, would sit on the side of the bed and phone his
wife in Palm Springs, where she was renting a house with Bappie. He
would yell, cajole, and weep until the sun rose. Ava, convinced he was

screwing around in Vegas, was resistant to the theatrics. Frank would emerge from his suite, dazed, in mid-afternoon, after a couple of hours' drug-induced slumber. Trying to placate his most valuable asset, Jack Entratter issued a memo on Frank's behalf to Sands staff on October 20: for the rest of Mr. Sinatra's engagement, Miss Gardner was banned from the premises should she attempt to show up, and under no circumstances should any phone calls from her be put through to him.

But Frank's attempt at face-saving was hollow: all the calls were going in the other direction, and Ava was immovable. Then came the call that did the trick. Unable to bear her coolness any longer, he took an old acquaintance to bed one night after the late show: a six-foot showgirl from Lou Walters's Folies Bergere revue (they'd met once before, in Boston). As she lay snoring afterward, Frank again phoned Palm Springs. Ava answered, sounding groggy.

Frank announced that he was in bed and he wasn't alone. He'd been drinking, a good bit; he was holding a glass now.

Silence on the other end.

Frank spoke a little too loudly. If Ava was going to accuse him all the time when he was innocent, he said, he might as well get the fun out of being guilty.

When Ava hung up, she remembered years later, she knew she and Frank had reached a point of no return.

"Hollywood's still betting the Ava Gardner–Frank Sinatra reconciliation ends in a divorce," Erskine Johnson wrote on the twenty-first.

Hollywood was betting on a sure thing. On October 29, Howard Strickling issued a memo on behalf of MGM: "Ava Gardner and Frank Sinatra stated today that having reluctantly exhausted every effort to reconcile their differences, they could find no mutual basis on which to continue their marriage. Both expressed deep regret and deep affection for each other. Their separation is final and Miss Gardner will seek a divorce."

In the meantime, Frank had brought record-breaking crowds to the Copa Room. True, these were still early days in Vegas—there were only seven hotels on the Strip; the tumbleweeds blew among them. The Sands had been open less than a year; the paint was barely dry. But a pattern had been set, thanks in no small part to the heat of *From Here to Eternity*: suddenly, in this two-horse town, Sinatra meant excitement, excitement meant crowds, crowds meant gambling, and gambling meant money for the casinos, especially the one where Frank was playing. Ten years later, Billy Wilder summed up the phenomenon: "When Sinatra is in Las Vegas, there is a certain electricity permeating the air. It's like Mack the Knife is in town, and the action is starting."

In a very real way, Sinatra built Vegas: not only was he present at the creation, but he was responsible for it. And the town's true owners—Meyer Lansky and Frank Costello and Joe Adonis and Doc Stacher—wanted him to feel welcome, to come back again and again, and to bring all those lovely crowds with him. "The object was to get him to perform there," Stacher said, "because there's no bigger draw in Las Vegas. When Frankie was performing, the hotel really filled up." The Sands's real owners wanted Frank to own a piece of the place, 2 percent, and they wanted it badly enough that they were glad to front him the money, a mere $54,000. The problem was the Nevada Tax Commission, which smelled a New York or Miami rat and used Sinatra's difficulties with the Internal Revenue Service as a club to beat him with.

The equity idea had first come up in March; Nevada newspapers had inveighed against it; the tax commission had tabled it. Now, however, for whatever reason, the wheel had turned. On October 31, Frank went before the commission, in Carson City, to plead his case, and though one out of the state's seven commissioners remained adamantly opposed,[4] wondering yet again why the $54,000 Sinatra supposedly had in hand shouldn't go straight to the IRS, the matter was put to a vote and he got his gambling license.

When he left the commission, the reporters were waiting, but it wasn't gaming licensure they wanted to discuss.

"Frank! Is your marriage to Ava over?"

He squinted behind his sunglasses. "I guess it's over if that's what she says."

"How do you feel about it?"

A long pause while Frank tried to think how he felt about something in whose reality he did not believe. "Well, it's very sad," he finally said. "It's tragic. I feel very badly about it."

"What about the rumors that you might get back together with Nancy?"

He waved the question off as he might have waved off a pesky housefly. Sanicola opened the car door for him and he got in.

In Los Angeles, at exactly the same time, a United Press reporter who had managed to get the private number at 320 North Carolwood was asking the same question of Frank's ex-wife.

"There is positively no chance of a reconciliation," she said. "All the rumors about Mr. Sinatra and me are false." She slammed down the phone and leaned on the kitchen counter for support, staring out the window for a long time.

Frank flew back to Las Vegas and, that night, hosted a Halloween party at the Sands. The next day, the New York papers carried an Associated Press photograph of the host standing between two chorus girls, wearing a clown costume. If his life was a kind of opera, at the moment it was *Pagliacci*.

Frank, hairline headed north, with the two Eddies: Cantor and Fisher.
Colgate Comedy Hour, November 29, 1953. Sinatra's cuff conceals the bandages
on his left wrist, the result of a suicide attempt two weeks before.

He'd been singing to many audiences, good, bad, and indifferent, over the past six months, but the songs he'd sung had shimmered out into the air and vanished: over that tumultuous period he hadn't committed a single tune to posterity. This all changed on Thursday, November 5, when Frank returned to Capitol's Melrose studios, shook hands with Nelson Riddle and Voyle Gilmore, and began recording what would become his first album for the label, *Songs for Young Lovers*.

There were only eleven musicians in Studio C that night: two reeds, four strings, piano, guitar, bass, drums, and harp. No brass. George Siravo, not Riddle, had written the arrangements, months before, for the even more stripped-down bands (eight players) that accompanied Sinatra at the 500 Club, the Riviera, and the Sands. On this night, Riddle was there only to conduct, a role he never had much taste for. But it was Sinatra, and Nelson was glad to receive Frank's warm greeting: he was now a known quantity.

Nelson Riddle heard, from the moment he lowered his baton, that something was different—that this was not the same Sinatra he'd recorded with the previous May. During that last session, Frank had sung beautifully but politely over the lushly orchestrated strings, muffling the promise of the great "I've Got the World on a String" he'd recorded just two days before. Now he fulfilled that promise. This time, with only half the number of musicians he'd had in May (and just four fiddlers rather than nine), his voice was more exposed. The band was hipper—Allan Reuss's electric guitar imparted a 1950s-modern sound on some numbers—and the songs were better: two Gershwins ("A Foggy Day" and "They Can't Take That Away from Me"), a Rodgers and Hart ("My Funny Valentine"), and Tom Adair and Matt Dennis's lovely (and gorgeously titled) "Violets for Your Furs."

This time, coming out from the protective cover of the orchestral backing, Sinatra was astonishing. On the first song, "A Foggy Day," he established dominance. The voice was as magnificent as ever, but now he showed a rhythmic ease, a sense of play, that he hadn't shown since he'd recorded the jazz-trio throwaways "That's How Much I Love You" and "You Can Take My Word for It, Baby," and his great "Sweet Lorraine," with the Metronome All-Stars, in 1946. His tossed-off, Hoboken-bratty lyrical improvisations ("I viewed the morning with much alarm/The British Museum—it lost its charm") showed the world that while Ira Gershwin might be Ira Gershwin, Sinatra was Sinatra.

He'd been loose in 1946 and he was loose now, but with a new component added: maturity. This year Frank had been through the crucible, emotionally and professionally. His "Foggy Day," from pensive verse ("I was a stranger in the city . . .") to joyous chorus, is an autobiography in miniature, a masterpiece of phrasing forged from Sinatra's inseparably intertwined life and art.

Frank had always been in impatient command in a recording studio—even with Mitch Miller. Nelson Riddle recalled: "If I wasn't conducting the orchestra to his liking, he'd shove me out of the way and take over. If he asked for diminuendo from the orchestra and didn't get it immediately, he'd take things into his own hands and you can believe that they damn well played softer for him than they did for me."

On "World on a String," Frank had brought a new kind of authority to the music itself. On "Foggy Day," he once more took charge, but with a chastened undertone. "Ava taught him how to sing a torch song," Riddle would say later. In this "Foggy Day," you can feel Frank and Ava's actual agonies and ecstasies in the real London, just three months before. His voice has such a plaintive tremolo that you worry for his emotional well-being. On the song's ultimate line, "and in foggy London town the sun was shining everywhere," Frank sings the word "shining" not once, not twice, but *five* times in a row—sings it so passionately that you can feel the deep dark in back of the sunlight.

The next night he recorded four more songs, and one of them, the first—a pretty Burke–Van Heusen tune called "Like Someone in Love"—had been arranged by Riddle. Siravo's charts were lovely, but this orchestration, with its Debussy/Ravel-esque flute passages (the flute would soon become a Riddle signature), was something special: a gift from one lover of impressionism to another, and a promise of more complex beauty to come.

Saturday night, November 7, wasn't just the loneliest night of the week, as Sammy Cahn and Jule Styne's great song had it, but the loneliest of

Sinatra's life: his second wedding anniversary, with his wife nowhere in sight. Accordingly, when Jimmy Van Heusen—Frank's master of revels, and the champ at getting him to Forget—picked him up at Beverly Glen, he announced in his wry voice that they were going to get Frank laid. But good. He was as good as his word.

The next night Chester accompanied Sinatra to the El Capitan Theatre on Hollywood Boulevard, where Frank was to do a guest spot on *The Colgate Comedy Hour,* with his old pal Jimmy Durante. If Frank was suffering over Ava, he hid it well, clowning it up with the Schnozzola, who kept interrupting him whenever he tried to sing—especially when he tried to sing "From Here to Eternity." The two did a musical quiz-show skit together; they sang a duet about how all comedians want to be singers and all singers want to be comedians. Frank even warbled the Halo Shampoo jingle, "Halo, Everybody, Halo."

Maybe he was able to feign good spirits so convincingly because he'd found a pleasant distraction: while he sang the jingle, a blond twenty-two-year-old beauty-pageant winner from North Dakota named Angeline Brown Dickinson smiled and showed off her silky tresses for the camera. Later, she and Frank—and then she and Frank and Jimmy—struck up a conversation backstage. Angie Dickinson was very young and, as she remembered vividly many years later, "bursting with awe" at being in Sinatra's presence. She had a humorous, easygoing presence about her that he liked a lot. She was witty, but not caustic; she knew how to talk, but she knew how to listen, too. It turned out she was married in an informal sort of way, yet she was also an extremely practical girl, and her sights were set firmly on Hollywood. Chester asked her for her number—for Frank, of course—and of course she gave it to him.

———

Ava was still wrangling with MGM over *The Barefoot Contessa.* The studio was demanding an exorbitant fee from Mankiewicz for her services—and proposing stingy terms for her end of the loan-out. She didn't give a rat's ass about the terms. She had just had it with Hollywood, a company town whose business she neither liked nor trusted, and she had had it with Frank. She wired Schenck himself:

> I AM DESPERATELY ANXIOUS TO DO THIS PICTURE . . . YOU
> MUST KNOW MY TERRIBLE DISAPPOINTMENT AT NOT BEING
> ABLE TO ACCUMULATE SOME MONEY AND SECURITY WHICH I
> HAD CONTEMPLATED WHEN I MADE MY NEW CONTRACT WITH
> METRO . . . AND I THINK THE LEAST THAT THE COMPANY CAN
> DO IS TO GIVE ME SOME MEASURE OF HAPPINESS IN DOING
> THE KIND OF PART I WANT TO DO AT THIS TIME AS I COULD
> LEAVE FOR EUROPE IMMEDIATELY.

Metro, of course, didn't give a good goddamn about its spoiled star's happiness, except insofar as it affected business. The right deal was all Schenck cared about. The horse-trading continued.

Frank knew how badly Ava wanted this role. What it really meant as far as he was concerned was that she wanted to return to Europe. Alone. And not just for a visit, but to stay, as long as she could. If she got the job—and she tended to get what she wanted—she would leave at the end of November for an indefinite period: three months of shooting in Rome, and then Spain, probably.

If she didn't get the job, she told the press, she might go to Spain anyway.

Frank knew who was in Spain, and he felt a kind of rising panic— *the end of November.* Maybe the two of them really were through; maybe she could resist him after all. There were times, at five or six in the morning, when he had to pour another Jack Daniel's and tell himself he must think of something to keep her here. He couldn't. He was constantly on edge: when he found out she'd had a drink with Peter Lawford at the Luau on Rodeo Drive (a totally innocent thing— Lawford's manager and Bappie were also present—but Hedda Hopper blared it as a date in her column the next day), Frank went nuts. He was not just a cuckold but a public cuckold, and in his own back-yard. He phoned Lawford and told him he was a dead man—his exact phrase. He screamed into the phone that he was sending somebody to break the actor's legs.

Now it was Lawford's turn to panic. He called his manager, Milt Ebbins—whose idea it had been in the first place to go have that drink with Ava—and begged him to call Sinatra and tell him that he was completely innocent.

Ebbins was glad to call Frank and try to set things straight, but there was a small problem: Frank had left town, and nobody knew where he was.

Hysterical with fear, Lawford begged his manager to find him.

═══

Ebbins found him, but it wasn't easy. It turned out Van Heusen had flown Sinatra to New York on his plane, and Frank was holed up at Chester's West Fifty-seventh Street apartment. Jimmy answered the phone, whispering hoarsely, his hand shielding the mouthpiece: "Yeah, he's here! Jesus Christ, and he's driving me crazy! Ava, Ava, Ava! A billion fucking broads in the world, and he's got to pick the one that can take him or leave him!"

"Eventually they got Frank onto the phone," Ebbins recalled.

And he started threatening me . . . I said, "Frank, Frank, listen to me, it wasn't Peter. *I* wanted to see Ava!" He said, "What?!" I said, "Listen, it was my idea to go to the Luau, I just wanted to meet Ava is all" . . . And it took some time to calm him down. I think he believed me. Well, he never said anything more. He never says that he's sorry. And when he got a hate on, forget it. He didn't talk to Peter for years.

He'd come to New York to begin yet another radio show for NBC: *To Be Perfectly Frank,* a fifteen-minute, twice-a-week broadcast on which Sinatra played DJ, spinning the records of other vocalists and singing a number or two of his own, backed by a five-piece combo. The show was a strangely mixed bag, reflecting both Frank's resurgent fortunes and the declining state of radio. At first a sponsor couldn't even be found. "Ten years ago, even five," wrote the critic Jack O'Brian, "such a show starring such a revivified 'hot' personality as 'The Voice' would have had 35 musicians, a 'name' conductor, a chorus of 16, several announcers and highly-paid guest stars. Now it's just Frank, five musicians, and recordings."

He was taping the shows for later broadcast on NBC affiliates, and during the ten days he spent in New York that November, he was in a kind of fever, consuming coffee and pills and cigarettes instead of food, recording episode after episode over the course of long days in the Rockefeller Center studios, stockpiling shows against the trip he knew he had to make to win back his wife.

In the meantime, he was a walking wreck, able at times to simulate his old charming self, but mostly obsessing about her, trying in vain to reach her on the phone (she and Bappie were lying low in another Palm Springs rental). Van Heusen took him out to Toots Shor's and "21," where Frank—still wearing his wedding ring, the gossips were interested to note—declined to sing when Chester sat down at the piano. Not in the mood, he said. A pretty blonde sitting nearby, "Melissa Weston Bigelow of New York and Southampton society," according to Kilgallen, found his moodiness attractive. After a couple of days it wore thin. When she left, Chester brought in the usual paid company (after an early experience with a pro who bore a slight resemblance to Billie Holiday, Frank had discovered a special fondness for black women), sometimes in twos and threes.

Jimmy Van Heusen indulged his friend as fully as his imagination and resources would allow, but even he, renowned for his heroic energy, was fraying out. He marshaled the usual reinforcements: Jule Styne and Sammy Cahn (though not together, just at the moment: they were having an idiotic feud), Manie Sacks, Ben Barton, Frank Military, Al Silvani.

Not Tami Mauriello, though. The old pug had actually gone and gotten a part—a pretty fair-sized one—in Kazan's fucking waterfront picture, which was just about to start shooting in Hoboken, where the populace was all agog at the arrival of the movie people with their trucks, lights, and cables. Not to mention the breathlessly awaited appearance of Marlon Brando.

After a few days, Frank stopped going out. He stiffed NBC, failing to appear for the premiere of *Perfectly Frank*, which was to be broadcast live; the network had to do a fast shuffle and throw one of the tapes he'd already stockpiled onto the air. The suits were not pleased—there were grumbles about legal action. Sinatra couldn't have cared less. He was walking around Jimmy's apartment in his pajamas, a drink in one hand and a cigarette in the other, gazing into space or out the window or at the flickering gray and white images on TV: Lucy and Ricky jabbering about this or that, to uproarious laughter. Husband-and-wife situation comedies were all the rage that fall, and a number of them featured actual couples—the Arnazes, Ozzie and Harriet, Burns and Allen, the Stu Erwins, Anne Jeffreys and Robert Sterling on *Topper*. When MGM announced the Frank-and-Ava split, some Hollywood wit cracked, "Well, that washes them up. They'll never get a TV situation comedy show now!"

On Monday, November 16, Mankiewicz and Schenck signed: Ava was to play the lead in *The Barefoot Contessa*. Mankiewicz would pay MGM $200,000 for her services; of this amount, Metro would pay Ava $60,000 for three months' work. It was well below her usual rate, but she didn't give a damn. All the trade papers carried the news. They also carried the news that Elia Kazan had started shooting *On the Waterfront* in Hoboken. Marlon Brando, wearing blue jeans and a red-and-black-checked hunting jacket, had slipped into town, listened attentively as Kazan explained the setup, done a couple hours' work, then slipped away in a black car. (He'd had it written into his contract that he could leave every afternoon to go see his psychiatrist in Manhattan.)

Across the river in Chester's place, Frank, still in his pajamas, sat and talked dully on the phone—to his agents, to Hank Sanicola. He had Sanicola read him the trades. Hank said he was sorry, about Ava, about *Waterfront*. Frank didn't answer.

He was due in St. Louis the next day, to rehearse for a week-before-Thanksgiving gig at the Chase Hotel. His bags still weren't packed. Chester looked at him. Would he please eat something, for fuck's sake? He looked like shit.

Frank stared into space. He would try.

Chester told him he had to go out. Could he get Frank anything? Blonde? Redhead? Brown sugar?

Frank didn't answer—not even a smile. Van Heusen left, exhaling with relief the second he walked out the door. He had had it, and so had the rest of Sinatra's friends. Frank had committed the worst sin, one of which he'd previously been incapable: he had finally bored them all to tears.

=====

Chester went home at 2:00 a.m. after attending another party at "21." It had been a gala occasion: he'd played the piano and sung, mostly his own songs, and he'd been a big hit. At forty, Jimmy Van Heusen wasn't anything like a good-looking man—tall, powerful, gravel voiced, he had a bullish presence enhanced by a thick neck and shaved head (he'd begun the ahead-of-his-time practice when he started losing his hair in his late twenties). "You would not pick him over Clark Gable any day," Angie Dickinson recalled. "But his magnetism was irresistible." He played piano beautifully, wrote gorgeously poignant songs about romance, and, quite straightforwardly if rather unromantically, loved to fuck. Women knew it at once by the look in his eye, the way he ran his fingers down a girl's arm—playing her like a piano!—and growled, in those W. C. Fields–ian tones, "Bee-yutiful." He had a fat wallet; he flew his own plane; he never went home alone.

Tonight, though, he did: he had a sick friend to tuck in. Van Heusen shook his head as he turned the key—and then stared at the spots of blood on the floor. He followed the red trail across the living room, his heart thudding. At the entrance to the kitchen, he saw Frank, his left pajama sleeve soaked deep scarlet, lying semiconscious on the linoleum.

———

Frantic when their star attraction failed to appear, the bookers at the Chase Hotel phoned everyone: Sinatra's agents, his lawyer, even Alan Livingston at Capitol Records. No one knew anything. Finally they called Morris Shenker. Shenker was a St. Louis defense attorney with a large and grateful clientele of men whose bona fides might not have stood up to scrutiny by the Kefauver Committee. An enormously powerful figure with ties to Vegas and the East Coast, the lawyer made it his business to know everyone and everything. And with one telephone call, he found out. Quickly and simply, he told the entertainment managers at the Chase Hotel that Sinatra had slit his wrists.

In truth, it had only been one wrist—his left. Van Heusen had paid his doorman $50 to get a cab fast and keep his mouth shut, then paid the cabbie $20 to run every red light on the way up to Mount Sinai Hospital. More money passed hands, and with great haste Frank was attended to and checked into a suite under his own name. The cover story was to be that he was exhausted. This was true enough. His weight was down to 118 pounds from 132, and he hadn't really slept for weeks. Though no official announcement had been made yet, the flowers and telegrams started arriving in great quantities the next morning.

After a drugged sleep, Sinatra awoke alert and agitated. He had to get out of there *now*, he kept repeating. Around his bed, his doctors, along with Van Heusen, Sacks, Styne, and Cahn (forgetting their feud), tried to reason with him. He was in no shape to move, let alone leave. Why not just put his feet up for a few days?

He had to get to California. Had to see her.

She was leaving him, he knew it. He'd tried to leave her, the only way he knew, but maybe he just didn't have the guts. Now he was pinning everything on looking her in the eye, holding her hand, and begging her to stay. He finally reached her on the phone—she'd returned to L.A. to go to the opera and see friends.

Oh Jesus, Francis.

She sounded both solicitous and slightly exasperated, but her voice was balm to his soul. He imagined her standing at his bedside, imagined the dimpled chin and lush lips and green eyes looking down at him.

His voice was weak. He was okay, but he had to see her right away.

She told him to just stay put until he was healthy. She wasn't going anywhere.

But he knew her: she probably had her bags packed already.

=====

"Sinatra's father says he went to Mt. Sinai hosp for a checkup," wrote Winchell, the All-Powerful. "But the rumors had it he tried to End It All."

Whenever Frank Sinatra taxed his patience to the utmost, Jimmy Van Heusen had to remind himself that this, after all, was Sinatra. A man who put his pants on one leg at a time, picked his nose, and told stupid jokes, but . . . Sinatra. As a songwriter of brilliance but not genius, Van Heusen was in an ideal position to understand what genius really was, and he recognized that Frank surely possessed it. It didn't excuse his excesses—only God could do that—but it began to explain them. Jimmy might bad-mouth Frank behind his back (and he meant it when he did), he might hate him at times and even fear him, yet he also loved him, as much as he could love anybody. And when the little bastard sang, Chester got more goose bumps than anyone else.

"I would rather write songs than do anything else—even fly," Van Heusen once told an interviewer. And he loved flying. He loved fucking, too, but the sublime pleasure of songwriting trumped all other joys—and made them possible. He had written some good songs for

Sinatra, and he hoped to write more. Staying as close as possible to Frank, Chester sensed, might just accelerate that process.

But Jimmy Van Heusen had another notable quality: he was a hypochondriac of the first order. He kept a Merck manual at his bedside, he injected himself with vitamins and painkillers, he had surgical procedures for ailments real and imagined. He was terrified of illness and death, and earlier that year, close to his fortieth birthday, he'd had what he'd felt might be a heart attack. The doctors weren't sure, but he was. Terrifyingly, over these last taxing weeks with Sinatra, Jimmy had begun to feel chest pains again.

Accordingly, while Frank got dressed in the hospital room, shooting his cuffs to cover the bandages (the doctor had just walked out, shaking his head, after warning Sinatra that he was leaving Against Medical Advice), Van Heusen looked his friend in the eye and told him he had to have a word with him.

The songwriter had already gone over in his mind what he wanted to say. If it meant the end of the friendship, so be it. But he'd come to the end of his rope. The two men looked at each other in the mirror as Frank looped his tie. And Jimmy, his voice serious, told Frank that he had to see a headshrinker when he got back to Los Angeles. He couldn't take this anymore.

Sinatra smiled a little. Why not?

———

Worried about their newly successful client's fragility, William Morris assigned Sinatra a shadow, in the person of the New York agent George E. Wood, a dapper, slightly shifty-eyed fellow who prided himself on his wide acquaintanceship among organized criminals of the top rank—many of whom functioned as a kind of show-business directorate. Wood relished the assignment. "When Frank ate, I ate; when he slept, I slept," the agent recalled. "When he felt like walking, I walked with him. When he took a haircut, I took a haircut. I loved the guy."

Wood bribed a TWA gate agent at La Guardia to let him walk his charge through a hangar so Frank could get on his L.A.-bound flight unmolested by the pack of reporters. He rode cross-country with him, watching him as he slept a drugged sleep, now and then glancing at the bandage on his left wrist. And Wood did his best to fend off the reporters who met the plane at Los Angeles International the next morning. It wasn't easy. The whole country was tuned in to what looked like the final act in the Frank-and-Ava saga.

RUMOR MILL IS MUM ON FRANKIE'S ROCKY ROMANCE, read a November 21 headline, punning lightly on the name of his radio show. "Whether skinny, harried Frank Sinatra would win back luscious Ava Gardner today prepared to be a matter known only to the principals," began the wire-service story, datelined Hollywood.

> Some of the couple's friends believed the crooner's estranged wife regarded their separation as "final." Others thought Sinatra's flying trip here from New York in defiance of his doctor's advice might "weaken" her stand.
>
> Several thought it was significant she did not meet him at the airport . . .
>
> Newsmen followed him to the baggage stand and again he growled:
>
> "Nothing. No comment."
>
> The crooner, down to 118 pounds from his normal 140, darted into a waiting limousine leaving still more questions unanswered.
>
> Will he follow Ava to Europe?
>
> Has she said she would talk to him?
>
> "No comment."

They'd made a plan to have dinner that night, at Bappie's place—Ava's big sister was now living with her husband, Charlie, in the Nichols Canyon cottage. Ava had insisted on a neutral location, with Bappie and Charlie present, so that Frank couldn't misconstrue the occasion.

She met him at the door, kissing him on the cheek and immedi- . ately noticing his bandaged wrist.

He deflected her concern, instantly sensing that vulnerability wouldn't play this time. It was nothing—a stupid accident. How was she?

Warm but cool at the same time, and nervous. He saw her hand shaking slightly as she held her cigarette. Frank was all charm, especially with Bappie, who'd once considered him an oily little dago (she didn't have much patience for Negroes or Jews, either) but now felt considerable warmth toward her brother-in-law.

It was too late, all of it. Ava had written him off. Not, of course, just for the one infidelity he'd boasted about, but for the hundreds he would never mention. Years later she would say, "I was happier married to Frank than ever before in my entire life. He was the most charming man I'd ever met—nothing but charm. Maybe, if I'd been willing to share him with other women we could have been happy."

She smiled at him now with a kind of relief: she'd worried before he came that she might not be able to resist him, that something would trigger her old susceptibilities. Nothing did. He looked like shit—that helped. Nor was she in the mood to mother him. She tapped her cigarette, she drank her drink, she looked at him and smiled, and all the while she was thinking of Rome, and Luis Miguel.

He saw it. He was endlessly intuitive—he could pick up a vibe from a room-service waiter or the second reporter from the left (though he didn't like the world to know what he knew), and he was, if anything, over-attuned to the love of his life. Early he had learned to watch Dolly closely, closely, to try to figure out whether she was going to hug him or hit him; early he'd learned to watch Ava closely, to see whether she was going to love him or leave him.

She was leaving him.

Her bags might as well have been sitting by the front door.

"F. Sinatra will spend Thanksgiving with Nancy and their tots," Winchell wrote the next morning.

Meanwhile, Ava came up with her own way to spend the holiday. "Ava Gardner on Thanksgiving morning boards the plane from Los Angeles to Rome, obviously in the hope of catching reporters and cameramen more interested in a turkey drumstick than in the Sinatras," Dorothy Manners wrote in her column. "One thing came out of her 'talks' with Frank—or at least one talk—they haven't seen each other since. She will not file for divorce (if she does at all) until she returns to this country in the spring."

The photographers caught up with her at Idlewild as she was about to board her Rome-bound connecting flight. She was standing on the aluminum steps in her big sunglasses, grinning in the November sun, holding a manila envelope containing a *Barefoot Contessa* script (she hadn't gotten around to reading it just yet) in her right hand and, with her left, waving to the cameras, showing the whole world that she was no longer wearing her wedding ring.

That night Frank was back at the El Capitan Theatre, once again guest starring on *The Colgate Comedy Hour,* along with Eddie Fisher, no less. The host, Eddie Cantor, brought Fisher out first, to croon a medley of his hits (including "I'm Walking Behind You," the number that had aced out Frank's version in the charts); Fisher then invited Cantor to appear on *his* TV show—the one with Axel Stordahl leading the band. A little later, as the great Harold Arlen himself suggestively tinkled the opening bars of "One for My Baby," Old Banjo Eyes said, "You know, Harold, there's one fella that sings your songs better than anyone else. Lately, he's become a dramatic actor—pretty good, too."

And out came Frank, to big *From Here to Eternity* applause, looking painfully thin in his tux. But if, as he walked onstage, he felt any hangover from the last ten terrible days, he lost it the instant he flared his nostrils and went into his own, all-Arlen medley: "Come Rain or Come Shine," "I've Got the World on a String," and Mercer and Arlen's "That Old Black Magic." This was, quite simply, a master class in American popular song, and Fisher, the perpetrator of "Oh, My Papa"—who was always deferential to Sinatra's infinitely greater gift—stood openmouthed in the wings. Frank was in magnificent voice, and his passion ("ev'ry time your lips meet mine, darling, down and down I go; round and round I go") was palpably, almost embarrassingly, real, blazing out sun-like from the little black-and-white screen.

Watching the old, scratchy kinescope and taking note of the way he seemed to favor his left arm, holding it slightly awkwardly at times, one can't help but wonder: Was he still wearing the bandages? Was that long tux-shirt cuff taped to prevent his accidentally revealing them?

———

SINATRA ADMITS HURTING WRIST BUT LAUGHS OFF SUICIDE RUMOR, ran the wire-service headline.

> Crooner Frank Sinatra admitted Tuesday he had "bruised and scratched" his wrist, but laughed off as gossip the rumors he had attempted suicide.
>
> The tempestuous singer, who recently reached a parting of ways with Ava Gardner, said he did not remember when or where the accident occurred.
>
> Rumors that Sinatra slashed his wrist started when a photograph taken during a conversation with Eddie Cantor revealed a mark on the singer's left wrist.
>
> Hollywood gossips immediately connected it with his recent hospitalization in New York.

———

Still feverishly plotting how he might win her back, he went into the Capitol studios again on two late nights in early December. For the first session, on the eighth, he recorded three swingers, trying to pick up the mood from the meditative note he'd ended on in November—and perhaps pick up his own mood as well. Most of all, though, he was trying to notch his first big hit for the label. But while Riddle's writing for the horns had all the wonderful lightness and sass of "World on a String," the songs themselves ("Take a Chance," "Ya Better Stop," and "Why Should I Cry over You?") were strictly grade-B stuff—a reminder to keepers of the pieties that Sinatra plus Riddle does not always equal magic.

The next night, though, singer and arranger returned to the studio with a string section and laid down three ballads, the second of which would turn into pure gold.

According to Nelson Riddle, Carolyn Leigh and Johnny Richards's "Young at Heart" had been floating around various record companies for a while without attracting a vocalist. Nat Cole had passed on it. "I think it's a good song," Riddle told Sinatra, "but nobody wants to do it."

"Let's do it," Frank said—according to legend (his), not even asking to hear it first. In fact, he had asked Jimmy Van Heusen for his opinion, and Chester had responded in his most clinical fashion that he thought "Young at Heart" could be a hit for Frank.

And so, on the night of December 9, Frank recorded it.

Sinatra, Riddle, and Gilmore convened at the KHJ studios at 8:30 p.m. They wrapped up at 1:00 in the morning—ninety minutes over-time, by the rules of Local 47 of the American Federation of Musicians. This meant that the costs for the studio time and the fees for the twenty-five players—costs that came out of Frank's pocket—doubled from $1,072.50 to $2,145 (some $17,000 today).

Clearly, Sinatra felt it was worth his while.

A great vocal recording of a popular song is an inseparable weave of words and melody, of the singer's work and the arranger's, and—of course—the musicians'. But also to be taken into account is the *meaning* of the song, which is not always what the lyrics say. "Young at Heart" was a paean to rebirth, the ideal soundtrack to Frank Sinatra's matchless comeback: "Fairy tales can come true; it could happen to you" was the perfect rejoinder to Swifty Lazar's "Even Jesus couldn't get resurrected in this town."

And everything about this recording was perfect. New high-fidelity recording tape and microphones brilliantly brought out Sinatra's diction, phrasing, and pitch-perfect tone, not to mention the gorgeousness of the musical background and Nelson Riddle's arrangement. From the opening fillip—a string passage announcing the melody in a

quizzical, slightly off-kilter way that draws the listener in irresistibly—
it was clear that a genius was at work. Riddle had brought impressionist sonorities to the American popular song for the first time, as well as
a complexity of sexual longing that would infuse the 1950s and provide
an antidote to the conventional pieties of the Eisenhower years.

And most to the point, he had brought a new level of art to Frank Sinatra. Once the singer began, it was apparent that Riddle had completely
understood Sinatra's lecture about overbusy orchestrations: the flutes
and strings shimmer over the gorgeous glide of Frank's ever-deepening
baritone; underneath lies the deep woof of the trumpetless brass section (featuring, for the first time, the bass trombonist George Roberts).
It was vintage Riddle—only the vintage had just ripened.

All at once, Sinatra and Riddle were a team. Frank had never sung
this way, and Nelson had never written this way. (The arrangements
he'd done for Nat Cole, while superb, were colorless by comparison.)
And what he and Frank were doing was inimitable: "Young at Heart"
is a wonderful number, but it's more a great moment than a great song
per se—it's difficult to imagine any other singer, no matter how skilled,
ever bringing as much to it as Sinatra brought to it that night, three
days from his thirty-eighth birthday.

As with Frank's acting in *From Here to Eternity*, his singing on
"Young at Heart" told the world that he truly had returned from the
dead. But as would be the case with the movie, the real fruits of the
recording would be delayed until the new year.

═══

The last song of the night, recorded in the wee small hours of December 10, never became nearly as well-known as "Young at Heart," but the
Jimmy Van Heusen number, with lyrics by Carl Sigman, was ravishing
all the same—and, as with all Sinatra's great ballads, a little too close
to home for comfort:

> *I could have told you she'd hurt you . . .*
> *But you were in love, and didn't want to know.*

Spain, May 1950. Jimmy Van Heusen shows Ava how to use his camera
while Frank and an expatriate couple named Frank and Doreen Grant look on.
Ava would take shelter with the Grants over the hard Christmas of 1953,
as Sinatra futilely tried to win her back.

The press was omnipresent in Sinatra's life: a third party in his marriage, a constant kibitzer on every aspect of his career. He could
never completely tune it out, because the reporters and columnists
were always checking in. Besides, he needed them as much as they
needed him.

Yet even if he'd turned a corner in his professional life, even if
he was behaving a little better than he used to, there were still those

journalists who felt honor-bound to attack him. Like Maggio, he was an uppity wop, proud even when he'd been beaten to a pulp. It didn't sit well with much of America—especially Middle America. An early-November editorial in Michigan's *Holland Evening Sentinel* read:

> The breakup of the sultry love affair of Frank Sinatra and Ava Gardner after only two years of what was euphemistically called marriage caused a critic to call the love affairs of the movie world "barnyard romance." The only trouble with that description is that it is insulting to the respectable domestic animals of the barnyard.

On the other hand, Edith Gwynn, in her Hollywood column, apostrophized rather feelingly:

> F. Sinatra is taking his usual beating from most of the press. He's often merited it in the past. But we don't dig how several reporters could chronicle as they did, when F.S. brushed 'em off at the airport here. Of him they front-paged, "he admitted he was upset"; "he said he is a sick man" (which he is!). They further itemed Frank was fresh out of a New York hospital, and then a few sentences later, beat his brains in because the guy wasn't all smiles, affable and gabby!
>
> Sinatra is on the verge of a whole new career—musically and dramatically. He is also on the verge of hysteria over "emotional problems." The fact that Ava Gardner is taking off for Europe again (to do "The Barefoot Contessa") won't be much help! Strikes us, The Voice rates at least half the break in print others in the spotlight might get!

That was certainly the way Frank felt. Christmas was coming and he wanted to spend it with his wife, but there was little evidence that his wife wanted to spend it with him. When he had talked to her in

Rome over the fucking transatlantic phone line, she'd been infuriatingly breezy, chattering on about the magic of the Eternal City, her wonderful new apartment, and her funny Italian maid . . .

The moment he told her he loved her, the connection was mysteriously severed.

The holiday blues descended on him early and heavily. And so, as Van Heusen had demanded, Frank began seeing a psychiatrist: Dr. Ralph Greenson, whose sister happened to be married to Sinatra's new lawyer, Milton "Mickey" Rudin. Like so many pilgrims to the Golden State, Ralph Greenson was a reinvented character: born Romeo Greenschpoon in Brooklyn forty-two years before, he had gravitated to Los Angeles after serving as an Army doctor in the war and quickly built a practice composed of movie stars and Beverly Hills housewives. Appropriately to the territory and to his great benefit, the darkly handsome doctor looked the part: with his square jaw and ironic (though sympathetic) Jewish (but not too Jewish) features, his black mustache and closely cropped graying hair, Greenson could have played a psychiatrist in a movie. Funnily enough, he almost had: a close friend, the writer Leo Rosten, had based the title character in *Captain Newman, M.D.*, his novel about an Army psychiatrist—eventually adapted for the screen, with Gregory Peck in the title role—directly on Greenson.

Ralph Greenson, who was to become Marilyn Monroe's psychoanalyst, would later gain notoriety in the therapeutic community for violating doctor-patient boundaries: he treated Monroe in his home, where she became virtually a part of his family, and eventually more or less took control of her life. Sinatra was no Monroe, but there is evidence that Greenson may have overstepped the bounds with him in a similar way. Since Frank would certainly have attracted unwanted notice by going to Greenson's Beverly Hills office, the psychiatrist offered to see him in his Spanish Mission–style house a stone's throw from the Brentwood Country Club.

The psychiatrist was titillated to be treating the most famous entertainer in the world. "Of all Greenson's interests," wrote Marilyn Monroe's biographer Donald Spoto, "it was the nature and burden of fame that seems to have most intrigued him and celebrities to whom he was most attracted. This was a recurring theme in his life's work." In a paper titled "Special Problems in Psychotherapy with the Rich and Famous," Greenson wrote: "I have found the impatience of the budding star and the fading film stars to be the most difficult with whom I have tried to work."

All Frank would have wanted to talk about, of course, was Ava, and the doctor would have been very interested—maybe a little too interested for Sinatra's taste. But there was another subject that Greenson also would certainly have wanted to discuss, behind the closed but not altogether soundproof door of his home study—one that would've made Frank quite uncomfortable: namely, the first woman in his life.

As for Marilyn Monroe: December 1953 was the closest she and Frank would ever come to working together. But having ground out a half-dozen pictures for 20th Century Fox over the past couple of years (most recently and unpleasantly, *River of No Return* and *There's No Business Like Show Business*), at what she considered wage-slave pay and always in the formulaic role of the Dumb Blonde, Monroe had decided to dig in her heels on *Pink Tights*. Her fame was rising; she wanted more money and better roles. She had seen the script, a silly remake of a silly 1943 Betty Grable movie called *Coney Island*: Monroe would play a turn-of-the-century cabaret singer, and Sinatra, a smooth-talking con man. It was a lark, but the only thing in it for her was the usual pouting and eye widening. To compound the insult, Fox had signed Sinatra for $5,000 a week, more than three times her $1,500 weekly salary as a contract player.

She was due at the studio on December 15 for the commencement of principal photography. She stayed home. So did Frank. But in truth, he was in a hurry to get out of town.

———

In the meantime, it was Christmas shopping season, sunny and in the seventies in Beverly Hills, and Louella Parsons was gratified to note that Frank had been spotted making the rounds of local shops with thirteen-year-old Nancy Sandra—who, Earl Wilson noted with mild horror, already had beaux.

A few days later, Louella gushed: "It wouldn't surprise me one mite if Frank Sinatra moved home. He's there all the time to see the children and they are just crazy about him."

She was in high officious-biddy mode, lobbying, as always, for uprightness and solid family values amid the swirling Gomorrah of Hollywood. Frank's kids were lobbying too, fighting hard to hold on to him, since he was around anyway and Christmas was coming.

But the smile on Big Nancy's face whenever he stopped by reminded him of that chick in the painting by da Vinci.

To try to calm down, he spent some money. He went into Teitelbaum's on Rodeo Drive and bought a white mink coat to take with him to Rome. Three weeks on *Pink Tights* would pay for it. He had the furrier stitch the initials AGS into the lining.

———

Except Ava wasn't going to be in Rome on Christmas. When he phoned her on Tuesday morning, the twenty-second (having gotten up at eleven—the crack of dawn, for him—to try to catch her before she headed out for cocktails at 8:00 p.m.), Ava informed him, somewhat testily, that she was going to Madrid for the holiday.

He responded just as testily. Who the fuck was in Madrid?

The Grants, if he must know. Frank and Doreen.

A long, pinging, staticky silence; the international operator straining to hear.

Ava finally spoke. She would be back in Rome on Saturday or Sunday.

He protested. But Christmas was Friday. Her birthday the day before.

She really had to get going.

United Press reached her the following morning to ask if she and Frank might be planning a holiday reconciliation.

She wasn't sure if she would put it that way.

Had she spoken to him?

She had. She proceeded to recount the conversation, in slightly different form. It had been entirely amicable, and she had arranged to cut her visit to Madrid short so she could meet Frank in Rome on Saturday or Sunday.

The reporter was scrawling, fast, in his notebook. So we could still say a holiday reconciliation.

"I'll be so happy to see him again," Ava said.

Frank had left Tuesday night, checking the two huge white suitcases that he took everywhere, but carrying the presents—an armful, including the big white Teitelbaum's box: he didn't want to risk some baggage handler snatching *that*. It was an overnight flight from Los Angeles to New York, a three-hour layover, then another ten-hour leg from Idlewild to Heathrow. Another layover, then three hours to Rome. These were the pre-jet days, propellers droning on the big Constellation, bumping along with the weather in the lower stratosphere, four hundred miles an hour tops, even with a tailwind. A lot of time to read, to try to sleep, to smoke and drink and worry. He chewed gum, he stared out the window, he drummed his fingers on the armrest. A lot of time to be impatient.

And to change his mind: he'd bought a ticket to Rome, but he had decided to go to Madrid.

The reporters were waiting at Heathrow.

"I'm going to spend Christmas with my wife," he said, walking fast toward customs as two redcaps laden with bags did their best to keep up. The pack of newsmen walked with him.

"I never talk about my personal affairs, but yes, my wife is expecting me."

The cheeky chap from *News of the World* chased him. Frank chewed his gum and walked straight ahead. A BOAC representative, tall with gray brushed-back hair and a large triangular nose, caught up with him.

"I gotta get to Madrid," Frank said. "The first flight, even if I have to stand all the way."

But he was ticketed to Rome, and the flights to Madrid were full.

While the customs people looked through his bags, he paced the terrazzo floor of the hall, back and forth, back and forth, for twenty, thirty, forty minutes. He sent a cable to Ava in Madrid, saying he would be there by evening. He was standing with his hands on his hips, tapping his foot, when the BOAC man finally returned. The flights were full.

Croydon Airport was fifteen miles away.

Chartering a twin-engine plane to Madrid would cost 160 pounds—about $440, a month's wages for a fairly well-off English office worker. Frank took out a thick wad of bills, pointed at one of the redcaps.

He grabbed a cab to Croydon.

———

Ava had spent her first couple of weeks in Rome preparing for *The Barefoot Contessa*: being fitted for costumes, finding an apartment, hiring a maid and an assistant, socializing with Bogart and Mankiewicz, making a splash on the Via Veneto. She even read that script—which, she was surprised to find, she loved. Not only was Mankiewicz a superbly witty writer, but her part was wonderful: she was to play Maria Vargas, an international woman of mystery who goes from dancing in a sleazy Madrid cabaret to marrying one of the richest men in the world. She would get to wear peasant costumes and ball gowns and seduce every man in sight.

The bit about Madrid caught her eye. It was as if Mankiewicz had been reading her mind. Spain was the place she now knew she loved most in the world, and she hadn't been able to stop thinking about the handsome bullfighter Domínguín since she'd met him in January. And so, since shooting wasn't to start till after the holidays, she made a beeline for the Spanish capital, to soak up some sun while she stayed at the villa of her expat friends Frank and Doreen Grant, but primarily to find Dominguín.

There was an urgency about Ava's actions over Christmas that year. She was about to turn thirty-one—then a far more advanced age for a woman (and especially a movie star) than now; also, as her biographer has written, she had been without a sexual partner for months. Frank's cable had come at a most unwelcome moment. "She was," Lee Server writes, "not a little distressed over Frank's pursuit, could not trust her resolve in the face of his determination, and so felt a pressing need to affirm a new romantic alliance right then, before anyone could do anything to stop it." She had edged out Dominguín's beautiful young girlfriend within hours of arriving in town—child's play—and in short order ("just hours before Sinatra's arrival," according to Server) had shacked up with the torero at the Hotel Wellington.

The newspapers always delighted in noting when Frank and Ava failed to meet each other at this or that airport, but her absence when Frank's chartered plane landed in Madrid on the afternoon of the twenty-fourth, her birthday, had nothing to do with pique: she was making love with Dominguín in their hotel suite at the time. The inopportune arrival of a lady's old beau just as she has taken up with a new one may seem like the stuff of commedia dell'arte or a farce by Feydeau, but the next few days were characterized less by romantic intrigue than by anger and sadness between the two former lovers, combined with the low-grade misery of keeping up appearances.

That night the two sat on the floor in the Grants' living room, exchanging presents and singing carols, Frank glancing at Ava, Ava avoiding Frank's glance. Right in the middle of the festivities United Press phoned. Frank gritted his teeth and took the call. "I hope to spend Christmas with my wife the same way millions of people [do] all over the world," he told the reporter.

Was he going back to Rome with Ava?

He couldn't say.

Did that mean Frank didn't know, or he wouldn't talk about it?

He couldn't say.

So great was the strain that he came down with a miserable cold the next morning. And she, in her fury at him for descending on her, fell ill, too.

She shouted an obscenity, sneezing and smashing her fist into the pillow. Dominguín didn't need a translation. And he understood when she explained she would have to go back to Rome with Sinatra. She would make sure he returned to America as soon as possible, then she would call for Luis Miguel to join her.

===

AVA GARDNER, SINATRA SILENT ON RECONCILIATION, read the December 30 wire-service headline, datelined Rome.

> Actress Ava Gardner, in bed with the flu shortly after resuming housekeeping with husband Frank Sinatra, was reported "feeling much better today."
>
> A doctor said she probably would be able to leave her apartment to keep several appointments later today.
>
> Miss Gardner went to bed yesterday several hours after she and Sinatra arrived in Rome from Madrid. He flew from the United States and followed her to Spain for Christmas, giving rise to reports of a reconciliation.
>
> On arrival here, they went straight to the actress' luxurious apartment on the fashionable Corso d'Italia, but neither would comment on whether she is abandoning her previously announced plans to get a divorce.
>
> Reached by telephone, Sinatra gave no hint of love or romance. Asked about a reconciliation, he snapped:
>
> "This doesn't concern anyone but us. This is nobody's business but our own."

Twentieth Century Fox was frantically trying to keep *Pink Tights* alive. Monroe's and Sinatra's salaries were being paid week after week, but nothing was happening. Darryl F. Zanuck was struggling to keep the film on track, but both stars were out of town and preoccupied: Marilyn holed up in San Francisco with the man she was about to marry, Joe DiMaggio; Frank in Rome, "trying to work things out" with his wife, as he kept cabling Fox.

With the press camped outside, Frank and Ava spent three days sequestered in her apartment, drinking, talking, shouting (not quite as loudly as they used to), even taking a shot at making up, without much success. She told him apologetically that she still felt like shit—but they both knew her health had nothing to do with it.

Rome, December 29, 1953. Sick, miserable, and about to be a couple no more.

They threw a New Year's Eve party—Ava's idea—at the Via Veneto cabaret run by Cole Porter's legendary muse Bricktop. Getting out of the apartment was a relief, as was being around other people—even if they barely knew the other guests: Eddie O'Brien and Rossano Brazzi plus some of the crew from her movie, dissolute Roman society nobs and equally dissolute expatriates and a few people from the embassy. Loud music, close quarters, lots of smoke; the usual requests for Frank to sing. He shook his head sadly. Sitting on his lap, Ava tried to cheer him up, amid the forced gaiety and phony sentimentality (1954! who knew what it would bring?). But when she and Frank kissed at the stroke of midnight, the tears running down her cheeks were quite real.

On Monday morning he sneaked off to the airport, leaving by a service entrance to avoid the reporters, and flew back to America alone.

Humphrey Bogart and Ava at a cocktail party for their film *The Barefoot Contessa,* Rome, early 1954. Frank was in Hollywood, 7,000 miles away, still pining for her.

While Frank was in the air, on Monday, January 4, Capitol released *Songs for Young Lovers* as a ten-inch LP, containing the eight songs from the November 5 and 6 sessions: "My Funny Valentine," "The Girl Next Door," "A Foggy Day," and "Like Someone in Love" on side one; "I Get a Kick Out of You," "Little Girl Blue," "They Can't Take That Away from Me," and "Violets for Your Furs" on side two. It was Frank's first album since *Sing and Dance with Frank Sinatra* on Columbia over three years earlier.

The cover of *Sing and Dance* had shown a hatless Frank (with a full head of hair), looking neat and collegiate in a striped necktie and light-colored jacket, smiling amiably against a bouncy pink background, complete with a couple's dancing feet. The cover of *Young Lovers* established a new, infinitely moodier Sinatra: against a dark background, the singer, in a dark suit and fedora, stood under a lamppost, a lonely figure with a cigarette, looking meditative while a pair of couples promenaded by. Sinatra and the young lovers were in separate universes—he was their serenader, not their friend.

George Siravo had arranged seven of the eight songs, but Nelson Riddle, the arranger of "Like Someone in Love"—a master at expressing emotional complexity and sexual tension—was poised to carry the baton forward.

Frank was living the reality of that figure on the album cover. Arriving back at his Los Angeles apartment, he found he couldn't eat, couldn't sleep, didn't feel like singing, and had little to do with his days besides see his headshrinker and do the radio show ("You may have heard it—if you've got a car," he told a television audience, which, like most of America, wasn't gathering around the radio in the living room anymore). On the movie front, Zanuck had suspended Monroe for noncompliance, and apart from pre-recording a couple of songs for *Pink Tights,* Frank didn't have much to do besides collect his paycheck. If he picked up a newspaper, he could read reports that Ava, who'd told him that she wasn't feeling well enough to see him off at the airport in Rome, had that very afternoon gone to the atelier of the sculptor Assen Peikov to begin posing, "in a chilly studio without much on," for a statue to be used in *The Barefoot Contessa*. Oh, and by the way, other reports said that she'd taken up with Shelley Winters's soon-to-be ex-husband, Vittorio Gassman.

Frank needed company, and fast, so he went to extreme measures: he moved Jule Styne into his apartment. "He *literally* moved me in," Styne recalled. Sinatra simply went to the Beverly Hills Hotel, where the recently divorced composer was renting a bungalow, and had Styne's belongings packed up and carted over to Beverly Glen.

The affable and energetic Styne was flattered—at first. The odd-couple arrangement would last for eight months in all, but it was a trial from the beginning. Frank thought and talked of little but Ava through the long days and nights. "I come home at night and the apartment is all dark," Styne remembered.

> I yell "Frank!" and he doesn't answer. I walk into the living room and it's like a funeral parlor. There are three pictures of Ava in the room and the only lights are three dim ones on the pictures. Sitting in front of them is Frank with a bottle of brandy. I say to him, "Frank, pull yourself together." And he says, "Go 'way. Leave me alone." Then all night he paces up and down and says, "I can't sleep, I can't sleep." At four o'clock in the morning I hear him calling someone on the telephone. It's his first wife, Nancy. His voice is soft and quiet and I hear him say, "You're the only one who understands me." Then he paces up and down some more and maybe he reads, and he doesn't fall asleep until the sun's up. Big deal. You can have it.

Frank was in a sleep-deprived daze. Driving his Cadillac convertible through Beverly Hills one afternoon, he crashed into a small English sports car at an intersection. It was a mismatch. The collision threw the other driver, one Mrs. Myrna McClees, out of her vehicle and onto the pavement: she was taken to the hospital unconscious, with a fractured skull and lacerations. Frank swore he had come to a full stop and looked both ways before proceeding. The woman recovered; Frank stumbled on.

His ex-wife, too, felt his pain. "Nancy Sinatra's pals are worried about the thin, drawn look that's replaced the bright, happy air sported by the crooner's ex for the last few years," Erskine Johnson wrote in his column. "They blame it on Nancy's involvement, through her kiddies, in Frank's current mental depression."

Maybe it also had something to do with those 4:00 a.m. phone calls. She was not only exhausted, but furious: She was propping him up, and for what? So he could make up for the thousandth time with that bimbo?

=====

There had been times when the membrane between his private sorrows and his onstage persona was porous: when his depression undermined his timing, his presence, his voice itself. Lately, though, the stage was more and more a refuge. On January 17 he returned to *The Colgate Comedy Hour*, singing "Young at Heart" and "The Birth of the Blues" in fine style and bantering easily with the audience about the romantic elopement of Joltin' Joe DiMaggio and Marilyn Monroe—which, unfortunately, had held up the movie Frank was supposed to be starring in with Miss Monroe, over at 20th Century Fox. He made a comically resigned face.

In the meantime, his new joke on *Rocky Fortune* was working the phrase "from here to eternity" into every episode, at least once, and often several times. Sometimes he wondered if anyone was listening.

Then, in the last week of the month, things began to pick up. Harry Cohn of Columbia Pictures, hearing the Oscar drumbeat grow louder for *From Here to Eternity*, called Frank in to discuss a multipicture deal. Louis Mayer's son-in-law Bill Goetz, who was leaving his job as production chief at Universal International to become an independent producer (and trying to get out of the long shadow of his brother-in-law David O. Selznick), called Frank in to talk about playing one of the leads in a screen adaptation of the hit musical *Guys and Dolls*.

Far more important than either of these calls was a talk Frank had with Ava.

He'd been phoning her every few days, not as often as he wanted, but more than her cool responses seemed to indicate he should. Then, one morning (Los Angeles time, just after the end of the workday in Rome), he caught her in a different mood: uncertain, agitated, needy. Mankiewicz and Bogart were giving her fits, she told him. She and the writer-director had been oil and water from the beginning: it turned out his witty script read better than it spoke, and Ava, having grown no less insecure about her acting ability, couldn't make it work. She needed to be propped up; the sharp-minded, sharp-tongued Mankiewicz wasn't a coddler. Early in the shoot, the cameraman, Jack Cardiff, asked Ava to perch on the arm of a sofa while he took measurements for lighting a close-up. Mankiewicz, happening to walk by, saw her there and griped, "You're the sittin'-est goddamn actress I've ever worked with."

"I was so surprised I couldn't even get my mouth open in time to say 'Go fuck yourself' to his departing back," Gardner later recalled. "And the truth is I was never able to give him my complete trust after that."

Unlike *Mogambo*'s John Ford, Mankiewicz was an intellectual; Ava felt she'd already failed that test with Artie Shaw. She couldn't win this filmmaker over with tough talk, and she was too mad to try to seduce him.

But Bogart was a bigger problem. Ava was intimidated in the first place by the fifty-four-year-old screen legend, and Bogie, who'd become pals with Sinatra over the past year, and was a world-class needler to boot ("I like a little agitation now and then," he said; "keeps things lively"), decided to give it to this broad, but good. "On the morning of the first day of shooting, Bogie came by his costar's dressing room to say hello," writes Lee Server.

> Stuffed into the tiny room were Ava, a makeup man, Ava's
> Italian secretary/translator . . . , Luis Miguel, and Bappie
> (who had recently arrived from California with an emergency
> replenishment of Ava's Larder: Hershey chocolate bars,
> chewing gum, marshmallows, popcorn, and Jack Daniel's
> whiskey). Bogart remarked that it looked like the circus was
> in town, and when introduced to Dominguín, he made a
> crack . . .

"I'll never figure you broads out," Bogart said. "Half the world's female population would throw themselves at Frank's feet, and here you are flouncing around with guys who wear capes and little ballerina slippers."

As Dominguín looked puzzled, Ava said, "Oh, mind your own goddamn business, Bogie." She wasn't smiling.

"It was to be the beginning of a rocky relationship," Server continues.

> Their rapport did not improve on the set. Ava's "stage fright" was still in place, and she found her confidence shriveling when confronted with Bogart's chronic irritability and what she perceived as his deliberate disruptions of her concentration with his complaints. Shooting one of their first scenes together, Bogie turned away from her during a take and shouted, "Hey, Mankiewicz, can you tell this dame to speak up? I can't hear a goddamn word she says!" To others he grumbled, "She's giving me nothing to work with." When not complaining, the sad fact was that Bogart ruined countless otherwise good takes with his racking coughs—warning heralds of the cancer that would kill him three years later.

The movie was a disaster, she told Frank. He listened carefully, then reassured her: Mankiewicz was puffed up with all those Oscars. She should just let him strut around a little bit, then look him in the eye and let him know she was the star of his movie. He'd change his tune. As for Bogie, he was probably pissed off that Ava's salary was twice as much as his.

But he was getting his whole salary, and Metro wasn't giving her shit.

Frank's tone was calm. It didn't matter. Bogie's pride was hurt. Ava should give him time. He was a good Joe.

They talked awhile longer, then she thanked Frank for the pep talk. She'd needed it.

It was easy. He loved her.

She loved him too. It was the first time she'd said it in weeks.

"I saw Frankie at Chasen's a few nights ago," Louella Parsons wrote at the end of January. "He looks so well these days, so everything must be okay with Ava Gardner. When he's unhappy he's a boy who shows it in his face."

Frank had started spending time with Bogart and Betty Bacall the year before, soon after he moved to the apartment on Beverly Glen. It was just one of those Hollywood things: Betty, driving by Holmby Park in her woody station wagon one afternoon, had spotted Sinatra taking one of his walks, head down, and called cheekily out the car window. There was a fella who looked like he could use a drink!

Frank looked up, smiling with surprise.

Betty smiled back. He should come on over sometime. The door was always open. And she drove off.

So he went over. The Bogarts lived just up the road, in a sprawling white-brick house on South Mapleton, and the door literally was open. There were small children and boxer dogs and shy Mexican maids: It was almost bourgeois, except that it wasn't. It was Hollywood. Frank had first met Betty and Bogie ten years before, when she was a girl of twenty and she and the married Bogart were seeing each other on the sly. Now they were the most glamorous couple in Hollywood, with a little boy and a little girl, a Holmby Hills mansion filled with a witty, glittering cast of characters who stopped by to drink and eat, but mostly drink, at all hours of the day and night: Spencer Tracy, Ira Gershwin, Ruth Gordon and Garson Kanin, Judy Garland and her husband Sid Luft, the David Nivens, Oscar Levant and Mike Romanoff and, of course, Bogart's agent, Swifty Lazar.

Bogart loved liquor ("The whole world is three drinks behind," he often said) and he loved company, but he didn't like to go out, and so the world came to him. Sinatra, who as George Jacobs said, "craved class like a junkie craves the needle," was agog at the Tinseltown aristocracy that gathered at Betty and Bogie's, but mostly he was agog at Bogart himself. "Sinatra was like a starstruck kid, in awe of Bogart, and watching his every move," Jacobs recalled.

> With all the people around, it was hard to be alone with Bogart, but Sinatra tended to shadow him, following him into the kitchen or out into the garden, hanging on everything he said. Sinatra saw Bogart as his mentor . . . [and] learned his lessons with straight A's. The two men had a lot of natural attributes in common. They were about the same size, short and skinny, and both men were losing their hair . . . Bogart had fabulous clothes, cashmere jackets, Italian shirts, and velvet slippers, and a certain cool and grace in the way he'd smoke, in the way he'd put away the Jack Daniel's, eventually a trademark taste Sinatra acquired from Bogart. Bogart had an effortless physical grace, which Sinatra only had when he sang. Otherwise, Sinatra was tense and jumpy, and remarkably insecure for someone used to playing to screaming fans. That they had stopped screaming was probably what made him this way. The Jack Daniel's definitely helped loosen him up. I noticed that he was much more "on" around Bogart than he was when I saw him at other gatherings.

To Frank, Bogart was that most magnetic of creatures: a great star who hated the phoniness of Hollywood but loved Sinatra. Bogie was also a genuine aristocrat, a Manhattan rich boy who'd flunked out of prep school, chucked it all, and had been spoiling for a fight ever since. He had a thing for strong women, just like Frank. Like Frank, he had a lifelong dislike of being touched by strangers. And he could wear a fedora like nobody else.

And then there was Betty. Now twenty-nine and the mother of two, Lauren Bacall was, if anything, even sexier than she'd been at twenty, her perfect skin still tawny, her blue feline eyes more insinuating. She was tall and long legged and, while not as heart-stoppingly beautiful as Ava, equally arresting. Also like Ava, she came from a humble background—the Bronx, in Betty's case—but she was watchful and quick-witted, and her modest beginnings didn't get in her way as much. Under the close tutelage of the director Howard Hawks, she'd found a character for her first film with Bogart, *To Have and Have Not*—slyly self-possessed, smoky voiced, tart tongued—and held on to it.

Nowadays she was spending more time at home with the kids than acting, and sometimes it frustrated her. She wouldn't have minded going out to kick up her heels every once in a while: the only place Bogie ever wanted to go was his goddamn sailboat, which made her seasick. She was crazy about Bogie, but like the rest of Hollywood she'd heard the whispers about him and his wig maker, Verita Peterson: since she refused to stoop to the role of jealous wife, though, she was trapped. And so now and then, when Frank was over, he would give Betty an appreciative look, and she didn't mind it a bit. She liked talking to him, too: they were much closer in age than she and her husband.

She was delighted to hear Sinatra's voice when he phoned her in New York. Betty was on her way to Rome, to join Bogie—and to make sure he was behaving himself. She and Frank chitchatted for a moment, then he paused and turned serious. Would she mind taking something to Ava for him?

Now it was her turn to pause. She was ever so slightly disappointed—and sorry for him, too.

Of course not. A little something from Cartier?

Not quite. He would have it delivered.

An hour later she opened her door to a small man holding a large white box: it was an orange-and-coconut cake, from Greenberg's Bakery on Madison Avenue. Frank had thought long and hard about the gift. The cake was Ava's favorite. And he had to consolidate his gains, so he'd decided to send something that would remind her of their sweetness together.

Betty took the cake with her in the car to Idlewild, carried the big box onto the plane, and parked it on the seat next to her. As she bounced over the dark Atlantic, every once in a while she adjusted the cake to keep it secure. "I stayed a night in London, and then Bogie was at the Rome airport to greet me," Bacall remembered.

> He took me and my cake box to the Excelsior Hotel and I asked him to tell Ava Gardner I had brought it. He told her— she did nothing about it—so two days later I decided to take it to her before it rotted. I didn't know her and felt very awkward about it—who knows what has happened between a man and a woman when it goes sour? Bogie had told me the picture was going well and that Ava had many people with her all the time, including her sister and a bullfighter named Luis Miguel Dominguin, with whom she was in love. I took the damn cake to the studio and knocked on her dressing-room door. After I had identified myself, the door opened. I felt like an idiot standing there with the bloody box—there were assorted people in the room and I was introduced to none of them. I said, "I brought this cake for you—Frank sent it to me in New York, he thought you'd like it." She couldn't have cared less. She wanted me to put it down on some table she indicated— not a thank-you, nothing.

Bacall was justifiably furious. With time, though, she realized that Ava's "reaction had only to do with Frank—she was clearly through with him, but it wasn't that way on his side. I never told Frank the coconut-cake saga, he would have been too hurt. Bogie always said the girls at MGM were so pampered, so catered to, that they were totally spoiled and self-indulgent. But she was professional about her work, and that's all he cared about."

Of course Ava was spoiled. She'd always admitted it. Frank, a prince since childhood, was spoiled too: it was a big difference between the two of them and the Bogarts, who tried to embody their tough screen personae in everyday life.

But Ava had rediscovered her professionalism. In a scene shot in an olive grove in Tivoli Gardens, she recalled, "I had to perform a flamenco-style dance wearing a tight sweater and a cheap satin skirt, enticing my partner, luring him closer, swirling out of his grasp, taunting him with my body." Her specialty. And she didn't have to say a word.

It came off splendidly. Mankiewicz was happy, Bogart was happy, Ava was happy. Back in California, Frank was finding it hard to get her on the phone again.

———

On Valentine's Day, a gloomy Sunday, Frank sent Ava a cable. He loved her and missed her and hoped she'd be coming back to him soon.

Then he went home and got drunk.

He'd called in a group of friends to play cards. "When we got there he was on the phone to Nancy," one of them recalled.

> But this time she was mad at him. She wouldn't talk to him.
>
> By the time we got the game started, he didn't even want to play anymore. He went into the den, opened a bottle, and started drinking alone. Okay. So we keep the game going awhile, and then Sammy Cahn gets up and he goes in to try to get Frank to join us. So what does he see?
>
> There's Frank drinking a toast to a picture of Ava with a tear running down his face. So Sammy comes back and we start playing again. All of a sudden we hear a crash. We all get up and run into the den, and there's Frank. He had taken the picture of Ava, frame and all, and smashed it. Then he had picked up the picture, ripped it into little pieces, and thrown it on the floor. So we tell him, "Come on, Frank, you've got to forget about all that. Come on and play some cards with us." He says,

"I'm through with her. I never want to see her again. I'm all right. I've just been drinking too much."

So we go back to the game and a little while later Sammy goes back to Frank, and there he is on his hands and knees picking up the torn pieces of the picture and trying to put it back together again. Well, he gets all the pieces together except the one for the nose. He becomes frantic looking for it, and we all get down on our hands and knees and try to help him.

All of a sudden the doorbell rings. It's a delivery boy with more liquor. So Frank goes to the back door to let him in, but when he opens it, the missing piece flutters out. Well, Frank is so happy, he takes off his gold wrist watch and gives it to the delivery boy.

The next day, the nominations for the 1953 Academy Awards were announced.

———

From Here to Eternity got thirteen nominations: for Best Picture, Best Director, Best Actress (Deborah Kerr), Best Actor (both Montgomery Clift and Burt Lancaster), Best Supporting Actress (Donna Reed), Best Screenplay, Best Cinematography, Best Costume Design (Black-and-White), Best Sound Recording, Best Film Editing, Best Music Scoring. And, of course, Best Supporting Actor (Frank Sinatra).

Ava was also nominated, as Best Actress in a Leading Role, for *Mogambo*. When she heard about it in Rome, she laughed out loud.

———

Frank, however, began to pray. We know this; what he said was between him and God. He could barely remember the last time he'd set foot in a church—every once in a great while, when he was in New York, he stopped by St. Patrick's and lit a candle for his sins (though he never dared to set foot in a confessional: where would he start?)—but that

Monday afternoon, before going to the airport (and several times in the weeks that followed), he drove over to the Good Shepherd Catholic Church, a lovely, Spanish Mission–style complex on Bedford and Santa Monica in Beverly Hills, went inside, and knelt in a pew.

The interior was cool and fragrant with the scents of incense and polished wood, the nave flanked with simple arches in smooth white stucco, the altar standing in a light-washed apse surrounded by tall stained-glass windows. He was alone in the sanctuary, except for one woman sitting a few rows ahead. Frank bowed his head.

Joe DiMaggio was advising his new bride to face down 20th Century Fox the way he'd faced down the New York Yankees: the studio owed her a raise, he told Marilyn, and something a hell of a lot better to do than *Pink Tights*. In the meantime, Zanuck looked for another female lead—maybe Jane Russell, maybe a sultry blond ingenue named Sheree North—and Sinatra consoled himself with the cash. "Frank Sinatra—who's collecting $50,000 for not working in 'Pink Tights'—grabs $23,000 for 9 nights at the Miami Beachcomber," Earl Wilson wrote in early February. And, a few days later: "There's a tug-of-war going on between La Vie en Rose and the Copacabana over Frank Sinatra's next NY singing date. Monte Proser of La Vie says Frank promised to appear for him. 'If he doesn't,' says Proser, 'I'll get out of the business.' Frank's also got a fat offer from the Copacabana, which has about twice the capacity of La Vie and could therefore pay him about twice as much."

Everybody wanted him except Ava. But everybody else wanted him a lot. All at once, he was hot as a pistol. There were nightclub dates, TV spots, and, most of all, all kinds of movie offers: Besides the role of Nathan Detroit in *Guys and Dolls* (for which a director had already been tapped—Joseph L. Mankiewicz), he'd been offered the title role in another adaptation of a Broadway musical, *Pal Joey*. And then there was a dark thriller, in which the lead role, a crazed presidential assassin, was a showpiece for a real actor. The script was called *Suddenly,* and Frank liked it a good deal.

———

While he rehearsed at the Beachcomber, the wire services ran, next to reports of Marilyn Monroe's spectacularly successful trip to entertain the U.S. Marines in Korea, a story picked up from New York's *Daily News.* QUADRANGLE: ROME COMIC SINATRA'S TOP RIVAL was the headline; the piece was datelined Rome, February 16.

> Walter Chiari, 28-year-old comedian known as the Danny Kaye of Italy, is the reason why Ava Gardner and Frankie Sinatra have not kissed and made up, according to the talk in Rome film circles today.
>
> Ava and Chiari have been seen together frequently, both before and since Frankie flew here for four days last month in a fruitless attempt at reconciliation.
>
> One Italian newspaper today named Ava as the fourth corner of a quadrangle, saying that Chiari had split with Lucia Bosé, Miss Italy of 1947, because of Miss Gardner.

It was all gossip, of course, but it was hard to ignore. And the quadrangle image, while picturesque, omitted a fifth leg, which complicated the romantic geometry considerably: the bullfighter Dominguín.[1]

———

Frank did a week at the Beachcomber, relaxed for a few days in the Florida Keys, then Chester flew him up to New York to try to put a smile on his face. While there, he had a brief but memorable encounter, as noted by Winchell on February 26: "Frank Sinatra and Artie Shaw met in Lindy's revolving door the other 2 a.m. Both took a coolish 5-second take and then walked away."

———

Frank kept busy. There was work and there was after work—paid company, chance encounters, old flames. The work made him happy, but it still left a lot of hours in the day. Winning the Oscar, he sometimes thought (knowing the thought was childish), would solve everything, would bring him work and wealth and maybe bring Ava back too.

At the same time, he felt pessimistic, superstitious. The other nominees—Eddie Albert and Robert Strauss and Jack Palance and Brandon De Wilde—were *actors*. What was he? (One thing he knew he wasn't, in an era when academy members voted only within their own categories, was popular among other performers. Albert and Palance were very popular.) Frank told Bob Thomas of the Associated Press that he probably wouldn't even be in Los Angeles for the Oscars. "I'm a saloon singer," he said plaintively. "I gotta go where the work is."

But remarkably, his wandering wife seemed discontent, too. In a lengthy syndicated interview at the end of the month, Laura Lee of the North American Newspaper Alliance sat down with Ava in Rome and found her in somber, regretful spirits. "What does Ava Gardner want most in the world? A baby," Lee wrote.

> She didn't have to think twice before answering. The thing she
> has wanted most in life for a long time is a couple of babies
> and a normal, happy marriage.
>
> What stands in the way?
>
> Miss Gardner swallows, bows her head and shakes it ever
> so slightly, as if to say, "Who knows?" . . ."Some day" is all she
> ventures by way of reply—"It must be some day."
>
> If she is putting on an act, Hollywood's No. 1 box-office star
> is a better actress even than her many fans believe.
>
> "Marriage for two people in the field of entertainment is a
> very difficult thing," Ava concedes. "Bogie . . . , who has been
> married to four actresses, and I were discussing this just this
> morning."

What they were discussing, no doubt, was the fact that the fourth and final actress Bogart had married, who had flown seven thousand miles to join him in Rome, was missing *her* couple of babies, badly, longing to fly back to them—and never forgetting the movie career she'd put in abeyance to be their mother.

"There isn't a single thing about this lousy business I like," Ava told Lee.

> I hate acting and hate not having a private life. You aren't allowed any privacy in this business.
>
> I haven't got a home. I haven't got a chauffeur or a car or even a mink coat [!]. I work for only one reason. The same rea-

Lauren Bacall carried a coconut cake from Frank to Ava when she went to Rome to visit her husband, Humphrey Bogart, on the set of *The Barefoot Contessa.* Ava ignored the cake. Bacall and Sinatra later formed a close friendship.

son everyone works, because I need the money and I can make more this way than any other I know of . . .

I could walk out of making pictures tomorrow and never have a moment's regret.

"A friend of Ava's," Lee wrote, "says she talks about Frankie constantly, but confesses that they 'Can't live together and can't live apart.' What the trouble is neither of them is willing to admit in public—if either really knows."

Frank escorts Frank Jr. and Little Nancy to the Academy Awards at the
Pantages Theatre, Hollywood, March 25, 1954.

Young at Heart" had entered the *Billboard* chart on February 13;
two weeks later, it climbed to the Top 10. *Songs for Young Lovers*
was also selling. Alan Livingston was ecstatic: time to start another
album. At the end of February, Sinatra flew back to Los Angeles; on
March 1, he went back to meet Nelson Riddle in the Capitol studios.

Frank recorded three numbers that Monday night: Johnny Mercer
and Rube Bloom's "Day In, Day Out," Harold Arlen and E. Y. Har-

burg's "Last Night When We Were Young," and a Sammy Cahn–Jule Styne title theme for an upcoming movie, "Three Coins in the Fountain." That insipid film, starring Louis Jourdan and Jean Peters, would premiere in June; Sinatra's singing over the title credits was the best part of it. Neither of the other two songs would be heard for a while, though. "Last Night When We Were Young" landed on Frank's *In the Wee Small Hours* album in 1955, but "Day In, Day Out" didn't officially resurface until 1991, when it appeared as a bonus track on a CD reissue of 1960's *Nice 'n' Easy*.

The lengthy obscurity of one of Sinatra's greatest recordings is something of a mystery. He had recorded the song, with an Axel Stordahl arrangement, on his first Capitol recording date the previous April. But the Stordahl version was problematic. On the one hand, there was Frank's vocal, which was sensational: tender, strong, and ardent. On the other, Axel's arrangement, to put a fine point on it, was corny, old-fashioned, and soporific, from the chimes-of-midnight pizzicato intro to the soupy wash of strings and harp glissandi that seem to want to recast this towering love song as the theme to a B movie. Alan Livingston's sharp young ears would have heard every bit of this, making his quest to link Sinatra and Riddle all the more urgent.

More important, though, Frank was eager to get the song right.

So he and Riddle made this magnificent recording, which languished in the Capitol vault for decades—in all likelihood, as the archivist Ed O'Brien has suggested, because Frank's concepts for each of his albums were so specific that there was simply no place to put "Day In, Day Out" until it resurfaced as an asterisk in the singer's seventy-sixth year. It was an astounding omission, but we are the beneficiaries of the correction, able to hear singer and arranger already at the apex of their powers. In the thirty-two-year-old Riddle's hands, "Day In, Day Out" became a hymn to passion, unashamedly romantic and forthrightly sexual. It is real drama rather than melodrama. And the arrangement's richness is greatly enhanced by the presence of a seventeen-piece string section, as contrasted to a mere nine for the Stordahl session.

In Riddle's hands, the fiddles pulse in waves, lilting and halting, with all the teasing hesitancy and onward rush of first love; his flutes and harps are shimmering moon glow rather than schmaltz. The great Mercer lyric, at first all daydreams and possibility, rises to a peak of ardor when the lovers meet and kiss ("an ocean's roar, a thousand drums"), and this is when Riddle finally brings on all the horns and timpani . . . but that's not the end. The music and the singing grow gentle again—

> Can there be any doubt
> When there it is, day in—day out

—before fading to a close. Riddle would later describe his methodology. "In working out arrangements for Frank," he said,

> I suppose I stuck to two main rules. First, find the peak of the song and build the whole arrangement to that peak, pacing it as he paces himself vocally. Second, when he's moving, get the hell out of the way. When he's doing nothing, move in fast and establish something. After all, what arranger in the world would try to fight against Sinatra's voice? Give the singer room to breathe. When the singer rests, then there's a chance to write a fill that might be heard.
>
> Most of our best numbers were in what I call the tempo of the heartbeat. That's the tempo that strikes people easiest because, without their knowing it, they are moving to that pace all their waking hours. Music to me is sex—it's all tied up somehow, and the rhythm of sex is the heartbeat. I usually try to avoid scoring a song with a climax at the end. Better to build about two-thirds of the way through, and then fade to a surprise ending. More subtle. I don't really like to finish by blowing and beating in top gear.

This is precisely the methodology of "Day In, Day Out." The heart-beat trips and quickens toward the climax, then eases back to a serene afterglow.

Sinatra was crazy about this arrangement, and his singing shows it. Here he is not only ardent and tender, as he was on the Stordahl record, but passionate. His emotional and sexual engagement with every syllable of the lyric, every note of the song, every bar of the arrangement, never wavers. This is not just a display of great singing but also a great work of art, rich with autobiographical meaning, shot through with longing and loss.

====

Infinitely restless, Frank flew to Palm Springs with Chester for fun and games, then, impatiently, flew back to Los Angeles. "Just for the record," Parsons sniffed possessively, two weeks to the day before the Oscars, "Frank Sinatra is here in town. He came in a few days ago from Palm Springs. He'll be on Bing Crosby's radio show, so the New York and Rome trips are canceled."

Rome: the world simply refused to stop believing—in much the same way the world couldn't stop believing in Santa Claus—that Frank and Ava would eventually get back together. But in the absence of hard news, writers were also coming up with their own material. Ava's new studio publicist, Dave Hanna, was probably responsible for the fanciful item Leonard Lyons used to lead his March 12 column—the subject, the famous coconut cake. "Ava was sure that a diamond ring, bracelet or necklace was inside the cake," Lyons wrote. "After all, a husband who is as carefree about money as Sinatra is wouldn't send an ordinary cake as a way of having a beautiful wife keep him in mind, 7,000 miles away.

"She therefore ate it all herself, chewing each bite carefully, in search of a hidden gem. 'I finished the whole cake,' she said, 'and all I found was that I couldn't get into my costume the next day.'"

Meanwhile, the real Frank and Ava behind the cartoonish images kept grabbing whatever pleasures they could, trying to keep the sadness at bay. Frank's method, as always, was ceaseless motion. Van Heusen kept the revels going, the plane warmed up. Just three days after she'd claimed Sinatra was staying put, Louella had to eat her words. "Frank Sinatra's excuse for missing the Look and Photoplay Magazine awards: 'I have business in New York' and the thought that Frankie's MOST important business is to attend all events furthering his career," she harrumphed, incoherent with indignation.

So there really had been a New York trip—was he on his way someplace else? Rome, perhaps? "Frank Sinatra off to Italy to escort Ava to the Academy Award doings—as though Ava couldn't find her way back to Hollywood," wrote Jimmie Fidler, who'd heard it from someone who'd heard it from someone else.

But it wasn't Rome; it was just New York. And it wasn't even business; it was just to keep moving.

===

Westbrook Pegler had laid off Frank for quite a while, not out of any merciful tendencies, but mainly because the Sinatra of the mid-1950s had fallen beneath the notice of the subversive-hunting columnist. For one thing, since Frank's Mafia scandals of the late 1940s, he had kept his contacts with the wiseguys as quiet as possible—not least because Ava hated the hoods even more than Pegler did. For another, Frank, with plenty to distract him, was no longer the liberal firebrand he had been in the 1940s. And in any case, the political climate of 1953 and 1954 was extremely unfriendly to liberalism. There was a Republican majority in Congress; Eisenhower was in the White House. It was one thing to rally for causes at Madison Square Garden when FDR was president; it was quite another to wear one's political heart on one's sleeve when the Hollywood blacklist was at its raging height. Even Bogart, who'd courageously gone to Washington to face down the House Un-American Activities Committee, felt compelled to distance himself from the Hollywood Ten.

In mid-March, though, Pegler had a halfhearted last whack at

Frank. The occasion was the arrival at San Quentin of Jimmy Tarantino, the New Jersey lowlife and co-founder (with Hank Sanicola) of
the short-lived scandal sheet *Hollywood Nite Life*. Under Tarantino's
guidance, *Hollywood Nite Life* had been nothing more than a vehicle
for shaking down film-colony denizens with sexual and pharmaceutical
idiosyncrasies: Frank had gone to lengths to distance himself, and to
make sure Sanicola distanced himself, from the whole business. Tarantino had kept up his extortionate ways, had been nabbed and convicted, and now Pegler, who'd gotten mileage from the subject back in
the day, was dredging up the past: "Frank Sinatra, an intimate friend
of Tarantino . . ."; "Sinatra's participation in an orgy of several days and
nights in a de luxe hotel in Havana with Lucky Luciano . . ."; "Willie
Moretti . . . Sinatra's original backer . . ."

It was a reminder to the Hearst-reading public that Frank had
once been down-and-out and a little bit dirty. (Why Pegler didn't dig
into Sinatra's recent investment in the Sands is a mystery.) The public
didn't care. The public wanted to know about Frank and Ava and
the Academy Awards. Pegler was growing more shrill and irrelevant
by the week; even Joe McCarthy was running out of gas. America was
in the mood to forgive Frank, and Frank had his eye on the brass ring.

═══

He went to prizefights and harness races and jazz clubs, and the whores
came to him. New York in the early spring of 1954 was a cavalcade
of pleasures, and Van Heusen and Sanicola were working overtime to
keep Frank away from the telephone, maybe even coax a smile from
him now and then. They were finally beginning to get some results.
His smile grew broader; his pals smiled back. Five nights in a row,
he ate with them at La Scala on West Fifty-fourth Street, Frank and
Hank and Jimmy and the music publisher Jackie Gale, plus whatever
hangers-on happened to be hanging on. And five nights in a row, they
all told Frank that he was going to take the Oscar. Every night they
closed the joint: late nights with cigarettes and anisette and gorgeous

broads and loud laughter. Frank would never let anyone else go near the check.

Then, very early in the morning of March 24, it was time to leave. Chester's plane was parked at Teterboro; the sun would be rising in an hour or two. As Frank and Hank and Jimmy left the restaurant, someone at the table called out: "Bring back that Oscar!"

Frank turned around to look at whoever it was, sitting there staring at him like he was God. He nodded. "I'm gettin' it," he said quietly.

===

He drove straight from Van Nuys Airport to 320 North Carolwood, for an Italian dinner. It was cool and rainy in Los Angeles, but the house was warm and smelled wonderful; after the kids jumped on him and he kissed Nancy on the cheek, Frank put *La Bohème* on the hi-fi and, just for a moment, with tomato sauce in his nostrils and Puccini in his ears, thought of another household long ago. He sat in the den— his den—and put his feet up and sipped Jack Daniel's and listened to the splendid music; Nancy came in and sat down, smoothing her skirt decorously, and they talked for a bit, for all the world like an old married couple, about how the kids were doing. Nancy Sandra, in the eighth grade, was loving school and had a ton of friends—male and female—but while Frankie was getting decent marks in fourth grade, he never *said* anything. He played with his planes and trains and cars and kept to himself. And little Tina's first-grade teacher said that she was daydreaming instead of paying attention (it would turn out that she had astigmatism).

When they sat down at the table, though, all four of them were smiling at him mysteriously.

He looked around the table—Tina giggled—and raised an eyebrow. Nancy ordered them all to eat before the food got cold.

They ate. Family chitchat, about school, about the coyotes they sometimes heard howling in the hills at night. Frank grilled his older daughter about boys; Frankie watched his father as if he were trying to memorize something. The maid cleared the table and put coffee cups at Nancy's and Frank's places. Frank's attention was distracted for a second; when he turned back, there was a small white box tied with blue ribbon sitting next to his cup.

He looked around the table at them.

It was a small gold medal on a thin chain, with Saint Genesius of Rome, the patron saint of actors, on one side and on the reverse a little Oscar statuette in bas-relief. "To Daddy—all our love from here to eternity," the inscription read.

Tears started to his eyes.

Frank looked at Big Nancy, for it had been her doing, of course: she was smiling that damn Mona Lisa smile of hers. He thanked her.

She just kept smiling.

The kids shouted for him to put it on.

He hung the chain around his neck and slid the medal under his shirt collar. He patted it twice as he looked at his family.

Then he went home alone.

———

The next day he awoke with a headache. It was still raining; the sky was the color of slate. George brought him the *Times* and the *Examiner* and yesterday afternoon's *Herald-Express* and made him coffee. Frank opened the papers and looked for his name. Louella had called late last night; she must have something. There he was in Winchell: "After being exiled too long, F. Sinatra rejoined the jukebox royalty. His balladandy, 'Young at Heart,' is among the Top Ten." Good. A headline caught his eye: NEWCOMER IS HOT FAVORITE FOR ANNUAL SCREEN AWARD. Good. But then, under Aline Mosby's byline, the piece, datelined Hollywood, March 24, began: "Audrey Hepburn, a newcomer to movies who says she's flat-chested and homely, is the hot favorite to reign as 1953's best actress at tomorrow night's 26th annual academy awards."

He read on:

This year's race of the celluloid kings and queens was turned into a $275,000 telecast that will make it the most gala, colorful

Oscar derby in 10 years. And by now the movie colonists, as eager as if this were a presidential election, have been predicting around their swimming pools who is likely to win the coveted gold statuettes.

His gaze roved restlessly down the column. Hepburn a cinch . . . Best Actor's contest a photo finish between Bill Holden, star of *Stalag 17*, and Burt Lancaster . . .

There.

" 'Eternity' is favored to be awarded the best picture honor by members of the Academy of Motion Picture Arts and Sciences, with 'Shane' a close rival," the piece continued.

Two stars of "Eternity," Donna Reed and Frank Sinatra, are popular choices for the supporting Oscars.

Miss Hepburn, Holden, Miss Reed, Sinatra and "From Here to Eternity" won the annual straw poll of academy voters released yesterday by Daily Variety, a show business trade paper. But Lancaster was only a handful of votes behind.

As usual, only eight of the 20 globe-trotting acting nominees will be in the audience of 2500 executives, fans and stars at the Pantages Theatre on busy Hollywood Boulevard.

Not one "best actress" nominee is in town. Miss Hepburn, Maggie McNamara and Deborah Kerr will be telecast at a branch meeting of nominees in New York. Ava Gardner is in Rome and Leslie Caron in Washington.

Holden will be on hand but Richard Burton is in England, Marlon Brando in New York, Montgomery Clift in Jamaica and Lancaster in Mexico. Miss Reed and Sinatra will be among many supporting nominees who will pull up in limousines before screaming fans outside the ornate theater.

Here was Louella. "Tonight's the night for Frank Sinatra," she wrote.

He'll either step up and get his Oscar for "From Here to Eternity," or else he and the rest of the audience will be surprised numb.

[But] whether Frankie wins or not, he's delighted with the St. Genesius medal given him by 13-year-old Nancy, Jr. and Frankie, Jr.

Was Parsons giving him the win or taking it away? He thought of the oracular pronouncement Chester had made when Frank had moaned that he didn't think he had a chance: *Anything can happen. There are a lot of upsets in these contests.*

═══

It was cold and drizzly, a night for keeping the Cadillac's convertible top up. He pulled in to the drive at 320 North Carolwood and walked to the front door, umbrella in hand. The door opened, and there they all were in the sweet-smelling foyer: behind, Nancy holding the baby's hand, and in front, Frank's two dates for the evening, Nancy junior in a white fur cape and Frankie in an overcoat and bow tie. Their eyes were big.

He exclaimed: how beautiful; how handsome. Little Nancy beamed; Frankie frowned.

Big Nancy was smiling her smile. *Good luck, Frank.*

He kissed her on the cheek and thanked her. Then he kissed the grinning Tina and thanked her too.

He patted the pocket of his tux jacket, where the medal sat. His right knee kept shaking, as if he were running in place.

Let's go.

═══

It was a long evening—ninety minutes, not nearly as long as the show is these days; but for Frank, endless. Donald O'Connor was the host, and he liked Donald; everyone did. But he couldn't pay attention while O'Connor made his jokes and the audience tittered and the band played and the film clips were shown and the show halted for commercials and started again and the endless awards were given out: his knee wouldn't stop shaking, and the only sound he could hear was white noise, a buzz in his head . . .

He was sitting on the left aisle, three-quarters of the way back. Little Nancy, beside him, was squeezing his arm; next to her, Frankie was leaning forward in his seat, his mouth slightly open, watching the proceedings avidly.

The buzz in Frank's head stopped for a moment when Donna Reed won for Best Supporting Actress. Then it began again. When William Holden won Best Actor instead of Monty, his daughter gave Frank's arm an extra squeeze. *Don't be too disappointed if you don't win, Daddy,* she whispered in his ear.

Don't you be, either, he whispered back.

An hour and a quarter into the show, close to the end, Mercedes McCambridge walked to the podium. The buzz in Frank's head stopped abruptly, and he watched her closely. She was a chunky little broad with a ringing voice and a short haircut, wearing an unflattering white strapless gown—not a looker, but she'd won Best Supporting Actress in 1949 for *All the King's Men.*

"Nominees for the best performance by an actor in a supporting role," she began, "are Eddie Albert, in *Roman Holiday,* Paramount; Brandon De Wilde, in *Shane,* Paramount; Jack Palance, in *Shane,* Paramount; Frank Sinatra, in *From Here to Eternity,* Columbia—"

Here, for the first time, there was applause.

"Robert Strauss, in *Stalag 17,* Paramount. And who, please, is the winner?" She turned and took the open envelope, saw the name on it before she returned to the microphone. With a gasp, she said, "The winner is Frank Sinatra, in *From Here to Eternity.*" And as the audience erupted, she hopped up and down, one small hop, like a little girl who'd just gotten exactly what she wanted for Christmas.

Barely anybody in the theater liked him, but at that moment everyone there felt exactly the way Mercedes McCambridge felt. A great gift had been given to them all: they had witnessed a miracle. Hollywood loves a show, and there was no show to compare to this. "A peculiar thing happened and I can't explain it," Louella Parsons wrote later. "I ran into person after person who said, 'He's a so-and-so but I hope he gets it. He was great!'"

Little Nancy burst into tears and couldn't stop crying. Frankie was gazing at his father in astonishment. Frank kissed his daughter's wet cheek, grasped his son's hand, and first walked, then trotted down the aisle. It was an easy, graceful trot, as though a great weight had been removed from his shoulders. The applause grew louder. Frank climbed the stage steps, shook Donald O'Connor's hand, and kissed him on the cheek. "Unbelievable," Frank said, shaking his head. He went to the podium, kissed McCambridge—she cooed with pleasure—and took his Oscar. He bowed deeply as the audience shouted bravos. Then he looked carefully at the gleaming statuette in his hands.

"Um—" he began, glancing up, then looking back down nervously.

"That's a clever opening," he said, to laughter. He smiled. The theater then went dead silent: nobody quite dared to breathe. "Ladies and gentlemen," Frank began, still finding it hard to face the crowd. He clearly hadn't prepared a speech. "I'm, I'm deeply thrilled," he stammered. "And, and very moved. And I really, really don't know what to say, because this is a whole new kind of thing. You know, I—song-and-dance-man-type stuff—" He grinned and glanced over at O'Connor. "And, uh, I'm terribly pleased, and if I start thanking everybody, I'll do a one-reeler up here, so I'd better not. And, uh, I'd just like to say, however, that, uh—" He smiled mischievously. "They're doing a lot of *songs* here tonight, but nobody asked me to—"

He didn't have to say the last word. He had now proved, definitively, that he could do something besides sing.

He was grinning broadly as the crowd laughed, looking around and seeming at ease for the first time. "I love you, though, thank you very much," he said, adding, as if further explanation were necessary, "I'm absolutely thrilled." And he blew the crowd a big kiss, took McCambridge's arm, and walked off.

═══

Watching on television in Santa Monica, Ralph Greenson turned to his wife. "That's it," the psychiatrist said. "We'll never see him again."

He was right.

═══

Several of the biographies say that Frank thanked Harry Cohn, Buddy Adler, and Fred Zinnemann that night. In fact, he cleverly thanked everybody by thanking nobody. At his brief press conference backstage, amid the grinning faces of Cohn, Adler, Zinnemann, and Donna Reed—*From Here to Eternity* had virtually swept the evening, winning eight Oscars and tying *Gone With the Wind*—Sinatra expressed his regret that the absent Montgomery Clift had failed to win the Academy Award he so deserved.[1] "I wanted to thank Monty Clift personally," Frank said. "I learned more about acting from Clift—it was equal to what I learned about musicals from Gene Kelly."

Then he posed for the cameras with Reed, both of them clutching their golden statuettes, both wearing the kinds of smiles that actors never smile in the movies. Frank had been photographed grinning like this once before, the time the cameras had caught him dancing with Lana Turner, the wedding band that joined him to Nancy clearly and indiscreetly visible on his left hand.

The woman he'd left Nancy (and Lana) for, the woman whose ring he still wore despite everything, the woman who had been largely responsible for getting him the role of Maggio, was the one person he never thanked. She was in Madrid, as busy in her way as he was in his.

═══

He drove his son and daughter home, and it was only the thought of them, warm in the car with him and unable to stop talking about the miracle of the evening, that kept Frank from driving the Cadillac into a light pole. The Oscar sat on the seat between him and Nancy Sandra, like a fourth passenger. The rain had stopped; the streets were black and slick; the streetlights had halos. He drove west on Hollywood, turned south on Fairfax to Sunset, turned right, and continued west. When he pulled up in front of 320 North Carolwood, all the lights in the house were on.

He knew people were waiting for him in the apartment on Beverly Glen: Jule Styne had thrown together a little congratulatory party, with Gene Kelly and Sammy Cahn and Betty Comden and Adolph Green and a few others. There would be a lot of champagne, and a fresh-faced starlet named Charlotte Austin. But Frank wasn't in the mood to see anybody—everybody who congratulated him seemed, in some small or large way, to take responsibility for his triumph. The one

Frank and Donna Reed hold their Oscars for *From Here to Eternity*.
Hollywood rejoiced in Sinatra's victory, the greatest career comeback ever.
Louella Parsons wrote later: "I ran into person after person who said,
'He's a so-and-so but I hope he gets it. He was great!'"

person who had somehow managed not to do this, who had seemed genuinely happy for him without having to take anything at all from him, had been his ex-wife.

So he turned left on Sunset instead of right, away from Beverly Glen, and guided the Cadillac over the slick black boulevard, driving carefully through the curves. He passed the Beverly Hills Hotel and turned off Sunset, among the dark, quiet streets with their tall palm trees and big, self-possessed houses. After a little while he pulled over and parked.

Sitting under a streetlight, he picked up the statuette and held it. He looked at it, ran his hand over its cool smoothness, turned it in the light. It was deliciously heavy: eight and a half pounds, the size of a newborn.

He opened the car door and got out, the statuette in his hand.

"I ducked the party, lost the crowds, and took a walk," he said years later. "Just me and Oscar! I think I relived my entire lifetime that night as I walked up and down the streets of Beverly Hills. Even when a cop stopped me, he couldn't bring me down to earth. It was very nice of him, although I did have to wait until his partner came cruising to assure him that I was who I said I was and that I had not stolen the statue I was carrying."

But he had not stolen the statue. He was Frank Sinatra.

ACKNOWLEDGMENTS

The true origin of this book was a slightly rowdy dinner at a Santa Monica restaurant called Guido's in September of 2004. I was finishing *Dean & Me*, the memoir I coauthored with Jerry Lewis; Jerry was in the midst of preparing his annual Muscular Dystrophy Association Telethon and in order to give some of the participants in the show a night off, his manager Claudia Stabile hosted an impromptu party. Present, among others, were the bandleader Jack Eglash, the guitarist (and Claudia's husband-to-be) Joe Lano, the pianist and arranger Vincent Falcone, the singer Jack Jones, and, to my great good fortune, me. The occasion was convivial and uninhibited and show-biz gossipy in a Vegas-centric way, and at a certain point in the evening the conversation turned to Frank Sinatra.

Several of the men present had worked with Sinatra; almost everyone at the table, myself excepted, had known him well. Given the atmosphere of boozy hilarity, it wouldn't have surprised me a bit if the talk had been mildly iconoclastic or gently scathing—the Old Man (as they all referred to him) had been dead for six years, after all—but, in fact, it was uniformly reverent.

These were musicians talking, they were speaking of Sinatra as a musician, and they spoke with awe—of his pitch, his incomparable way with a lyric, his transcendent professionalism, his collegiality. And even his vulnerability. At one point Vinnie Falcone, who was Sinatra's conductor and accompanist toward the end of the singer's career, spoke of his fruitless efforts to get Frank to record the great and legendarily difficult Billy Strayhorn classic "Lush Life." "Come on, Boss, just you and me and a piano," Vinnie said. Sinatra shook his head. Even the gods know their limits.

The evening stayed with me. Here was a vision of Frank Sinatra as a man and an artist, without the traps and trappings of celebrity, without a trace of the bad behavior for which he was so celebrated and which so often seemed to be the main, if not the only, topic of conversation. Sinatra lived and breathed in the talk of these awed colleagues. And so when yet another major biography of him came out just months after that dinner at Guido's—an apparently exhaustively researched book, in which, remarkably, the subject (and certainly the great artist) neither lived nor breathed—my interest was piqued.

The book you hold in your hands would have never existed without Phyllis Grann, great editor and—I am proud to say—great friend. To encourage a first-time biographer to take on Sinatra—not only a gigantic subject but also, perhaps, the most chronicled human in modern history—might have looked like sheer folly to most people (including, often, the biographer himself) but never to Phyllis, who evinced a mysteriously deep and abiding belief in me from the first time we met.

From the word go with *Frank*, it was starkly clear to me that I was far out of my depth, miles out at sea where my limited expertise was concerned. I proceeded with maximum misgivings, even with terror. But I worked hard at it, slowly and steadily; and the one thing I never lost sight of was that dinner at Guido's. Here was a genius and a great artist, a man who had changed—shaped—the twentieth century, and I owed him his due. If I wasn't qualified to provide it, I owed it to Sinatra to qualify myself. My affection for him may have wavered—he had a genius, too, for making himself dislikable—but the one note I could never find within myself was the condescension, even the contempt, on which so many other writers based their narratives. Frank always brought me back. I dreamed of him, spoke to him, even, saw him plain in all his electric variability.

Idolatry, too, was out. Idolatry was fine for the idolators, but, once again, I felt I owed my subject more: I owed him a biography he deserved. If he continued to hold my affection despite his considerable, even spectacular, flaws, that was all well and good. It would sustain me. It did sustain me.

But I had help, and I needed every bit of it.

There are four men whose loyalty and perspicacity lifted me from sloughs of despond and ignorance and gave Bernoulli-like loft to a much-heavier-than-air project. First I must single out Peter Bogdanovich, a man who, quite simply, I am lucky to know, and who, luckily for me, knew Frank Sinatra. As my earliest reader, and as a first-rate writer himself, Peter literally kept me going, chapter by chapter, with his heartfelt enthusiasm and incomparable cultural-historical perspective.

That Will Friedwald and Michael Kraus, who both know as much about Sinatra as anyone has a right to know, gave freely of their time and steadily approved of what I was doing still amazes me. I will always remember their generosity. I was wildly fortunate to have these two frighteningly learned, gimlet-eyed men parsing every sentence of the book.

To a great editor of another sort, my brother and friend, Peter W. Kaplan, I owe more than I can say.

As I do to my longtime literary agent, Joy Harris, my ally, advocate, and friend through thick and thin—and sometimes a lot of thin. From our first day working together, I have felt that Joy understood me completely and was able to wait almost indefinitely for me to do what we both felt I could do. She also has never put a foot wrong. A writer can ask for no more.

To Karen Cumbus, and to Aaron, Avery, and Jacob Kaplan, I owe the greatest debt of all: the blessing of having someone for whom to do my work and to whom to give my work; a safe harbor in a tempest-tossed world.

I would also like to extend deep gratitude to Damian Da Costa, Ted Panken, and Katherine Bang.

And to the following: Monty Alexander, Peggy Alexander, Bette Alexander, Iris Hiskey Arno, Ajay Arora, George Avakian, Brook Babcock, Jean Bach, Adam Begley, A. Scott Berg, Tony Bill, Bill Boggs, Ernest Borgnine, Shannon E. Bowen, Laurie Cahn, Mariah Carey, Jeanne Carmen, Christopher Cerf, Iris Chester, Jonathan Cohen, Jeffrey Collette, Frank Collura, Kenny Colman, Peggy Connelly, Stan Cornyn, Neil Daniels, Houstoun Demere, Angie Dickinson, Frank DiGiacomo, John Dominis, Renée Doruyter, Todd Doughty, Bob Eckel, Chris Erskine, Vincent Falcone, Michael Feinstein, John Fontana, Dan Frank, Gloria Delson Franks, Mitchell Freinberg, Bruce J. Friedman, Drew Friedman, Gary Giddins, Vince Giordano, Steve Glauber, Irwin Glusker, Starleigh Goltry, Bob Gottlieb, Chuck Granata, Mary Edna Grantham, Connie Haines, Betsy Duncan Hammes, Bruce Handy, Bill Harbach, Lee Herschberg, Suzanne Herz, Don Hewitt, Rebecca Holland, Anne Hollister, George Jacobs, Bruce Jenkins, John Jenkinson, Jack Jones, Mearene Jordan, Robert Kaplan, Kitty Kelley, Ed Kessler, Steve Khan, Andreas Kroniger, Suzy Kunhardt, Theodora Kuslan, Andrew Lack, Claudia Gridley Stabile Lano, Joe Lano, Peter Levinson, Jerry Lewis, Richard Lewis, Abbey Lincoln, George Lois, Mark Lopeman, Carmel Malin, Karyn Marcus, Gene McCarthy, Barbara McManus, Sonny Mehta, David Michaelis, Bill Miller, Mitch Miller, Jackeline Montalvo, Pat Mulcahy, Leonard Mustazza, Eunice Norton, Dan Okrent, Ed O'Brien, Tony Oppedisano, Neal Peters, Saint Clair Pugh, Mario Puzo, Alison Rich, Jenny Romero, Andrew Rosenblum, Frankie Randall, Adam Reed, Mickey Rooney, Andrew Rosenblum, Ric Ross, Steve Rubin, Mike Rubino, Jane Russell, George Schlatter, Gary Shapiro, Mike Shore, Liz Smith, Tyler Smith, Ted Sommer, Joe Spieler, William Stadiem, Jo Stafford, Nancy Steiner, Karen Svobodny, Laura Swanson, Gay Talese, Bill Thomas, Thomas Tucker, Sarah Twombly, Roberta Wennik-Kaplan, Tim Weston, Virginia Wicks, Bud Yorkin, and Sidney Zion.

And, it does not go without saying, effusive thanks to the great team at Doubleday, from copy editing to design to marketing to production.

If I have inadvertently omitted anyone from the list, I ask them to forgive me and know that they reside in my heart, if not my short-term memory.

PHOTO CREDITS

Cover: Ken Veeder/Capitol/MPTV
Frontispiece: Bill Dudas/MPTV

3   AP/Wide World Photos
12   © Academy of Motion Picture Arts
     and Sciences
14   Neal Peters Collection
27   Michael Ochs Archives/Getty Images
42   CBS Photo Archive/Getty Images
56   Neal Peters Collection
66   Michael Ochs Archives/Getty Images
71   Frank Driggs Collection
84   Metronome/Getty Images
99   © Academy of Motion Picture Arts
     and Sciences
112 Hulton Archive/Getty Images
113 Gene Lester/Getty Images
132 Photofest
133 Hulton Archive/Getty Images
150 CBS/Landov
153 © Bettmann/Corbis
167 Herbert Gehr/Life Magazine/Time &
     Life Pictures/Getty Images
168 Herbert Gehr/Life Magazine/Time &
     Life Pictures/Getty Images
190 Frank Driggs Collection
191 Everett Collection/Rex USA
205 © Bettmann/Corbis
206 © Bettmann/Corbis
222 Michael Ochs Archives/Getty Images
223 AP/Wide World Photos
236 © Bettmann/Corbis
237 Frank Driggs Collection
259 Photofest
260 © Bettmann/Corbis
272 © Bettmann/Corbis
275 Everett Collection/Rex USA
290 CBS Photo Archive/Getty Images
292 © SNAP/Zuma Press

313 CBS Photo Archive/Getty Images
314 CBS Photo Archive/Getty Images
338 © Bettmann/Corbis
340 Everett Collection
355 Gene Lester/Getty Images
357 Silver Screen Collection/Getty
     Images
380 © Bettmann/Corbis
382 The Kobal Collection
401 © Bettmann/Corbis
417 MPTV
419 Frank Driggs Collection
435 Frank Driggs Collection
437 CBS Photo Archive/Getty Images
455 Popperfoto/Getty Images
456 Bob Costello/N.Y. Daily News
478 Hulton Archive/Getty Images
494 Everett Collection
496 Hulton Archive/Getty Images
515 Bert Hardy/Picture Post/Getty
     Images
533 Everett Collection/Rex USA
555 © Bettmann/Corbis
574 Hulton Archive/Getty Images
579 © Academy of Motion Picture Arts
     and Sciences
597 AP/Wide World Photos
599 Frank Driggs Collection
619 Sid Avery/MPTV
621 © ANSA/Corbis
642 Michael Ochs Archives/Getty
     Images
658 AP/Wide World Photos
676 Rex USA
685 Photofest
687 © Bettmann/Corbis
702 M. Garrett/Getty Images
704 Hulton Archive/Getty Images
717 Hulton Archive/Getty Images

NOTES AND SOURCES

CHAPTER 1

1. The filial proxies for Mrs. Sinatra and Mrs. Puzo (also in a sense representing the two visions of godfatherhood) would have a memorable encounter in a Santa Monica restaurant in the 1970s, not long after the release of the movie version of *The Godfather*. In the film, of course (as in the novel), a down-on-his-luck Sinatra-like singer wins a crucial movie role through the vivid intercession of Don Corleone. Horse's head and all, it made for a terrific story—one that, naturally enough, Sinatra resented. The worlds-colliding confrontation between the singer and the novelist/screenwriter was colorful enough that Puzo recounted it afterward in a letter to his close friend the novelist Bruce Jay Friedman. "As told to me by Mario," Friedman recalled, "he was having dinner with a female acquaintance—and spotted Sinatra at a distant table. Thinking he might impress his friend, he decided to walk over and introduce himself. 'The second I got to my feet, I saw that I had made a mistake. Sinatra was surrounded by "necks." For insurance, I stuck a fork in my pocket.' Thus fortified, he walked over, introduced himself to Sinatra, who cursed him out for five minutes straight. 'I accepted this calmly,' said Puzo, 'and noted that he never once looked me in the eye. And what amused me was the preposterous notion of a skinny *Northern* Italian daring to curse out an Italian from the South.'" (Friedman to author, e-mail, Jan. 15, 2007).

SOURCE NOTES

1   **"The only two":** Peter Bogdanovich, in discussion with the author, Feb. 2009.

5   **"I really don't think":** Peggy Connelly, in discussion with the author, May 2006.

7   **"Sometimes I'd be":** Hamill, *Why Sinatra Matters*, p. 83.

9   **"When I would get":** Ibid., p. 84.

10   **"She was a pisser":** MacLaine, *My Lucky Stars*, p. 82.

10   **"I think my dad":** Tina Sinatra, *My Father's Daughter*, p. 14.

11   **"Honest and truly":** Lyrics from "Honest and Truly," words and music by Fred Rose (New York: Leo Feist, 1924).

11   **"He was a hijacker":** Summers and Swan, *Sinatra*, p. 21.

CHAPTER 2

1. Or maybe just having seen the writing on the wall: Marty O'Brien, "a tough battler from Hoboken," according to boxrec.com, nevertheless compiled an unspectacu-

lar 1–6 lifetime record, losing his last fight, on June 6, 1921, to Johnny Dohan, by a knockout in the fifth round. In all, Marty was knocked out in three of his seven prizefights.

2. One must understand the succession of immigrations to appreciate the true power of the ethnic pecking order in early-twentieth-century America. Mario Puzo used the German-Irishness of Don Corleone's adoptive son Tom Hagen to signal that he was one classy consigliere. Likewise, the German-Irishness of Hoboken's Park Avenue was a sign that the Sinatras had, at last, well and truly Arrived.

3. In his monumental biography *Mozart: A Life*, Maynard Solomon tells us how "[i]n several of Mozart's most characteristic adagios and andantes a calm, contemplative, or ecstatic condition gives way to a troubled state—is penetrated by hints of storm, dissonance, anguish, anxiety, danger—and this in turn is succeeded by a restoration of the status quo ante, now suffused with and transformed by the memory of the turbulent interlude . . . The felicitous states that frame Mozart's excursions into anxiety may [psychologically] represent a variety of utopian modalities, and the impinging, disturbing materials may be taken to represent a variety of fearful things—the hidden layers of the unconscious, the terrors of the external world, a principle of evil, the pain of loss, or the irrevocability of death. An argument can be made, however, that in the last analysis we bring to the entire continuum of such states derivatives of feelings having their origin in early stages of our lives, and in particular the preverbal state of symbiotic fusion of infant and mother, a matrix that constitutes an infancy-Eden of unsurpassable beauty but also a state completely vulnerable to terrors of separation, loss, and even fears of potential annihilation . . . Not without good reason, the British psychoanalyst D. W. Winnicott described a baby as 'an immature being who is all the time *on the brink of unthinkable anxiety*,' an anxiety that is kept at bay only through a mother's ongoing, mirroring validation of the infant's existence. It may be such a precarious moment where inexpressible ecstasy collides with unthinkable anxiety that we sense in the Andante of Mozart's A-minor Sonata, which, reduced to its simplest essence, tells a story about trouble in paradise" (p. 187).

   If ever there was a story about trouble in paradise, it is the sixty-two-year story of Frankie and Dolly.

4. The story of Sinatra's naming is, with mythological aptness, clouded. Sinatra family history would have it that he was Francis Albert at birth, period. The truth doesn't seem to be so simple. By some accounts, the big baby was purposely named for his godfather, Frank Garrick, who was triply qualified, being (a) Marty's close friend; (b) Irish-American, and therefore classy; and (c) (best of all) the nephew of a Hoboken police captain. According to other accounts, Dolly and Marty meant to name their son for Marty, but at the christening (poor Dolly, still recuperating, was absent) the priest, mistaking Garrick for the dad, asked *his* name, and Marty, staring at his tattoos, or just too flummoxed to speak up, left himself uncommemorated for the ages. (And a good thing, too: "Marty Sinatra" wouldn't have looked nearly as good on all those great Capitol albums.) The name on the birth certificate was rendered, by some ethnically clueless clerk, as "Frank Sinestro" (Clarke, *All or Nothing At All*, p. 6).

   Frank, not Francis.

   An equally careless census clerk in 1920 listed the family name as "Sonatri," and the three residents of the cold-water flat on Monroe Street as twenty-five-year-old Tony (occupation: boilermaker), twenty-three-year-old Della (occupation: none), and four-year-old just plain Frank. (Interestingly, another "Sonatri" family also resided at 415 Monroe, also with a son—aged seven—named Frank.) The 1930 census lists the inhabitants of 705 Park Avenue, Hoboken, as Anthony (not Martin), Natalie (not Dolly), and Frank (not Francis) Sinatra (not Sonatri).

5. Rosebud alert: in his adult years, Sinatra's favorite color scheme was . . . orange and black.

6. "There are singers in my family but not any professionals," he told the *Los Angeles Times*'s music columnist in 1943. "I've been so busy singing since I left off being a sports reporter on a little New Jersey paper . . . that I haven't had time to study."

SOURCE NOTES

14 **"Uncle Vincent"**: Tina Sinatra, *My Father's Daughter*, p. 162.
17 **"a small grand piano"**: Kelley, *His Way*, p. 26.
19 **"The thing you have"**: Giddins, *Bing Crosby*, p. 259.
20 **"Bing Crosby is the only"**: Ibid., p. 56.
21 **"I've learned the meaning"**: Lyrics from "Just One More Chance," words and music by Sam Coslow and Arthur Johnson (New York: Famous Music, 1931).
22 **"I think it was at some"**: Thomas Thompson, "Frank Sinatra's Swan Song," *Life*, June 25, 1971.
22 **"If you think you're going"**: Kelley, *His Way*, p. 28.
22 **"Her way of thinking"**: Summers and Swan, *Sinatra*, p. 25.
24 **"Like Dolly"**: Tina Sinatra, *My Father's Daughter*, p. 16.
24 **"Frank, sporting the T-shirt"**: Nancy Sinatra, *American Legend*, p. 20.

CHAPTER 3

1. Frank had pursued Marie, the younger sister of his close friend Billy Roemer, but since he wasn't doing very well in school and didn't seem to be going anywhere generally, Marie had spurned his attentions. Whatever he sang at the joint recital appears not to have changed her mind.

2. But not for the same reason. Crosby started wearing hats in publicity stills, and then in the movies, to cover up his premature baldness—a little preview of the future for Sinatra, whose hairline at this point was still lush and low.

3. Yet Frank went a good deal further: he had a lifelong obsession with cleanliness and neatness—many friends and acquaintances have mentioned his need to clean ashtrays, line up bottles of liquor on a bar, and so forth—that verged on the pathological.

4. They could also be unkind. A cousin of a friend of the author, a man who had a lively dance-band business in Hoboken in the 1930s, recalled telling young Sinatra to beat it.

5. Picasso, who falsely claimed to have been able to draw like Raphael from the moment he first picked up a pencil, was guilty of the same peccadillo.

6. Earlier in 1935, during breaks in the Lindbergh-baby-kidnapping trial of Bruno Hauptmann, WNEW's announcer Block had begun the revolutionary practice of playing records on the air—an idea that caught on and became *The Make-Believe Ballroom*. The station would become increasingly important in Frank Sinatra's career, culminating in the arrival in the early 1960s of William B. Williams, the disc jockey who dubbed Sinatra "the Chairman of the Board."

7. Although he well might have. In a clip from a Hollywood musical that came out a couple of years later (1937's *Manhattan Merry-Go-Round*), the moviemakers have one of their characters refer unashamedly—and in a complimentary context!—to the new Yankee phenom Joe DiMaggio, who appears briefly, as a guinea (www.youtube.com/watch?v=pgrCCc12sFc).

8. Sinatra actually wound up recording the thing in 1961, in a blisteringly up-tempo Billy May chart—an exercise in redemptive revisionism—on *Swing Along with Me*.

9. The big and dreaded gong, which—when the Major gave the high sign to the gong striker—tolled like John Donne's church bell right in the middle of a failed act, sending the aspirant not just off the show (that would have been bad enough) but in many cases back to destitution on America's hard Depression streets. Major Bowes, fearful of physical attack by disappointed contestants, had a large body-

guard on hand to hustle off the losers before they said or did anything unfortunate.

SOURCE NOTES

28   **"[A] New Year's Eve party"**: Kelley, *His Way*, p. 31.

30   **"When she saw Crosby's"**: Ibid., p. 33.

30   **"I remember the moment"**: Frank Sinatra, interview with Bill Boggs, *Midday Live with Bill Boggs*, Sept. 22, 1975 (broadcast Nov. 30, 1975).

31   **"It was when I left"**: Douglas-Home, *Sinatra*, p. 21.

31   **"On Christmas Eve"**: Frank Sinatra, interview with Sidney Zion, Yale University, April 15, 1986.

34   **"All life's grandeur"**: Lowell, *Near the Ocean*, p. 19.

34   **"It was a lucky"**: Lyrics from "I Found a Million-Dollar Baby," words by Billy Rose and Mort Dixon, music by Harry Warren (New York: Remick Music, 1931).

36   **"You'd better quit"**: Kelley, *His Way*, p. 34.

37   **"The NEWest Thing"**: Jaker, Sulek, and Kanze, *Airwaves of New York*, p. 134.

41   **"Oh, he never worked"**: Kelley, *His Way*, p. 36.

CHAPTER 4

1.   The draconian terms of the Bowes contract dictated that the name of the show not be used to promote any professional appearances on the part of former *Amateur Hour* contestants. In addition, former contestants were to pay 15 percent of subsequent professional fees straight to the Major. Frank Sinatra did not lose sleep about hewing to the letter of the agreement.

2.   And also, apparently, of the Hoboken mobster Angelo "Gyp" DeCarlo's. DeCarlo, an underling of the North Jersey boss Willie Moretti, was an avuncular executioner with a soft spot for sponsoring young Italian-American singers. In later years he would keep a large portrait of Sinatra in the barnlike structure in Mountainside he used as his headquarters. Just like *The Sopranos*.

SOURCE NOTES

43   **"Just because"**: Lyrics from "Shine," words by Lew Brown and Cecil Mack, music by Ford T. Dabney (New York: Shapiro, Bernstein, 1924).

43   **"walked right into"**: Kelley, *His Way*, p. 36.

46   **"There's only ten"**: Higham, *Ava*, p. 133.

46   **"I hate your husband"**: Kelley, *His Way*, p. 131.

48   **"panic period"**: Frank Sinatra, interview with Sidney Zion, Yale University, April 15, 1986.

53   **"I don't want you"**: Lyrics from "Between the Devil and the Deep Blue Sea," words by Ted Koehler, music by Harold Arlen (New York: Mills Music, 1931).

CHAPTER 5

SOURCE NOTES

60   **"being then and there"**: Kelley, *His Way*, p. 6.

61   **"He looked like"**: Ibid., p. 7.

64   **"On a Sunday evening"**: Frank Sinatra, interview with Sidney Zion, Yale University, April 15, 1986.

65   **"Cheech, could I go"**: Kevin Coyne, "Sinatra's First, Freed at Last," *New York Times*, Oct. 22, 2006.

65   **"Our love, I feel it"**: Lyrics from "Our Love," words and music by Larry Clinton, Buddy Bernier, and Bob Emmerich (New York: Chappell, 1939).

67   **"So, I woke Harry"**: Levinson, *Trumpet Blues*, p. 67.

CHAPTER 6

1.   The record wouldn't be released until the following June—when it would sell a disappointing eight thousand copies—but the song, performed live by the Music Makers with Sinatra, was broadcast several times that fall, and heard (as we'll soon discover) by some very important people.

SOURCE NOTES

72   **"Hey, Connie Haines":** Connie Haines, in discussion with the author, Jan. 2006.

73   **"bedlam. Gene Krupa":** Jenkins, *Goodbye*, p. 3.

74   **"We don't have a singer":** Levinson, *Trumpet Blues*, p. 67.

74   **"It's an interesting thing":** Michael Feinstein, in discussion with the author, April 2007.

75   **"Frank told Harry":** Haines, discussion.

76   **"The Irish Kids":** Gay Talese, in discussion with the author, May 2007.

76   **"Can you imagine?":** Hamill, *Why Sinatra Matters*, p. 71.

76   **"After the first show":** Levinson, *Trumpet Blues*, p. 69.

77   **"Please give the new boy":** Kelley, *His Way*, p. 49.

77   **"sensational, intense style":** Ibid.

78   **"He sounded somewhat":** George T. Simon, "The Sinatra Report," *Billboard*, Nov. 20, 1965.

78   **"I'll never forget":** Levinson, *Trumpet Blues*, p. 76.

79   **"the torchy ballads":** Kelley, *His Way*, p. 49.

80   **"Here comes the night":** Lyrics from "Here Comes the Night," words by Frank Loesser, music by Hilly Edelstein and Carl Hohengarten (New York: Paramount Music, 1939).

80   **"half a love":** Lyrics from "All or Nothing At All," words and music by Jack Lawrence and Arthur Altman (New York, Leeds Music, 1940).

81   **"an institute you can't":** Lyrics from "Love and Marriage," words by Sammy Cahn, music by James Van Heusen (New York: Barton Music, 1955).

CHAPTER 7

1.   At virtually the same moment, Jack Kapp, the brilliant but tunnel-visioned producer who single-handedly created Bing Crosby's recording career, was pushing Crosby, hard, to abandon his scat-singing ways for a more commercially palatable vocal style. Kapp won, Bing became an enormously wealthy musical demigod, and we lost a great jazz artist. Tommy Dorsey, it might be argued, possessed his own inner Jack Kapp.

SOURCE NOTES

86   **"He could do something":** Levinson, *Tommy Dorsey*, p. 42.

87   **"the Dorsey band":** Ibid., p. 108.

87   **"the greatest melodic":** Friedwald, *Sinatra!* p. 80.

89   **"Have you heard":** Levinson, *Tommy Dorsey*, p. 110.

90   **"Yes, I remember":** Douglas-Home, *Sinatra*, p. 23.

91   **"Fame and fortune":** *Tommy Dorsey–Frank Sinatra: The Song Is You* (RCA, 1994). Set of five compact discs.

91   **"On a night like this":** Lyrics from "Marie," words and music by Irving Berlin (New York: Irving Berlin, 1928).

92   **"Hell, if we don't":** Levinson, *Tommy Dorsey*, p. 111.

92   **"learned a lot from Harry":** Friedwald, *Sinatra!* p. 75.

93   **"he dozed":** Ibid., p. 74.

93   **"The bus pulled":** Levinson, *Trumpet Blues*, p. 79.

94   **"The first time":** Jo Stafford, in discussion with the author, Feb. 2006.

94   **"The only problem"**: Jo Stafford, interview with Michael Feinstein, *Ballad of the Blues* (Feinery, 2003). Compact disc.

94   **"Never even heard"**: Ibid.

96   **"Frank really loved"**: Ibid.

96   **"Sinatra knew this"**: Daniel Okrent, "A Season of Song: Saint Francis of Hoboken," *Esquire*, Dec. 1987.

97   **"Well, see"**: Stafford, discussion.

97   **"Young"**: Ibid.

97   **"I want you"**: Tormé, *Traps, the Drum Wonder*, p. 53.

CHAPTER 8

1.   He was in a Chicago studio with the band just days after he joined Dorsey, recording "The Sky Fell Down" and "Too Romantic."

SOURCE NOTES

100   **"I can still"**: Jo Stafford, in discussion with the author, Feb. 2006.

100   **"For maybe"**: Frank Sinatra, interview with Sidney Zion, Yale University, April 15, 1986.

101   **"Once, Sinatra"**: Friedwald, *Sinatra!* p. 88.

101   **"Tommy was a very"**: Douglas-Home, *Sinatra*, p. 24.

103   **The producer George**: George Avakian, in discussion with the author, Oct. 2006.

103   **"I used to watch"**: Summers and Swan, *Sinatra*, p. 65.

104   **"Tommy sometimes"**: Friedwald, *Sinatra!* p. 86.

105   **"You can have"**: Stafford, discussion.

106   **"I was never"**: Sinatra, interview.

106   **"calisthenics for the throat"**: Summers and Swan, *Sinatra*, p. 66.

106   **"Frank can hold"**: Ibid.

106   **"The audience wouldn't"**: Levinson, *Tommy Dorsey*, p. 114.

107   **"He had something"**: Ibid.

107   **"When I say"**: Ibid., p. 115.

107   **"It was at the Meadowbrook"**: Ibid., p. 119.

108   **"I take a sheet"**: Steve Wynn, from "Remembering Frank Sinatra," *USA Weekend*, May 4, 2008.

109   **"Go ahead, do your thing"**: Kelley, *His Way*, p. 53.

110   **"When you sing"**: Stafford, interview.

110   **"He wound it up"**: Friedwald, *Sinatra!* p. 90.

111   **"Just call out"**: Levinson, *Tommy Dorsey*, p. 125.

111   **"Next thing I know"**: Friedwald, *Sinatra!* p. 91.

111   **"I'll never smile again"**: Lyrics from "I'll Never Smile Again," words and music by Ruth Lowe (New York: Sun Music, 1939).

CHAPTER 9

1.   He would finish it, in a way, forty years later, when, his voice crackling with age and emotion, he recorded a monumentally powerful version of "Soliloquy," on *Sinatra 80th: Live in Concert.*

2.   The name of the city had very different connotations in the early 1940s, when Las Vegas was still a sleepy desert burg with sand on the streets and hitching posts for horses, from what it would have fifteen or twenty years later, when Sinatra, with the help of organized crime, had turned the town into, well . . . *Vegas.*

3.   Jean Bach knew Sinatra before he wore those floppy bow ties, and believes she knows where he got the idea: her. She used to sew ties like that for her husband,

Shorty Sherock, she said. "I remember this particular print, I thought Shorty was brave to wear it—and he came home one day, and he'd been in the elevator at the Brill Building, and Frank got on and looked at Shorty and menacingly said, 'Who wrote the lyrics to that tie?' And the next thing we know, we saw photographs of him with a kind of artist-looking bow tie" (Bach, in discussion with the author, March 30, 2006).

SOURCE NOTES

113 **"Dad was in"**: Nancy Sinatra, *American Legend*, p. 43.

114 **"I hated missing"**: Frank Sinatra, interview with Sidney Zion, Yale University, April 15, 1986.

114 **"Frank would tap"**: Summers and Swan, *Sinatra*, p. 69.

115 **"It must have been"**: Kelley, *His Way*, p. 56.

115 **"Tommy Dorsey came"**: Ed Kessler, in discussion with the author, May 2006.

115 **"They were in"**: Ibid.

116 **"I remember him"**: Ibid.

117 **"they got at it"**: Jo Stafford, in discussion with the author, Feb. 2006.

117 **"went at each other"**: Tormé, *Traps, the Drum Wonder*, p. 62.

117 **"I can live"**: Ibid., p. 63.

118 **"coldly efficient"**: Ibid.

119 **"If Tommy Dorsey"**: Cahn, *I Should Care*, p. 131.

124 **"Nothing meant anything"**: Levinson, *September in the Rain*, p. 114.

124 **"I kept thinking"**: Sinatra, interview.

124 **"All they wanted"**: E. J. Kahn, "The Voice," *New Yorker*, Nov. 9, 1946.

125 **"This boy's going"**: Wilson, *Sinatra*, p. 31.

125 **"a shy boy"**: Summers and Swan, *Sinatra*, p. 58.

125 **"Match me"**: Kelley, *His Way*, p. 111.

126 **"I used to stand"**: Hanna, *Sinatra*, p. 16.

127 **"He was hanging"**: Connie Haines, in discussion with the author, Jan. 2006.

CHAPTER 10

1. As would be another important Sinatra arranger, Quincy Jones.

2. And, a couple of years later, it would be *hasta la vista* to Lana. The way was paved one night during that same fateful January 1942, when Sinatra stopped in at the brand-new, star-studded L.A. nightclub Mocambo (palm fronds, cockatoos in cages), where he once again encountered the gorgeous Ava Gardner, nineteen and newly married to Mickey Rooney. When Rooney "introduced" her to the singer—both she and Sinatra remembered, but failed to mention, the earlier meeting at MGM—Sinatra said, flirtatiously, "Why didn't I meet you first?" She blushed at the inside joke, and both filed away the compliment (Server, *Ava Gardner*, p. 174).

3. Sinatra had registered for the draft in December 1940 but, as a married father, was granted a deferment. The loophole protected him from the draft—but not the contempt of much of the public and many men in uniform—until the fall of 1943, when the deferments were ended and he was reclassified 1-A. Shortly afterward, to nationwide hoots, he was reclassified yet again, to 4-F, for a punctured eardrum.

   In August 1942, after Lana Turner impulsively married a Hollywood wannabe named Steve Crane (who, it would inconveniently turn out, was already married at the time), a heartbroken Buddy Rich enlisted in the Marines and left Dorsey.

4. Although Hoboken lives on robustly in his dentalization of the *t*'s in the lyric: "I hear music when I look at you/A beautiful theme of ev'ry dream I ever knew." His pronunciation of "beautiful" sounds like something that might come out of the mouth of a sensitive gunsel in an old Warner Brothers gangster picture.

5. In appearance and bearing, Goodman was almost Dorsey's Jewish counterpart:

bespectacled, tough, egomaniacal. Musically, though, he was deeper and more virtuosic: Goodman was esteemed as both a classical and a jazz musician. In the late 1940s, as Dorsey continued to wax sentimental, Goodman even developed an interest in bebop.

SOURCE NOTES

135 **"Lucky Strike green"**: Jones, *From Here to Eternity,* pp. 754–55.
137 **"almost tubercular"**: Kelley, *His Way*, p. 60.
137 **"Frank was not like"**: Shaw, *Twentieth-Century Romantic*, p. 30.
138 **"He was so excited"**: Levinson, *Tommy Dorsey*, p. 151.
138 **"Frank sat on a stool"**: Summers and Swan, *Sinatra*, p. 73.
138 **"Lana was the love"**: Tormé, *Traps, the Drum Wonder*, p. 74.
139 **"Now, in the story"**: Frank Sinatra, interview with Sidney Zion, Yale University, April 15, 1986.
140 **"He's such a damn"**: Levinson, *Tommy Dorsey*, p. 152.
140 **"I gotta do it"**: Ibid., p. 155.
141 **"I was sitting with Sinatra"**: Friedwald, *Sinatra!* p. 110.
141 **"Tommy was a good"**: Levinson, *Tommy Dorsey*, p. 155.
142 **"I'll wake each"**: Lyrics from "Just as Though You Were Here," words by Edgar De Lange, music by John B. Brooks (New York: Yankee Music, 1942).
143 **"The curtains drawn"**: Nancy Sinatra, *My Father*, p. 35.
143 **"[Tommy] said, 'No' "**: Sinatra, interview.
144 **"Let him go"**: Wilson, *Sinatra*, p. 35.
145 **"Don't worry"**: Levinson, *Tommy Dorsey*, p. 156.
145 **"After tonight"**: Tommy Dorsey, *The Sentimental Gentleman of Swing: Centennial Collection* (RCA, 2005). Set of three compact discs.
145 **"Well, Frank"**: Ibid.
146 **"was literally crying"**: Summers and Swan, *Sinatra*, p. 74.
146 **"I hope you fall"**: Nancy Sinatra, *American Legend*, p. 51.
147 **"I was now free"**: Sinatra, interview.
148 **"this skinny kid"**: Shaw, *Twentieth-Century Romantic*, p. 40.
148 **"He said, 'What are you' "**: Sinatra, interview.
149 **"I was in New York"**: Nancy Sinatra, *My Father*, p. 44.
149 **"There were about five"**: Ibid., p. 45.
150 **"What the fuck"**: Kelley, *His Way*, p. 40.

CHAPTER 11

1. Including the band's girl singer, a blond, pug-nosed twenty-two-year-old from North Dakota named Norma Deloris Egstrom, a.k.a. Peggy Lee.
2. Interestingly, one of the first buyers of the new and improved Sinatra age was none other than E. J. Kahn Jr. in "Phenomenon," the three-part 1946 *New Yorker* profile— prepared with the aid of that magazine's legendary fact-checking department—that was the basis for his 1947 book, *The Voice.*
3. Or, as the announcer would intone: "*Your Hit Parade* survey checks the best sellers on sheet music and phonograph records, the songs most heard on the air and most played on the automatic coin machines, an accurate, authentic tabulation of America's taste in popular music" (Brooks and Marsh, *TV's Greatest Hits*, p. 280).

SOURCE NOTES

153 **"EXTRA ADDED ATTRACTION"**: Friedwald, *Sinatra!* p. 123.
156 **"Be careful, it's my heart"**: Lyrics from "Be Careful, It's My Heart," words and music by Irving Berlin (New York: Irving Berlin, 1942).

158 **"a kid was given a ticket"**: Kahn, *Voice*, p. 67.
158 **"certain things were"**: Ibid.
159 **"George was a *genius*"**: Jerry Lewis, in discussion with the author, March 2008.
159 **"in case a patron"**: Kelley, *His Way*, p. 67.
160 **"I saw fans run"**: Nancy Sinatra, *My Father*, p. 47.
162 **"I'd look out my bedroom"**: Nancy Sinatra, *American Legend*, p. 54.
162 **"People call me an overnight"**: Frank Sinatra, interview with Sidney Zion, Yale University, April 15, 1986.
163 **"Frankie is a product"**: Kelley, *His Way*, p. 75.

CHAPTER 12

1. Another hypothesis, lip-wise: starting in the early 1940s and until the end of his career, Sinatra had a habit, during vocalization, of periodically pulling his mouth to the right and lowering his eyelids—an expression that signaled emotional transport, but that also might have been his version of the corner-of-the-lips pinhole that Tommy Dorsey used to sneak a breath.

2. In fact he was the president of his congregation, Temple Beth Israel in Philadelphia.

3. Ben Barton, as a young supplicant, had brought the song to Frank backstage at the Paramount, initiating a thirty-year business and personal relationship.

4. The figure isn't universally accepted: some have pointed out that "All" never won a gold record, as, for example, Glenn Miller's "Chattanooga Choo Choo" had the year before. Still, sales were brisk. And, it should be noted, the fact that Harry James himself had broken through in a big way didn't hurt a bit. Not long after Sinatra made his big splash at the Riobamba, James—now divorced from Louise Tobin and dating Betty Grable—and the Music Makers, now twenty-seven strong (including an eight-piece string section and two French horns), opened at the Paramount, causing almost the same kind of hysteria that Frankie had.

5. The studio's pointed new slogan: "Entertainment, not genius."

6. Very chivalrous of Frank, as long as he was fudging his age by two years, to make Nancy two years younger, too!

7. One of which, Harold Adamson and Jimmy McHugh's "I Couldn't Sleep a Wink Last Night," was nominated for an Oscar.

8. Though the general hoity-toitiness was somewhat ruffled by the highly conspicuous ringside presence of Dolly (attending not with Marty but with a gaggle of Hoboken girlfriends). Mama Sinatra cheered lustily throughout Frankie's performance, then came backstage afterward to pose for pictures and brief reporters: "You know, my son has broken just about every record that bastard Bing Crosby ever set. Write *that* down in your goddamn notepad" (Taraborrelli, *Sinatra*, p. 67).

9. Some men reluctant to go into military service during World War II are known to have had an eardrum punctured. However, the FBI file on Sinatra notes that "the perforation of the drum (tympanum) was a disease perforation so far as Captain WEINTROB could tell and not the result of an incision by human hands" (Kuntz and Kuntz, *Sinatra Files*, p. 19).

10. The following year he would acknowledge his fears, with only partial irony, by recording a novelty number called "Dick Haymes, Dick Todd, and Como." The V-Disc, a unique collaboration among Sammy Cahn, Johnny Burke, and Jimmy Van Heusen, contained lines such as "I'll soon become a wreck/they're breathin' on my neck" and "They're really comin' fast/Who knows, I may be past." Where Haymes and Como were concerned, Sinatra's fears were not misplaced. One suspects Todd, the so-called Canadian Crosby (he sounded exactly like Bing played at a slightly slower speed), was thrown in for joke value. And as always with Frank, his best jokes were written by others.

SOURCE NOTES

170 **"You better push"**: Kelley, *His Way*, p. 72.

170 **"SPECIALLY ADDED"**: Shaw, *Twentieth-Century Romantic*, p. 43.

170 **"Frank was in"**: Wilson, *Sinatra*, p. 44.

170 **Many years later**: Frank Sinatra, interview with Sidney Zion, Yale University, April 15, 1986.

170 **"If you're not scared"**: Jerry Lewis, in discussion with the author, March 2008.

171 **"Three times an evening"**: George Frazier, "Frank Sinatra," *Life*, May 3, 1943.

171 **"When I came"**: Summers and Swan, *Sinatra*, p. 81.

171 **"I'm flying high"**: Kelley, *His Way*, p. 79.

171 **"was a sensation"**: Cahn, *I Should Care*, p. 132.

172 **"He had them"**: Friedwald, *Sinatra!* p. 130.

172 **"Jimmy Van Heusen once canceled"**: Kelley, *His Way*, p. 574.

174 **"He was a very unusual-looking"**: George Avakian, in discussion with the author, Oct. 2006.

175 **"He is acutely aware"**: Goddard Lieberson, liner notes for *Frank Sinatra Conducts the Music of Alec Wilder* (Columbia Records, 1946).

176 **"Traveling by train"**: Nancy Sinatra, *American Legend*, p. 57.

177 **"SECRET OF LURE"**: Isabel Morse Jones, "Secret of Lure Told by Crooner— It's Love," *Los Angeles Times*, Aug. 12, 1943.

179 **"Noah Webster forgive"**: Parsons, *Tell It to Louella*, p. 147.

179 **"Dear Sir"**: Kuntz and Kuntz, *Sinatra Files*, p. 4.

181 **"It's Dorsey"**: Friedwald, *Sinatra!* p. 112.

182 **"The next day"**: Puzo, *Godfather*, p. 43.

182 **"The man who straightened"**: Sinatra, interview.

183 **"Frank told me years"**: Lewis, discussion.

183 **"*Bergen Record* entertainment"**: Levinson, *Tommy Dorsey*, p. 161.

184 **"vividly remembers her"**: Ibid.

184 **"not real underworld"**: Taraborrelli, *Sinatra*, p. 65.

185 **"It wasn't much"**: Ibid.

186 **"Hey, Wop"**: Wilson, *Sinatra*, p. 79.

186 **"Frank Albert Sinatra is physically"**: Kuntz and Kuntz, *Sinatra Files*, p. 11.

187 **"Dear Mr. Winchell"**: Ibid., p. 5.

188 **"The diagnosis"**: Weintrob to Commanding General, Dec. 28, 1943, FBI, 25-244122 7.

188 **"stated that no one"**: Kuntz and Kuntz, *Sinatra Files*, p. 20.

189 **"What physical or mental"**: Ibid., p. 11.

CHAPTER 13

1. It must have been a different group of soldiers and sailors who attended a show at the Hollywood Canteen in January 1944. Not just Sinatra, but Hope, Crosby, Ginger Rogers, and Fibber McGee and Molly were present. "When it was [Sinatra's] turn to sing," Nancy Sinatra writes, "the ovations kept him on stage for over an hour. At the end of his performance, it was reported that servicemen swarmed onto the stage, lifted him to their shoulders and paraded him throughout the Canteen, cheering so loudly that it could be heard blocks away" (Nancy Sinatra, *American Legend*, p. 59).

2. The "Franklin" was, of course, for FDR; "Emanuel" was in honor of the soon-to-be-dishonored Manie Sacks. The "Wayne" remains a mystery—perhaps a tribute to a New Jersey town where Frank once spent a pleasant hour? In any case, the emotionally snakebit and eternally paternally disregarded F. W. E. Sinatra would eventually—in a classic case of identifying with the oppressor—change his name to

Frank junior. (And would be immortalized, on *The Sopranos*, as the Chairboy of the
Board.)

3. "The artist agrees to conduct himself with due regard to public conventions and morals and agrees that he will not do or commit any act or thing that will degrade him in
society, or bring him into public hatred, contempt, scorn, or ridicule, that will tend
to shock, insult, or offend the community or ridicule public morals or decency, or
prejudice the producer (MGM) or the motion picture industry in general" (Leff and
Simmons, *Dame in the Kimono*, p. 5).

4. Proser was Frank Costello's legit partner, and would gradually—and then not so
gradually—be edged out.

SOURCE NOTES

192 **"There's a lot of griping"**: Summers and Swan, *Sinatra*, p. 93.

192 **"It is not too much"**: Manchester, *The Glory and the Dream*, p. 309.

193 **"Take a minute"**: Vimms Vitamins radio advertisement, MP3, www.oldtime
radiofans.com/old_radio_commercials/vimms_vitamins.php.

193 **"Dad was on the air"**: Nancy Sinatra, *American Legend*, p. 59.

196 **"This love of mine"**: Lyrics from "This Love of Mine," words and music by
Sol Parker, Hank Sanicola, and Frank Sinatra (New York: Barton Music/Warner
Bros. Music, 1953).

197 **"Who wants to hire"**: White, *You Must Remember This*, p. 304.

197 **"I was at Lockheed"**: James Kaplan, "The King of Ring-a-Ding-Ding," *Movies
Rock* (a supplemental publication of *Vanity Fair*), Dec. 2007.

200 **"Niggers all work"**: Lyrics from "Ol' Man River," words by Oscar Hammerstein, music by Jerome Kern (New York: T. B. Harms, 1927).

200 ***"I want that boy"***: Nancy Sinatra, *My Father*, p. 64.

201 **"I have just received"**: Columbia Records Archive, Sony Music Corporation.

202 **"it was in complete innocence"**: Ibid.

204 **"Joe E. Lewis, the only"**: Ibid.

CHAPTER 14

1. There was also the far from negligible matter of broad new sexual horizons. From
the beginning of Sinatra's tenure at Metro springs the legend—impossible to sub-
stantiate but too delicious to ignore—of the to-do list of female fellow luminaries
he posted on his dressing-room wall and checked off one by one as he proceeded
through.

2. The effect of Lady May's unique child rearing on her son's maturing psyche was
understandably complex. Getting wind that the young Englishman had certain
sexual eccentricities, Mayer assumed that Lawford was simply gay and, with fatherly
concern, sent him to get testosterone injections. Lawford, whom the author knew
slightly, told the story on himself with great amusement.

3. And Hope and Crosby both belonged to the ritzy Lakeside Golf Club, just across the
street: No Jews Allowed, and as for Italian-American entertainers, why, the question
had never even come up before, but now that it was being asked . . . Despite Bob
and Bing's sponsorship, Lakeside turned Sinatra down, and he thereby became the
first gentile ever to join the ranks of Groucho Marx, Jack Benny, and George Burns at
Hillcrest Country Club, in Beverly Hills.

SOURCE NOTES

206 **"Sinatra 1-A"**: Spencer Leigh, "What Did the FBI Make of Top Pop Stars?"
Independent, Dec. 13, 2005, www.independent.co.uk/arts-entertainment/music/
features/what-did-the-fbi-make-of-top-pop-stars-519323.html.

207 **"bugle-deaf Frankie-boy"**: Kuntz and Kuntz, *Sinatra Files*, p. 21.

207 **"Even I grow humble"**: Shaw, *Twentieth-Century Romantic*, p. 78.

209 **"Dateline New York"**: Columbia Records Archive, Sony Music Corporation.

213 **"On the golf course"**: Lyrics from "I Can't Get Started," words by Ira Gershwin, music by Vernon Duke (New York: Chappell, 1935).

214 **"I'll forget my sins"**: Lyrics from "San Fernando Valley," words and music by Gordon Jenkins (New York: Mayfair Music, 1943).

214 **framed quotation**: Shaw, *Twentieth-Century Romantic*, p. 71.

215 **"When I arrived"**: Nancy Sinatra, *American Legend*, p. 61.

216 **"It came to such"**: Cahn, *I Should Care*, p. 134.

216 **"Frank thought Fred"**: Bud Yorkin, in discussion with the author, Feb. 2006.

218 **"I was born with"**: Nancy Sinatra, *American Legend*, p. 61.

218 **"quickly apologized"**: Ibid.

218 **"Because I didn't think"**: Ibid.

219 **"We used to play"**: Silverman, *Dancing on the Ceiling*, p. 78.

219 **"Listen, I'm not supposed"**: Wilson, *Sinatra*, p. 62.

220 **"Pictures stink"**: Kelley, *His Way*, p. 98.

220 **"Naturally he was tired"**: Ibid.

220 **"It's easy for a guy"**: Ibid.

222 **"In Sinatra's singing spot"**: Nancy Sinatra, *American Legend*, p. 63.

CHAPTER 15

SOURCE NOTES

225 **"Could I bring"**: Wilson, *Sinatra*, p. 63.

226 **"Mac, imagine this guy"**: Ibid.

228 **"Then let's see"**: Kelley, *His Way*, p. 95.

230 **"SINATRA HIT BY EGGS"**: Ibid.

230 **"He may be famous"**: Ibid., p. 96.

230 **"[It] was always jammed"**: Ibid., p. 95.

232 **"Let's go down"**: Shaw, *Twentieth-Century Romantic*, p. 80.

232 **"Peg was inside"**: Ibid.

232 **"I was in my room"**: Ibid.

232 **"In the company of Orson"**: Kelley, *His Way*, p. 99.

233 **"No indictment was found"**: Ibid., p. 100.

234 **"Though she'd love to work"**: Lyrics from "(I Got a Woman Crazy for Me) She's Funny That Way," words by Richard A. Whiting, music by Neil Moret (San Francisco: Villa Moret, 1928).

234 **"I fall in love"**: Lyrics from "I Fall in Love Too Easily," words by Sammy Cahn, music by Jule Styne. From *Anchors Aweigh* (MGM, 1945).

CHAPTER 16

1. Nancy was clearly trying to butter Manie up by writing out Frankie junior's middle name, but—fascinatingly—got her own son's given first name (Franklin) wrong. It could have been that (just for a change) her husband was on her mind, but I think it more likely that she didn't think of Frank as Francis, either. Ava Gardner, as we'll see, would be the one who started all that.

2. Still, it must be noted that the Sinatra of 1945 was a very different man from the one who had been a punching bag for his Hoboken Four partners back in the Major Bowes days. Fame, money, and power had pumped up his physical confidence and sense of entitlement (and would continue to do so until the onset of old age); it never hurt his confidence, either, that the beefy retainers with whom he surrounded himself jumped at his every command and flinched at each unkind word.

SOURCE NOTES

241 **"They tell me you"**: Nancy Sinatra, *American Legend*, p. 66.

241 **"What blazing new"**: Parsons, *Tell It to Louella*, p. 151.

243 **"necessary to the national"**: Kelley, *His Way*, p. 101.

243 **"IS CROONING ESSENTIAL?"**: Ibid.

243 **"I miss the times"**: Lyrics from "Homesick, That's All," words and music by
     Gordon Jenkins (Columbia Records, 1945). V-Disc recording.

243 **"MR. FRANK SINATRA"**: Columbia Records Archive, Sony Music
     Corporation.

245 **Frank's daughter Nancy has written:** Nancy Sinatra, *American Legend*,
     p. 58.

246 **"There might be"**: George Benjamin, "Who Says Sinatra's a 'Sad Sack'? They
     Loved Him Overseas—and 150,000 GIs Can't Be Wrong!" *Modern Screen*, Jan.
     1946, www.songsbysinatra.com/reprints/ms_0146.html

247 **"Go away, boy"**: Ibid.

247 **"The singer kidded"**: Kelley, *His Way*, p. 104.

247 **"Are you a tenor"**: Wilson, *Sinatra*, p. 337.

247 **"Shoemakers in uniform"**: Kelley, *His Way*, p. 104.

247 **"Mice make women"**: Kahn, *Voice*, p. 114.

248 **"joy ride"**: Kelley, *His Way*, p. 105.

248 **"the Apollonian marvel"**: Bosley Crowther, "Anchors Aweigh," *New York
     Times*, July 20, 1945.

249 **"Sinatra came down"**: Summers and Swan, *Sinatra*, p. 111.

250 **"George and I were"**: Kelley, *His Way*, p. 107.

251 **"GARY HIGH SCHOOL"**: *Edwardsville (Ill.) Intelligencer*, Nov. 2, 1945.

251 **"outstanding efforts"**: Kelley, *His Way*, p. 109.

252 **"You could reach"**: Summers and Swan, *Sinatra*, p. 110.

252 **"What's he got?"**: *The House I Live In* (RKO, 1945).

253 **"a darling of"**: Kuntz and Kuntz, *Sinatra Files*, p. 40.

254 **"FRANK SINATRA, well known"**: Ibid., p. 45.

255 **"they called Shirley Temple"**: Summers and Swan, *Sinatra*, p. 12.

255 **"I don't like Communists"**: Kelley, *His Way*, p. 110.

255 **"We're bigger than"**: Moquin and Van Doren, *American Way of Crime*,
     p. viii.

258 **"Phil and Frank were"**: Kelley, *His Way*, p. 111.

CHAPTER 17

SOURCE NOTES

261 **"August 1, 1945"**: Columbia Records Archive, Sony Music Corporation.

261 **"Dear Frank. For the past six"**: Ibid.

263 **"Dear Frank: I received"**: Ibid.

266 **"They were tough-minded"**: George Avakian, in discussion with the author,
     Oct. 2006.

268 **"These should be recorded"**: Friedwald, *Sinatra!* p. 176.

268 **"We don't have enough"**: Ibid.

268 **"Sinatra gave us"**: Ibid.

268 **"I don't know the first thing"**: Ibid.

268 **"That was a very strange"**: Avakian, discussion.

268 **"Sinatra was then"**: Friedwald, *Sinatra!* p. 176.

268 **"Sinatra wasn't so bad"**: Avakian, discussion.

269 **Frank Sinatra Conducts:** *Frank Sinatra Conducts the Music of Alec Wilder*
     (Columbia Records, 1946).

269 **"If you don't know"**: Columbia Records Archive, Sony Music Corporation.

CHAPTER 18

1. Although, as Will Friedwald points out, the long American Federation of Musicians strike, during which the big bands couldn't record, deprived the bands of vital revenue.

2. Technically, Sinatra was beaten to the punch by the great Lee Wiley, who, beginning in the late 1930s, made a series of limited-edition, one-composer (Gershwin, Porter, Rodgers and Hart) albums for New York's Liberty Music Shops, which catered exclusively to Manhattan's first-nighting and cabaret-going elite.

3. The bureau continued watching the Mafia closely, but doing little about it, until J. Edgar Hoover's death in 1972. Officially—since the Mob was aware that Hoover was a deeply closeted cross-dresser and a passionate racetrack bettor who may have financed his gambling habit in unorthodox ways—the director was of the opinion that the Mob was an exaggerated problem.

SOURCE NOTES

276 **"How sweet the way":** Lyrics from "One Love," words by Leo Robin, music by David Rose (Sydney: Chappell, 1946).

277 **"As Shaw put it":** Friedwald, *Sinatra!* p. 155.

277 **"I take great pride":** Ibid., p. 156.

279 **"I was working":** Ibid., p. 153.

282 **"The day after our marriage":** Summers and Swan, *Sinatra*, p. 124.

282 **"If I had as many":** Kelley, *His Way*, p. 471.

283 **"Yes, light an Old Gold":** *Songs by Sinatra*, radio broadcast, Jan. 2, 1946, transcript at emruf.webs.com/sinatra.htm

283 **"featured songs for the ages":** Friedwald, *Sinatra!* p. 160.

284 **"As a symptom":** Kuntz and Kuntz, *Sinatra Files*, p. 25.

285 **"I got a break":** Kelley, *His Way*, p. 126.

285 **"Company had early":** Ibid., p. 127.

286 **"Frank was born":** Shaw, *Twentieth-Century Romantic*, p. 74.

288 **"The New York Office":** Kuntz and Kuntz, *Sinatra Files*, p. 28.

CHAPTER 19

1. Pablo Picasso felt much the same way: see John Richardson's superb biography.

2. This unique but completely successful meeting with jazz immortals occurred at a particularly significant juncture in the history of America's single indigenous art form, while the young titans Dizzy Gillespie and Charlie Parker were in the process of creating jazz's version of cubism, bebop. A few months later, twenty-one-year-old Mel Tormé, having heard Ella Fitzgerald sing scat syllables on "Lady Be Good," would begin trying it out himself, with great success. Sinatra, however, would keep being Sinatra (he could do nothing else), developing in parallel to jazz, never in its thrall. He was a representational artist to his core: abstraction never tempted him.

3. A recent biography quotes Avakian as saying the singer and his henchmen walked down the hall "like five diamonds" (Summers and Swan, *Sinatra*, p. 86). Which makes no sense at all until you realize what the producer was actually saying: that they resembled the playing card the five of diamonds.

4. Hilliard would also later co-write the great Sinatra anthem about the other end of the day, "In the Wee Small Hours."

5. He had acquired the nickname after surviving a 1929 "ride" in which he had been stabbed in the face.

SOURCE NOTES

292 **"I haven't much":** Summers and Swan, *Sinatra*, p. 127.

293 **"Sinatra arrived":** Kelley, *His Way*, p. 127.

293 **"an over-festive vacation"**: Wilson, *Sinatra*, p. 66.

294 **"You get word"**: Lyrics from "There's No Business Like Show Business," words and music by Irving Berlin (New York: Irving Berlin, 1946).

295 **"Sinatra telephoned in"**: Columbia Records Archive, Sony Music Corporation.

296 **"Good evening, ladies"**: Wilson, *Sinatra*, p. 66.

297 **"SINATRA'S STOOGERY"**: Shaw, *Twentieth-Century Romantic*, p. 101.

297 **"Bobby Burns phoned"**: Kelley, *His Way*, p. 127.

297 **"Called Sinatra for rehearsal"**: Columbia Records Archive, Sony Music Corporation.

298 **"Sinatra only worked part"**: Ibid.

298 **"many times"**: "Sinatras Split; Frankie Turns to Lana Turner," *Chester (Pa.) Times*, Oct. 7, 1946.

299 **"It's just a family"**: "Sinatra 'Hiding' in Marital Rift," *Oakland Tribune*, Oct. 7, 1946.

299 **"He did not report"**: Kelley, *His Way*, p. 127.

302 **"Let me welcome you"**: Havers, *Sinatra*, p. 115.

303 **"The only thing"**: Lana Turner, *Lana*, p. 42.

303 **"I am not in love"**: Kelley, *His Way*, p. 131.

303 **"I think Frank has done his best"**: Louella Parsons, *Los Angeles Examiner*, Oct. 7, 1946.

305 **"left at 2:30 to appear"**: Columbia Records Archive, Sony Music Corporation.

305 **"NO CONSENT"**: Kelley, *His Way*, p. 129.

305 **"I won't be surprised"**: Barbas, *First Lady of Hollywood*, p. 269.

306 **"SUGGEST YOU READ"**: Kelley, *His Way*, p. 129.

306 **"JUST CONTINUE TO PRINT"**: Ibid., p. 130.

307 **George Avakian remembers:** George Avakian, in discussion with the author, Oct. 2006.

308 **"was relatively tense"**: Ibid.

308 **"He used to call me 'kid' "**: Ibid.

309 **"He did them very quickly"**: Ibid.

309 **"Hard work"**: Shaw, *Twentieth-Century Romantic*, p. 100.

310 **"You must be glad"**: Ibid., p. 104.

311 **"There can rarely have been"**: Friedrich, *City of Nets*, p. 262.

CHAPTER 20

1. The Brooklyn gangster born Giuseppe Doto had thus renamed himself, in the belief that he was as handsome as the Greek god. He was not.

2. As opposed to Dean Martin, who was far more confident of his strength and masculinity than Sinatra, and had little use for glad-handers of every variety, especially mobsters. As a young man, Dino Crocetti had worked as a dealer in gambling joints along the Ohio River, and knew exactly which characters to avoid.

3. Peter J. Levinson told the author that in the mid-1960s, over the course of many conversations with Hank Sanicola—the two were working on a book that didn't pan out—Sanicola said he had helped Sinatra pack a suitcase full of cash to take to Luciano in Havana.

4. Thirty years later, he himself would tell Pete Hamill, "It was one of the dumbest things I ever did" (Hamill, *Why Sinatra Matters*, p. 145).

SOURCE NOTES

314 **"Well, Frankie and I"**: Louella Parsons, *Middletown (N.Y.) Times Herald*, Jan. 27, 1947.

315 **"wanted Nancy to have"**: Summers and Swan, *Sinatra*, p. 129.

315 **"to protect personal funds"**: Ibid.
318 **"A freakish accident"**: Robert Ruark, "He Remembers Lucky Luciano," *Winona (Minn.) Daily News*, Feb. 25, 1962.
319 **"Shame, Sinatra"**: Shaw, *Twentieth-Century Romantic*, p. 108.
319 **"Sinatra was here for four days"**: Ibid.
319 **"a good kid"**: Taraborrelli, *Sinatra*, p. 90.
320 **"Luciano was very"**: Kelley, *His Way*, p. 133.
320 **"In addition to Mr. Luciano"**: Shaw, *Twentieth-Century Romantic*, p. 108.
321 **"It was a pretty story"**: Ibid.
321 **"I was brought up"**: Ibid., p. 109.
321 **"the complete story"**: Summers and Swan, *Sinatra*, p. 131.
322 **"Picture me, skinny Frankie"**: Shaw, *Twentieth-Century Romantic*, p. 110.
323 **"WILL YOU BE"**: *Modern Screen*, May 1947.
323 **"She found a doctor"**: Tina Sinatra, *My Father's Daughter*, p. 8.
324 **"Don't you *ever*"**: Ibid., p. 9.
324 **"Dad made a dramatic"**: Ibid.
326 **"This excellent and well-produced"**: Shaw, *Twentieth-Century Romantic*, p. 115.
327 **"known in the cafés"**: Earl Wilson, "Frankie's Fight," *Zanesville (Ohio) Times Recorder*, April 18, 1947.
328 **"shit heel"**: Summers and Swan, *Sinatra*, p. 142.
328 **"degenerate"**: Kelley, *His Way*, p. 136.
328 **"I'll kill you"**: Ibid.
328 **"For two years"**: Ibid.
329 **"Every time Frank"**: Ibid., p. 135.
329 **"Jeez, I think"**: Ibid., p. 137.
330 **"SINATRA ARRESTED"**: *Los Angeles Times*, April 10, 1947.
331 **"Frankie . . . was met"**: Ibid., Jan. 31, 1947.
332 **"Frank came in"**: Wilson, *Sinatra*, p. 72.
333 **"[giving] the story headlines"**: "Words & Music," *Time*, April 21, 1947.
334 **"1. Mr. Mortimer said he had"**: Kuntz and Kuntz, *Sinatra Files*, p. 26.
335 **"arrest on a sex offense"**: Ibid., p. 31.
335 **"I talked this afternoon"**: Ibid.
336 **"It was a right-hand punch"**: Wilson, *Sinatra*, p. 73.
337 **"Frank taught me to swim"**: Gloria Delson Franks, in discussion with the author, May 2006.

CHAPTER 21

1. She would name names to HUAC in 1952, and regret it the rest of her life.
2. Weirdly enough, considering Sinatra's future history, Tarantino's first brush with the law in California revolved around the apparently staged 1945 kidnapping of his son, James junior, and his wife. Tarantino charged that the kidnapping had been engineered by the right-wing demagogue Gerald L. K. Smith in retaliation for Tarantino's bold editorial stands against anti-Semitism and Fascism in . . . *Hollywood Nite Life*. Sinatra telegraphed the district attorney on his behalf.
3. Mostly. A photograph from a late-1940s Los Angeles radio appearance shows Frank and Nat "King" Cole sitting and looking at each other: while Sinatra is grinning with undisguised pleasure at being in Cole's presence, the latter's expression is wary and haughty.

SOURCE NOTES

342 **"I couldn't stand kissing"**: Kelley, *His Way*, p. 141.
343 **"I wanna house"**: Christopher Reed, "E. Stewart Williams: Architect Whose

Design for Frank Sinatra's House Launched a Style of Desert Modernism," www. guardian.co.uk/news/2005/nov/01/.

344 **"The show is alternately dull"**: Havers, *Sinatra*, p. 126.

345 **"A campaign of propaganda"**: Westbrook Pegler, King Features Syndicate, Sept. 10, 1947.

345 **"I insist the 'Communist Party' "**: Victor Riesel, "Plot—Not a Party," *Chester (Pa.) Times*, Sept. 10, 1947.

346 **"of many writers"**: Westbrook Pegler, King Features Syndicate, Sept. 10, 1947.

346 **"impugned the professional integrity"**: Ibid.

346 **"Sinatra has several"**: Kahn, *Voice*, p. 23.

347 **"Kahn writes also"**: Westbrook Pegler, King Features Syndicate, Sept. 11, 1947.

347 **"From time to time"**: Westbrook Pegler, King Features Syndicate, Dec. 8, 1947.

349 **"The crooner"**: Shaw, *Twentieth-Century Romantic*, p. 116.

349 **"Broadway whispers"**: Ibid., p. 115.

351 **"I hurried around"**: Davis, *Yes I Can*, p. 82.

352 **"I can speak"**: Ibid., p. 86.

352 **"always has a colored act"**: Ibid., p. 106.

353 **"There's a kid"**: Ibid., p. 110.

CHAPTER 22

1. In fact, this may have been the moment when, as a tribute to the great love of his life, Frank Albert became Francis Albert for all time.

2. He had rewritten the script for *Gone With the Wind* on the same condition.

3. Yes, the very tune with which Dean Martin would score a huge hit sixteen years later, toppling the Beatles from the number-1 spot on the *Billboard* charts.

SOURCE NOTES

358 **"I don't want her"**: Lyrics from "Too Fat Polka," words and music by Ross MacLean and Arthur Richardson (New York: Shapiro, Bernstein, 1947).

359 **"If you looked down"**: Cahn, *I Should Care*, p. 95.

360 **"I looked at him"**: Gardner, *Ava*, p. 219.

360 **"one of the greatest"**: Ibid.

363 **"On this trip"**: Nancy Sinatra, *My Father*, p. 59.

364 **"We'd had a few other governesses"**: Ibid.

364 **"When the Crosby kids"**: Gary Giddins, in discussion with the author, Oct. 2006.

364 **"I remember her"**: Crosby and Firestone, *Going My Own Way*, p. 76.

365 **"When Bing realized"**: Giddins, discussion.

365 **"Right now"**: Shaw, *Twentieth-Century Romantic*, p. 125.

367 **"Pompous and funereal"**: Bosley Crowther, "Miracle of the Bells," *New York Times*, March 17, 1948.

368 **"Frank Sinatra, looking"**: "The New Pictures," *Time*, March 29, 1948.

369 **"a hunk of religious"**: Santopietro, *Sinatra in Hollywood*, p. 100.

369 **"the worst single"**: "Last Year's Movies," *Life*, March 8, 1948.

370 **"I just couldn't"**: *60 Greatest Old-Time Radio Shows Starring Frank Sinatra and Friends* (Radio Spirits, 2000). Set of thirty compact discs.

373 **"It's been a long time"**: Gardner, *Ava*, p. 220.

375 **"A lot of silly stories"**: Ibid., p. 221.

375 **"We drank, we laughed"**: Ibid.

376 **"We met for dinner"**: Ibid.

377 **"How you feeling"**: *Spotlight Review 48* (Radio Spirits, 2000). Set of thirty compact discs.

377 **"Mr. Sinatra's performance"**: Bosley Crowther, "Frank Sinatra, Kathryn Grayson Head Cast of Lavish 'Kissing Bandit' at the Capitol," *New York Times*, Nov. 19, 1948.

377 **"Frank and my father"**: Arthur Marx, interview with Steve Glauber, *CBS Sunday Morning*, October 2007.

378 **"It was nothing"**: Jane Russell, in discussion with the author, Sept. 2009.

378 **"IS SINATRA FINISHED?"**: *Modern Television & Radio*, Dec. 1948.

378 **"so many things"**: Nancy Sinatra, *American Legend*, p. 87.

379 **"not only can't"**: Shaw, *Twentieth-Century Romantic*, p. 124.

379 **"to be nearer"**: Nancy Sinatra, *American Legend*, p. 91.

379 **"up in the world"**: Tina Sinatra, *My Father's Daughter*, p. 20.

380 **"It seems my friends"**: Lyrics from "Comme Ci Comme Ça," words by Alex Charles Kramer and Joan Whitney, music by Bruno Coquatrix (New York: Paris Music, 1949).

381 **"It wasn't a very"**: Nancy Sinatra, *American Legend*, p. 87.

CHAPTER 23

1. Yet another easy target. Frank may have convinced Buddy Rich that he could handle himself pretty well, but that was long before Rich—who was as diminutive as Sinatra—had earned his black belt in karate.

SOURCE NOTES

383 **"One day while"**: Nancy Sinatra, *My Father*, p. 75.

383 **"The moment Candy"**: Tormé, *It Wasn't All Velvet*, p. 64.

384 **"I found [him]"**: Wilson, *Sinatra*, p. 83.

385 **"Okay, kids, the part's"**: Gardner, *Ava*, p. 217.

385 **"a car sped"**: Ibid.

386 **"I'm going to marry"**: Kelley, *His Way*, p. 138.

386 **"I'd say"**: Jerry Lewis, in discussion with the author, March 2008.

387 **"How can I be"**: Ibid.

387 **"Don't be surprised"**: Bosley Crowther, "Frank Sinatra and Gene Kelly in 'Take Me Out to the Ball Game,' at Loew's State," *New York Times*, March 10, 1949.

387 **"He just didn't"**: Kelley, *His Way*, p. 131.

388 **"He just can't bear"**: Shaw, *Twentieth-Century Romantic*, p. 127.

388 **"They don't quite get"**: Ibid., p. 126.

388 **"M, N, O, P"**: Lyrics from "A—You're Adorable," words and music by Buddy Kaye, Fred Wise, and Sidney Lippman (New York: Laurel Music, 1948).

389 **"The voice is better at night"**: Frank Sinatra Jr., interview with Michael Bourne, WBGO, Nov. 5, 2009.

389 **"The recording date"**: Granata, *Sessions with Sinatra*, p. 52.

391 **"The sometimes unruly crooner"**: *Newsweek*, vol. 34, 1949.

391 **"On the island of Stromboli"**: Lyrics from "(On the Island of) Stromboli," words and music by Ken Lane and Irving Taylor (1949).

392 **"Check this"**: Columbia Records Archive, Sony Music Corporation.

392 **"Dear Frank"**: Ibid.

393 **"Deep down"**: Flamini, *Ava*, chapter 8.

394 **"We met in the ladies' room"**: Gardner, *Ava*, p. 222.

394 **"October 30, 1949"**: Nancy Sinatra, *American Legend*, p. 91.

395 **"The Swoon is real gone"**: Shaw, *Twentieth-Century Romantic*, p. 125.

396 **"Both Frank and I"**: Gardner, *Ava*, p. 226.

396 **"All my life"**: Ibid.

396 **"Bobby and I"**: Kelley, *His Way*, p. 154.

397 **"She was like a Svengali"**: Server, *Ava Gardner*, p. 187.

399 **"Quentin Reynolds and Heywood Broun's"**: Walter Winchell on Broadway, syndicated column, Dec. 14, 1949.

400 **"You're the salt in my stew"**: Lyrics from "You're the Cream in My Coffee," words and music by Lew Brown, Buddy Gard DeSylva, and Ray Henderson (New York: DeSylva, Brown, and Henderson, 1928).

400 **"I said that"**: *1949: Lite Up Time Shows by Frank Sinatra* (Jazz Band, 1993). Compact disc.

CHAPTER 24

1. The motto of Metro's production manager, J. J. Cohn: "A rock is a rock, a tree is a tree, shoot it in Griffith Park" (Silverman, *Dancing on the Ceiling*, p. 104).

2. A man destined to be one of history's footnotes, Clark (né Samuel Goldberg) had been one of Columbia's biggest recording stars until his untimely death in an airplane crash the previous October. "He was a real rival to Crosby," recalled the Columbia producer George Avakian. "But he also had the handicap of not being able to appeal to people visually because he wasn't good-looking. He was a slightly overweight, slightly undersized person of very drab appearance. Everything was drab about him. So the quality of his voice was terrific, but nothing else happened. He would have been a disaster in the television era, because he looked like your father's younger brother" (Avakian, in discussion with the author, Oct. 2006).

3. A remarkable booking, given Sinatra's odor at the moment. The Copa was the crème de la crème of nightclubs, and bookings for even the biggest stars were usually four weeks. How to explain? As tempting as it is to look for organized crime behind every potted plant in Sinatra's life, the Mob really does seem to have stuck with him through the roughest patches in his career, and Frank Costello owned the Copa.

4. Later the author of *The Manchurian Candidate*, which of course became a movie starring Sinatra.

SOURCE NOTES

402 **"Never before has"**: Shaw, *Twentieth-Century Romantic*, p. 130.

404 **"I'm quite sure"**: Ed Sullivan, Little Old New York, syndicated column, Feb. 1, 1950.

405 **"She arrived late"**: Server, *Ava Gardner*, p. 182.

406 **"Frank Sinatra squired"**: United Press, Feb. 7, 1950.

406 **"a major mistake"**: Shaw, *Twentieth-Century Romantic*, p. 133.

407 **"I am very much"**: Kelley, *His Way*, p. 157.

407 **"Ava Gardner's current travels"**: Sheilah Graham, Hollywood Today, syndicated column, Feb. 10, 1950.

407 **"FRANK SINATRA'S WIFE"**: *Los Angeles Times*, Feb. 15, 1950.

408 **"the shit really hit the fan"**: Gardner, *Ava*, p. 225.

408 **"I am very glad"**: Louella Parsons, International News Service, syndicated column, Feb. 24, 1950.

409 **"romantic episode"**: *Los Angeles Times*, Feb. 15, 1950.

409 **"I have here"**: Herman, *Joseph McCarthy*, p. 99.

409 **"Ava Gardner's lines"**: Erskine Johnson, In Hollywood, syndicated column, March 10, 1950.

409 **"apostle of degradation"**: See Spoto, *Notorious*, p. 296.

411 **"Items-We-Doubt"**: Walter Winchell on Broadway, syndicated column, March 14, 1950.

411 **"I found myself"**: Summers and Swan, *Sinatra*, p. 155.

411 **"Every single night"**: Ibid., p. 157.

412   **"Someone told Sinatra"**: Kelley, *His Way*, p. 160.
412   **"Sam, Frank"**: Friedwald, *Sinatra!* p. 183.
413   **"I'm adored, I'm adored"**: Lyrics from "I Am Loved," words and music by Cole Porter (New York: Hal Leonard, 1950).
413   **"My voice was"**: Kelley, *His Way*, p. 160.
413   **"After the opening"**: Friedwald, *Sinatra!* p. 183.
413   **"Whether temporarily"**: Shaw, *Twentieth-Century Romantic*, p. 135.
413   **"Frank was nervous"**: Gardner, *Ava*, p. 228.
413   **"Did you have to sing"**: Wayne, *Ava's Men*, p. 119.
414   **"We took a plain"**: Artie Shaw, interview with Ted Panken, April 2, 2002.
414   **"Artie solved"**: Gardner, *Ava*, p. 230.
416   **"It was Frank"**: Ibid., p. 231.
418   **"It's like being"**: Server, *Ava Gardner*, p. 267.
418   **"Every artist is a woman"**: Richardson, *A Life of Picasso: The Triumphant Years, 1917–1932*, p. 341.

CHAPTER 25

SOURCE NOTES
420   **"As you know"**: Columbia Records Archive, Sony Music Corporation.
420   **"Mitch, we've got"**: Ibid.
420   **"What makes you"**: Friedwald, *Sinatra!* p. 78.
420   **"Daisy is darling"**: Lyrics from "American Beauty Rose," words and music by Arthur Altman, Hal David, and Redd Evans (1950).
421   **"irresistible"**: Friedwald, *Sinatra!* p. 179.
422   **"Oh, God"**: Gardner, *Ava*, p. 220.
423   **"extreme cruelty"**: Associated Press, April 27, 1950.
423   **"neither of us"**: International News Service, April 27, 1950.
423   **"Frank Sinatra, cast loose"**: "Sinatra Breaks with M-G-M; Will Free-Lance," *Long Beach (Calif.) Independent*, April 29, 1950.
424   **"Hey, did you"**: Nancy Sinatra, *My Father*, p. 87.
424   **"I hear you"**: Ibid.
425   **"Listen, Sinatra had"**: Server, *Ava Gardner*, p. 187.
426   **"I can say this now"**: Nancy Sinatra, *American Legend*, p. 95.
426   **"You couldn't do that"**: Lee Herschberg, in discussion with the author, May 2006.
427   **"he would send off"**: Server, *Ava Gardner*, p. 187.
428   **"was tragic and terrifying"**: Shaw, *Twentieth-Century Romantic*, p. 137.
428   **"BALI TOO H'AI"**: International News Service, May 4, 1950.
429   **"Yes, I'll probably see"**: Kelley, *His Way*, p. 166.
430   **"I remember one time"**: Server, *Ava Gardner*, p. 197.
430   **"A very, very wild spirit"**: Ibid., p. 201.
431   **" 'Ava,' Bappie said"**: Gardner, *Ava*, p. 241.
431   **"thought she was the most"**: Server, *Ava Gardner*, p. 197.
431   **"Someone had passed"**: Gardner, *Ava*, p. 246.
432   **"it just got into her blood"**: Server, *Ava Gardner*, p. 187.
432   **"Oh, what a lovely surprise"**: Ibid., p. 205.
433   **"Of course, I knew"**: Ibid., p. 207.
433   **"They can't make this"**: Shaw, *Twentieth-Century Romantic*, p. 139.
433   **"This bullfighter is nothing"**: Server, *Ava Gardner*, p. 207.
435   **"Eiffel Tower and stuff"**: Shaw, *Twentieth-Century Romantic*, p. 139.

CHAPTER 26

1. The incident rhymes strangely with the 1970 visit by Elvis Presley to President
   Richard M. Nixon, in which Presley volunteered to be a "Federal Agent-at-Large"
   in the Bureau of Narcotics and Dangerous Drugs. Like Sinatra, Presley cited his
   ability to mix with undesirables—in this case, hippies. And like Sinatra, Elvis got the
   brush-off—though in a nicer way (for one thing, Nixon took the meeting).

SOURCE NOTES

438 **"It takes real courage"**: Richmond, *Fever*, p. 177.

438 **"Sinatra, astoundingly thin"**: Ibid.

439 **"If TV is his oyster"**: Havers, *Sinatra*, p. 148.

441 **"Sipping tea on stage"**: Nancy Sinatra, *American Legend*, p. 96.

441 **"I watched mass hysteria"**: Shaw, *Twentieth-Century Romantic*, p. 141.

442 **"Bless me, he's GOOD"**: Ibid.

442 **"People who simply put"**: Ibid.

443 **"pleasant throwaways"**: George Avakian, in discussion with the author, Oct.
    2006.

443 **"a cute little novelty"**: Frank Sinatra, interview with Ben Heller, WMID,
    Atlantic City, N.J., Sept. 4, 1950.

444 **"There's no sign of life"**: Wilson, *Sinatra*, p. 94.

445 **"I don't think Frank"**: Nancy Sinatra, *American Legend*, p. 97.

445 **"Bright, with good"**: Friedwald, *Sinatra!* p. 185.

445 **"DATE: SEPTEMBER 7, 1950"**: Kuntz and Kuntz, *Sinatra Files*, p. 67.

447 **"the Hollywood–Los Angeles underworld"**: *Dixon (Ill.) Evening Telegraph*,
    May 29, 1950.

447 **"Sinatra's decline"**: Ibid.

448 **"heard the whispered"**: Server, *Ava Gardner*, p. 215.

449 **"a tear or so"**: "Frank Sinatras Legally Parted by Court Action," *Los Angeles
    Times*, Sept. 29, 1950.

450 **"I don't feel much"**: Ibid.

450 **"I would see her faint"**: Nancy Sinatra, *My Father*, p. 74.

451 **"Frank Sinatra walked off"**: Shaw, *Twentieth-Century Romantic*, p. 144.

451 **"a surprisingly good actor"**: Ibid.

451 **"bad pacing, bad scripting"**: Ibid.

452 **"Frank was always late"**: Kelley, *His Way*, p. 171.

452 **"Frank was always washing"**: Ibid.

453 **"Frank was insanely jealous"**: Ibid., p. 170.

CHAPTER 27

1. There are some who claim that it was Frank himself who came up with the idea to
   do a record with Dagmar: he was always a willful, often shrewd, manager of his own
   career—though sometimes he was more headstrong than wise. In any case, desperate
   times call for desperate measures, and if the duet was Frank's idea, we should probably applaud him for his audacity, if not his perspicacity.

2. In fact, there is a famous list of some two hundred important popular songs that
   Sinatra never recorded, out of either sheer neglect or (far more likely) fear that they
   wouldn't sell.

3. Miller threatened to terminate Clooney's contract if she didn't record "Come On-a
   My House." And as the producer Paul Weston, Jo Stafford's husband, told Charles
   L. Granata, "You can't believe the crap that he had Jo record, tunes like 'Underneath
   the Overpass,' stuff that just died. He would be very persuasive, and the artist didn't
   have much choice. They'd say, 'This is a piece of crap,' and Mitch would say, 'Oh, it's
   gonna be a hit,' so they'd do it" (Friedwald, *Sinatra!* p. 193).

SOURCE NOTES

456 **"We like Eddie Fisher":** Ed O'Brien, in discussion with the author, March 2007.

457 **"You had to":** Havers, *Sinatra*, p. 169.

457 **"Singer Eddie Fisher":** Fisher, *Been There, Done That*, p. 42.

457 **"The cash customers":** Ibid.

457 **"I became the hottest":** Ibid., p. 43.

459 **"I almost fell off my chair":** Philip Nobile, "Sinatra: Crooner or Canary?"
     Gallery, Sept. 1978.

460 **"like a lost kitten":** Ibid.

461 **"Van Heusen was a wild man":** James Kaplan, "The King of Ring-a-Ding-
     Ding," *Movies Rock* (a supplemental publication of *Vanity Fair*), Dec. 2007.

461 **"We have information":** Nobile, "Sinatra."

468 **"He's not going to admit any":** Ibid.

471 **"That's a heartbreaking":** George Avakian, in discussion with the author, Oct.
     2006.

471 **"That's bullshit":** Friedwald, *Sinatra!* p. 192.

471 **"when they played":** Ibid., p. 191.

472 **"A love that's there for others too":** Lyrics from "I'm a Fool to Want You,"
     words and music by Jack Wolf, Joel Herron, and Frank Sinatra. From *Where Are
     You?* (Capitol Records, 1957).

472 **"Dolly showed me":** Gardner, *Ava*, p. 267.

473 **"quieter, withdrawn":** Ibid.

473 **"[looked] at me very carefully":** Ibid., p. 269.

473 **"Stagehands running in and out":** Server, *Ava Gardner*, p. 225.

474 **"Please nobody sit":** Ibid., p. 227.

474 **"The only autographs":** Ibid., p. 225.

474 **Featured on the stage":** Bosley Crowther, *New York Times*, April 26, 1951.

475 **"I growled and barked":** Nancy Sinatra, *My Father*, p. 80.

475 **"Great stuff, Frank":** O'Brien, discussion.

476 **"She had a dark and roving":** Lyrics from "Roving Kind," words and music
     by Arnold Stanton, Jessie Cavanaugh, and James Cavanaugh (New York: Hollis
     Music, 1950).

476 **"My heart *cries* for you":** Lyrics from "My Heart Cries for You," words and
     music by Percy Faith and Carl Sigman (New York: Massey Music, 1950).

476 **"Frank looks at Miller":** O'Brien, discussion.

476 **"You're a nice guy":** Lawrence Staig, "Obituaries: Guy Mitchell," *Independent*,
     July 5, 1999, www.independent.co.uk/arts-entertainment/obituaries-guy-mitchell
     -1104390.html.

477 **"the worst thing":** Friedwald, *Sinatra!* p. 76.

477 **"You look so lovely":** Lyrics from "Mama Will Bark," words and music by Dick
     Manning (Columbia Records, 1951).

477 **Friedwald points out:** Friedwald, *Sinatra!* p. 187.

CHAPTER 28

1. Pevney, a journeyman who would go on to direct Dean Martin and Jerry Lewis in 3
    Ring Circus, was known for being organized, precise, and relaxed on set—qualities
    that both Sinatra and the feuding Martin and Lewis tested to the full.

2. Fortunately, Sinatra would get over his distaste for the great song, recording memo-
    rable versions of it with Nelson Riddle in 1953 and Neal Hefti in 1962.

SOURCE NOTES

478 **"If I can't get a divorce":** Kelley, *His Way*, p. 182.

479 **"This is what Frank wants":** Ibid.

479 **"I don't think a woman"**: Ibid.
479 **"Frank Sinatra was the happiest"**: Shaw, *Twentieth-Century Romantic*, p. 155.
480 **"I too had sat"**: Winters, *Shelley*, p. 319.
481 **"His children were"**: Kelley, *His Way*, p. 181.
481 **"Frank was losing"**: Winters, *Shelley*, p. 320.
481 **"I can't remember what"**: Ibid.
482 **"Mr. Sinatra is going"**: Kelley, *His Way*, p. 181.
482 **"I'll have a cup of coffee"**: Ibid., p. 182.
482 **"Shelley, if Frank"**: Ibid.
483 **"pleasantly tune-filled"**: *New York Times*, March 27, 1952.
483 **"GET THE FUCK"**: Server, *Ava Gardner*, p. 229.
483 **"Crooner Frankie Sinatra"**: United Press, Aug. 3, 1951.
484 **"The two movie queens"**: United Press, "Ava, Back Out of Seclusion, Gets Snub from Hedy Lamarr," Aug. 5, 1951.
484 **"If you don't give"**: Shaw, *Twentieth-Century Romantic*, p. 148.
485 **"It was dark"**: Gardner, *Ava*, p. 271.
486 **"Kill the light"**: Shaw, *Twentieth-Century Romantic*, p. 148.
486 **"Next time I'll kill you"**: Ibid.
486 **"I hope I'm going"**: Ibid., p. 149.
486 **"I'm sorry to"**: Ibid.
487 **"Grossly exaggerated"**: Ibid.
487 **"I honestly don't know"**: Ibid.
488 **"It doesn't really"**: Gardner, *Ava*, p. 274.
488 **"I suppose you wish"**: Ibid.
489 **"It was about"**: Ibid., p. 275.
490 **"Just a few"**: Ibid.
490 **"Oh my God"**: Nancy Sinatra, *American Legend*, p. 99.
491 **"I did not try"**: Shaw, *Twentieth-Century Romantic*, p. 150.
491 **"Tuesday night"**: Ibid.
493 **"Ava was chatting"**: Server, *Ava Gardner*, p. 232.
493 **"Every time I"**: Ibid.
494 **"I like the way"**: Bill Miller, in discussion with the author, May 2006.
494 **"Sinatra's my pal"**: Ibid.
495 **"Speaking of getting laid"**: Ibid.

CHAPTER 29

1. True to egocentric and vindictive form, for several weeks Frank ended every show by looking the camera straight in the eye and saying, not in a warm and fuzzy way, "I leave you with two words . . . SHELLEY WINTERS." He continued the practice until Winters's lawyer sent CBS and Sinatra's lawyer a cease-and-desist letter threatening a large lawsuit (Winters, *Shelley*, p. 323).

2. Of course in real life, Bing too was the anti-Crosby, but that, as they say, is another story.

3. This seems as good a place as any to note that for whatever unknown reason, almost all Sinatra books, including some of the most trustworthy and authoritative, insistently misspell Sacks's surname with an *h* instead of a *k*. The mistake is so widespread that during the course of my research I kept having to refer back to photocopies I had made of letters from Sacks to Sinatra, on the record executive's stationery, with typed and handwritten signatures, to assure myself that the majority opinion, in this case at least, was wrong. The moral being that any and every convincing assertion about Frank Sinatra's life should always be examined carefully.

4. And still retains a weird charm after fifty-plus years.

SOURCE NOTES

498 **"Everything is a racket":** Associated Press, Dec. 14, 1950.

499 **"spotty, taking full":** Jim Davidson's Classic TV Info, www.classictvinfo. com/Sinatra/SinatraShow1.htm.

499 **"a very real":** Jack Gould, "C.B.S. Presents Its No. 1 Competitor to Milton Berle in the Person of Frank Sinatra," *New York Times*, Oct. 12, 1951.

502 **"The wedding is off":** Gardner, *Ava*, p. 284.

502 **"Now the bedlam began":** Ibid.

503 **"They were giggly":** Wilson, *Sinatra*, p. 96.

504 **"How did those creeps":** Kelley, *His Way*, p. 187.

504 **"Frank was so angry":** Summers and Swan, *Sinatra*, p. 161.

505 **"Wonderful designer":** Ibid.

505 **"Well, we finally":** Ibid.

505 **"This marriage is blessed":** Kelley, *His Way*, p. 189.

505 **"Who sent this":** Shaw, *Twentieth-Century Romantic*, p. 154.

506 **"Look after him":** Kelley, *His Way*, p. 190.

506 **"All I had with me":** Gardner, *Ava*, p. 286.

506 **"It was a chilly day":** Shaw, *Twentieth-Century Romantic*, p. 154.

507 **"Naturally a photographer":** Gardner, *Ava*, p. 286.

507 **"We drank a lot":** Ibid., p. 287.

507 **"Frank and I didn't start":** Summers and Swan, *Sinatra*, p. 162.

508 **"SNARLING FRANK":** Shaw, *Twentieth-Century Romantic*, p. 155.

508 **"WHAT A BORE":** Ibid.

508 **"Frank Sinatra evidently":** Wilson, *Sinatra*, p. 97.

509 **"By every ordinary standard":** Swan, *Twentieth-Century Romantic*, p. 158.

509 **"Come on-a my house":** Lyrics from "Come On-a My House," words and music by Ross Bagdasarian and William Saroyan (1939).

509 **"Chief beef hinges":** Friedwald, *Sinatra!* p. 196.

510 **"Kidding each other's":** Jim Davidson's Classic TV Info.

510 **"Mr. Gardner":** Summers and Swan, *Sinatra*, p. 163.

510 **"We're going to redecorate":** Shaw, *Twentieth-Century Romantic*, p. 155.

511 **"I lost control":** Ibid., p. 157.

512 **"Even the most":** Bosley Crowther, "Six Newcomers on Holiday Fare," *New York Times,* Dec. 26, 1951.

513 **"a tiny curly-headed":** James Jones, *From Here to Eternity*, p. 37.

514 **"Cohn's Folly":** Zinnemann, *Life in the Movies*, p. 171.

514 **"No wonder Sinatra":** Santopietro, *Sinatra in Hollywood*, p. 138.

CHAPTER 30

1. The practice prevented a studio from losing money on a contract player temporarily lying fallow: when studio A had nothing going for a star, it would loan said star to studio B for one picture, at a rate above the salary it was paying the player, and pocket the difference.

2. An intriguing parallel is Dean Martin, Ava's male counterpart as a (platonic, of course) love object for Frank, who possessed many of these same qualities, and· whose extreme masculine beauty was not dissimilar to hers.

3. And who would drop dead of a heart attack eleven years later, at fifty-eight, just a couple of years too soon to see his daughter Mia become Frank Sinatra's third wife.

SOURCE NOTES

515 **"It was like":** Gloria Delson Franks, in discussion with the author, May 2006.

516 **"Neither gave an inch":** Kelley, *His Way*, p. 192.

517 **"Just so you know"**: Lyrics from "Walking in the Sunshine," words and music by Bob Merrill (New York: Chappell, 1952).

518 **"What are you"**: Wilson, *Sinatra*, p. 99.

518 **"I sold Fox"**: Gardner, *Ava*, p. 293.

518 **"Cynthia, from Montparnasse"**: Server, *Ava Gardner*, p. 239.

519 **"SINATRA SCRAMBLES TO RECOVER"**: *Oakland Tribune*, March 20, 1952.

520 **"I'll always be"**: Shaw, *Twentieth-Century Romantic*, p. 159.

520 **"Nodding, he became"**: Ibid.

521 **"As one of his"**: Wilson, *Sinatra*, p. 99.

521 **"somewhat subdued"**: *New York Times*, March 27, 1952.

521 **"GONE ON FRANKIE"**: Shaw, *Twentieth-Century Romantic*, p. 160.

522 **"If your sweetheart sends"**: Lyrics from "Cry," words and music by Churchill Kohlman (New York: Mellow Music, 1951).

522 **"JOHNNIE'S GOLDEN RAYS"**: Shaw, *Twentieth-Century Romantic*, p. 160.

523 **"Do you folks suffer"**: *Syracuse (N.Y.) Herald Journal*, March 12, 1952.

523 **"I'd like to tell you"**: Wilson, *Sinatra*, p. 99.

523 **"These people have"**: Shaw, *Twentieth-Century Romantic*, p. 161.

525 **"What do you want"**: Havers, *Sinatra*, p. 161.

526 **"Frank didn't want"**: Friedwald, *Sinatra!* p. 187.

527 **"was known for making"**: Granata, *Sessions with Sinatra*, p. 73.

527 **"Today is our"**: Summers and Swan, *Sinatra*, p. 165.

528 **"I don't know"**: *Lethbridge (AB) Herald*, June 10, 1952.

528 **"Under present conditions"**: Ibid.

528 **"She is unwilling"**: Shaw, *Twentieth-Century Romantic*, p. 163.

528 **"Ava had a reckless look"**: Nancy Sinatra, *My Father*, p. 77.

530 **"Services of Frank Sinatra"**: Kelley, *His Way*, p. 194.

531 **"the asshole of creation"**: Server, *Ava Gardner*, p. 243.

531 **"Frankly Speaking"**: Kelley, *His Way*, p. 195.

532 **"Well, there it is"**: Ibid.

532 **"That should have"**: Ibid., p. 196.

532 **"When I recently"**: Nancy Sinatra, *American Legend*, p. 104.

CHAPTER 31

1. Miller, Marden's postwar successor as owner of the gorgeous nightclub atop the Jersey Palisades, was no relation to Sinatra's pianist—but was the father of the controversial *New York Times* reporter Judith Miller.

2. Lana would soon have Lamas fired from *Latin Lovers* (to be replaced by Ricardo Montalban) and would take up with Lex Barker—whom she would marry a year later, and whom Turner's daughter Cheryl Crane would later accuse of having sexually abused her when she was ten.

SOURCE NOTES

533 **"Ava Gardner, upon"**: Hedda Hopper, In Hollywood, syndicated column, Sept. 8, 1952.

534 **"After all"**: Gardner, *Ava*, p. 200.

534 **"Whatever Sinatra ever"**: Shaw, *Twentieth-Century Romantic*, p. 163.

535 **"He sang onstage"**: Kelley, *His Way*, p. 198.

535 **"I'll never come back"**: Ibid.

535 **"There were twenty thousand"**: Cannon, *Grabtown Girl*, p. 99.

535 **"Don't you remember"**: Lyrics from "Why Try to Change Me Now," words and music by Cy Coleman (New York: Hal Leonard, 1952).

536 **"That's it, Frank"**: Granata, *Sessions with Sinatra*, p. 76.

536 **"Well! What whorehouse"**: Cannon, *Grabtown Girl*, p. 100.

536 **"Breakfast with the Sinatras"**: On Broadway with Earl Wilson, syndicated column, Sept. 19, 1952.

537 **"The battles between"**: Newspaper Enterprise Association, Aug. 1, 1952.

537 **"You're all that I desire"**: Lyrics from "Love Me," words and music by Victor Young and Ned Washington (New York: Helene Blue Musique). First recorded by Jack Teagarden, 1933.

537 **"nearly broke"**: Cannon, *Grabtown Girl*, p. 101.

538 **"a crackup of their marriage"**: Associated Press, Oct. 7, 1952.

538 **"We're having oral battles"**: Ibid.

539 **"Harry, I want"**: Wilson, *Sinatra*, p. 108.

539 **"You must be out"**: Ibid.

539 **"About the money"**: Ibid.

541 **"God, Ava"**: Kelley, *His Way*, p. 203.

541 **"I want you to get Harry"**: Ibid., p. 185.

542 **"You know who's right"**: Nancy Sinatra, *My Father*, p. 96.

542 **"We bumped into Frank"**: Hedda Hopper's Hollywood, syndicated column, Oct. 17, 1952.

543 **"By the time"**: Gardner, *Ava*, p. 192.

545 **"I want to have"**: Aline Mosby, United Press, Oct. 3, 1952.

545 **"a hollow success"**: Lana Turner, *Lana*, p. 158.

546 **"to catch Frank"**: Gardner, *Ava*, p. 305.

546 **"looking lovely as ever"**: Ibid., p. 306.

547 **"Everybody wants to"**: Eliot, *Cary Grant*, p. 1.

547 **"It is true"**: Wilson, *Sinatra*, p. 105.

547 **"Ah, Frank"**: Gardner, *Ava*, p. 195.

548 **"We did what we could"**: Lana Turner, *Lana*, p. 168.

548 **"Frank seemed to approve"**: Gardner, *Ava*, p. 309.

549 **"For God's sake"**: Ibid., p. 310.

549 **"NOT CONFIRMED"**: *Los Angeles Times*, Oct. 21, 1952.

550 **"the Palm Springs police"**: Wilson, *Sinatra*, p. 101.

550 **"COLUMNIST SAYS SINATRA"**: Associated Press, Oct. 21, 1952.

550 **"Frank's in the bathroom throwing up"**: Wilson, *Sinatra*, p. 102.

551 **"The problems were never in bed"**: Kelley, *His Way*, p. 175.

551 **"FRANKIE READY TO SURRENDER"**: Shaw, *Twentieth-Century Romantic*, p. 165.

551 **"I can't do anything myself"**: Ibid.

552 **"Hey, Ava"**: Server, *Ava Gardner*, p. 249.

552 **"So, Frank"**: Ibid.

553 **"Sinatra smelled like"**: Kelley, *His Way*, p. 188.

554 **"Frank was very nice"**: Mary Edna Grimes, in discussion with the author, Nov. 2008.

554 **"Goodbye, Dolly"**: United Press, Oct. 3, 1952.

CHAPTER 32

1. She's also said to have won him over with another variant of her most famous remark: when Ford introduced Ava to the English governor of Kenya and the governor's wife, the director is alleged to have said, "Ava, why don't you tell the governor what you see in this one-hundred-twenty-pound runt you're married to," and Ava is alleged to have replied, "Well, there's only ten pounds of Frank but there's one hundred and ten pounds of cock!" "Ford wanted to kill her," one Sinatra biographer wrote—but given the fact (according to Maureen O'Hara) that the director constantly doodled pictures of penises, he probably would've been more intrigued than upset (Kelley, *His Way*, p. 190).

SOURCE NOTES

555 **"It was quite"**: Higham, *Ava*, p. 133.

556 **"Clark's the kind"**: Server, *Ava Gardner*, p. 253.

556 **"on safari"**: Gardner, *Ava*, p. 316.

556 **"The movie company"**: Ibid.

556 **"once we settled"**: Ibid.

557 **"Make the spaghetti"**: Bogdanovich, *Who the Hell's in It*, p. 404.

558 **"Why don't you"**: Peter Bogdanovich, in discussion with the author, May 2009.

560 **"I had the strongest"**: Gardner, *Ava*, p. 319.

560 **"I often felt"**: Ibid.

561 **"The truth is"**: Ibid.

561 **"Let's put it"**: *Los Angeles Times*, Nov. 23, 1952.

561 **"You're damn good"**: Gardner, *Ava*, p. 324.

561 **"For someone with"**: Ibid.

562 **"Jack Ford tried"**: Ibid., p. 327.

563 **"I don't need this"**: Shaw, *Twentieth-Century Romantic*, p. 170.

563 **"He's such a comical"**: James Jones, *From Here to Eternity*, p. 246.

563 **"Frank had never"**: Gardner, *Ava*, p. 199.

563 **"scared to death"**: Shaw, *Twentieth-Century Romantic*, p. 170.

564 **"The [screen] test"**: Summers and Swan, *Sinatra*, p. 172.

564 **"Since [Sinatra's] was"**: Shaw, *Twentieth-Century Romantic*, p. 170.

565 **"CONFIDENTIAL"**: Kelley, *His Way*, p. 214.

566 **"AVA GARDNER STRICKEN"**: Server, *Ava Gardner*, p. 259.

567 **"Frank, give the earrings"**: Ibid., p. 260.

568 **"When I was on my lecture tour"**: Hedda Hopper, In Hollywood, syndicated column, Oct. 4, 1952.

569 **"Spent a pleasant"**: Edith Gwynn, Hollywood, syndicated column, Oct. 25, 1952.

569 **"Where's your wife"**: Hedda Hopper, In Hollywood, syndicated column, Oct. 26, 1952.

569 **"At the end"**: Mark Rotella, "Simply Red," *New York Times*, Aug. 10, 2003.

570 **"A funny thing happened"**: Leonard Lyons, The Lyons Den, syndicated column, Dec. 3, 1952.

570 **"Is he good"**: Hy Gardner, It Happened Last Night, syndicated column, Dec. 8, 1952.

570 **"It's pretty lonesome"**: Hy Gardner, It Happened Last Night, syndicated column, Dec. 4, 1952.

570 **"It's all right"**: Server, *Ava Gardner*, p. 257.

570 **"Ava couldn't be alone"**: Ibid., p. 258.

570 **"he has a prior"**: Hy Gardner, It Happened Last Night, Dec. 8, 1952.

570 **"was given a birthday cake"**: *Zanesville (Ohio) Times Recorder*, Dec. 16, 1952.

571 **"Frank came back"**: Gardner, *Ava*, p. 209.

571 **"Then came the death wait"**: Kelley, *His Way*, p. 191.

572 **"Fred Zinnemann . . . has gone"**: Hedda Hopper's Hollywood, syndicated column, Dec. 3, 1952.

573 **"Frank's still in there"**: Hedda Hopper's Hollywood, syndicated column, Dec. 10, 1952.

575 **"When Frank Sinatra"**: Wilson, *Sinatra*, p. 108.

CHAPTER 33

1. Though for the average American family in 1953, $1,000 was over two months' income.

2. In the novel, Woltz's racist rant is subtly different and less florid, to wit: "I don't

care how many guinea Mafia goombahs come out of the woodwork." (Period, not exclamation point.) Strikingly, the word "Mafia" never occurs once in the movie of *The Godfather*, due to an agreement struck between the producer Al Ruddy and the crime-family chief Joe Colombo, the figurehead of the Italian-American Civil Rights League.

3. Appearing on *Texaco Star Theater* on February 3, Sinatra showed a horrified Uncle Miltie a shrunken head he had brought back from Africa. "It was Clark Gable," Frank said. "Do you think I would leave him there with Ava?" (Server, *Ava Gardner*, p. 406).

4. Including the May 1952 miscarriage.

5. Ironically, in his turn as Nathan Detroit in the 1955 *Guys and Dolls*, Frank would find himself in a sense imitating himself imitating Maggio imitating Runyon's original 1930s characters.

SOURCE NOTES

580 **"He was delighted"**: Summers and Swan, *Sinatra*, p. 170.

581 **"Frank Sinatra, needing"**: Earl Wilson on Broadway, syndicated column, Jan. 23, 1953.

581 **"I wanted to tell"**: Wilson, *Sinatra*, p. 110.

582 **"Pearl, they've offered"**: Levinson, *September in the Rain*, p. 111.

583 **"Cohn hated Sinatra"**: Rappleye and Becker, *All American Mafioso*, p. 132.

583 **"Now listen to me"**: *The Godfather* (Paramount Pictures, 1972).

583 **"Frank Sinatra and Harry Cohn"**: Thomas, *King Cohn*, p. 305.

584 **"It was the first time"**: Ibid., p. 306.

584 **"He doesn't look"**: Kelley, *His Way*, p. 210.

585 **"Frank Sinatra has been"**: International News Service, Feb. 3, 1953.

585 **"Talked to Frank Sinatra"**: International News Service, Feb. 4, 1953.

586 **"Chums say Frankie"**: Dorothy Kilgallen, The Voice of Broadway, syndicated column, Feb. 20, 1953.

587 **"I didn't think"**: Gardner, *Ava*, p. 210.

588 **"He never got over it"**: Server, *Ava Gardner*, p. 260.

588 **"MONTGOMERY CLIFT"**: Kelley, *His Way*, p. 215.

589 **"DEAR HARRY"**: Ibid.

589 **"a kind of intensity"**: James Jones, *From Here to Eternity*, p. 776.

589 **"Because I want"**: Bosworth, *Montgomery Clift*, p. 247.

589 **"His scenes bristled"**: Ibid., p. 130.

590 **"Good dialogue"**: Kelley, *His Way*, p. 217.

590 **"We had a mutual"**: Santopietro, *Sinatra in Hollywood*, p. 137.

591 **"Monty really coached"**: Kelley, *His Way*, p. 217.

591 **"By his intensity"**: Zinnemann, *Life in the Movies*, p. 122.

591 **"As a singer"**: Santopietro, *Sinatra in Hollywood*, p. 137.

592 **"Sinatra here took"**: Santopietro, *Sinatra in Hollywood*, p. 137.

592 **"This outfit"**: *From Here to Eternity* (MGM, 1953).

593 **"He was scared"**: Ernest Borgnine, in discussion with the author, Feb. 2009.

594 **"The three of them"**: Bosworth, *Montgomery Clift*, p. 252.

594 **"got so used to carrying"**: Buford, *Burt Lancaster*, p. 129.

594 **"After we filmed"**: Ernest Borgnine, in discussion with the author, Dec. 2009.

595 **"box office insurance"**: Wood Soanes, syndicated column, March 27, 1953.

595 **"a smash success"**: Ibid.

595 **"We concocted a little"**: Frank Morriss, syndicated column, March 26, 1953.

596 **"Crooner Frank Sinatra"**: International News Service, April 7, 1953.

596 **"I told him"**: Kelley, *His Way*, p. 216.

598 **"Isn't Frank Sinatra"**: Earl Wilson, syndicated column, March 2, 1953.

CHAPTER 34

1. Not to be confused with Lucy's El Adobe Café, which opened just a few doors away on Melrose, years after the original Lucey's closed.

2. A decade later, Dexter would go on to another form of infamy when, as head of the label's Capitol of the World division, he turned down the Beatles—twice—as Capitol artists.

SOURCE NOTES

600 **"Alan, we've just":** Friedwald, *Sinatra!* p. 206.

600 **"Really?":** Havers, *Sinatra*, p. 171.

600 **"He was meek":** Friedwald, *Sinatra!*, p. 207.

602 **"Frank Sinatra was signed":** Associated Press, March 14, 1953.

602 **"We had every salesman":** Friedwald, *Sinatra!* p. 207.

603 **"All hair restorers":** Newspaper Enterprise Association, March 16, 1953.

603 **"Salient factors":** Harold Heffernan, syndicated column, April 2, 1953.

605 **"It was late":** Havers, *Sinatra*, p. 174.

605 **"Could they have been":** Hedda Hopper, syndicated column, April 2, 1953.

606 **"Sinatra appears":** Hal Humphrey, syndicated column, April 15, 1953.

606 **"The singer said":** Associated Press, April 15, 1953.

607 **"Deborah Kerr and me":** Nancy Sinatra, *American Legend*, p. 109.

608 **"Sinatra was at his best":** Zinnemann, *Life in the Movies*, p. 124.

608 **"Frank was very":** Wagner, *Pieces of My Heart*, p. 123.

608 **"Every night, after work":** Nancy Sinatra, *My Father*, p. 97.

609 **"Frank Sinatra, who tossed":** Dorothy Kilgallen, The Voice of Hollywood, syndicated column, April 24, 1953.

610 **"He was very, very good":** Zinnemann, *Life in the Movies*, p. 130.

611 **"Frank and Monty":** Kelley, *His Way*, p. 218.

611 **"His fervor, his anger":** Nancy Sinatra, *American Legend*, p. 112.

612 **"I was on the sidelines":** Kelley, *His Way*, p. 218.

612 **"Sinatra delivered":** Zinnemann, *Life in the Movies*, p. 130.

613 **"I can't blame him":** Ibid.

616 **"got the string":** Lyrics from "I've Got the World on a String," words by Ted Koehler, music by Harold Arlen (1932).

616 **"Who wrote that":** Levinson, *September in the Rain*, p. 113.

618 **"He couldn't help":** Ibid., p. 24.

618 **"Riddle was still":** Friedwald, *Sinatra!* p. 216.

619 **"Now we have":** Ibid., p. 217.

620 **" 'South of the Border'—I thought":** Havers, *Sinatra*, p. 176.

620 **"Jesus Christ":** Levinson, *September in the Rain*, p. 113.

CHAPTER 35

1. The previous December, while she and the children were away, she'd received a visit of another kind: from a burglar, who took some $30,000 worth of her jewelry.

2. Though some people were listening. "What are they talking about in Hollywood?" wrote Bob Thomas of the Associated Press, on July 18. "The amazing comeback of Frank Sinatra on his new records. He sings zingy like the old Frankie-boy."

3. One wonders if he was thinking, consciously or unconsciously, about the magic Sinatra had once worked at the Capitol with *Miss Grant Takes Richmond*.

SOURCE NOTES

622 **"Sinatra was at his":** Friedwald, *Sinatra!* p. 218.

622 **"Nelson was standing":** Ibid.

623 **"Crooner Frank Sinatra"**: Associated Press, May 4, 1953.
624 **"Nancy Sinatra's steadfast date"**: Walter Winchell, syndicated column, Nov. 4, 1953.
625 **"There was no way"**: Jacobs and Stadiem, *Mr. S*, p. 50.
626 **"I'd rather swim the Channel"**: Kelley, *His Way*, p. 222.
627 **"Sinatra has been a flop"**: Havers, *Sinatra*, p. 177.
627 **"Agence France Presse"**: International News Service, May 31, 1953.
627 **"FRANK SINATRA HAS COLLAPSE"**: United Press, June 1, 1953.
629 **"We came back"**: Gardner, *Ava*, p. 336.
629 **"Sinatra is still"**: Shaw, *Twentieth-Century Romantic*, p. 176.
629 **"Imagine"**: Friedrich, *City of Nets*, p. 90.
630 **"Cohn had decided"**: Zinnemann, *Life in the Movies*, p. 131.
631 **"came up from the lobby"**: Wilson, *Sinatra*, p. 111.
632 **"Dialogue between Ava"**: Frank Morriss, syndicated column, Aug. 12, 1953.
633 **"Looking through my"**: Jimmie Fidler, syndicated column, Aug. 19, 1953.
633 **"For the first time"**: Shaw, *Twentieth-Century Romantic*, p. 177.
634 **"ACADEMY AWARD RACE"**: Lubbock *(Tex.) Avalanche-Journal*, Aug. 30, 1953.
634 **"Frank Sinatra has been receiving"**: Jimmie Fidler, syndicated column, Aug. 31, 1953.
635 **"Those dark cheaters"**: Lee Mortimer, syndicated column, Aug. 31, 1953.
635 **"Ava, honey, you do know"**: Gardner, *Ava*, p. 336.
636 **"A close friend"**: United Press, Sept. 9, 1953.
637 **"FRANKIE AND AVA FEUDING"**: United Press, Sept. 10, 1953.
637 **"I saw a picture"**: Kelley, *His Way*, p. 224.
637 **"You start with love"**: Ibid.
638 **"Every big star"**: Earl Wilson, syndicated column, Sept. 11, 1953.
638 **"Electrifying"**: Fisher, *Eddie*, p. 226.
638 **"Frank let loose"**: Havers, *Sinatra*, p. 182.
639 **"Frank Sinatra's intimates"**: Dorothy Kilgallen, syndicated column, Sept. 16, 1953.
639 **"As a Cupid"**: Earl Wilson, syndicated column, Sept. 12, 1953.
640 **"She kissed me"**: Kelley, *His Way*, p. 224.
641 **"The Voice unleashed a torrent"**: Server, *Ava Gardner*, p. 226.

CHAPTER 36

1. Humphrey Bogart had given Lazar the slightly needling nickname—which the agent hated—as a double-edged tribute to the rapidity with which Lazar executed his not always strictly kosher deals.
2. The apartments have long since been razed.
3. Although apparently the switch had been effected with the tacit cooperation of Lazar, the ultimate cynic when Sinatra was down and the ultimate sycophant when he rose again.
4. Perhaps thinking or saying some variation of the Nevada senator Pat Geary's speech to Michael Corleone in *The Godfather, Part II*: "I don't like your kind of people. I don't like to see you come out to this clean country in your oily hair, dressed up in those silk suits, and try to pass yourselves off as decent Americans."

SOURCE NOTES
642 **"Isn't it a little late"**: Kelley, *His Way*, p. 225.
643 **"When he was down"**: Shaw, *Twentieth-Century Romantic*, p. 175.
643 **"Almost since their marriage"**: Dorothy Kilgallen, syndicated column, Sept. 30, 1953.
643 **"devastating"**: Dorothy Kilgallen, syndicated column, Oct. 1, 1953.

644 **"Together again"**: Associated Press, Oct. 2, 1953.

644 **"Don't believe a word"**: Server, *Ava Gardner*, p. 267.

644 **"They're together"**: Shaw, *Twentieth-Century Romantic*, p. 178.

644 **"If Frankie goes"**: Harrison Carroll, syndicated column, Oct. 12, 1953.

645 **"Two intimates of Frank Sinatra"**: Jimmie Fidler, syndicated column, Oct. 6, 1953.

645 **"a footloose and fancy-free"**: Dunning, *Encyclopedia of Old-Time Radio*, p. 582.

646 **"Hi, I don't know"**: Havers, *Sinatra*, p. 183.

646 **"He was always"**: Jacobs and Stadiem, *Mr. S*, p. 90.

647 **"For Chrissakes"**: Ibid., p. 53.

648 **"Politics has nothing"**: Bosworth, *Marlon Brando*, p. 141.

648 **"Frank Sinatra would"**: Ibid., p. 153.

649 **"Frank Sinatra's now practically"**: Earl Wilson, syndicated column, Sept. 30, 1953.

649 **"Frank Sinatra has decided"**: Louella Parsons, syndicated column, Oct. 10, 1953.

649 **"In what would become"**: Jacobs and Stadiem, *Mr. S*, p. 90.

650 **"I slept in the same *room*"**: George Jacobs, in discussion with the author, March 2009.

651 **"He's a dead man"**: Jacobs and Stadiem, *Mr. S*, p. 21.

651 **"head down, all alone"**: Ibid., p. 36.

652 **"When I opened"**: Ibid., p. 46.

653 **"who didn't seem ex"**: Ibid., p. 48.

653 **"rococo New Jersey style"**: Ibid.

653 **"The correct way"**: Ibid.

654 **"There's nothing like"**: Associated Press, Oct. 12, 1953.

654 **"Everything is fine"**: Louella Parsons, syndicated column, Oct. 20, 1953.

654 **"I can't eat"**: Kelley, *His Way*, p. 225.

655 **"Hollywood's still betting"**: Erskine Johnson, syndicated column, Oct. 21, 1953.

655 **"Ava Gardner and Frank Sinatra"**: Kelley, *His Way*, p. 226.

656 **"When Sinatra is in Las Vegas"**: Pignone, *Sinatra Treasures*, p. 104.

656 **"The object was"**: Kelley, *His Way*, p. 241.

656 **"Frank! Is your marriage"**: Ibid., p. 227.

657 **"There is positively"**: Shaw, *Twentieth-Century Romantic*, p. 180.

CHAPTER 37

SOURCE NOTES

660 **"I was a stranger"**: Lyrics from "Foggy Day," words by Ira Gershwin, music by George Gershwin (New York: Gershwin, 1937).

660 **"If I wasn't conducting"**: Kelley, *His Way*, p. 232.

660 **"Ava taught him"**: Hamill, *Why Sinatra Matters*, p. 177.

662 **"I AM DESPERATELY"**: Server, *Ava Gardner*, p. 270.

663 **"Yeah, he's here"**: Ibid., p. 272.

663 **"Eventually they got"**: Ibid.

664 **"Ten years ago"**: International News Service, Nov. 9, 1953.

664 **"Melissa Weston Bigelow"**: Dorothy Kilgallen, syndicated column, Nov. 13, 1953.

665 **"Well, that washes"**: Hal Humphrey, syndicated column, Nov. 11, 1953.

666 **"You would not pick"**: James Kaplan, "The King of Ring-a-Ding-Ding," *Movies Rock* (a supplemental publication of *Vanity Fair*), Dec. 2007.

668 **"Sinatra's father says"**: Walter Winchell, syndicated column, Nov. 24, 1953.

668 **"I would rather write"**: Kaplan, "King of Ring-a-Ding-Ding."

669 **"When Frank ate"**: Kelley, *His Way*, p. 229.

670 **"RUMOR MILL IS MUM"**: Wire service report, Nov. 21, 1953, transcribed from *Huntington (Pa.) Daily News*, Nov. 23, 1953.

671 **"I was happier"**: Jordan, "Living with Miss G."

671 **"F. Sinatra will spend"**: In New York with Walter Winchell, syndicated column, Nov. 19, 1953.

672 **"Ava Gardner on Thanksgiving"**: Dorothy Manners, syndicated column, Nov. 26, 1953.

672 **"You know, Harold"**: *The Golden Years of Classic Television: The Colgate Comedy Hour, Vol. 1* (Miracle Picture, 2005), DVD.

673 **"ev'ry time your lips"**: Lyrics from "That Old Black Magic," words by Johnny Mercer, music by Harold Arlen (New York: Famous Music, 1942).

673 **"SINATRA ADMITS HURTING WRIST"**: *Lubbock (Tex.) Morning Avalanche*, Dec. 10, 1953.

674 **"I think it's a good song"**: Nancy Sinatra, *American Legend*, p. 114.

674 **"Fairy tales"**: Lyrics from "Young at Heart," words by Carolyn Leigh, music by Johnny Richards (New York: Sunbeam Music, 1954).

675 **"I could have told you"**: Lyrics from "I Could Have Told You So," words by Carl Sigman, music by James Van Heusen (New York: Music Sales, 1953).

CHAPTER 38

SOURCE NOTES

677 **"The breakup of the sultry"**: *Holland (Mich.) Evening Sentinel*, Nov. 11, 1953.

677 **"F. Sinatra is taking"**: Edith Gwynn, syndicated column, Dec. 1, 1953.

678 **"Of all Greenson's"**: Spoto, *Marilyn Monroe*, p. 427.

679 **"Special Problems in Psychotherapy"**: Ibid., p. 426.

680 **"It wouldn't surprise me"**: Louella Parsons, syndicated column, Dec. 16, 1953.

681 **"I'll be so happy"**: United Press, Dec. 23, 1953.

681 **"I'm going to spend"**: Ibid.

683 **"She was not a little"**: Server, *Ava Gardner*, p. 283.

684 **"AVA GARDNER"**: *Newport (R.I.) Daily News*, Dec. 30, 1953.

685 **"trying to work"**: Shaw, *Twentieth-Century Romantic*, p. 182.

CHAPTER 39

1. Who, to complete the slightly absurd polygon, would marry Walter Chiari's former fiancée, Lucia Bosé, later that year.

SOURCE NOTES

688 **"You may have heard"**: Earl Wilson, syndicated column, transcribed from *Zanesville (Ohio) Times Recorder*, Jan. 23, 1954.

688 **"in a chilly studio"**: Wilson, *Sinatra*, p. 115.

688 **"He *literally* moved"**: Kelley, *His Way*, p. 233.

689 **"I come home"**: Ibid., p. 235.

689 **"Nancy Sinatra's pals"**: Erskine Johnson, syndicated column, Jan. 24, 1954.

691 **"You're the sittin'-est"**: Gardner, *Ava*, p. 221.

691 **"I like a little"**: Server, *Ava Gardner*, p. 284.

691 **"On the morning"**: Ibid.

693 **"I saw Frankie"**: Louella Parsons, syndicated column, Jan. 30, 1954.

693 **"craved class"**: Jacobs and Stadiem, *Mr. S*, p. 50.

694 **"Sinatra was like"**: Ibid., p. 40.

696 **"I stayed a night"**: Bacall, *By Myself and Then Some*, p. 241.

697 **"I had to perform"**: Gardner, *Ava*, p. 348.

697 **"When we got there"**: Sciacca, *Sinatra*, p. 171.

699 **"Frank Sinatra—who's collecting"**: Earl Wilson, syndicated column, Feb. 8, 1954.

699 **"There's a tug-of-war"**: Earl Wilson, syndicated column, Feb. 12, 1954.

700 **"QUADRANGLE"**: *New York Daily News* wire report, Feb. 16, 1954.

700 **"Frank Sinatra and Artie Shaw"**: Walter Winchell, syndicated column, Feb. 26, 1954.

701 **"I'm a saloon singer"**: Bob Thomas, syndicated column, March 14, 1954.

701 **"What does Ava"**: Laura Lee, syndicated column, March 14, 1954.

CHAPTER 40

1. Fred Zinnemann, who had won the Best Director Oscar, also said as much: "The picture never could have won these honors without Montgomery Clift. He was the heart of the whole movie" (United Press, March 26, 1954).

SOURCE NOTES

706 **"an ocean's roar"**: Lyrics from "Day In, Day Out," words by Johnny Mercer, music by Rube Bloom (New York: Bregman, Vocco, and Conn, 1939).

706 **"In working out"**: Shaw, *Entertainer*, p. 27.

707 **"Just for the record"**: Louella Parsons, syndicated column, March 11, 1954.

707 **"Ava was sure"**: Leonard Lyons, syndicated column, March 15, 1954.

708 **"Frank Sinatra's excuse"**: Louella Parsons, syndicated column, March 14, 1954.

708 **"Frank Sinatra off to Italy"**: Jimmie Fidler, syndicated column, March 18, 1954.

709 **"Frank Sinatra, an intimate"**: *Wisconsin State Journal*, March 16, 1954.

709 **"Sinatra's participation"**: Westbrook Pegler, syndicated column, March 16, 1954.

709 **"Willie Moretti"**: Ibid.

710 **"Bring back that Oscar"**: Kelley, *His Way*, p. 238.

711 **"To Daddy—all our love"**: Ibid., p. 237.

711 **"After being exiled"**: Walter Winchell, syndicated column, March 23, 1954.

711 **"NEWCOMER IS HOT FAVORITE"**: *El Paso Herald-Post*, March 24, 1954.

712 **"Tonight's the night"**: Louella Parsons, syndicated column, March 25, 1954.

714 **"Nominees for the best"**: Twenty-sixth Academy Awards broadcast, 1954.

715 **"A peculiar thing"**: Shaw, *Twentieth-Century Romantic*, p. 185.

715 **"Unbelievable"**: Twenty-sixth Academy Awards broadcast, 1954.

716 **"That's it"**: Kelley, *His Way*, p. 239.

716 **"I wanted to thank"**: Hopper and Brough, *Whole Truth and Nothing But*, p. 47.

718 **"I ducked the party"**: Shaw, *Entertainer*, p. 32.

BIBLIOGRAPHY

Bacall, Lauren. *By Myself and Then Some*. New York: HarperCollins, 2005.

Bacon, Francis. *The Essays*. Edited by John Pitcher. New York: Penguin, 1985.

Balliett, Whitney. *Alec Wilder and His Friends: The Words and Sounds of Marian McPart-land, Mabel Mercer, Marie Marcus, Bobby Hackett, Tony Bennett, Ruby Braff, Bob and Ray, Blossom Dearie, and Alec Wilder*. New York: Houghton Mifflin, 1974.

Barbas, Samantha. *The First Lady of Hollywood: A Biography of Louella Parsons*. Berkeley: University of California Press, 2006.

Bogdanovich, Peter. *Who the Devil Made It: Conversations with Legendary Film Directors*. New York: Knopf, 1997.

———. *Who the Hell's in It: Portraits and Conversations*. New York: Knopf, 2004.

Bosworth, Patricia. *Marlon Brando*. New York: Viking, 2001.

———. *Montgomery Clift: A Biography*. New York: Harcourt Brace Jovanovich, 1978.

Brooks, Tim, and Earle Marsh. *TV's Greatest Hits: The 150 Most Popular TV Shows of All Time*. New York: Ballantine, 1985.

Buford, Kate. *Burt Lancaster: An American Life*. Cambridge, Mass.: Da Capo, 2001.

Cahn, Sammy. *I Should Care: The Sammy Cahn Story*. New York: Arbor House, 1974.

Cannon, Doris Rollins. *Grabtown Girl: Ava Gardner's North Carolina Childhood and Her Enduring Ties to Home*. Asheboro, N.C.: Down Home Press, 2001.

Cerf, Bennett. *At Random: The Reminiscences of Bennett Cerf*. New York: Random House, 2002.

Clarke, Donald. *All or Nothing At All: A Life of Frank Sinatra*. New York: Macmillan, 1997.

Cornyn, Stan. *Exploding: The Highs, Hits, Hype, Heroes, and Hustlers of the Warner Music Group*. New York: HarperEntertainment, 2002.

Crane, Cheryl, with Cliff Jahr. *Detour*. New York: Arbor House, 1988.

Crosby, Gary, and Ross Firestone. *Going My Own Way*. Garden City, N.Y.: Doubleday, 1983.

Dannen, Fredric. *Hit Men: Power Brokers and Fast Money Inside the Music Business*. New York: Vintage, 1991.

Davis, Sammy, Jr., with Burt Boyar and Jane Boyar. *Yes I Can: The Story of Sammy Davis Jr.* New York: Farrar, Straus and Giroux, 1972.

DeRoos, Robert. Unpublished biography of Jimmy Van Heusen. MS.

Douglas-Home, Robin. *Sinatra*. New York: Grosset and Dunlap, 1962.

Dunning, John. *The Encyclopedia of Old-Time Radio*. New York: Oxford University Press, 1998.

Eames, John Douglas. *The MGM Story: The Complete History of over Fifty Roaring Years*. New York: Crown, 1976.

Eliot, Marc. *Cary Grant: A Biography*. New York: Three Rivers, 2005.

Exner, Judith, as told to Ovid Demaris. *My Story*. New York: Grove, 1977.

Falcone, Vincent, and Bob Popyk. *Frankly, Just Between Us: My Life Conducting Frank Sinatra's Music*. Milwaukee: Hal Leonard, 2005.

Farrow, Mia. *What Falls Away*. New York: Bantam, 1997.

Fisher, Eddie. *Eddie: My Life, My Loves*. New York: Harper and Row, 1981.

Fisher, Eddie, with David Fisher. *Been There, Done That*. New York: St. Martin's, 2000.

Flamini, Roland. *Ava: A Biography*. New York: Coward, McCann and Geoghegan, 1983.

Freedland, Michael. *All the Way: A Biography of Frank Sinatra, 1915–1998*. New York: St. Martin's, 1998.

Friedrich, Otto. *City of Nets*. Berkeley: University of California Press, 1997.

Friedwald, Will. *Jazz Singing: America's Great Voices from Bessie Smith to Bebop and Beyond*. New York: Da Capo, 1999.

———. *Sinatra! The Song Is You: A Singer's Art*. New York: Scribner, 1995.

———. *Stardust Melodies: A Biography of Twelve of America's Most Popular Songs*. New York: Pantheon, 2002.

Fuchs, Jeanne, and Ruth Prigozy. *Frank Sinatra: The Man, the Music, the Legend*. Rochester, N.Y.: University of Rochester Press, 2007.

Gabler, Neal. *Winchell: Gossip, Power, and the Culture of Celebrity*. New York: Vintage, 1995.

Gardner, Ava. *Ava: My Story*. New York: Bantam, 1990.

Giddins, Gary. *Bing Crosby: A Pocketful of Dreams: The Early Years, 1903–1940*. Boston: Little, Brown, 2001.

———. *Natural Selection: Gary Giddins on Comedy, Film, Music, and Books*. New York: Oxford University Press, 2006.

———. *Visions of Jazz: The First Century*. New York: Oxford University Press, 2000.

Goodman, Ezra. *The Fifty-Year Decline and Fall of Hollywood*. New York: Simon and Schuster, 1961.

Granata, Charles L. *Sessions with Sinatra: Frank Sinatra and the Art of Recording*. Chicago: Chicago Review Press, 1999.

Grudens, Richard. *Snootie Little Cutie: The Connie Haines Story*. New York: Celebrity Profiles, 2000.

Grun, Bernard. *The Timetables of History*. New York: Touchstone, 1991.

Hamill, Pete. *Why Sinatra Matters*. Boston: Little, Brown, 1998.

Hanna, David. *Sinatra*. New York: Gramercy, 1990.

Havers, Richard. *Sinatra*. New York: DK, 2004.

Haygood, Wil. *In Black and White: The Life of Sammy Davis Jr*. New York: Knopf, 2003.

Herman, Arthur. *Joseph McCarthy: Reexamining the Life and Legacy of America's Most Hated Senator*. New York: Free Press, 1999.

Hersh, Burton. *Bobby and J. Edgar: The Historic Face-Off Between the Kennedys and J. Edgar Hoover That Transformed America*. New York: Basic Books, 2007.

Hersh, Seymour. *The Dark Side of Camelot*. Boston: Little, Brown, 1998.

Higham, Charles. *Ava: A Life Story*. New York: Delacorte, 1974.

Hopper, Hedda, and James Brough. *The Whole Truth and Nothing But*. Garden City, N.Y.: Doubleday, 1963.

Ingham, Chris. *The Rough Guide to Frank Sinatra*. New York: Rough Guides, 2005.

Jacobs, George, and William Stadiem. *Mr. S: My Life with Frank Sinatra*. New York: HarperCollins, 2004.

Jaker, Bill, Frank Sulek, and Peter Kanze. *The Airwaves of New York: Illustrated Histories of 156 AM Stations in the Metropolitan Area, 1921–1996*. Jefferson, N.C.: McFarland, 1998.

Jenkins, Bruce. *Goodbye: In Search of Gordon Jenkins*. Berkeley, Calif.: Frog, 2005.

Jones, James. *From Here to Eternity*. New York: Scribner, 1951.

Jones, Quincy. *Q: The Autobiography of Quincy Jones*. New York: Harlem Moon, 2002.

Jordan, Mearene. "Living with Miss G." Unpublished memoir about Ava Gardner. MS.

Kahn, E. J., Jr. *The Voice: The Story of an American Phenomenon*. New York: Harper and Brothers, 1946.

Kaye, Lenny. *You Call It Madness: The Sensuous Song of the Croon*. New York: Villard, 2005.

Kelley, Kitty. *His Way: The Unauthorized Biography of Frank Sinatra*. New York: Bantam, 1986.

Kierkegaard, Søren. *Either/Or: A Fragment of Life, Vol. 1*. Translated by David F. Swenson and Lillian Marvin Swenson. Princeton, N.J.: Princeton University Press, 1949.

Kuntz, Tom, and Phil Kuntz, eds. *The Sinatra Files: The Secret FBI Dossier*. New York: Three Rivers, 2000.

Lahr, John. *Sinatra: The Artist and the Man*. New York: Random House, 1997.

Lawford, Patricia Seaton. *The Peter Lawford Story: Life with the Kennedys, Monroe, and the Rat Pack*. New York: Carroll and Graf, 1988.

Leff, Leonard J., and Jerold Simmons. *The Dame in the Kimono: Hollywood, Censorship, and the Production Code from the 1920s to the 1960s*. New York: Anchor, 1991.

Levinson, Peter J. *September in the Rain: The Life of Nelson Riddle*. New York: Watson-Guptill, 2001.

———. *Tommy Dorsey: Livin' in a Great Big Way*. Cambridge, Mass.: Da Capo, 2005.

———. *Trumpet Blues: The Life of Harry James*. New York: Oxford University Press, 1999.

Levy, Shawn. *Rat Pack Confidential*. New York: Doubleday, 1998.

Lowell, Robert. *Near the Ocean*. New York: Noonday, 1971.

MacLaine, Shirley. *My Lucky Stars: A Hollywood Memoir*. New York: Bantam, 1995.

Manchester, William. *The Glory and the Dream: A Narrative History of America, 1932–1972*. New York: Bantam, 1984.

Moquin, Wayne, and Charles Lincoln Van Doren. *The American Way of Crime: A Documentary History*. New York: Praeger, 1976.

Mustazza, Leonard. *Ol' Blue Eyes: A Frank Sinatra Encyclopedia*. Westport, Conn.: Praeger, 1999.

———. ed. *Frank Sinatra and Popular Culture: Essays on an American Icon*. Westport, Conn.: Praeger, 1998.

Mustazza, Leonard, and Steven Petkov, eds. *The Frank Sinatra Reader*. New York: Oxford University Press, 1997.

O'Brien, Ed, with Robert Wilson. *Sinatra 101: The 101 Best Recordings and the Stories Behind Them*. New York: Berkley Trade, 1996.

Parsons, Louella Oettinger. *Tell It to Louella*. New York: Putnam, 1961.

Pignone, Charles. *Frank Sinatra: The Family Album*. New York: Little, Brown, 2007.

———. *The Sinatra Treasures: Intimate Photos, Mementos, and Music from the Sinatra Family Collection*. New York: Bulfinch, 2004.

Prager, Joshua. *The Echoing Green: The Untold Story of Bobby Thomson, Ralph Branca, and the Shot Heard Round the World*. New York: Pantheon, 2006.

Puzo, Mario. *The Godfather*. New York: Putnam, 1969.

Rappleye, Charles, and Ed Becker. *All American Mafioso: The Johnny Rosselli Story*. New York: Doubleday, 1991.

Reeves, Richard. *President Nixon: Alone in the White House*. New York: Simon and Schuster, 2002.

Richardson, John. *A Life of Picasso*. 3 vols. New York: Random House, 1996.

Richmond, Peter. *Fever: The Life and Music of Miss Peggy Lee*. New York: Henry Holt, 2006.

Riddle, Nelson. *Arranged by Nelson Riddle*. New York: Alfred, 1985.

Rockwell, John. *Sinatra: An American Classic*. New York: Random House, 1984.

Santopietro, Tom. *Sinatra in Hollywood*. New York: St. Martin's Griffin, 2009.

Schoemer, Karen. *Great Pretenders: My Strange Love Affair with 50s Pop Music*. New York: Free Press, 2007.

Schwartz, Jonathan. *All in Good Time: A Memoir*. New York: Random House, 2005.

Sciacca, Tony. *Sinatra*. New York: Pinnacle, 1976.

Server, Lee. *Ava Gardner: "Love Is Nothing."* New York: St. Martin's Griffin, 2006.

———. *Robert Mitchum: "Baby, I Don't Care."* New York: Macmillan, 2002.

Shaw, Arnold. *Sinatra: The Entertainer*. New York: Delilah, 1984.

———. *Sinatra: Twentieth-Century Romantic*. New York: Pocket Books, 1969.

Sheed, Wilfrid. *The House That George Built: With a Little Help from Irving, Cole, and a Crew of About Fifty*. New York: Random House, 2008.

Sifakis, Carl. *The Mafia Encyclopedia: From Accardo to Zwillman*. New York: Facts on File, 1999.

Silverman, Stephen M. *Dancing on the Ceiling: Stanley Donen and His Movies*. New York: Knopf, 1996.

Sinatra, Nancy. *Frank Sinatra, My Father*. New York: Pocket Books, 1986.

———. *Frank Sinatra, 1915–1998: An American Legend*. Santa Monica, Calif.: General Publishing Group, 1998.

Sinatra, Tina, with Jeff Coplon. *My Father's Daughter: A Memoir*. New York: Simon and Schuster, 2000.

Smith, Liz. *Natural Blonde*. New York: Hyperion, 2000.

Solomon, Maynard. *Mozart: A Life*. New York: HarperCollins, 1996.

Spoto, Donald. *Marilyn Monroe: The Biography*. New York: HarperCollins, 1993.

———. *Notorious: The Life of Ingrid Bergman*. Cambridge, Mass.: Da Capo, 2001.

Summers, Anthony, and Robbyn Swan. *Sinatra: The Life*. New York: Knopf, 2005.

Taraborrelli, J. Randy. *Sinatra: Behind the Legend*. New York: Carol, 1997.

Thomas, Bob. *King Cohn: The Life and Times of Harry Cohn*. New York: Putnam, 1967.

Tormé, Mel. *It Wasn't All Velvet*. New York: Viking, 1998.

———. *Traps, the Drum Wonder: The Life of Buddy Rich*. New York: Oxford University Press, 1991.

Tosches, Nick. *Dino: Living High in the Dirty Business of Dreams*. New York: Doubleday, 1992.

Turner, John Frayn. *Frank Sinatra*. New York: Taylor, 2004.

Turner, Lana. *Lana: The Lady, the Legend, the Truth*. New York: Dutton, 1982.

U.S. Treasury Department Bureau of Narcotics. *Mafia: The Government's Secret File on Organized Crime*. New York: Norton, 2009.

Wagner, Robert J., with Scott Eyman. *Pieces of My Heart: A Life*. New York: HarperEntertainment, 2008.

Wayne, Jane Ellen. *Ava's Men: The Private Life of Ava Gardner*. New York: St. Martin's, 1990.

———. *Lana: The Life and Loves of Lana Turner*. New York: St. Martin's, 1995.

White, Mark. *You Must Remember This: Popular Songwriters, 1900–1980*. New York: Scribner, 1985.

Wilder, Alec. *American Popular Song: The Great Innovators, 1900–1950*. New York: Oxford University Press, 1990.

Wilson, Earl. *Sinatra: An Unauthorized Biography*. New York: Signet, 1976.

Winters, Shelley. *Shelley, Also Known as Shirley*. New York: William Morrow, 1980.

Zehme, Bill. *The Way You Wear Your Hat*. New York: Harper Perennial, 1999.

Zinnemann, Fred. *A Life in the Movies: An Autobiography*. New York: Scribner, 1992.

INDEX

—

Page numbers in *italics* refer to illustrations.